ERISA PRINCIPLES

ERISA, the detailed and technical amalgam of labor law, trust law, and tax law, directly governs trillions of dollars spent on retirement savings, health care, and other important benefits for more than 100 million Americans. Despite playing this central role in the US economy and social insurance systems, the complexities of ERISA are understood by only a few specialists. *ERISA Principles* elucidates employee benefit law from a policy perspective, concisely explaining how common themes apply across a wide range of benefit plans and factual contexts. The book's non-technical language and cross-cutting conceptual organization reveal latent similarities and rationalize differences between the regulatory treatment of apparently disparate programs, including traditional pensions, 401(k) retirement savings plans, and health care plans. Important legal developments – whether statutory, judicial, or administrative – are framed and analyzed in an accessible, principles-centric manner, explaining how ERISA functions as a coherent whole.

PETER J. WIEDENBECK is the Joseph H. Zumbalen Professor of the Law of Property at Washington University in St. Louis School of Law. He has written numerous books and articles on federal tax law and the tax- and labor-law regulation of employee benefit plans, and has coauthored casebooks on federal income taxation, employee benefits, and partnership taxation. In 2022, he chaired the Advisory Council on Employee Welfare and Pension Benefit Plans.

BRENDAN S. MAHER is Professor of Law at Texas A&M University School of Law and the Director of the Health Law, Policy and Management Program. He was formerly the Connecticut Mutual Professor of Law at the University of Connecticut, where he ran the school's Insurance Law Center. He retired in 2020 from Stris & Maher LLP, where he handled multiple ERISA matters before the United States Supreme Court.

ERISA Principles

PETER J. WIEDENBECK
Washington University School of Law

BRENDAN S. MAHER
Texas A&M University School of Law

CAMBRIDGE
UNIVERSITY PRESS

Shaftesbury Road, Cambridge CB2 8EA, United Kingdom

One Liberty Plaza, 20th Floor, New York, NY 10006, USA

477 Williamstown Road, Port Melbourne, VIC 3207, Australia

314–321, 3rd Floor, Plot 3, Splendor Forum, Jasola District Centre, New Delhi – 110025, India

103 Penang Road, #05-06/07, Visioncrest Commercial, Singapore 238467

Cambridge University Press is part of Cambridge University Press & Assessment, a department of the University of Cambridge.

We share the University's mission to contribute to society through the pursuit of education, learning and research at the highest international levels of excellence.

www.cambridge.org
Information on this title: www.cambridge.org/9781107167032
DOI: 10.1017/9781316711507

© Peter J. Wiedenbeck and Brendan S. Maher 2024

This publication is in copyright. Subject to statutory exception and to the provisions of relevant collective licensing agreements, no reproduction of any part may take place without the written permission of Cambridge University Press & Assessment.

First published 2024

A catalogue record for this publication is available from the British Library.

Library of Congress Cataloging-in-Publication Data
NAMES: Wiedenbeck, Peter J., 1953– author. | Maher, Brendan S., author.
TITLE: ERISA principles / Peter J. Wiedenbeck, Washington University School of Law; Brendan S. Maher, Texas A&M University School of Law.
OTHER TITLES: Employee Retirement Income Security Act principles Description: Cambridge, United Kingdom ; New York, NY : Cambridge University Press, 2024. | Includes index.
IDENTIFIERS: LCCN 2023018386 (print) | LCCN 2023018387 (ebook) | ISBN 9781107167032 (hardback) | ISBN 9781316617786 (paperback) | ISBN 9781316711507 (epub)
SUBJECTS: LCSH: United States. Employee Retirement Income Security Act of 1974. | Pension trusts–Law and legislation–United States. | Deferred compensation–Taxation–Law and legislation–United States.
CLASSIFICATION: LCC KF3512 .W5325 2023 (print) | LCC KF3512 (ebook) | DDC 344.7301/252–dc23/eng/20230724
LC record available at https://lccn.loc.gov/2023018386
LC ebook record available at https://lccn.loc.gov/2023018387

ISBN 978-1-107-16703-2 Hardback
ISBN 978-1-316-61778-6 Paperback

Cambridge University Press & Assessment has no responsibility for the persistence or accuracy of URLs for external or third-party internet websites referred to in this publication and does not guarantee that any content on such websites is, or will remain, accurate or appropriate.

Contents

Acknowledgments		*page* ix
Table of Cases		xi
Table of Legislation		xxvii
Table of Rules and Regulations		lxxv

PART I GENERAL CONSIDERATIONS		1
1	**Overview of ERISA**	3
	A Benefit Plan Varieties	5
	B ERISA's Pattern of Regulation	12
	C ERISA's Principal Policies	15
	D ERISA's Relation to Tax Qualification	22
	E Note on Coverage	25
2	**ERISA's Coverage**	28
	A The "Plan" Prerequisite	29
	B "Employee" Status	40
	C The Pension–Welfare Dichotomy	44
	D Exceptions: Top Hat, Government, and Church Plans	51
	E Conclusion	57
PART II CONDUCT CONTROLS: WELFARE AND PENSION PLANS		59
3	**Disclosure**	61
	A Statutory Disclosure Obligations	62
	B SPD Contents and Consequences	71
	C Non-SPD Communications	103
	D Conclusion	112

vi Contents

4 Fiduciary Obligations 116

A Definition of Fiduciary 117
B Fiduciary Duties 127
C Prohibited Transactions 139
D Participant-Directed Investments 145
E Conclusion 157

5 Enforcement 160

A Standing 161
B Scope of Review 167
C Causes of Action 176
D Remedies 182
E Conclusion 191

6 Preemption 193

A The Architecture of Express Preemption 195
B The Puzzle of ERISA's "Relate to" Clause 196
C General State Laws 199
D Costs and Preemption Policy 211
E The Role of Federal Common Law 216
F The Insurance Savings Clause 218
G Conclusion 222

PART III CONTENT CONTROLS: PENSION PLANS 225

7 Accumulation 227

A Participation 228
B Benefit Accrual 237
C Vesting 250
D Conclusion 261

8 Distribution 263

A Timing 263
B Anti-alienation 265
C Spousal Rights 279
D Conclusion 285

9 Security 288

A Minimum Funding Standards 289
B PBGC Termination Insurance 299
C Overfunded Plan Termination 306
D Conclusion 311

Contents

vii

PART IV TAX CONTROLS: QUALIFIED RETIREMENT SAVINGS		313
10	**Taxes and Retirement Saving**	315
	A Taxation of Deferred Compensation	317
	B Targeting the Tax Subsidy	333
	C Limiting the Tax Subsidy	380
	D Reorienting Private Pensions	406
	E Conclusion	425
PART V HEALTH PLAN CONTENT CONTROLS		429
11	**Employment-Based Health Care**	431
	A Health Care Finance and Employment	432
	B ERISA and Health Regulation	438
	C The ACA and Employment-Based Health Regulation	447
	D States in the Post-ACA World	457
	E Future Health Reform	460
	F Conclusion	462
Appendix		463
Index		465

Acknowledgments

We thank Matt Gallaway, Law Publisher of Cambridge University Press, for his support of this work and the patience he displayed when the project was repeatedly and extensively delayed.

This book has a long, complex history. A prior edition was published by Oxford University Press as Peter J. Wiedenbeck, *ERISA: Principles of Employee Benefit Law* (2010). Samantha L. H. Cassetta guided the proposal through the Oxford University Press acquisition process. We are grateful to her and the anonymous peer reviewers who graciously shared their time and expertise. That book, in turn, was a revised and expanded version of Peter J. Wiedenbeck, *ERISA in the Courts* (GPO 2008), written for the Federal Judicial Center (FJC). Kris Markarian, FJC legal editor, deserves special thanks for her unstinting support and skillful editing of Chapters 1–9. Earlier versions of parts of the FJC book appeared in: Peter J. Wiedenbeck, *Implementing ERISA: Of Policies and "Plans,"* 72 WASH. U. L.Q. 559 (1994); Peter J. Wiedenbeck, *ERISA's Curious Coverage*, 76 WASH. U. L.Q. 311 (1998); and Peter J. Wiedenbeck & Russell K. Osgood, *Employee Benefits* 132–37, 389–96, 443–46, 787–832 (West Pub. Co. 1996), reprinted with permission of West, a Thomson Reuters business.

Thanks also to the many individuals who reviewed prior drafts of parts of this book, including the participants at several faculty workshops at Washington University School of Law. In particular, we are grateful for thoughtful reviews and comments received from Merton Bernstein, Cheryl D. Block, Jonathan Barry Forman, John O. Haley, Daniel I. Halperin, Daniel L. Keating, Pauline Kim, John H. Langbein, Shaun P. Martin, Dana M. Muir, Russell K. Osgood, Radha Pathak, Joel S. Seligman, Norman P. Stein, Kent S. Syverud and Robert B. Thompson.

We are also indebted to Thomas E. Clark (Washington University J.D. 2007, LL.M. 2008) of the Wagner Law Group for his advice on updating the book, especially his suggestions concerning ERISA fiduciary law and participant-directed investments.

For research assistance we thank Phillip Clifton of the Washington University School of Law Class of 2021, Jacob Cogdill of the Washington University School of Law Class of 2024, Josue Barron of the Texas A&M School of Law Class of 2023, and Meaganne Lewellyn of the Texas A&M School of Law Class of 2022.

Brendan Maher would like to also thank his sons William and Hank Maher, his wife Lisa Maher, and his mother Tina Maher for their love and support.

Table of Cases

Abatie v. Alta Health & Life Insurance Co., 458 F.3d 955 (9th Cir. 2006) 174n64

Ablamis v. Roper, 937 F.2d 1450 (9th Cir. 1991) 205n52, 270n27

Aetna Health Inc. v. Davila, 542 U.S. 200 (2004) 96, 101n176, 123, 191n149, 207n63, 220n119, 440n53

Ahmed v. Ahmed, 158 Ohio App. 3d 527 N.E.2d 424 (2004) 277n55

Aiken v. Policy Management Systems Corp., 13 F.3d 138 (4th Cir. 1993) 81n91, 84n106

Albertson's Inc. v. Commissioner, 42 F.3d 537 (9th Cir. 1994) 23n84

Albertson's Inc. v. Commissioner, 95 T.C. 415 (1990) 323n24

Alday v. Container Corp. of America, 906 F.2d 660 (11th Cir. 1990) 90n128, 104n182, 105n187

Alessi v. Raybestos-Manhattan, Inc., 451 U.S. 504 (1981) 21n78, 197n13, 199n18, 203n41, 212

Alexander v. Brigham & Women's Physicians Organization, Inc. 513 F.3d 37 (1st Cir. 2008) 53n133

Alexander v. Primerica Holdings, Inc., 967 F.2d 90 (3d Cir. 1992) 88n120

Allen v. GreatBanc Trust Co., 835 F.3d 670 (7th Cir. 2016) 157n170

Allen v. Wells Fargo & Co., 967 F.3d 767 (8th Cir. 2020) 157n170

Allis-Chalmers Corp. v. Lueck, 471 U.S. 202 (1985) 195n8

Amara v. CIGNA Corp., 925 F. Supp. 2d 242 (D. Connecticut 2012) 75n68, 76n69, 79n86, 97n157, 187n136

American Council of Life Insurers v. Ross, 558 F.3d 600 (6th Cir. 2009) 221n127

American Federation of Grain Millers v. International Multifoods Corp., 116 F.3d 976 (2d Cir. 1997) 90n130

American Medical Security, Inc. v. Bartlett, 111 F3d 358 (4th Cir. 1997) 444

Ames v. America National Can Co., 170 F.3d 751 (7th Cir., 1999) 69n39

Amschwand v. Spherion Corp., 505 F.3d 342 (5th Cir. 2007) 187n133, 190n147

Andochick v. Byrd, 709 F.3d 296 (4th Cir. 2013) 279n64

Andre v. Salem Technical Services Corp., 797 F. Supp. 1416 (N.D. Illinois 1992) 166n27

Angst v. Mack Trucks, Inc., 969 F.2d 1530 (3d Cir. 1992) 30n12

Armistead v. Vernitron Corp., 944 F.2d 1287 (6th Cir. 1991) 105n186

Arndt v. Sec. Bank S.S.B. Employees' Pension Plan, 182 F.3d 538 (7th Cir. 1999) 246n78

Arnold v. Arrow Transportation Co. of Delaware, 926 F.2d 782 (9th Cir. 1991) 102n176

Association of Data Processing Services Organizations v. Camp, 397 U.S. 150 (1970) 162n8

Atwood v. Newmont Gold Co., 45 F.3d 1317 (9th Cir. 1995) 81n91

Baetens v. Commissioner, 777 F.2d 1160 (6th Cir. 1985) 403n293

Bakri v. Venture Manufacturing Co., 473 F.3d 677 (6th Cir. 2007) 53n133

Ballone v. Eastman Kodak Co., 109 F.3d 117 (2d Cir. 1997) · 108n201, 109n203

Barker v. America Mobil Power Corp., 64 F.3d 1397 (9th Cir. 1995) 111n215

Barker v. Ceridian Corp., 122 F.3d 628 (8th Cir. 1997) 90n130

Barnes v. Lacy, 927 F.2d 539 (11th Cir. 1991) 107n191

Barnhart v. N.Y. Life Insurance Co., 141 F.3d 1310 (9th Cir. 1998) 42n81

Barrowclough v. Kidder, Peabody & Co., 752 F.2d 923 (3d Cir. 1985) 51n124–126, 66n25

Bartling v. Fruehauf Corp., 29 F.3d 1062 (6th Cir. 1994) 70n45

Beach v. Commonwealth Edison Co., 382 F.2d 656 (7th Cir. 2004) 107n91, 109n203

Beck v. Pace International Union, 427 F.3d 668 (9th Cir. 2005) 137n83–84

Belanger v. Wyman-Gordon Co., 71 F.3d 451 (1st Cir. 1995) 30n12, 37n50

Belka v. Rowe Furniture Co., 571 F. Supp. 1249 (D. Md. 1983) 52n128

Bellas v. CBS, Inc., 221 F.3d 517 (3d Cir. 2000) 246n78

Benbow v. Commissioner, 774 F.2d 740 (7th Cir. 1985) 403n293

Benefit Recovery, Inc. v. Donelon, 521 F.3d 326 (5th Cir. 2008) 221n127

Benenson v. Commissioner, 887 F.3d 511 (1st Cir. 2018) 330n51

Bergt v. Retirement Plan for Pilots Employed by Mark Air, Inc., 293 F.3d 1139 (9th Cir. 2002) 81n91, 82n98, 86n113

Berlin v. Michigan Bell Telephone Co., 858 F.2d 1154 (6th Cir. 1988) 107, 107n191–192, 110, 110n208

Biggers v. Wittek Industries., Inc., 4 F.3d 291 (4th Cir. 1993) 39n64

Bilello v. JPMorgan Chase Retirement Plan, 592 F. Supp. 2d 654 (S.D.N.Y. 2009) 166n26

Bill Gray Enterprises, Inc. Employee Health and Welfare Plan v. Gourley, 248 F.3d 206 (3d Cir. 2001) 444n79

Bins v. Exxon Co. U.S.A., 220 F.3d 1042 (9th Cir. 2000) 107n191

Bixler v. Central Pennsylvania Teamsters Health & Welfare Fund, 12 F.3d 1292 (3d Cir. 1993) 111n212

Table of Cases

Black & Decker Disability Plan v. Nord, 538 U.S. 822 (2003) 170n44

Black v. TIC Investment Corp., 900 F.2d 112 (7th Cir. 1990) 105n186

Blatt v. Marshall & Lassman, 812 F.2d 810 (2d Cir. 1987) 119n10

Blau v. Del Monte Corp., 748 F.2d 1348 (9th Cir. 1984) 35n40

Blaw Knox Retirement Plan v. White Consolidated Industries, 998 F.2d 1185
(3d Cir. 1993) 304n80

Board of Trustees of the CWA/ITU Negotiated Pension Plan v. Weinstein, 107 F.3d
139 (2d Cir. 1997) 68n37, 70n45

Boggs v. Boggs, 520 U.S. 833 (1997) 200n23, 204n44, 205, 205n54, 208, 208n64,
217, 266n7, 270n27, 284, 284n92, 285n95–97

Bogue v. Ampex Corp., 976 F.2d 1319 (9th Cir. 1992) 30–31, 30n16, 31n17, 32n19

Branco v. UFCW-Northern California Employers Joint Pension Plan, 279 F.3d
1154 (9th Cir. 2002) 285n97

Bridges v. America Electric Power Co., 498 F.3d 442 (6th Cir. 2007) 166n26

Brines v. XTRA Corp., 304 F.3d 699 (7th Cir. 2002) 33n30, 34n38

Bristol SL Holdings, Inc. v. Cigna Health & Life Insurance Co., 22 F.4th 1086 (9th
Cir. 2022) 166n29

Browe v. CTC Corp., 15 F.4th 175 (2d Cir. 2021) 52n130, 53n133

Brown v. American Life Holdings, Inc., 190 F.3d 856 (8th Cir. 1999) 68n37, 69n39

Brown v. Ampco-Pittsburgh Corp., 876 F.2d 546 (6th Cir. 1989) 35n40

Brown v. J. B. Hunt Transport Services, Inc., 586 F.3d 1079 (8th Cir. 2009) 70n45

Buce v. Allianz Life Insurance Co., 247 F.3d 1133 (11th Cir. 2001) 84n106

Burke v. Kodak Retirement Income Plan, 336 F.3d 103 (2d Cir. 2003) ...86n114,
87n115

Burke v. Pitney Bowes Inc. Long-Term Disability Plan, 544 F.3d 1016 (9th Cir.
2008) 174n64

Burstein v. Retirement Account Plan for Employees of Allegheny Health Education
& Research Foundation, 334 F.3d 365 (3d Cir. 2003) 74n60, 85n107, 90n126

Burwell v. Hobby Lobby Stores, Inc., 573 U.S. 682 (2014) 450n122, 455,
455n143–145

California Division of of Labor Standards Enforcement v. Dillingham
Construction, N.A., Inc., 519 U.S. 316 (1997) 200n22, 201n31, 202, 203n40,
208n65–66, 210n73

Callery v. U.S. Life Insurance Co. in City of N.Y., 392 F.3d 401 (10th Cir.
2004) ....,.... 187n133

Calogera Abbruscato v. Empire Blue Cross & Blue Shield, 274 F.3d 90 (2d Cir.
2001) 243

Carollo v. Cement & Concrete Workers District Council Pension Plan, 964 F.
Supp. 677 (E.D.N.Y. 1997) 243

Central Laborers' Pension Fund v. Heinz, 541 U.S. 739 (2004) 246

Champion v. Black & Decker (U.S.) Inc., 550 F.3d 353 (4th Cir. 2008) · 171n51

Chao v. Day, 436 F.3d 234 (D.C. Cir. 2006) 32n23, 120n13

Table of Cases

Chao v. Merino, 452 F.3d 174 (2d Cir. 2006) 102n176

Chastain v. AT & T, 558 F.3d 1177 (10th Cir. 2009) 165n20

Chiles v. Ceridian Corp., 95 F.3d 1505 (10th Cir. 1996) 84n106, 88n118

Christopher v. Mobil Oil Co., 950 F.2d 1209 (5th Cir.) 165n20

Cicio v. Does, 321 F.3d 83 (2d Cir. 2003) 123n34

CIGNA Corp. v. Amara, 563 U.S. 421 (2011) 74, 74n61, 75n68, 76n69–70, 78n81,
79n86, 82n96, 87, 87n116–117, 90n126, 92n137, 93n142, 96, 97n157, 112,
187, 187n136, 189n143, 439n49

Citigroup Pension Plan ERISA Litigation, In re, 470 F. Supp. 2d 323 (S.D.N.Y.
2006) 240n61

Citizens to Preserve Overton Park v. Volpe, 401 U.S. 402 (1971) 36n48

Citrus Valley Estates, 49 F.3d 1410 (9th Cir. 1995) 295n28–29, 389n233

Coar v. Kamizir, 990 F.2d 1413 (3d Cir. 1993) 268n20

Coldesina v. Estate of Simper, 407 F.3d 1126 (10th Cir. 2005) 120n13

Cole v. Permanente Medical Group, Inc., 609 F. App'x 445 (9th Cir.
2015) 180n97

Collins v. Ralston Purina Co., 147 F.3d 592 (7th Cir. 1998) 31n17

Commissioner v. Keystone Consolidated Industries, Inc., 508 U.S. 152
(1993) 139n90

Community for Creative Non-Violence v. Reid, 490 U.S. 730 (1989) 42n80

Conkright v. Frommert, 559 U.S. 506 (2010) 135n76, 168, 174n66, 439n47,
440n53

Consolidated Litigation Concerning International Harvester's Disposition of
Wisconsin Steel, In re, 681 F. Supp. 512 (N.D. Illinois 1988) 304n81

Coomer v. Bethesda Hospital, Inc., 370 F.3d 499 (6th Cir. 2004) 180n96

Cooper v. IBM Personal Pension Plan, 457 F.3d 636 (7th Cir. 2006) 240, 240n60

Cowden v. Commissioner, 289 F.2d 20 (5th Cir. 1961) 321n16

Cunningham v. Wawa, Inc., 387 F. Supp. 3d 529 (E.D. Pa. 2019) 77n76

Curcio v. John Hancock Mutual Life Insurance Co., 33 F.3d 226 (3d Cir. 1994)
104n184

Curtiss-Wright Corp. v. Schoonejongen, 514 U.S. 73 (1995) 61n1, 67n33,
121n18, 182n104, 440n54

Cutaiar v. Marshall, 590 F.2d 523 (3d Cir. 1979) 139n90

Cvelbar v. CBI Illinois, Inc., 106 F.3d 1368 (7th Cir. 1997) 31n17, 39n64

D.C. v. Greater Washington. Board of Trade, 506 U.S. 125 (1992) 194n6,
201n28

Davidson v. Canteen Corp., 957 F.2d 1404 (7th Cir. 1992) 250n96

De Buono v. NYSA-ILA Med. & Clinical Services Fund, 520 U.S. 806
(1997) 200n22, 204n46, 210n72

De Nobel v. Vitro Corp., 885 F.2d 1180 (4th Cir. 1989) 81n91

Deibler v. United Food and Commercial Workers International Union 23, 973 F.2d
206 (3d Cir. 1992) 35n41

Table of Cases

Delaye v. Agripac, Inc., 39 F.3d 235 (9th Cir. 1994) 31n16

Demer v. IBM Corp. LTD Plan, 835 F.3d 893 (9th Cir. 2016) 192n151

Demery v. Extebank Deferred Compensation Plan (B), 216 F.3d 283 (2d Cir. 2000) 52n130, 322n22

Denmark v. Liberty Life Assurance Co., 566 F.3d 1 (1st Cir. 2009) 173n58, 174n64

Devlin v. Empire Blue Cross & Blue Shield, 274 F.3d 76 (2d Cir.2001) · 85n109

Diak v. Dwyer, Costello & Knox, P.C., 33 F.3d 809 (7th Cir. 1994) ·· 35n44, 37, 37n52

Diehl v. Twin Disc, Inc., 102 F.3d 301 (7th Cir. 1996) 90n129

DiFelice v. U.S. Airways, Inc., 497 F.3d 410 (4th Cir. 2008) 150n136

Dister v. Continental Group, Inc., 859 F.2d 1108 (2d Cir. 1988) 180n97

District of Columbia v. Greater Washington Board of Trade, 506 U.S. 125 (1992) 202

Divane v. Northwestern University, 953 F.3d 980 (7th Cir. 2020) ········ 151n142

Doe v. Travelers Insurance Co., 167 F.3d 53 (1st Cir.1999) ········ 68n37, 70n45

Don E. Williams Co. v. Commissioner, 429 U.S. 569 (1977) ·············· 385n221

Donovan v. Bierwirth, 680 F.2d 263 (2d Cir. 1982) ························ 135–36

Donovan v. Dillingham, 668 F.2d 1196 (11th Cir. 1982) ············· 34, 34n32–34

Doyle v. Liberty Life Assurance Co., 542 F.3d 1352 (11th Cir. 2008) ····· 171n51

Drutis v. Quebecor World (USA) Inc., 459 F. Supp. 2d 580 (E.D. Ky. 2006) 240n61

Drutis v. Rand McNally & Co., 499 F.3d 608 (6th Cir. 2007) ·············· 240n62

Duggan v. Hobbs, 99 F.3d 307 (9th Cir. 1996) ····················· 52n130, 53n133

Dwyer v. Galen Hospital Illinois, Inc., No. 94-C-544, 1996 U.S. Dist. LEXIS 2921 (N.D. Ill. Mar. 11, 1996) 35n41

Eddy v. Colonial Life Insurance Co., 919 F.2d 747 (D.C. Cir. 1990) ····· 110–11

Edes v. Verizon Communications, Inc., 417 F.3d 133 (1st Cir. 2005) ······ 228n4

Edgar v. Avaya, Inc., 503 F.3d 340 (3d Cir. 2007) ·························· 155n160

Edwards v. State Farm Mutual Automobile Insurance Co., 851 F.2d 134 (6th Cir. 1988) 74n60, 81n91

Egelhoff v. Egelhoff, 532 U.S. 141 (2001) ······· 274–77, 275n46–50, 276n51–54, 285n97

Ehlmann v. Kaiser Foundation Health Plan of Tex., 198 F.3d 552 (5th Cir. 2000) 111n215

Eller v. Bolton, 168 Md. App. 96, 895 A.2d 382 (Md. Ct. Spec. App 2006) 285n97

Elmore v. Cone Mills Corp., 23 F.3d 855 (4th Cir. 1994) ···················· 33n30

Emmenegger v. Bull Moose Tube Co., 197 F.3d 929 (8th Cir. 1999) ···· 47n106

ERISA Industry Committee v. City of Seattle, 840 F. App'x 248 (9th Cir. 2021) 459

Estate of Altobelli v. IBM, 77 F.3d 78 (4th Cir. 1996) ······················· 278n58

Estate of Kensinger v. URL Pharma, Inc., 674 F.3d 131 (3d Cir. 2012) ·· 279n64

Table of Cases

Estate of Ritzer v. National Organization of Industrial Trade Unions Insurance Trust Fund Hosp., Med., Surgical Health Benefit, 822 F. Supp. 951 (E.D.N.Y.1993) 86n14

Evans v. Akers, 534 F.3d 65 (1st Cir. 2008) 166n26

Faircloth v. Lundy Packing Co., 91 F.3d 648 (4th Cir. 1996) 68n37, 70n45

Feifer v. Prudential Insurance Co., 306 F.3d 1202 (2d Cir. 2002) 35n38

Felix v. Lucent Technologies, Inc., 387 F.3d 1146 (10th Cir. 2004) 161n8

Fifth Third Bancorp v. Dudenhoeffer, 573 U.S. 409 (2014) ·21n79, 154n55, 155, 155n160–161

Files v. ExxonMobil Pension Plan, 428 F.3d 478 (3d Cir. 2005) 271n33

Firestone Tire & Rubber Co. v. Bruch, 489 U.S. 101 (1989) 32n22, 101n176, 102, 133n65, 164–71, 176, 255n116, 276n52, 439n47

Fischer v. Philadelphia Electric Co., 96 F.3d 1533 (3d Cir. 1996) (Fischer II) 107n191, 108n197–199

Fischer v. Philadelphia Electric Co., 994 F.2d 130 (3d Cir. 1993), (Fischer I) 107n191

FMC Corp. v. Holliday, 498 U.S. 52 (1990) 201n27, 204n43, 219n114, 222n130, 443n72, 445n86

Foltz v. U.S. News & World Rep., Inc., 865 F.2d 364 (D.C. Cir. 1989) ·· 130n60

Fontaine v. Metropolitan Life Insurance Co., 800 F.3d 883 (7th Cir. 2015) 221, 221n126

Fontenot v. NL Industries, Inc., 953 F.2d 960 (5th Cir. 1992) 30, 30n12

Fort Halifax Packing Co. v. Coyne, 482 U.S. 1 (1987) 29–33, 116n1, 201n29, 211–13, 276n51

Fox v. Blue Cross & Blue Shield of Florida Inc., 517 F. App'x 754 (11th Cir. 2013) 70n45

Fox Valley & Vicinity Construction Workers Pension Fund v. Brown, 897 F.2d 275 (7th Cir. 1990) 278n58, 278n62

Franklin v. First Union Corp., 84 F. Supp. 2d 720 (E.D. Va. 2000) 150n136

Frommert v. Conkright, 433 F.3d 254 (2d Cir. 2006) 86n114, 96

Frommert v. Conkright, 738 F.3d 522 (2d Cir. 2013) 250n96

Fry v. Exelon Corp. Cash Balance Pension Plan, 571 F.3d 644 (7th Cir. 2009) 241n63

Fugarino v. Hartford Life & Accident Insurance Co., 969 F.2d 178 (6th Cir. 1992) 28n2

Gable v. Sweetheart Cup Co., 35 F.3d 851 (4th Cir. 1994) ·····90n128, 104n182

Gables Insurance Recovery, Inc. v. Blue Cross & Blue Shield of Florida, Inc., 813 F.3d 1333 (11th Cir. 2015) 167n29

Gabriel v. Alaska Electrical Pension Fund, 773 F.3d 945 (9th Cir. 2014) ······85n109, 86n113

Gallione v. Flaherty, 70 F.3d 724 (2d Cir. 1995) 52n130

Gavalik v. Continental Can Co., 812 F.2d 834 (3d Cir. 1987) 181

Table of Cases

xvii

Gearlds v. Entergy Services, Inc., 709 F.3d 448 (5th Cir. 2013) ⋯79n85, 187n133, 190n147

Gilbert v. Burlington Industrial, Inc., 765 F.2d 320 (2d Cir. 1985) ⋯⋯⋯⋯ 30n9

Gilbertson v. Allied Signal, Inc., 328 F.3d 625 (10th Cir. 2003) ⋯⋯⋯⋯⋯ 169n43

Gilmore v. Silgan Plastics Corp., 917 F. Supp. 686 (E.D. Mo. 1996) ⋯⋯⋯ 37n52

Gimeno v. NCHMD, Inc., 38 F.4th 910 (11th Cir. 2022) ⋯⋯⋯⋯⋯⋯⋯⋯79n85

Gobeille v. Liberty Mutual Insurance Co., 577 U.S. 312 (2016) ⋯⋯ 206, 206n58, 207n59, 216n99, 457n156, 458, 458n165–167, 459

Godwin v. Sun Life Assurance Co. of Canada, 980 F.2d 323, 328 (5th Cir. 1992) ⋯⋯⋯⋯⋯⋯⋯⋯⋯⋯⋯⋯⋯⋯⋯⋯⋯⋯⋯⋯⋯⋯⋯⋯⋯⋯⋯⋯⋯⋯⋯⋯⋯⋯ 84n106

Golden Gate Resaurant Ass'n v. City & County of San Francisco, 546 F.3d 639 (9th Cir. 2008) ⋯⋯⋯⋯⋯⋯⋯⋯⋯⋯⋯⋯⋯⋯⋯⋯⋯⋯⋯⋯⋯⋯⋯⋯⋯⋯⋯⋯ 446–47, 459

Govoni v. Bricklayers, Masons & Plasterers International Union, Local 5 Pension Fund, 732 F.2d 250 (1st Cir. 1984) ⋯⋯⋯⋯⋯⋯⋯⋯⋯⋯ 84n104, 84n106

Graden v. Conexant Systems Inc., 496 F.3d 291 (3d Cir. 2007) ⋯⋯⋯⋯⋯ 166n26

Greany v. Western Farm Bureau Life Insurance Co., 973 F.2d 812 (9th Cir. 1992) ⋯⋯⋯⋯⋯⋯⋯⋯⋯⋯⋯⋯⋯⋯⋯⋯⋯⋯⋯⋯⋯⋯⋯⋯⋯⋯⋯⋯⋯⋯⋯⋯⋯ 106n188

Great–West Life & Annuity Insurance Co. v. Knudson, 534 U.S. 204 (2002) 94n144–145, 167n31, 185, 191n149, 439n50, 440n52

Greenberg v. H & H Music Co., 506 U.S. 981 (1992) ⋯⋯⋯⋯⋯⋯⋯⋯ 180n96

Grindstaff v. Green, 133 F.3d 416 (6th Cir. 1998) ⋯⋯⋯⋯⋯⋯⋯⋯⋯⋯ 123n31

Guidry v. Sheet Metal Workers National Pension Fund, 493 U.S. 365 (1990) · 266n8, 267, 267n15

Haberern v. Kaupp Vascular Surgeons Ltd. Defined Benefit Pension Plan & Trust Agreement, 24 F.3d 1491 (3d Cir. 1994) ⋯⋯⋯⋯⋯⋯⋯⋯⋯⋯⋯⋯ 180n96

Hagel v. United Land Co., 759 F. Supp. 1199 (E.D. Va. 1991) ⋯⋯⋯⋯⋯ 46n105

Hagwood v. Newton, 282 F.3d 285 (4th Cir. 2002) ⋯⋯⋯⋯⋯⋯⋯⋯⋯⋯ 281n78

Hamilton v. Allen-Bradley Co., 244 F.3d 819 (11th Cir. 2001) ·111n212, 119n10

Hancock v. Metropolitan Life Insurance Co., 590 F.3d 1141 (10th Cir. 2009) 218n111, 219n117, 221n127

Hansen v. Continental Insurance Co., 940 F.2d 971 (5th Cir. 1991) 80n90, 81n91

Harris Trust & Savings Bank v. Salomon Smith Barney, Inc., 530 U.S. 238 (2000) ⋯⋯⋯⋯⋯⋯⋯⋯⋯⋯⋯⋯⋯⋯⋯⋯⋯⋯⋯⋯⋯⋯⋯⋯⋯⋯⋯⋯ 179, 179n92

Harzewski v. Guidant Corp., 489 F.3d 799 (7th Cir. 2007) ⋯⋯⋯⋯⋯⋯ 99n168

Hawkins v. Commissioner, 86 F.3d 982 (10th Cir. 1996) ⋯⋯⋯⋯ 270n28, 270n30

Heady v. Dawn Food Products, Inc., 2003 U.S. Dist. LEXIS 21634 (W.D. Ky. Nov. 25, 2003) ⋯⋯⋯⋯⋯⋯⋯⋯⋯⋯⋯⋯⋯⋯⋯⋯⋯⋯⋯⋯⋯⋯⋯⋯⋯⋯⋯⋯ 99n168

Heath v. Varity Corp., 71 F.3d 256 (7th Cir. 1995) ⋯⋯⋯⋯⋯⋯⋯⋯⋯182n103

Hecker v. Deere & Co., 556 F.3d 575 (7th Cir. 2009) ⋯⋯⋯⋯⋯⋯⋯⋯149n134

Heidgerd v. Olin Corp., 906 F.2d 903 (2d Cir. 1990) ⋯⋯⋯⋯⋯⋯ 71n49, 81n91

Heimeshoff v. Hartford Life & Accident Insurance Co., 571 U.S. 99 (2013) 20n72, 175n69

Henglein v. Informal Plan for Plant Shutdown Benefits for Salaried Employees, 974 F.2d 391 (3d Cir. 1992) 34n38, 35n42, 37
Hepple v. Roberts & Dybdahl, Inc., 622 F.2d 962 (8th Cir. 1980) 254n113
Herberger v. Shanbaum, 897 F.2d 801 (5th Cir. 1990) 268n20
Herman v. S.C. National Bank, 140 F.3d 1413 (11th Cir. 1998) 178n88
Hill v. AT&T Corp., 125 F.3d 646 (8th Cir. 1997) 278n58
Hirt v. Equitable Retirement Plan for Employees, Managers and Agents, 441 F. Supp. 2d 516 (S.D.N.Y. 2006) 240n61
Hirt v. Equitable Retirement Plan for Employees, Managers and Agents, 533 F.3d 102 (2d Cir. 2008) 240n62
Hockett v. Sun Co., 109 F.3d 1515 (10th Cir. 1997) 107n191
Hogan v. Raytheon Co., 302 F.3d 854 (8th Cir. 2002) 272n33
Holland v. Burlington Industrial, Inc., 772 F.2d 1140 (4th Cir. 1985) 30n9
Hopkins v. AT&T Global Information Solutions. Co., 105 F.3d 153 (4th Cir. 1997) 271n33
Horvath v. Keystone Health Plan East, Inc., 333 F.3d 450 (3d Cir. 2003) 111n215
Howard Jarvis Taxpayers Ass'n v. California Secure Choice Retirement Savings Program, 443 F. Supp.3d 1152 (E.D. Cal. 2020) 234n29
Hozier v. Midwest Fasteners, Inc., 908 F.2d 1155 (3d Cir. 1990) 20n73
Hughes Aircraft Co. v. Jacobson, 525 U.S. 432 (1999) 121n18, 248n90
Hughes Salaried Retirees Action Committee v. Administrator of Hughes Non-Bargaining Retirement Plan, 72 F.3d 686 (9th Cir. 1995) 68n37, 69n40
Hughes v. 3M Retiree Medical Plan, 281 F.3d 786 (8th Cir. 2002) 68n37, 69n40
Hughes v. Northwestern University, 142 S. Ct. 737 (2022) 150, 150n137, 151n142
Hummell v. S.E. Rykoff & Co., 634 F.2d 446 (9th Cir. 1980) 254n114, 255n115
Hurlic v. Southern California Gas Co., 539 F.3d 1024 (9th Cir. 2008) ... 240n62
Hurwitz v. Sher, 982 F.2d 778 (2d Cir. 1992) 283n87
Ince v. Aetna Health Management, Inc., 173 F.3d 672 (8th Cir. 1999) ..111n216
Ingersoll-Rand Co. v. McClendon, 498 U.S. 133 (1990) 177n79, 196n10, 204n45, 204n47, 207n60–63, 208
Inter-Modal Rail Employees Association v. Atchison, Topeka and Santa Fe Railway Co., 520 U.S. 510 (1991) 181–82, 255n118, 256n120
IT Corp. v. General America Life Insurance Co., 107 F.3d 1415 (9th Cir. 1997) 32n23, 120n13
James v. National Business Systems, Inc., 924 F.2d 718 (7th Cir. 1991) 33n30
Jammal v. American Family Insurance Co., 914 F.3d 449 (6th Cir. 2019) .42n81
Jander v. Retirement Plans Committee of IBM, 910 F.3d 620 (2d Cir. 2018) 157n170
Jander v. Retirement Plans Committee of IBM, 962 F.3d 85 (2d Cir. 2020) 157n170
Jenkins v. Yager, 444 F.3d 916 (7th Cir. 2006) 147n125
Jensen v. SIPCO, Inc., 38 F.3d 945 (8th Cir. 1994) 88n118
Jerome Mirza & Associates v. United States, 882 F.2d 229 (7th Cir. 1989) 295, 389n233
Jervis v. Elerding, 504 F. Supp. 606 (C.D. Cal. 1980) 39n65

Table of Cases

John Hancock Mutual Life Insurance Co. v. Harris Trust & Savings Bank, 510 U.S. 86 (1993) 15n51, 104n184, 218n111

Jordan v. Federal Express Corp., 116 F.3d 1005 (3d Cir.1997) 69n38

J.P. Morgan Chase Cash Balance Litigation, In re, 460 F. Supp. 2d 479 (S.D.N.Y. 2006) 240n61

Kane v. Aetna Life Insurance Co., 893 F.2d 1283 (11th Cir. 1990), 192Kelly v. Honeywell International, Inc., 933 F.3d 173 (2d Cir. 2019) 106n188

Kemmerer v. ICI Americas, Inc., 70 F.3d 281 (3d Cir.1995) 51n126, 52n127

Kemp v. International Business Machines Corp., 109 F.3d 708 (11th Cir. 1997)48n112

Kennedy v. Plan Administrator for DuPont Savings and Investment Plan, 555 U.S. 285 (2009) 217, 277n56, 278

Kenney v. Roland Parson Contracting Corp., 28 F.3d 1254 (D.C. Cir. 1994) · 34n32

Kenseth v. Dean Health Plan, Inc., 722 F.3d 869 (7th Cir. 2013) 79n85, 190n147

Kentucky Association of Health Plans, Inc. v. Miller, 538 U.S. 329 (2003) 220, 221n128

King v. Blue Cross and Blue Shield of Illinois, 871 F.3d 730 (9th Cir. 2017) ·91n131, 95

King v. Burwell, 576 U.S. 473 (2015) 447n107, 449n115

Kinstler v. First Reliance Standard Life Insurance Co., 181 F.3d 243 (2d Cir. 2000) 169n43

Koehler v. Aetna Health, Inc., 683 F.3d 182 (5th Cir. 2012) 96, 101n176

Kolentus v. Avco Corp., 798 F.2d 949 (7th Cir. 1986) 81n91

Krishna v. Colgate Palmolive Co., 7 F.3d 11 (2d Cir. 1993) 278n58

Krohn v. Huron Memorial Hospital, 173 F.3d 542 (6th Cir. 1999) 102n176, 111n212

Kulinski v. Medtronic Bio-Medicus, Inc., 21 F.3d 254 (8th Cir. 1994) 31n18

Kuntz v. Reese, 785 F.2d 1410 (9th Cir. 1986) 164

Kurz v. Philadelphia Electrical Co., 96 F.3d 1544 (3d Cir.1996) 85n109

Laborers' Pension Fund v. Miscevic, 880 F.3d 927 (7th Cir. 2018) 276n55

Lackey v. Whitehall Corp., 704 F. Supp. 201 (D. Kan. 1988) 39n65

Land v. CIGNA Healthcare of Florida, 381 F.3d 1274 (11th Cir. 2004) ·· 123n34

Landwehr v. DuPree, 72 F.3d 726 (9th Cir. 1995) 178n88

Lanfear v. Home Depot, Inc., 536 F.3d 1217 (11th Cir. 2008) 166n26

Langbecker v. Electronic Data Systems Corp., 476 F.3d 299 (5th Cir. 2007) 149n134, 150n136

Langston v. Wilson McShane Corp., 828 N.W.2d 109 (Minn. 2013) 271n33

Larsen v. American Medical Security, Inc., 524 U.S. 936 (1998) 445n89

LaRue v. DeWolff, Boberg & Associates, 450 F.3d 570 (4th Cir. 2006) 188

LaRue v. DeWolff, Boberg & Associates, 552 U.S. 248 (2008) ·· 166n26, 175n67, 184n114

Laurent v. PriceWaterhouseCoopers LLP, 448 F. Supp. 2d 537 (S.D.N.Y. 2006) 240n61

Table of Cases

Laurent v. PriceWaterhouseCoopers LLP, 794 F.3d 272 (2d Cir. 2015) ·· 241n63

Laurent v. PricewaterhouseCoopers LLP, 945 F.3d 739 (2d Cir. 2019) ····· 78n80

Law v. Ernst & Young, 956 F.2d 364 (1st Cir. 1992) ························· 106n188

LeBlanc v. Cahill, 153 F.3d 134 (4th Cir. 1998) ························· 178n88

Lee v. Union Electric Co., 789 F.2d 1303 (8th Cir. 1986) ················· 84n106

Lehman Bros. Inc., In re, 2020 WL 3264058 (Bankr. S.D.N.Y. June 15, 2020) 320n15

Leuthner v. Blue Cross & Blue Shield Northeastern Pennsylvania, 454 F.3d 120 (3d
Cir. 2006) ···161n8, 165n19

Little Sisters of the Poor Saints Peter and Paul Home v. Pennsylvania,140 S. Ct.
2367 (2020) ··· 456

Lloyd M. Garland, M.D., F.A.C.S., P.A. v. Commissioner, 73 T.C. 5 (1979) 351n99

Lockheed Corp. v. Spink, 517 U.S. 882 (1996) 121n18, 139n90, 182n104, 248n90

Loffredo v. Daimler AG, 500 F. App'x 491 (6th Cir. 2012) ················· 320n15

Lojek v. Thomas, 716 F.2d 675 (9th Cir. 1983) ························· 254n113

Luby v. Teamsters Health, Welfare & Pension Trust Funds, 944 F.2d 1176 (3d Cir.
1991) ·· 170n45

M & G Polymers USA, LLC v. Tackett, 574 U.S. 427 (2015) ··· 49n117, 88n120

Mackey v. Lanier Collection Agency & Services, Inc., 486 U.S. 825 (1988) ·196n10,
200n22, 201n29, 203n40, 204n47, 206n58, 215

Malone v. White Motor Corp., 435 U.S. 497 (1978) ························· 195n8

Maniance v. Commerce Bank, 40 F.3d 264 (8th Cir. 1994) ················· 120n14

Manning v. Hayes, 212 F.3d 866 (5th Cir. 2000) ························· 278n58

Marks v. Watters, 322 F.3d 316 (4th Cir. 2003) ························· 123n30

Martin Fireproofing Profit-Sharing Plan and Trust v. Commissioner, 92 T.C. 1173
(1989) ·· 381n206

Martinez v. Schlumberger, Ltd., 338 F.3d 407 (5th Cir. 2003) 107n191, 109n203,
111n217

Martone v. Robb, 902 F.3d 519 (5th Cir. 2018) ························· 157n170

Maryland Stop Loss Insurance Litigation, In re, No. MIA-370-12195 (Dec. 8,
1995) ··· 444n80

Massachusetts v. Morash, 490 U.S. 107 (1989) ························· 201n29

Massachusetts Mutual Life Insurance Co. v. Russell, 473 U.S. 134 (1985) ···· 73n57,
82n97, 183

Mattias v. Computer Sciences Corp. 34 F. Supp. 2d 120 (D.R.I. 1999) ······98–100,
102

Matz v. Household International Tax Reduction Investment Plan, 774 F.3d 1141
(7th Cir. 2014) ·································· 256n121, 257n123

Mayeaux v. Louisiana Health Service & Indemnity Co., 376 F.3d 420 (5th Cir.
2004) ·· 124n34

Mazzei v. Commissioner, 150 T.C. 138 (2018) ························· 330n51

McAuley v. IBM Corp., 165 F.3d 1038 (6th Cir. 1999) ········ 107n191, 108n198

McBride v. PLM International, Inc., 179 F.3d 737 (9th Cir. 1999) ············· 165

Table of Cases

McCauley v. First Unum Life Insurance Co., 551 F.3d 126 (2d Cir. 2008) · 171n51

McCravy v. Metropolitan Life Insurance Co., 690 F.3d 176 (4th Cir. 2012) · 79n85, 190n147

McGann v. H & H Music Co., 946 F.2d 401 (5th Cir. 1991) 180n96

McGath v. Auto-Body North Shore, Inc., 7 F.3d 665 (7th Cir. 1993) 180n96

McGovern v. Commissioner, T.C. Summary Op. 2003-137 (2003) 401n283

McGowan v. NJR Service Corp., 423 F.3d 241 (3d Cir. 2005) ·· 79n85, 190n147

McKinsey v. Sentry Insurance, 986 F.2d 401(10th Cir. 1993) 47n106

McKnight v. Southern Life & Health Insurance Co., 758 F.2d 1566 (11th Cir. 1985) 72n52, 80n90

McMillan v. Parrott, 913 F.2d 310 (6th Cir. 1990) 278n58

Meguerditchian v. Aetna Life Insurance Co., 999 F. Supp. 2d 1180 (C.D. Cal. 2014) 96n151

Mello v. Sara Lee Corp., 431 F.3d 440 (5th Cir. 2005) 85n107

Mers v. Marriott International Group Accidental Death & Dismemberment Plan, 144 F.3d 1014 (7th Cir. 1998) 172n56

Mertens v. Hewitt Associates, 508 U.S. 248 (1993) 20n73, 21n78, 94, 94n144–145, 178, 184, 186–87, 191n149, 192, 439n49

Metlife Life & Annuity Co. of Connecticut v. Akpele, 886 F.3d 998 (11th Cir. 2018) 279n64

Metropolitan Life Insurance Co. v. Glenn, 554 U.S. 105 (2008) 101n174, 135n76, 171–74, 192, 439n47

Metropolitan Life Insurance Co. v. Hanslip, 939 F.2d 904 (10th Cir. 1991) · 278n58

Metropolitan Life Insurance Co. v. Massachusetts, 471 U.S. 724 (1985) 443n69

Metropolitan Life Insurance Co. v. Wheaton, 42 F.3d 1080 (7th Cir. 1994)   270n30

Michaelis v. Deluxe Financial Services, Inc., 446 F. Supp. 2d 1227 (D. Kan. 2006) 188n138

Miller v. Rite Aid Corp., 334 F.3d 335 (3d Cir. 2003) 161n8

Millsap v. McDonnell Douglas Corp., 368 F.3d 1246 (10th Cir. 2004) ·· 188n137

Moench v. Robertson, 62 F.3d 553 (3d Cir. 1995) 154–57

Mondry v. American Family Mutual Insurance Co., 557 F.3d 781 (7th Cir. 2009) 69n38

Montanile v. Board of Trustees of the National Elevator Industrial Health Benefit Plan, 136 S. Ct. 651 (2016) 94n145, 186, 186n132, 190n148, 439n50

Moore v. Metropolitan Life Insurance Co., 856 F.2d 488 (2d Cir. 1988) 104n182, 105n187

Morse v. Stanley, 732 F.2d 1139 (2d Cir. 1984) 130n59

Motor Vehicle Manufacturers Association v. State Farm Mutual Automobile Insurance Co., 463 U.S. 29 (1983) 173n62

Moyle v. Liberty Mutual Retirement Benefit Plan, 823 F.3d 948 (9th Cir. 2016) 79n86

Mullins v. Pfizer, Inc., 23 F.3d 663 (2d Cir. 1994) 107n191

Table of Cases

Murphy v. Inexco Oil Co., 611 F.2d 570 (5th Cir. 1980) 46n105

Murphy v. Verizon Communications, Inc., 587 F. App'x 140 (5th Cir. 2014) · 68n37

Muse v. IBM Corp., 103 F.3d 490 (6th Cir. 1996) 107n191, 108n196

Mushalla v. Teamsters Local No. 863 Pension Fund, 300 F.3d 391 (3d Cir. 2002) 108n198

Musmeci v. Schwegmann Giant Super Markets., Inc., 332 F.3d 339 (5th Cir. 2003) 45n100

N.Y. State Conference of Blue Cross & Blue Shield Plans v. Travelers Insurance Co., 514 U.S. 645 (1995) 194n5, 199n18, 200n22, 203n38, 205n48, 206n58, 208n65, 209, 210n72, 214n93

Nachman Corp. v. PBGC, 446 U.S. 359 (1980) 300n60, 315n1

Nachwalter v. Christie 805 F.2d 956 (11th Cir. 1986) 104, 105n186–187, 106n188

Nationwide Mutual Insurance Co. v. Darden, 503 U.S. 318 (1992) ···· 41, 42n85

Nedrow v. McFarlane & Hays Co. Profit Sharing Plan & Trust, 476 F. Supp. 934 (E.D. Mich. 1979) 254n114

Nemeth v. Clark Equipment Co., 677 F. Supp. 899 (W.D. Mich. 1987) 256n119

New Orleans Electrical Pension Fund v. Newman, 784 F. Supp. 1233 (E.D. La. 1992) 277n55

New Valley Corp., Re 89 F.3d 143 (3d Cir. 1996) 52n130

NLRB v. United Insurance Co. of America, 390 U.S. 254 (1968) 42n81

Nolan v. Detroit Edison Co., 991 F.3d 697 (6th Cir. 2021) 97n157

North Cypress Medical Center Operating Co. v. Cigna Healthcare, 781 F.3d 182 (5th Cir. 2015) 221n129

Odom v. Microsoft Corp., 486 F.3d 541 (9th Cir. 2007) 166n29

O'Halloren v. Marine Cooks & Stewards Union, 730 P.2d 616 (Or. App. 1986) 39n65

Osberg v. Foot Locker, Inc., 862 F.3d 198 (2d Cir. 2017) 76n76, 97n157, 97n159

Palmisano v. Allina Health Systems, 190 F.3d 881 (8th Cir. 1999) 84n106

Pane v. RCA Corp., 667 F. Supp. 168, 170–71 (D.N.J. 1998) 31n18

Patterson v. Shumate, 504 U.S. 753 (1992) 267n16

Patton v. Denver Post Corp., 326 F.3d 1148 (10th Cir. 2003) 271n33

Paul v. Detroit Edison Co. & Michigan Consolidated Gas Co. Pension Plan, 642 F. App'x 588 (6th Cir. 2016) 85n109

PBGC v. Ouimet Corp., 630 F.2d 4, 12 (1st Cir. 1980) 304n79

PBGC v. White Consolidated Industries, 998 F.2d 1192 (3d Cir. 1993) ·· 304n80

Pearce v. Chrysler Group LLC Pension Plan, 893 F.3d 339 (6th Cir. 2018) 77n77, 77n80, 85n112, 187n136

Pegram v. Herdrich, 530 U.S. 211 (2000) 122–23, 207n61

Pennsylvania (Commonwealth of) v. Nelson, 350 U.S. 497 (1956) 197n12

Perlman v. Swiss Bank Corp. Comprehensive Disability Protection Plan, 195 F.3d 975 (7th Cir. 1999) 173n56

Peterson v. America Life & Health Insurance Co., 48 F.3d 404 (9th Cir. 1995) 43n87

Table of Cases

Pettaway v. Teachers Insurance & Annuity Association of America, 644 F.3d 427 (D.C. Cir. 2011) ·· 71n49

Phillips v. Brandess Home Builders, Inc., 1995 U.S. Dist. LEXIS 14496 (N.D. Ill. Oct. 2, 1995) ·· 34n38

Pierce v. Security Trust Life Insurance Co., 979 F.2d 23 (4th Cir. 1992) ·· 81n91

Pierre v. Connecticut General Life Insurance Co., 502 U.S. 973 (1991) · 169n43

Pilot Life Insurance Co. v. Dedeaux, 481 U.S. 41 (1987) 73n57, 82n97, 177n79, 183n112, 191n150, 201n26, 204n45, 207n60, 220n119, 276n52, 439n46, 440n53

Pinto v. Reliance Standard Life Insurance Co., 214 F.3d 377 (3d Cir. 2000) 174n65

Pisciotta v. Teledyne Industries, Inc., 91 F.3d 1326 (9th Cir. 1996) ······· 85n107

PM Group Life Insurance Co. v. W. Growers Assurance Trust, 953 F.2d 543 (9th Cir. 1992) ·· 217n105

Pocchia v. NYNEX Corp., 81 F.3d 275 (2d Cir. 1996) ····················· 111n217

Pritzker v. Merrill Lynch, Pierce, Fenner & Smith, Inc., 7 F.3d 1110 (3d Cir. 1993) ··· 51n124, 66n21, 66n25

Provident Life & Accident Insurance Co. v. Sharpless, 364 F.3d 634 (5th Cir. 2004) 221n129

Public Employees Retirement System v. Betts, 492 U.S. 158 (1989) ······· 241n64

Rathbun v. Qwest Communications International, Inc., 458 F. Supp. 2d 1238 (D. Colo. 2006) ··· 45n100

Raymond B. Yates, M.D., P.C. Profit Sharing Plan v. Hendon, 541 U.S. 1 (2004) 24n90, 28n2, 41, 42n85, 53n132

Raymond v. Mobil Oil Co., 983 F.2d 1528 (10th Cir. 1993) ··············· 165n20

Raytech Corp. v. PBGC, 241 B.R. 790 ···························· 304n80

Register v. PNC Financial Services Group, Inc., 477 F.3d 56 (3d Cir. 2007) ··· 240n62

Reich v. Compton, 57 F.3d 270 (3d Cir. 1995) ···························· 178n87

Reich v. Continental Casualty Co., 33 F.3d 754 (7th Cir. 1994) ·········· 178n87

Reich v. Rowe, 20 F.3d 25 (1st Cir. 1994) ································ 178n87

Reich v. Stangl, 73 F.3d 1027 (10th Cir. 1996) ·························· 178n87

Retail Industry Leaders Association v. Fielder, 475 F.3d 180 (4th Cir. 2007) 446–47

Rhoades, McKee & Boer v. United States, 43 F.3d 1071 (6th Cir. 1995) ······ 294n24, 295n28–29

Rhorer v. Raytheon Engineers & Constructors, Inc., 181 F.3d 634, 642 (5th Cir. 1999) ·· 96n153

Rice v. Santa Fe Elevator Corp., 331 U.S. 218 (1947) ······················ 197n12

Richards v. Fleet Boston Financial Corp., 427 F. Supp. 2d 150 (D. Conn. 2006) ·· 240n61

Ritter v. Hughes Aircraft Co., 58 F.3d 454 (9th Cir. 1995) ················· 180n97

Rivers v. Central & S.W. Corp., 186 F.3d 681 (5th Cir. 1999) ·············· 271n33

Rose v. Long Island Railroad Pension Plan, 828 F.2d 910 (2d Cir. 1987) ·· 12n34

Rud v. Liberty Life Assurance Co., 438 F.3d 772 (7th Cir. 2006) 173n56
Rush Prudential HMO, Inc. v. Moran, 536 U.S. 355 (2002) ... 207n62, 219n116, 442n66, 457n157
Rutledge v. Pharmaceutical Care Management Association, 141 S. Ct. 474 (2020) 200n22, 214n95, 216n100
Ruttenberg v. U.S. Life Insurance Co., 413 F.3d 652 (7th Cir. 2005) 42–43
Sakol v. Commissioner, 574 F.2d 694 (2d Cir. 1978) 318n10
Saladino v. I.L.G.W.U. National Retirement Fund, 754 F.2d 473 (2d Cir. 1985) 164
Samaroo v. Samaroo, 193 F.3d 185 (3d Cir. 1999) 271n33
Sandy v. Reliance Standard Life Insurance Co., 222 F.3d 1202 (9th Cir. 2000) 169n43
Saporito v. Combustion Engineering Inc., 843 F.2d 666 (3d Cir. 1988) 162n8
Schmidt v. Sheet Metal Workers' National Pension Fund, 128 F.3d 541 (7th Cir. 1997) 104n184, 126n43
Schonholz v. Long Island Jewish Medical Trust, 87 F.3d 72 (2d Cir. 1996) 31n17
Scott v. Gulf Oil Co., 754 F.2d 1499 (9th Cir. 1985) 34n38
Securities & Exchange Commission v. Capital Gains Bureau, 375 U.S. 180 (1963) 78n80, 83n101
Securities & Exchange Commission v. Variable Annuity Life Insurance Co. of America, 359 U.S. 65 (1959) 442n68
Senkier v. Hartford Life & Accident Insurance Co., 948 F.2d 1050 (7th Cir. 1991) 81n91
Sereboff v. Mid Atlantic Medical Services, Inc., 547 U.S. 356 (2006) ··94n145, 186, 439n50
Sgro v. Danone Waters of North America, Inc., 532 F.3d 940 (9th Cir. 2008) 221n129
Shaw v. Delta Air Lines, Inc., 463 U.S. 85 (1983) 199n17, 200n21, 201n30, 203n39, 204n43, 210n73
Shea v. Esensten, 107 F.3d 625 (8th Cir. 1997) 111
Sikora v. UPMC, 876 F.3d 110 (3d Cir. 2017) 53n133
Silkwood v. Kerr-McGee Corp., 464 U.S. 238 (1984) 220n118
Silva v. Metropolitan Life Insurance Co., 762 F.3d 711 (8th Cir. 2014) 79n85
Simas v. Quaker Fabric Corp. of Fall River, 6 F.3d 849 (1st Cir. 1993) 32n19
Simon v. Value Behavioral Health, Inc., 208 F.3d 1073 (9th Cir. 2000) .. 166n29
Simpson v. Ernst & Young, 100 F.3d 436 (6th Cir. 1996) 44n91
Simpson v. Ernst & Young, 850 F. Supp. 648 (S.D. Ohio 1994) 44n93
Skinner v. Northrop Grumman Retirement Plan B, 673 F.3d 1162 (9th Cir. 2012) 78n80, 79n85, 187n136
Slice v. Sons of Norway, 34 F.3d 630 (8th Cir. 1994) 106n188
Spanos v. Continental Publishing Services, Inc., 1994 U.S. Dist. LEXIS 6695 (N.D. Cal. May 17, 1994) 36n45
Spink v. Lockheed Corp., 125 F.3d 1257 (9th Cir. 1997) 86n113, 107n188

Table of Cases

Sprague v. General Motors Corp., 133 F.3d 388 (6th Cir. 1998)   88n118, 90n127

Standard Insurance Co. v. Morrison, 537 F.Supp.2d 1142 (D. Mont. 2008) 221n125, 221n127

Standard Oil Co. v. Agsalud, 633 F.2d 760 (9th Cir. 1980) 212n86

Stearns v. NCR Corp., 97 F. Supp. 2d 954 (D. Minn. 2000) 90n129

Stewart v. Thorpe Holding Co. Profit Sharing Plan, 207 F.3d 1143 (9th Cir. 2000) 270n30

Strzelecki v. Schwarz Paper Co., 824 F. Supp. 821 (N.D. Ill. 1993) 35n38, 39n64

Sullivan v. LTV Aerospace & Defense Co., 82 F.3d 1251 (2d Cir. 1996)   171n51

Sullivan-Mestecky v. Verizon Communications Inc., 961 F.3d 91 (2d Cir. 2020) 79n85

Summers v. State Street Bank & Trust Co., 104 F.3d 105 (7th Cir. 1997) 131n61

Swinney v. GMC, 46 F.3d 512 (6th Cir. 1995) 165n19

Thole v. U.S. Bank N.A., 140 S. Ct. 1615 (2020) 162n9

Tibble v. Edison International, 575 U.S. 523 (2015) 150–51, 152n147

Tibble v. Edison International, 729 F.3d 1110 (9th Cir. 2013) 151n143

Tolbert v. RBC Capital Markets Corp., 758 F.3d 619 (5th Cir. 2014) 47n106

Tomlinson v. El Paso Corp., 653 F.3d 1281 (10th Cir. 2011) 240n62

Trustees of the Directors Guild of America—Producer Pension Benefits Plans v. Tise, 234 F.3d 415 (9th Cir. 2000) 272n33

Tull v. United States, 481 U.S. 412 (1987) 188n138

Unisys Corp. Retiree Medical Benefit "ERISA" Litigation, In re, 58 F.3d 896 (3d Cir. 1995) 88n118, 90, 90n129, 92n133, 104n184

Unisys Savings Plan Litigation, In re, 74 F.3d 420 (3d Cir. 1996) 149n134

United Paperworkers International Union, Local 1468 v. Imperial Home Decor Group., 76 F. Supp. 2d 179 (D.R.I. 1999) 32n19

United States v. Ricciardi, 357 F.2d 91 (2d Cir. 1966) 28n2

UNUM Life Insurance Co. of America v. Ward, 526 U.S. 358 (1999) 208n63, 219n116, 220n119–120

US Airways, Inc. v. McCutcheon, 569 U.S. 88 (2013) .. 94n145, 439n50, 444n79

US Airways, Inc. v. McCutcheon, 663 F.3d 671 (3d. Cir. 2011) 444n79

Vallone v. CNA Financial Corp., 375 F.3d 623 (7th Cir. 2004) . 85n107, 88n118

Varity Corp. v. Howe, 516 U.S. 489 (1996) 20n75, 69n42, 83n102, 103n179, 107n189, 110n207, 122n24, 129n57, 130n59, 184n115, 191n149, 440n51

Vartanian v. Monsanto Co., 131 F.3d 264 (1st Cir. 1997) 107n191

Vartanian v. Monsanto Co., 14 F.3d 697 (1st Cir. 1994) 162n8, 164n18

Vaughn v. Bay Environmental Management Inc., 544 F.3d 1008 (9th Cir. 2008) 166n26

Veilleux v. Atochem North America, Inc., 929 F.2d 74 (2d Cir. 1991) 96n151

Vinson & Elkins v. Commissioner, 7 F.3d 1235 (5th Cir. 1993)., ... 295n27

Virginia ex rel. Cuccinelli v. Sebelius, 2010 WL 1038397 (E.D. Va.) 436n34

Vizcaino v. Microsoft Corp., 120 F.3d 1006 (9th Cir. 1997) 43n88

Wachtell, Lipton, Rosen & Katz v. Commissioner, 26 F.3d 291 (2d Cir.
 1994) 295n25, 295n28–29
Wal–Mart Stores, Inc. v. Dukes, 564 U.S. 338 (2011) 79n86
Wangberger v. Janus Capital Group, Inc., 529 F.3d 207 (4th Cir. 2008) . 166n26
Wayne v. Pacific Bell, 238 F.3d 1048 (9th Cir. 1999) 109n203
Weinreb v. Hospital for Joint Diseases Orthopaedic Inst., 404 F.3d 167 (2d Cir.
 2005) 87n115
Wells v. General Motors Corp., 881 F.2d 166 (5th Cir. 1989) 30n12, 31
White Farm Equipment Co., Re 788 F.2d 1186 (6th Cir. 1986) 88n120
Williams v. Commissioner, 28 T.C. 1000 (1957) 321n16
Williams v. Wright, 927 F.2d 1540 (11th Cir. 1991) 39n64
Wilson v. Safelite Group, Inc., 930 F.3d 429 (6th Cir. 2019) 47n106
Wilson v. Southwestern Bell Telephone Co., 55 F.3d 399 (8th Cir. 1995) 107n191
Wolfe v. J. C. Penney Co., 710 F.2d 388 (7th Cir. 1983) 66n21
Wolk v. UNUM Life Insurance of America, 186 F.3d 352 (3d Cir. 1999) ·· 43n87
Wright v. R. R. Donnelley & Sons Co. Group Benefits Plan, 402 F.3d 67 (1st Cir.
 2005) 173n56
Young v. Washington Gas Light Co., 206 F.3d 1200 (D.C. Cir. 2000) 30n12
Zubik v. Burwell, 578 U.S. 403 (2016) 455, 455n147

Table of Legislation

FEDERAL LAW

United States Code (USC)

1 USC - General Provisions

§ 1 .... 38n54

4 USC - Flag and Seal, Seat of Government, and the States

§ 114 .... 325n35

§ 114(b)(1)(I)(i) 325n35

5 USC - Government Organizations and Employees

§ 701(a)(2) 36n47

11 USC - Bankruptcy

§ 104(a) 306n89

§ 507(a)(4) 306n89

§ 507(a)(5) 306n89

§ 541(c)(2) 267n16

18 USC - Crimes and Criminal Procedure

§ 664 .... 160n3

§ 1027 .... 160n3

§ 1954 .... 160n3

26 USC - Internal Revenue Code 4

§ 21 .... 11f

§ 22 .... 11f

§ 25B 412n320

§ 36B(b)(a)(A)(i) 450n120

§ 36B(c)(2)(B)-(C) 450n123, 451n126

§ 36B(c)(2)(C)(i) 451n126, 451n127

§ 36B(c)(2)(C)(i)(II) 451n126, 451n127

26 USC - Internal Revenue Code (cont.)

§ 36B(c)(2)(C)(ii) 451n126, 451n127, 453n134
§ 45E 413n322
§ 45E(e)(4) 413n323
§ 45E(f) 413n324
§ 61 .... 11f
§ 62(a) 450n123
§ 63(b) 450n123
§ 72 .... 10f, 421n349
§ 72(p) 267n14, 402n287
§ 72(p)(1)(A) 402n290
§ 72(p)(2) 267n14
§ 72(p)(2)(B) 402n288
§ 72(t) 24n89, 264n3, 267n14, 402n290
§ 72(t)(1) 399n272, 400n281, 404n295
§ 72(t)(2) 415n328
§ 72(t)(2)(A) 399n273
§ 72(t)(2)(A)(i) 399n272
§ 72(t)(2)(A)(vii) 267n15
§ 72(t)(2)(B) 399n274
§ 72(t)(2)(C) 399n274
§ 72(t)(2)(D)-(G) 401n282
§ 72(t)(2)(H) 399n275
§ 72(t)(2)(I) 400n280
§ 72(t)(2)(J) 236n38
§ 72(t)(2)(K) 400n276
§ 72(t)(2)(L) 400n276
§ 72(t)(2)(M) 400n279
§ 72(t)(2)(N) 399n271
§ 72(t)(3)(B) 399n273
§ 72(t)(4) 399n273
§ 72(t)(7) 401n282
§ 72(t)(8) 401n282
§ 72(t)(10)(B) 238n53
§ 72(t)(11) 400n279
§ 79 .... 6n16, 11f
§ 83 .... 10f, 318n12, 319–23
§ 83(a) 45n98, 52n131, 317n9, 318n10, 320, 357n122
§ 83(a)(1) 318n10
§ 83(c)(1) 318n11
§ 83(c)(2) 317n9
§ 83(e)(2) 22n82, 325n31, 325n35, 357n122

Table of Legislation

§ 83(i) 318n12

§ 101 .... 11f

§ 101(a) 6n16

§ 104(a)(3) 11f

§ 105(a) 11f

§ 105(b) 6n16, 11f

§ 106 .... 11f, 434n26

§ 106(a) 6n16, 450n124

§ 106(d)(1) 11f

§ 125 .... 11f

§ 127 .... 6n17

§ 129 .... 11f

§ 132(a) 6n17

§ 132(f) 6n17

§ 162(a)(1) 386n223

§ 213 .... 11f

§ 213(a) 450n123

§ 213(d) 11f, 450n123

§ 219(a) 328n44

§ 219(b) 328n44, 329n49

§ 219(b)(5) 379n199

§ 219(b)(5)(C) 328n44

§ 219(d)(I) 330n53

§ 219(g) 328n45, 330n51, 413n325, 416n331

§ 223 .... 11f

§ 263 .... 386n223

§ 401 .... 332n60

§ 401-33 .... 4n6

§ 401(a) 10f, 22, 25n99, 54n134, 342n76, 344n81

§ 401(a)(1) 325n31

§ 401(a)(2) 127n50, 163n12, 309n109, 309n111, 315n2, 325n31

§ 401(a)(3) 24n91, 226n4, 337n70, 343n77, 384n214

§ 401(a)(4) 24n91, 226n4, 337n70, 347n89, 358n128, 359

§ 401(a)(5) 226n4, 337n70, 367n151

§ 401(a)(5)(B) 362n137

§ 401(a)(5)(C) 24n91, 368n155

§ 401(a)(5)(D) 371n168

§ 401(a)(5)(G) 10f, 25n99, 54n134, 342n76

§ 401(a)(7) 256n121

§ 401(a)(9) 24n89, 332n63, 391, 391n239, 396n259

§ 401(a)(9)(A) 392n243

§ 401(a)(9)(A)(ii) 392n244

xxx *Table of Legislation*

26 USC - Internal Revenue Code (cont.)

§ 401(a)(9)(B)(ii) 394n251
§ 401(a)(9)(B)(iii) 393n247
§ 401(a)(9)(B)(iv) 393n248
§ 401(a)(9)(C) 392n242
§ 401(a)(9)(D) 393n247
§ 401(a)(9)(E)(ii) 393n247, 394n249
§ 401(a)(9)(E)(iii) 394n249
§ 401(a)(9)(G) 392n244
§ 401(a)(9)(H) 393n246
§ 401(a)(9)(H)(i) 394n250
§ 401(a)(9)(H)(ii) 393n247, 394n250
§ 401(a)(11) 13n43
§ 401(a)(11)(A)(i) 279n65
§ 401(a)(11)(A)(ii) 279n66
§ 401(a)(11)(B) 280n70
§ 401(a)(11)(B)(iii) 280n72
§ 401(a)(11)(D) 280n73
§ 401(a)(13) 13n44, 19n69
§ 401(a)(13)(A) 248n85, 265n6, 266n12, 267n13, 401n285, 402n286
§ 401(a)(13)(B) 13n43, 269n26, 269n27
§ 401(a)(13)(C) 268n21
§ 401(a)(14) 265n4, 265n5
§ 401(a)(16) 380n205
§ 401(a)(16)(A) 379n196
§ 401(a)(16)(D)(ii) 379n199
§ 401(a)(17) 359n132, 381n208
§ 401(a)(19) 251n100
§ 401(a)(20) 422n356
§ 401(a)(23) 1of, 21n79, 45n100, 70n44
§ 401(a)(26) 226n4, 355n115, 356n120
§ 401(a)(26)(G) 1of, 54n134
§ 401(a)(26)(H) 356n118
§ 401(a)(27) 1of
§ 401(a)(28) 1of, 21n79, 45n100
§ 401(a)(29) 297n39, 301n65, 304n83
§ 401(a)(31) 326n36, 405n298
§ 401(a)(31)(B) 406n302
§ 401(a)(31)(B)(ii) 403n292
§ 401(a)(31)(C) 404n294
§ 401(a)(31)(E) 405n298
§ 401(a)(33) 297n38, 297n39, 327n41

Table of Legislation

§ 401(a)(35) 21n79, 127n52, 128n52, 141n96

§ 401(a)(36) 264n1, 398n265

§ 401(a)(39) 399n269

§ 401(b)(1)(C) 344n83

§ 401(b)(2) 344n83

§ 401(b)(6)(B) 344n81, 349n91

§ 401(f) 10f

§ 401(k) 8, 10f, 331n57

§ 401(k)(1) 10f

§ 401(k)(2)(B) 399n268, 415n328

§ 401(k)(2)(B)(i)(VII) 399n270

§ 401(k)(2)(D) 233n25

§ 401(k)(3)(A) 375n182

§ 401(k)(3)(A)(i) 374n178

§ 401(k)(3)(A)(ii) 376n186

§ 401(k)(3)(B) 375n183

§ 401(k)(3)(C) 375n181

§ 401(k)(3)(D) 375n183, 399n268, 415n328

§ 401(k)(3)(D)(ii) 376n184

§ 401(k)(3)(E) 376n186

§ 401(k)(3)(G) 10f

§ 401(k)(8) 377n187

§ 401(k)(8)(B)(ii) 377n187

§ 401(k)(8)(C) 377n187

§ 401(k)(11) 377n188

§ 401(k)(11)(A) 377n188

§ 401(k)(11)(C) 377n188

§ 401(k)(11)(D)(i) 377n188

§ 401(k)(12) 377n188, 410n315

§ 401(k)(12)(A)(i) 378n189

§ 401(k)(12)(D) 378n189

§ 401(k)(12)(E)(i) 399n268

§ 401(k)(12)(F) 378n190

§ 401(k)(13) 378n191, 407n304

§ 401(k)(13)(C)(iii) 378n192

§ 401(k)(13)(D) 378n193

§ 401(k)(13)(D)(iii) 399n268

§ 401(k)(14) 399n268

§ 401(k)(15) 233n25

§ 401(k)(15)(B) 234n26

§ 401(k)(16) 379

§ 401(k)(16)(B) 379n195

xxxii · *Table of Legislation*

26 USC - Internal Revenue Code (cont.)

§ 401(k)(16)(C) ·· 379n196
§ 401(k)(16)(D) ·· 379n198
§ 401(k)(16)(D)(i)(I) ·· 379n197
§ 401(k)(16)(E)(i) ·· 379n197
§ 401(*l*) ··· 24n91, 226n4, 368n155, 369–70
§ 401(*l*)(2) ·· 368n157
§ 401(*l*)(2)(A)(ii) ··· 368n158
§ 401(*l*)(3)(A) ··· 368n157
§ 401(*l*)(4)(A) ·· 368n157, 368n158
§ 401(*l*)(4)(C) ··· 368n156
§ 401(*l*)(5)(A) ··· 368n156
§ 401(*l*)(5)(E) ··· 368n156
§ 401(m) ·· 10f
§ 401(m)(4) ·· 399n268
§ 401(m)(4)(A)(iii) ·· 235n36
§ 401(m)(4)(C) ·· 376n184, 415n328
§ 401(m)(4)(D) ··· 235n36
§ 401(m)(13) ·· 235n36
§ 402A ·································· 10f, 332n60, 374n177, 384n217
§ 402(a) ····················· 22n82, 309n106, 325n35, 357n122, 421n349
§ 402A(a)(1) ·· 332n61, 374n177
§ 402A(a)(2) ··· 374n177
§ 402A(a)(3) ··· 374n177
§ 402A(c)(1) ·· 332n62, 374n177
§ 402A(c)(3) ··· 332n63
§ 402A(c)(3)(A) ·· 332n63
§ 402A(c)(4)(A)(ii) ·· 332n63
§ 402A(c)(4)(E)(i) ·· 332n63
§ 402A(d) ··· 332n61
§ 402A(d)(1) ··· 374n177
§ 402A(d)(5) ··· 332n63
§ 402A(e) ·· 50n120, 236n38, 397n261
§ 402A(e)(1)(A)(i) ·· 236n43
§ 402A(e)(1)(C) ·· 332n60
§ 402A(e)(2)(A)(ii) ··· 236n39
§ 402A(e)(3)(A)(i) ·· 236n39
§ 402A(e)(3)(B)(i) ·· 236n41
§ 402A(e)(4)(A) ·· 236n39
§ 402A(e)(6)(A) ·· 236n40
§ 402A(e)(7)(A) ·· 236n42
§ 402A(e)(7)(B) ·· 236n43

Table of Legislation xxxiii

§ 402A(e)(8)(A) 236n44
§ 402(b) 10f, 45n98, 52n131
§ 402(b)(1) 357n123
§ 402(b)(4)(A) 358n126
§ 402(b)(4)(B) 358n127
§ 402(b)(4)(C) 358n126
§ 402(c) 22n83, 248n87, 264n3, 326n36, 403n293
§ 402(c)(1) 309n106, 394n253, 404n294
§ 402(c)(1)(A) 404n294, 404n296
§ 402(c)(1)(C) 404n296
§ 402(c)(2) 332n63, 404n294
§ 402(c)(4) 394n253
§ 402(c)(4)(A) 403n293
§ 402(c)(6) 404n297
§ 402(c)(8)(B) 393n246
§ 402(c)(11) 394n253, 403n293
§ 402(e)(3) 8n28, 331n57, 331n58, 380n203, 384n214
§ 402(e)(4) 326n37
§ 402(e)(6) 326n36, 405n298
§ 402(f) 405n300, 407n304
§ 402(f)(2)(B) 405n300
§ 402(g)(1) 380n203, 384n214, 387n228
§ 402(g)(1)(C) 384n215
§ 403(a) 332n60
§ 403(a)(1) 325n35, 357n122, 391n239
§ 403(a)(4) 326n36, 404n294
§ 403(a)(4)(A)(iii) 404n296
§ 403(a)(4)(B) 394n253, 404n294, 404n297
§ 403(a)(5) 326n36, 405n298
§ 403(a)(6) 399n270
§ 403(a) 9n29, 10f
§ 403(b) 25n99, 25n100, 394n253
§ 403(b)(1) 331n58
§ 403(b)(7)(A)(i) 399n268
§ 403(b)(7)(A)(i)(VII) 399n270
§ 403(b)(7)(D) 399n268
§ 403(b)(8)(A) 404n294
§ 403(b)(8)(A)(iii) 404n296
§ 403(b)(8)(B) 394n253, 403n293, 404n297, 405n300
§ 403(b)(10) 391n239, 406n302
§ 403(b)(11) 399n268
§ 403(b)(11)(E) 399n270

26 USC - Internal Revenue Code (cont.)

§ 403(b)(12)(A) 235n36
§ 403(b)(12)(D) 234n26
§ 403(b)(15) 233n23
§ 403(b)(16) 379n195
§ 403(b)(17) 399n268
§ 403(b) 9n29, 10f
§ 403(c) 10f, 357n123
§ 404(a)(1) 289n3, 386n222, 386n227
§ 404(a)(1)-(3) 6n15, 22n80, 325n33, 385n220
§ 404(a)(1)(A) 293n15, 386n227, 390n234
§ 404(a)(1)(A)(i) 386n227
§ 404(a)(1)(E) 289n3, 386n225
§ 404(a)(2) 325n31, 332n60, 391n239, 405n298, 406n302
§ 404(a)(2) 9n29, 10f
§ 404(a)(3) 386n227
§ 404(a)(3)(A) 386n226
§ 404(a)(3)(A)(i)(I) 386n227
§ 404(a)(3)(A)(ii) 386n225
§ 404(a)(3)(A)(v) 386n227
§ 404(a)(5) 6n15, 23n84, 323, 357n124, 357n125
§ 404(a)(6) 385n221
§ 404(a)(7) 289n3
§ 404(a)(7)(A) 383n213
§ 404(a)(7)(A)(i) 386n227
§ 404(a)(7)(C)(i) 383n213
§ 404(a)(7)(C)(iii) 383n213
§ 404(a)(7)(C)(iv) 383n213
§ 404(a)(27) 8n27
§ 404(a)(36) 7n24
§ 404(b)(2) 390n238
§ 404(c) 407n304
§ 404(j) 386n226
§ 404(l) 386n226
§ 404(o) 289n3, 293n15, 390n236
§ 404(o)(2)(A) 390n237
§ 404(o)(3) 390n238
§ 408(a)(6) 248n87, 391n239
§ 408(b)(3) 391n239
§ 408(d) 248n87
§ 408(d)(1) 328n46
§ 408(d)(3) 331n55, 403n293

Table of Legislation

§ 408(d)(3)(A) 404n296
§ 408(d)(3)(A)(i) 404n294
§ 408(d)(3)(A)(ii) 404n294
§ 408(d)(3)(C) 394n253
§ 408(d)(3)(D) 404n294
§ 408(e)(1) 328n46, 328n47
§ 408(g) 280n69
§ 408(o) 330n51
§ 408(p)(2)(C)(i) 377n188
§ 408(p)(2)(F) 235n36
§ 408A(a) 328n47
§ 408A(c)(1) 328n47
§ 408A(c)(2) 329n49, 331n54
§ 408A(c)(3) 330n51, 413n325, 416n331
§ 408A(c)(3)(B) 330n52
§ 408A(c)(4) 330n53, 332n63, 391n240
§ 408A(c)(5) 331n55
§ 408A(c)(5)(B) 330n51
§ 408A(c)(6) 403n293
§ 408A(d) 332n61
§ 408A(d)(1) 328n47
§ 408A(d)(2) 330n51
§ 408A(d)(2)(B) 332n61
§ 408A(d)(3) 330n51, 403n293
§ 408A(d)(3)(A) 331n55
§ 408A(d)(3)(B) 331n55
§ 408A(d)(3)(C) 331n56
§ 408A(e) 331n55
§ 409(h) 21n79, 45n100, 70n44
§ 409A 10f, 324–25
§ 409A(a)(1)(A) 324n28
§ 409A(a)(1)(B) 324n29
§ 409A(a)(2)-(4) 324n27
§ 409A(b)(1) 324n28
§ 410 .... 163n14
§ 410(a) 13n41
§ 410(a)(1)(B)(i) 252n104
§ 410(a)(1)(B)(ii) 228n2
§ 410(a)(2) 228n3
§ 410(a)(3) 228n5
§ 410(a)(4) 163n14, 230n11
§ 410(a)(5) 228n6, 229n10

xxxvi   *Table of Legislation*

26 USC - Internal Revenue Code (cont.)

§ 410(a)(5)(B) 229n7
§ 410(a)(5)(C) 229n8
§ 410(a)(5)(D) 229n9
§ 410(a)(5)(D)(iii) 229n9
§ 410(a)(17) 386n226
§ 410(b) 24n91, 226n4, 337n70, 367n151, 368n155, 373
§ 410(b)(1)(B) 343n77
§ 410(b)(2)(ii) 376
§ 410(b)(2)(A)(ii) 346n85
§ 410(b)(2)(B) 346n87
§ 410(b)(2)(C) 346n86
§ 410(b)(2)(D) 354n109
§ 410(b)(3)(A) 353n106
§ 410(b)(3)(C) 353n105
§ 410(b)(4) 353n108
§ 410(b)(4)(A) 230n12
§ 410(b)(5) 352n101, 353n104
§ 410(b)(5)(B) 352n103, 353n104
§ 410(b)(6)(B) 347n89, 355n116
§ 410(b)(6)(E) 374n178
§ 410(b)(6)(F) 343n80
§ 410(c) 10f, 342n76
§ 410(c)(2) 54n134
§ 411 .... 13n42, 25n99, 163n14
§ 411(a) 252n105
§ 411(a)(1) 250n99, 283n90
§ 411(a)(2) 229n9
§ 411(a)(2)(A) 251n101
§ 411(a)(2)(B) 251n102
§ 411(a)(3)(A) 253n111, 273n38
§ 411(a)(3)(A)-(G) 253n110
§ 411(a)(3)(D) 251n100
§ 411(a)(4) 252n107
§ 411(a)(5) 252n106
§ 411(a)(6) 252n106
§ 411(a)(6)(A) 228n6
§ 411(a)(7) 247n83, 279n65
§ 411(a)(7)(A)(i) 237n50
§ 411(a)(7)(A)(ii) 237n49
§ 411(a)(8) 237n50, 238n51
§ 411(a)(10)(A) 252n108

Table of Legislation

§ 411(a)(10)(B) 253n109
§ 411(a)(11) 308n105, 403n292
§ 411(a)(13) 10f, 237n50
§ 411(b) 14n45
§ 411(b)(1)(A) 242n67
§ 411(b)(1)(B) 243n68
§ 411(b)(1)(C) 243n69, 244n73
§ 411(b)(1)(G) 239n57, 241n64
§ 411(b)(1)(H) 239n55
§ 411(b)(1)(H)(ii) 239n56
§ 411(b)(1)(H)(iv) 241n64
§ 411(b)(2) 239n54
§ 411(b)(4)(A) 229n10
§ 411(b)(4)(B) 237n47
§ 411(b)(4)(C) 237n46
§ 411(b)(5) 10f, 239n55, 240n63
§ 411(c) 250n99
§ 411(c)(3) 237n50
§ 411(c)(7) 297n37
§ 411(d)(3) 256n121, 301
§ 411(d)(4) 251n103
§ 411(d)(5) 309n108
§ 411(d)(6) 63n8, 105n186
§ 411(d)(6)(A) 245n75, 245n77, 297n36
§ 411(d)(6)(B) 247n83
§ 411(d)(6)(D) 248n88
§ 411(d)(6)(E) 248n88
§ 411(e) 10f, 54n134, 342n76
§ 411(f) 238n52
§ 412 .... 14n46, 70n43, 289n3, 298n47
§ 412(a) 290n6, 292n11, 293n16
§ 412(a)(2)(A) 390n235
§ 412(a)(2)(B) 290n7, 388n232
§ 412(a)(2)(C) 25n101
§ 412(a)(2)(D) 288n1
§ 412(b) 292n11
§ 412(b)(2) 298n42
§ 412(b)(2)(B)(iii) 294n20
§ 412(c) 296n32, 304n82
§ 412(c)(1) 292n11
§ 412(c)(3) 292n13
§ 412(c)(4) 296n34, 304n87

xxxviii *Table of Legislation*

26 USC - Internal Revenue Code (cont.)

§ 412(c)(4)(B) 296n33
§ 412(c)(5) 292n13
§ 412(c)(5)(A) 291n9
§ 412(c)(5)(B) 296n32
§ 412(c)(6) 296n33
§ 412(c)(7) 293n15, 390n234, 390n238
§ 412(d)(2) 245n77
§ 412(d)(3) 298n42
§ 412(e) 54n134
§ 412(e)(2) 388n232
§ 412(e)(3) 14n50
§ 412(*l*)(1)(B) 304n83
§ 412(*l*)(5)(A) 304n83
§ 413(e) 233n23
§ 414A 235n32, 407n304, 408n310
§ 414A(b)(1) 235n34
§ 414A(b)(2) 235n34
§ 414A(b)(3) 235n33
§ 414A(b)(4) 235n34
§ 414A(c) 235n32
§ 414(a) 249n93
§ 414(b) 226n4, 303n79, 350n95
§ 414(c) 6n18, 226n4, 303n79, 350n95
§ 414(cc) 378n193
§ 414(d) 54n138, 342n76
§ 414(e) 342n76
§ 414(e)(3)(B)(ii) 56n143
§ 414(e)(3)(B)(I) 57n149
§ 414(e)(3)(C) 56n143
§ 414(e)(3)(D) 56n144
§ 414(e)(4) 57n150
§ 414(f) 12n30
§ 414(h)(1) 250n99
§ 414(i) 237n49, 239n58
§ 414(j) 6n19, 10f, 237n50, 239n58
§ 414(*l*) 10f
§ 414(*l*)(2) 310n114
§ 414(m) 226n4, 351n99
§ 414(n) 226n4, 351n100
§ 414(p) 13n43, 26n104
§ 414(p)(1) 270n28

Table of Legislation

§ 414(p)(1)(A)(i) 271n31, 277n56
§ 414(p)(2) 270n29
§ 414(p)(3) 27n32, 271n31
§ 414(p)(4) 272n35
§ 414(p)(5) 273n37
§ 414(p)(7) 27n32
§ 414(p)(8) 270n28
§ 414(p)(11) 271n31
§ 414(q) 53n132, 226n4, 368n155
§ 414(q)(1) 354n111
§ 414(q)(1)(b)(ii) 354n112
§ 414(q)(2) 355n113
§ 414(q)(3) 354n112
§ 414(q)(5) 354n112
§ 414(r) 352n101, 352n102, 353n104
§ 414(r)(2) 352n103
§ 414(r)(8) 352n101
§ 414(s) 362n137
§ 414(v)(2) 384n215
§ 414(v)(2)(A) 384n215
§ 414(v)(2)(B) 384n216
§ 414(v)(2)(E) 384n216
§ 414(v)(3)(A) 384n215
§ 414(v)(7) 384n217
§ 414(w) 235n32
§ 414(y) 288n1
§ 415 411
§ 415(a) 380n205, 381n206
§ 415(b) 380n205
§ 415(b)(5) 389n233
§ 415(c) 381n206, 384n215
§ 415(c)(3) 362n137
§ 415(e) 383n212, 383n213
§ 415(f) 380n205
§ 415(f)(1)(B) 381n206
§ 416(c) 367n154
§ 416(e) 367n154
§ 416(g)(H) 234n26
§ 416(i)(1)(B) 355n113, 392n242
§ 417 .... 13n43
§ 417(a) 281n76, 281n78
§ 417(a)(1)(A) 281n77

26 USC - Internal Revenue Code (cont.)

§ 417(a)(1)(A)(i) 281n79
§ 417(a)(1)(A)(iii) 282n81
§ 417(a)(2) 274n42, 283n85
§ 417(a)(2)(A) 283n84
§ 417(a)(3)(A) 281n79
§ 417(a)(3)(B) 282n82
§ 417(a)(3)(B)(ii) 282n82
§ 417(a)(4) 283n88
§ 417(a)(5) 281n78
§ 417(a)(6) 282n83
§ 417(a)(6)(A) 281n79, 282n81
§ 417(a)(6)(B) 282n83
§ 417(b) 279n65
§ 417(c)(1)(A) 279n68
§ 417(c)(1)(A)(i) 279n67
§ 417(c)(1)(B) 279n67
§ 417(c)(2) 279n68
§ 417(d) 280n73
§ 417(e) 283n90, 308n105, 403n292
§ 417(f)(2) 282n80
§ 417(g) 281n77
§ 420 .... 70n43, 311n118
§ 420(c)(3) 311n118
§ 430 .... 289n3, 298n47
§ 430-32 .... 14n46
§ 430(a) 293n16, 304n83, 390n235
§ 430(a)(1)(B) 290n6, 294n19
§ 430(b) 293n17, 293n18, 390n235
§ 430(c) 304n83
§ 430(c)(1)-(4) 390n235
§ 430(d)(1) 293n17, 304n83, 390n235
§ 430(h)(1) 291n10, 294n22, 295n26
§ 430(h)(2) 294n21
§ 430(h)(3) 294n21
§ 430(i) 296n30, 296n31
§ 430(j) 297n40, 297n41
§ 430(k) 298n43, 304n86
§ 430(*l*) 311n118
§ 431 .... 25n101
§ 432 .... 12n32
§ 432(e)(9) 245n77

§ 433 .... 288n1
§ 436 .... 14n46, 297n39, 298n47
§ 436(a) 304n83
§ 436(b) 301n65, 304n83
§ 446(a) 317n6
§ 446(e) 291n9
§ 451(a) 317n6
§ 457 .... 12n34, 25n100, 323n25
§ 457A 323n25
§ 457(b) 10f, 235n36, 332n60
§ 457(b)(5) 391n239
§ 457(d)(1) 405n298
§ 457(d)(1)(A) 399n268
§ 457(d)(1)(A)(v) 399n270
§ 457(d)(1)(C) 405n298, 406n302
§ 457(d)(2) 391n239
§ 457(d)(4) 399n268
§ 457(e)(10) 403n293
§ 457(e)(16) 403n293
§ 457(e)(16)(A) 404n294
§ 457(e)(16)(A)(iii) 404n296
§ 457(e)(16)(B) 394n253, 404n297, 405n300
§ 457(f) 10f
§ 457(g) 10f
§ 501(a) 22n81, 325n34, 357n121
§ 501(c)(3) 10f
§ 529(a) 332n64
§ 529A(b)(1) 333n65
§ 529A(e)(1)-(3) 333n65
§ 529(c)(1) 332n64
§ 529(c)(3)(B)(ii) 332n64
§ 529(c)(3)(E) 332n64
§ 529(c)(6) 332n64
§ 530(a) 332n64
§ 530(d)(2)(A) 332n64
§ 530(d)(4) 332n64
§ 1401-1403 .... 420n345
§ 1411(c)(5) 325n35
§ 1563(a) 350n95
§ 1563(a)(1) 351n96
§ 1563(d) 351n98
§ 1563(e) 351n98

xlii Table of Legislation

26 USC - Internal Revenue Code (cont.)

§ 1563(f) 351n98
§ 1563(f)(5) 350n95
§ 1563(f)(5)(A) 351n97
§ 3101(a) 325n32
§ 3101(b)(1) 325n32
§ 3101(b)(2) 325n32
§ 3111(a) 325n32
§ 3111(b) 325n32
§ 3121(a)(1) 325n32, 367n151
§ 3121(a)(5) 325n32
§ 3121(a)(5)(D) 325n32
§ 3121(v)(1) 325n32
§ 3301 .... 325n32
§ 3306(b)(1) 325n32
§ 3306(b)(5) 325n32
§ 3306(b)(5)(D) 325n32
§ 3306(r)(1) 325n32
§ 3405(c) 405n299
§ 3405(e)(1) 405n299
§ 3405(e)(5) 405n299
§ 4971 .... 298n48
§ 4972 .... 289n3, 293n15, 386n225
§ 4974(a) 392n241
§ 4974(c) 400n281
§ 4974(e) 392n241
§ 4975 .... 145n114, 146n124, 315n3
§ 4975(a) 144n112
§ 4975(a)(6) 145n114
§ 4975(b) 144n112
§ 4975(d)(1) 267n13, 402n286
§ 4975(d)(12) 309n111
§ 4975(d)(17) 143n105
§ 4975(d)(25) 406n303
§ 4975(e)(1) 145n114
§ 4975(e)(2)-(6) 144n112
§ 4975(e)(2)(A) 144n112
§ 4975(e)(2)(H) 144n112
§ 4975(e)(7) 10f, 70n44
§ 4975(f)(8) 143n105
§ 4975(f)(12) 406n303
§ 4975(g) 145n114

Table of Legislation

§ 4980 .... 163*n*12
§ 4980(a) 310*n*115
§ 4980(d) 310*n*116
§ 4980A 383*n*213
§ 4980B 26*n*102, 27*n*107, 225*n*1
§ 4980B(f) 26*n*103
§ 4980D 225*n*1
§ 4980D(c)-(d) 27*n*107
§ 4980F 63*n*8, 249*n*94
§ 4980H 450*n*122
§ 4980H(a) 451*n*126
§ 4980H(a)(2) 451*n*126, 451*n*129
§ 4980H(b) 451*n*126
§ 4980H(b)(1)(B) 451*n*126, 451*n*130
§ 4980H(c)(2)(A) 451*n*125
§ 4980H(c)(2)(D) 451*n*129
§ 5000A 450*n*118
§ 5000A(c)(3)(A) 450*n*121
§ 6058 .... 64*n*11
§ 6075 .... 64*n*11
§ 6433 .... 413*n*321
§ 7701(a)(37) 401*n*282
§ 7701(a)(46) 353*n*106
§ 9801 .... 26*n*105
§ 9801-9803 .... 225*n*1
§ 9801-9833 .... 27*n*107
§ 9802 .... 26*n*105
§ 9802(c)-(f) 27*n*106
§ 9811-9813 .... 27*n*106
§ 9815 .... 225*n*1
§ 9831-9834 .... 26*n*105, 225*n*1
§ 9831(d) 452*n*132
§ 9834 .... 27*n*107

29 USC - Labor 4

§ 186(c) 49*n*114
§ 186(c)(7)(C) 49*n*116
§ 215(a)(3) 179*n*94
§ 623(f)(2)(B)(ii) 241*n*64
§ 623(i)(1) 239*n*54, 239*n*55
§ 623(i)(2) 239*n*56
§ 623(i)(9) 239*n*56
§ 623(i)(10) 239*n*55, 240*n*63

xliv　　　　　　　　*Table of Legislation*

29 USC - Labor (cont.)

§ 623(*l*)(1)(A)(ii) 241n64

§ 660(c) 179n94

§ 1001 .... 438n39

§ 1001(a) 18n64, 259n129, 260n134, 288n2

§ 1001(a)(1) 48n111

§ 1001(b) 175n69, 182n107

§ 1001(c) 288n2

§ 1002(1) 29n3, 33n28, 38n54, 40n69, 44n96, 47n108, 48n110, 48n111, 48n112, 232n21, 438n40

§ 1002(1)-(3) 234n29, 236n38

§ 1002(1) 5n12, 5n14, 11f

§ 1002(2) 5n11, 5n14, 33n28

§ 1002(2)(A) 7n24, 13n39, 29n3, 38n54, 40n68, 44n95, 45n98, 45n101, 46n102, 49n115, 232n21, 246n78, 318n12, 380n202, 398n265

§ 1002(2)(B) 49n115

§ 1002(2)(C) 233n23

§ 1002(3) 5n10, 5n14, 29n3, 44n94

§ 1002(3)(a) 13n40

§ 1002(3)(C)(ii)(I) 57n149

§ 1002(3)(D) 57n150

§ 1002(5) 232n21

§ 1002(6) 40n71

§ 1002(7) 40n70, 41n75, 134n73, 163n13, 182n106

§ 1002(8) 42n84, 134n73, 167n30, 273n39, 285n94

§ 1002(11) 28n2

§ 1002(12) 28n2

§ 1002(14) 133n68, 144n112

§ 1002(14)(A) 144n112

§ 1002(14)(A)-(E) 140n92

§ 1002(14)(B) 142n101

§ 1002(14)(C) 143n103

§ 1002(14)(F) 140n93

§ 1002(14)(G) 140n92

§ 1002(14)(H) 140n93, 143n103, 144n112

§ 1002(14)(I) 140n93

§ 1002(15) 140n93, 144n112

§ 1002(16)(A) 62n3, 124n38

§ 1002(16)(B) 62n3

§ 1002(19) 245n76, 253n112, 300n60

§ 1002(21)(A) 17n58, 32n21, 100n171, 100n172, 103n179, 117n5, 122n21

§ 1002(21)(A)(i) 32n23, 118n6

§ 1002(23) 237n49, 237n50, 247n83, 279n65

Table of Legislation

§ 1002(24) 237n50, 238n51
§ 1002(31) 292n11
§ 1002(32) 12n34, 25n98, 54n137, 54n138
§ 1002(33) 12n34, 54n134
§ 1002(33)(C)(i) 56n147
§ 1002(33)(C)(ii)(II) 56n143
§ 1002(33)(C)(iii) 56n143
§ 1002(33)(C)(iv) 56n144
§ 1002(34) 6n18, 162n11, 237n49, 239n58
§ 1002(35) 6n19, 237n50, 239n58
§ 1002(36) 12n34, 291n8, 291n9
§ 1002(37) 12n30
§ 1002(41) 12n31
§ 1002(43) 233n23
§ 1002(43)(A) 233n23
§ 1002(44) 233n23
§ 1002(45) 50n120, 397n261
§ 1002(b) 47n108
§ 1003(1) 29n4
§ 1003(2) 236n38
§ 1003(2)(A) 29n4
§ 1003(a) 5n9, 29n4, 44n94, 236n38
§ 1003(b) 25n98, 54n134, 271n31, 342n76
§ 1003(b)(1) 12n34
§ 1003(b)(2) 12n34
§ 1003(b)(5) 12n34, 291n8
§ 1021 .... 62n3, 124n38
§ 1021-1025 .... 439n44
§ 1021-1031 .... 13n36
§ 1021(a)(2) 64n15, 65n18, 298n50
§ 1021(e) 311n118
§ 1021(f) 65n18, 298n50
§ 1021(i) 67n28
§ 1021(j) 298n50
§ 1021(m) 67n28
§ 1022 .... 40n74
§ 1022(a) 71n47, 72n51, 73n55, 94n147, 100n170, 101n176, 105n185
§ 1022(a)(1) 16n54, 91n132
§ 1022(b) 71n48, 81n92, 94n146, 101n175, 101n176, 114n223
§ 1022(b)(1) 105n185
§ 1023 .... 64n11, 64n12
§ 1023(b)(3)(D) 17n61
§ 1024 .... 62n3, 124n38

xlvi   *Table of Legislation*

29 USC - Labor (cont.)

§ 1024(a) 64n11

§ 1024(a)(2) 62n2

§ 1024(a)(3) 62n2

§ 1024(b)(1) 63n7, 249n95

§ 1024(b)(2) 62n5, 68n34, 73n58

§ 1024(b)(3) 64n15

§ 1024(b)(4) 62n5, 67n31, 67n32, 68n35, 73n58

§ 1025 .... 62n3, 66n24, 66n27, 124n38

§ 1025(a)(1)(A) 66n26

§ 1025(a)(2)(B)(i) 66n26

§ 1025(a)(2)(B)(iii) 66n26

§ 1025(a)(2)(D) 66n26

§ 1030 .... 51n125, 62n2

§ 1031(a)(1) 28n2

§ 1040 .... 255n117, 265n120

§ 1051-1061 .... 13n40

§ 1051(1) 88n119, 246n78, 275n49

§ 1051(2) 39n67, 45n98, 51n122, 51n123, 226n2, 318n12

§ 1052 .... 43n89

§ 1052(a)(1) 228n2

§ 1052(a)(1)(A) 13n41

§ 1052(a)(1)(B)(i) 252n104

§ 1052(a)(1)(B)(ii) 228n2

§ 1052(a)(2) 228n3

§ 1052(a)(3) 228n5

§ 1052(a)(4) 163n14, 230n11

§ 1052(b)(1) 228n6

§ 1052(b)(2) 229n7

§ 1052(b)(3) 229n8

§ 1052(b)(4) 229n9

§ 1052(b)(4)(C) 229n9

§ 1052(b)(5) 229n10

§ 1052(c) 233n23

§ 1053 .... 13n42

§ 1053(a) 88n119, 252n105, 322n18

§ 1053(a)(1) 250n99

§ 1053(a)(2) 229n9

§ 1053(a)(2)(A) 251n101

§ 1053(a)(2)(B) 251n102, 318n12

§ 1053(a)(3) 253n110

§ 1053(a)(3)(A) 253n111, 273n38

Table of Legislation

§ 1053(a)(3)(D) 251n100
§ 1053(b)(1) 252n107
§ 1053(b)(2) 252n106
§ 1053(b)(3) 252n106
§ 1053(b)(3)(A) 228n6
§ 1053(c)(1)(A) 252n108
§ 1053(c)(1)(B) 253n109
§ 1053(c)(3) 251n103
§ 1053(d) 252n104
§ 1053(e) 283n90, 403n292
§ 1053(e)(1) 308n105
§ 1053(f) 237n50
§ 1054 .... 14n45
§ 1054(b)(1)(A) 242n67, 245n74
§ 1054(b)(1)(B) 243n68
§ 1054(b)(1)(C) 243n69, 244n73
§ 1054(b)(1)(G) 239n57, 241n64
§ 1054(b)(1)(H) 239n55
§ 1054(b)(1)(H)(ii) 239n56
§ 1054(b)(1)(H)(v) 241n64
§ 1054(b)(2) 239n54
§ 1054(b)(4)(A) 229n10
§ 1054(b)(4)(B) 237n47
§ 1054(b)(4)(C) 237n46
§ 1054(b)(5) 240n63
§ 1054(c) 237n50, 250n99
§ 1054(c)(4) 309n108
§ 1054(g) 63n8, 252n108
§ 1054(g)(1) 105n186, 245n75, 245n77, 248n88, 297n36
§ 1054(g)(2) 247n83
§ 1054(g)(4) 248n88
§ 1054(h) 63n8, 86n114, 249n94
§ 1054(h)(6) 249n94
§ 1054(i) 297n38
§ 1054(j) 128n52
§ 1054(j)(3) 141n96
§ 1054(k) 238n52
§ 1055 .... 13n43
§ 1055(a)(1) 279n65
§ 1055(a)(2) 279n66
§ 1055(b)(1) 280n70
§ 1055(b)(1)(C) 280n72

xlviii

Table of Legislation

29 USC - Labor (cont.)

§ 1055(b)(4) ·· 280n73
§ 1055(c) ··· 281n76, 281n78
§ 1055(c)(1)(A) ·· 281n77
§ 1055(c)(1)(A)(i) ·· 281n79
§ 1055(c)(1)(A)(iii) ·· 282n81
§ 1055(c)(2) ··· 274n42, 283n85
§ 1055(c)(2)(A) ·· 283n84
§ 1055(c)(3)(A) ·· 281n79
§ 1055(c)(3)(B) ·· 282n82
§ 1055(c)(3)(B)(ii) ··· 282n82
§ 1055(c)(4) ··· 283n88
§ 1055(c)(5) ··· 281n78
§ 1055(c)(7) ··· 282n83
§ 1055(c)(7)(A) ··· 281n79, 282n81
§ 1055(c)(7)(B) ·· 282n83
§ 1055(c)(8)(A) ·· 281n79
§ 1055(d) ··· 279n65
§ 1055(d)(2) ··· 281n77
§ 1055(e) ··· 279n66
§ 1055(e)(1)(A) ·· 279n68
§ 1055(e)(1)(A)(i) ·· 279n67
§ 1055(e)(1)(B) ·· 279n67
§ 1055(e)(2) ··· 279n68
§ 1055(f) ·· 280n73
§ 1055(g) ··· 283n90, 308n105, 403n292
§ 1055(h)(2) ··· 282n80
§ 1056(a) ·· 265n4, 265n5
§ 1056(c) ··· 251n100
§ 1056(d)(1) ·················· 13n44, 19n69, 166n28, 248n85, 265n6, 275n49, 285n95
§ 1056(d)(2) ··· 266n12, 267n13, 401n285
§ 1056(d)(3) ··· 13n43, 26n104, 269n26
§ 1056(d)(3)(B) ·· 270n28
§ 1056(d)(3)(B)(i)(I) ·· 277n56
§ 1056(d)(3)(C) ·· 270n29
§ 1056(d)(3)(D) ··· 271n31, 271n32
§ 1056(d)(3)(E) ·· 272n35
§ 1056(d)(3)(F) ·· 273n37
§ 1056(d)(3)(H) ·· 271n32
§ 1056(d)(3)(K) ·· 270n28
§ 1056(d)(4) ··· 268n21
§ 1056(d)(5) ··· 268n21

Table of Legislation

§ 1056(g) 297n39, 301n65, 304n83
§ 1056(h) 185n121, 249n93
§ 1057 .... 258n126
§ 1060(f) 288n1
§ 1081-1085 .... 13n40
§ 1081(1)(8) 14n46
§ 1081(a) 290n7
§ 1081(a)(1) 290n7
§ 1081(a)(2) 14n50
§ 1081(a)(2)(B) 290n7
§ 1081(a)(3) 39n67, 51n122, 51n123, 226n2, 291n8, 322n23
§ 1081(a)(8) 290n7, 322n23, 388n232
§ 1081(a)(9) 291n8
§ 1081(b) 14n50
§ 1082 .... 70n43
§ 1082-1085 .... 14n46
§ 1082(a) 290n6, 292n11, 293n16, 322n23
§ 1082(a)(2)(B) 388n232
§ 1082(a)(2)(C) 25n101
§ 1082(a)(2)(D) 288n1
§ 1082(b) 292n11
§ 1082(b)(2) 298n42
§ 1082(b)(2)(B)(iii) 294n20
§ 1082(c) 296n32, 304n82
§ 1082(c)(1) 292n11
§ 1082(c)(3) 292n13
§ 1082(c)(4) 296n34, 305n87
§ 1082(c)(4)(B) 296n33
§ 1082(c)(5) 292n13
§ 1082(c)(5)(A) 291n9
§ 1082(c)(5)(B) 296n32
§ 1082(c)(6) 296n33
§ 1082(c)(7) 297n37
§ 1082(d) 291n9
§ 1082(d)(1)(B) 304n83
§ 1082(d)(2) 245n77, 297n36
§ 1082(d)(3) 298n42
§ 1082(d)(5)(A) 304n83
§ 1083 .... 70n43
§ 1083(a) 293n16, 304n83
§ 1083(a)(1)(B) 290n6, 294n19
§ 1083(b) 293n17, 293n18

l   *Table of Legislation*

29 USC - Labor (cont.)

§ 1083(c) 290n6, 294n19, 304n83
§ 1083(d) 290n6
§ 1083(d)(1) 293n17, 304n83
§ 1083(h)(1) 291n10, 294n22, 295n26
§ 1083(h)(2) 294n21
§ 1083(h)(3) 294n21
§ 1083(i) 296n30, 296n31
§ 1083(j) 297n40, 297n41
§ 1083(k) 298n43, 305n86
§ 1083(l) 311n118
§ 1084 .... 25n101
§ 1085(a)(2)(D) 288n1
§ 1085(e)(9) 245n77
§ 1101(a) 13n37
§ 1101(a)(1) 39n67, 51n122, 51n123, 226n2, 322n19, 322n20
§ 1101(b)(2) 15n51
§ 1102(a)(1) 68n36, 124n35, 124n36
§ 1102(a)(1)(D) 275n49
§ 1102(a)(2) 124n35
§ 1102(b)(2) 126n44
§ 1102(b)(3) 89n122, 124n37, 168n36, 248n91
§ 1102(b)(4) 36n49, 275n49
§ 1102(c)(3) 149n135
§ 1103(a) 124n37, 149n135
§ 1103(a)(1) 124n37, 125n39, 149n135
§ 1103(a)(2) 124n37, 149n135
§ 1103(b)(4) 145n118
§ 1103(c)(1) 133n67, 163n12, 309n109, 309n111, 322n18
§ 1104 .... 13n37, 315n3
§ 1104(a) 32n20
§ 1104(a)(1) ··· 40n74, 103n179, 112n220, 134n73, 179n89, 308n103, 309n111
§ 1104(a)(1)(A) 100n172, 121n20, 127n50, 133n66
§ 1104(a)(1)(B) 100n172, 128n51
§ 1104(a)(1)(C) 128n52, 141n96
§ 1104(a)(1)(D) 126n45, 128n53, 132n63, 149n135
§ 1104(a)(2) 21n79, 128n52, 153n151, 154n154
§ 1104(c) 130n58
§ 1104(c)(1) 124n37, 145n119
§ 1104(c)(1)(A) 146n124
§ 1104(c)(3) 406n302
§ 1104(c)(5) 379n193, 407n304

Table of Legislation

§ 1104(c)(6) 50n120
§ 1104(d) 310n117
§ 1104(e) 395n254
§ 1105 .... 315n3
§ 1105(a) 125n40
§ 1105(a)(2) 126n45, 149n135
§ 1105(b)(2) 149n135
§ 1105(b)(3)(B) 149n135
§ 1105(c) 125n39, 125n41
§ 1105(c)(1) 124n36, 149n135
§ 1105(c)(2)(A)(i) 126n45
§ 1105(c)(3) 149n135
§ 1105(d)(1) 124n37
§ 1106 .... 13n37, 32n20, 179n89, 315n3
§ 1106(a)(1) 141n98
§ 1106(a)(1)(A)-(D) 140n91
§ 1106(a)(1)(B) 143n103
§ 1106(a)(1)(C) 142n101
§ 1106(a)(1)(E) 140n95
§ 1106(a)(2) 140n95, 141n98, 153n152
§ 1106(b) 141n97, 141n98
§ 1107 .... 315n3
§ 1107(a) 140n95, 153n152
§ 1107(a)(2) 136n80
§ 1107(b) 141n96
§ 1107(b)(1) 21n79, 153n152
§ 1107(b)(2) 153n153
§ 1107(c)(3) 141n96
§ 1107(d)(1) 140n95
§ 1107(d)(2) 140n95
§ 1107(d)(3) 21n79, 153n151
§ 1107(d)(3)-(6) 128n52
§ 1107(d)(4) 140n95, 153n151
§ 1107(d)(5) 140n95
§ 1107(d)(6) 153n151
§ 1107(c) 140n95
§ 1108 .... 315n3
§ 1108(a) 141n98, 143n106
§ 1108(b)(1) 143n104
§ 1108(b)(2) 142n102
§ 1108(b)(9) 309n111
§ 1108(b)(13) [USCA] 311n118

lii   *Table of Legislation*

29 USC - Labor (cont.)

§ 1108(b)(14) 143n105
§ 1108(c)(1) 122n22
§ 1108(c)(3) 100n174, 122n22, 133n68
§ 1109 .... 73n56, 75n63, 161n6
§ 1109(a) 117n3, 127n48, 142n99, 143n108, 149n135
§ 1109(b) 127n49
§ 1110(a) 17n59, 100n174, 132n63, 149n135, 168n38
§ 1111(b) 160n3
§ 1122 .... 162n10
§ 1131 .... 62n4, 160n3
§ 1132 .... 13n38, 160n2, 163n12, 439n45
§ 1132(a) 4n4, 40n74, 82n97, 176n75
§ 1132(a)(1) 67n29, 67n32
§ 1132(a)(1)-(3) 73n56
§ 1132(a)(1)(A) 62n4, 65n19, 161n4, 311n118
§ 1132(a)(1)(B) 74n59, 97n160, 161n5, 168, 256n122
§ 1132(a)(2) 75n63, 117n4, 143n108, 161n6, 162n9
§ 1132(a)(3) 62n4, 72n53, 103n180, 113n222, 117n4, 143n108, 161n7,
                      162n9, 176n76, 190n147, 256n122, 298n44, 388n232
§ 1132(a)(4) 62n4
§ 1132(a)(5) 62n4, 72n53, 161n7, 298n45, 388n232
§ 1132(a)(6) 62n4, 67n30, 145n115, 161n4, 298n50
§ 1132(a)(8) 65n19
§ 1132(a)(9) 308n102, 308n103
§ 1132(b)(1) 161n7
§ 1132(c) 62n4, 161n4
§ 1132(c)(1) 65n19, 67n29, 67n32, 311n118
§ 1132(c)(4) 298n50
§ 1132(c)(7) 67n30
§ 1132(d)(2) 189n144
§ 1132(i) 145n115
§ 1132(*l*) 145n116
§ 1132(*l*)(4) 145n117
§ 1133 .... 66n20
§ 1134(b)(1)(D) 162n10
§ 1140 .... 18n63, 179n93, 179n95, 181n100
§ 1141 .... 160n3
§ 1144 .... 13n38, 73n57, 190n145, 442n61, 442n62, 457n155
§ 1144(a) 13n35, 177n82, 196n11, 234n29, 274n44
§ 1144(b)(2) 15n52
§ 1144(b)(2)(A) 122n110, 442n64

§ 1144(b)(2)(B)	122*n*112, 442*n*65
§ 1144(b)(4)	200*n*20
§ 1144(b)(7)	26*n*104, 269*n*27
§ 1144(d)	267*n*15
§ 1154(j)	21*n*79
§ 1161	26*n*102
§ 1161-1169	225*n*1, 441*n*57
§ 1161(b)	441*n*57
§ 1162	26*n*103
§ 1162(1)	441*n*58
§ 1162(3)	441*n*58
§ 1163	26*n*102, 441*n*59
§ 1164	26*n*103
§ 1169	26*n*104, 27*n*107
§ 1181	26*n*105
§ 1181-1183	225*n*1
§ 1182	26*n*105, 43*n*89
§ 1182(b)(1)	436*n*33
§ 1182(c)-(e)	27*n*106
§ 1185-1185b	438*n*41
§ 1185-1185e	27*n*106
§ 1185b	27*n*107
§ 1185d	27*n*108, 63*n*10, 225*n*1, 448
§ 1185d(a)(1)	448*n*110
§ 1191-91e	26*n*105
§ 1191-1191c	225*n*1
§ 1191b	448*n*111
§ 1191b(a)(1)	448*n*111
§ 1191b(b)(2)	448*n*111
§ 1191d	458, 459*n*169
§ 1193-1193c	397*n*261
§ 1193(b)(1)(B) [USCA]	236*n*39
§ 1193(c)(1) [USCA]	236*n*42
§ 1193(d)(1)(A) [USCA]	236*n*39
§ 1193(d)(1)(B)(i) [USCA]	236*n*41
§ 1193(d)(2)(A) [USCA]	236*n*39
§ 1193(e)(4)(A) [USCA]	236*n*40
§ 1193(e) [USCA]	236*n*44
§ 1204(a)	64*n*11
§ 1231	54*n*135
§ 1301(a)(8)	300*n*59
§ 1301(a)(13)	303*n*79

liv *Table of Legislation*

29 USC - Labor (cont.)

§ 1301(a)(14) ·· 303n79
§ 1301(a)(16) ·· 105n186
§ 1301(a)(18) ·· 105n186
§ 1301(a)(21) ·· 307n96
§ 1301(b)(1) ·· 303n79
§ 1302(a) ·· 299n55
§ 1302(g)(2) ·· 300n57
§ 1303(e) ·· 298n46
§ 1305(b)(1) ·· 300n56
§ 1306(a)(3)(A)(vii) ·· 288n1
§ 1306(a)(8)(E) ·· 288n1
§ 1307(a) ·· 300n56
§ 1307(e) ·· 300n56
§ 1321(a) ·· 14n47, 299n52
§ 1321(b) ·· 54n134
§ 1321(b)(1) ·· 14n47
§ 1321(b)(1)-(5) ·· 299n52
§ 1321(b)(6) ·············· 39n67, 51n122, 51n123, 226n2, 299n53
§ 1321(b)(7) ·· 299n52
§ 1321(b)(8) ·· 299n53
§ 1321(b)(9) ·· 299n53
§ 1321(b)(13) ·· 299n54, 383n213
§ 1321(c)(2) ·· 299n54
§ 1321(c)(3) ·· 299n54
§ 1321(d) ·· 299n53
§ 1322(a) ·· 300n58, 301n66
§ 1322(b)(1) ·· 301n65, 301n69
§ 1322(b)(3)(A) ·· 301n68
§ 1322(b)(3)(B) ·· 301n67
§ 1322(b)(5) [USCA] ·· 302n70
§ 1322(b)(6) ·· 301n66
§ 1322(b)(7) ·· 301n65, 301n69
§ 1322(b)(8) ·· 301n65
§ 1341 ·· 14n48
§ 1341a ·· 14n48
§ 1341(a) ·· 307n94
§ 1341(a)(1) ·· 303n74
§ 1341(a)(2) ·· 307n95, 307n96, 307n99
§ 1341(b) ·· 307n94
§ 1341(b)(1)(A) ·· 307n95

Table of Legislation

§ 1341(b)(1)(B) 307n97, 307n98
§ 1341(b)(2)(A) 307n98
§ 1341(b)(2)(B) 307n97
§ 1341(b)(2)(C) 308n100
§ 1341(b)(2)(C)(ii) 308n100
§ 1341(b)(2)(D) 308n101
§ 1341(b)(3)(A)(ii) 308n104
§ 1341(b)(3)(B) 309n107
§ 1341(c)(1)(C) 303n74
§ 1341(c)(2)(B) 303n74
§ 1341(d)(1) 308n100
§ 1342 .... 306n91
§ 1342(a) 303n75
§ 1343 .... 306n92
§ 1343(b) 306n93
§ 1344(a) 302n71
§ 1344(b)(2) 302n72
§ 1344(b)(3) 302n72
§ 1344(b)(4) 302n72
§ 1344(b)(7) 302n72
§ 1344(d) 302n71
§ 1344(d)(1) 163n12, 309n109
§ 1344(d)(2) 309n110
§ 1344(d)(3) 309n108
§ 1345 .... 305n84
§ 1350 .... 308n104
§ 1362(a) 105n186, 303n79
§ 1362(b) 105n186
§ 1362(b)(1)(A) 303n76
§ 1365 .... 64n11
§ 1368 .... 305n85
§ 1369(a) 304n80
§ 1381-1461 .... 25n101
§ 1441 .... 245n77

42 USC - Public Health and Welfare

§ 300gg 27n108, 448n111
§ 300gg(a)(1) 448n111
§ 300gg(a)(1)(A) 450n116
§ 300gg-300gg-28 448
§ 300gg-1 .... 448n111, 450n117
§ 300gg-2 .... 448n111

lvi   *Table of Legislation*

42 USC - Public Health and Welfare (cont.)

§ 300gg-3 .... 448n111
§ 300gg-4 .... 448n111, 455n140
§ 300gg-5 .... 448n111
§ 300gg-6 .... 448n111, 457n159
§ 300gg-6(a) 448n111, 454n136
§ 300gg-7 .... 448n111
§ 300gg-8 .... 448n111
§ 300gg-9 .... 448n111
§ 300gg-11 .... 448n111
§ 300gg-11(a) 454n139
§ 300gg-11(b) 454n139
§ 300gg-12 .... 448n111
§ 300gg-13 .... 448n111, 455n142, 455n144
§ 300gg-13(a)(1)-(5) 455n144
§ 300gg-14 .... 448n111, 455n141
§ 300gg-15 .... 63n10, 448n111
§ 300gg-15a 448n111
§ 300gg-15(d)(4) 63n7
§ 300gg-16 .... 448n111
§ 300gg-17 .... 448n111
§ 300gg-18 .... 448n111
§ 300gg-19 .... 448n111
§ 300gg-19a 448n111
§ 300gg-19b 448n111, 457n157
§ 300gg-21 .... 448n111
§ 300gg-22 .... 448n111
§ 300gg-23 .... 448n111
§ 300gg-23(a) 457n156
§ 300gg-25 .... 448n111
§ 300gg-26 .... 448n111
§ 300gg-27 .... 448n111
§ 300gg-28 .... 448n111
§ 300gg-91(a)(1) 447n108
§ 300gg-91(b)(2) 447n108
§ 300gg-91(b)(4) 447n108
§ 300gg-91(e)(1)(A) 447n108
§ 300gg-91(e)(2) 447n108
§ 300gg-91(e)(3) 447n108
§ 300gg-91(e)(4) 447n108
§ 300gg-91(e)(5) 447n108

Table of Legislation

§ 18011(a) 447*n*108
§ 18011(e) 447*n*108
§ 18022(b)(1) 454*n*137
§ 18031 .... 450*n*119
§ 18031(d)(3)(B)(i)-(ii) 458*n*163
§ 18041(d) 457*n*158

Federal Acts by Popular Name

Achieving a Better Life Experience Act 2014 (Pub L No 113-295) (ABLE Act)
§ 101 .... 333*n*65
§ 103 .... 333*n*65
Administrative Procedure Act 1946 (Pub L No 79-404, 60 Stat 237) 36
Age Discrimination in Employment Act 1967 (Pub L No 90-202, 80 Stat 202)
238–39
§ 4(f)(2)(B)(ii) 241*n*64
§ 4(i)(1) 239*n*54, 239*n*55
§ 4(i)(2) 239*n*56
§ 4(i)(9) 239*n*56
§ 4(i)(10) 239*n*55, 240*n*63
§ 4(*l*)(1)(A)(ii) 241*n*64
Church Plan Parity and Entanglement Protection Act 1999 (Pub L No 106-244,114
Stat 499) 12*n*34
Civil Rights Act 1964 (Pub L No 88-352, 78 Stat 241)
§ 701-718 180
Congressional Review Act Disapproval (Pub L No 115-35, 131 Stat 848) .. 234*n*29
Consolidated and Further Continuing Appropriations Act 2015 (Pub L No 113-235,
128 Stat 2130) 12*n*32
Consolidated Appropriations Act 2021 (Pub L No 11-260, 134 Stat 2877)
§ 115(b) 459*n*168
Consolidated Omnibus Reconciliation Act 1985 (Pub L No 99-272, 100 Stat 82)
(COBRA) 26, 225*n*1, 441–42
§ 10,001-10,003 .... 441*n*56
Coronavirus Aid, Relief, and Economic Security Act 2020 (Pub L No 116-136, 134
Stat 281) (CARES Act)
§ 2202 .... 400*n*277
§ 2202(a)(6)(B) 400*n*277
§ 2203 .... 393*n*245
§ 2206(b) 402*n*289
§ 3608 .... 297*n*40

Table of Legislation

Employee Retirement Income Security Act 1974 (Pub L No 93-406, 88 Stat 829)

§ 2 .... 438n39
§ 2(a) 18n64, 259n129, 260n134, 288n2
§ 2(b) 175n69, 182n107
§ 2(c) 288n2
§ 3(1) 5n12, 5n14, 10f, 11f, 29n3, 29n4, 33n28, 38n54, 40n69, 44n96,
                47n108, 48n110, 48n111, 48n112, 232n21, 438n40
§ 3(1)-(3) 234n29, 236n38
§ 3(2) 5n14, 10f, 11f, 33n28
§ 3(2)(A) 5n11, 13n39, 29n3, 29n4, 38n54, 40n68, 44n95, 45n98, 45n101,
            46n102, 49n115, 232n21, 246n78, 318n12, 380n202, 398n265
§ 3(2)(B) 11f, 47n108, 49n115
§ 3(2)(C) 233n23
§ 3(3) 5n10, 5n14, 10f, 13n40, 29n3, 29n4, 44n94
§ 3(5) 232n21, 233n22
§ 3(6) 40n71
§ 3(7) 40n70, 41n75, 134n73, 163n13, 182n106
§ 3(8) 42n84, 134n73, 167n30, 273n39, 285n94
§ 3(11) 28n2
§ 3(12) 28n2
§ 3(14) 133n68, 144n112
§ 3(14)(A) 144n112
§ 3(14)(A)-(E) 140n92
§ 3(14)(B) 142n101
§ 3(14)(C) 143n103
§ 3(14)(F) 140n93
§ 3(14)(G) 140n92
§ 3(14)(H) 140n93, 143n103, 144n112
§ 3(14)(I) 140n93
§ 3(15) 140n93, 144n112
§ 3(16)(A) 62n3, 124n38
§ 3(16)(B) 62n3
§ 3(19) 245n76, 253n112, 300n60
§ 3(21) 117
§ 3(21)(A) 17n58, 32n21, 100n171, 100n172, 103n179, 117n5, 122n21
§ 3(21)(A)(i) 32n23, 119n8
§ 3(23) 237n49, 237n50, 240n60, 247n83, 279n65
§ 3(24) 237n50, 238n51
§ 3(31) 292n11
§ 3(32) 10f, 11f, 12n34, 54n134, 54n137, 54n138
§ 3(33) 10f, 11f, 54n134
§ 3(33)(C)(ii)(I) 57n149

§ 3(33)(C)(ii)(II) 56n143
§ 3(33)(C)(iii) 56n143
§ 3(33)(C)(iv) 56n144
§ 3(33)(D) 57n150
§ 3(34) 6n18, 10f, 162n11, 237n49, 239n58
§ 3(35) 6n19, 10f, 237n50, 239n58
§ 3(36) 12n34, 291n8
§ 3(37) 12n30
§ 3(41) 12n31
§ 3(43) 233n23
§ 3(43)(A) 233n23
§ 3(44) 233n23
§ 3(45) 50n120, 236n38, 397n261
§ 4(a) 5n9, 5n14, 10f, 11f, 13n40, 28n1, 29n4, 44n94, 236n38
§ 4(b) 10f, 11f, 25n98, 54n134, 271n31, 342n76
§ 4(b)(5) 12n34, 291n8
§ 14(b)(2) 11f
§ 101 .... 62n3, 124n38
§ 101-105 .... 439n44
§ 101-111 .... 13n36
§ 101(a)(2) 64n15, 65n18, 298n50
§ 101(a)(f) 298n50
§ 101(e) 311n118
§ 101(f) 65n18
§ 101(i) 67n28
§ 101(j) 298n50
§ 101(m) 67n28
§ 102 .... 40n74
§ 102(a) 71n47, 72n51, 73n55, 94n147, 100n170, 105n185
§ 102(a)(1) 16n54, 91n132
§ 102(b) 71n48, 81n91, 94n146, 101n175, 114n223
§ 103 .... 64n11, 64n12
§ 103(b)(3) 17n61
§ 104 .... 62n3, 124n38
§ 104(a) 64n11
§ 104(a)(2) 62n2
§ 104(a)(3) 62n2
§ 104(b)(1) 63n7, 105n185, 249n95
§ 104(b)(2) 62n5, 68n34, 70n45, 73n58
§ 104(b)(3) 64n15
§ 104(b)(4) 62n5, 67n31, 67n32, 68n35, 68n37, 69n42, 73n58
§ 105 .... 62n3, 66n27, 124n38

Table of Legislation

Employee Retirement Income Security Act 1974 (Pub L No 93-406, 88 Stat 829) (cont.)

§ 105(a)(1)(A) 66n26
§ 105(a)(2)(B)(i) 66n26
§ 105(a)(2)(B)(iii) 66n26
§ 105(a)(2)(D) 66n26
§ 110 .... 51n125, 62n2
§ 111(a)(1) 28n2
§ 201-211 .... 13n40
§ 201(1) 88n119, 246n78, 275n49
§ 201(2) 1of, 39n67, 45n98, 51n122, 51n123, 318n12, 322n20, 322n22
§ 202 .... 43n89
§ 202(1) 226n2
§ 202(a)(1) 228n2
§ 202(a)(1)(A) 13n41
§ 202(a)(1)(B)(i) 252n104
§ 202(a)(1)(B)(ii) 228n2
§ 202(a)(2) 228n3
§ 202(a)(3) 228n5
§ 202(a)(4) 163n14, 230n11
§ 202(b)(1) 228n6
§ 202(b)(2) 229n7
§ 202(b)(3) 229n8
§ 202(b)(4) 229n9
§ 202(b)(4)(C) 229n9
§ 202(b)(5) 229n10
§ 202(c) 233n25
§ 203 .... 13n42
§ 203(a) 88n119, 252n105, 322n18
§ 203(a)(1) 250n99
§ 203(a)(2) 229n9
§ 203(a)(2)(A) 251n101
§ 203(a)(2)(B) 251n102, 318n12
§ 203(a)(3) 253n110
§ 203(a)(3)(A) 253n111, 273n38
§ 203(a)(3)(D) 251n100
§ 203(b)(1) 252n107
§ 203(b)(2) 252n106
§ 203(b)(3)(A) 228n6
§ 203(c)(1)(A) 252n108
§ 203(c)(1)(B) 253n109
§ 203(c)(3) 251n103

§ 203(d)	252n104
§ 203(e)	283n90
§ 203(e)(1)	308n105, 402n292
§ 203(f)	237n50
§ 204	14n45
§ 204(b)(1)(A)	242n67, 245n74
§ 204(b)(1)(B)	243n68, 244n73
§ 204(b)(1)(C)	243n69, 244n73
§ 204(b)(1)(G)	239n57, 241n64
§ 204(b)(1)(H)	239n55
§ 204(b)(1)(H)(i)	240n60
§ 204(b)(1)(H)(ii)	239n56
§ 204(b)(1)(H)(v)	241n64
§ 204(b)(2)	239n54
§ 204(b)(4)(A)	229n10
§ 204(b)(4)(B)	237n47
§ 204(b)(4)(C)	237n46
§ 204(b)(5)	239n55, 240n63
§ 204(c)	237n50, 250n99
§ 204(c)(4)	309n108
§ 204(g)	63n8, 252n108
§ 204(g)(1)	105n186, 245n75, 245n77, 297n36
§ 204(g)(2)	247n83
§ 204(g)(4)	248n88
§ 204(g)(5)	248n88
§ 204(h)	63n8, 86n114, 249n94
§ 204(h)(6)	249n94
§ 204(i)	297n38
§ 204(j)	21n79
§ 204(j)(3)	141n96
§ 204(k)	238n52
§ 205	13n43, 284–85
§ 205(a)(1)	279n65
§ 205(a)(2)	279n66
§ 205(b)(1)	280n70
§ 205(b)(1)(C)	280n72
§ 205(b)(4)	280n73
§ 205(c)	281n76, 281n78
§ 205(c)(1)(A)	281n77
§ 205(c)(1)(A)(i)	281n79
§ 205(c)(1)(A)(iii)	282n81
§ 205(c)(2)	274n42, 283n85

lxii　　　　　　　　　*Table of Legislation*

Employee Retirement Income Security Act 1974 (Pub L No 93-406, 88 Stat 829) (cont.)

§ 205(c)(2)(A) 283n84
§ 205(c)(3)(A) 281n79
§ 205(c)(3)(B) 282n82
§ 205(c)(3)(B)(ii) 282n82
§ 205(c)(4) 283n88
§ 205(c)(5) 281n78
§ 205(c)(5)(1)(A)(i) 281n79
§ 205(c)(7) 282n83
§ 205(c)(7)(A) 281n79, 282n81
§ 205(c)(7)(B) 282n83
§ 205(c)(8)(A) 281n79
§ 205(d) 279n65
§ 205(d)(2) 281n77
§ 205(e) 279n66
§ 205(e)(1)(A)(i) 279n67
§ 205(e)(1)(B) 279n67, 279n68
§ 205(e)(2) 279n68
§ 205(f) 280n73
§ 205(g) 283n90, 308n105, 402n292
§ 205(h)(2) 282n80
§ 206(a)(3) 265n4, 265n5
§ 206(c) 251n100
§ 206(d)(1) 13n44, 19n69, 166n28, 248n85, 265n6, 275n49, 285n95
§ 206(d)(2) 266n12, 267n13, 268, 401n285
§ 206(d)(3) 13n43, 26n104, 269n26
§ 206(d)(3)(B) 270n28
§ 206(d)(3)(B)(i)(I) 277n56
§ 206(d)(3)(C) 270n29
§ 206(d)(3)(D) 271n31, 271n32
§ 206(d)(3)(F) 273n37
§ 206(d)(3)(H) 271n32
§ 206(d)(3)(K) 270n28
§ 206(d)(4) 268n21
§ 206(d)(5) 268n21
§ 206(g) 297n39, 301n65, 304n83
§ 206(h) 185n121, 249n93
§ 207 .... 258n126
§ 207(j) 128n52
§ 210(f) 288n1
§ 301-305 .... 13n40

Table of Legislation

§ 301(a) 290n7

§ 301(a)(1) 290n7

§ 301(a)(2) 14n50

§ 301(a)(3) ·········· 10f, 39n67, 51n122, 51n123, 226n2, 291n8, 322n22, 322n23

§ 301(a)(8) 14n46, 322n23, 388n232

§ 301(a)(9) 291n8

§ 301(b) 14n50

§ 302 .... 70n43

§ 302-305 .... 14n46

§ 302(a) 290n6, 292n11, 293n16, 322n23

§ 302(a)(2)(B) 290n7, 388n232

§ 302(a)(2)(C) 26n101

§ 302(a)(2)(D) 288n1

§ 302(a)(8) 290n7

§ 302(b) 292n11

§ 302(b)(2) 298n42

§ 302(b)(2)(B)(iii) 294n20

§ 302(c) 296n32, 304n82

§ 302(c)(1) 292n11

§ 302(c)(3) 292n13

§ 302(c)(4) 296n34, 305n87

§ 302(c)(4)(B) 296n33

§ 302(c)(5) 292n13

§ 302(c)(5)(A) 291n9

§ 302(c)(5)(B) 296n32

§ 302(c)(6) 296n33

§ 302(c)(7) 297n37

§ 302(d) 291n9

§ 302(d)(1)(B) 304n83

§ 302(d)(2) 245n77, 297n36

§ 302(d)(3) 298n42

§ 302(d)(5)(A) 304n83

§ 303 .... 70n43

§ 303(a) 293n16, 304n83

§ 303(a)(1)(B) 290n6, 291n19

§ 303(b) 293n17, 293n18

§ 303(c) 290n6, 294n19, 304n83

§ 303(d) 290n6

§ 303(d)(1) 293n17, 304n83

§ 303(h)(1) 291n10, 294n22, 295n26

§ 303(h)(2) 294n21

§ 303(h)(3) 294n21

lxiv   *Table of Legislation*

Employee Retirement Income Security Act 1974 (Pub L No 93-406, 88 Stat 829)
(cont.)

§ 303(i) 296n30, 296n31
§ 303(j) 297n40, 297n41
§ 303(k) 298n43, 305n86
§ 303(*l*) 311n118
§ 305(e)(9) 246n77
§ 306 .... 288n1
§ 401(a) 13n37, 17n59, 38n61
§ 401(a)(1) 10f, 39n67, 48n111, 51n122, 51n123, 226n2, 322n19,
                                                    322n20, 322n22
§ 401(b)(2) 15n51
§ 402(a)(1) 38n61, 68n36, 124n35, 124n36, 124n37
§ 402(a)(2) 124n35, 124n37
§ 402(b) 70n46
§ 402(b)(2) 126n44
§ 402(b)(3) 89n122, 124n37, 168n36, 248n91
§ 402(b)(4) 36n49, 275n49
§ 402(c) 70n46
§ 402(c)(1) 124n36
§ 402(c)(3) 149n135
§ 403 .... 149n135
§ 403(a) 124n37, 149n135
§ 403(a)(1) 125n39, 149n135
§ 403(a)(2) 149n135
§ 403(c)(1) 133n67, 163n12, 309n109, 309n111, 322n18
§ 404 .... 13n37, 439n45
§ 404(a) 32n20
§ 404(a)(1) 40n74, 75n63, 103n179, 112n220, 134n73, 179n89,
                                                    308n103, 309n111
§ 404(a)(1)(A) 100n172, 121n20, 127n50, 133n66
§ 404(a)(1)(B) 100n172, 128n51
§ 404(a)(1)(C) 128n52, 141n96
§ 404(a)(1)(D) 126n45, 128n53, 128n55, 132n63, 149n135, 275n49
§ 404(a)(2) 21n79, 128n52, 153n151, 154n154, 158
§ 404(c) 130n58, 147–53, 148n133, 149n134, 149n135, 152n150, 158–59
§ 404(c)(1) 124n37, 145n119
§ 404(c)(1)(a) 146n124
§ 404(c)(3) 406n302
§ 404(c)(5) 379n193, 407n304
§ 404(d) 310n117
§ 404(e) 395n254
§ 405 .... 149n135

§ 405(a)	125*n*40
§ 405(a)(1)	127*n*47
§ 405(a)(2)	126*n*45, 127*n*47, 149*n*135
§ 405(a)(3)	127*n*47
§ 405(b)(1)(B)	149*n*135
§ 405(b)(3)(B)	149*n*135
§ 405(c)	125*n*39, 125*n*41
§ 405(c)(1)	149*n*135
§ 405(c)(1)(B)	117
§ 405(c)(2)(A)	127*n*47
§ 405(c)(2)(A)(ii)	126*n*45
§ 405(d)(1)	124*n*37, 149*n*135
§ 406	13*n*37, 32*n*20, 139, 179*n*89, 315*n*3
§ 406(a)(1)	141*n*98
§ 406(a)(1)(A)-(D)	140*n*91
§ 406(a)(1)(C)	141*n*96, 142*n*101
§ 406(a)(1)(E)	140*n*95
§ 406(a)(2)	140*n*95, 141*n*98, 153*n*152
§ 406(b)	141*n*97, 141*n*98
§ 406(c)	50*n*120
§ 407	315*n*3
§ 407(a)	140*n*95, 153*n*152
§ 407(a)(2)	136*n*80
§ 407(b)	141*n*96
§ 407(b)(1)	21*n*79
§ 407(b)(2)	153*n*153
§ 407(c)(3)	141*n*96
§ 407(d)(1)	140*n*95
§ 407(d)(2)	140*n*95
§ 407(d)(3)	1*of*, 21*n*79, 153*n*151
§ 407(d)(3)-(6)	128*n*52
§ 407(d)(4)	140*n*95, 153*n*151
§ 407(d)(5)	140*n*95
§ 407(d)(6)	153*n*151
§ 407(e)	140*n*95
§ 408	315*n*3
§ 408(a)	141*n*98
§ 408(b)(1)	143*n*104
§ 408(b)(2)	142*n*102
§ 408(b)(3)	1*of*
§ 408(b)(9)	309*n*111
§ 408(b)(13)	311*n*118
§ 408(b)(14)	143*n*105

lxvi   *Table of Legislation*

Employee Retirement Income Security Act 1974 (Pub L No 93-406, 88 Stat 829) (cont.)

§ 408(c)(1) 122n22
§ 408(c)(3) 100n174, 122n22, 133n68, 135n75
§ 408(g) 143n105
§ 409 .... 73n56, 75n63, 161n6, 189–90
§ 409(a) 117n3, 127n48, 142n99, 143n108, 149n135
§ 409(b) 127n49
§ 410(a) 100n174, 128n55, 149n135, 168n38
§ 411(b) 160n3
§ 501 .... 62n4, 160n3
§ 502 .... 13n38, 160–61, 160n2, 163n12, 439n46
§ 502(a) 4n7, 40n74, 82n97, 161n8, 176n75, 177, 182–84, 190–91,
                                                                        190n145
§ 502(a)(1) 67n29, 67n32, 161n8, 177
§ 502(a)(1)-(3) 73n56
§ 502(a)(1)(A) 62n4, 65n19, 161n4, 311n118
§ 502(a)(1)(B) 74–75, 74n59, 97n160, 161n5, 168, 175n67, 189–90,
                                                                189n144, 256n122
§ 502(a)(2) 75n63, 117n4, 143n108, 161n6, 177–78, 183–84, 184n115,
                                                            189, 190n146, 191n149
§ 502(a)(3) 62n4, 72n53, 75, 103n180, 113n222, 117n4, 143n108, 144,
                            144n111, 161n7, 176n76, 177–79, 180, 184–90, 189n143,
                            191n149, 192, 256n122, 298n44, 388n232
§ 502(a)(4) 62n4
§ 502(a)(5) 62n4, 72n53, 161n7, 298n45, 388n232
§ 502(a)(6) 62n4, 67n30, 145n115, 145n116, 161n4, 298n50
§ 502(a)(8) 65n19
§ 502(a)(9) 308n102, 308n103
§ 502(b)(1) 161n7
§ 502(c) 62n4, 161n4
§ 502(c)(1) 65n19, 67n29, 67n32, 311n118
§ 502(c)(4) 298n50
§ 502(c)(7) 67n30
§ 502(d)(2) 189n144
§ 502(i) 145n115
§ 502(*l*) 145n116, 161n4
§ 502(*l*)(4) 145n117
§ 502(m) 161n4
§ 503 .... 66n20, 66n24
§ 503(b)(4) 145n118

Table of Legislation

§ 510 ....18*n*63, 165, 179, 179*n*93, 179*n*94, 179*n*95, 180–82, 181*n*100, 188, 255*n*117, 256*n*120

§ 511 ....160*n*3

§ 514 ....13*n*38, 73*n*57, 190*n*145, 442, 442*n*61, 442*n*62, 457

§ 514(a) 13*n*35, 177*n*82, 194, 196–204, 196*n*11, 197*n*13, 209, 214*n*93, 222, 234*n*29, 274*n*44

§ 514(b) 196*n*9

§ 514(b)(2) 15*n*52, 218

§ 514(b)(2)(A) 195, 218*n*110

§ 514(b)(2)(B) 195–96, 218*n*112

§ 514(b)(4) 200*n*20

§ 514(b)(7) 26*n*104, 269*n*27

§ 514(c) 177*n*82

§ 514(d) 267*n*15

§ 601 ....26*n*102

§ 601-609 ....225*n*1, 441*n*57

§ 602 ....26*n*103

§ 602(1) 441*n*58

§ 602(3) 441*n*58

§ 603 ....26*n*102, 441*n*59

§ 604 ....26*n*103

§ 609 ....26*n*104, 27*n*107

§ 701 ....26*n*105

§ 701-703 ....225*n*1

§ 702 .... 26*n*105, 43*n*89

§ 702(b)(1) 436*n*33

§ 702(c)-(f) 27*n*106

§ 711-713 ....438*n*41

§ 711-714 ....27*n*106

§ 713 ....27*n*107

§ 715 .... 27*n*108, 225*n*1, 448*n*110

§ 715(a) 448

§ 715(a)(1) 63*n*10

§ 715(b) 448*n*111

§ 731-734 .... 26*n*105, 225*n*1

§ 733 ....448*n*111

§ 733(a)(1) 448*n*111

§ 733(b)(2) 448*n*111

§ 735 ....458–59, 459*n*169

§ 801-804 .... 50*n*120, 397*n*261

§ 801(b)(1)(B) 236*n*39

lxviii   *Table of Legislation*

Employee Retirement Income Security Act 1974 (Pub L No 93-406, 88 Stat 829)
(cont.)

§ 801(c)(1) 236n42
§ 801(d)(1)(A)(i) 236n39
§ 801(d)(1)(B)(i) 236n41
§ 801(d)(2)(A) 236n39
§ 801(e) 236n44
§ 801(e)(4)(A) 236n40
§ 3004(a) 64n11
§ 3031 .... 54n135
§ 4001(a)(8) 300n59
§ 4001(a)(13) 303n79
§ 4001(a)(14) 303n79
§ 4001(a)(16) 105n186
§ 4001(a)(18) 105n186
§ 4001(a)(21) 296n33, 307n96
§ 4001(b)(1) 303n79
§ 4002(a) 299n55
§ 4002(g)(2) 300n57
§ 4003(e) 298n46
§ 4005(b)(1) 300n56
§ 4006(a)(3)(A)(vii) 288n1
§ 4006(a)(8)(E) 288n1
§ 4007(a) 300n56
§ 4007(e) 300n56, 300n57
§ 4011 .... 65n18
§ 4021(a) 14n47, 299n52
§ 4021(b) 54n134
§ 4021(b)(1) 14n47
§ 4021(b)(1)-(5) 299n52
§ 4021(b)(6) 39n67, 51n122, 51n123, 226n2, 299n53
§ 4021(b)(7) 299n52
§ 4021(b)(8) 299n53
§ 4021(b)(9) 299n53
§ 4021(b)(13) 299n54, 383n213
§ 4021(c)(2) 299n54
§ 4021(c)(3) 299n54
§ 4021(d) 299n53
§ 4022 .... 162n10
§ 4022(a) 300n58, 301n66
§ 4022(b)(1) 301n65, 301n69
§ 4022(b)(3)(A) 301n68

Table of Legislation

§ 4022(b)(3)(B) 301n67
§ 4022(b)(5) 302n70
§ 4022(b)(5)(A) 299n53
§ 4022(b)(6) 301n66
§ 4022(b)(7) 301n65, 301n69
§ 4022(b)(8) 301n65
§ 4041 .... 14n48
§ 4041A 14n48
§ 4041(a) 105n186, 307n94
§ 4041(a)(1) 303n74
§ 4041(a)(2) 307n95, 307n96, 307n99
§ 4041(b) 105n186, 307n94
§ 4041(b)(1)(A) 307n95
§ 4041(b)(1)(B) 307n97, 307n98
§ 4041(b)(1)(D) 162n10
§ 4041(b)(2)(A) 307n98
§ 4041(b)(2)(B) 307n97
§ 4041(b)(2)(C) 308n100
§ 4041(b)(2)(C)(ii) 308n100
§ 4041(b)(2)(D) 308n101
§ 4041(b)(3)(A)(ii) 308n104
§ 4041(b)(3)(B) 309n107
§ 4041(c)(1)(A) 303n74
§ 4041(c)(2)(B) 303n74
§ 4041(d)(1) 308n100
§ 4042 .... 306n91
§ 4042(a) 303n75
§ 4043 .... 306n92
§ 4043(b) 306n93
§ 4044(a) 302n71
§ 4044(b)(2) 302n72
§ 4044(b)(3) 302n72
§ 4044(b)(4) 302n72
§ 4044(b)(7) 302n72
§ 4044(d) 302n71
§ 4044(d)(1) 163n12, 309n109
§ 4044(d)(2) 309n110
§ 4044(d)(3) 309n108
§ 4045 .... 305n84
§ 4062(a) 105n186, 303n79
§ 4062(b) 105n186, 303n78
§ 4062(b)(1)(A) 303n76

Table of Legislation

Employee Retirement Income Security Act 1974 (Pub L No 93-406, 88 Stat 829) (cont.)

§ 4065 ....64n11
§ 4068 ....305n85
§ 4069 ....304n81
§ 4069(a) 304n80
§ 4104(a) 132n63
§ 4201-4402 ....25n101
§ 4281 ....245n77

Fair Labor Standards Act 1938 (Pub L No 75-718, 52 Stat 1060)

§ 215(a)(3) 179n94

Federal Insurance Contributions Act 1935

(68A Stat 415) (FICA) 325n32, 368n157

Federal Unemployment Tax Act 1954 (Pub L No 86-778, 68A Stat 439)

(FUTA) 325n32

Health Care and Education Reconciliation Act 2010 (Pub L No 111-152, 24 Stat

1029) 431n1

Health Insurance Portability and Accountability Act 1996 (Pub L No 104-191, 110

Stat 1936) (HIPAA) 431n1, 442
§ 101 ....442n60
§ 102 ....442n60

Katrina Emergency Tax Relief Act 2005 (Pub L No 109-73, 119 Stat 2016)

§ 101 ....400n278

Labor Management Relations Act (Pub L No 80-101, 61 Stat 136) (Taft-Hartley Act)

....49, 67, 167, 267n15, 268
§ 142(1) 28n2
§ 301 ....190n145
§ 302(c) 47n108, 49n114, 49n116

Multiemployer Pension Reform Act 2014 (Pub L No 113-235, 128

Stat 2132) 12n32, 245n77

No Surprises Act 2020 (Pub L No 116-260, 134 Stat 2877)

§ 115(b) 458–59

Occupational Safety and Health Act 1974 (Pub L No 91-596, 84

Stat 1590) 179n94

Older Workers Benefit Protection Act 1990 (Pub L No 101-433, 104

Stat 978) 241n64

Patient Protection and Affordable Care Act 2010 (Pub L No 111-148, 124 Stat 119)

(ACA) 27, 63, 95, 176, 193–94, 225n1, 431, 431n1, 431n2, 447–62
§ 1302(b) 453n134
§ 1302(b)(2)(A) 453n134
§ 1302(d)(2) 453n134
§ 1562(e) 448n109

Table of Legislation

Pension Protection Act 2006 (Pub L No 109-280, 120 Stat 780) 240, 292, 294, 390

§ 706(d) 240n63

§ 706(e)(1) 240n63

§ 1102 .... 405n300

Public Health Service Act 1944 (Pub L No 78-410, 58 Stat 682)

§ 2715(d)(4) 63n7

Religious Freedom Restoration Act 1993 (Pub L No 103-141, 107 Stat. 1488) 455–56

Retirement Equity Act 1984 (Pub L No 98-397, 98 Stat 1426)··· 229n9, 247, 269, 286–87

Setting Every Community Up for Retirement Enhancement Act 2019 (Pub L No 116-94, 133 Stat 2534) (SECURE Act) 396n259

§ 101 .... 233n23

§ 112(b) 233n25

Setting Every Community Up for Retirement Enhancement Act 2020 (Pub L No 117-328, 136 Stat 4459) (SECURE 2.0 Act) 185n121, 235

§ 102(c) 235n32

§ 106 .... 233n23

§ 120 .... 406n303

§ 121 .... 379n194

§ 127 .... 236n38

§ 127(g) 236n38

§ 202 .... 396n258

§ 304 .... 308n105

§ 305 .... 374n176

Social Security Act Medicare Amendment 1965 (Pub L No 89-97, 79 Stat 286) 434n23

Taft-Hartley Act (Pub L No 80-101, 61 Stat 136) ········· 49, 67, 167, 267n15, 268

§ 142(1) 28n2

§ 301 .... 190n145

§ 302(c) 47n108, 49n114, 49n116

Taxpayer Relief Act 1997 (Pub L No 105-34, 111 Stat 788)

§ 1505(a)(1) 342n76

§ 1505(d)(2) 342n76

Tax Cuts and Jobs Act 2017 (Pub L No 115-97, 131 Stat 2054)

§ 11081(a)(2) 450n121

Tax Reform Act 1986 (Pub L No 99-514, 100 Stat 2085) 251n101

21st Century Cures Act 2016 (Pub L No 114-255, 130 Stat 1033)

§ 18001 .... 452n132

Welfare and Pension Plans Disclosure Act 1958 (Pub L No 85-836, 72 Stat 997) 38n55, 48–49, 198

lxxii   *Table of Legislation*

Welfare and Pension Plans Disclosure Act 1958 (Pub L No 85-836, 72 Stat 997) (cont.)

§ 3(1) 38n58

§ 3(2) 38n58

§ 3(10) 28n2

§ 3(a)(1) 49n113

§ 4(b)(4) 38n56

Welfare and Pension Plans Disclosure Act Amendments 1962 (Pub L No 87-420, 76 Stat 35) 28n2, 38n56

State Law

Oregon Revised Statutes

§ 178.210(1) 380n203

§ 178.215 .... 380n203

Uniform Partnership Act 1914 44

Uniform Probate Code

§ 1-201(18) 273n40, 273n41, 274n43

§ 2-803 .... 273n41

§ 2-804 .... 273n40

Washington Revised Code

§ 11.07.010(2)(a) 275n47

§ 11.07.010(5)(a) 275n46

Restatements of the Law (American Law Institute)

Restatement of Contracts (1932)

§ 236(c) 92n133

Restatement (Second) of Contracts (1981)

§ 90(1) 104n184

§ 203(c) 92n133

Restatement (Second) of Torts (1977)

§ 537 .... 93n140

§ 540 .... 93n140

§ 546 .... 83n100-1

§ 551 .... 81n93, 93n139

Restatement (Second) of Trusts (1959)

§ 74 .... 119n11

§ 108 .... 124n35

§ 155(2) 269n23

§ 157 .... 269n24

§ 157(a) 269n25

§ 164	128n55
§ 167	154n158
§ 170	135n75, 142n100
§ 170(1)	127n50
§ 171	126n45
§ 173	69n42
§ 174	128n51
§ 183	128n54
§ 184	126n45
§ 205(c)	188n140
§ 205(i)	188n140
§ 211	188n140
§ 222	13n62
§ 222(2)	135n75
§ 223	127n49
§ 224	127n47
§ 224(2)(b)	126n45, 127n47
§ 225	126n42
§ 225(2)(b)	126n45
§ 228	128n52
§ 284	144n111
§ 289	179n92
§ 291	144n111
§ 292	179n92
§ 294	144n111

Restatement (Third) of Trusts (2007)

§ 2	119n11
§ 31	124n35
§ 76	128n55
§ 76(1)	128n53
§ 77	128n51, 128n55, 131n62
§ 78	127n50, 135n75, 142n100
§ 78(1)	128n55, 131n62, 131n74
§ 79	128n54, 130n59
§ 80	126n45
§ 81	127n47
§ 82(2)	69n42
§ 87	131n62
§ 90	130n59
§ 90(a)	128n52, 137n83
§ 90(b)	128n52
§ 95	78n81

Table of Rules and Regulations

FEDERAL RULES AND REGULATIONS

Code of Federal Regulations (CFR)

Title 26 - Treasury Regulations

§ 1.36B-2(c)(5) 452n132
§ 1.72(p)-1 .... 402n290
§ 1.83-1(a)(1) 318n12
§ 1.83-1(a)(1)(i) 318n10
§ 1.83-3(c) 318n11
§ 1.83-3(c)(2) 318n11
§ 1.83-3(e) 319n13, 321n16
§ 1.83-3(h) 318n10
§ 1.83-3(i) 318n10
§ 1.83-5(a) 318n10
§ 1.401-1(a)(2) 360n134
§ 1.401-1(a)(2)(i) 10f, 264n2
§ 1.401-1(a)(2)(ii) 10f
§ 1.401-1(a)(2)(iii) 10f
§ 1.401-1(b)(1)(i) 7n23, 8n25, 10f, 264n1, 360n134, 398n263, 398n264
§ 1.401-1(b)(1)(ii) 6n20, 7n24, 8n26, 10f, 264n2, 360n134, 398n266
§ 1.401-1(b)(4) 134n73, 273n39
§ 1.401(a) 3 (prop) 264n1
§ 1.401-4(b) 367n151
§ 1.401(a)(4)-1(c)(4)(i) 349n91
§ 1.401(a)(4)-2(b)(2) 362n138
§ 1.401(a)(4)-2(b)(2)(ii) 369n159
§ 1.401(a)(4)-2(b)(3)(i)(A) 362n141
§ 1.401(a)(4)-2(b)(3)(i)(B) 362n141

lxxv

lxxvi   *Table of Rules and Regulations*

Title 26 - Treasury Regulations (cont.)

§ 1.401(a)(4)-2(c) 360n133
§ 1.401(a)(4)-2(c)(1) 361n135, 362n139, 362n140
§ 1.401(a)(4)-2(c)(2)(iv) 369n162
§ 1.401(a)(4)-2(c)(2)(v) 365n146
§ 1.401(a)(4)-2(c)(2)(v)(A) 365n146
§ 1.401(a)(4)-2(c)(3)(i) 362n139
§ 1.401(a)(4)-2(c)(3)(ii) 364n142
§ 1.401(a)(4)-2(c)(3)(iii) 364n144
§ 1.401(a)(4)-3(b) 362n138, 366n147
§ 1.401(a)(4)-3(b)(3) 369n161
§ 1.401(a)(4)-3(b)(6)(ii) 369n160
§ 1.401(a)(4)-3(c) 366n148
§ 1.401(a)(4)-3(c) (prop) 360n133
§ 1.401(a)(4)-3(c)(1)(i) (prop) 361n135
§ 1.401(a)(4)-3(d) 366n149
§ 1.401(a)(4)-3(d)(3)(i) 369n162
§ 1.401(a)(4)-4 .... 359n131
§ 1.401(a)(4)-4(c)(1) 359n131
§ 1.401(a)(4)-4(e) 359n131
§ 1.401(a)(4)-5 .... 358n129, 360n134, 410n314
§ 1.401(a)(4)-5(2) 360n134
§ 1.401(a)(4)-5(3) 360n134
§ 1.401(a)(4)-7 369
§ 1.401(a)(4)-7(a) 369n163
§ 1.401(a)(4)-7(b)(1) 370n164
§ 1.401(a)(4)-7(c)(1) 370n165
§ 1.401(a)(4)-8 .... 360n133
§ 1.401(a)(4)-11(g)(2) 373n171
§ 1.401(a)(4)-11(g)(3)(ii)-(v) 373n172
§ 1.401(a)(4)-11(g)(3)(iii) 373n174
§ 1.401(a)(4)-11(g)(3)(iv) 373n174
§ 1.401(a)(4)-11(g)(4) 373n173
§ 1.401(a)(5)-1(e) 371n168
§ 1.401(a)(9)-3(c)(3) (prop) 394n250
§ 1.401(a)(9)-5 .... 395n255, 395n256
§ 1.401(a)(9)-5(b)(1) (prop) 395n255
§ 1.401(a)(9)-5(b)(4) (prop) 395n256, 395n257
§ 1.401(a)(9)-5(d)(1)(i) 394n250
§ 1.401(a)(9)-5(e)(1) 394n250
§ 1.401(a)(9)-5(e)(2) 394n250
§ 1.401(a)(9)-6 .... 392n244, 395n257

§ 1.401(a)(9)-6(b)(2)(iii) (prop) 392n244
§ 1.401(a)(9)-6(q) (prop) 395n257
§ 1.401(a)-11(b)(2) 281n75
§ 1.401(a)-11(g)(2)(ii) 281n75
§ 1.401(a)-13(b)(2) 267n15
§ 1.401(a)-13(d)(1) 266n12
§ 1.401(a)-13(d)(2) 402n286
§ 1.401(a)-13(d)(2)(iii) 267n13
§ 1.401(a)-14(c) 265n5
§ 1.401(a)-20 ······ 279n66, 280n71, 280n72, 281n74, 281n75, 281n78, 282n82,
282n83, 283n84, 283n86, 283n87, 283n88
§ 1.401(a)(26)-1(b)(1) 356n119
§ 1.401(a)(26)-2(d)(1)(iii) 356n118
§ 1.401(a)(26)-3 .... 356n118
§ 1.401(k)-1(d)(3) 415n328
§ 1.401(k)-2(a)(2) 375n183
§ 1.401(k)-2(a)(3) 375n183
§ 1.401(k)-2(a)(3)(i) 376n185
§ 1.401(k)-2(b) 377n187
§ 1.401(k)-2(c)(1) 375n182
§ 1.401(k)-3 .... 410n315
§ 1.401(k)-6 .... 374n178
§ 1.401(l)-2(d)(4) 368n156
§ 1.401(l)-3(d)(9) 368n156
§ 1.402A-1 .... 332n61
§ 1.402(a)-1(a)(1)(ii) 403n293
§ 1.402(a)-1(a)(2) 309n106
§ 1.402(a)-2(a)(2) 315n2
§ 1.402(b)-1(a) 357n123
§ 1.402(b)-1(a)(2) 357n124
§ 1.402(b)-1(b) 357n123
§ 1.402(f)-1 .... 405n300
§ 1.403(c)-1 .... 357n123
§ 1.404(a)-12(b)(3) 357n124
§ 1.408-2(b)(8) 280n69
§ 1.410(a)-1(b)(2)(i) 238n52
§ 1.410(a)-1(b)(2)(ii)-(v) 238n53
§ 1.410(a)(4) 230n11
§ 1.410(a)(4)-1(b)(3) 344n82
§ 1.410(a)(4)-1(c)(4)(i) 344n82
§ 1.410(a)(4)-2(c)(2)(ii) 343n79
§ 1.410(a)-4(b) 163n14, 230n11

lxxviii   *Table of Rules and Regulations*

Title 26 - Treasury Regulations (cont.)

§ 1.410(a)-4(b)(1) 230n11
§ 1.410(a)-4(b)(2) 230n11
§ 1.410(a)-4(b)(3) 230n11
§ 1.410(a)-4(b)(4) 230n11
§ 1.410(a)-7 .... 228n5
§ 1.410(b)-2(b)(2) 343n78
§ 1.410(b)-2(b)(3) 344n83
§ 1.410(b)-2(b)(5) 343n80
§ 1.410(b)-3(a)(1) 343n79
§ 1.410(b)-3(a)(2)(i) 374n178
§ 1.410(b)-4(c)(4) 345n84, 364n143
§ 1.410(b)-5(d)(3) 347n89
§ 1.410(b)-6(b) 353n108
§ 1.410(b)-6(b)(2) 354n109
§ 1.410(b)-6(b)(3) 354n109
§ 1.410(b)-6(c) 353n105
§ 1.410(b)-6(d) 353n106
§ 1.410(b)-6(d)(2)(iii)(B) 353n106
§ 1.410(b)-6(e) 353n104
§ 1.410(b)-6(f) 237n48, 354n110
§ 1.410(b)-7(c)(3) 354n109
§ 1.410(b)-7(d) 344n81, 349n91
§ 1.410(b)-7(d)(1) 344n82
§ 1.410(b)-7(d)(5) 347n89
§ 1.410(b)-7(e)(1) 347n89
§ 1.410(b)-9 .... 343n78, 353n106
§ 1.411(a)-4(a) 253n112
§ 1.411(a)-4T(a) 253n112
§ 1.411(a)-7(a) 247n83
§ 1.411(a)-7(a)(1) 246n78
§ 1.411(a)-8T(b) 253n109
§ 1.411(a)-8T(b)(2) 253n109
§ 1.411(b)-1(b)(1)(ii)(A) 242n67
§ 1.411(b)-1(b)(2)(ii)(F) 243n71
§ 1.411(b)-1(b)(3)(ii)(A) 243n69
§ 1.411(b)-1(b)(3)(iii) 243n69
§ 1.411(b)(5)-1 .... 239n55, 240n63
§ 1.411(b)(5)-1(f)(1) 240n63
§ 1.411(d)-2(b)(1) 256n121
§ 1.411(d)-3(a)(1) 247n83
§ 1.411(d)-3(a)(3)(i) 246n81

Table of Rules and Regulations

§ 1.411(d)-3(b) 247n84
§ 1.411(d)-3(b)(3)(i) 246n78
§ 1.411(d)-3(b)(3)(ii) 246n78
§ 1.411(d)-3(b)(4) 246n78
§ 1.411(d)-3(c)-3(6) 247n83
§ 1.411(d)-3(g)(2) 246n78
§ 1.411(d)-3(g)(14) 247n83
§ 1.411(d)-3(g)(15) 247n83
§ 1.411(d)-4 .... 246n78, 247n83, 248n88
§ 1.411(d)-5 .... 251n103
§ 1.412(b)-1(h)(1) (prop) 294n23
§ 1.412(b)-1(h)(3) (prop) 294n24
§ 1.412(b)-1(h)(4) (prop) 294n24
§ 1.412(i)-1(a) 14n50
§ 1.414(c)-2(c) 351n97
§ 1.414(q)-1T 355n114
§ 1.414(r)-0(c) 352n102
§ 1.414(r)-2(b)(3)(iv) 352n101
§ 1.414(r)-8(b) 352n103
§ 1.414(s)-1 .... 362n137
§ 1.451-1(a) 317n7
§ 1.451-2(a) 317n8
§ 54.4980F-1 .... 63n8, 249n94
§ 54.9802-4(a)-(c) 452n132
§ 54.9802-4(c)(i)(ii) 452n132

Title 29 - Labor

§ 2509.75-5 .... 118n6
§ 2509.75-8 .... 112n218, 120n15
§ 2510.3-1(a)(2) 47n108
§ 2510.3-1(a)(3) 11f, 49n115
§ 2510.3-1(j) 55n141
§ 2510.3-1(k) 11f, 48n111, 50n119
§ 2510.3-2(b) 47n109, 49n115
§ 2510.3-2(c) 45n99, 47n106
§ 2510.3-2(d) 234n29, 380n202
§ 2510.3-2(f) 380n202
§ 2510.3-3(b) 38n63, 40n72, 44n90
§ 2510.3-3(b)-3(c)(2) 44n90
§ 2510.3-3(d)(1)(i)(B) 163n15, 182n106
§ 2510.3-3(d)(2)(i)(A) 164n16
§ 2510.3-21(c)(1)(ii)(B) 118n7
§ 2510.3-55 .... 232n22

Title 29 - Labor (cont.)

§ 2510.3-104b-10 ·· 64*n*17
§ 2520.102-2(a) ····································· 94*n*147, 100*n*171
§ 2520.102-2(b) ································· 91*n*132, 94*n*147
§ 2520.102-3(*l*) ·················· 91*n*132, 94*n*146, 114*n*223
§ 2520.103-1 ·· 64*n*12
§ 2520.103-1(c) ·· 64*n*13
§ 2520.104-20 ·· 62*n*2
§ 2520.104-23 ································· 51*n*125, 62*n*2
§ 2520.104-41 ·· 64*n*13
§ 2520.104-46 ·· 64*n*13
§ 2520.104a-2 ·· 64*n*14
§ 2520.104a-5 ·· 64*n*14
§ 2520.104b-10(d) ···································· 64*n*15
§ 2520.105-3 ··· 66*n*26
§ 2530.200a-2 ··· 163*n*14
§ 2530.200b-1(b) ······································ 237*n*48
§ 2530.200b-2 ··· 228*n*5
§ 2530.200b-3 ··· 228*n*5
§ 2530.204-1(a) ······································· 237*n*47
§ 2530.204-1(b)(1) ······················· 237*n*45, 237*n*46
§ 2530.204-2(c)(1) ······················· 237*n*46, 237*n*47
§ 2550 ·· 148*n*133
§ 2550.404a-1(b)(1) ·································· 137*n*83
§ 2550.404a-1(b)(2) ·································· 137*n*83
§ 2550.404a-1(c)(1) ·································· 138*n*87
§ 2550.404a-1(c)(2) ·································· 139*n*88
§ 2550.404a-2 ··· 406*n*302
§ 2550.404c ·································· 147*n*125, 148*n*133
§ 2550.404c-1 ································ 124*n*37, 130*n*58
§ 2550.404c-1(a)(2) ·································· 147*n*125
§ 2550.404c-1(b)(1) ·································· 147*n*126
§ 2550.404c-1(b)(2)(i)(B) ···························· 148*n*130
§ 2550.404c-1(b)(2)(i)(B)(1) ························· 147*n*129
§ 2550.404c-1(b)(2)(i)(B)(3) ························· 148*n*131
§ 2550.404c-1(b)(2)(ii)(B) ·························· 152*n*151
§ 2550.404c-1(b)(2)(ii)(C) ·························· 147*n*128
§ 2550.404c-1(b)(3) ·································· 147*n*127
§ 2550.404c-1(c)(2) ·································· 147*n*129
§ 2550.404c-1(d)(2)(i) ······························ 148*n*132
§ 2550.404c-1(d)(2)(ii)(E)(4) ·············· 148*n*131, 152*n*151
§ 2550.404c-1(d)(2)(iv) ······························ 148*n*133

§ 2550.404c-1(d)(3) 146n124
§ 2550.404c-5 .... 235n34, 379n193, 407n304
§ 2560.503-1 .... 175n67
§ 2560.503-1(a) 176n74
§ 2560.503-1(d) 176n74
§ 2560.503-1(f) 66n20
§ 2560.503-1(g) 66n20
§ 2560.503-1(g)(1)(iii) 66n21
§ 2560.503-1(i)(5) 66n22
§ 2560.503-1(j) 66n22
§ 2560.503-1(j)(4) 66n23
§ 2560.503-1(m)(8) 66n22
§ 2570.46 .... 141n98
§ 2570.48 .... 143n107
§ 2575.2(f) 67n30
§ 2575.502c-1 .... 65n19, 67n29
§ 2590.715-2711 .... 225n1
§ 2590.715-2712 .... 225n1
§ 2590.715-2713 .... 225n1
§ 2590.715-2714 .... 225n1
§ 2590.715-2719(b) 176n72
§ 2590.715-2719(b)(2) 439n47
§ 2590.715-2719(b)(2)(F)(1) 176n73
§ 4022.2 .... 300n62, 301n64, 301n65
§ 4022.3 .... 301n64, 301n65
§ 4022.3(a) 300n61, 300n62
§ 4022.4(a)(1) 300n61, 301n65
§ 4022.4(a)(3) 300n61, 301n64
§ 4022.6(a) 300n61
§ 4022.7(a) 301n63
§ 4022.7(c)(1) 301n63
§ 4022.22(a) 301n67, 301n68
§ 4022.25 .... 301n69
§ 4022.62(b)(2) 390n238
§ 4041.21 .... 307n94
§ 4041.23 .... 307n95
§ 4041.23(b)(5) 307n99
§ 4041.23(b)(9) 308n102
§ 4041.23(c) 310n114
§ 4041.24 .... 307n97
§ 4041.24(a) 307n98
§ 4041.24(f) 310n114

lxxxii *Table of Rules and Regulations*

Title 29 - Labor (cont.)

§ 4041.25(a) 307n97, 307n98
§ 4041.26(a)(2) 308n100
§ 4041.27 .... 307n99
§ 4041.27(a)(2) 310n114
§ 4041.28 .... 308n101
§ 4041.28(c)(3) 308n103
§ 4041.29 .... 309n107
§ 4041.31(a) 308n100
§ 4044.13(a) 302n73
§ 4044.17(a) 302n72

Title 45 - Public Welfare

§ 147.131 .... 456n149
§ 147.132 .... 456n149
§ 156.100-156.155 .... 454n138
§ 156.111 .... 454n138
§ 156.145(a) 453n134

Federal Rules of Civil Procedure

§ 23(b)(3) 83n99

PART I

General Considerations

1

Overview of ERISA

The stakes are high in the regulation of employee benefit plans. The aggregate assets held by qualified private retirement savings plans reached $11.9 trillion by the close of 2020, a greater than nine-fold increase in real terms since the passage of the Employee Retirement Income Security Act of 1974 (ERISA).[1] Employer spending for employee health care coverage is now more than $814 billion *annually*.[2] Retirement and savings plan contributions constitute about 3.4 percent of total compensation costs in private industry, while employer-provided health insurance costs constitute 7.1 percent of total compensation.[3] In 2021, 51 percent of private-sector workers were retirement plan participants, while some 71 percent of Americans working full-time were covered by an employer- or union-sponsored group health care plan, of which 54 percent participated.[4]

---

[1] U.S. Dept. of Labor, Private Pension Plan Bulletin Abstract of 2020 Form 5500 Annual Report, 3, 7 (2022), www.dol.gov/sites/dolgov/files/EBSA/researchers/statistics/retirement-bulletins/private-pension-plan-bulletins-abstract-2020.pdf. In comparison, total assets in private trusteed plans in 1975 were reported as $260 billion (nominal dollars). U.S. Dep't of Labor, Private Pension Plan Bulletin Historical Tables and Graphs 1975-2020 13 (2022) www.dol.gov/sites/dolgov/files/ebsa/researchers/statistics/retirement-bulletins/private-pension-plan-bulletin-historical-tables-and-graphs.pdf. From 1975 through 2020, the consumer price index increased by a factor of about 5.0 according to the CPI Inflation Calculator of the Bureau of Labor Statistics.

[2] Kelsey Waddill, *Employer-Sponsored Health Plans Spent $814B on 2019 Benefits*, Xtelligent Healthcare Media, (July 21, 2021), https://healthpayerintelligence.com/news/employer-sponsored-health-plans-spent-814b-on-2019-benefits [https://perma.cc/7KMY-2M7A].

[3] U.S. Dept. of Labor, Bureau of Lab. Stat., Employer Costs for Employee Compensation – September 2022, 4 (2022) www.bls.gov/news.release/pdf/ecec.pdf .

[4] U.S. Bureau of Labor Statistics, *68 Percent of Private Industry Workers Had Access to Retirement Plans in 2021*, TED: The Economics Daily (Nov. 1, 2021), www.bls.gov/opub/ted/2021/68-percent-of-private-industry-workers-had-access-to-retirement-plans-in-2021.htm [https://perma.cc/7PKU-KBPC]; U.S. Bureau of Labor Statistics, *Health Care Benefits Take-Up Rate Was 77 Percent for Private Industry Workers in March 2021*, TED: The Economics

General Considerations

This book provides an overview of the regulation of employee benefit plans under federal labor and tax laws. Part I explores the structure, policy, and scope of federal benefit plan regulation (Chapters 1 and 2). Part II addresses those aspects of benefit plan regulation that are common to both pension plans, which provide employees with deferred compensation, and welfare plans, which provide employees with medical insurance, dental insurance, life insurance, or other benefits. The four common concerns of pension and welfare plan regulation – disclosure, fiduciary obligations, enforcement, and preemption (Chapters 3–6) – have been the focus of much litigation that evinces unresolved conflicts between several fundamental policies. Part III examines the minimum standards required of certain key terms of the pension contract, specifically those relating to plan participation and vesting, pension distributions, and defined benefit plan funding and termination rules (Chapters 7–9). Part IV traces the influence of federal tax law on retirement savings (in Chapter 10). Part V addresses health plan content controls, offering a broad overview of the history and operation of select policy concepts and legal rules that – after the passage (and partial repeal) of the Patient Protection and Affordable Care Act (ACA) now largely define the state of "employment-based health care" in the United States (Chapter 11).

The labor-law aspects of ERISA are codified in Title 29 of the United State Code.[5] Counterparts to several important labor provisions appear in the Internal Revenue Code as conditions on the favorable income tax treatment accorded "qualified" (i.e., tax-subsidized) pension, annuity, profit-sharing, and stock bonus plans (collectively known as qualified retirement plans). In particular, many of the minimum standards governing pension plan content (Part III) are reproduced (verbatim or nearly so) in Subchapter D of the tax Code.[6] This overlap is attributable to a paternalistic or protective policy that is common to some of the tax and labor provisions of ERISA, and in those instances the interpretation of the qualified plan rules offers guidance for the application of ERISA's labor provisions. Other objectives of the two bodies of law are not shared, and their administration and enforcement are markedly different.[7]

DAILY (Sept. 30, 2021), www.bls.gov/opub/ted/2021/health-care-benefits-take-up-rate-was-77-percent-for-private-industry-workers-in-march-2021.htm [https://perma.cc/XY8L-VPMN].

[5] Employee Retirement Income Security Act of 1974 (ERISA), Pub. L. No. 93-406, 88 Stat. 829 (codified as amended in scattered sections of 26 and 29 U.S.C.). ERISA as used herein refers only to the labor-law provisions of the statute even though Title II of the original legislation contained extensive amendments to the Internal Revenue Code.

[6] I.R.C. §§ 401–33 (2018). Throughout this book, citations to the Internal Revenue Code will be provided where there is a close tax-law counterpart to ERISA's labor provisions.

[7] In contrast to unified public administration of the qualified plan rules by the Internal Revenue Service (IRS), suits by plan participants and beneficiaries (i.e., private enforcement) are the dominant mode of implementing ERISA. See ERISA § 502(a), 29 U.S.C. § 1132(a). ERISA disputes are extremely common in the federal courts. In the twelve-month period ending March 31, 2021, 4,897 civil actions under ERISA were commenced in the U.S. district courts, constituting 1.1 percent of all new civil cases and 2.7 percent of all new actions brought under

A BENEFIT PLAN VARIETIES[8]

Employee benefit plans are categorized in a number of different ways, according to the characteristics of the program. Those characteristics determine the extent of governmental regulation of the program under both ERISA and the tax Code, and so a brief benefit plan typology is essential background.

The type of benefit available under the plan affords the most fundamental basis for classification. ERISA applies only to certain employee benefit plans.[9] The statute defines an employee benefit plan as "an employee welfare benefit plan or an employee pension benefit plan or a plan which is both an employee welfare benefit plan and an employee pension benefit plan."[10] A program that systematically defers compensation until termination of employment (or longer) is an *ERISA pension plan*,[11] while a program that provides any of certain specifically listed benefits is a *welfare plan*, whether the benefit is provided on a current or deferred basis.[12] Health insurance is by far the most costly welfare benefit; other types of welfare benefits include life insurance, disability insurance, and severance pay.[13] Because the definitions of "pension plan" and "welfare plan" are not exhaustive, there is a third category of employee benefits entirely beyond ERISA's reach – any nonpension employee benefit that is not enumerated in the definition of welfare plan.[14]

Whether the program receives preferential income tax treatment provides a second ground for classification. A *qualified* deferred compensation plan obtains the advantage of tax deferral by satisfying numerous conditions; if those conditions are not met, the program is a *nonqualified* arrangement and the employer's

---

a federal statute. U.S. COURTS, TABLE C-2. U.S. DISTRICT COURTS – CIVIL CASES FILED, BY JURISDICTION AND NATURE OF SUIT–DURING THE 12-MONTH PERIODS ENDING MARCH 31, 2020 AND 2021 (2021), www.uscourts.gov/statistics/table/c-2/federal-judicial-caseload-statistics/2021/03/31 [https://perma.cc/V6HM-Q67S]. Over the same twelve-month period, ERISA cases contributed about 2.1 percent of the civil appeals filed in the U.S. Courts of Appeals. U.S. COURTS, TABLE B-7. U.S. COURTS OF APPEALS – CIVIL AND CRIMINAL CASES FILED, BY CIRCUIT AND NATURE OF SUIT OR OFFENSE – DURING THE 12-MONTH PERIOD ENDING MARCH 31, 2021 (2021), www.uscourts.gov/statistics/table/b-7/federal-judicial-caseload-statistics/2021/03/31 [https://perma.cc/ZB57-FYSP] (assuming the "Other Labor" category of private cases involving federal question jurisdiction is predominantly composed of ERISA suits).

[8] The discussion in this section is adapted from Peter J. Wiedenbeck & Russell K. Osgood, *Cases and Materials on Employee Benefits* 62-70 (2nd ed. 2013), and is reprinted with permission of West, a Thomson Reuters business.

[9] ERISA § 4(a), 29 U.S.C. § 1003(a) (2018).

[10] ERISA § 3(3), 29 U.S.C. § 1002(3) (2018).

[11] ERISA § 3(2)(A), 29 U.S.C. § 1002(2)(A) (2018); *see infra* Chapter 2C.

[12] ERISA § 3(1), 29 U.S.C. § 1002(1) (2018); *see infra* Chapter 2C.

[13] Some welfare benefits, such as employer-provided group-term life insurance, are received by more workers than health care but are far less expensive. For a comparison of the cost and coverage of health care and other benefits, *see* BUREAU OF LAB. STAT, *supra* Chapter 1 note 3.

[14] ERISA §§ 3(1)–(3), 4(a), 29 U.S.C. §§ 1002(1)–(3), 1003(a) (2018); *see infra* Chapter 2C.

6 *General Considerations*

deduction must await inclusion of the benefits in the employee's gross income.[15] Certain types of welfare benefits can also receive preferential tax treatment, typically in the form of outright tax exemption rather than deferral. Both the value of the insurance coverage and the amount of any proceeds received under an employer-provided health care plan may be entirely tax free; employer-provided group-term life insurance may qualify for similarly advantageous treatment.[16] In addition to such "qualified" welfare benefits, tax exemption is granted to some benefits that ERISA does not regulate, such as educational assistance programs and employer-provided parking or transportation benefits.[17] In each instance, favorable tax treatment does not depend solely on the type of benefit; it is also conditioned on satisfaction of various criteria prescribed by the Internal Revenue Code. Consequently, benefits provided under a program that fails to meet the tax law's requirements are taxable in-kind compensation.

Turning specifically to deferred compensation, the most important determinant of both labor-law and tax-law regulation is the plan's status as either a "defined benefit" or a "defined contribution" plan. A *defined contribution plan* (also known as an "individual account plan" in ERISA's lexicon) means a plan "which provides for an individual account for each participant and for benefits based solely on the amount contributed to the participant's account, and any income, expenses, gains and losses, and any forfeitures of accounts of other participants which may be allocated to such participant's account."[18] Any other sort of deferred compensation program is a *defined benefit plan*.[19] Contributions or benefits need not be set at a stated dollar amount to be "defined"; rather, the plan need only specify a definite formula (which may depend on compensation level, length of service, age, or other factors) for allocating contributions among participants (in the case of a defined contribution plan) or for determining benefits (in the case of a defined benefit plan).[20] The distinction between defined contribution and defined benefit plans is keyed to an important practical difference – whether the employee or the employer (respectively) bears the risk of investment performance.

Under a defined contribution plan, the employee is entitled only to the balance in her account. Accordingly, the amount of deferred compensation received is

---

[15] *Compare* I.R.C. § 404(a)(1)–(3) (2018) (current deduction for contributions to qualified pension, annuity, profit-sharing, or stock bonus plans) *with id.* § 404(a)(5) (nonqualified arrangement). For an overview of the tax treatment of qualified deferred compensation, *see infra* Chapter 1D. The intricate qualification conditions that must be satisfied to obtain favorable tax treatment are explored in Chapter 10.

[16] I.R.C. § 106(a) (2018) (health care coverage); *id.* § 105(b) (health care proceeds) (2018); *id.* § 79 (group-term life insurance coverage) (2018); *id.* § 101(a) (life insurance proceeds) (2018).

[17] I.R.C. § 127 (educational assistance programs) (2018); *id.* §§ 132(a), (f) (qualified transportation fringe) (2018).

[18] ERISA § 3(34), 29 U.S.C. § 1002(34) (2018); *see* I.R.C. § 414(c) (2018).

[19] ERISA § 3(35), 29 U.S.C. § 1002(35) (2018); *see* I.R.C. § 414(j) (2018).

[20] *See* Treas. Reg. § 1.401–1(b)(1)(ii) (as amended in 2020).

Under a defined benefit plan, in contrast, the risks and rewards of investment performance fall primarily on the employer.[21] That is, a defined benefit plan is an employer's commitment to make specified future payments; the employer is contractually obligated to make those payments even if the assets set aside to finance them prove inadequate. In many respects, defined benefit plans are subject to much more intensive regulation than defined contribution plans.[22]

diminished by low contribution rates, poor rates of return, and declines in asset values (possibly impairing her standard of living in retirement), while high contribution rates, high yields and asset appreciation increase her wealth.

Under a defined benefit plan, in contrast, the risks and rewards of investment performance fall primarily on the employer.[21] That is, a defined benefit plan is an employer's commitment to make specified future payments; the employer is contractually obligated to make those payments even if the assets set aside to finance them prove inadequate. In many respects, defined benefit plans are subject to much more intensive regulation than defined contribution plans.[22]

The broad categories of defined benefit and defined contribution plans are subdivided further. The Internal Revenue Code provides for qualified pension, profit-sharing, stock bonus, and annuity plans. It is essential to understand that a pension plan within the meaning of the tax laws is *not* the same as a pension plan as defined by ERISA. A *pension plan* in tax usage "is a plan established and maintained by an employer primarily to provide systematically for the payment of . . . benefits to his employees over a period of years, usually for life, after retirement";[23] therefore, it is also a pension plan under ERISA. The ERISA category, however, is broader, also including most profit-sharing, stock bonus, and annuity plans. Compounding confusion is the fact that a pension plan (tax Code sense) may be of either the defined benefit or defined contribution type. A fundamental difference between a pension plan (tax Code sense) and a profit-sharing or stock bonus plan has to do with the timing of distributions: pension plans must be designed to provide retirement income, while profit-sharing and stock bonus plans may permit in-service distributions after the passage of a fixed number of years or the attainment of a stated age.[24] Today, profit-sharing and stock bonus plans generally provide for distributions upon separation from service or retirement, and so they too are pension plans in the ERISA sense. But as originally conceived by the tax laws, pension plans were

---

[21] In the case of an underfunded plan of an insolvent employer, the Pension Benefit Guaranty Corporation (PBGC) will make good on most pension promises (by cost-spreading through an insurance mechanism), but employees with large or recently enhanced pension claims may bear part of the loss. And when an overfunded, qualified plan is terminated, as much as 50 percent of the excess assets may be claimed by the IRS or the participants. *See infra* Chapter 9.

[22] These additional requirements are addressed in Chapters 7B and 9 *infra*.

[23] Treas. Reg. § 1.401–1(b)(1)(i) (as amended in 2020).

[24] *Compare id* (describing employee payments with pension plans), *with* § 1.401–1(b)(1)(ii) (describing employee payments with profit-sharing plans). The rule that in-service distributions are prohibited under a pension plan, as defined for tax purposes, is subject to a statutory exception, which was enacted as I.R.C. § 401(a)(36) in 2006 to facilitate phased retirement programs. The statute further provides that a pension plan can be qualified even if it permits distributions to be made to an employee who has attained age sixty-two and is still employed. Corresponding language was added to the definition of a pension plan for purposes of ERISA as the final sentence in 29 U.S.C. § 1002(2)(A) (2018). But because of the greater breadth of the ERISA category, this amendment was probably unnecessary.

General Considerations

conceived as retirement savings vehicles, while profit-sharing and stock bonus plans were seen as shorter-term deferred compensation programs.

A *money purchase pension plan* is a defined contribution plan that requires specified annual contributions (usually a percentage of each participant's compensation) regardless of the employer's profits.[25] The money purchase plan is, in most respects, the simplest qualified deferred compensation arrangement, the "plain vanilla" retirement plan. A *profit-sharing plan* is also a defined contribution arrangement, but the amount contributed may be geared to profits or left to the discretion of the board of directors; indeed, annual contributions are not required, and contributions can be made even if the employer has no current or accumulated profits or is a tax-exempt (nonprofit) organization.[26] The plan must, however, provide a definite formula for allocating any contributions among participants' accounts. A *stock bonus plan* can be a discretionary contribution arrangement like a profit-sharing plan, except that it provides distributions in the form of employer stock.[27] A profit-sharing or stock bonus plan may include a *cash-or-deferred arrangement* (commonly known as a CODA or *401(k) plan*) allowing participants to contribute a portion of their pay to the deferred compensation plan or take it all in cash. If the plan is properly structured (i.e., if it meets the requirements of a "qualified" cash-or-deferred arrangement, specified in I.R.C. § 401(k)), participants are not treated as having constructively received amounts they contribute, and so tax is deferred until distribution.[28]

Two types of formulas are commonly used to specify the amount of the retirement annuity due (i.e., to "define" the benefit) under a defined benefit pension plan. A *unit credit plan* explicitly takes into account job tenure with a three-factor formula: the benefit at retirement age is defined as the product of (1) a service factor (usually either the participant's total years of service with the employer or years of participation in the plan), (2) a stated percentage (typically in the range of 1 percent to 3 percent), and (3) a specified measure of compensation. The compensation measure is sometimes career-average compensation, but more often it is computed over a shorter period – frequently three to five years – that yields the maximum average (called highest average compensation) or that immediately precedes separation from service (called final average compensation). In contrast, a *flat benefit plan* uses a two-factor formula, specifying the benefit at normal retirement age as the product of (1) a specified measure of compensation (which again may be career average, highest average, or final average), and (2) a stated percentage (typically in the range of 40 percent to 60 percent). The difference between flat benefit and unit credit formulas is really only a matter of degree,

---

[25] Treas. Reg. § 1.401–1(b)(1)(i) (as amended in 2020).

[26] *Id.* § 1.401–1(b)(1)(ii); I.R.C. § 401(a)(27) (2018).

[27] Treas. Reg. § 1.401–1(b)(1)(iii) (as amended in 2020); I.R.C. §§ 401(a)(23), 409(h) (2018).

[28] I.R.C. § 402(e)(3) (2018).

Overview of ERISA

however, because under a flat benefit plan a minimum period of service (typically ten years or more) is invariably required to qualify for the full stated benefit, and the "flat" benefit is reduced proportionately for participants with fewer years of service.

Defined benefit plans present special problems relating to funding. ERISA requires that the employer's commitment to pay specified benefits in the future be backed up by a systematic savings program in the present. Because the amount that will become due is generally contingent on future events (such as final or career-average compensation, total length of service, and survival to retirement), the total amount that will become due must be estimated based on reasonable predictions of such factors, and a method must be used to allocate that estimated total cost over the participants' working years. That is, contributions under a defined benefit plan are not specified in the plan (as in a defined contribution plan), but must be determined actuarially. Another important feature of defined benefit plans is the ability to grant or increase benefits retroactively; benefits may be granted based on periods of service prior to institution of the plan. For example, the service factor under a unit credit formula may use total years of service with the employer, both before and after the plan is established, rather than years of participation. The grant of such *past service credit* necessarily creates an immediate unfunded liability, which the plan's actuarial funding method, as regulated by ERISA's minimum funding rules, must redress.

An *annuity plan* is, in effect, a pension plan (tax-law meaning) that is funded by the purchase of annuity contracts from an insurance company rather than by contributions to a trust. Accordingly, to receive preferential tax treatment, an annuity plan must, in general, satisfy all the qualification requirements applicable to pension plans other than those pertaining to the terms and funding of the trust.[29]

The organizational chart in Figure 1.1 presents an overview of the main types of employee benefit arrangements, focusing on retirement arrangements and categorized according to distinctions in treatment under ERISA and the Internal Revenue Code. (It is oversimplified in some respects; for example, similar subcategories apply to nonqualified pension plans.) The statutory citations provide support for the indicated classifications; they are not intended to designate the regulatory regime that applies to each category (the subject of the remainder of this book). Special shading is applied to defined benefit pension plans to indicate that this type of retirement savings program is subject to intensive regulation to ensure that adequate funds will be available to pay promised benefits (see Chapter 9). A similar organizational chart that focuses on welfare benefit arrangements, Figure 1.2, follows immediately thereafter.

---

[29] I.R.C. §§ 403(a), 404(a)(2) (2018). A qualified annuity plan of the sort described in the text is a generally available qualified plan. It must be distinguished from a "403(b) annuity" (also known as a "tax-sheltered annuity"), which is a special retirement savings program subject to relaxed requirements that may be offered to employees of tax-exempt educational or charitable organizations, as well as state and local government educational organization (e.g., public school) employees. *Id.* § 403(b).

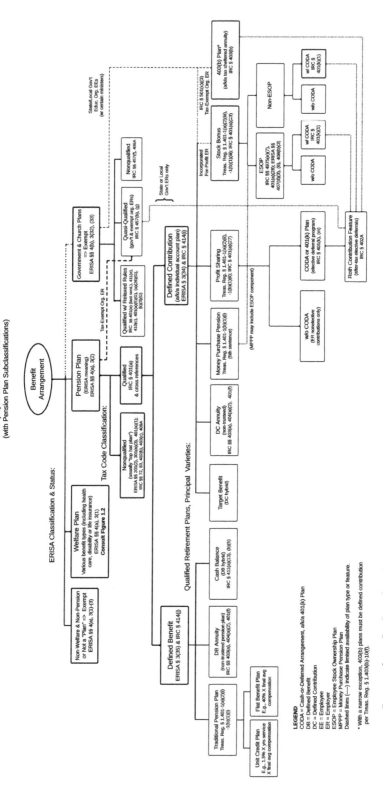

FIGURE 1.1 Pension benefit plan classification

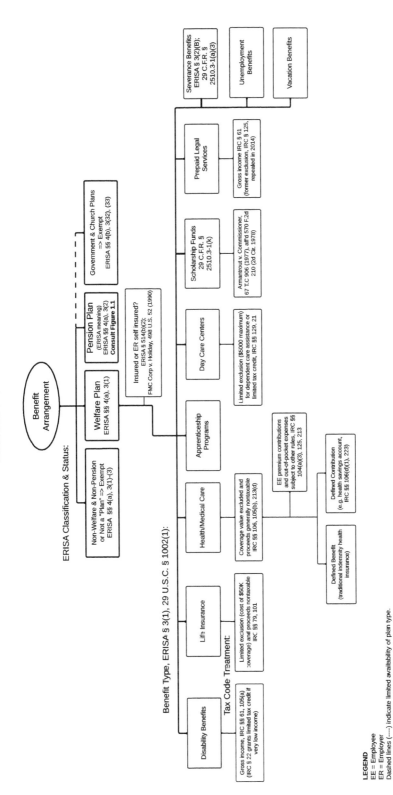

FIGURE 1.2 Welfare benefit plan classification

12   *General Considerations*

Another important characteristic used to categorize benefit plans is the distinction between single-employer plans and multiemployer plans. A *multiemployer plan* is a plan to which more than one employer is required to contribute that is maintained pursuant to a collective bargaining agreement with more than one employer. For this purpose, all businesses that are under common control are treated as one employer.[30] Any plan that is not a multiemployer plan is called a *single-employer plan*, even if several legally distinct entities contribute.[31] A plan may be classified as a single-employer plan because it is, in fact, maintained by only one employer; because it is maintained by multiple employers under common control; or because unrelated multiple employers contribute to a plan that is not the product of collective bargaining. Multiemployer plans grant contributions or benefits for service with any participating employer and are frequently sponsored by unions representing workers in industries such as the construction trades, where workers change employers frequently. Multiemployer plans, although well adapted to employment patterns in certain industries, present special challenges for funding.[32]

B ERISA'S PATTERN OF REGULATION

ERISA implicitly prescribes four levels of employee benefit regulation. First, certain employer-provided benefits are exempt from federal regulation, either because they are not provided pursuant to a "plan, fund or program," or because they are of a kind that does not fit the description of a pension or welfare benefit.[33] Congress also stipulated that governmental and church plans are to be free of federal oversight, presumably to ease intergovernmental relations (comity) and prevent entanglement.[34] Although entirely beyond ERISA's reach, benefits in this first category are

---

[30] ERISA § 3(37), 29 U.S.C. § 1002(37) (2018); *see* I.R.C. § 414(f) (2018).

[31] ERISA § 3(41), 29 U.S.C. § 1002(41) (2018).

[32] Israel Goldowitz, *Funding of Public Sector Pension Plans: What Can Be Learned from the Private Sector*, 23 CONN. INS. L.J. 143, 158, 163–64 (2016) (discussing funding issues that plague multiemployer pension plans resulting in a $52 billion deficit). Congress addressed these issues through enacting the Multiemployer Pension Reform Act of 2014; Consolidated and Further Continuing Appropriations Act, 2015, Pub. L. No. 113-235, 128 Stat. 2130, 2773-822 (codified as 26 U.S.C. § 432).

[33] *See infra* Chapter 2.

[34] ERISA §§ 3(32), (33), 4(b)(1)–(2), 29 U.S.C. §§ 1002(32), (33), 1003(b)(1)–(2) (2018); Church Plan Parity and Entanglement Protection Act, Pub. L. No. 106-244, 114 Stat. 499 (2000); Advocate Health Care Network v. Stapleton, 137 S.Ct. 1652, 1658–62 (2017) (providing further context to the definition of church plans). In addition to its federalism concerns, Congress also observed that underfunded governmental plans pose less threat to workers' financial security, since public employers have recourse to the tax power to make good on their benefit promises. *See* Rose v. Long Island R.R. Pension Plan, 828 F.2d 910, 914 (2d Cir. 1987). In 1996, however, Congress imposed advance funding as a condition on the favorable tax treatment of certain state and local government retirement plans. I.R.C. § 457 (g) (2018). Also expressly excepted from ERISA are unfunded excess benefit plans, which are arrangements maintained for the exclusive purpose of providing pension benefits that exceed

Overview of ERISA

permissible subjects of state or local regulation because ERISA's preemption clause also does not apply.[35]

The lowest level of federal regulation constrains the administration of all employee benefit plans, both pension and welfare, in three respects. First, reporting and disclosure rules mandate the collection and dissemination of information concerning plan terms and finances to the Secretary of Labor and the participants and beneficiaries.[36] Second, plan fiduciaries are held to exacting standards of conduct derived from trust law.[37] Third, state regulation of pension and welfare plans is preempted, and federal courts are granted exclusive jurisdiction to enforce ERISA's requirements (including fiduciary duties), as well as jurisdiction concurrent with state courts over suits by a participant or beneficiary to enforce the terms of the plan.[38]

Additional requirements apply to pension plans, which provide retirement income or the deferral of income until the termination of covered employment or beyond.[39] These plans are subject to complex, intensive regulation, including minimum standards governing certain terms of the deferred compensation program.[40] The minimum standards generally prevent employers from imposing age or service conditions on plan membership that are more exacting than the attainment of age twenty-one and completion of one year of service.[41] The minimum standards also demand (among other things) that benefits derived from employer contributions become nonforfeitable within a reasonable period (often five years),[42] that a participant's spouse receive certain protections in the event of death or divorce,[43] and that a participant's interest in the plan be inalienable.[44]

The most stringent regulation is reserved for defined benefit pension plans. Over and above the foregoing, defined benefit pension plans must provide minimum

---

the Internal Revenue Code's limits on the amount of deferred compensation that may be provided under a qualified retirement plan. ERISA §§ 3(36), 4(b)(5), 29 U.S.C. §§ 1002(36), 1003(b)(5) (2018).

[35] ERISA § 514(a), 29 U.S.C. § 1144(a) (2018).

[36] ERISA §§ 101–11, 29 U.S.C. §§ 1021–31 (2018).

[37] ERISA §§ 401(a), 404, 406, 29 U.S.C. §§ 1101(a), 1104, 1106 (2018).

[38] ERISA §§ 502, 514, 29 U.S.C. §§ 1132, 1144 (2018).

[39] ERISA § 3(2)(A), 29 U.S.C. § 1002(2)(A) (2018).

[40] ERISA §§ 3(3), 4(a), 201–11, 301–305, 29 U.S.C. §§ 1002(3), 1003(a), 1051–61, 1081–85 (2018).

[41] ERISA § 202(a)(1)(A), 29 U.S.C. § 1052(a)(1)(A) (2018); *see* I.R.C. § 410(a) (corresponding tax qualification condition) (2018). Exceptions are discussed *infra* Chapter 7 notes 2, 26, and accompanying text.

[42] ERISA § 203, 29 U.S.C. § 1053 (2018); *see* I.R.C. § 411 (2018) (corresponding tax qualification condition).

[43] ERISA §§ 205, 206(d)(3), 29 U.S.C. §§ 1055, 1056(d)(3) (2018); *see* I.R.C. §§ 401(a)(11), (a)(13)(B), 414(p), 417 (2018) (corresponding tax qualification conditions).

[44] ERISA § 206(d)(1), 29 U.S.C. § 1056(d)(1) (2018); *see* I.R.C. § 401(a)(13) (2018) (corresponding tax qualification condition).

rates of benefit accrual,[45] satisfy minimum funding standards,[46] and comply with the Pension Benefit Guaranty Corporation (PBGC) termination insurance program,[47] which includes restrictions on plan termination.[48]

The morphogenesis of this graduated system of regulation is straightforward. Congress was primarily concerned about pensions and was persuaded to impose detailed substantive regulation of certain key terms of deferred compensation programs (hereafter, pension content controls). Among pension plans, defined benefit arrangements required greater oversight because of the actuarial funding challenge. Absent systematic advance funding, payment of the stipulated retirement annuity is contingent on the long-term financial health of the employer; funding rules and the PBGC insurance system secure the employer's pension promise. With a defined contribution plan, such security is unnecessary because full performance is rendered upon contribution to the participant's account (i.e., the participant bears the investment risk). Welfare plans generally involve current, rather than deferred, compensation, and so the risks of defeated expectations and employer default are less severe. Consequently, Congress declined to regulate the content of welfare plans in ERISA,[49] but mandated disclosure of plan terms and finances, imposed uniform fiduciary obligations, and promulgated a detailed scheme of federal judicial enforcement. This three-pronged approach equips participants with tools to safeguard their own interests. Thus, ERISA facilitates private monitoring of privately constituted welfare plans, while pension plans are subject to both private monitoring and limited content regulation.

ERISA's four-tiered system of regulation is modified in two instances, to adapt federal law to the special characteristics of (1) executive deferred compensation programs (discussed *infra* Chapter 2D), and (2) insurance-funded pension and welfare plans. Insurance-funded plans get special treatment to accommodate federal benefit plan regulation to paramount state insurance law. ERISA's minimum funding requirements do not apply to a pension plan funded *exclusively* by the purchase of level-premium individual or group insurance or annuity contracts under which benefits are guaranteed by a state-licensed insurance company.[50] If pension benefits are partially insurer-guaranteed, then funding rules apply, but ERISA's

---

[45] ERISA § 204, 29 U.S.C. § 1054 (2018); *see* I.R.C. § 411(b) (2018) (corresponding tax qualification condition).

[46] ERISA §§ 301(a)(8), 302–05, 29 U.S.C. §§ 1081(a)(8), 1082–85 (2018); *see* I.R.C. §§ 412, 430–32, 436 (2018) (corresponding tax-law funding rules).

[47] ERISA § 4021(a), (b)(1), 29 U.S.C. § 1321(a), (b)(1) (2018).

[48] ERISA §§ 4041, 4041A, 29 U.S.C. §§ 1341, 1341a (2018).

[49] *But see* Section E, *infra* (discussing health care regulation). Prior to the passage of the ACA, on limited occasions Congress had responded to public concern over gaps in health insurance coverage by amending ERISA to impose certain limited content controls on health care plans. *See infra* Part III note 1, and Chapter 11B.

[50] ERISA § 301(a)(2), (b), 29 U.S.C. § 1081(a)(2), (b) (2018); *see* I.R.C. § 412(e)(3); Treas. Reg. § 1.412(i)–1(a) (1980).

Overview of ERISA

fiduciary responsibility standards do not cover the insurance company's investment and asset-management activities under such a "guaranteed benefit policy."[51] In the case of an insured welfare plan (a health plan financed by the employer's purchase of a group medical insurance policy, for example), federal welfare standards (i.e., reporting and disclosure, fiduciary responsibility, and enforcement) are not relaxed, with states retaining (some) power to regulate plans indirectly via regulation of the insurance companies that service the plans.[52]

C ERISA'S PRINCIPAL POLICIES

The pattern of benefit plan regulation described above is a response to a number of perceived injustices and breakdowns in the delivery of retirement and insurance benefits as employment compensation. The tax-subsidized but largely unregulated regime that preceded ERISA frequently frustrated workers' expectations, if not their legal rights.

ERISA, one key participant has observed, "was, at its core, a 'reasonable expectations' bill. It gave an ordinary employee the assured right to receive what a reasonable person in his boots would have expected in the circumstances. Primarily, it was a consumer protection bill."[53] This goal of consumer protection is advanced by three of ERISA's general policies: promoting informed financial decision making; preventing mismanagement and abuse of benefit programs; and protecting the reliance interests of plan participants and beneficiaries. At the same time, Congress embraced a fourth policy: preserving substantial employer control over plan sponsorship and design. These four principal policies are briefly described in this section. The tensions among them, however, are not so easily resolved. Subsequent chapters will show that ERISA litigation frequently calls on the federal courts to reconcile conflicts among these competing policies.

Promoting Informed Financial Decision Making

Mandatory disclosure rules are a central component of ERISA. Disclosure of plan terms and finances promotes economic efficiency by giving participants and beneficiaries the information they need to accommodate their personal financial affairs to the employer's program, as, for example, in determining their needs for additional savings or insurance. ERISA requires that the plan administrator supply participants

---

[51] ERISA § 401(b)(2), 29 U.S.C. § 1101(b)(2) (2018). *See* John Hancock Mut. Life Ins. Co. v. Harris Tr. & Sav. Bank, 510 U.S. 86, 106 (1993) (construing "guaranteed benefit policy" as requiring the allocation of investment risk to the insurer, and concluding that ERISA's fiduciary rules apply to assets held in an insurance company's general account under a participating group annuity contract).

[52] ERISA § 514(b)(2), 29 U.S.C. § 1144(b)(2) (2018) (the insurance "savings clause"). ERISA preemption is notoriously broad and complicated, a state of affairs for which both the courts and Congress share blame. We discuss preemption in greater detail in Chapter 6, *infra*.

[53] Frank Cummings, *ERISA: The Reasonable Expectations Bill*, 65 TAX NOTES 880, 881 (1994).

General Considerations

and beneficiaries with a summary plan description (SPD), which "shall be written in a manner calculated to be understood by the average plan participant, and shall be sufficiently accurate and comprehensive to reasonably apprise such participants and beneficiaries of their rights and obligations under the plan."[54] Congress made the SPD the participants' principal source of information on plan content for the following reasons:

> It is grossly unfair to hold an employee accountable for acts which disqualify him from benefits, if he had no knowledge of these acts, or if these conditions were stated in a misleading or incomprehensible manner in plan booklets. Subcommittee findings were abundant in establishing that an average plan participant, even where he has been furnished an explanation of his plan's provisions, often cannot comprehend them because of the technicalities and complexities of the language used.[55]

Facilitating informed decision making is a pervasive goal of ERISA, extending far beyond the mandatory disclosure rules. Many of ERISA's core requirements of pension plan content (e.g., minimum standards governing vesting and funding) can be understood as a response to the problem of information overload (Chapters 7 and 9).

> For most workers, the cost of evaluating the specialized terms and particular finances of numerous alternative plans (associated with different employment opportunities) may exceed the benefit of a marginally more valuable pension. Information costs may be reduced by limited standardization (i.e., restricting the variance) of key contract terms. By reducing job search costs, content regulation may increase economic efficiency.

> From the information cost perspective, pension content controls complement the disclosure regime. Disclosure provides access to information, while content controls limit the volume of information to a manageable level. Together, they facilitate career and financial planning.[56]

---

[54] ERISA § 102(a)(1), 29 U.S.C. § 1022(a)(1) (2018).

[55] S. REP. NO. 93-127, at 11 (1973), *reprinted in* 1 SUBCOMM. ON LABOR OF THE S. COMM. ON LABOR AND PUBLIC WELFARE, 94TH CONG., LEGISLATIVE HISTORY OF THE EMPLOYEE RETIREMENT INCOME SECURITY ACT OF 1974, at 587, 597 (Comm. Print 1976) [hereinafter ERISA LEGISLATIVE HISTORY].

In *Cent. Laborers' Pension Fund v. Heinz*, 541 U.S. 739, 744 (2004), the Court construed a plan amendment placing additional restrictions on the receipt of pension benefits as a prohibited reduction in benefits, in part to protect retirement planning decisions:

"Heinz worked and accrued retirement benefits under a plan with terms allowing him to supplement retirement income by certain employment, and he was being reasonable if he relied on those terms in planning his retirement. The 1998 amendment undercut any such reliance, paying retirement income only if he accepted a substantial curtailment of his opportunity to do the kind of work he knew." *Id.* at 744–45.

[56] Peter J. Wiedenbeck, *Implementing ERISA: Of Policies and "Plans,"* 72 WASH. U. L.Q. 559, 574 (1994).

Overview of ERISA 17

ERISA standardizes certain *express* terms of the pension promise, but does not stop there. In effect, all *implied* terms of *both* pension and welfare plans are standardized as well. By imposing uniform fiduciary obligations and authorizing the development of a federal common law of benefit plans to replace preempted state law, the unwritten terms of the benefit program are standardized as well (Chapters 4 and 6).[57]

Preventing Mismanagement and Abuse

ERISA imposes uniform federal fiduciary obligations to control mismanagement and abuse of employee benefit programs. While drawing on general principles of trust law, ERISA's fiduciary standards include two fundamental departures from prevailing state law. First, the statutory definition of fiduciary extends far beyond state law trustees, imposing standards of competence and fair dealing on anyone who has or exercises any discretionary authority in the administration of the plan, or who exercises any control in the management of its assets, and on paid investment advisers as well.[58] Second, ERISA voids any attempt to relax its stringent fiduciary obligations through the inclusion of exculpatory clauses in the plan,[59] even though such indulgences are common and effective under state law.

Federal fiduciary standards were designed to work in combination with improved disclosure of plan finances and powerful enforcement tools to stem misconduct in plan administration.[60] Particularized reporting of transactions between the plan and certain related parties would give participants and the Labor Department information needed to assert workers' rights,[61] while the federal courts, armed with broad remedial powers and supported by nationwide service of process, would grant

---

[57] By "federal common law," we essentially mean "decisional law filling the gaps in ERISA with respect to the many subjects which Congress did not expressly address."

[58] ERISA § 3(21)(A), 29 U.S.C. § 1002(21)(A) (2018). E.g., S. Rep. No. 93-127, at 29, *reprinted in* 1 ERISA Legislative History, *supra* Chapter 1 note 55, at 587, 615 (fiduciary responsibility provisions deemed necessary because "[I]t is unclear whether the traditional law of trusts is applicable . . . . [to certain] . . . plans, such as insured plans, which do not use the trust form as their mode of funding."). While the extension of fiduciary obligations to insurance and annuity plans was deliberate and well understood, including as fiduciaries all persons with any discretionary authority in plan administration (in addition to those who have a role in the management or disposition of assets) seems to have escaped congressional attention.

[59] ERISA § 410(a), 29 U.S.C. § 1110(a) (2018). *See* S. Rep. No. 93-127, at 29, *reprinted in* 1 ERISA Legislative History, *supra* Chapter 1 note 55, at 587, 615.

[60] E.g., S. Rep. No. 93-127, at 29, *reprinted in* 1 ERISA Legislative History, *supra* Chapter 1 note 55, at 587, 615 ("[W]ithout provisions . . . allowing ready access to both detailed information about the plan and to the courts, and without standards by which a participant can measure the fiduciary's conduct . . . he is not equipped to safeguard either his own rights or the plan assets.").

[61] *Id.* at 27–28; *see* ERISA § 103(b)(3)(D), 29 U.S.C. § 1023(b)(3)(D) (2018).

18 *General Considerations*

effective relief.[62] Moreover, employees would be free to assert their rights without fear of employer retaliation by discharge, demotion, or other adverse employment action.[63] That, at least, was the idea.

Protecting Reliance

In the case of pension plans, ERISA goes beyond disclosure and regulation of fiduciary conduct to impose minimum standards for certain plan terms. Such substantive regulation ensures that the promise of a pension has some minimum content. Limited content control of pension plans has traditionally been justified as necessary to protect employee reliance interests.[64] But under a regime of mandatory disclosure, is reliance worthy of protection? If, for example, participants are made aware that the plan does not allow for vesting, no legitimate expectation is defeated when a pension is denied an employee terminated before retirement age, however long their service.

Minimum standards of pension plan content "protect" reliance only in the sense that they *prevent* reliance that might often be unwarranted. Hence, the justification for content regulation must lie in a concern that substantial numbers of plan participants would not make proper use of the information available to them. That concern may be well founded, for workers may misevaluate pension promises as a result of an innate bias in human judgment. Investigations in cognitive psychology yield evidence that people systematically underestimate the likelihood of the occurrence of low-probability long-delayed events.[65] Underestimation of the risk of pension loss from factors such as forfeiture conditions, underfunding, fiduciary misconduct, or employer insolvency would cause workers to overvalue unregulated pension promises. Consistent overvaluation would permit employers to charge more for pension plan coverage, via reduced wages or other benefits, than such contingent retirement savings are really worth. Substantive regulation to reduce the

---

[62] *E.g.*, S. REP. NO. 93-127, at 35, *reprinted in* 1 ERISA LEGISLATIVE HISTORY, *supra* Chapter 1 note 55, at 587, 621 ("remove jurisdictional and procedural obstacles which in the past appear to have hampered effective enforcement of fiduciary responsibilities under state law"); Cummings, *supra* Chapter 1 note 53, at 881–82 (draftsman of ERISA recounts service-of-process problems under prior law).

[63] *See* ERISA § 510, 29 U.S.C. § 1140 (2018).

[64] The congressional findings include: "many employees with long years of employment are losing *anticipated* retirement benefits owing to lack of vesting provisions in such plans" and "owing to the termination of plans before requisite funds have been accumulated, employees and their beneficiaries have been deprived of *anticipated* benefits; and that it is therefore desirable in the interests of employees and their beneficiaries, ... that minimum standards be provided assuring the equitable character of such plans and their financial soundness." ERISA § 2(a), 29 U.S.C. § 1001(a) (2018) (emphasis added).

[65] *E.g.*, Cass R. Sunstein, *Legal Interference with Private Preferences*, 53 U. CHI. L. REV. 1129, 1167 (1986); Cass R. Sunstein, *The Laws of Fear*, 115 HARV. L. REV. 1119, 1125–28 (2002) (reviewing PAUL SLOVIC, THE PERCEPTION OF RISK (2000)).

Overview of ERISA

risk of pension loss might bring the real worth of plan coverage into line with workers' inflated estimation, increasing their welfare and improving overall economic efficiency. From this standpoint, ERISA's pension plan content controls could be fairly viewed as an instance of consumer protection legislation;[66] disclosure being ineffective in this area, protection took the form of minimum standards of product quality, similar to automobile safety standards.

There is a second strand to ERISA's worker protections that is distinct from the effort to align expectations and reality. Curiously, ERISA contains elements of a forced savings system, even though plan sponsorship is voluntary, and public subsidy is available only through the Internal Revenue Code. ERISA's restriction on certain age and service conditions[67] ensures that employees who are otherwise eligible begin participation early, making it more likely that they will accumulate adequate retirement savings in spite of any youthful proclivity to overdiscount future support needs.[68] In addition, the antialienation requirement invalidates the sale or transfer of rights under the plan in an effort to prevent participants and beneficiaries from dissipating their savings prior to retirement.[69]

These two protective policies (preventing unwarranted reliance and forcing retirement savings) are fundamentally paternalistic. Paternalism is the conventional understanding of ERISA's primary purpose. Yet there is an alternative justification for limiting the variability of certain plan terms: promoting better decision making. As noted earlier, some standardization of key contract terms, such as vesting or funding, may be necessary to avoid information overload.[70] This information cost perspective views much of ERISA as an effort to facilitate individual career and financial planning, not override it. Many particular rules are subject to wildly divergent interpretations, according to whether they are understood as efforts to liberate or confine employee decision making.

Preserving Employer Autonomy

ERISA itself does not infringe on employers' freedom to choose whether or not to sponsor employee benefit programs.[71] Because pension and welfare benefit plans are voluntary employment-based programs, employers will decline to offer retirement or health benefits if costs become too high. By virtue of this opt out, the regulation of employee benefits entails a delicate balance – measures intended to

---

[66] See supra text accompanying Chapter 1 note 53.

[67] See supra text accompanying Chapter 1 note 42.

[68] See H.R. Rep. No. 93-807, at 43–44 (1974), as reprinted in 2 ERISA LEGISLATIVE HISTORY, supra Chapter 1 note 55, at 3115, 3163–64.

[69] ERISA § 206(d)(1), 29 U.S.C. § 1056(d)(1); see I.R.C. § 401(a)(13) (2018).

[70] See supra text accompanying Chapter 1 notes 54–57.

[71] For a discussion of how the Affordable Care Act impacts the obligations of ERISA plans, see infra Section E and Chapter 11.

improve the quality of pension and welfare benefit programs, if taken too far, deter some employers from providing such benefits at all. Hence the imposition of higher and higher standards, while ensuring first-rate coverage for some workers, would cause a larger and larger proportion of the US labor force to receive nothing.[72] This cost/coverage trade-off sets the limits of legislation in this field, as the courts have recognized.[73]

The "minimum standards" approach sets a reliable baseline content for certain key pension plan provisions, such as vesting, that had repeatedly brought workers to grief. These lower bounds can be surpassed or not as the sponsor chooses, while other plan terms and practices are unconstrained. Most notably, neither the extent of workforce coverage nor the level of plan benefits is fixed by law.

The virtue of the minimum standards approach is the flexibility it preserves for plan sponsors – flexibility to tailor the plan to the unique needs and objectives of the business.[74] With flexibility comes variation and complexity, attended by increased costs of plan administration and compliance. This is the vice of the minimum standards approach.[75] (In contrast, the lockstep, take-it-or-leave-it approach to deferred compensation – mandatory plan terms with voluntary employer participation – at least has the virtue of simplicity.) Many experts are worried that the costs of compliance with ERISA's minimum funding and termination insurance rules,

---

[72] *See, e.g.,* M&G Polymers USA, LLC v. Tackett, 574 U.S. 427, 434–36 (2015) (discussing cost tradeoffs); Heimeshoff v. Hartford Life & Accident Ins. Co., 571 U.S. 99, 108 (2013) (same). This point was also made forcefully during Senate debate on ERISA. 119 Cong. Rec. 30,375 (1973), *reprinted in* 2 ERISA LEGISLATIVE HISTORY, *supra* Chapter 1 note 55, at 1776 (remarks of Sen. Harrison Williams, principal Democratic cosponsor of ERISA).

[73] *See, e.g.,* Hozier v. Midwest Fasteners, Inc., 908 F.2d 1155, 1160 (3d Cir. 1990) ("Having made a fundamental decision not to require employers to provide *any* benefit plans, Congress was forced to balance its desire to regulate extant plans more extensively against the danger that increased regulation would deter employers from creating such plans in the first place."). *See also* Mertens v. Hewitt Assocs., 508 U.S. 248, 262–63 (1993).

[74] As a result, plans can be designed to promote different personnel policies. Some employers may wish to provide an incentive to increase job tenure, thereby reducing recruitment and training costs, while other businesses (especially since the elimination of mandatory retirement) may want to limit job tenure, using the pension plan to ease out superannuated workers. Some pension plans are geared to providing a secure source of retirement income by accumulating regular contributions in a diversified investment portfolio for periodic distribution over the employee's retirement years, while others – such as profit-sharing and stock bonus plans – may provide a productivity incentive by making contributions dependent on firm output or profits, or by investing heavily in employer securities. *See* TERESA GHILARDUCCI, LABOR'S CAPITAL: THE ECONOMICS AND POLITICS OF PRIVATE PENSIONS 15–16, 20 (1992) (discussing how flexibility is the main attraction of pensions for employers).

[75] *See e.g.,* Varity Corp. v. Howe, 516 U.S. 489, 496–97 (1996). In interpreting ERISA's fiduciary duties "courts may have to take account of competing congressional purposes, such as Congress' desire to offer employees enhanced protection for their benefits, on the one hand, and, on the other, its desire not to create a system that is so complex that administrative costs, or litigation expenses, unduly discourage employers from offering welfare benefit plans in the first place." *Id.* at 497.

Overview of ERISA 21

which have been repeatedly tightened since the mid-1980s, have contributed to a marked decline in prevalence of defined benefit pension plans.[76]

Supersession of state regulation – federal preemption (discussed in Chapter 6, *infra*) – is an indispensable counterpart to the minimum standards approach. If state and local governments were permitted to impose additional controls on pension or welfare plans, benefit costs would increase under many plans, while their utility in serving employer personnel policies would diminish.

Policy Interactions

The importance of ERISA's four principal policies varies with the context, as shown by the increasing levels of regulation applied to welfare plans, defined contribution pension plans, and defined benefit pension plans. The absence of welfare plan content controls, for example, indicates that the protective policy (paternalism) has little force in this arena.[77] The disclosure of plan terms and finances serves employees' information needs (as do uniform fiduciary standards), while preemption shields the employer from the costs of state-mandated benefits. With these tools, Congress promotes informed contracting with respect to welfare benefits, thereby facilitating private autonomy rather than restricting it.

The regulatory implications of these policy concerns are sometimes remarkably consistent. Preemption, for example, is arguably supported both by the employer's interest in controlling costs and the employee's planning interest (via the standardization of implicit plan terms). Frequently, however, ERISA's policies interfere with rather than reinforce one another.[78] Where important problems were foreseen, Congress specially adjusted the balance between competing concerns. For instance, ERISA accommodates the traditional use of profit-sharing and stock bonus plans as a productivity incentive by relaxing generally applicable fiduciary duties (prudence and diversification) to permit concentrated investment in employer securities.[79] Other tensions must be resolved by the courts.

---

[76] Virginia Doelgast, Matthew Bidwell & Alexander J. S. Colvin, *New Directions in Employment Relations Theory: Understanding Fragmentation, Identity, and Legitimacy*, 74 ILR Rev.: J. Work & Pol'y 555, 563–64 (2021).

[77] For certain health plans, the passage of the Affordable Care Act modified this in a limited way. *See infra* Section E and Chapter 11.

[78] *E.g., Mertens*, 508 U.S. at 262–63 (1993): "There is, in other words, a 'tension between the primary [ERISA] goal of benefiting employees and the subsidiary goal of containing pension costs.'" (quoting Alessi v. Raybestos-Manhattan, Inc., 451 U.S. 504, 515 (1981)).

[79] ERISA §§ 404(a)(2), 407(b)(1), (d)(3), 29 U.S.C. §§ 1104(a)(2), 1107(b)(1), (d)(3) (2018); Fifth Third Bancorp v. Dudenhoeffer, 573 U.S. 409, 411–12 (2014). In 2006, however, Congress altered the balance between retirement security and employer autonomy by requiring most defined contribution plans holding publicly traded employer securities to allow a participant who has at least three years of service to switch the investment of his account from employer securities to a diversified investment vehicle. Regardless of length of service, a participant must be given similar investment control over the portion of his account balance

D ERISA'S RELATION TO TAX QUALIFICATION

ERISA's graduated regulatory regime (*supra* Section B) applies to welfare and pension plans regardless of whether the program qualifies for preferential tax treatment. Most pension and health care plans are intended to garner special tax benefits – deferral in the case of pensions, and outright exemption in the case of health care. Such favored status is provided to encourage widespread pension and health insurance coverage, but the tax concessions come with strings attached. Numerous conditions must be satisfied to "qualify" for special tax treatment. In the case of retirement savings, some of those qualification conditions track ERISA's pension plan content controls. Indeed, apart from the PBGC insurance system, all the major substantive components of federal pension regulation are reproduced in the Internal Revenue Code, where they function as conditions on the preferential tax treatment granted qualified retirement plans. This section focuses on the overlap between ERISA's pension regulation and the tax Code's qualification criteria, with emphasis on the cause and extent of that correspondence.

The definition of a qualified plan is set forth in IRC § 401(a) – the longest subsection of the Internal Revenue Code – which incorporates by reference much of the remainder of Subchapter D. Directly or indirectly, the definition of a qualified plan imposes hundreds of conditions. Although the qualification requirements are quite intricate, the operational tax rules are actually very simple. There are three major components of the preferential tax treatment of qualified deferred compensation. First, the employer receives a current deduction (subject to certain limits) for amounts actually contributed to the plan.[80] Second, the trust that holds the plan assets is generally exempt from taxation on its investment income.[81] Third, any amount contributed on behalf of an individual employee is not included in gross income until actually distributed by the plan; upon distribution, trust earnings are taxable to the recipient as well.[82] In some circumstances, distributions may be eligible for further tax deferral if they are promptly reinvested in another qualified plan or an individual retirement account (IRA).[83] Because the employer is allowed a deduction even though the employee does not simultaneously report income, deferral is the essence of the qualified plan tax preference. In contrast, nonqualified

---

that is attributable to employee contributions or elective contributions under a 401(k) plan. ERISA § 204(j), 29 U.S.C. § 1054(j) (2018); *see* I.R.C. § 401(a)(35) (2018); *see also* I.R.C. §§ 401(a)(23), (a)(28), 409(h) (2018) (outlining additional diversification requirements for qualified stock bonus and employee stock ownership plans).

[80] I.R.C. § 404(a)(1)-(3) (2018).

[81] *Id.* § 501(a) (2018). Qualified trusts are subject to tax on any unrelated business taxable income. *Id.* § 511–14.

[82] *Id.* §§ 83(e)(2), 402(a) (2018).

[83] *Id.* § 402(c) (2018).

Overview of ERISA

plan contributions are subject to the "matching principle" – the employer's deduction must await inclusion by the employee.[84]

The magnitude of the tax deferral accorded qualified retirement plans is staggering. According to the Treasury, the net cost of the preferential treatment of qualified retirement plans is projected to be approximately $176 billion in fiscal year 2022 ($229 billion if IRAs and Keogh plans are included).[85] Going by congressional estimates, the figure is $288 billion for employer plans ($325 billion if IRAs and Keogh plans are included).[86] By either measure, the tax subsidy for qualified retirement savings is certainly one of the top two federal tax expenditures (the other being the exclusion of employer-provided health care benefits), and it may well be the largest. Presumably, tax deferral on such a grand scale is granted for some compelling public purpose. That purpose, principally, is to provide workers an incentive to accumulate an adequate level of retirement income.[87] Social Security alone affords only a base-level or subsistence-level standard of living in retirement; middle- and upper-income workers must supplement their Social Security benefits in order to maintain their pre-retirement standard of living. Instead of relying on supplementation via private saving, the government intervenes to encourage accumulation through qualified plans in order to counteract an assumed bias in favor of current consumption.[88] Secondarily, Congress hopes that the qualified plan tax subsidy will promote economic growth by increasing investment and capital formation.

A subsidy is justifiable only to the extent that it induces behavior that would not otherwise occur – in this case, additional savings. The myriad conditions on the preferential tax treatment of qualified retirement savings represent attempts to properly target the tax subsidy to avoid wasted revenue. Some of those conditions ensure that the tax allowance benefits employees rather than the employer; some try to direct the subsidy to the group of employees who would not save on their own (generally lower-paid workers); and some try to restrict subsidized saving to use as

---

[84] *Id.* § 404(a)(5) (2018); Albertson's Inc. v. Comm'r, 42 F.3d 537, 543 (9th Cir. 1994), *cert. denied*, 516 U.S. 807 (1995).

[85] EXECUTIVE OFFICE OF THE PRESIDENT, ANALYTICAL PERSPECTIVES, BUDGET OF THE UNITED STATES GOVERNMENT, FISCAL YEAR 2023, at 153, 160 (2022), www.govinfo.gov/content/pkg/BUDGET-2023-PER/pdf/BUDGET-2023-PER-5-3.pdf.

[86] STAFF OF THE JOINT COMM. ON TAXATION, ESTIMATES OF FEDERAL TAX EXPENDITURES FOR FISCAL YEARS 2022–2026, at 42, www.jct.gov/publications/2022/jcx-22-22/.

[87] *See* U.S. GOV'T PRINTING OFFICE, 95TH CONG., NATIONAL PENSION POLICIES: PRIVATE PENSION PLANS, HEARINGS BEFORE THE SUBCOMMITTEE ON RETIREMENT INCOME AND EMPLOYMENT OF THE HOUSE SELECT COMMITTEE ON AGING 228–50 (Comm. Print 1978) (statement of Daniel I. Halperin, tax legislative counsel, U.S. Department of the Treasury).

[88] Deborah M. Weiss, *Paternalistic Pension Policy: Psychological Evidence and Economic Theory*, 58 U. CHI. L. REV. 1275, 1279 (1991); Peter J. Wiedenbeck, *Paternalism and Income Tax Reform*, 33 U. KAN. L. REV. 675, 684–85, 689–91 (1985).

retirement income (instead of being used to buy a house or send a child to college, for example).[89] The first of these objectives is shared with ERISA and explains the duplication of ERISA's pension provisions in the tax Code's qualification requirements.[90] The latter two objectives, which try to channel public assistance into additional *retirement* funds for that portion of the workforce that would not otherwise save enough, explain the many qualification conditions that have no ERISA counterparts.

The anti-discrimination norm is the paramount means to this end. A qualified retirement plan cannot discriminate in favor of highly compensated employees, either with respect to plan membership or the proportion of each participant's compensation provided as contributions or benefits.[91] This nondiscrimination principle is the central criterion for qualification because it attempts, through a covert redistribution mechanism, to channel the tax allowance into retirement savings that would not otherwise occur.[92] The nondiscrimination rules are a complex, awkward, and imperfect means of targeting the tax subsidy, however, because their efficacy depends upon variables to which they are not attuned, particularly the composition of the employer's workforce (factors such as the age, pay level, and savings proclivity of each worker).[93] In addition to nondiscrimination, other tax rules restrict the amount and duration of tax deferral in an effort to minimize wasted revenue, and some regulate the timing of pension plan distributions so that public assistance is devoted to *retirement* support instead of saving for other goals.[94] Because responsible stewardship of public money is the objective, this network of qualified retirement plan tax controls is distinct from and applies in addition to ERISA's pension content controls (and the tax qualification criteria that reiterate them), which protect workers whether or not their pension is subsidized.

Preferential tax treatment has also shaped the contours of US health care financing, as considered in Chapter 11. The tax expenditure associated with the exclusion of employer contributions for medical insurance premiums and medical care is

---

[89] Various tax rules restrict the timing of qualified plan distributions in an attempt to ensure that subsidized savings are neither dissipated before retirement nor amassed as a legacy to the next generation. E.g., I.R.C. § 72(t) (2018) (additional tax on early distributions); *id.* § 401(a)(9) (2018) (minimum distributions required to prevent excessive deferral).

[90] Conversely, preexisting tax qualification rules sometimes have a bearing on the interpretation of ERISA's labor-law rules. Raymond B. Yates, M.D., P.C. Profit Sharing Plan v. Hendon, 541 U.S. 1, 3 (2004) ("Congress' objective was to harmonize ERISA with long-standing tax provisions.").

[91] I.R.C. §§ 401(a)(3), 410(b) (coverage nondiscrimination) (2018); *id.* §§ 401(a)(4), (a)(5)(C), (*l*) (2018) (nondiscrimination in contributions or benefits).

[92] *See infra* Chapters 10A, 10B. Bruce Wolk, *Discrimination Rules for Qualified Retirement Plans: Good Intentions Confront Economic Reality*, 70 Va. L. Rev. 419, 429–33 (1984); Peter J. Wiedenbeck, *Nondiscrimination in Employee Benefits: False Starts and Future Trends*, 52 Tenn. L. Rev. 167, 246–49 (1985).

[93] *See infra* Chapter 10B.

[94] *Id.*

Overview of ERISA

estimated by the Treasury at $211.5 billion in fiscal year 2022, or $187.4 billion according to congressional staff.[95]

E NOTE ON COVERAGE

Before commencing an in-depth examination of employee benefit plan regulation, the limits on the scope of this study should be highlighted.

The subject of this book is the *federal* regulation of employee benefits. State or local law is not systematically addressed. As already noted, a benefit arrangement that does not satisfy ERISA's definition of either a welfare plan or a pension plan is a permissible subject of state or local regulation.[96] Thanks to preemption, state and local law is ordinarily irrelevant to welfare and pension plans, but some general state laws survive, and insured plans must contend with state insurance regulation.[97] In addition, under ERISA's governmental plan exception, welfare and pension benefit programs for employees of a state or local government are also left to the protection of state or local law.[98] On the tax side, special rules (including relaxed or alternative qualification requirements) apply to governmental deferred compensation plans.[99] While sometimes mentioned in Chapter 10, these special tax regimes for government retirement programs are not examined comprehensively.

Apart from churches and church affiliates, charitable organizations are subject to ERISA's labor-law requirements. Their deferred compensation programs may, however, obtain favorable tax treatment under somewhat more lenient standards than apply to taxable employers (see Figure 1.1).[100] As with state and local government retirement plans, these rules are alluded to in Chapter 10 but not explored thoroughly.

The special rules applicable to multiemployer plans, both welfare and pension, are also beyond the scope of this book. In particular, multiemployer defined benefit

---

[95] EXECUTIVE OFFICE OF THE PRESIDENT, ANALYTICAL PERSPECTIVES, BUDGET OF THE UNITED STATES GOVERNMENT, FISCAL YEAR 2022, at 111 (2022), www.govinfo.gov/content/pkg/BUDGET-2022-PER/pdf/BUDGET-2022-PER.pdf; STAFF OF THE JOINT COMM. ON TAXATION, ESTIMATES OF FEDERAL TAX EXPENDITURES FOR FISCAL YEARS 2022–2026, at 41, www.jct.gov/publications/2022/jcx-22-22/.

[96] *See supra* text accompanying Chapter 1 notes 35–37.

[97] *See infra* Chapter 6B, 6E.

[98] ERISA §§ 4(b), 3(32), 29 U.S.C. §§ 1003(b), 1002(32) (2018). The governmental plan exception also extends to Indian tribal governments and their subdivisions, agencies, and instrumentalities, provided that all plan participants are employees substantially all of whose services involve the performance of essential governmental function and who are not engaged in commercial activities. *Id.* § 1002(32).

[99] *E.g.*, I.R.C. §§ 401(a) (2018); § 411; § 401(a)(5)(G) (relaxed qualification criteria) (2018); *id.* § 403(b) (tax-sheltered annuities for public school employees) (2018); *id.* § 457 (alternative rules for deferred compensation plans of state and local governments) (2018).

[100] *E.g.*, I.R.C. § 403(b) (tax-sheltered annuities for educational organization employees) (2018); *id.* § 457 (alternative rules for deferred compensation plans of tax-exempt organizations) (2018).

26 *General Considerations*

pension plans are subject to minimum funding obligations that are distinct from the rules for single-employer plans, and the PBGC termination insurance program operates differently.[101] In most other important respects, however, multiemployer plans are governed by the same federal labor and tax-law rules as single-employer plans.

Finally, it was observed in the description of ERISA's pattern of regulation that Congress mandated disclosure of plan terms and finances, imposed uniform fiduciary obligations, and promulgated a detailed scheme of federal judicial enforcement, but generally declined to regulate the content of welfare plans. Since the late 1980s health care plans have become an exception to the laissez faire approach to welfare plan content.

As health care prices grew by leaps and bounds and non-group health insurance became almost unaffordable, the Consolidated Omnibus Reconciliation Act of 1985 (COBRA) added Part 6 of ERISA Title I, which requires sponsors of group health plans that normally cover twenty or more employees to provide continued access to health plan coverage to workers who would otherwise lose coverage due to termination of employment or reduction of hours. Beneficiaries who would lose coverage due to the death of the employee or certain changes in dependency or family status are also granted a right to elect continuation coverage.[102] In each case COBRA continuation coverage is for a limited period (typically eighteen or thirty-six months) and may be made contingent on payment of a premium that cannot exceed 102 percent of the plan's cost of covering similarly situated employees or beneficiaries.[103]

Health care plan content regulation under COBRA was soon followed by further major inroads. Starting in 1993 group health plans were required to provide benefits to a child of the plan participant in accordance with the terms of a qualified medical child support order, so that children of divorced or separated parents would have reliable access to continued health care coverage.[104] Then in 1996 Congress added Part 7 of ERISA Title I, which limits exclusions from group health plan coverage based on preexisting health conditions and prohibits certain health status discrimination.[105] Subsequent amendments to Part 7 have expanded its reach to prohibit

---

[101] ERISA §§ 302(a)(2)(C), 304, 29 U.S.C. §§ 1082(a)(2)(C), 1084 (2018) (minimum funding standard for multiemployer plans); I.R.C. §§ 412(a)(2)(C), 431 (2018). ERISA §§ 4201–4402, 29 U.S.C. §§ 1381–1461 (2018) (special termination insurance provisions for multiemployer plans).

[102] ERISA §§ 601, 603, 29 U.S.C. §§ 1161, 1163 (2018) ; *see* I.R.C. § 4980B (2018).

[103] ERISA §§ 602, 604, 29 U.S.C. §§ 1162, 1164 (2018); *see* I.R.C. § 4980B(f) (2018).

[104] ERISA §§ 514(b)(7), 609, 29 U.S.C. §§ 1144(b)(7), 1169 (2018). The qualified medical child support order is modeled after the qualified domestic relations order, which provides a mechanism for family law claimants to obtain access to a participant's pension if certain conditions designed to protect the plan and other participants are satisfied. *See infra* Chapter 8B; ERISA § 206(d)(3), 29 U.S.C. § 1056(d)(3) (2018); I.R.C. § 414(p) (2018).

[105] ERISA §§ 701, 702, 731–34, 29 U.S.C. §§ 1181, 1182, 1191–91c (2018); *see* I.R.C. §§ 9801, 9802, 9831–34 (2018).

Overview of ERISA

discrimination on the basis of genetic information, mandate coverage of a minimum hospital stay following the birth of a child, cover post-mastectomy reconstructive surgery, continue coverage of college students while on medical leave of absence, and provide parity in mental health benefits.[106] As with ERISA's pension plan content regulation, the Internal Revenue Code reinforces the health plan content message by imposing a parallel set of tax rules.[107]

This brings us to the elephant that has been in the room since 2010: the Patient Protection and Affordable Care Act (ACA). The ACA imposed some notable content controls on employment-based health insurance as a part of the legislation's larger project of expanding access to health care by reforming the health insurance markets in the United States.[108] Those specific legislative choices are subject to continuing judicial and political challenges. In part because of that contestation, Chapter 11 will survey the broad terrain of employment-based health care today without exhaustively inventorying the details of the ACA.

---

[106] ERISA §§ 702(c)–(f), 711–14, 29 U.S.C. §§ 1182(c)–(f), 1185–85c (2018); *see* I.R.C. §§ 9802 (c)–(f), 9811–13 (2018).

[107] Most of the group health plan content requirements of Part 7 of ERISA Title I appear in I.R.C. §§ 9801–33 (2018). Violation of these rules exposes the employer (or the plan in the case of a multiemployer plan or a multiple employer welfare arrangement) to an excise tax of $100 per day for each individual affected by the violation for each day that it persists. *Id.* §§ 9834, 4980B. Certain exceptions or limitations of the penalty tax may apply if the failure to comply was due to reasonable cause rather than willful neglect. *Id.* § 4980D(c)–(d).

Similarly, the tax version of the COBRA continuation coverage requirements appear in I.R.C. § 4980B (2018).

ERISA's required recognition of qualified medical child support orders (*supra* Chapter 1 note 103 and accompanying text), and ERISA § 713, which mandates coverage of post-mastectomy reconstructive surgery, do not have tax Code counterparts. *See* ERISA §§ 609, 713, 29 U.S.C. §§ 1169, 1185b (2018).

[108] ERISA § 715, 29 U.S.C. § 1185d (2018), incorporates by reference many of the health insurance reforms of the ACA, making them applicable to some employer-provided group health plans. *See, e.g.,* 42 U.S.C. § 300gg (2018) (premium rate regulation applicable to individual and some group plans). Important ACA-specific reforms will be discussed in Chapter 11, *infra.*

2

ERISA's Coverage

Congress relied on the Commerce Clause as the basis for regulating employee benefit plans. The labor provisions of ERISA apply to any "employee benefit plan" established or maintained by an employer "engaged in commerce or in any industry or activity affecting commerce," as well as to plans established or maintained by unions representing employees so engaged.[1] The statute broadly defines "commerce" and "industry or activity affecting commerce" to reach almost any employer or union, regardless of size.[2]

Enterprise size does not seriously restrict ERISA's scope, but federal controls come into play only if there is an "employee benefit plan." The definition of employee benefit plan imposes three important limitations on ERISA's coverage. First, the arrangement for the provision of benefits must constitute a "plan, fund, or program." Second, the plan must provide benefits to employees or their beneficiaries. Third, the benefits provided must be of a type specified in either the definition

---

[1] ERISA § 4(a), 29 U.S.C. § 1003(a) (2018).

[2] ERISA § 3(11), (12), 29 U.S.C. § 1002(11), (12) (2018). *See* Fugarino v. Hartford Life & Accident Ins. Co., 969 F.2d 178, 183 (6th Cir. 1992) (group health insurance provided by small family-owned restaurant subject to ERISA notwithstanding the business's trivial impact on commerce), *cert. denied*, 507 U.S. 966 (1993), *overruled on other grounds by* Raymond B. Yates, M.D., P.C. Profit Sharing Plan v. Hendon, 541 U.S. 1 (2004).

ERISA's definitions of "commerce" and "industry or activity affecting commerce" were carried over verbatim from a predecessor statute, the Welfare and Pension Plans Disclosure Act of 1958, Pub. L. No. 85-836, § 3(10), (11), 72 Stat. 997, *amended by* Pub. L. No. 87-420, 76 Stat. 35 (repealed by ERISA § 111(a)(1), 29 U.S.C. § 1031(a)(1) (2018)). Those definitions were in turn taken from the jurisdictional provision of the Taft-Hartley Act, 29 U.S.C. § 142(1) (2018). 104 CONG. REC. 16,437–38 (1958) (remarks of Reps. Barden, Frelinghuysen, and Green). Under Taft-Hartley, it is sufficient if the industry as a whole affects commerce; it is not necessary that the particular enterprise in which the employer or unionized employees are engaged affects commerce. *E.g.*, United States v. Ricciardi, 357 F.2d 91, 95 (2d Cir. 1966) (relevant industry "comprises all business activities in the same field").

ERISA's Coverage

of a "welfare plan" or a "pension plan."[3] Each of these criteria implicates fundamental interpretive and policy issues that are examined below. The chapter concludes with an exploration of legislative exceptions that render certain employee benefit plans largely or completely exempt from federal regulation.

A THE "PLAN" PREREQUISITE

To be subject to ERISA, an arrangement for the provision of benefits must be a "plan, fund, or program."[4] The statute offers no definition of those terms. Courts regularly encounter three types of challenges to the existence of a plan: namely that the benefit arrangement is too transient, too indefinite, or too restricted in coverage.

Transience[5]

Where an employee benefit can be provided without establishing an ongoing administrative apparatus, there is no "plan," provided that the obligation is unfunded and nondiscretionary. This conclusion follows from a line of cases that has *Fort Halifax Packing Co. v. Coyne* as its source.[6] There, the Supreme Court held that a Maine law requiring one-time severance payments in the event of a plant closing was not preempted by ERISA because it "neither establishes, nor requires the employer to maintain, an employee welfare benefit 'plan.'"[7]

In *Fort Halifax* the Court equated an ERISA plan with an "ongoing administrative program for processing claims and paying benefits."[8] That definition was supported by the policy of preemption: conforming a benefit program to a patchwork of state regulation would forfeit the advantages of uniform administrative practice. The Maine law, in contrast, imposed only a contingent one-time obligation to make nondiscretionary lump-sum payments, and so entailed no such inefficiency. The Court acknowledged that it had previously affirmed decisions holding an unfunded severance program subject to ERISA, but in that instance, payments were due whenever covered workers left employment. Such an ongoing commitment to pay benefits required a continuing administrative scheme, unlike the

---

[3] ERISA § 3(3), (1), (2)(A), 29 U.S.C. § 1002(3), (1), (2)(A) (2018).
[4] ERISA §§ 4(a), 3(3), (1), (2)(A), 29 U.S.C. §§ 1003(a), 1002(3), (1), (2)(A) (2018).
[5] Much of the following discussion is derived from Wiedenbeck, *supra* Chapter 1 note 56, at 586–89, 591–93.
[6] 482 U.S. 1 (1987).
[7] *Id.* at 6.
[8] *Id.* at 12. The *Fort Halifax* majority observed that "Congress intended pre-emption to afford employers the advantages of a uniform set of administrative procedures governed by a single set of regulations." *Id.* at 11. Yet employers could secure the cost advantages of a single set of administrative procedures by including a choice-of-law provision in their benefit plans. This consideration suggests that it is workers who benefit, through lower information costs, from having all plans subject to the *same* set of supplementary rules. See *supra* Chapter 1C.

General Considerations

one-time obligation in *Fort Halifax*, the case at hand.[9] The Court also observed that the Maine plant-closing law "not only fails to implicate the concerns of ERISA's preemption provision, it fails to implicate the regulatory concerns of ERISA itself."[10] Looking to the legislative history of ERISA's fiduciary responsibility rules (which apply to both pension and welfare plans), the Court concluded that "[t]he focus of the statute thus is on the administrative integrity of benefit plans – which presumes that some type of administrative activity is taking place."[11]

Lower court decisions involving employer-initiated severance programs have fleshed out the scope of *Fort Halifax*. Arrangements to make a readily determinable lump-sum cash payment have been found not to constitute an ERISA plan.[12] Yet some short-term commitments calling for payment in a lump sum have been subjected to federal regulation, notwithstanding the Supreme Court's search for an ongoing administrative program. Comparison of the decisions demonstrates that if there is no continuing administrative apparatus, then ERISA's application turns on the presence or absence of *discretion* in processing benefit claims.

Many of the leading cases involve *unfunded* executive severance ("golden parachute") programs. In *Fontenot v. NL Industries, Inc.*,[13] the employer adopted, as one component of a takeover defense, a plan providing that if the employment of selected senior executives was terminated for any reason within two years of a change in control of the corporation, the affected individuals would receive lump-sum cash severance payments equal to three times their highest annual compensation over the preceding three years.[14] The plaintiff, who was not included in the program, was terminated one year after the takeover; he sued for benefits under federal law. The district court granted summary judgment in favor of the employer on the ground that ERISA did not apply, and the court of appeals affirmed.[15]

In contrast, ERISA has been applied to some golden parachute programs. It is startling and perhaps a little ironic that a labor law enacted to protect workers' interests is sometimes invoked to protect managers in the event of a change in corporate control. Cases such as *Bogue v. Ampex Corp.*[16] vividly illustrate the

---

[9] *Fort Halifax*, 482 U.S. at 17–19 (distinguishing Holland v. Burlington Indus., Inc., 772 F.2d 1140 (4th Cir. 1985), *summarily aff'd*, 477 U.S. 901 (1986); Gilbert v. Burlington Indus., Inc., 765 F.2d 320 (2d Cir. 1985), *summarily aff'd*, 477 U.S. 901 (1986)).

[10] *Fort Halifax*, 482 U.S. at 15.

[11] *Id.*

[12] Young v. Wash. Gas Light Co., 206 F.3d 1200 (D.C. Cir. 2000); Belanger v. Wyman-Gordon Co., 71 F.3d 451 (1st Cir. 1995); Angst v. Mack Trucks, Inc., 969 F.2d 1530 (3d Cir. 1992); Fontenot v. NL Indus., Inc., 953 F.2d 960 (5th Cir. 1992); Wells v. Gen. Motors Corp., 881 F.2d 166 (5th Cir. 1989), *cert. denied*, 495 U.S. 923 (1990).

[13] 953 F.2d 960 (5th Cir. 1992).

[14] *Id.* at 961, 963.

[15] *Id.* at 961.

[16] 976 F.2d 1319 (9th Cir. 1992), *cert. denied*, 507 U.S. 1031 (1993). The Ninth Circuit subsequently distinguished *Bogue* in holding that an individually negotiated executive employment contract that called for readily determinable severance payments in the event of

ERISA's Coverage

breadth of the statute. The program in *Bogue* promised severance pay to any of ten executives of a subsidiary that was slated for sale, if the executive was not offered "substantially similar employment" within ten months after the sale.

> In this case, Allied-Signal, the program's administrator, remained obligated to decide whether a complaining employee's job was "substantially equivalent" to his pre-acquisition job. Although the program, like the plans in *Fort Halifax* and *Wells*, was triggered by a single event, that event would occur more than once, at a different time for each employee. There was no way to carry out that obligation with the unthinking, one-time, nondiscretionary application of the plan administrators in *Fort Halifax* and *Wells*. Although its application was uncertain, its term was short, and the number of its participants was small, the program's administration required a case-by-case, discretionary application of its terms. Whether or not Allied-Signal ever thought [that the program would be subject to ERISA] does not matter . . . . We hold that Allied-Signal was obligated to apply enough ongoing, particularized, administrative, discretionary analysis to make the program in this case a "plan."[17]

Similarly, an arrangement that required a separate determination of each covered executive's eligibility for benefits (specifically, whether post-merger termination was for reasons other than cause) was an ERISA plan.[18] And a Massachusetts "tin parachute" statute, mandating lump-sum severance payments to certain employees who are eligible for unemployment compensation when discharged within twenty-four months after takeover of their employer, was held preempted because, in contrast to *Fort Halifax*, the payment obligation is triggered separately (by termination) for each worker, and eligibility for unemployment compensation requires a

---

termination "without cause" did not establish an ERISA plan. According to the court, this single discretionary determination – unlike the ten decisions possible in *Bogue* – did not require "ongoing discretionary analysis." Delaye v. Agripac, Inc., 39 F.3d 235, 238 (9th Cir. 1994). This analysis conflates the search for continuing (nondiscretionary) administrative activity with the search for discretionary decision making. ERISA's policies of preventing employer abuse and protecting participants indicate that a single judgment call should result in plan classification, so that federal fiduciary oversight is triggered. See discussion of restricted coverage, *infra* text accompanying Chapter 2 notes 53–67.

[17] *Bogue*, 976 F.2d at 1323. *Accord* Schonholz v. Long Island Jewish Med. Ctr., 87 F.3d 72, 76 (2d Cir.), *cert. denied*, 519 U.S. 1008 (1996); Cvelbar v. CBI Ill., Inc., 106 F.3d 1368, 1376 (7th Cir. 1997); Collins v. Ralston Purina Co., 147 F.3d 592, 595–97 (7th Cir. 1998).

[18] Pane v. RCA Corp., 667 F. Supp. 168, 170–71 (D.N.J. 1998), *aff'd*, 868 F.2d 631 (3d Cir. 1989). *Cf.* Kulinski v. Medtronic Bio-Medicus, Inc., 21 F.3d 254, 257 (8th Cir. 1994) (agreement calling for severance pay in the event of resignation for good reason within one year of a hostile takeover did not create an ERISA plan because it gave the *employee* unfettered discretion to decide whether he had good reason to resign; the court noted that a plan exists where the *employer* "must analyze each employee's particular circumstances in light of the appropriate criteria" to determine benefit eligibility or amount).

General Considerations

potentially controversial factual determination that the worker was not discharged for cause.[19]

This focus on administrative discretion seems sensible in light of the *Fort Halifax* policy analysis: if preventing mismanagement and abuse by fiduciaries is the central tenet of ERISA, perhaps ERISA should not apply where there are no judgment calls to oversee. ERISA's fiduciary-duty and prohibited-transactions rules apply only to fiduciaries,[20] and the statute provides a broad functional definition that classifies as a fiduciary any person who has or exercises "any discretionary authority" in the management or administration of the plan.[21] This approach is also consistent with the limited abuse-of-discretion standard of review that is applied to benefit claim denials where the plan gives the fiduciary discretionary authority to determine eligibility for benefits or to construe the terms of the plan.[22]

Mishandling of plan assets is as much a threat to the integrity of benefit plans as abusive decision making. ERISA's fiduciary responsibility provisions were intended to prohibit outright thievery and looting of benefit funds by anyone with access to the fund, however exalted or subordinate that person's position. Accordingly, oversight of discretionary decision making alone is not enough to protect workers' interests. ERISA should apply *either* if the benefit obligation involves the exercise of discretion *or* if it is advance funded. ERISA's drafters apparently understood this point: if the plan is funded, any person who "exercises any authority or control respecting management or disposition of its assets" is a fiduciary, whether or not that authority involves the exercise of discretion.[23] Yet the protection Congress intended to afford in the definition of fiduciary becomes illusory if the statute fails to apply for want of a plan. To safeguard workers from *both* oppressive decisions *and* looting of the fund, the core jurisdictional principle should be: where there is a fiduciary, there is a plan.

The severance payments required by the Maine plant-closing statute in *Fort Halifax* were unfunded and nondiscretionary; the employer's obligation could be discharged without the service of an ERISA fiduciary. Yet the Court's opinion indicates that ERISA would apply if there were "an ongoing administrative program for processing claims and paying benefits."[24] Apparently, then, a regular or continuing benefit obligation would trigger ERISA even if it were unfunded and

---

[19] Simas v. Quaker Fabric Corp. of Fall River, 6 F.3d 849, 853–54 (1st Cir. 1993) (relying on *Bogue*). *Accord* United Paperworkers Int'l Union, Loc. 1468 v. Imperial Home Decor Grp., 76 F. Supp. 2d 179 (D.R.I. 1999) (Rhode Island tin parachute statute preempted).

[20] ERISA §§ 404(a), 406, 29 U.S.C. §§ 1104(a), 1106 (2018).

[21] ERISA § 3(21)(A), 29 U.S.C. § 1002(21)(A) (2018). *See infra* Chapter 4A.

[22] Firestone Tire & Rubber Co. v. Bruch, 489 U.S. 101 (1989). *See infra* Chapter 5B.

[23] ERISA § 3(21)(A)(i), 29 U.S.C. § 1002(21)(A)(i) (2018). E.g., Chao v. Day, 436 F.3d 234, 235–37 (D.C. Cir. 2006) (taking pains to note that "the 'discretion' requirement – which is repeated twice in the discretionary clause – is conspicuously omitted altogether from the disposition clause"); IT Corp. v. Gen. Am. Life Ins. Co., 107 F.3d 1415, 1419–21 (9th Cir. 1997) (holding that any control over the disposition of plan assets, discretionary or not, establishes fiduciary status). *See generally infra* Chapter 4A.

[24] *Fort Halifax*, 482 U.S. at 12.

ERISA's Coverage

nondiscretionary.[25] This connotation of "plan" may take into account that, although "ERISA's central focus [is on] administrative integrity,"[26] fiduciary responsibility is not the only component of federal benefit plan regulation. In particular, workers must be informed of the extent of the benefit obligation (coverage, amount, and timing) and the method for "processing claims and paying benefits" in order to take full advantage of the program. Ongoing administration by itself implicates informational interests, and so should trigger ERISA's reporting and disclosure regime.[27]

This judicially developed definition of plan (requiring either ongoing administration or the presence of a fiduciary) is informed by the goals of ERISA and is moored to the statute's text. Recall that ERISA defines both a welfare plan and a pension plan as a "plan, *fund*, or *program*."[28] Use of the term "fund" indicates that ERISA applies whenever the obligation is advance funded. Funding, of course, requires continuing oversight and ensures that there will be someone with fiduciary status. "Program" implies an ordered sequence of events (such as a procedure for processing claims and paying benefits), which lends credence to the distinction between ongoing administration and a one-time lump-sum payment.

Indefiniteness

To be subject to federal regulation, a welfare or pension plan must be "established or maintained by an employer or by an employee organization."[29] That is, the plan must already have come into existence. A tentative or projected benefit arrangement is not a "plan" or (equivalently) has not been "established."[30]

---

[25] *Id.* at 18 nn.10 & 12 (distinguishing a benefit obligation that entails "regularity of payment").

[26] *Id.* at 18.

[27] In discussing why the Maine plant-closing statute "fails to implicate the regulatory concerns of ERISA itself," *Fort Halifax*, 482 U.S. at 15, the Court considered *both* fiduciary responsibility and reporting and disclosure. The opinion observes that there was no "administrative activity potentially subject to employer abuse" and that "[n]o financial transactions take place that would be listed in an annual report, and no further information regarding the terms of the severance pay obligation is needed because the statute itself makes these terms clear." *Id.* at 16.

[28] ERISA § 3(1), (2), 29 U.S.C. § 1002(1), (2) (2018) (emphasis added).

[29] *Id.*

[30] Brines v. XTRA Corp., 304 F.3d 699, 701 (7th Cir. 2002), *cert. denied*, 538 U.S. 978 (2003) ("The statement in the plan that 'The company will develop and implement an appropriate separation program' did not create a legally enforceable promise." "And the vagueness of the 'will develop' statement is a strong indication that it was not *intended* to be a promise, but merely a prediction, which creates no rights.") (citations omitted); Elmore v. Cone Mills Corp., 23 F.3d 855, 862 (4th Cir. 1994) (employer's preliminary statements of its intentions concerning the terms of a new employee stock ownership plan do not constitute an enforceable plan); James v. Nat'l Bus. Sys., Inc., 924 F.2d 718, 720 (7th Cir. 1991) (Posner, J.) (stating that for ERISA to come into play the plan must be "intended to be in effect, and not just be something for future adoption" and that documents describing a plan as being tentative, contingent, or in futuro should be considered as evidence that no plan was in effect).

34 *General Considerations*

Donovan v. Dillingham[31] is the leading authority on the proof required to demonstrate that a plan has been created.[32] The case involved the purchase of health insurance by small employers through a group insurance trust in order to obtain more favorable rates. The Secretary of Labor argued that even if the purchase of health insurance was not itself sufficient to trigger ERISA, the separate determination of each employer to provide benefits to its employees by subscribing to the group trust established a plan.[33] The court held that a plan is not "established" merely by virtue of a *decision* to provide benefits of a type specified in ERISA; rather, the program must have become a reality.[34] A decision implemented by the purchase of insurance, however, creates a plan.[35] Employers who purchased insurance through the group trust were found to have established ERISA welfare plans if the insurance was obtained to fulfill a collective bargaining agreement or under circumstances indicating an intent to provide continuing coverage to a class of employees.[36] More generally, the court observed that "[i]n determining whether a plan, fund, or program (pursuant to a writing or not) is a reality a court must determine whether from the surrounding circumstances a reasonable person could ascertain the intended [1] benefits, [2] beneficiaries, [3] source of financing, and [4] procedure for receiving benefits," recognizing that some of these essential criteria can be incorporated from sources outside the plan, such as an insurance claims procedure.[37]

As the *Dillingham* definition suggests, no particular formality is required to show the existence of a plan. Most importantly, compliance with ERISA is not essential. (If compliance were a condition of plan classification, then ERISA's standards, which were intended to be mandatory, would be made elective.)[38] Oral

---

[31] 688 F.2d 1367 (11th Cir. 1982) (en banc).

[32] "Every circuit that has since been required to decide whether, on the particular facts before it, a pension plan has come into being has adopted the *Dillingham* approach." Kenney v. Roland Parson Contracting Corp., 28 F.3d 1254, 1257 (D.C. Cir. 1994) (Ginsburg, J.) (citing authorities).

[33] Donovan v. Dillingham, 668 F.2d 1196, 1198 (11th Cir. 1982) (opinion before rehearing en banc).

[34] *Dillingham*, 688 F.2d at 1373.

[35] *Id*. at 1375.

[36] *Id*. at 1374–75.

[37] *Id*. at 1373.

[38] *Id*. at 1372 ("it would be incongruous for persons establishing or maintaining informal or unwritten employee benefit plans, or assuming the responsibility of safeguarding plan assets, to circumvent the Act merely because an administrator or other fiduciary failed to satisfy reporting or fiduciary standards"). *Accord* Brines v. XTRA Corp., 304 F.3d 699, 701 (7th Cir. 2002) (dicta, explaining cases), *cert. denied*, 538 U.S. 978 (2003); Scott v. Gulf Oil Co., 754 F.2d 1499, 1503–04 (9th Cir. 1985) (unwritten plan); Henglein v. Informal Plan for Plant Shutdown Benefits for Salaried Emps., 974 F.2d 391, 400–01 (3d Cir. 1992) (same, but emphasizing that oral representations cannot modify a valid written plan); Phillips v. Brandess Home Builders, Inc., No. 95-C-204, 1995 U.S. Dist. LEXIS 14496, at *6 (N.D. Ill. Oct. 2, 1995) ("The applicability of ERISA standards cannot turn on an employer's

ERISA's Coverage

35

arrangements can be plans even though ERISA requires almost all welfare and pension plans to be in writing.[39] Similarly, unpublicized (secret) benefit programs can trigger the statute, bringing its fundamental tenet of employee disclosure into play.[40] Moreover, if the intended benefits and beneficiaries are clear but the employer is silent as to funding or claims procedure, some decisions find a plan based on the inference that benefits are to be paid out of the employer's general funds, or that application for benefits should be made to the company's personnel department.[41]

Can an informal policy of providing a benefit in individually determined amounts to selected employees be a plan? Arguably the intended benefits and beneficiaries of such a policy are "unascertainable." When faced with evidence that a large employer maintained a long-standing system of ad hoc individualized grants of severance benefits, the Third Circuit held that "the discretionary nature of benefits ... does not alone deprive a document or program of its status as an employee benefit plan under the *Dillingham* standard, so long as a reasonable person can ascertain the contingent benefit and contingent beneficiaries."[42] The discretionary nature of the benefit would not prevent a disappointed employee from obtaining review of the denial of the benefit, but that review would be limited to the deferential abuse-of-discretion standard.[43] In contrast, the Seventh Circuit has refused to apply ERISA to an accounting firm's informal pension arrangement, where only three of twenty-five retirees received benefits and the amount was determined ad hoc rather than according to an established formula. The court observed that "[w]ith only this evidence, we could not begin to fashion appropriate relief for [plaintiff], since we do not know whether he was the type of employee [the firm] intended to cover, or what benefits are due."[44] Similarly, a district court found

---

compliance with them."); Strzelecki v. Schwarz Paper Co., 824 F. Supp. 821, 826 (N.D. Ill. 1993) ("If an employer could avoid ERISA coverage of its benefit plan simply by violating ERISA's requirements and then claiming that the plan did not function the way ERISA plans typically function, the whole purpose of the statute – to protect employees from employers' mismanagement of benefit plans – would be defeated.") (citations omitted). *See also* Feifer v. Prudential Ins. Co., 306 F.3d 1202, 1209–10 (2d Cir. 2002) (informal program summary constituted the plan during the period before plan instruments were drafted despite attempted disclaimer; crediting disclaimer would permit employers to opt out of ERISA's requirements).

[39] E.g., *Dillingham*, 688 F 2d at 1372; Scott v. Gulf Oil Co., 754 F.2d 1499, 1503–04 (9th Cir. 1985).

[40] E.g., Brown v. Ampco-Pittsburgh Corp., 876 F.2d 546, 550–51 (6th Cir. 1989) (confidential memorandum to management created severance pay plan); Blau v. Del Monte Corp., 748 F.2d 1348 (9th Cir. 1984), *cert. denied*, 474 U.S. 865 (1985) (same, and refusing to interpret secret plan with reference to the employer's secret intentions or past course of conduct).

[41] E.g., Deibler v. United Food & Com. Workers' Loc. Union 23, 973 F.2d 206, 210 (3d Cir. 1992); Dwyer v. Galen Hosp. Ill., Inc., No. 94-C-544, 1996 U.S. Dist. LEXIS 2921, at *26–27 (N.D. Ill. Mar. 11, 1996).

[42] *Henglein*, 974 F.2d at 401.

[43] *Id.*

[44] Diak v. Dwyer, Costello & Knox, P.C., 33 F.3d 809, 813 (7th Cir. 1994).

36   *General Considerations*

that a chief executive officer's practice of occasionally granting severance pay in amounts determined by the application of largely undefined criteria was too unsystematic and indefinite to constitute a plan.[45]

The principle that discretionary authority brings ERISA's fiduciary standards into play to safeguard employees,[46] clashes with the cases holding that too much discretion negates the existence of a plan by making the intended benefits or beneficiaries unascertainable. If standards or guidelines for the exercise of discretion can be gleaned from the employer's representations, past practice, or surrounding circumstances, then the courts have a basis to review benefit determinations to prevent employer abuse, and the policy of ERISA demands such review. But what if there are no standards, so that discretion is unbounded and benefits are awarded by a series of individualized ad hoc determinations? When discretion becomes prerogative, is there any role for a reviewing court to play?

Under the federal Administrative Procedure Act, there is no jurisdiction to review bureaucratic action where the decision is "committed by law to agency discretion."[47] The Supreme Court interprets this exception to the general rule of reviewability narrowly, holding that judicial review is precluded only where there is "no law to apply" – that is, preclusion applies only where there is no basis for a court to police the exercise of discretion because there is no indication of any standards or guidelines that the agency must use in making the decision.[48] A similar futility concern seems to be at play in cases holding that too much discretion negates the existence of a plan by making the intended benefits or beneficiaries unascertainable. ERISA requires that every employee benefit plan "specify the basis on which payments are made to and from the plan."[49] "Plan" is a broader category than "fund," and this rule applies to nearly all plans, including unfunded welfare plans. Where there is no fund, specifying "the basis on which payments are made . . . from the plan" necessarily requires that the plan either expressly define its intended beneficiaries and benefits (either by specification, class description, or formula), or set forth meaningful guidelines to inform the fiduciary's exercise of discretion.

Should a benefit arrangement that does not comply with this aspect of ERISA be exempt from ERISA, any more than, for instance, a program that violates the writing requirement? Because ERISA was designed to protect employees' reasonable expectations, the answer apparently depends on the information available to employees. If the employer's actions or omissions have created a reasonable expectation that benefits might be awarded, a plan might be held to exist, but covering only that

---

[45] Spanos v. Cont'l Pub'g Servs., Inc., No. C-93-1624 MHP, 1994 U.S. Dist. LEXIS 6695, at *7–11 (N.D. Cal. May 17, 1994).

[46] *See supra* text accompanying Chapter 2 notes 12–22.

[47] 5 U.S.C. § 701(a)(2) (2018).

[48] Citizens to Pres. Overton Park v. Volpe, 401 U.S. 402 (1971). *See generally* Ronald M. Levin, *Understanding Unreviewability in Administrative Law*, 74 Minn. L. Rev. 689 (1990).

[49] ERISA § 402(b)(4), 29 U.S.C. § 1102(b)(4) (2018).

ERISA's Coverage

group of employees as to which such a reasonable expectation could arise.[50] Using reasonable expectations as a guide, ad hoc grants of severance or pension benefits that are unknown to the continuing workforce would not trigger ERISA. On the other hand, if workers become aware (whether by employer information or recurrent practice) that such benefits are granted to selected managerial employees, a plan covering management could be found to exist. This approach would distinguish *Henglein v. Informal Plan for Plant Shutdown Benefits*,[51] in which a plan was held to exist where the employer was aware that salaried employees believed there was an ongoing discretionary severance program but made no effort to dispel that impression, from *Diak v. Dwyer, Costello & Knox, P.C.*, in which the court held there was no plan, and where there was no evidence that the claimant was aware of ad hoc unfunded pension payments to three retirees.[52]

Restricted Coverage[53]

Restricted coverage constitutes the third ground on which the existence of a plan is frequently challenged. Where a benefit is provided to one or a very small number of employees, the arrangement may be intended only as a "special deal" contained in individual employment contracts and not part of a general program. But does the meaning of "plan" necessarily entail a general program? ERISA's policies strongly

---

[50] Belanger v. Wyman-Gordon Co., 71 F.3d 451 (1st Cir. 1995), held that severance pay granted under a series of four time-limited early retirement offers made within four years did not create an ongoing severance pay plan because each offer involved only an unfunded nondiscretionary one-time payment that was independent on its face, and the company never represented that there was any linkage or continuing commitment. *Id.* at 456. The court observed that in determining the existence of a plan, "[o]ne very important consideration is whether, in light of all the surrounding circumstances, a reasonable employee would perceive an ongoing commitment by the employer to provide employee benefits." *Id.* at 455.

[51] Henglein v. Informal Plan for Plant Shutdown Benefits for Salaried Emps., 974 F.2d 391, 396 (3d Cir. 1992) (describing relevant evidence of the existence of a plan, including the employer's oral representations, "a deliberate failure to correct known perceptions of a plan's existence, [and] the reasonable understanding of employees." *Id.* at 400).

[52] Diak v. Dwyer, Costello & Knox, P.C., 33 F.3d 809, 813 (7th Cir. 1994) (no evidence that claimant expected a pension; he was told that the firm had no pension plan and that payments to a retiree were compensation for services). The *Diak* court reached the right result, but the decision would have been better founded on the lack of employee reliance rather than the difficulty in ascertaining the intended benefits or beneficiaries. *See also* Gilmore v. Silgan Plastics Corp., 917 F. Supp. 686 (E.D. Mo. 1996), in which an announced company policy of granting severance benefits to employees approved by the plant manager was held not to create a plan, even though the manager's discretionary decision was shown to have been based on production needs. Under the analysis suggested in the text, the *Gilmore* facts are enough to constitute a plan. Had ERISA been applied, the plaintiffs should nevertheless have been denied relief because they were not challenging any discretionary (i.e., fiduciary) decision. Instead, they had been denied benefits pursuant to company announcements (informal plan amendments) that clearly limited program eligibility to employees in other job classifications.

[53] Parts of the following discussion are derived from Wiedenbeck, *supra* Chapter 1 note 56, at 576–85.

38 *General Considerations*

suggest that the answer should be no, although the statutory text offers scant guidance.[54]

Legislative history suggests that a benefit arrangement covering one or a few employees can be a plan. ERISA's reporting and disclosure rules and its definitions of welfare and pension plans are drawn from the Welfare and Pension Plans Disclosure Act of 1958 (WPPDA),[55] which exempted plans covering twenty-five or fewer participants from disclosure obligations.[56] However, ERISA did not carry forward any such small-plan exemption.[57] The alteration made to the predecessor definitions of welfare and pension plans is also telling. The WPPDA required that the plan be "communicated or its benefits described in writing to the employees."[58] This writing requirement was designed to "eliminate informal or personal arrangements from the scope of the [WPPDA]," because "[i]ndividual arrangements with executives for benefits are not contemplated as being covered by the [WPPDA]."[59] Under ERISA, certain executive compensation arrangements are excluded in a more targeted fashion, as described below.[60] And while ERISA requires nearly all plans to be "established and maintained pursuant to a written instrument,"[61] the writing requirement is now a consequence of plan classification, not a predicate of it.[62]

A regulation in effect since 1975 indicates that a single-employee arrangement can be a plan subject to ERISA,[63] and several courts

---

[54] The welfare and pension plan definitions refer in the plural to "participants" and "employees." ERISA § 3(1), (2)(A), 29 U.S.C. § 1002(1), (2)(A) (2018). *But see* 1 U.S.C. § 1 (2018) ("In determining the meaning of any Act of Congress, unless the context indicates otherwise ... words importing the plural include the singular."). On the other hand, in common usage the term "plan" normally conveys a sense of prearrangement or design, not generality. *E.g.*, Random House College Dictionary 1014 (rev. ed. 1975); American Heritage College Dictionary 1045 (3d ed. 1993); Webster's New Universal Unabridged Dictionary 1372 (2d ed. rev. 1983).

[55] Pub. L. No. 85-836, 72 Stat. 997 (1958) (repealed 1975).

[56] *Id.* § 4(b)(4), 72 Stat. at 999, *amended by* Pub. L. No. 87-420, 76 Stat. 35 (1962).

[57] Early versions of pension reform legislation did exempt plans covering not more than twenty-five employees. *E.g.*, S. 4, 93d Cong. § 104(b)(4) (1973), *reprinted in* 1 ERISA Legislative History, *supra* Chapter 1 note 55, at 93, 112; S. Rep. No. 93-127, at 18–19 (1973) (stating small plans exempted to avoid inhibiting growth of pension coverage), *reprinted in* 1 ERISA Legislative History, *supra* Chapter 1 note 55, at 604–05.

[58] Welfare and Pension Plans Disclosure Act of 1958, Pub. L. No. 85-836, § 3(1), (2), 72 Stat. 997, *amended by* Pub. L. No. 87-420, 76 Stat. 35 (1962).

[59] S. Rep. No. 85-1440, at 25 (1958), *reprinted in* Office of the Solicitor, U.S. Department of Labor, Legislative History of the Welfare and Pension Plans Disclosure Act of 1958, at 206 (1962) [hereinafter WPPDA Legislative History]; H.R. Rep. No. 85-2283, at 11 (1958), *reprinted in* WPPDA Legislative History, at 207.

[60] *See infra* text accompanying Chapter 2 notes 67, 122–133.

[61] ERISA §§ 401(a), 402(a)(1), 29 U.S.C. §§ 1101(a), 1102(a)(1) (2018).

[62] *See supra* Chapter 2 notes 38–39.

[63] 29 C.F.R. § 2510.3-3(b) (2021) ("[A] Keogh plan under which one or more common-law employees, in addition to the self-employed individuals, are participants covered under the plan, will be covered under title I.").

ERISA's Coverage

agree.[64] Other cases hold that restricted coverage bars ERISA's application, but many of them can be traced to some early Labor Department advisory opinions that announced (without support) that an individual employment contract is not subject to ERISA[65] – a position the Department has since recanted.[66] Cases may also proceed from the assumption that Congress could not have intended to work such a sweeping transformation of employment relations. Applied to individualized benefit commitments, ERISA might seem to swallow up the common law of employment contracts. But this concern is misplaced, because ERISA only reaches post-employment compensation (i.e., pensions) and enumerated welfare benefits, not all terms and conditions of employment.

The objection that ERISA's protective policy is unnecessary when a benefit arrangement is specially designed (perhaps even separately bargained for) to meet the needs of one or a few employees is more weighty. In those circumstances, it can be assumed that participation is fully informed and deliberate, and key personnel typically have the education, judgment, and bargaining power necessary to protect themselves. Because such special arrangements grow out of competition for highly skilled labor, the firm's interest is aligned with the participant's, which minimizes the risk of employer abuse.

But restricted coverage by itself does not ensure that the program is designed and administered to meet the needs of participants. Consider a financially strapped small firm that promises a pension to one or a few rank-and-file employees in lieu of paying higher wages – the business may fail while the benefit is unfunded, but the participants are not in a position to gauge that risk. As this example illustrates, the identity of the promisees is a better indicator of the need for regulation than mere breadth of coverage. In fact, ERISA excepts unfunded deferred compensation plans for "a select group of management or highly compensated employees" from its fiduciary oversight and pension content controls.[67] This targeted exclusion of

---

[64] E.g., Cvelbar v. CBI Ill., Inc., 106 F.3d 1368, 1376 (7th Cir. 1997); Biggers v. Wittek Indus., Inc., 4 F.3d 291, 298 (4th Cir. 1993); Strzelecki v. Schwarz Paper Co., 824 F. Supp. 821, 827 (N.D. Ill. 1993); Williams v. Wright, 927 F.2d 1540, 1545 (11th Cir. 1991).

[65] E.g., Jervis v. Elerding, 504 F. Supp. 606 (C.D. Cal. 1980); Lackey v. Whitehall Corp., 704 F. Supp. 201 (D. Kan. 1988); O'Halloren v. Marine Cooks & Stewards Union, 730 P.2d 616 (Or. App. 1986).

[66] E.g., Letter to Mr. Joel P. Bennet (Oct. 19, 1985) (ERISA coverage is "not affected by the fact that the arrangement is limited to covering a single employee, is negotiated between the employer and the employee, or is not intended by the employer–plan sponsor to be an employee benefit plan for purposes of [ERISA]"); U.S. Dep't of Lab., Pension & Welfare Benefits Admin., ERISA Opinion Letter 91-20A (July 2, 1991).

[67] ERISA § 201(2), 29 U.S.C. § 1051(2) (2018) (participation, benefit accrual, vesting, spousal rights, and antialienation); ERISA § 301(a)(3), 29 U.S.C. § 1081(a)(3) (2018) (funding); ERISA § 401(a)(1), 29 U.S.C. § 1101(a)(1) (2018) (fiduciary responsibility); ERISA § 4021 (b)(6), 29 U.S.C. § 1321(b)(6) (2018) (termination insurance). This "top hat plan" exception is examined *infra* Chapter 2D.

40   *General Considerations*

certain executive compensation arrangements confirms that an individual employment contract or small-plan exception was not intended and is not necessary.

B "EMPLOYEE" STATUS

ERISA applies only to plans that provide pension benefits to "employees"[68] or welfare benefits to "participants or their beneficiaries."[69] Where the statute applies it confers rights and remedies on participants and beneficiaries. "Participant" is defined by reference to employee status,[70] but the statute defines employee circularly, as "any individual employed by an employer."[71] Perhaps incorporation of the common-law meaning was expected, but the legislative history offers no clear guidance, and other definitional approaches are plausible. The resulting ambiguity has forced the courts to decide whether federal law governs the benefit rights of certain categories of workers, including business owners and independent contractors.

Working Owners

Labor Department regulations provide that a benefit program that covers *only* individuals who own, or whose spouses own, an interest in an unincorporated business (as partner or proprietor) is not a "plan" subject to federal regulation, but ERISA applies if one or more common-law employees are participants.[72] If a corporation is *wholly* owned by an individual (or by an individual and his or her spouse), a benefit program that does not cover anyone else is also exempt from ERISA, even if the owner is also a common-law employee of the corporation.[73]

ERISA applies if a benefit plan covers at least one common-law employee along with business owners. In that situation, do ERISA's protections extend to the owners? ERISA grants rights and remedies to "participants" and their beneficiaries,[74] and the

---

[68] A pension plan is defined as a program that provides retirement income to employees or results in a deferral of income by employees until the termination of employment or later. ERISA § 3(2)(A), 29 U.S.C. § 1002(2)(A) (2018).

[69] ERISA § 3(1), 29 U.S.C. § 1002(1) (2018).

[70] ERISA § 3(7), 29 U.S.C. § 1002(7) (2018).

[71] ERISA § 3(6), 29 U.S.C. § 1002(6) (2018).

[72] 29 C.F.R. § 2510.3-3(b), (c) (2021). To trigger ERISA the program must cover a common-law employee who is not an owner's spouse.

[73] *Id.* This rule was apparently designed to avoid distortions in the choice-of-business form, but it does not extend to cases where the corporation is closely held and all plan participants are shareholder–employees. Leckey v. Stephano, 263 F.3d 267 (3d Cir. 2001) (ERISA applies to pension plan of corporation wholly owned by participant, his spouse, and his stepdaughter). Accordingly, the incorporation of a sole proprietorship does not affect ERISA's coverage, but the incorporation of a partnership often does.

[74] E.g., ERISA § 102, 29 U.S.C. § 1022 (2018) (disclosure); ERISA § 404(a)(1), 29 U.S.C. § 1104 (a)(1) (2018) (fiduciary duties); ERISA § 502(a), 29 U.S.C. § 1132(a) (2018) (civil enforcement).

ERISA's Coverage

statute defines "participant" as an "employee or former employee of an employer . . . who is or may become eligible to receive a benefit" under the plan.[75] Reliance on the traditional common-law understanding of the employment relationship would suggest that partners and proprietors cannot be participants and so cannot qualify for ERISA's protections, even if they are covered under a plan that includes common-law employees. If so, their rights and obligations would be defined and enforced by state, not federal, law. Having different bodies of law apply to employees and owners who work side-by-side in an unincorporated business and participate in the same benefit programs seems a strangely inefficient result, yet a circuit split developed on the question. *Raymond B. Yates, M.D., P.C. Profit Sharing Plan* v. *Hendon* put the matter to rest, holding that:

> If a plan covers one or more employees other than the business owner and his or her spouse, the working owner may participate on equal terms with other plan participants. Such a working owner, in common with other employees, qualifies for the protections ERISA affords plan participants and is governed by the rights and remedies ERISA specifies.[76]

Yates involved a sole shareholder and president of a professional corporation, but the Court's holding and reasoning apply with equal force to working owners of unincorporated businesses, such as partners, limited liability company members, and sole proprietors.[77] *Yates* avoids the inefficiency, confusion, and perception of unfairness that would flow from letting state law govern the rights and obligations of partners or proprietors, while federal law, with its more limited set of remedies,[78] controls the fate of common-law employees who are covered by the same plan and involved in the same transaction. *Yates* does not preclude another curious result: the benefit rights of the owners of an unincorporated business are given by state law so long as the owners are the only plan participants, but the inclusion of a single employee in the program instantly modifies the owners' rights, making them a creature of federal law.

Independent Contractors

Nationwide Mutual Insurance Co. v. *Darden*[79] involved a benefit arrangement set up by an insurance company for its independent commission agents. In determining ERISA's reach, the Supreme Court construed the term "employee" to incorporate the traditional test of employee status under the general common law of agency:

---

[75] ERISA § 3(7), 29 U.S.C. § 1002(7) (2018).
[76] Raymond B. Yates, M.D., P.C. Profit Sharing Plan v. Hendon, 541 U.S. 1, 6 (2004).
[77] The Court's opinion consistently addresses the status of "working owners," not just "shareholder–employees." *See, e.g., id.,* at 11, 17.
[78] *See infra* Chapter 5D.
[79] 503 U.S. 318 (1992).

General Considerations

In determining whether a hired party is an employee under the general common law of agency, we consider the hiring party's right to control the manner and means by which the product is accomplished. Among the other factors relevant to this inquiry are the skill required; the source of the instrumentalities and tools; the location of the work; the duration of the relationship between the parties; whether the hiring party has the right to assign additional projects to the hired party; the extent of the hired party's discretion over when and how long to work; the method of payment; the hired party's role in hiring and paying assistants; whether the work is part of the regular business of the hiring party; whether the hiring party is in business; the provision of employee benefits; and the tax treatment of the hired party.[80]

Conceding that the common law offers "no paradigm of determinacy," the Court explained that "all of the incidents of the relationship must be assessed and weighed with no one factor being decisive."[81] The Court rejected the argument that ERISA's broad remedial purposes support a more expansive reading of the term, in part because the purposive approach would engender even greater uncertainty.[82]

In spite of *Darden*, the Seventh Circuit, in *Ruttenberg v. US Life Insurance Co.*,[83] held that a disability insurance policy covering independent commodities traders was subject to ERISA rather than state law. Although the trader was an independent contractor of the trading firm that arranged the insurance, he was named to receive benefits by the policy, and so the court concluded that he fit the statutory definition of a beneficiary, a "person designated by a participant, *or by the terms of an employee benefit plan*, who is or may become eligible to receive a benefit thereunder."[84] If taken seriously, this definition of beneficiary would allow a plan to extend coverage to anyone it wants, perhaps even selling its package of health or disability insurance to individuals unrelated to the employer or union sponsor. The rights and obligations of those unrelated (but named) plan "beneficiaries" would then be governed exclusively by ERISA, potentially obliterating a large swath of state insurance law.[85] Before the Supreme Court's decision in *Yates*,[86] some lower courts ruled that sole

---

[80] *Id.* at 323–24 (quoting Cmty. for Creative Non-Violence v. Reid, 490 U.S. 730, 751–52 (1989)).

[81] *Darden*, 503 U.S. at 324 (quoting NLRB v. United Ins. Co. of Am., 390 U.S. 254, 258 (1968)). Accord Barnhart v. N.Y. Life Ins. Co., 141 F.3d 1310, 1312–13 (9th Cir. 1998). *See, e.g.*, Jammal v. Am. Fam. Ins. Co., 914 F.3d 449, 457–60 (6th Cir. 2019), *cert. denied*, 140 S. Ct. 643 (2019) (applying the *Darden* factors but reversing the district court for applying those factors incorrectly).

[82] *Darden*, 503 U.S. at 326–27.

[83] 413 F.3d 652, 662 (7th Cir. 2005).

[84] *Id.*; ERISA § 3(8), 29 U.S.C. § 1002(8) (2018) (emphasis added).

[85] In an amicus brief to the Supreme Court, the Justice Department argued that this interpretation of beneficiary "has no logical stopping point, because it would allow a plan to cover anyone it chooses, including independent contractors excluded by [*Nationwide Mut. Ins. Co. v. Darden*]." Raymond B. Yates, M.D., P.C. Profit Sharing Plan v. Hendon, 541 U.S. 1, 11 n.2 (2004).

[86] *See supra* Chapter 2 notes 76–78 and accompanying text.

proprietors or partners covered by a welfare plan were employers, not employees, and could not be participants. As such, state law rather than ERISA would apply to such owners, unless they could somehow be treated as beneficiaries.[87] To avoid the inefficiency of having different bodies of law apply to owners and employees who work side-by-side in an unincorporated business under the same benefit program, some courts seized upon the fact that covered workers were named in the policy as payees of disability and certain other insurance benefits, and hence working owners could be seen as beneficiaries even if they were not participants. This line of authority was rendered irrelevant by the holding in *Yates*, that working owners covered by a plan are participants subject to ERISA (i.e., employer and employee are not mutually exclusive categories). The idea that there can be a beneficiary when there is no corresponding participant was a convenient but anomalous construct. Having outlived its usefulness, this idea should be disavowed, not used as the foundation for an extension of ERISA's jurisdiction to independent contractors, as was done in *Ruttenberg*.

The increase in the contingent workforce and the rise of telecommuting has blurred the worker classification distinction between employee and independent contractor. Where a plan by its terms covers some or all categories of "employees" (meaning common-law employees), or expressly excludes independent contractors, errors in worker classification can cause wrongful denial of benefits.[88] ERISA, however, does not mandate universal coverage; it allows employees to be excluded from participation based on their mode of payment, job type, or work location, or for other reasons.[89] Consequently, workers who are found to have been mistakenly treated as independent contractors are not automatically entitled to participate by virtue of their employee status; plans may, and commonly do, impose other more restrictive conditions.

---

[87] E.g., Peterson v. Am. Life & Health Ins. Co., 48 F.3d 404 (9th Cir.), *cert. denied*, 516 U.S. 942 (1995); Wolk v. UNUM Life Ins. of Am., 186 F.3d 352, 356–58 (3d Cir. 1999), *cert. denied*, 528 U.S. 1076 (2000). These cases decline to treat partners as "participants" because ERISA restricts that term to employees or former employees. Instead, they hold that a partner who is covered by a benefit program along with one or more common-law employees falls within ERISA's definition of "beneficiary" because the partner is designated by the terms of the plan as a person who may be entitled to benefits. *Peterson*, 48 F.3d at 408–09; *Wolk*, 186 F.3d at 356–58

[88] *See* Vizcaino v. Microsoft Corp., 120 F.3d 1006 (9th Cir. 1997) (en banc) (unless excluded by another provision, ERISA plan that by its terms applies to "common-law employees" must cover a large staff of "freelance" software developers that the company erroneously treated as independent contractors for employment tax purposes, despite the fact that freelancers were hired under the understanding that they were not eligible for benefits), *cert. denied*, 522 U.S. 1098 (1998). Besides plan coverage, the worker classification distinction is important because fees paid to independent contractors are not subject to income tax withholding, nor is the payer liable for Social Security taxes or the federal unemployment tax.

[89] The only eligibility conditions outlawed by ERISA are certain age and service conditions in the case of pension plans and specified health status factors in the case of group health plans. ERISA §§ 202, 702, 29 U.S.C. §§ 1052, 1182 (2018).

44 General Considerations

Nominal Partners

ERISA does not apply to retirement plans that cover only partners.[90] Yet an appellate court has held that a nominal partner in one of the world's largest accounting firms was more properly classified as an employee for purposes of ERISA and was therefore entitled to statutory protection against discharge intended to prevent pension vesting.[91] While recognizing that the partner–employee distinction is governed by common-law principles codified in the Uniform Partnership Act and successor statutes, the court's analysis was heavily influenced by the traditional test of employee status under the general common law of agency (as enunciated in *Darden*), with particular emphasis on the plaintiff's inability to participate in the management and control of the business.[92] The case presented an extreme example of a partner being frozen out by a self-perpetuating management committee.[93]

C THE PENSION–WELFARE DICHOTOMY

ERISA applies only to an "employee benefit plan," defined as either an employee welfare benefit plan or an employee pension benefit plan.[94] Consequently, in addition to requiring a "plan" in which at least one "employee" participates, federal regulation comes into play only if the arrangement provides either welfare or pension benefits. A program that provides retirement income or systematically defers compensation until termination of covered employment or beyond qualifies as a pension plan.[95] A program that provides any of certain *specifically listed benefits* is a welfare plan, whether the benefit is provided on a current or deferred basis.[96] Welfare benefits may be provided in kind, but far more commonly they take the form of cash payments or reimbursements of the cost of designated expenses (e.g., medical care). Any nonpension employee benefit that is not enumerated in the definition of "welfare plan" is wholly exempt from federal regulation. This section examines some curious features of this statutory benefit taxonomy, beginning with pension benefits.

Pension Benefits

Pension plans are subject to the most intensive federal regulation because of the long-term nature of the benefit promise and the resulting potential for changed

---

[90] 29 C.F.R. § 2510.3-3(b), -3(c)(2) (2021).
[91] Simpson v. Ernst & Young, 100 F.3d 436 (6th Cir. 1996), *cert. denied*, 520 U.S. 1248 (1997).
[92] *Id.* at 443.
[93] See the district court's fuller recitation of facts, Simpson v. Ernst & Young, 850 F. Supp. 648, 650–53 (S.D. Ohio 1994).
[94] ERISA §§ 4(a), 3(3), 29 U.S.C. §§ 1003(a), 1002(3) (2018).
[95] ERISA § 3(2)(A), 29 U.S.C. § 1002(2)(A) (2018).
[96] ERISA § 3(1), 29 U.S.C. § 1002(1) (2018).

ERISA's Coverage

circumstances and defeated expectations.[97] Because a worker's employment or family circumstances may change, ERISA requires that pension benefits become nonforfeitable (vest) upon the completion of no more than seven years of service and normally provides survivor annuity protection to the participant's spouse. Because the employer's financial condition may take an unexpected turn for the worse, ERISA contains safeguards against default, requiring systematic advance funding and Pension Benefit Guaranty Corporation (PBGC) insurance of defined benefit plans. Although deferral creates the risks to which these rules respond, the statutory definition of a pension plan is not simply keyed to the duration of the commitment. To be a pension plan, the program must "provide retirement income to employees, or result[ ] in a deferral of income by employees for periods extending to the termination of covered employment or beyond."[98] Consequently, deferral of compensation, even for an extended period, does not necessarily create a pension plan (absent special circumstances) if the deferred amounts are payable during the continuance of the employment relationship.[99] Indeed, such in-service deferred compensation arrangements do not even meet the definition of a welfare plan, and therefore are also exempt from federal disclosure and fiduciary obligations.

Retirement income need not be paid in cash,[100] and annuity distribution is not required. A lump-sum payment can be used for support in retirement, and a plan that provides retirement income is a pension plan regardless of "the method of distributing benefits from the plan."[101] The other prong of the statutory definition is

---

[97] See supra Chapter 1B, C.

[98] ERISA § 3(2)(A), 29 U.S.C. § 1002(2)(A) (2018). ERISA is not a tax statute, and so the definitional references to "retirement income" and "deferral of income" should not be construed as conditioning pension plan classification on the time at which compensation is includible in gross income. Funded nonqualified deferred compensation is taxable upon the elimination of any substantial risk of forfeiture, I.R.C. §§ 402(b), 83(a) (2018), which may occur well in advance of retirement or separation from service, yet such plans were clearly intended to be subject to ERISA, see, e.g., ERISA § 201(2), 29 U.S.C. § 1051(2) (2018) (only certain unfunded executive deferred compensation plans are subject to relaxed regulation). Hence the references to income in the pension plan definition should be interpreted according to the timing of the distribution of deferred compensation – in accordance, that is, with the common understanding that the term "income" has reference to receipt.

[99] A Labor Department regulation provides that the term "pension plan" does not include "payments made by an employer to some or all of its employees as bonuses for work performed, unless such payments are systematically deferred to the termination of covered employment or beyond, or so as to provide retirement income to employees." 29 C.F.R. § 2510.3-2(c) (2021). But see infra Chapter 2 note 106 (examining recent appellate decisions on the subject).

[100] See Musmeci v. Schwegmann Giant Super Mkts., Inc., 332 F.3d 339 (5th Cir. 2003) (vouchers for groceries provided to retired supermarket employees), cert. denied, 540 U.S. 1110 (2004); I.R.C. §§ 401(a)(23), (a)(28), 409(h) (2018) (stock bonus plans and employee stock ownership plans must permit distribution in form of employer securities); but see Rathbun v. Qwest Commc'ns Int'l, Inc., 458 F. Supp. 2d 1238 (D. Colo. 2006) (program reimbursing active and retired employees' local telephone expenses does not provide retirement income, distinguishing Musmeci).

[101] ERISA § 3(2)(A), 29 U.S.C. § 1002(2)(A) (2018) (final clause); U.S. Dep't of Lab., Pension & Welfare Benefits Admin., ERISA Opinion Letter 75-12 (July 17, 1975) (profit-sharing plan

General Considerations

even more expansive, for a plan that defers income only to the "termination of covered employment" – that is, until separation from service – is a pension plan, although departing employees may be years away from retirement, in the sense of permanent withdrawal from the labor force. Moreover, a plan that does not "by its express terms" provide retirement income or defer compensation until separation from service is nevertheless a pension plan if it does so "as a result of surrounding circumstances."[102] Under this rule, a deferred compensation arrangement can be a pension plan if distributions are skewed toward the last years of participants' careers,[103] and even relatively short-term deferral can trigger pension classification if the program's coverage is tilted in favor of older workers nearing retirement.[104] Absent such surrounding circumstances, the mere fact that a fixed-term deferred compensation agreement calls for earlier payment in the event of death, disability, or other termination of employment does not turn it into a pension plan because termination-based distributions are incidental, rather than being the focus of the program.[105]

If a participant is given the option of taking payment of deferred compensation after a specified period of time or allowing the amount to remain on deposit for distribution (with earnings) upon separation from service, is it a pension plan? Provided that early payment is not penalized nor delayed distribution subsidized (by the tax law or the employer) so as to bias the participant's choice, the program

---

calling for lump-sum distribution on termination of employment is a pension plan under ERISA). A pair of Fourth Circuit decisions can be read as finding long-term payout important to pension classification, but that conclusion is suspect. Wiedenbeck, *supra* Chapter 1 note 56, at 579–81.

[102] ERISA § 3(2)(A), 29 U.S.C. § 1002(2)(A) (2018).

[103] U.S. Dep't of Lab., Pension & Welfare Benefits Admin., ERISA Opinion Letter 83-46A (Sept. 8, 1983) (late-career distributions and long payout schedule are factors to be considered in determining whether a deferred compensation arrangement is a pension plan as a result of surrounding circumstances).

[104] E.g., U.S. Dep't of Lab., Pension & Welfare Benefits Admin., ERISA Opinion Letter 89-07A (Apr. 27, 1989) (bonus program under which employee must continue to be employed for five years to receive payment is not a pension plan unless the selection of bonus recipients is skewed toward employees nearing retirement); U.S. Dep't of Lab., Pension & Welfare Benefits Admin., ERISA Opinion Letter 81-16A (Jan. 23, 1981) (ten-year payout could make oil and gas royalty fund a pension plan, depending on the likelihood that employees permitted to participate will retire or separate from service within that period).

[105] Hagel v. United Land Co., 759 F. Supp. 1199, 1202 (E.D. Va. 1991) (bonus that provided for payment in five equal annual installments or earlier in the event of death, permanent disability, or change in control of employer held not pension plan because ERISA requires that a plan "generally defer the receipt of income to the termination of employment," which is not satisfied where "under the facts of a particular case, a portion of the withheld income happens to become due after termination"); U.S. Dep't of Lab., Pension & Welfare Benefits Admin., ERISA Opinion Letter 83-46A (Sept. 8, 1983) ("mere fact that a plan provides that payments which would otherwise be made on a specified date may be paid earlier in the event an employee terminates employment does not automatically mean that the arrangement is a pension plan by its express terms," but is a factor to be considered in conjunction with surrounding circumstances). *See* Murphy v. Inexco Oil Co., 611 F.2d 570 (5th Cir. 1980).

würde not cause compensation to be *systematically* deferred until the termination of employment, and is exempt from ERISA.[106] If, however, the employer administers the program in a way that discourages participants from taking early payment, then it is a pension plan as a result of surrounding circumstances. These circumstances may include the employer's communications (or lack thereof) concerning the program, such as the failure to publicize the early withdrawal option.[107]

Severance pay plans present a unique classification challenge under ERISA. Severance pay is, by definition, compensation deferred until the termination of employment. Thus it would automatically fall into the pension category, but for a special dispensation. That dispensation takes the form of statutory authorization for the Secretary of Labor to write regulations treating some or all severance pay arrangements as welfare plans rather than pension plans.[108] Pursuant to that authority, if severance payments that do not exceed twice the employee's annual pre-termination compensation are completed within two years, the program will not be treated as a pension plan, provided that the payments are not conditioned, directly or indirectly, on retirement.[109]

---

[106] 29 C.F.R. § 2510.3-2(c) (2021) (bonus program does not constitute a pension plan unless "payments are systematically deferred to the termination of covered employment or beyond, or so as to provide retirement income to employees"); McKinsey v. Sentry Ins., 986 F.2d 401, 406 (10th Cir. 1993). Recent decisions seem to turn on whether the program in question is (either explicitly or via surrounding circumstances) one intended to defer compensation until termination (in which case it is a pension plan, even if the plan permits in-service distributions by election of the participant) or whether the aim is to provide bonus payments for superior performance (in which case it is not an ERISA plan at all, regardless of whether the bonus can, at the election of the participant, be deferred until termination of employment). *See* Wilson v. Safelite Grp., Inc., 930 F.3d 429 (6th Cir. 2019) (distinguishing between deferred compensation and bonus plans); Tolbert v. RBC Cap. Mkts. Corp., 758 F.3d 619 (5th Cir. 2014) (finding a deferred compensation "wealth accumulation program" to be a covered plan and distinguishing Emmenegger v. Bull Moose Tube Co., 197 F.3d 929 (8th Cir. 1999) as involving an exempt "bonus" program).

[107] U.S. Dep't of Lab., Pension & Welfare Benefits Admin., ERISA Opinion Letter 81-18A (Feb. 2, 1981) (employee stock purchase plan under which participants had the right to sell their stock but were not always given share certificates could be a pension plan if it is administered or communicated in a way that discourages participants from receiving or selling the stock); U.S. Dep't of Lab., Pension & Welfare Benefits Admin., ERISA Opinion Letter 90-17A (June 25, 1990) (employee stock purchase plan could be pension plan if communications to participants suggest that it is intended to provide retirement income or defer income until separation from service); U.S. Dep't of Lab., Pension & Welfare Benefits Admin., ERISA Opinion Letter 83-46A (Sept. 8, 1983) (same).

[108] ERISA § 3(2)(B), 29 U.S.C. § 1002(2)(B) (2018). Severance pay is also a welfare benefit by virtue of the cross-reference to benefits described in section 302(c) of the Labor Management Relations Act in ERISA's definition of a welfare plan. ERISA § 3(1), 29 U.S.C. § 1002(1) (2018); 29 C.F.R. § 2510.3-1(a)(2) (2021). But recall that ad hoc separation payments to selected employees may be so indefinite that the arrangement does not constitute a "plan." *See supra* Chapter 2 notes 29–52 and accompanying text.

[109] 29 C.F.R. § 2510.3-2(b) (2021). The Labor Department has taken the position that severance pay may be indirectly conditioned on retirement and so subject to stringent pension plan

48 General Considerations

Welfare Benefits

Welfare plans are subject to reporting and disclosure requirements, fiduciary responsibility standards, and a federal enforcement mechanism that includes broad preemption of state law. To be classified as a welfare plan, the program must provide one or more statutorily enumerated benefits, namely:

> (A) medical, surgical, or hospital care benefits, or benefits in the event of sickness, accident, disability, death or unemployment, or vacation benefits, apprenticeship or other training programs, or day care centers, scholarship funds, or prepaid legal services, or (B) any benefit described in section 302(c) of the Labor Management Relations Act, 1947 (other than pensions on retirement or death, and insurance to provide such pensions).[110]

In general, ERISA applies without regard to whether benefits are financed by the purchase of insurance (group-term life insurance is commonly used to provide employee death benefits, for example) or are paid out of the general assets of the employer (i.e., self-insurance).[111] While a welfare plan may provide benefits of more than one type, a benefit that is not described in ERISA does not become subject to federal regulation merely because it is included with pension or welfare benefits in a multi-benefit plan.[112] Federal preemption does not apply, and employees' rights to such non-ERISA benefits are determined by state courts under state law.

The benefit types included in the welfare plan definition seem haphazard and unsystematic. In fact, the statute reflects the scope of two earlier pieces of federal legislation. The Welfare and Pension Plans Disclosure Act of 1958 (WPPDA) provided the starting point for ERISA's definition of a welfare plan, but it reached only "medical, surgical, or hospital care or benefits, or benefits in the event of

---

regulation if the program is limited to employees with many years of service (a group for whom termination of employment is likely to mean withdrawal from the labor force, i.e., retirement) or is conditioned on taking distribution from the company's retirement plan. U.S. Dep't of Lab., Pension & Welfare Benefits Admin., ERISA Opinion Letter 84-15A (Mar. 20, 1984) (severance arrangement limited to employees with eighteen or more years of service); U.S. Dep't of Lab., Pension & Welfare Benefits Admin., ERISA Opinion Letter 83-47A (Sept. 13, 1983) (severance pay conditioned on employee taking lump-sum distribution from defined benefit pension plan).

[110] ERISA § 3(1), 29 U.S.C. § 1002(1) (2018).

[111] The fiduciary responsibility provisions (Part 4, Title I) contain an exception for unfunded executive deferred compensation plans, ERISA § 401(a)(1), 29 U.S.C. § 1101(a)(1) (2018) (discussed *infra* Chapter 2D), but not for unfunded welfare plans. The welfare plan definition, however, lists "scholarship *funds*," ERISA § 3(1), 29 U.S.C. § 1002(1) (2018) (emphasis added), not scholarships generally, and so unfunded educational assistance programs are not covered. 29 C.F.R. § 2510.3-1(k) (2021).

[112] ERISA § 3(1), 29 U.S.C. § 1002(1) (2018), provides that a benefit program is a welfare plan only "to the extent that" it provides one of the statutorily listed benefits. Kemp v. Int'l Bus. Machs. Corp., 109 F.3d 708 (11th Cir. 1997).

ERISA's Coverage

sickness, accident, disability, death, or unemployment."[113] Presumably, this definition responded to the perceived prevalence of various sorts of employee benefit programs at the time of its enactment. ERISA expanded upon this definition by directly listing most of the benefits then described in paragraphs (6) through (8) of section 302(c) of the Labor Management Relations Act (the Taft-Hartley Act),[114] while incorporating the rest by reference. In 1974, the cross-reference to section 302 (c) reached only severance and holiday benefits,[115] but a 1990 amendment of the Taft-Hartley Act brought "financial assistance for employee housing" within the ambit of welfare plan regulation.[116]

The welfare plan definition looks only to the type of benefit. A promise of *deferred* welfare benefits is just a welfare plan, not a pension plan (the benefit is not retirement income). Consequently, retiree health care benefits are subject only to reporting and disclosure, fiduciary obligations, and federal enforcement. Because no vesting requirement applies, employers are generally free to terminate such programs at any time to stem escalating costs or for other reasons, regardless of an employee's length of service or level of need.[117] The employer may, of course, voluntarily obligate itself to provide lifelong health care benefits to retirees, and

---

[113] WPPDA § 3(a)(1), Pub. L. No. 85-836, 72 Stat. 997.

[114] Labor Management Relations (Taft-Hartley) Act, § 302(c), 29 U.S.C. § 186(c) (2018).

[115] 29 C.F.R. § 2510.3-1(a)(3) (2021) (1975 regulation observes that Taft-Hartley Act cross-reference expands ERISA's statutory list of welfare benefits only by adding holiday, severance, and similar benefits). As noted earlier, severance programs can also be classified as pension plans because benefits are deferred until "the termination of covered employment." ERISA § 3 (2)(A), 29 U.S.C. § 1002(2)(A) (2018). Nevertheless, most severance pay plans are subject only to welfare plan requirements because the Labor Department has exercised its authority to exempt designated severance pay plans from pension controls by regulation. ERISA § 3(2)(B), 29 U.S.C. § 1002(2)(B) (2018); 29 C.F.R. § 2510.3-2(b) (2021). Under that regulation, if severance benefits do not exceed two years' pay and are fully distributed within two years, pension plan treatment is avoided, and almost all severance programs are written to conform to those conditions.

[116] 29 U.S.C. § 186(c)(7)(C) (2018). ERISA's reliance on the Taft-Hartley Act's list of benefits apparently stems from the fact that notorious abuses in the management of employee benefit funds created the impetus for ERISA's fiduciary standards, and those abuses involved trusts to provide benefits to unionized employees under the Taft-Hartley Act. That act makes it a crime for an employer to contribute to a trust for unionized employees if the trust provides any type of benefit not specifically permitted by section 302(c), and so the Taft-Hartley Act's list of permissible benefits may have been assumed to cover the field of lawful employee benefits. Unfortunately, there are two problems with this assumption. First, other types of benefits may be provided to unionized employees if they are not funded through a trust, and, in general, ERISA was intended to apply regardless of funding. (Even if there is no pot of money to steal, ERISA makes a fiduciary's discretionary decisions subject to oversight.) Second, employers may unilaterally establish benefit plans (funded or not) for their nonunionized workers, and these programs are not constrained by the Taft-Hartley Act's list of permissible benefits. Accordingly, if ERISA's definition of a welfare plan was intended to cover the universe of nonpension benefits – or even if it was meant to cover all *funded* nonpension benefits – its drafters were mistaken.

[117] M & G Polymers USA, LLC v. Tackett, 574 U.S. 427, 434–35 (2015).

50 *General Considerations*

many cases are founded on the assertion that such a contractual undertaking was made,[118] but such a commitment exceeds ERISA's minimum standards for welfare plans.

Other Benefits

ERISA's pension and welfare plan definitions fail to reach several types of compensation that can be significant to workers' career and financial planning, such as the decision whether to accept or continue employment, or the determination of the necessary amount of household saving. Or, from a paternalistic perspective, the statute fails to cover a number of benefits that can induce substantial reliance. In-service deferred compensation is among the most glaring omissions. Employer financial assistance that is targeted to dependent care or college costs is usually also exempt.[119] Because such arrangements escape classification as pension or welfare plans, federal preemption does not apply. Consequently, this third category of employee benefits, while exempt from federal oversight, is a permissible subject of state and local regulation.

Formerly, emergency savings programs epitomized the gap in ERISA's benefit coverage. Short-term precautionary saving does not satisfy the statutory pension plan definition (it provides neither retirement income nor deferral to the termination of employment). Precautionary saving might well be used to pay unexpected medical expenses or for support during a period of layoff or unemployment. Those are common welfare benefits, but if the account can also be used to pay the rent or fix the car when money is tight, then the arrangement is not "for the purpose of providing" enumerated welfare benefits. In 2022 Congress amended ERISA and the Code to regulate employer-sponsored pension-linked emergency savings accounts.[120] Limited emergency savings programs for nonhighly compensated employees, with built-in worker notifications and protections, ready access to amounts saved and favorable tax treatment, are designed to encourage greater participation by low-income workers in 401(k) and other defined contribution retirement plans.[121]

---

[118] *See infra* Chapter 3B, C.

[119] The Labor Department takes the position that the welfare plan definition comprehends dependent care benefits only when the employer provides care *in kind* (on-premises child care facilities, for example) or when financed through a trust, not when the company provides financial assistance out of its general assets for employee-arranged care. ERISA Op. Ltrs., 88-10A (Dep't of Labor Aug. 12, 1988), 91-25A (Dep't of Labor July 2, 1991). Similarly, the welfare plan definition catches "scholarship *funds*" but misses more common unfunded employer promises to provide education benefits. 29 C.F.R. § 2510.3-1(k) (2021) (unfunded scholarship programs exempt).

[120] ERISA §§ 3(45), 404(c)(6), 801–04, 29 U.S.C. §§ 1002(45), 1104(c)(6), 1193–1193c (West Supp. 2023); I.R.C. § 402A(e) (West Supp. 2023).

[121] *See infra* Chapter 7A.

D EXCEPTIONS: TOP HAT, GOVERNMENT, AND CHURCH PLANS

A few benefit arrangements that fit the statutory definition of an employee benefit plan (either pension or welfare) are nevertheless excepted from most or all of ERISA's requirements. The most important exceptions are for unfunded executive deferred compensation arrangements (so-called top hat plans), and for plans sponsored by governmental or religious organizations.

Top hat plans are unfunded plans "maintained by an employer primarily for the purpose of providing deferred compensation for a select group of management or highly compensated employees."[122] Although they would otherwise be classified as pension plans (the deferral invariably extends at least to the termination of employment), top hat plans are exempt from all the minimum standards applied to pension plans and are even excused from ERISA's generally applicable fiduciary obligations.[123] Consequently, only the reporting and disclosure rules and the federal enforcement mechanisms (including preemption) apply.[124] Of these, the reporting and disclosure obligations of top hat plans have been relaxed by regulation,[125] so ERISA's principal effect on unfunded executive deferred compensation arrangements is to provide a mechanism for federal judicial enforcement of the terms of the plan, which (as a result of the ouster of state law) must be interpreted and applied according to federal common law.[126] Congress exempted top hat plans from ERISA's requirements because high-level executives have the bargaining power to negotiate particular terms and monitor their interest under the plan, and therefore do not need substantive protections (the minimum standards of pension plan content) or fiduciary obligations. If bargaining and informal oversight break down,

---

[122] ERISA § 201(2), 29 U.S.C. § 1051(2) (2018). Language is repeated at ERISA §§ 301(a)(3), 401 (a)(1), 4021(b)(6), 29 U.S.C. §§ 1081(a)(3), 1101(a)(1), 1321(b)(6) (2018).

[123] ERISA §§ 201(2) (accrual, vesting, spousal rights, and antialienation), 301(a)(3) (funding), 401 (a)(1) (fiduciary responsibility), 4021(b)(6) (plan termination insurance), 29 U.S.C. §§ 1051 (2), 1081(a)(3), 1101(a)(1), 1321(b)(6) (2018).

[124] Barrowclough v. Kidder, Peabody & Co., 752 F.2d 923, 929–31 (3d Cir. 1985) (limited application to top hat plans), *overruled as to an unrelated point by* Pritzker v. Merrill Lynch, Pierce, Fenner & Smith, Inc., 7 F.3d 1110 (3d Cir. 1993) (arbitrability of ERISA claims).

[125] ERISA § 110, 29 U.S.C. § 1030 (2018), permits the Labor Department to prescribe an alternate method of compliance with the statutory reporting and disclosure obligations for any category of pension plans that meet certain criteria. Pursuant to that authority, the Labor Department allows an employer to satisfy its informational obligations by filing a single statement of the number of unfunded top hat plans it maintains and the number of employees in each, and providing plan documents to the Department on request. 29 C.F.R. § 2520.104-23 (2021); *Barrowclough*, 752 F.2d at 931–34 (relaxed disclosure requirements).

[126] *Barrowclough*, 752 F.2d at 935–37 (federal enforcement mechanism and federal common law apply to claim for breach of the plan's terms); Kemmerer v. ICI Ams., Inc., 70 F.3d 281, 287 (3d Cir.) ("breach of contract principles, applied as a matter of federal common law, govern disputes arising out of [top hat] plan documents" and such plans should be "interpreted in keeping with the principles that govern unilateral contracts"), *cert. denied*, 116 U.S. 1826 (1995).

General Considerations

however, these executives must have access to judicial enforcement to vindicate their rights, or the plan becomes an illusory promise.[127]

The definition of a top hat plan leaves the scope of this exemption unclear. The plan must be unfunded and "maintained by an employer primarily for the purpose of providing deferred compensation for a select group of management or highly compensated employees." Whether "primarily" refers to the type of benefits provided or to the composition of participants was an unsettled issue until the Labor Department issued an opinion in 1990.[128] The Labor Department announced its view that "primarily" refers to the benefits provided under the plan and not to the participant composition,[129] so that the exemption may be lost if any participant is not a member of the "select group." Case law since then has generally followed this approach,[130] which is more consonant with ERISA's informational and protective policies, although in mixed-membership plans it may "safeguard" executives in ways that they do not need or want.[131]

In order to apply a rule that top hat status is lost if any member fails to qualify as "management" or a "highly compensated employee," those categories must be

---

[127] *Kemmerer*, 70 F.3d at 288. *See* Wiedenbeck, *supra* Chapter 1 note 56, at 581.

[128] Early decisions and rulings seemed to follow the latter approach, looking to the percentage of employees covered by the plan and comparing their *average* pay with the rest of the workforce, so that the exemption could apply even if a few rank-and-file employees were covered by the plan. E.g., Belka v. Rowe Furniture Co., 571 F. Supp. 1249 (D. Md. 1983). *See generally* Vincent Amoroso et al., *SERP Sponsors Beware*, 24 Pens. & Ben. Rep. (BNA) 1001 (1997); Edward J. Rayner, *ERISA's Top-Hat Plan Exemption: A Primer*, 99 Tax Notes 107 (2003).

[129] U.S. Dep't of Lab., Pension & Welfare Benefits Admin., ERISA Opinion Letter 90-14A (May 8, 1990).

[130] E.g., Gallione v. Flaherty, 70 F.3d 724, 726–28 (2d Cir. 1995) (union plan covering full-time officers, who were responsible for setting policy and negotiating labor contracts, exempt because limited to upper-echelon of union management); Duggan v. Hobbs, 99 F.3d 307, 312–13 (9th Cir. 1996) (unfunded pension provided under individually negotiated severance agreement was an exempt top hat plan because departing employee had sufficient clout to influence the design and operation of the plan); In re New Valley Corp., 89 F.3d 143, 148 (3d Cir. 1996) (holding that "[i]n character, the plan must cover *only* high level employees") (emphasis added). *But see* Demery v. Extebank Deferred Comp. Plan (B), 216 F.3d 283, 288 (2d Cir. 2000) (finding that the inclusion of "two or three employees who were arguably not 'highly compensated' or 'a select group of management'" employees is *not* an obstacle to top hat status) and Browe v. CTC Corp., 15 F.4th 175, 194, 197 (2d Cir. 2021) (noting early in the opinion that the plan "must cover only high-level employees" to qualify as a top hat plan but then describing the reason the plan at bar was not a top hat plan was because, inter alia, it involved "the inclusion of a *significant number* of employees who lacked any indicia of 'management' status) (emphasis added). It appears the courts largely follow the DOL view but with a potential "de minimis" exception, that is, if the plan includes one or two stray employees who are not highly compensated or managerial, the top hat exemption may still be attainable.

[131] If the top hat plan exemption is forfeited because of the inclusion of rank-and-file employees, then ERISA's pension funding and vesting requirements would come into play, which (in the case of a nonqualified plan) would cause the participants to be taxed in advance of distribution. *See infra* Chapter 10 notes 18–24 and accompanying text; I.R.C. §§ 402(b), 83(a) (2018).

ERISA's Coverage 53

specified with precision. Yet the statute leaves both terms undefined. Some practitioners have assumed that satisfaction of the tax law's quantitative definition of the term "highly compensated employee" suffices for top hat status, but that definition serves other purposes.[132] The Labor Department's 1990 opinion seems to take the view that "the ability to affect or substantially influence, through negotiation or otherwise, the design and operation of their deferred compensation plan" provides a functional definition of "management or highly compensated employees"; and several (but not all) courts have followed that reasoning.[133] Under this approach, many plans that extend coverage to middle-management ranks could be found to violate ERISA's substantive provisions, even though all participants satisfy the tax law's definition of "highly compensated employee." That may be appropriate in light of ERISA's protective policy, but the functional approach requires a fact-intensive inquiry, the outcome of which is far less predictable than bright-line criteria keyed to compensation levels.

Government and church plans, both pension and welfare, are exempt from all of ERISA's labor-law requirements, including the reporting and disclosure and federal

---

[132] I.R.C. § 414(q) (2018) (definition of highly compensated employee for purposes of the coverage and amount nondiscrimination rules). *See* Raymond B. Yates, M.D., P.C. Profit Sharing Plan v. Hendon, 541 U.S. 1, 13–14 (2004) (looking to the tax Code's definition of highly compensated employee for guidance in interpreting the top hat plan exception to ERISA's fiduciary responsibility rules).

[133] *See generally* Peter Wiedenbeck & Norman Stein, *The Executive Compensation Threat to Retirement*, 26 FLA. TAX REV. ____ (2023). The courts of appeal disagree on the role the ability of participants to negotiate plan terms or operation plays with respect to a top hat determination. *Compare, e.g.,* Browe v. CTC Corp., 15 F.4th 175, 196 (2d Cir. 2021) (reaffirming that "the ability to negotiate plan terms is an important component of top hat plans"); Bakri v. Venture Mfg. Co., 473 F.3d 677, 678–79 (6th Cir. 2007) (holding that the ability of individual participants to "influence" plan terms and operation is a key part of determining whether the plan is a top hat plan); *Duggan*, 99 F.3d 307 (adopting DOL position on importance of negotiation ability); *with* Sikora v. UPMC, 876 F.3d 110, 116 (3d Cir. 2017) (finding that "plan participants' bargaining power is not a substantive element of a top-hat plan" and attempting to distinguish decisions that suggest otherwise) and Alexander v. Brigham & Women's Physicians Org., Inc., 513 F.3d 37, 47 (1st Cir. 2008) (holding that top hat plans lack any "requirement of individual bargaining power"). The disagreement is one of status versus substance. The pro-negotiation circuits reason that participants should only lose a portion of ERISA's protections if they in fact have bargaining power to protect themselves. The anti-negotiation circuits do not dispute the underlying idea that the top hat plan exemption only makes sense for employees with some heightened ability to protect themselves; instead they argue that the way the statute is written means that Congress concluded that the certain highly compensated and/or managerial employees can do so "by virtue of their position or compensation level" alone, without any further inquiry into whether participants possess actual bargaining power. *Sikora* at 114–16. The pro-negotiation view seems more consistent with ERISA's general preference for keying regulation to function rather than form. Fiduciary obligations, for example, arise under ERISA based on actual or potential conduct, rather than because of the title an actor holds. *See generally infra* Chapter 4A. If some highly compensated managerial employees lack de facto power to protect themselves, it seems odd that ERISA would rob them of protection merely by virtue of their salaries or titles.

enforcement provisions.[134] Unlike the top hat plan exceptions, these exclusions are not conditioned on the plan being unfunded or limited to executives. This is unsurprising, for the absence of need for regulation was not the primary justification for excluding government and church plans from coverage. Government plans were exempted primarily out of concern that the imposition of the new standards "[might] entail unacceptable cost implications to governmental entities."[135] Costs to state and local governments were the focus of concern, and so the governmental plan exception is founded on principles of federalism, in the sense of comity or noninterference.[136]

A governmental plan is defined generally as a plan that is "established or maintained for its employees by the Government of the United States, by the government of any State or political subdivision thereof, or by any agency or instrumentality of any of the foregoing."[137] The concept of an agency or instrumentality of a state or political subdivision is broad, but not limitless. The tax law's definition of qualified deferred compensation plans contains corresponding exceptions for government and church plans, and the IRS has ruled that a volunteer fire company providing fire protection services by contract with local municipalities was not an agency or instrumentality of the government where the company was under the exclusive control of a board of trustees elected by the volunteer firefighters, was not affiliated with the state under any specific legislation, and was financed by community donations and contract fees rather than tax revenue.[138] The IRS announced a

---

[134] ERISA §§ 4(b), 3(32), 3(33), 4021(b), 29 U.S.C. §§ 1003(b), 1002(32), 1002(33), 1321(b) (2018). In addition, government and church pension plans are excused from compliance with the tax-law counterparts of ERISA's minimum standards for pension plan content; they must, however, satisfy pre-ERISA vesting rules to be treated as qualified plans. I.R.C. § 401(a) (2018) (final sentence); *id.* § 411(e) (accrual and vesting), § 412(e) (2018) (funding exception and pre-ERISA vesting requirement), § 4975(g) (2018) (prohibited-transaction excise tax exception). Church plans, but not state and local government plans, must also satisfy the pre-ERISA nondiscrimination rules. I.R.C. §§ 410(c)(2), 401(a)(5)(G), (a)(26)(G) (2018).

[135] H.R. REP. NO. 93-807, at 165 (1974), *reprinted in* 2 ERISA LEGISLATIVE HISTORY, *supra* Chapter 1 note 55, at 3115, 3285. ERISA did, however, mandate further congressional study of the adequacy of participant protections under governmental retirement plans. ERISA § 3031, 29 U.S.C. § 1231 (2018). Reports by the labor and tax committees of the House and Senate were due by the end of 1976, but no legislation came out of efforts to develop a "Public Employee Retirement Income Security Act."

[136] Rose v. Long Island R.R. Pension Plan, 828 F.2d 910, 914 (2d Cir. 1987). *See* H.R. REP. NO. 93-533, at 9 (1973) *reprinted in* 2 ERISA LEGISLATIVE HISTORY, *supra* Chapter 1 note 55, at 2356-57.

[137] ERISA § 3(32), 29 U.S.C. § 1002(32) (2018). Governmental plan also comprehends plans established and maintained by an Indian tribal government or a subdivision, agency, or instrumentality thereof, provided that substantially all of the services of all the participant-employees entail performance of essential governmental functions, not commercial activities. *Id.*

[138] Rev. Rul. 89-49, 1989-1 C.B. 117. The tax Code's definition of a governmental plan is identical to ERISA's except that it requires the plan to be "established and maintained" by a governmental organization rather than "established or maintained." *Compare* I.R.C. § 414(d) (2018),

ERISA's Coverage

multifactor test that emphasizes the extent of public control over the organization's operations:

> A plan will not be considered a governmental plan merely because the sponsoring organization has a relationship with a governmental unit or some quasi-governmental power. One of the most important factors to be considered in determining whether an organization is an agency or instrumentality of the United States or any state or political subdivision is the degree of control that the federal or state government has over the organization's everyday operations. Other factors include: (1) whether there is specific legislation creating the organization; (2) the source of funds for the organization; (3) the manner in which the organization's trustees or operating board are selected; and (4) whether the applicable governmental unit considers the employees of the organization to be employees of the applicable governmental unit. Although all of the above factors are considered in determining whether an organization is an agency of a government, the mere satisfaction of one or all of the factors is not necessarily determinative.[139]

Although the Department of Labor has not adopted this test as an interpretation of ERISA's definition of a governmental plan, it appears to follow a similar approach.[140]

While the test focuses on operational control over the plan sponsor, day-to-day operational control *over the plan* is not required. A plan can be "established or maintained" by a unit of government for its employees without being governmentally administered; a health care plan for state employees is a government plan even though benefits are provided via contractual arrangements with one or more health maintenance organizations, for example.[141] Similarly, welfare and pension plans established by collective bargaining between a governmental unit and a union representing public employees are treated as established or maintained by the

---

with ERISA § 3(32), 29 U.S.C. § 1002(32) (2018). This unexplained and apparently inadvertent discrepancy is discussed in *Rose*, 828 F.2d at 918–21.

[139] Rev. Rul. 89-49, 1989-1 C.B. 117. Contrast I.R.S. Priv. Ltr. Rul. 9414007 (Apr. 8, 1994), which applied the same standards to find that a volunteer fire protection district created under specific state legislation was an instrumentality of state government where the bulk of its revenues were received from property taxes, and three of the seven members of the district's board of trustees were elected by property owners or appointed by public officials.

[140] E.g., U.S. Dep't of Lab., Pension & Welfare Benefits Admin., ERISA Opinion Letter 86-06A (Feb. 3, 1986) (City of Milwaukee Firemen's Relief Association's death benefit plan is a governmental plan because the association was established by state statute and municipal charter, its membership is limited to current and former public employees, and the plan is subsidized by the city).

[141] Silvera v. Mut. Life Ins. Co. of N.Y., 884 F.2d 423 (9th Cir. 1989); Simac v. Health All. Med. Plans, Inc., 961 F. Supp. 216 (C.D. Ill. 1997). Limiting the governmental plan exemption to cases of direct public administration of employee benefit plans would violate the principle of economic neutrality for no apparent purpose. Private employers cannot escape ERISA by contracting out the provision of benefits. *See* 29 C.F.R. § 2510.3-1(j) (2021) (employer may establish or maintain a benefit plan by paying premiums to provide coverage under group insurance arrangements selected by the employees).

56   *General Considerations*

government even if they are administered by a board that is not controlled by the public employer; the exemption is not limited to plans created by the unilateral action of a governmental body.[142]

ERISA also exempts church plans, apparently out of concern for separation of church and state. The exception precludes First Amendment challenges based on entangling government regulation. ERISA accommodates the complex institutional structure of some churches by including as a church any related tax-exempt organization. The related organization need not have a primary religious purpose. As a result, the church plan definition is remarkably expansive. As amended in 1980, it goes far beyond exempting plans covering religious personnel or church employees, exempting plans covering employees of religiously *affiliated* charitable organizations such as hospitals, schools, and group homes. An employee of a tax-exempt organization is treated as the employee of a church, and his employer is deemed to be a church if the organization is "controlled by or associated with a church or a convention or association of churches,"[143] and sharing "common religious bonds and convictions with the church" is sufficient to show association.[144] Accordingly, benefit plans covering employees of Catholic hospitals or parochial schools (for instance) may be exempt from ERISA, even though their tax-exempt but nonsectarian counterparts must contend with the full force of federal regulation.[145]

In 2017, litigation on the scope of the church plan exemption reached the Supreme Court.[146] In contrast to the "established *or* maintained" statutory language regarding (covered) private plans and (exempt) government plans, the church exemption speaks of plans "established *and* maintained ... by a church."[147] At issue in *Advocate Health Care Network* was whether the church exemption reached plans that were not only "maintained" by (as explained above) church-affiliated organizations but were also never "established" by a church proper in the first place. Put differently, the question before the Court was: could a plan that was *neither* established nor maintained by a church be exempt as a church plan? The Court unanimously answered yes, on textual grounds. Congress amended the statute in 1980 to expand the group of the plans that fell within the church exemption. The resulting statutory language, the Court reasoned, plainly encompassed plans that

---

[142] U.S. Dep't of Lab., Pension & Welfare Benefits Admin., ERISA Opinion Letter 79-36A (June 11, 1979) (equal numbers of employer and union trustees); U.S. Dep't of Lab., Pension & Welfare Benefits Admin., ERISA Opinion Letter 86-22A (Sept. 9, 1986) (governmental plan even if administered solely by union representatives).

[143] ERISA § 3(33)(C)(ii)(II), (33)(C)(iii), 29 U.S.C. § 1002(33)(C)(ii)(II), (33)(C)(iii) (2018); *see* I.R.C. § 414(e)(3)(B)(ii), (e)(3)(C) (2018).

[144] ERISA § 3(33)(C)(iv), 29 U.S.C. § 1002(33)(C)(iv) (2018); *see* I.R.C. § 414(e)(3)(D) (2018).

[145] E.g., U.S. Dep't of Lab., Pension & Welfare Benefits Admin., ERISA Opinion Letter 86-03A (Jan. 13, 1986) (plan covering Catholic school employees); U.S. Dep't of Lab., Pension & Welfare Benefits Admin., ERISA Opinion Letter 94-11A (Mar. 23, 1994) (plan covering employees of Mennonite hospital).

[146] Advocate Health Care Network v. Stapleton, 137 S. Ct. 1652 (2017).

[147] 29 U.S.C. § 1002(33)(C)(i) (2018).

were *maintained* by church-affiliated organizations, irrespective of whether such plans were established by a church.[148]

The church plan definition is expansive in two further respects. First, all ministers or clergy engaged in religious work are treated as church employees even if they are technically independent contractors or are actually employed by another institution (e.g., army, prison, or hospital chaplains, or teachers of religious studies at an unrelated university).[149] Second, a retroactive correction mechanism is provided for plans that fail to meet the exemption criteria.[150]

E CONCLUSION

The scope of federal benefit regulation is remarkably broad – it can reach an oral promise made to a single employee. Yet ERISA's coverage also has significant limitations. Some of those limitations are consistent with the statute's objectives; others are quite anomalous.

It takes a "plan" to trigger the statute. The goal of preventing mismanagement and abuse requires the oversight of discretionary decision making, and so the courts have rightly concluded that the presence of discretion is sufficient to justify finding that there is a plan. Stringent fiduciary obligations were also meant to apply to anyone who handles benefit funds, and so advance funding should be enough to find a plan, even absent discretion. In contrast, an unfunded nondiscretionary benefit obligation does not require fiduciary oversight, but in that case another statutory goal may come into play. ERISA promotes economic efficiency by providing workers with the information they need to make better career and financial planning decisions. Where disclosure of the principal features of an ongoing benefit commitment would facilitate planning, that alone should be enough to find a plan.

Uncertainty as to the amount of benefits or the identity of beneficiaries has led some courts to hold that no enforceable plan exists. Often that is the right result. But ERISA was intended to protect employees' reasonable expectations, so if the employer's acts create a reasonable expectation of benefits, that expectation should be enforced notwithstanding documents or practices that purport to give the employer uncontrolled discretion over who will benefit or in what amount.

ERISA was enacted to inform and protect employees An "employee" must participate in a benefit program for the law to apply, which the Supreme Court

---

[148] As Justice Kagan wrote, with her customary precision:
"ERISA provides (1) that a 'church plan' means a 'plan established and maintained ... by a church' and (2) that a 'plan established and maintained ... by a church' is to 'include [ ] a plan maintained by' a principal-purpose organization. Under the best reading of the statute, a plan maintained by a principal-purpose organization therefore qualifies as a 'church plan,' regardless of who established it." 137 S. Ct. at 1663.

[149] ERISA § 3(33)(C)(ii)(I), 29 U.S.C. § 1002(33)(C)(ii)(I) (2018); *see* I.R.C. § 414(e)(3)(B)(I) (2018); 126 CONG. REC. 20,245 (remarks of Sen. Long).

[150] ERISA § 3(33)(D), 29 U.S.C. § 1002(33)(D) (2018); *see* I.R.C. § 414(e)(4) (2018).

construes to mean common-law employee. Where working owners of an unincorporated business are covered under the same program as their common-law employees, the owners' rights as plan participants are controlled by ERISA rather than state law, even though the owners also sometimes act as employer with respect to the plan. An individual may act in more than one capacity – wear multiple hats – in relation to an employee benefit plan, with distinct rights and obligations flowing from those different roles.

The applicability and intensity of federal regulation is also keyed to the nature of the program's benefits; only plans providing employees with "welfare" or "pension" benefits are covered. Arguably, ERISA's goals would be best served by classifying deferred compensation of any sort as a pension benefit, with current in-kind compensation designated as a welfare benefit if the compensation is of a sort that is important enough to warrant federal oversight. The history of political and legal attention to employee benefits produced less functional categories, however. Pension controls come into play only if the program is designed to provide retirement income or compensation is deferred to the termination of employment; welfare plans may offer substantial deferred compensation without concern for vesting or funding; and some important fringe benefits, including employer financial assistance with child care or college costs, are exempt from ERISA.

Three important exceptions from ERISA are also surprising in the light of the legislative objectives. Unfunded executive deferred compensation arrangements must use ERISA's enforcement mechanism, but are otherwise exempt from all federal and state regulation. Top managers typically have access to information and the power to protect themselves, but why limit this exception to *unfunded* deferred compensation? Executives who arrange a special trust fund for their retirement hardly need federal safeguards to reign in their hand-picked trustee. In addition, government and church plans, both pension and welfare, are entirely excluded from ERISA, regardless of the employees' need for information or protection. Although the legal rationales and political expediency of those exclusions are clear, many workers are left without protection, and in some industries ERISA's coverage is quite erratic. Retirement plans of both state and church-affiliated institutions of higher education are exempt from federal oversight, for example, while private nonsectarian colleges and universities must toe the line.

Any comprehensive new statute is bound to contain some mistakes and political compromises. ERISA has its share. ERISA's coverage, while not capricious, is in several ways quite curious.

PART II

Conduct Controls: Welfare and Pension Plans

ERISA entails two very different approaches to the regulation of employee benefits. The administration of all employee benefit plans is subject to federal oversight to promote informed participation, ensure compliance with plan terms, and prevent misconduct in plan administration. To protect the interests of participants and their beneficiaries (the paternalistic policy), pension plans are also subject to minimum standards governing certain terms of the deferred compensation program. Thus, ERISA monitors only the administration or *conduct* of most welfare plans, while it subjects pension plans to both *conduct* and limited *content* regulation. Although they are welfare plans, some content controls apply to certain group health plans, mostly because of Affordable Care Act amendments of ERISA, as will be explored in Chapter 11.

ERISA's *conduct* controls constrain the administration of all employee benefit plans, both pension and welfare, in four respects. First, reporting and disclosure rules mandate the collection and dissemination of information concerning plan terms and finances to the Secretary of Labor and plan participants and beneficiaries (Chapter 3). Second, plan fiduciaries are held to exacting standards of conduct derived from trust law (Chapter 4). Third, a federal enforcement mechanism prescribes remedies and gives the federal courts exclusive jurisdiction to enforce ERISA's requirements (including fiduciary duties), as well as jurisdiction concurrent with state courts over suits to enforce the terms of the plan (Chapter 5). And fourth, state regulation of pension and welfare plans is broadly pre-empted (Chapter 6).

3

Disclosure

"This may not be a foolproof informational scheme, although it is quite thorough."[1]

This chapter analyzes the major themes that have emerged from the case law on disclosure obligations. ERISA grants claimants a private right of action to recover benefits due to them or to obtain "appropriate equitable relief" to enforce statutory obligations, including disclosure requirements and fiduciary duties. This robust civil enforcement mechanism puts teeth in the disclosure regime, as the courts have found that an incomplete or erroneous description of plan terms can sometimes bind the plan or trigger fiduciary liability. The result has been an explosion of disclosure litigation.

There is an obvious functional relationship between disclosure and the other components of ERISA's conduct regulation. Reporting and disclosure of plan finances may deter fiduciary misconduct. Should deterrence fail, disclosure provides plan participants and beneficiaries the information they need to monitor the plan's administration to enforce their rights.

Besides working to control mismanagement and abuse of benefit funds, disclosure gives workers the information they need to evaluate their employment and retirement options, and allows them to accommodate their personal financial affairs to the employer's program. Appreciating the limits of a pension plan enables participants to determine the extent of additional individual savings they may need to provide sufficient resources in retirement. And knowledge about welfare benefit plans can assist workers in making good decisions about whether they need to save for health care expenses that are not covered by the employer's plan, or to secure additional life insurance or disability income protection. This planning function serves the goal of increasing economic efficiency.

---

[1] Curtiss-Wright Corp. v. Schoonejongen, 514 U.S. 73, 84 (1995).

62   *Conduct Controls: Welfare and Pension Plans*

A STATUTORY DISCLOSURE OBLIGATIONS

The statutory disclosure obligations imposed by Part 1 of Title I of ERISA apply to all employee benefit plans, both pension and welfare, although they are relaxed by regulation for certain types of plans, including unfunded or fully insured welfare plans that cover fewer than 100 participants, and unfunded or insured pension or welfare plans covering "a select group of management or highly compensated employees."[2] Disclosure obligations are imposed on the plan administrator, a person so designated by the terms of the plan; absent such designation, the plan sponsor is the administrator by default.[3] The obligations run in favor of plan participants and beneficiaries and the Secretary of Labor. Disclosure obligations are enforceable by injunction or civil penalties, and in the case of willful violations, by criminal penalties.[4]

Routine disclosure is required of three kinds of information: (1) the terms of the plan, (2) the current financial status of the plan, and (3) the participant's current entitlement to benefits under a pension plan. In addition, the instruments under which the plan is operated must be available for examination, and a copy must be provided by the administrator upon written request from a participant or beneficiary.[5] These four general information-sharing obligations are described here, but ERISA also imposes many highly particularized disclosure requirements.[6]

---

[2] ERISA § 104(a)(2), (3), 29 U.S.C. § 1024(a)(2), (3) (2018) (authority to relax certain information requirements by regulation); ERISA § 110, 29 U.S.C. § 1030 (2018) (authority to prescribe alternative method of compliance for pension plans that is consistent with the statute's purposes and provides adequate disclosure); 29 C.F.R. § 2520.104-20 (2022) (small unfunded or insured welfare plans), *id.* §§ 2520.104-23, -24 (unfunded or insured pension or welfare plans for a select group of management or highly compensated employees).

[3] ERISA §§ 101, 104, 105, 29 U.S.C. §§ 1021, 1024, 1025 (2018) (administrator's obligations); ERISA § 3(16)(A), 29 U.S.C. 1002(16)(A) (2018) (administrator defined). The sponsor is the employer in the case of a single-employer plan, the union in the case of a union plan, or the trustees in the case of a jointly administered Taft-Hartley plan. ERISA § 3(16)(B), 29 U.S.C. 1002(16)(B) (2018).

[4] ERISA § 502(a)(3), (a)(5), 29 U.S.C. § 1132(a)(3), (a)(5) (2018) (injunctions); ERISA § 502(a) (1)(A), (a)(4), (a)(6), (c), 29 U.S.C. § 1132(a)(1)(A), (a)(4), (a)(6), (c) (2018) (civil penalties); ERISA § 501, 29 U.S.C. § 1131 (2018) (criminal penalties).

[5] ERISA § 104(b)(2), (4), 29 U.S.C. § 1024(b)(2), (4) (2018).

[6] Since ERISA's enactment the number of required notifications and reporting obligations has proliferated. The September 2017 edition of a Labor Department guide to information obligations contains a chart, "Overview of ERISA Title I Basic Disclosure Requirements," that runs to 14 pages, and is followed by a three-page chart giving an "Overview of Basic PBGC Reporting and Disclosure Requirements." U.S. DEPARTMENT OF LABOR, REPORTING AND DISCLOSURE GUIDE FOR EMPLOYEE BENEFIT PLANS (2017), at https://www.dol.gov/sites/dolgov/files/ebsa/about-ebsa/our-activities/resource-center/publications/reporting-and-disclosure-guide-for-employee-be nefit-plans.pdf. Similarly, an IRS guide of tax reporting obligations nearly fills fifteen pages. IRS RETIREMENT PLAN REPORTING AND DISCLOSURE REQUIREMENTS (2018), at https://www .irs.gov/pub/irs-pdf/p5411.pdf.

Disclosure 63

1 *Plan Terms*

Participants' principal source of information about the terms of the plan is the summary plan description (SPD). The SPD must be furnished to each participant and to each beneficiary receiving benefits under the plan within ninety days after the employee becomes a participant or the beneficiary first receives benefits. A summary of any material modification (SMM) of the information required to be presented in the SPD must be distributed to participants and beneficiaries within 210 days after the close of the plan year in which the change is adopted. In the case of a material reduction in covered services or benefits under a group health plan, notification must be made no later than sixty days *before* the change.[7] Similarly, notice of a plan amendment that significantly reduces the *rate* of future benefit accrual under a defined benefit or money purchase pension plan must be provided within a reasonable time before the effective date of the amendment.[8] This *advance notice* requirement gives affected employees an opportunity to lobby their employer, seek alternative employment, or take other steps to protect their interests.[9]

In addition to the SPD, the Affordable Care Act requires group health plans to furnish participants a summary of benefits and coverage (SBC) prior to enrollment or reenrollment. The SBC provides a condensed overview of plan benefits and coverage in a uniform format, using common definitions of standard insurance and medical terms, to facilitate comparison of cost, coverage, benefits, and exceptions. The SBC must utilize terminology understandable by the average plan enrollee, include examples of coverage for common benefit scenarios, and be presented in a standardized template that does not exceed four double-sided pages in length, and does not include print smaller than 12-point font.[10] The SBC, which functions as a sort of summary summary plan description, does *not* substitute for the SPD.

2 *Plan Finances*

The Labor Department, in conjunction with the Internal Revenue Service (IRS) and the Pension Benefit Guaranty Corporation (PBGC), has developed a joint

---

[7] Public Health Services Act § 2715(d)(4), 42 U.S.C. § 300gg-15(d)(4) (2018). This advance notice effectively supersedes ERISA § 104(b)(1), 29 U.S.C. § 1024(b)(1) (2012), which requires only that a description of the change be furnished within sixty days *after* the date of adoption of the change.

[8] ERISA § 204(h), 29 U.S.C. § 1054(h) (2018); *see* I.R.C. § 4980F (006) (excise tax for failure to give advance notice); Treas. Reg. § 54.4980F-1 Q&A-9 (as amended in 2012) (reasonable time generally means forty-five days). An amendment that decreases any participant's *total* accrued benefit violates ERISA's minimum standards on pension plan content. ERISA § 204(g), 29 U.S.C. § 1054(g) (2018); *see* I.R.C. § 411(d)(6) (2018). *See infra* Chapter 7B, text accompanying notes 62–73.

[9] *See infra* Chapter 7B, text accompanying notes 80–83.

[10] ERISA § 715(a)(1), 29 U.S.C. § 1185d (2018), 42 U.S.C. § 300gg-15 (2018).

annual reporting instrument, Form 5500, the "Return/Report of Employee Benefit Plan."[11] The annual report is designed to give each of the participating agencies the information needed to monitor plan operations and enforce compliance with the laws it administers. Form 5500 and the accompanying schedules provide extensive information on the financial condition of the plan, including a complete set of audited financial statements and, in the case of a defined benefit pension plan, an actuarial statement detailing the funding status of the plan.[12] (Simplified reporting requirements apply to certain plans, including those covering fewer than 100 participants and unfunded or insured welfare plans.[13]) The plan administrator must file Form 5500 electronically within seven months after the close of the plan year.[14]

Some of the information contained in the annual report must be shared with plan participants and beneficiaries via a summary annual report (SAR). The SAR provides basic information on the financial condition of the plan. It is a short document (typically one page) that discloses aggregate plan expenses and benefit payments for the year, the number of participants, the value of net assets at the beginning and end of the year, as well as plan income and employer and employee contributions. The SAR also notifies participants of their right to receive, without charge, a copy of the plan's balance sheet and income statement (with notes), or a copy of the full annual report and schedules thereto upon payment of a reasonable copying charge.[15] The SAR was apparently intended to serve the same function under ERISA as the traditional trust law duty to periodically render an accounting to beneficiaries: providing the information necessary to monitor and enforce compliance with fiduciary obligations.[16] By itself, however, the contents of the SAR are so generic and abbreviated that they cannot alert participants and beneficiaries to potential problems or questionable practices in plan administration, and for that reason some advocate revising or eliminating this disclosure obligation.[17]

---

[11] Annual reporting obligations are prescribed by: (1) ERISA §§ 103, 104(a), 29 U.S.C. §§ 1023, 1024(a) (2018), for employee benefit plans subject to ERISA; (2) I.R.C. §§ 6057, 6058, for funded deferred compensation plans; and (3) ERISA § 4065, 29 U.S.C. § 1365, for PBGC-insured defined benefit pension plans. See ERISA § 3004(a), 29 U.S.C. § 1204(a) (2018) (Labor–Treasury consultation and coordination in the development of forms and regulations under ERISA); ERISA § 4065, 29 U.S.C. § 1365 (similar coordination mandate applied to PBGC).

[12] ERISA § 103, 29 U.S.C. § 1023 (2018), 29 C.F.R. § 2520.103-1 (2022).

[13] 29 C.F.R. §§ 2520.103-1(c), 2520.104-41, -44, -46 (2022).

[14] 29 C.F.R. §§ 2520.104a-2, -5 (2022).

[15] ERISA §§ 101(a)(2), 104(b)(3), 29 U.S.C. §§ 1021(a)(2), 1024(b)(3) (2018) (summary annual report requirement); 29 C.F.R. § 2520.104b-10(d) (2022) (contents of summary annual report).

[16] See RESTATEMENT (THIRD) OF TRUSTS § 83 & cmt. a (2007); RESTATEMENT (SECOND) OF TRUSTS § 172 (1959); 2A AUSTIN W. SCOTT & WILLIAM F. FRATCHER, SCOTT ON TRUSTS § 172 (4th ed. 1987) (hereinafter SCOTT ON TRUSTS).

[17] In 2005, for example, a working group of the ERISA Advisory Council concluded "The current model SARs in the Labor Regulations do not provide useful information to retirement plan participants." Advisory Council Report of the Working Group on Communications to Retirement Plan Participants, at www.dol.gov/agencies/ebsa/about-ebsa/about-us/erisa-advis

Because of the risk presented by underfunding, additional notification requirements apply to defined benefit pension plans subject to ERISA Title IV, the plan termination insurance program. After the close of each plan year, the administrator of an insured plan must provide a plan funding notice to the PBGC, to each plan participant and beneficiary, and to each union representing participants or beneficiaries; this notice must be written so as to be understandable by the average plan participant. The plan funding notice for a single-employer plan must state whether the plan met its funding target in each of the past three plan years, report the funding target attainment percentage if less than 100 percent in any of those years, and report the assets and liabilities of the plan for each of those years. If any amendment or event having a material effect on plan liabilities (e.g., a plant closing) took effect during the year, the notice must explain the change and provide a projection of its impact on plan liabilities as of the end of the plan year. The funding notice must also summarize the rules governing defined benefit plan termination, describe the nature and limits of the PBGC's guarantee of benefits, explain how to get a copy of the plan's annual report, and alert recipients if the sponsor and members of its controlled group were required to provide detailed financial information to the PBGC as a result of specified indicia of serious underfunding.[18] If the required funding notice is not timely provided, each affected participant and beneficiary may seek a civil penalty of up to $110 per day.[19]

3 *Individual Status*

ERISA requires that any participant or beneficiary whose claim for benefits is denied be given individualized notice of the specific reasons therefor, written "in a manner calculated to be understood by the participant," along with a description of the steps

---

ory-council/2005-communications-to-retirement-plan-participants. The issue of effectiveness was considered by the ERISA Advisory Council again in 2017. See Mandated Disclosure for Retirement Plans – Enhancing Effectiveness for Participants and Sponsors, at www.dol.gov/sites/dolgov/files/EBSA/about-ebsa/about-us/erisa-advisory-council/2017-mandated-disclosure-for-retirement-plans.pdf.

The standard form SAR does at least notify recipients of the type of information contained in the annual report and of their right to examine or obtain a copy of it. 29 C F R § 2520.104b-10 (d)(3), (4) (2022). In certain respects even the full annual report has limited utility as an indicator of financial risks, because the underlying identity of the investments of funded plans is frequently impossible to determine. See Peter J. Wiedenbeck et al., *Invisible Pension Investments*, 32 VA. TAX. REV. 591 (2013).

[18] ERISA § 101(a)(2), (f), 29 U.S.C. § 1021(a)(2), (f) (2018) (effective for plan years beginning after 2007; for prior years, ERISA § 4011 (repealed 2012) imposed less stringent notice requirements).

[19] ERISA § 502(a)(1)(A), (c)(1), 29 U.S.C. § 1132(a)(1)(A), (c)(1) (2018); 29 C.F.R. § 2575.502c-1 (2022) (inflation adjustment). The funding notice requirement may also be enforced by injunction. ERISA § 502(a)(8), 29 U.S.C. § 1132(a)(8) (2018).

to be taken to obtain review of the claim denial.[20] The notice must indicate what type of information would support the claim and explain why it is necessary, so that the claimant has a reasonable opportunity to perfect his claim.[21] If the claimant invokes the plan's mechanism for review of the benefit denial and the appeal proves unsuccessful, the plan administrator must provide copies of documents, records and information relevant to evaluation of the claim.[22] This disclosure equips the disappointed participant or beneficiary to decide whether to pursue a civil enforcement action.[23]

Particularized status reports must be provided to pension plan participants and beneficiaries at specified periods or upon written request.[24] These pension benefit statements must report total accrued benefits (i.e., benefits earned by service to date) and either the portion that is nonforfeitable ("vested") or the earliest date on which they will become nonforfeitable. Invoking both the planning and anti-abuse objectives of the statute, one court observed that, were a participant unable to obtain this information on request, "his or her financial planning would be impaired and his or her effort to enforce the rights and fiduciary obligations imposed by ERISA would be severely hampered."[25] In the case of a defined contribution plan, the statement must also report the most recent valuation of any assets in which the participant's account is invested, and since 2021 must annually include a lifetime income disclosure: a report of the monthly payment under a life annuity equal in actuarial value to the participant's current account balance.[26] If the participant has the right to direct the investment of his or her individual account, then the statement must also describe any limitations on that right, explain the importance of diversification to retirement security, warn of the risk of investing more than 20 percent of a portfolio in one entity, and direct attention to investment information on the Labor Department's website.[27] Similarly, defined contribution plan participants and beneficiaries are also generally entitled to advance notice of (1) any blackout period during which

---

[20] ERISA § 503, 29 U.S.C. § 1133 (2018); 29 C.F.R. § 2560.503-1(f), (g) (2022) (timing and contents of notice).

[21] 29 C.F.R. § 2560.503-1(g)(1)(iii) (2022); Wolfe v. J.C. Penney Co., 710 F.2d 388 (7th Cir. 1983), *overruled on other grounds by* Pritzker v. Merrill Lynch Pierce Fenner & Smith, Inc., 7 F.3d 1111 (1993).

[22] 29 C.F.R. § 2560.503-1(i)(5), -1(j) (2022); *id.* -1(m)(8) (definition of relevant information).

[23] *See* 29 C.F.R. § 2560.503-1(j)(4) (2022) (notice of adverse decision on review must include statement informing claimant of right to bring a civil enforcement action).

[24] ERISA § 105, 29 U.S.C. § 1025 (2018).

[25] Barrowclough v. Kidder, Peabody & Co., 752 F.2d 923, 934 (3d Cir. 1985), *overruled on other grounds by* Pritzker v. Merrill Lynch Pierce Fenner & Smith, Inc., 7 F.3d 1111 (1993).

[26] ERISA § 105(a)(1)(A), (a)(2)(B)(i), (iii), (a)(2)(D), 29 U.S.C. § 1025(a)(1)(A), (a)(2)(B)(i), (iii), (a)(2)(D) (Supp. 2020). The lifetime income equivalent must be reported both as the monthly amount of: (i) a single life annuity commencing at age sixty-seven (or the participant's age, if older); and (ii) a 100 percent joint and survivor annuity commencing at age sixty-seven (or the participant's age, if older), assuming a spouse of the same age. 29 C.F.R. § 2520.105-3 (2022).

[27] ERISA § 105, 29 U.S.C. § 1025 (2018).

Disclosure

their right to direct the investment of their accounts or obtain distributions or plan loans will be suspended, and (2) their right to divest their holdings of employer securities.[28] If a pension benefit statement is not timely provided, each affected participant and beneficiary may seek civil penalty of up to $110 per day.[29] In the event of a plan administrator's failure or refusal to provide timely advance notice of blackout periods or divestment rights, a per-day civil penalty runs in favor of the Labor Department.[30]

4 Plan Instruments

Upon written request and the payment of a reasonable charge for copying, any participant or beneficiary may also obtain a copy of "the latest updated summary plan description, and the latest annual report, any terminal report, the bargaining agreement, trust agreement, contract, or other instruments under which the plan is established or operated."[31] Failure or refusal to send the material by mail within thirty days exposes the plan administrator to a civil penalty of up to $110 per day, payable to the requesting participant or beneficiary.[32] This disclosure obligation clearly applies to the plan document and any trust agreement, as well as the collective bargaining agreement in the case of a jointly administered plan under the Taft-Hartley Act. But what about a request for other documents that may be prepared or used in the process of plan administration? Examples include actuarial valuation reports of defined benefit plans, statements of investment policy, proxy voting guidelines, minutes of trustee meetings, schedules of usual and customary charges for reimbursable medical services, and contracts with third-party administrators. Benefit denials typically trigger broad requests for supporting documents, and when a benefit dispute proceeds to litigation the complaint frequently contains a claim for civil penalties based on allegedly inadequate or untimely disclosure. Consequently, federal courts have repeatedly been called upon to define "other instrument[s] under which the plan is established or operated."

"[O]ne of ERISA's central goals," the Supreme Court observed, "is to enable plan beneficiaries to learn their rights and obligations at any time."[33] Disclosure upon

---

[28] ERISA § 101(i), (m), 29 U.S.C. § 1021(i), (m) (2018).

[29] ERISA § 502(a)(1), (c)(1), 29 U.S.C. § 1132(a)(1), (c)(1) (2018); 29 C.F.R. § 2575.502c-1 (2022) (inflation adjustment).

[30] ERISA § 502(a)(6), (c)(7), 29 U.S.C. § 1132(a)(6), (c)(7) (2018), 29 C.F.R. § 2575.2(f) (2022) (for penalties assessed after Aug. 1, 2016, cap on civil penalty adjusted for inflation to $131 per day).

[31] ERISA § 104(b)(4), 29 U.S.C. § 1024(b)(4) (2018).

[32] ERISA §§ 104(b)(4), 502(a)(1), (c)(1), 29 U.S.C. §§ 1024(b)(4), 1132(a)(1), (c)(1) (2018); 29 C.F.R. § 2575.502c-1 (2022) (inflation adjustment).

[33] Curtiss-Wright Corp. v. Schoonejongen, 514 U.S. 73, 83 (1995).

request of instruments under which the plan is established or operated is a key component of the statute's "elaborate scheme" to that end.[34] Accordingly, it comprehends "a set of all currently operative, governing plan documents."[35]

Although ERISA demands that a plan be "established and maintained pursuant to a written instrument,"[36] a single plan document is not required. Frequently, recourse to a multiplicity of documents is necessary to define the terms of a welfare or pension plan. This proliferation creates uncertainty as to the scope of the catch-all category, "other instruments under which the plan is established or operated." Most circuits have adopted a narrow reading of the phrase, holding that "formal legal documents that govern or confine a plan's operations" must be provided upon request, but not "routine documents with which or by means of which the plan conducts its operations."[37] Several opinions distinguish documents that must be supplied under threat of civil penalty from the broader group of documents that may have to be

---

[34] *Id.* at 84 (discussing ERISA § 104(b)(2), 29 U.S.C. § 1024(b)(2)).

[35] *Id.* (dictum). The quoted language refers directly to the obligation of the plan administrator to make such documents available for inspection at the administrator's principal office and other designated locations. The cognate obligation to furnish a copy upon written request, ERISA § 104(b)(4), 29 U.S.C. § 1024(b)(4), includes the same list of documents (with the addition of "any terminal report") and the same catch-all reference to other instruments under which the plan is established or operated. The Court noted the parallelism between inspection and copying with a "see also" citation. *Schoonejongen*, 514 U.S. at 84.

[36] ERISA § 402(a)(1), 29 U.S.C. § 1102(a)(1) (2012).

[37] Bd. of Trustees of the CWA/ITU Negotiated Pension Plan v. Weinstein, 107 F.3d 139, 142 (2d Cir. 1997) (holding release of actuarial report not required); Faircloth v. Lundy Packing Co., 91 F.3d 648, 654–55 (4th Cir. 1996) (holding that ESOP funding and investment policies must be disclosed, but not the ESOP's IRS determination letter, fiduciary insurance policy, nor appraisal reports because ERISA § 104(b)(4) does not encompass any documents that would assist participants and beneficiaries in determining whether a plan is being properly administered); Hughes Salaried Retirees Action Comm. v. Adm'r of Hughes Non-Bargaining Ret. Plan, 72 F.3d 686, 691 (9th Cir. 1995) (en banc) (refusing to penalize withholding of names and addresses of retired plan participants because "§ 104(b)(4) requires the disclosure of only the documents described with particularity and 'other instruments' similar in nature"); Murphy v. Verizon Commc'ns, Inc., 587 Fed. App'x 140, 144–45 (5th Cir. 2014) (investment guidelines need not be provided where plaintiffs never alleged them to be binding on the plans); Doe v. Travelers Ins. Co., 167 F.3d 53, 60 (1st Cir. 1999) (holding mental health guidelines not within "other instruments" because the plan administrator "was not bound to use them, nor did patients have any legal rights under them"); Brown v. Am. Life Holdings, Inc., 190 F.3d 856, 861–62 (8th Cir. 1999) (corporate actions replacing members of the ESOP Administrative Committee, minutes of Administrative Committee meetings, and written communications with trustee evidence the day-to-day operations; they are not governing plan documents); Ames v. Am. Nat'l Can Co., 170 F.3d 751, 758–59 (7th Cir., 1999) (in dispute concerning benefits available following sale of corporate division, request for sale contract, minutes of board meetings at which the plans were adopted or amended, and documents reporting the identity and corporate position of the individual members of retirement committee, the named fiduciary, not required to be provided under ERISA § 104(b)(4)).

Disclosure

released to provide full and fair review of a claim denial,[38] and from documents discoverable in litigation.[39]

Documents that specify benefit entitlements or impose *binding obligations* on plan administrators are a clear case for disclosure. In contrast, records and forms used in day-to-day plan operations – such as meeting minutes, claim forms, enrollment forms, and lists of participants' names and addresses – need not be supplied upon request. Implementation data of this sort are not determinative of the rights and obligations of participants and beneficiaries, and so do not control or govern plan operation.[40] But what about documents that do not fully control plan operations but limit or constrain *decision making*?[41] And what of documents that, although purely advisory, are *intended to influence* or guide fiduciary judgment, such as the opinions of lawyers, accountants, and other professionals?[42]

---

[38] Mondry v. American Family Mut. Ins. Co., 557 F.3d 781, 798–99 (7th Cir. 2009); Jordan v. Tyson Foods, Inc., 312 Fed. Appx. 726, 735–36 (6th Cir. 2006) (civil penalty does not apply to violations of claims procedure regulation); Groves v. Modified Retirement Plan for Hourly Paid Employees of Johns Manville Corp. and Subsidiaries, 803 F.2d 109, 116–18 (3d Cir. 1986) (same).

[39] Ames v. American Nat. Can Co., 170 F.3d 751, 759 (7th Cir. 1999) ("affirmative obligation to disclose materials under ERISA, punishable by penalties, extends only to a defined set of documents. If litigation comes along, then ordinary discovery rules under the management of the district court provide the limits on what must be produced."); Brown v. American Life Holdings, Inc., 190 F.3d 856, 861 (8th Cir. 1999) (same, refusing to impose civil penalty for failure to provide documents relating to changes in the members of ESOP Administrative Committee, resolutions and minutes of the Administrative Committee, and written communications regarding investments between the employer or the Administrative Committee and ESOP trustee). Huss v. IBM Med. & Dental Plan, 418 F. App'x 498, 510–11 (7th Cir. 2011).

[40] *E.g., Brown*, 190 F.3d at 861–62 (corporate actions replacing members of the ESOP Administrative Committee, minutes of Administrative Committee meetings, and written communications with trustee evidence the day-to-day operations, they are not governing plan documents); Allinder v. Inter-City Prods. Corp., 152 F.3d 544, 549 (6th Cir. 1998) ("other instruments" does not include "documents used in the ministerial day-to-day processing of individual claims"); *Weinstein*, 107 F.3d at 142; *Hughes Salaried Retirees Action Comm.*, 72 F.3d at 691 (refusing to penalize withholding of names and addresses of retired plan participants).

[41] Standards that limit discretion rule out certain actions and thereby control plan operations to that extent. Consider investment guidelines (e.g., a maximum percentage of the fund's portfolio that may be invested in common stock), or a list of circumstances that are not sufficient to support a hardship distribution from a profit-sharing plan.

[42] Typical of this category are reports or memoranda setting out factors that should (or should not) be considered by a fiduciary in making a decision. Such factors may not be outcome-determinative standing alone. Realistically, such advice or instruction from the fiduciary's supervisor or from a professional with special expertise will be taken seriously. De facto, guidance of this sort establishes a protocol for decision making which, although it does not control the outcome, is certainly intended to influence it.

    Section 104(b)(4) is ERISA's counterpart to a trustee's duty to furnish information to beneficiaries upon request, and that duty extends to inspection of opinions of counsel obtained by the trustee to assist in the administration of the trust. RESTATEMENT (THIRD) OF TRUSTS § 82(2) & cmt. f (2007); RESTATEMENT (SECOND) OF TRUSTS § 173 (1959); 2A SCOTT ON TRUSTS, *supra* Chapter 3 note 16, § 173. *See* Varity Corp. v. Howe, 516 U.S. 489, 497 (1996)

Conduct Controls: Welfare and Pension Plans

Employee benefit plan administration commonly utilizes more or less limiting decision protocols or advice. Defined benefit pension plan funding depends upon regular actuarial reports.[43] Employee stock ownership plans of private companies obtain periodic stock valuations.[44] Health care plans cover medically necessary treatments and services that are not experimental and not specifically excluded, with "medical necessity" typically elaborated by detailed internal guidelines specified in technical medical terms. Moreover, the amount paid for covered treatment may be limited to "usual and customary charges," the mechanism for determining which is not specified in the plan. Most courts allow such documents to be withheld without penalty, despite the integral role they may play in determinations concerning benefit eligibility or amount.[45] The Labor Department disagrees.[46]

("[T]he law of trusts often will inform, but will not necessarily determine the outcome of, an effort to interpret ERISA's fiduciary duties.").

[43] An actuarial report effectively determines a defined benefit plan's minimum funding obligation by virtue of the actuary's determination of actuarial assumptions, experience gains and losses, accrued liability, and the actuarial value of plan assets. Those determinations affect the extent to which participants bear a risk of underfunding. Funding in excess of ERISA's minimum standards is left to the discretion of the employer, and to that extent an actuarial report can be fairly characterized as advisory. *See* ERISA §§ 302, 303, 29 U.S.C. §§ 1082, 1083 (2018); *see also* I.R.C. §§ 412, 430 (2018).

[44] An ESOP of a closely held corporation must give participants the right to take cash instead of stock distributions, with the amount determined under a fair valuation formula. I.R.C. § 4975 (e)(7) (2018) (ESOP definition), *id.* §§ 401(a)(23), 409(h) (2018) (put option). Hence an ESOP stock valuation report measures participants' account values, and may fix the level of plan benefits.

[45] Brown v. J.B. Hunt Transp. Servs., Inc., 586 F.3d 1079, 1089 (8th Cir. 2009) (even if long-term disability plan claims manuals must be disclosed pursuant to ERISA's claims procedure regulation, they are not "other instruments" for purposes of ERISA § 104(b)(2), therefore civil penalty does not apply); Fox v. Blue Cross & Blue Shield of Fla. Inc., 517 F. App'x 754, 757 (11th Cir. 2013) (refusal to provide documents used to determine amount to be paid for out-of-network services pursuant to health plan promising payment of 100 percent of the "allowed amount" does not trigger per diem civil penalty even though plan paid less than 10 percent of the actual charge for participant's brain surgery); Doe v. Travelers Ins. Co., 167 F.3d 53, 60 (1st Cir.1999) (mental health guidelines not within "other instruments" because the plan administrator "was not bound to use them, nor did patients have any legal rights under them"); Faircloth v. Lundy Packing Co., 91 F.3d 648, 655 (4th Cir. 1996) (release of ESOP stock valuation report not required); Bd. of Trustees of the CWA/ITU Negotiated Pension Plan v. Weinstein, 107 F.3d 139, 142 (2d Cir. 1997) (release of actuarial report not required). *Contra* Bartling v. Fruehauf Corp., 29 F.3d 1062, 1070 (6th Cir. 1994) (requiring release of actuarial report and observing that in light of the objective of disclosure, "all other things being equal, courts should favor disclosure where it would help participants understand their rights"); *see* Mondry v. American Family Mut. Ins. Co., 557 F.3d 781, 800 (7th Cir. 2009) (internal guidelines erroneously treated as binding must be disclosed).

[46] ERISA Advisory Op. 96-14A (U.S. Dep't of Labor, 1996) (schedule of usual and customary fees used as the basis for determining the dollar amount to be paid for health claims must be disclosed upon request). As a general standard, the Labor Department advised that a document which establishes or amends the plan in question, establishes a claims procedure, specifies formulas, methodologies, or schedules to be applied in determining or calculating a participant's or beneficiary's benefit entitlement, or does any of the other things described in sections

Disclosure

B SPD CONTENTS AND CONSEQUENCES

ERISA requires that participants and beneficiaries be furnished with a summary plan description (SPD) "written in a manner calculated to be understood by the average plan participant [that is] sufficiently accurate and comprehensive to reasonably apprise such participants and beneficiaries of their rights and obligations under the plan."[47] In particular, the SPD must contain information concerning "the plan's requirements respecting eligibility for participation and benefits; a description of the provisions providing for nonforfeitable pension benefits; [and] circumstances which may result in disqualification, ineligibility, or denial or loss of benefits."[48] The SPD was intended to serve as workers' primary source of information about the plan, supplying accessible, reliable information on which to base decisions.[49] As ERISA's mechanism to facilitate career and financial planning, the SPD was expected to promote economic efficiency. In that role, it has failed.

Enhanced economic efficiency requires some sacrifice of comprehensiveness. Employee benefit plans are long, complex legal instruments. Full disclosure, as by distributing all operative plan documents, would be meaningless to virtually all participants.[50] Excessive detail inhibits utilization and so operates to obscure the principal features, conditions, and limitations of the benefit plan. Abridgment and simplified expression are needed to make information accessible, but distillation fosters the impression that general explanations and illustrations are not subject to qualification or exceptions in special circumstances.

To achieve ERISA's objectives, disclosures must be both: (1) understandable – because otherwise they *will not* be used; and (2) sufficiently accurate and comprehensive to reasonably apprise participants and beneficiaries of their rights and obligations – because incorrect or dangerously incomplete information *should not* be used. Rather

---

402(b) and 402(c) of ERISA, [] would have to be furnished in accordance with the terms of section 104(b)(4).

ERISA Advisory Op. 97-11A (U.S. Dep't of Labor, 1997) (ruling that a contract between the plan and a third-party administrator need not be disclosed unless it supplies such terms, procedures, or formulas). *See also* ERISA Advisory Op. 87-10A (U.S. Dep't of Labor, 1987) (minutes of trustees' meetings need not be released where they concern a review of the investment manager's performance and do not specify plan terms or procedures); ERISA Advisory Op. 82-33A (U.S. Dep't of Labor, 1982) (distinguishing minutes of trustees' meetings that must be disclosed).

[47] ERISA § 102(a), 29 U.S.C. § 1022(a) (2018).

[48] ERISA § 102(b), 29 U.S.C. § 1022(b) (2018).

[49] *E.g.*, Pettaway v. Teachers Ins. & Annuity Ass'n of Am., 644 F.3d 427, 433 (D.C. Cir. 2011) (observing that the SPD is an "ERISA-mandated, plain-language document upon which plan participants may rely to understand their benefits"); Heidgerd v. Olin Corp., 906 F.2d 903, 907 (2d Cir.1990) (noting that the SPD "will be an employee's primary source of information regarding employment benefits, and employees are entitled to rely on the descriptions contained in the summary.").

[50] As mentioned above, participants are entitled to receive the operative plan documents, but only upon request *See supra* Chapter 3 notes 31–46 and accompanying text.

72 *Conduct Controls: Welfare and Pension Plans*

than demanding full disclosure, the SPD aims to achieve *optimal* disclosure, which requires a sensitive balance between "understandable" and "accurate and comprehensive" (i.e., reliable). The governing principle, "to reasonably apprise such participants and beneficiaries of their rights and obligations under the plan,"[51] is acutely sensitive to context, including the specific terms of the plan and the experience and capabilities of participants. Thoughtful compromises between understandability (SPD utility) and reliability must be made to improve worker career and financial planning. The SPD standard anticipates such trade-offs, but the incentive structure required to produce balanced, optimal disclosures is lacking. In the administrative and judicial implementation of ERISA reliability was enforced, while understandability was neglected.

Judicial enforcement of the reliability norm led to the demise of understandability. By the mid-1980s complaints that disclosures were inaccurate or incomplete were coming before the courts, and plan members were starting to win monetary recoveries based on the failure of an SPD to warn of circumstances causing disqualification, ineligibility, denial or loss of benefits, or where the SPD promised benefits that the language of the plan did not support.[52] That unexpected liability triggered the natural defensive response: plan sponsors remade their SPDs into extended full-disclosure disclaimer documents, and the SPD morphed into a liability shield. Understandability was jettisoned because it could be: no civil penalty is geared to understandability defects, nor does ERISA's limited set of civil enforcement actions supply leverage.[53] Importantly, employers are able to use other

---

[51] ERISA § 102(a), 29 U.S.C. § 1022(a) (2018).

[52] Zittrouer v. Uarco Inc. Group Ben. Plan, 582 F. Supp. 1471 (N.D. Ga. 1984) (failure to warn of convalescent care exclusion); Hillis v. Waukesha Title Co., 576 F. Supp. 1103, 1109 (E.D. Wis. 1983) (failure to warn of forfeiture for competition); McKnight v. Southern Life & Health Ins. Co., 758 F.2d 1566 (11th Cir. 1985) (participant entitled to benefit accrual under SPD's version of break-in-service rules even if the underlying plan document denied service credit; alternative holding). *McKnight* appears to be the case that brought the risk of liability for disclosure violations to the attention of a broad group of benefits law practitioners. It seems to have been the first appellate holding to impose liability. Its conclusion – that in cases of conflict between the plan and the SPD, the purpose of the summary required protection of an employee who reasonably relied on the summary – received coverage in the leading specialty news service. *Breaks in Service Do Not Cancel Employee's Past Service Credits*, 12 PENS. REP. (BNA) 672 (May 13, 1985). These three cases, *Zittrouer, Hillis,* and *McKnight,* were highlighted in an influential treatise's discussion of equitable relief for misstatements and omissions in an SPD, STEPHEN R. BRUCE, PENSION CLAIMS 391 (1988), which seems to have stimulated or at least contributed to the explosion of disclosure litigation. (The author, Stephen Bruce, represented the employees before the Supreme Court in *CIGGA Corp. v. Amara,* 563 U.S. 421, 424 (2011).) And by 1988 *Hillis* and *McKnight* were also being cited by the leading treatise on qualified retirement plans, MICHAEL J. CANAN, QUALIFIED RETIREMENT AND OTHER EMPLOYEE BENEFIT PLANS §11.2 at 382–83 (1988 ed.).

[53] In principle an injunction mandating issuance of a comprehensible explanation is available as a prospective remedy. *See* ERISA § 502(a)(3), (5), 29 U.S.C. § 1132(a)(3), (5) (plan participants, beneficiaries, fiduciaries, and Secretary of Labor authorized to bring civil action for appropriate equitable relief to enforce and provision of ERISA Title I). Instead of bringing a lawsuit with no prospect of monetary recovery, however, the natural response to impenetrable

Disclosure   73

methods of publicizing the advantages of the plan via non-SPD communications, and in doing so they may face minimal risk of liability for inaccurate or misleading representations.[54]

In contrast to understandability, the command that the summary be "sufficiently accurate and comprehensive to reasonably apprise ... participants and beneficiaries of their rights and obligations under the plan"[55] was taken seriously. This part examines the judicial elaboration of this reliability norm and shows that it is enforced with restrictions that limit access to effective relief. Plan sponsors persuaded courts that relief is available through equity, not contract law, which poses obstacles to monetary recovery and collective litigation.

Redressable SPD defects fall into three categories. First, the SPD may err by contradicting the underlying terms of the plan (the inaccurate SPD). Second, the SPD may contradict itself. Third, the mistake may lie in an SPD omission, by failing to warn plan participants and beneficiaries of important qualification criteria, for example. We begin with the inaccurate SPD, which illustrates how ERISA's limited array of causes of action and remedies has shaped disclosure case law.

1 *The Inaccurate SPD*

ERISA grants participants and beneficiaries the right to sue for specified civil penalties, for benefits due, to redress breaches of fiduciary obligations, and for appropriate equitable relief to enforce ERISA's requirements or the terms of the plan.[56] The statutory enforcement mechanism is exclusive – ERISA pre-empts state law causes of action, including tort claims for fraud, deceit, or misrepresentation.[57] Therefore, workers harmed by deficient communications must fashion their claim to fit within one of ERISA's limited grounds for judicial intervention.

If the SPD is inaccurate, workers complain that promised benefits were denied based on legal technicalities of which they were unaware. (Although any participant or beneficiary can obtain access to the underlying plan documents, governing instruments are difficult to understand and are not routinely distributed.[58]) The SPD is intended to give participants accessible and reliable information about the

---

gobbledygook is to ask someone for an informal translation, as by consulting a supervisor or the benefits department.

[54] *See infra* Chapter 3C.

[55] ERISA § 102(a), 29 U.S.C. § 1022(a) (2018).

[56] ERISA §§ 502(a)(1)-(3), 409, 29 U.S.C. §§ 1132(a)(1)-(3), 1109 (2018).

[57] ERISA § 514, 29 U.S.C. § 1144 (2018); *see* Pilot Life Ins. Co. v. Dedeaux, 481 U.S. 41, 57 (1987) (holding that ERISA pre-empts state common law tort and contract actions founded on an insurer's bad faith refusal to pay claims, relying on "the clear expression of congressional intent that ERISA's civil enforcement scheme be exclusive"); Massachusetts Mut. Life Ins. Co. v. Russell, 473 U.S. 134, 147 (1985).

[58] ERISA § 104(b)(2), (4), 29 U.S.C. § 1024(b)(2), (4) (2018). See the discussion of plan instruments, text accompanying Chapter 3 notes 31–46, *supra*.

Conduct Controls: Welfare and Pension Plans

plan, and to serve as their primary source of information concerning the plan's terms. The planning function requires accurate disclosure of the most important aspects of the benefit program, so that workers can make wise use of it. From that perspective, the SPD defines the core deal between the employer and participating employees. As such, the SPD arguably *is* the plan: the SPD's terms, as far as they go, could sensibly be understood as the terms of the contract. That argument suggests that refusal to pay benefits based on a discrepancy between the SPD and underlying formal plan documents constitutes a breach of contract, redressable by suit "to recover benefits due ... under the terms of his plan [or] to enforce his rights under the terms of the plan."[59] Hence, if the SPD is understood to embody the crux of the deal, then recovery on the contract should be available in a suit for benefits, without proof of reliance.

In contrast, if an inaccurate SPD merely *describes* but does not itself comprise "the plan," then a suit to recover benefits will fail, for the terms of the plan as set forth in the governing documents have not been breached. Consequently, instead of enforcing the plan, recovery is limited to "appropriate equitable relief" to enforce ERISA in contravention of the plan. A claim of promissory estoppel is equitable in nature and may be brought to redress a violation of the statutory requirement that the SPD be accurate. Estoppel is conditioned on proof of reliance, but proof of reliance can be difficult and costly in the employee benefit context. Often the employee's claim – that she rejected another job offer, failed to save, or declined to purchase additional insurance because of her understanding of a plan's promised benefits – lacks objective corroboration. Conditioning recovery on convincing proof of detrimental reliance risks under-enforcement of the norm that the SPD provide accurate information. That laxity would reduce the sponsor's incentive to take precautions to ensure accuracy.

The Courts of Appeals uniformly concluded that the language of the SPD could trump contradictory plan documents, but the circuits split over whether the SPD's binding force followed from contract or estoppel.[60] In *CIGNA Corp. v. Amara*[61] the Supreme Court resolved the matter, concluding "that the summary documents, important as they are, provide communication with beneficiaries about the plan, but that their statements do not themselves constitute the *terms* of the plan for purposes

---

[59] ERISA § 502(a)(1)(B), 29 U.S.C. § 1132(a)(1)(B) (2018).

[60] *Compare* Health Cost Controls of Ill., Inc. v. Washington, 187 F.3d 703 (7th Cir. 1999) (if "the plan and the summary plan description conflict, the former governs ... unless the plan participant or beneficiary has reasonably relied on the summary plan description to his detriment"); Andersen v. Chrysler Corp., 99 F.3d 846 (7th Cir. 1996); Branch v. G. Bernd Co., 955 F.2d 1574, 1579 (11th Cir. 1992), *with* Edwards v. State Farm Mut. Auto. Ins. Co., 851 F.2d 134, 137 (6th Cir. 1988) (reliance not required); Helwig v. Kelsey-Hayes Co., 93 F.3d 243, 249–50 (6th Cir. 1996) (*Edwards'* principle that defective SPD trumps inconsistent language in plan documents applies to welfare as well as pension plans); Burstein v. Ret. Account Plan for Employees of Allegheny Health Educ. & Research Found., 334 F.3d 365, 380–82 (3d Cir. 2003) (reliance not required; SPD furnishes plan's terms to the extent that it conflict with the language of the formal plan document).

[61] CIGNA Corp. v. Amara, 563 U.S. 421 (2011).

Disclosure 75

of §502(a)(1)(B)," ERISA's contract-like cause of action.[62] Consequently, remedies for an inaccurate SPD must be sought under §502(a)(3), as a claim for appropriate equitable relief to enforce ERISA's requirements.[63]

The Court's *Amara* opinion then pivoted to explore the prerequisites for equitable relief under §502(a)(3). The *Amara* Court indicated that in appropriate circumstances estoppel, reformation, or surcharge might support monetary recovery for harms caused by disclosure violations.[64] Each of those remedies is subject to distinct conditions, and while estoppel requires showing detrimental reliance, individualized proof of reliance may not be a necessary condition for reformation or surcharge.[65] The opinion explains that "any requirement of harm must come from the law of equity" and the requisite standard turns upon the equitable remedy sought.[66]

> [T]he standard of prejudice must be borrowed from equitable principles, as modified by the obligations and injuries identified by ERISA itself. Information-related circumstances, violations, and injuries are potentially too various in nature to insist that harm must always meet that more vigorous "detrimental harm" [*sic*, reliance] standard when equity imposed no such strict requirement.[67]

Amara was litigated as a class action and the record did not address reliance. The observation that some other showing of harm might support reformation or surcharge allowed the case to continue.[68]

---

[62] *Id.* at 438 (emphasis in original).

[63] An inaccurate SPD is generally the product of a fiduciary breach. The plan administrator is a fiduciary tasked with furnishing an adequate SPD, and any material error therein typically proceeds from disloyalty or neglect. The resulting violation or ERISA § 404(a)(1) is not redressable under ERISA § 502(a)(2), 29 U.S.C. § 1132(a)(2) (2018), however, because that cause of action is limited to appropriate relief under ERISA § 409, 29 U.S.C. § 1109. Section 409 renders the breaching fiduciary personally liable *to the plan*, not to the individual participant or beneficiary harmed by the breach.

[64] 563 U.S. at 439–42.

[65] *Id.* at 443 ("Looking to the law of equity, there is no general principle that 'detrimental reliance' must be proved before a remedy is decreed. To the extent any such requirement arises, it is because the specific remedy being contemplated imposes such a requirement.")

[66] *Id.* at 443.

[67] *Id.* at 445.

[68] In an opinion concurring in the judgment, Justice Scalia, joined by Justice Thomas, complained that the Court's entire discussion of estoppel, reformation, and surcharge was unwarranted. Moreover, "[e]ven if we adhere to our dicta" that these are distinctly equitable remedies, "it is far from clear that they are available remedies in this case." *Id.* at 449 (Scalia, J., concurring in the judgment). Noting that CIGNA admitted that misled workers might be able to recover under an equitable estoppel theory, Justice Scalia observed that "it presumably makes this concession only because questions of reliance would be individualized and potentially inappropriate for class-action treatment. Surcharge (which CIGNA does not concede and which is not briefed) may encounter the same problem." *Id.* at 450; *see* Transcript of Oral Argument at 20–24, 53, 54, CIGNA Corp. v. Amara 563 U.S. 421 (2011) (No. 09-804).

The differing views of Justices Breyer and Scalia on the susceptibility of the surcharge remedy to class-based resolution led the lower courts on remand to avoid the uncertainty by adopting reformation as the relief mechanism. Amara v. CIGNA Corp., 925 F. Supp. 2d 242, 263–64 (D. Conn. 2012), *aff'd* 775 F.3d 510, 518 (2d Cir. 2014).

a Reformation

In proceedings following remand in *Amara* the Second Circuit addressed the availability of reformation.[69] In connection with the transition from a traditional defined benefit pension plan to a cash balance plan, CIGNA Corporation had falsely assured participants that the new arrangement would significantly enhance their retirement program, that the initial credit to workers' new cash balance accounts would include the full actuarial value of their previously earned benefits, and that the changes would not save CIGNA money.[70] The Supreme Court had observed that "[t]he power to reform contracts (as contrasted with the power to enforce contracts as written) is a traditional power of an equity court, not a court of law, and was used to prevent fraud."[71] Accepting that invitation, the Second Circuit found reformation justified where clear and convincing evidence established that "defendants committed fraud or similar inequitable conduct and that such fraud reasonably caused plaintiffs to be mistaken about the terms of the pension plan."[72] The record revealed that CIGNA had sought to avoid workforce dissatisfaction by misrepresenting the terms of the new cash balance plan both in SPDs and other general notices, and "actively prevented employees from learning the truth",[73] including by instructing benefits department staff and consultants *not* to provide quantitative comparisons between the old and new plans, despite employees' requests. Those factors adequately established entitlement to reformation on a class-wide basis, the appellate court concluded,[74] rendering CIGNA liable to pay the benefits as advertised.[75] Other cases have reached similar conclusions.[76]

---

[69] Amara v. CIGNA Corp., 775 F.3d 510 (2d Cir. 2014).

[70] 563 U.S. at 428–30. Because the adoption, amendment, or termination of a plan is a nonfiduciary act (a so-called settlor function), CIGNA was entirely within its rights to substitute a lower-cost plan. Nevertheless, the cost misrepresentation is relevant and problematic because it reinforced the prior falsehoods (that participants' benefits would be enhanced and that their initial cash balances captured the full value of their accrued benefits), inducing workers to acquiesce in the changes.

[71] *Id.* at 440.

[72] 775 F.3d at 526.

[73] *Id.*

[74] *Id.* at 530–31.

[75] The Supreme Court had refused to order benefit payments based solely on the terms of the SPD – the Court rejected the view that the SPD is the contract. Yet following remand the ultimate outcome of the litigation was an order to pay benefits in line with the SPD representations. The impact of the reformation analysis was to impose two additional conditions on that result: (1) a required showing of employer fraud or inequitable conduct, (2) causing employee mistake about the terms of the underlying plan. *Id.* at 525. The Second Circuit rejected CIGNA's argument that reformation also requires a separate showing of actual harm as a third element. Instead, the mistaken party's failure to receive the expected advantages of the agreement suffices. *Id.* at 525 n.12.

[76] Osberg v. Foot Locker, Inc., 862 F.3d 198, 212–13 (2d Cir. 2017) (holding, on facts similar to *Amara*, that detrimental reliance need not be shown to support the remedy of plan reformation,

Disclosure

CIGNA's finely tooled prevarication might suggest that reformation will be available to enforce SPD representations over contradictory plan terms only in extreme situations. That may be true, but a 2018 reformation case from the Sixth Circuit indicates that fraud or inequitable conduct is a flexible concept that does not always require intent to deceive.[77] The controversy concerned eligibility for subsidized early retirement ("30-and-out" benefits) under Chrysler's pension plan. The SPD said that a plan participant who had satisfied the age and service requirements for 30-and-out benefits did not need to be actively employed at retirement to qualify, but the plan document said that an employee who was terminated by the company was ineligible.[78] After the plaintiff was terminated in connection with a reduction in force his application for 30-and-out benefits was denied, despite the fact that he had recently and repeatedly been advised to consult the SPD for details about his pension.[79] Starting from the settled doctrine that contract reformation is justified where one party is mistaken and the other commits fraud or engages in inequitable conduct, the question on appeal was whether the worker needed to prove Chrysler's intent to deceive in order to demonstrate fraud or inequitable conduct. The court rejected an intentional deception requirement, remanding the case with instructions to consider certain guideposts indicative of wrongful conduct or constructive fraud.[80]

---

and that proof of mistake to support class-wide reformation need not be individualized, but can be "through generalized circumstantial evidence in appropriate cases").

In Cunningham v. Wawa, Inc., 387 F. Supp. 3d 529 (E.D. Pa. 2019), defendants opposed class certification of claims based upon fiduciary misrepresentations and a misleading SPD, arguing that individual evidence of detrimental reliance is required to support relief. Relying on *Osberg*, 862 F.2d at 211–12, the district court held that in light of *Amara* plaintiffs need not show detrimental reliance to seek reformation or surcharge in an action under ERISA § 502(a)(3). 387 F. Supp. 3d at 540–42, 545. Defendants were granted permission to appeal class certification, and the Secretary of Labor filed a brief supporting the district court's ruling that detrimental reliance is not necessary to support reformation or surcharge. Brief of the Secretary of Labor as Amicus Curiae in Support of Plaintiffs-Appellees, Cunningham v. Wawa Inc., *appeal docketed*, No. 19-2930 (3d Cir. Dec. 11, 2019), 2019 WL 6837265. *See* Jacklyn Wille & Lydia Wheeler, *Wawa Retirees Get Labor Department Support in Stock Plan Battle*, BLOOMBERG BEN. & EXEC. COMP. NEWS, Dec. 12, 2019. Shortly after the Labor Department's brief was filed the parties reached a settlement. Martina Barash, *Wawa, Ex-Employees Agree to Settle Stock Sell-Off Class Action*, BLOOMBERG BEN. & EXEC. COMP. NEWS, Dec. 30, 2019.

[77] Pearce v. Chrysler Grp. LLC Pension Plan, 893 F.3d 339 (6th Cir. 2018).

[78] *Id.* at 343.

[79] *Id.* at 343–44. Pearce responded to the denial of benefits by asking the benefit manager to show him where in the SPD "he could find what you have stated" but he apparently received no response.

[80] *Id.* at 347–48. The Labor Department filed an amicus brief in *Pearce* arguing that precedent and treatises on equitable jurisdiction show that "fraud" has a broader meaning in equity than at law, and that intent to deceive is not a necessary element for reformation. Brief for the United States as Amicus Curiae in Support of the Plaintiff-Appellant, Pearce v. Chrysler Grp. LLC Pension Plan, 893 F.3d 339 (6th Cir. 2018), 2017 WL 3263553.

b Surcharge

An SPD error not attributable to fraud or inequitable conduct cannot be remedied by reformation. The *Amara* Court observed that monetary relief in the form of equitable compensation or "surcharge" is a historic remedy for breach of fiduciary duty.

> Equity courts possessed the power to provide relief in the form of monetary "compensation" for a loss resulting from a trustee's breach of duty, or to prevent the trustee's unjust enrichment. ... Indeed, prior to the merger of law and equity this kind of monetary remedy against a trustee, sometimes called a "surcharge," was "exclusively equitable."[81]

"The surcharge remedy extended to a breach of trust committed by a fiduciary encompassing any violation of a duty imposed upon that fiduciary."[82] Consequently, violations involving no bad faith – including prudence missteps, such as negligent drafting of the SPD – might be redressable via surcharge provided that actual harm caused by the breach is proven.[83] The required showing of injury, the Court observed, could consist of detrimental reliance, but a less demanding standard, such as proof of likely harm flowing from undisclosed detrimental plan changes, could suffice.[84]

"In some jurisdictions it is held that there can be no estoppel unless the misrepresentations were designedly made, or were designed to deceive the same party who relied on them. The weight of authority is against both of these propositions; a party may be estopped to deny representations made when he had no knowledge of their falsity, or which he made without any intent to deceive the party now setting up the estoppel. A better statement of the principle is that the fraud consists in the inconsistent position subsequently taken, rather than in the original conduct. It is the subsequent inconsistent position, and not the original conduct that operates to the injury of the other party." Henry L. McClintock, Handbook on the Law of Equity § 31 (2d ed. 1948) (footnotes omitted). De Funiak, Handbook of Modern Equity 235 (2d ed. 1956) ("Fraud has a broader meaning in equity [than at law] and intention to defraud or to misrepresent is not a necessary element."); SEC v. Capital Gains Bureau, 375 U.S. 180, 193–95 (1963).

The *Pearce* court also rejected Chrysler's argument that the plan could be reformed only if the fraud or inequitable conduct occurred in drafting the plan. *Id.* at 349 (distinguishing Skinner v. Northrup Grumman Ret. Plan B, 673 F.3d 1162, 1166–67 (9th Cir. 2012), and emphasizing that "the basis of [Pearce's] mutual agreement with Chrysler was the SPD").

Moreover, the Second Circuit held that reformation is categorically available as a remedy, even absent proof of mistake, fraud or inequitable conduct, where it is shown that the terms of the plan violate ERISA. Laurent v. PricewaterhouseCoopers LLP, 945 F.3d 739, 749 (2d Cir. 2019).

[81] CIGNA Corp. v. Amara, 563 U.S. at 441–42 (citations omitted); *see* Restatement (Third) of Trusts § 95 & cmt. b (2012);

[82] *Id.* at 442.

[83] *See id.* at 444.

[84] *Id.*

Disclosure 79

Lower courts followed the invitation to apply surcharge to award monetary relief for disclosure harms.[85] Whether surcharge will support effective class-wide relief remains unclear, however. As of 2022, cases imposing surcharge have involved individual plaintiffs and clear evidence of detrimental reliance, not the sort of widespread misinformation disseminated in *Amara*.[86]

c Estoppel

Provided that the conditions for estoppel are satisfied, monetary relief can be obtained based on the terms of an inaccurate SPD. For equity to intervene, however, reliance must be reasonable or justifiable, as well as detrimental.[87] Challenges to the reasonableness of reliance on an inaccurate SPD can arise if the SPD: (1) contains a warning that plan terms control in the event of inconsistency (SPD disclaimer clauses); or (2) fails to address an important issue (reliance on silence).

---

[85] *E.g.*, Gimeno v. NCHMD, Inc., 38 F.4th 910, 914–15 (11th Cir. 2022) (where employer failed to notify participant of required evidence of insurability form but withheld for supplemental life insurance premiums and provided benefits summary listing coverage, insurance proceeds may be recovered via surcharge); Sullivan-Mestecky v. Verizon Commc'ns Inc., 961 F.3d 91, 102–03 (2d Cir. 2020); Silva v. Metro. Life Ins. Co., 762 F.3d 711, 720–22 (8th Cir. 2014); Gearlds v. Entergy Servs., Inc., 709 F.3d 448, 452 (5th Cir. 2013) (surcharge supported claim for medical benefits where plaintiff was induced to take early retirement by negligent oral and written assurances that he would continue to receive medical benefits); McCravy v. Metro. Life Ins. Co., 690 F.3d 176, 181 (4th Cir. 2012) (plaintiff, who paid life insurance premiums for several years for her child only to learn upon the child's death that the child had been ineligible for dependent coverage, could potentially recover insurance proceeds via surcharge, not just refund of premiums mistakenly paid); *see also* Kenseth v. Dean Health Plan, Inc., 722 F.3d 869, 883 (7th Cir. 2013) (discussing *McCravy* and *Gearlds*). *But see* Skinner v. Northrop Grumman Ret. Plan B, 673 F.3d 1162, 1167 (9th Cir. 2012) (surcharge unavailable where retirees failed to show they changed positions due to inaccurate SPD).

[86] On remand the district court in *Amara* grounded relief in reformation out of concern that Wal–Mart Stores, Inc. v. Dukes, 564 U.S. 338 (2011), created "thornier issues" for certification of a class seeking monetary damages via surcharge. Amara v. CIGNA Corp., 925 F. Supp. 2d 242, 263–64 (D. Conn. 2012), aff'd, 775 F.3d 510 (2d Cir. 2014). *See supra* Chapter 3 note 68. *But see* Moyle v. Liberty Mut. Ret. Benefit Plan, 823 F.3d 948, 964–65 (9th Cir. 2016) (concluding that individual issues of reliance do not preclude class certification if representations allegedly made on uniform classwide basis and suit seeks reformation or surcharge).

[87] Pomeroy's treatise on equity lists six essential elements of equitable estoppel. One of them is that the party asserting estoppel must not know the true facts (for present purposes, the actual terms of the plan) at the time the false representation (here, the erroneous SPD) was made and when it was acted upon. 3 SPENCER W. SYMONS, POMEROY'S EQUITY JURISPRUDENCE § 805 (5th ed. 1941). More than simple ignorance of the true facts (good faith) is demanded, however: the party asserting estoppel must also lack a reason to know the truth. Reasonable diligence is required, "otherwise no equity will arise in his favor." *Id.* § 813, at 236. *Accord* JAMES W. EATON, HANDBOOK OF EQUITY JURISPRUDENCE 169 (1901); 2 JOSEPH STORY, COMMENTARIES ON EQUITY JURISPRUDENCE § 1553b, at 785 (12th ed., Jairus W. Perry ed., 1877) ("A party setting up an equitable estoppel is himself bound to the exercise of good faith and due diligence to ascertain the truth" (footnote omitted)).

80 *Conduct Controls: Welfare and Pension Plans*

Regarding inconsistency, the SPD was envisioned as workers' primary source of information about the terms of the plan, a ready reference serving as the foundation for career and financial planning.[88] Congress was acutely aware that plan documents are complex legal instruments that do not speak to the typical employee: to advance economic efficiency, the highlights or key provisions of the program must be translated into actionable information.[89] In most instances, therefore, it would be patently *unreasonable* to expect workers to check assertions made in the SPD against the highly technical language of underlying plan documents. Indeed, such confirmation would be both frustrating and counterproductive: workers would be expending resources to replicate the plan administrator's vernacular communication efforts.[90] But does that conclusion hold if the SPD contains an express warning that, in the event that the SPD conflicts with plan document(s) or is incomplete or ambiguous,

---

[88] *See supra* Chapter 3 note 49 and accompanying text. Observe that the SPD is distributed to plan participants and beneficiaries routinely and automatically – unlike operative plan instruments, no request is necessary to trigger SPD disclosure.

[89] By 1972, comprehensive pension reform legislation introduced by Senators Harrison Williams and Jacob Javits called for furnishing understandable summaries to participants as a matter of course. Retirement Income Security for Employees Act of 1972, S. 3598, 92d Cong. §§ 505, 507(b), 118 CONG. REC. 16,908, 16,915, 16,916 ("administrator shall furnish to every participant upon his enrollment in the plan ... a summary of the plan's important provisions ... written in a manner calculated to be understood by the average participant"). The report of the Senate Committee on Labor and Public Welfare explained:

"An important issue relates to the effectiveness of communication of plan contents to employees. Descriptions of plans furnished to employees should be presented in a manner that an average and reasonable worker participant can understand intelligently. It is grossly unfair to hold an employee accountable for acts which disqualify him from benefits, if he had no knowledge of these acts, or if these conditions were stated in a misleading or incomprehensible manner in plan booklets. Subcommittee findings were abundant in establishing that an average plan participant, even where he has been furnished an explanation of his plan provisions, often cannot comprehend them because of the technicalities and complexities of the language used." S. Rep. No. 92-1150, at 10 (1972). *Accord id.* at 37–38.

John Erlenborn, Republican House manager of the bill that became ERISA, observed:

"[I]f people do have this sort of meaningful information made available to them, I think some of the unwarranted expectations that gave rise to the horror stories that people were not getting what they anticipated will be a thing of the past, because many of them are based on what people anticipated getting that they never were entitled to, because they did not honestly know what was in their pension plan; they did not honestly know what their rights would be." 120 CONG. REC. 4284 (1974). *See id.* 29,195–96 (remarks of Rep. Dent) (reporting that Rep. Erlenborn "insisted from the very beginning that a complete and full disclosure of a pension participant's standing within the pension plan be made available, and that it should be written in such a way that individuals would understand exactly what his position was," calling this "one of the cornerstones of reform").

[90] *See Hansen v. Cont'l Ins. Co.*, 940 F.2d 971, 981 (5th Cir. 1991) ("Of course, if a participant has to read and understand the [insurance] policy in order to make use of the summary, then the summary is of no use at all."); *McKnight v. Southern Life and Health Ins. Co.*, 758 F.2d 1566, 1570 (11th Cir. 1985) (observing that it would defeat the purpose of the SPD "to publish and distribute a plan summary booklet designed to simplify and explain a voluminous and complicated document, and then proclaim that any inconsistencies will be governed by the plan.").

the terms of the plan document(s) control? What effect, if any, should be accorded such an SPD disclaimer clause? Should workers be expected to look behind the SPD? There is long-standing and nearly unanimous agreement in the case law that the purposes of disclosure demand that the SPD be given controlling legal effect in the event it conflicts with the terms of the plan, even if the SPD contains a disclaimer clause.[91] Absent actual awareness of an error, reliance on the mandated communication vehicle is justified per se.

Regarding silence, the SPD was envisioned as an accessible *summary*. To be useful to the *average* plan participant it cannot convey all information that is potentially relevant to *any* participant. That necessarily means that some employees must sometimes be expected to inquire further. But that does not mean estoppel should apply *only* to express declarations contained in the SPD. Congress demands that the SPD "shall contain [among other information] the plan's requirements respecting eligibility for participation and benefits [and] circumstances which may result in disqualification, ineligibility, or denial or loss of benefits."[92] SPD silence in the face of a duty to reveal such conditions and limitations would reasonably be understood as confirmation that the plan does not impose a restrictive criterion.[93] Accordingly, reliance on an SPD's failure to warn of a situation that could trigger

---

[91] *E.g., Hansen*, 940 F.2d at 981–82; Atwood v. Newmont Gold Co., 45 F.3d 1317, 1321 (9th Cir. 1995) (dicta); Aiken v. Policy Mgmt. Sys. Corp., 13 F.3d 138, 140–41 (4th Cir. 1993); Senkier v. Hartford Life & Accident Ins. Co., 948 F.2d 1050, 1051 (7th Cir. 1991) (dicta); Heidgerd v. Olin Corp., 906 F.2d 903, 907–08 (2d Cir. 1990); Edwards v. State Farm Mut. Auto. Ins. Co., 851 F.2d 134, 136 (6th Cir. 1988); McKnight v. S. Life & Health Ins. Co., 758 F.2d 1566, 1571 (11th Cir. 1985) (alternative holding). *Contra* Kolentus v. Avco Corp., 798 F.2d 949, 958 (7th Cir. 1986); *see* De Nobel v. Vitro Corp., 885 F.2d 1180, 1195 (4th Cir. 1989) (disclaimer effective, but that conclusion subsequently treated as dictum by Pierce v. Security Trust Life Insurance Co., 979 F.2d 23, 28 n.4 (4th Cir. 1992)); *cf.* Bergt v. Ret. Plan for Pilots Employed by Mark Air, Inc., 293 F.3d 1139, 1145 (9th Cir. 2002) (if SPD contradicts plan document and plan document is more favorable to employees, then plan document controls).

[92] ERISA § 102(b), 29 U.S.C. § 1022(b) (2018).

[93] To state the principle another way, participants and beneficiaries would reasonably expect that a document purporting to be an SPD satisfies ERISA's requirements for an SPD (i.e., is legally sufficient). Their reliance on the plan administrator not violating the law should be protected. The principle has long been recognized: "These [equitable] estoppels may be created by the acts of a party, by his express declaration, and in many cases by his silence – by his not speaking when he had a duty to speak. 'If a man was silent when he ought to have spoken, he shall not speak when he ought to be silent.'" ELIAS MERWIN, THE PRINCIPLES OF EQUITY AND EQUITY PLEADING 515 (1896) (footnotes omitted) (the exact source of the quoted equitable maxim is unclear); *accord* EATON *supra* Chapter 3 note 87, § 61 at 170 ("[M]isleading silence, where there is a duty to speak, is as effectual to create an estoppel as a direct representation"); POMEROY, *supra* Chapter 3 note 87, at § 808a (estoppel by silence or inaction must be predicated on an obligation or duty to speak). The principle is likewise well-established in tort law liability for nondisclosure. RESTATEMENT (SECOND) OF TORTS § 551 (1977).

Conduct Controls: Welfare and Pension Plans

disqualification, ineligibility, denial, or loss of benefits is as justified as reliance on the (reasonable meaning) of the SPD's text itself.[94]

Detrimental reliance is another key element of estoppel.[95] The *Amara* Court declared that "when a court exercises its authority under §502(a)(3) to impose a remedy equivalent to estoppel, a showing of detrimental reliance must be made."[96] Estoppel's detrimental reliance element often involves highly specific proof. Did an understanding of a plan's promised benefits cause the plaintiff employee to reject another job offer, fail to save, or decline to purchase additional insurance? As these examples suggest, reliance in the employee benefit context typically takes the form of inaction. Inaction, however, might flow from ignorance or indifference. How does a plan member prove that his complacency was SPD-based? Is independent confirmation required? Some people may discuss their circumstances and decision making with coworkers or benefits staff, but frequently there will be no objective evidence to corroborate the worker's own (possibly sincere, possibly self-serving) assertion.

Conditioning estoppel on objective evidence of reliance – evidence that is often unavailable – will cause under-enforcement of the norm that the SPD provide accurate information.[97] Under-enforcement reduces the administrator's incentive to take adequate precautions.[98] Insufficient care in SPD preparation undermines the planning function, decreasing the probability that the economic efficiency benefits envisioned for the SPD will be fully realized. Moreover, rigidly insisting

---

[94] See the discussion of failure-to-warn cases, *infra* Chapter 3 notes 149–163 and accompanying text.

[95] *See* Robert A. Hillman, *Questioning the "New Consensus" on Promissory Estoppel: An Empirical and Theoretical Study*, 98 COLUM. L. REV. 580, 597–600 (1998) (presenting data showing that reliance continues to be a key substantive element of promissory estoppel).

[96] CIGNA Corp. v. Amara, 563 U.S. 421, 443 (2011).

[97] Economic theory suggests that a damage multiplier could be employed to counteract perverse incentives created by under-detection or under-enforcement. *See* FRANK H. EASTERBROOK & DANIEL R. FISCHEL, THE ECONOMIC STRUCTURE OF CORPORATE LAW 320–23, 332–33 (1991); *see also* Alan Schwartz, *The Myth That Promisees Prefer Supracompensatory Remedies: An Analysis of Contracting for Damage Measures*, 100 YALE L.J. 369, 395–98, 401–03 (1990) (public action to reduce promisee litigation costs, as by an award of attorneys' fees, is economically superior to punitive damages as a solution to the problem of contract under-enforcement). ERISA remedies are strictly limited, however, and do not condone consequential or punitive damages or any such multiplier. ERISA § 502(a), 29 U.S.C. § 1132(a) (2018); Massachusetts Mut. Life Ins. Co. v. Russell, 473 U.S. 134 (1985); Pilot Life Ins. Co. v. Dedeaux, 481 U.S. 41 (1987) (holding ERISA pre-empts state law cause of action for bad faith insurance claims processing under an insured employee benefit plan).

[98] *See* Bergt v. Ret. Plan for Pilots Employed by MarkAir, Inc., 293 F.3d 1139, 1145 (9th Cir. 2002) ("[T]he law should provide as strong an incentive as possible for employers to write the SPDs so that they are consistent with the ERISA plan master documents, a relatively simple task.").

Disclosure 83

on objective evidence of reliance would effectively prevent the award of estoppel-based relief on a consolidated or class-wide basis.[99]

The element of reliance functions as estoppel's causation requirement. If the defective communication was not relied upon, then it has not produced injury to the plaintiff, and the defendant is not responsible for the harm complained of by the plaintiff. Yet the miscommunication need not be the sole cause of the harm, however. It is enough that the representation materially *contributed* to the injurious course of conduct.[100] Moreover, "a rigorous showing of causation is not [always] required" in equity.[101] This traditional equitable flexibility suggests receptivity to a pragmatic approach to proof of causation if justice so requires.

Equity's historic flexibility, combined with the indispensable role of an accurate SPD in accomplishing ERISA's economic efficiency objectives, counsel judicial receptivity to adaptation in applying estoppel's detrimental reliance requirement in the SPD context.[102] But adjustment of equitable estoppel principles to the ERISA

---

[99] *See supra* Chapter 3 note 68. The class action condition that "questions of law or fact common to class members predominate over any questions affecting only individual members," Fed. R. Civ. Proc. 23(b)(3), will be difficult to satisfy where success on the merits demands proof of how a misrepresentation impacted individual decision making.

[100] J.D. Heydon et al., Meagher, Gummow and Lehane's Equity: Doctrines and Remedies 541 (5th ed. 2015) ("it suffices that the representation has materially contributed to the representee's course of conduct. The fact that other causes contributed to the representee's course of conduct does not prevent an estoppel from arising.").

Justifiable reliance is likewise the factual causation element of the common law tort of deceit. Restatement (Second) of Torts § 546 (1977). In that context, it is not "necessary that his reliance upon the truth of the fraudulent misrepresentation be the sole or even the predominant or decisive factor in influencing his conduct. It is not even necessary that he would not have acted or refrained from acting as he did unless he had relied on the misrepresentation." *Id.* cmt. b. Instead, "[i]t is enough that the representation has played a substantial part, and so has been a substantial factor, in influencing his decision." *Id.*

[101] Samuel L. Bray, *Fiduciary Remedies, in* Oxford Handbook of Fiduciary Law (E. Criddle et al. eds. 2018) ("[o]ne difference [from damages at law] is that a rigorous showing of causation is not required in equitable compensation"); Heydon, *supra* Chapter 3 note 100, at 817–35; *see* SEC v. Capital Gains Bureau, 375 U.S. 180, 193 (1963) (observing that "[i]t is not necessary in a suit for equitable or prophylactic relief to establish all the elements required" in a common law fraud suit, citing Harold Greville Hanbury & Ronald Harling Maudsley, Modern Equity 643 (8th ed. 1962)); *see also* Restatement (Second) of Torts § 546 cmt. b (1977) (justifiable reliance on a fraudulent misrepresentation means that the representation must have been a substantial factor influencing the decision, but it is not "necessary that he would not have acted or refrained from acting as he did unless he had relied on the misrepresentation"). In contrast, a stricter standard of causation is generally required for negligence. *Id.* § 432(1) & cmt. a ("the actor's negligent conduct is not a substantial factor in bringing about harm to another if the harm would have been sustained even if the actor had not been negligent").

[102] *See* Varity Corp. v. Howe, 516 U.S. 489, 496–97 (1996) (observing that, while the common law of trusts offers a starting point that informs interpretation of ERISA's fiduciary regime, in some instances trust law must be adapted to serve statutory purposes). Legal scholarship on equitable remedies, and estoppel in particular, demonstrates that such an adaptation of estoppel's requirements to the employee benefit plan context would be entirely consistent with the traditions of the field. History "shows that equity's established emphasis on the public

84 Conduct Controls: Welfare and Pension Plans

context (sometimes called "ERISA estoppel" in the courts) has been episodic and haphazard. As currently applied in ERISA appellate cases, estoppel is a mess – variable, unstable, and confused. ERISA estoppel was not produced by thoughtful, conscious evolution.

The full story is told elsewhere.[103] Two examples will show the mass of contradictions: one suggests relaxation of the stringency of estoppel's detrimental reliance requirement, while the other dramatically amplifies that stringency.

In an early estoppel case before the First Circuit, Judge (later Justice) Stephen Breyer cited three district court cases as authority for the one-sentence announcement that to secure relief a worker allegedly misled by a faulty SPD "must show some significant reliance upon, or possible prejudice flowing from, the faulty plan description."[104] Neither was present in the record evidence,[105] nor did the opinion acknowledge that the traditional detrimental reliance standard demands *both* reliance *and* prejudice (i.e., a change of position causing harm). Nevertheless, as an appellate case of first impression, the reliance-or-prejudice formulation was picked up by some other circuits.[106] Compared with detrimental reliance, the reliance-or-prejudice test offers broader scope for application of estoppel in ERISA cases.

---

interest and judicial discretion intersect in refining the application of these doctrines" including estoppel. T. Leigh Anenson, *Equitable Defenses in the Age of Statutes*, 36 REV. LITIG. 659, 664 (2018). Equitable principles are expanded or contracted in service of the public interest, and the Supreme Court has equated the public interest with the purposes or objectives of governing legislation. *Id.* at 672–78. In some contexts, courts have adjusted estoppel's reliance element when needed to promote fair play and protect weaker parties. T. Leigh Anenson, *The Triumph of Equity: Equitable Estoppel in Modern Litigation*, 27 REV. LITIG. 377, 389–98 (2008).

[103] Peter J. Wiedenbeck, *Unbelievable: ERISA's Broken Promise*, (Aug. 6, 2021). Washington University in St. Louis Legal Studies Research Paper No. 21-08-01, Available at SSRN: https://ssrn.com/abstract=3900735.

[104] Govoni v. Bricklayers, Masons & Plasterers Int'l Union, Local 5 Pension Fund, 732 F.2d 250, 252 (1st Cir. 1984). *See* Dale Joseph Gilsinger, Annotation, *Showing of Reliance on or Prejudice from Summary Plan Description (SPD) by Party Seeking to Enforce Terms of SPD in Preference to Terms of Plan*, 31 A.L.R. FED. 2d 363, § 5 & cmt. (2008 & Supp.) (noting that despite brevity and weakness of its analysis, *Govini* is frequently cited by courts both within and outside the First Circuit).

[105] *Id.*

[106] Aiken v. Policy Mgmt. Sys. Corp., 13 F.3d 138, 141 (4th Cir. 1993) (relying on *Govoni* and explicitly endorsing the disjunctive nature of the conditions); Chiles v. Ceridian Corp., 95 F.3d 1505, 1519 (10th Cir. 1996) (relying on *Aiken*); Godwin v. Sun Life Assur. Co. of Canada, 980 F.2d 323, 328 (5th Cir. 1992) *Cf.* Buce v. Allianz Life Ins. Co., 247 F.3d 1133, 1156 n.1 (11th Cir. 2001) (referring to the reliance or prejudice standard as a "somewhat cryptic requirement").

The Eighth Circuit also adheres to this standard, at least in cases involving a "faulty" SPD (one that does not contain all the information required by the statute and regulations). Palmisano v. Allina Health Systems, 190 F.3d 881, 887–88 (8th Cir. 1999). That position can likewise be traced back to *Govoni*. *See* Lee v. Union Electric Co., 789 F.2d 1303, 1308 (8th Cir. 1986) (dicta) (paraphrasing and citing *Govoni*).

Disclosure

Other courts have modified estoppel in ERISA cases in the other direction, by engrafting additional limitations on the doctrine's operation. Most prominent is a line of decisions restricting estoppel to situations in which the claimant can show, in addition to reasonable and detrimental reliance on a material misrepresentation, the presence of "extraordinary circumstances."[107] According to the Third Circuit, extraordinary circumstances "generally involve acts of bad faith on the part of the employer, attempts to actively conceal a significant change in the plan, or commission of fraud."[108] The Sixth Circuit does not insist on bad faith, but finds extraordinary circumstances if "the balance of equities strongly favors the application of estoppel."[109] The extraordinary circumstances condition was originally imposed in cases where the claimant sought to hold the administrator to representations made in communications *other* than the SPD. In that context it may be appropriate to limit relief to egregious circumstances, in order to maintain and promote the primacy of the SPD.[110] That concern is not implicated when participants rely to their injury on a mistaken SPD: the SPD, after all, was intended to provide an accessible, reliable foundation for workers' career and financial planning.[111] Nevertheless, in the Sixth Circuit the extraordinary circumstances limitation has carried over into estoppel claims founded on inaccurate SPDs.[112] The Ninth

---

[107] E.g., Mello v. Sara Lee Corp., 431 F.3d 440, 444–45 (5th Cir. 2005); Burstein v. Retirement Account Plan for Emps. of Allegheny Health Educ. & Research Found., 334 F.3d 365, 383 (3d Cir. 2003); *see also* Pisciotta v. Teledyne Indus., Inc., 91 F.3d 1326, 1331 (9th Cir. 1996); Vallone v. CAN Fin. Corp., 375 F.3d 623 (emphasizing "narrow scope" of ERISA estoppel and noting that only extreme circumstances justify such claims).

[108] Jordan v. Federal Express Corp., 116 F.3d 1005, 1011 (3d Cir.1997).

[109] Paul v. Detroit Edison Co. & Michigan Consol. Gas Co. Pension Plan, 642 F. App'x 588, 594 (6th Cir. 2016) (holding estoppel conditions satisfied where worker was given repeated written and oral assurances of the correctness of the projected amount of early retirement benefits, and would suffer substantial economic harm by reduction of pension and repayment of more than $17,000 of erroneous overpayments). Similarly, the Ninth Circuit has observed:
"Although we have not defined "extraordinary circumstances" in this context, courts have held that making "a promise that the defendant reasonably should have expected to induce action or forbearance on the plaintiff's part," Devlin v. Empire Blue Cross & Blue Shield, 274 F.3d 76, 86 (2d Cir.2001), as well as "conduct suggesting that [the employer] sought to profit at the expense of its employees," a "showing of repeated misrepresentations over time," or evidence "that plaintiffs are particularly vulnerable," Kurz v. Phila. Elec. Co., 96 F.3d 1544, 1553 (3d Cir.1996), can constitute extraordinary circumstances." Gabriel v. Alaska Elec. Pension Fund, 773 F.3d 945, 957 (9th Cir. 2014).

[110] *See infra* Chapter 3C.

[111] The "extraordinary circumstances" condition might arguably be appropriate, as a matter of policy, in a small subset of defective SPD cases. If the alleged SPD defect involves a mistaken implication (*not* the omission of a required warning), then to avoid incentivizing ever-more-lengthy and detailed SPDs (that is, to avoid undermining the summary nature of the document), perhaps relief should generally be denied. This category of cases is discussed below as an incomplete SPD of the material omission type.

[112] Pearce v. Chrysler Group LLC Pension Plan, 893 F.3d 339, 351 (6th Cir. 2018). The plaintiff argued that additional estoppel elements, including the extraordinary circumstances requirement, should not be applied to him because they had been developed for non-SPD communications, and

86   *Conduct Controls: Welfare and Pension Plans*

Circuit seems poised to make a similar hash of estoppel as applied to an SPD that contradicts the plan.[113]

Impulses to expand (reliance-or-prejudice) or contract (extraordinary circumstances) estoppel in the ERISA context are at once poorly reasoned and irreconcilable. In contrast, the Second Circuit developed a promising adaptation of traditional estoppel principles to the ERISA environment. After reviewing the confusion in the appellate courts, the Second Circuit rejected a rigid detrimental reliance requirement because it "imposes an insurmountable hardship on many plaintiffs," and "hardly advances the Congressional purpose of protecting the beneficiaries of ERISA plans by insuring that employees are fully and accurately apprised of their rights under the plan."[114] Concluding that the "consequences of an inaccurate SPD

> in an era when the Sixth Circuit held that the SPD's provisions controlled by contract if they were in conflict with the plan. *Id.* at 350. Admitting that this argument was logical, the court nevertheless found it foreclosed by circuit precedent applying those restrictive estoppel requirements in several cases decided after the Supreme Court decided *Amara*. *Id.* None of the four cited post-*Amara* Sixth Circuit cases, however, involved an inaccurate SPD. Rather than distinguishing them, the *Pearce* court apparently felt bound by the assertion in earlier opinions that the restrictive approach to estoppel applies whenever the plaintiff is attempting to invoke equitable estoppel to avoid unambiguous pension plan provisions.

[113] *See Gabriel*, 773 F.3d at 955–57, 958–61. Like the Sixth Circuit, the Ninth Circuit developed additional restrictions on estoppel claims based upon non-SPD communications: "to maintain a federal equitable estoppel claim in the ERISA context, the party asserting estoppel must not only meet the traditional equitable estoppel requirements, but must also allege: (1) extraordinary circumstances; (2) 'that the provisions of the plan at issue were ambiguous such that reasonable persons could disagree as to their meaning or effect'". *Id.* at 957 (quoting Spink v. Lockheed Corp., 125 F.3d 1257, 1262 (9th Cir.1997)). Also like the Sixth Circuit, pre-*Amara* the Ninth Circuit treated an inaccurate SPD as binding under a contract theory, without regard to estoppel or reliance. Bergt v. Retirement Plan for Pilots Employed by MarkAir, Inc., 293 F.3d 1139, 1143 (9th Cir. 2002) (deciding based on the purpose of the SPD to "follow the other courts that have held that the SPD is part of the ERISA plan", but "conclud[ing] that when the plan master document is more favorable to the employee than the SPD, and unambiguously allows for eligibility of an employee, it controls, despite contrary unambiguous provisions in the SPD", *id.* at 1145). Post-*Amara*, the insistence that estoppel can never be applied when "recovery on the claim would contradict written plan provisions", *Gabriel*, 773 F.3d at 956, implies that workers who reasonably rely to their detriment on an inaccurate SPD will be afforded no relief. Estoppel will be available only if the underlying unknown and undisclosed plan terms are ambiguous, and only in the face of extraordinary circumstances. It seems that in the wake of *Amara* the Ninth Circuit has not simply retreated from characterizing the SPD's terms as the core of the benefit contract, it has stripped the SPD of any special legal significance: for estoppel purposes; it is just another written communication that participants and beneficiaries should treat as suspect and unreliable.

[114] Burke v. Kodak Ret. Income Plan, 336 F.3d 103, 112 (2d Cir. 2003) (quoting Estate of Ritzer v. Nat'l Org. of Indus. Trade Unions Ins. Trust Fund Hosp., Med., Surgical Health Benefit, 822 F. Supp. 951, 955–56 (E.D.N.Y.1993)). The *Burke* court expressly declined to use "harsh common law principles to defeat employees' claims based on a federal law designed for their protection," 336 F.3d at 113–14. *See* Frommert v. Conkright, 433 F.3d 254, 267 (2d Cir. 2006) (applying likely harm standard as predicate for relief under ERISA § 204(h), 29 U.S.C. § 1054 (h) (2018), in cases of failure to provide adequate advance notice of a significant reduction in the rate of future benefit accrual).

Disclosure

must be placed on the employer," the court opted to require a showing "that a plan participant or beneficiary was *likely* to have been harmed as a result of a deficient SPD. Where a participant makes this initial showing, however, the employer may rebut it through evidence that the deficient SPD was in effect a harmless error."[115]

It was a challenge to the validity of this "likely harm" standard that led the Supreme Court to grant certiorari in *CIGNA Corp. v. Amara*.[116] During oral argument Justice Breyer suggested that the sensible way to proceed in a class action seeking redress under ERISA section 502(a)(3) for injuries allegedly due to misinformation would be to require the defendant to respond to plaintiffs' preliminary showing of likely harm by presenting evidence that particular class members were not injured by the faulty communication. Indeed, he speculated that the outcome of that burden-shifting approach would not differ much from enforcing the SPD as a contract under section 502(a)(1).[117] That "likely harm" might offer a policy-sensitive substitute for individualized proof of detrimental reliance on an inaccurate SPD has been forgotten in the wake of *Amara* – the opinion's sweeping endorsement of reformation and surcharge moved litigators and lower courts to pursue alternatives to an estoppel remedy that, as it then existed, was not well-adapted to many ERISA contexts.

2 The Self-Contradictory SPD

a Perceptible Conflicts

If, instead of contradicting the underlying plan documents, the SPD contradicts itself, courts generally refuse to impose liability, on the view that reliance is unjustified. If a reasonable participant's careful reading of the SPD alone reveals an inconsistency, further investigation would seem to be the prudent response. Faced with an obviously defective SPD, common sense would counsel participants to take additional steps to inform themselves, such as by calling the contradiction to the attention of the plan administrator or consulting the terms of the underlying plan

---

[115] 336 F.3d at 113 (emphasis in original). *See* Weinreb v. Hosp. for Joint Diseases Orthopaedic Inst., 404 F.3d 167, 171–72 (2d Cir. 2005) (following *Burke*, but finding presumption rebutted by actual knowledge of plan requirement).

[116] 563 U.S. 421, 425 (2011) ("We agreed to decide whether the District Court applied the correct legal standard, namely, a 'likely harm' standard, in determining that CIGNA's notice violations caused its employees sufficient injury to warrant legal relief.").

[117] Transcript of Oral Argument at 15–17, 23–24, CIGNA Corp. v. Amara, 563 U.S. 421 (2011) (No. 09-804). Defendant's counsel insisted that the equitable remedy for such misinformation lay in estoppel, and that relief requires plaintiff to present individualized proof of detrimental reliance. *Id.* at 17, 18, 24, 54–55. In addition, defendants' counsel suggested a very restrictive view of the evidence that would be sufficient to demonstrate detrimental reliance: proof that a participant who had decided to leave the company reacted to faulty information by continuing employment. *Id.* at 24. The Chief Justice responded skeptically to the assertion that each plan member must individually show injury and causation. *Id.* at 20.

documents. Failure to do so would defeat an estoppel claim, for want of reasonable reliance. Taking the initiative to investigate, in contrast, advances collaboration and promotes rapid identification and correction of communication gaffes.

Such self-help is feasible only in instances where the SPD contradiction is readily apparent to the workers, i.e., where apparent internal conflicts cry out for correction or further explanation. Many SPD discrepancies, however, are imperceptible ex ante to the average plan participant. ERISA policies counsel greater receptivity to estoppel claims founded upon apparent promises belied by imperceptible (or latent) internal conflicts.

The self-contradictory SPD problem received a great deal of attention during the 1990s and early 2000s in a series of cases involving SPDs that seemingly promised no-cost, life-long retiree health care, but also reserved to the employer the unrestricted right to amend or terminate the plan.[118] ERISA does not require vesting of welfare benefits,[119] and retiree health care is classified as a welfare benefit, even though the plan provides valuable long-term deferred compensation. The employer is free, however, to make a vesting commitment.[120] The employer may, as a matter of contract, unconditionally obligate itself to provide future welfare benefits, or it can extend such benefits subject to any conditions or limitations it chooses.[121] Employers providing retiree health care plans typically condition eligibility for benefits on retirement at specified ages, and may require completion of an extended period of service. In addition, the plan documents invariably reserve the right to

---

[118] *E.g.*, Vallone v. CNA Fin. Corp., 375 F.3d 623 (7th Cir. 2004); Sprague v. Gen. Motors Corp., 133 F.3d 388, 403 (6th Cir. 1998) (*Sprague V*) (en banc); Chiles v. Ceridian Corp., 95 F.3d 1505 (10th Cir. 1996); In re Unisys Corp. Retiree Med. Benefit "ERISA" Litig., 58 F.3d 896 (3d Cir. 1995); Jensen v. SIPCO, Inc., 38 F.3d 945 (8th Cir. 1994). *See also* Calogera Abbruscato v. Empire Blue Cross & Blue Shield, 274 F.3d 90 (2d Cir. 2001) (life insurance benefits).

[119] ERISA §§ 201(1), 203(a) 29 U.S.C. §§ 1051(1), 1053(a) (2018).

[120] *E.g.*, Kelly v. Honeywell Int'l, Inc., 933 F.3d 173 (2d Cir. 2019) (retiree medical benefits vested by contract); Jensen v. SIPCO, Inc., 38 F.3d at 951–52 (same); Alexander v. Primerica Holdings, Inc., 967 F.2d 90, 95 (3d Cir. 1992); In re White Farm Equip. Co., 788 F.2d 1186, 1193 (6th Cir. 1986) ("The parties may themselves set out by agreement or by private design, as set out in plan documents, whether retiree welfare benefits vest, or whether they may be terminated.").

In M & G Polymers USA, LLC v. Tackett, 574 U.S. 427 (2015), the Supreme Court held that the decision whether a collective bargaining agreement establishing a retiree health care plan includes a commitment to vesting benefits must be made "according to ordinary principles of contract law," *id.* at 435. A prominent scholar concluded that the suggested interpretive approach is actually quite misguided from a contract law perspective. Robert A. Hillman, *The Supreme Court's Application of "Ordinary Contract Principles" to the Issue of the Duration of Retiree Healthcare Benefits: Perpetuating the Interpretation/Gap-Filling Quagmire*, 32 A.B.A. J. Lab. & Emp. L. 299 (2017). The *Tackett* majority's approach could be understood as imposing a clear statement rule to support the vesting of welfare benefits – in effect, a presumption against vesting. *See* Peter J. Wiedenbeck, *Untrustworthy: ERISA's Eroded Fiduciary Law*, 58 Wm. & Mary L. Rev. 1007, 1058–63 (2018).

[121] The highly conditional – and typically evanescent – character of promised welfare benefits is explained in Wiedenbeck, *supra* Chapter 3 note 120, at 1044–51.

Disclosure 89

amend or terminate the plan, for ERISA requires every employee benefit plan to contain a procedure for amending the plan.[122] Read broadly, such a reservation-of-rights clause imposes a crucial additional condition on eligibility for benefits: the plan sponsor must not alter or disavow its commitment before the health care is sought. The real issue in the retiree health plan cutback cases is how broadly *should* such a reservation-of-rights clause be read?

The matter is noncontroversial if the SPD clearly warns that the employer is obligated to provide retiree health care for the time being only, and although the employer expects to continue the program, it may be altered or discontinued at any time for any reason. Plan sponsors are seldom so forthright, however, for they have an interest in obtaining the maximum advantage from benefit programs, which requires that workers place a high value on them. To obtain that advantage (typically in the form of reduced worker turnover or lower current compensation), employers want to tout the benefits of the program, and lifetime, no-cost health care coverage is a considerable benefit.

b Imperceptible Conflicts

This is all well and good, for benefit plans are voluntary programs that must serve the employer's interest as well as the interests of the participants and beneficiaries.[123] But if the touting appears in the SPD itself, there is cause for concern. And if the glowing description crosses the line to puffing or deliberate deception – as where the SPD makes strong representations as to the future continuance of the program (explicit promises of lifetime medical care, for instance), with the only hint that benefits could be reduced or employee costs increased appearing as an inconspicuous statement concerning generic amendment authority located in a remote part of the document – then that concern should turn to alarm.[124]

---

[122] ERISA § 402(b)(3), 29 U.S.C. § 1102(b)(3) (2018).

[123] For discussion of ERISA's policy of preserving employer autonomy, see *supra* Chapter 1C; Daniel Fischel & John H. Langbein, *ERISA's Fundamental Contradiction: The Exclusive Benefit Rule*, 55 U. Chi. L. Rev. 1105 (1988); Wiedenbeck, *supra* Chapter 3 note 120, at 1018–21.

[124] *See* James F. Stratman, *Contract Disclaimers in ERISA Summary Plan Documents: A Deceptive Practice?*, 10 Indus. Rel. L.J. 350, 364 (1988) (finding 85 percent of the subjects in an experiment on SPD comprehension did not even notice an SPD disclaimer clause printed in a smaller typeface near the end of the document); *Benefit Eligibility is Misunderstood by Plan Participants, GAO Report Says*, 14 Pens. Rep. (BNA) 1287 (1987) ("GAO report suggested that many SPDs may be too technical for workers to fully comprehend"). The problem examined here arises only when the SPD is internally inconsistent, and its resolution depends upon the special status of the plan summary. Where the promise of continued benefits does not appear in the SPD, but is made through other oral or written communications, participants may be similarly misled, but the problem should be analyzed in terms of the binding effect of informal communications. *See infra* Chapter 3C.

Two circuits have squarely held that a reservation-of-rights clause in the SPD insulates the plan sponsor from liability for lifetime benefits promised elsewhere in the SPD. *In re Unisys Corporation Retiree Medical Benefit "ERISA" Litigation*[125] involved an SPD that stated, "When you retire ... the comprehensive medical expense benefits then in force for you and your eligible dependents under this plan will be continued for the rest of your life," with a reservation-of-rights clause in another location. The Third Circuit dismissed the retirees' estoppel claim "because it cannot be reconciled with the unqualified reservation of rights clauses in the plan."[126] Estoppel generally requires reasonable or justifiable reliance, and it is foolish to credit either of two contradictory statements. The Sixth Circuit, which then (pre-*Amara*) enforced the SPD as a matter of contract, also refused relief, holding that an unambiguous reservation-of-rights clause implicitly qualifies representations that the program will be maintained as is in the future.[127] Under either approach, the message is, let the participant beware.[128]

Other courts have criticized these decisions in dicta.[129] The Eighth Circuit, for example, held that an internal SPD conflict between a promise of benefit continuation and reserved amendment rights makes the benefit contract ambiguous, allowing resort to extrinsic evidence to resolve the confusion, and preventing summary judgment for the employer.[130]

---

[125] 58 F.3d 896 (3d Cir. 1995).

[126] *Id.* at 907 (3d Cir. 1995). *Unisys*, which is founded on estoppel principles, predates *Burstein v. Retirement Account Plan for Employees of Allegheny Health Education & Research Foundation*, 334 F.3d 365 (3d Cir. 2003), in which the Third Circuit repudiated estoppel in the inaccurate SPD context. In the aftermath of CIGNA Corp. v. Amara, 563 U.S. 421 (2011), holding that the SPD is not the plan and does not govern as a matter of contract, the *Unisys* estoppel approach is presumably reinstated.

[127] Sprague v. Gen. Motors Corp., 133 F.3d at 400–01.

[128] Several other decisions are routinely cited for the proposition that a reservation-of-rights clause overrides a promise of lifetime benefits. In those cases, however, the vesting language appeared in informal communications, not in the SPD. Hughes v. 3M Retiree Med. Plan, 281 F.3d 786 (8th Cir. 2002); Gable v. Sweetheart Cup Co., 35 F.3d 851 (4th Cir. 1994); Alday v. Container Corp. of Am., 906 F.2d 660 (11th Cir. 1990).

[129] Diehl v. Twin Disc, Inc., 102 F.3d 301, 307 (7th Cir. 1996) (calling *Unisys* a "forced construction" and "interpretive gymnastics"); Stearns v. NCR Corp., 97 F. Supp. 2d 954, 963 (D. Minn. 2000) ("[T]he *Sprague* decision in effect gives [employers] carte blanche license to offer inducements to employees to waive their rights and then to renege on their promises after the employees have irrevocably done so. Nothing in ERISA requires courts to sanction such an unfair result."), *rev'd*, 297 F.3d 706, 712 (8th Cir. 2002) (holding that "there must be an affirmative indication of vesting in the plan documents to overcome an unambiguous reservation of rights").

[130] Barker v. Ceridian Corp., 122 F.3d 628, 638 (8th Cir. 1997). *See also* Am. Fed'n of Grain Millers v. Int'l Multifoods Corp., 116 F.3d 976, 981 (2d Cir. 1997) ("In this Circuit, to reach a trier of fact, an employee does not have to 'point to unambiguous language to support [a] claim. It is enough [to] point to written language capable of reasonably being interpreted as creating a promise on the part of [the employer] to vest [the recipient's] ... benefits.'").

Disclosure 91

Should notice of retained amendment authority negate an SPD's apparent promise of lifetime benefits? Three important considerations suggest that it should not.

First, the contradiction in the SPD, however apparent to judges and lawyers, is seldom obvious to – and never highlighted for – participants. It is not as if one paragraph of the summary flatly announces "X" while the following paragraph declares "*not* X." Instead, the summary typically emphasizes an apparently unequivocal benefit promise, while another section of the document – usually at the end, and often grippingly labeled "Regulatory Notices" or "General Provisions" – includes a boilerplate incantation of the sponsor's retained right to modify or terminate. Hence the inconsistency between representations concerning the value of the plan in the future and a reserved power to pull the plug has very low salience and may be imperceptible to the average plan participant.[131] Indeed, it may be practically invisible to any non-lawyer reader, especially if the SPD is accompanied by other employer representations touting generous plan benefits.

Second, focusing on the conscientiousness (or skepticism) of the participant overlooks ERISA's policies. An SPD containing such a hidden ambiguity is defective: it fails to "reasonably apprise [] participants and beneficiaries of their rights and obligations under the plan."[132] It accordingly seems odd to say that participants must bear an additional burden (the costs of investigation or the risks of failing to investigate) because the administrator has violated ERISA. Instead of forcing participants to look behind the SPD when faced with inconsistent terms, they could be permitted to rely on a reasonable interpretation of the document. A reservation-of-rights clause can be read, as some courts do, to qualify representations that the program will be maintained as is in the future; alternatively, the lifetime benefit representations can be understood as creating exceptions to the sponsor's retained amendment authority

---

[131] The leading understandability case, King v. Blue Cross and Blue Shield of Illinois, 871 F.3d 730 (9th Cir. 2017), entailed failure to effectually warn. *See infra* Chapter 3 notes 150–151 and accompanying text. Alternatively, *King* can be understood to involve a contradiction imperceptible to the participant. Unlike *Sprague* and the lifetime healthcare cases, the contradiction in *King* was not deliberate.

[132] ERISA § 102(a)(1), 29 U.S.C. § 1022(a)(1) (2018). An SPD which apparently promises ongoing benefits must do more than include a boilerplate recitation of retained amendment authority: "Any description of exceptions, limitations, reductions, and other restrictions of plan benefits shall not be minimized, rendered obscure or otherwise made to appear unimportant." 29 C.F.R. § 2520.102-2(b) (2002). If the sponsor retains unconditional authority to terminate a welfare plan but the SPD makes representations concerning future benefits, it must clearly disabuse workers of the notion that they have legally enforceable rights to continued coverage or benefits. *See* 29 C.F.R. § 2520.102-3(*l*) (2022) (both pension and welfare plan SPDs must contain "a statement clearly identifying circumstances which may result in ... loss, forfeiture ... of any benefits that a participant or beneficiary might otherwise reasonably expect the plan to provide on the basis of the [SPD's] description of benefits"). For a discussion of failure to warn liability, see *infra* Chapter 3 notes 149–163 and accompanying text.

Conduct Controls: Welfare and Pension Plans

(reservation of rights).[133] Where the covert conflict in the SPD appears in the context of an employer campaign promoting the promise of lifetime benefits, the latter accommodation seems far the more natural reading.

Finally, consider the employer's conduct and its consequences. Avoiding a self-contradictory SPD is a straightforward task – it requires only a careful review of the summary description by a well-informed plan official or experienced professional. The minimal cost of prevention raises a strong inference that any such latent repugnancy is the product of a deliberate effort to mislead. Where the SPD contradicts plan documents, employers are not allowed to expressly disclaim inadvertent misstatements;[134] reading a reservation-of-rights clause broadly permits employers to implicitly disavow deceit and profit by inducing workers to overvalue benefit plans. Workers presented with an equivocal SPD may use it or ignore it, but either way society bears the cost of suboptimal career and financial planning.[135] Alternatively, workers may investigate further, which is duplicative and wasteful.[136]

When viewed in this light, an SPD that promises lifetime benefits but also contains an unqualified reservation of amendment authority is at best an attractive nuisance, if not a guileful snare. Attention to the origin of the contradiction, its lack of salience to the average plan participant, and the relative costs that the employer and workers would have to incur to avoid harm, shows that ERISA's policies call for a remedy when the sponsor reneges on the commitment to future benefits. Does ERISA condone such a bait and switch? Or do "equitable principles, as modified by the obligations and injuries identified by ERISA itself" authorize relief?[137]

---

[133] This argument was made explicit in *Unisys*: "According to the retirees, the plans were ambiguous because they were susceptible to either of two interpretations: the retirees' interpretation that the lifetime language limited the scope of the reservations of rights, or the company's interpretation that the reservation of rights limited the lifetime language." *Unisys*, 58 F.3d at 903. The opinion concludes, without explanation, that where a reservation-of-rights clause is "broad and unequivocal, it will prevail over a promise of lifetime benefits." *Id.* at 904 n.11. That proposition is at odds with the principle of contract interpretation declaring that "[w]here there is an inconsistency between general provisions and specific provisions, the specific provisions ordinarily qualify the meaning of the general provisions." RESTATEMENT OF CONTRACTS § 236(c) (1932); *see* RESTATEMENT (SECOND) OF CONTRACTS § 203(c) & cmt. e (1981).

  A distinction might plausibly be drawn between a reservation-of-rights clause that contains explicit overriding language (like "notwithstanding anything in this document to the contrary") and one that does not, because such overriding language technically eliminates the contradiction. But here again the role of the SPD indicates that the presence of an ambiguity should be determined from the viewpoint of a reasonable participant, not a businessperson, lawyer, or judge.

[134] *See supra* Chapter 3 note 91 and accompanying text.

[135] Imposition of liability in this context works as an anti-fraud rule, allowing workers to distinguish plan quality and firms to compete on the basis of benefit packages, thereby avoiding unravelling of the labor market. *See infra* Chapter 3 notes 204–06 and accompanying text.

[136] *See* EASTERBROOK & FISCHEL, *supra* Chapter 3 note 97, at 280–81, 287 (disclosure by the firm prevents redundant production of information), 290–92 (free-rider and standardization problems support mandatory disclosure).

[137] CIGNA Corp. v. Amara, 563 U.S. 421, 445 (2011).

Disclosure 93

The *Amara* majority opinion telegraphs an affirmative answer: equitable relief should be forthcoming in cases involving latent SPD contradictions, and without individualized proof of detrimental reliance, because the conditions for plan reformation would be satisfied. Contract reformation, as observed earlier, is authorized where one party is mistaken about the terms of the undertaking and the other commits fraud or inequitable conduct.[138] That aptly describes the situation in which an SPD promises future health or welfare benefits but inconspicuously negates that commitment by inclusion of a reservation-of-rights clause. The contradiction, being undetectable by the average plan participant, causes mistaken belief in future entitlement, and even if the plan administrator did not craft a deliberately misleading SPD (fraudulent concealment), the administrator breached his fiduciary duty to warn (negligent concealment, or "constructive fraud").[139] Reformation could be ordered in equity, the *Amara* Court noted, even in circumstances where the complaining party (here, mistaken plan members) "was negligent in not realizing its mistake."[140]

The surcharge remedy might also be available.[141] In particular, *Amara* suggested that actual harm might be adequately established for plan participants generally even those who did not consult or even see the faulty SPD or SMM – if circumstances indicate that the terms of the summary documents were a topic of general workforce interest and discussion.[142] The susceptibility of the surcharge remedy to

[138] *See supra* Chapter 3 notes 69–80 and accompanying text.

[139] 3 POMEROY, *supra* Chapter 3 note 87, at §§ 900–02 (fraudulent concealment), 943, 955, 956 (constructive fraud by fiduciary). *See Amara*, 563 U.S. at 437 (plan administrator a "trustee-like fiduciary"), 439 (emphasizing that suit brought against plan fiduciary supports resort to equitable remedies); *see also* RESTATEMENT (SECOND) OF TORTS § 551(1) (1977), which provides liability for nondisclosure as follows:

"One who fails to disclose to another a fact that he knows may justifiably induce the other to act or refrain from acting in a business transaction is subject to the same liability to the other as though he had represented the nonexistence of the matter that he has failed to disclose, if, but only if, he is under a duty to the other to exercise reasonable care to disclose the matter in question."

A fiduciary relationship between the parties establishes such a duty. *Id.* § 551(2).

[140] 563 U.S. at 443 (citing 3 POMEROY, *supra* Chapter 3 note 87, at § 856b). *See also* 3 POMEROY, *supra* Chapter 3 note 87, at §§ 955–56b (transaction between persons in fiduciary relationship presumptively invalid absent full and fair explanation by fiduciary, and in some cases presumption can be overcome only by showing that the beneficiary acted upon independent advice). It is noteworthy that this position is also reflected in the elements of the common law tort of deceit. The recipient of a fraudulent misrepresentation can recover for pecuniary loss if he justifiably relies on the falsehood, but he "is justified in relying upon its truth, although he might have ascertained the falsity of the representation had he made an investigation." RESTATEMENT (SECOND) OF TORTS §§ 537, 540 (1977).

[141] 563 U.S. at 444.

[142] *Id.* During oral argument in *Amara* Justice Kagan observed:

"Very few people read their SPDs, but you only need one person to read the SPD to come in and say, by the way, folks, 21,000 of us are not getting our retirement benefits for the next few years, and within a day every employee in the workplace is going to know about that." Transcript of Oral Argument at 55, CIGNA Corp. v. Amara 563 U.S. 421 (2011) (No. 09-804).

94 *Conduct Controls: Welfare and Pension Plans*

class-based resolution, however, remains an unsettled question.[143] *Amara's* remedial discussion sent a message that in 2011 the Court stood ready to disavow the notion that *Mertens* v. *Hewitt Associates* excludes all monetary awards from the category of equitable relief.[144] Subsequently, the Court has since distanced itself from the view that *Amara* "all but overrul[es] *Mertens*."[145] An increasingly pro-business majority may not be ready to countenance a proliferation of class actions seeking large pecuniary awards against major corporate employers based on ERISA disclosure violations.

3 *The Incomplete SPD*

The SPD controls where it flatly contradicts the underlying plan documents. Where the SPD is silent on an issue that the plan documents address, more nuanced analysis is required.

Claims faulting an SPD for communicating insufficient information are of two sorts. Some cases assert that the summary is defective because it lacks the required description of all "circumstances which may result in disqualification, ineligibility, or denial or loss of benefits."[146] This failure-to-warn characterization invites comparisons to hidden defects and dangerous consumer products. Alternatively, the complaint may contend that participants or beneficiaries were led astray because the SPD was not "sufficiently ... comprehensive to reasonably apprise such participants and beneficiaries of their rights and obligations under the plan."[147] Here the assertion is that the summary, being too abbreviated, implied that benefits would be available in circumstances not authorized by the plan. This portrayal candidly laments that the SPD is a *summary* – or rather, that it is *too* summary. By inviting review of the balance struck between utility and reliability, this framing exposes the tension inherent in the SPD formulation. Acknowledged or not, incomplete SPD

---

[143] *See supra* Chapter 3 notes 68, 86, and accompanying text.

[144] 508 U.S. 248 (1993). The *Amara* Court pointedly distinguished *Mertens* as a claim against a non-fiduciary. 563 U.S. at 439 ("plaintiff [in *Mertens*] sought 'nothing other than compensatory damages' against a nonfiduciary" while *Amara* "concerns a suit by a beneficiary against a plan fiduciary"). This undermining of *Mertens* may have provoked the separate opinion of Justice Scalia, who authored the Courts' opinion in *Mertens*. *See generally* John H. Langbein, *What ERISA Means by "Equitable": The Supreme Court's Trail of Error in Russell, Mertens, and* Great-West, 103 COLUM. L. REV. 1317 (2003).

[145] Montanile v. Board of Trustees of the National Elevator Indus. Health Benefit Plan, 136 S. Ct. 651, 660 & n.3 (2016) (citing US Airways, Inc. v. McCutcheon, 569 U.S. 88, 94–95 (2013)) (asserting that "our interpretation of 'equitable relief' in *Mertens, Great-West,* and Sereboff v. Mid Atlantic Medical Services, Inc., 547 U.S. 356 (2006), remains unchanged").

[146] ERISA § 102(b), 29 U.S.C. § 1022(b) (2018); *see* 29 C.F.R. § 2520.102-3(*l*) (2022) (SPD must "clearly identify[]" such disqualifying circumstances); *id.* -3(m) (required warning of limits of PBGC guarantee of pension plan benefits).

[147] ERISA § 102(a), 29 U.S.C. § 1022(a) (2018); *see* 29 C.F.R. § 2520.102-2(a), (b) (2022).

Disclosure

claims implicate the goal of *optimal* disclosure.[148] If not handled sensitively, this category of disclosure litigation threatens to hamper career and financial planning rather than improve it.

The planning function demands trade-offs between completeness and usability. Abridgment and simplified expression make information accessible, but often create the impression that general explanations and illustrations are not subject to qualification or exceptions in special circumstances. In contrast, excessive detail inhibits utilization and obscures the principal features, conditions, and limitations of the benefit plan. Congress meant the SPD to get this central trade-off right.

SPD omissions run the gamut. Some foreseeably impose widespread and acute injury, and these failure-to-warn cases, like personal injuries from defective products, demand redress. In other instances a plaintiff in special circumstances might suffer avoidable harm for want of information, but the rest of the SPD audience – typical participants and beneficiaries – could be dissuaded by length and complexity from using an expanded document. The palpably injured plaintiff presents a sympathetic claim, while the average worker's interest in getting a usable synopsis goes unrepresented before the court. In such cases the temptation to impose liability — the impetus to conclude that the SPD should have said more – ought to be resisted. At this end of the spectrum allowances must be made for the summary function of the SPD: to preserve utility, many omissions should be treated as necessary or acceptable. These two categories, we shall see, blend into one another. Drawing a workable line between them that serves ERISA's policies presents a challenge.

a Failure to Warn

It must be emphasized that failure to warn of potential hazards (circumstances that may cause disqualification, ineligibility, denial or loss of benefits) really means failure to *effectually* warn. In line with ERISA's planning function, required SPD warnings must be written to be understood by average plan participants. Subtle caveats discernible by lawyers or judges are insufficient: economic efficiency demands that the intended audience be alerted to possible pitfalls.[149]

This principle is illustrated by *King v. Blue Cross and Blue Shield of Illinois*.[150] There, a summary of material modifications (SMM, functionally an SPD amendment) was issued to disclose health plan alterations that were made to comply with the Affordable Care Act. The SMM reported the elimination of lifetime benefit caps in a way that made it appear that the change applied not just to the plan for active employees, but also to the company's retiree health plan (which it did not). The Ninth Circuit concluded that the SMM violated ERISA's disclosure requirements because it "does not reasonably apprise the average plan participant that the lifetime

---

[148] *See supra* Chapter 3 notes 47–51 and accompanying text.
[149] See the discussion of imperceptible SPD contradictions, *supra* Chapter 3B2b.
[150] 871 F.3d 730 (9th Cir. 2017).

Conduct Controls: Welfare and Pension Plans

benefit maximum continues to apply to the Retiree Plan."[151] Similarly, *Koehler v. Aetna Health, Inc.* involved a health maintenance organization (HMO) SPD that required approval for out-of-network referrals, but did not clearly disclose that *advance* authorization for the services at issue was also required.[152] The Fifth Circuit found the SPD ambiguous concerning whether preapproval was required for coverage and held that ERISA's understandability standard requires that ambiguities *in the SPD* be resolved in favor of participants and beneficiaries, even if the plan administrator is expressly given discretion to interpret *the plan*.[153] And in *Frommert v. Conkright*, the Second Circuit (after remand from the Supreme Court) held that an SPD which did not explain the amount of a pension offset triggered by a previous lump sum distribution failed to warn of "circumstances which may result in disqualification, ineligibility, or denial or loss of benefits," and concluded that equitable relief under ERISA § 502(a)(3) would be warranted if plaintiffs could establish the standard of harm required by the equitable remedy they seek.[154]

The failures to warn in *King, Koehler*, and *Frommert* resulted from inattention to clarity or simple oversight. Sometimes, failure to warn is deliberate, proceeding from a calculatedly misleading SPD.

CIGNA Corp. v. Amara[155] was essentially a deliberate failure-to-warn case. The conversion of CIGNA's traditional defined benefit pension plan to a cash balance plan was accomplished by freezing each active participant's accrued benefit under the traditional pension plan and instituting a notional account, with an initial balance determined by reference to the actuarial present value of the worker's accrued pension benefit, to which compensation and interest credits would be added each year following conversion. Upon separation from service the plan provided that the outgoing employee would receive the more valuable of her accrued benefit under the frozen pension plan and the amount indicated by her cash balance account. CIGNA failed to reveal, however, that the manner in which the initial balance to workers' notional accounts was determined would in many cases cause the frozen accrued benefit under the traditional pension plan to exceed the cash balance account for several years after the switch, despite the fact that

---

[151] 871 F.3d at 740. *Accord* Meguerditchian v. Aetna Life Ins. Co., 999 F. Supp. 2d 1180, 1188 (C.D. Cal. 2014), *aff'd*, 648 F. App'x 605 (9th Cir. 2016) (holding short-term disability plan SPD not understandable where 60-day period for filing notice of disability was defined in terms of absence from work, but employer maintained mandatory 90-day temporary part-time return to work program); Veilleux v. Atochem N. Am., Inc., 929 F.2d 74, 76 (2d Cir. 1991) (holding SPD of severance pay plan inadequate where explanation that employees transferred to new employer upon sale of their division were not eligible for benefits appeared under the heading "Leaves of Absence" and within the "Maternity" subsection).

[152] 683 F.3d 182 (5th Cir. 2012).

[153] *Id.* at 187–89 (citing Rhorer v. Raytheon Eng'rs & Constructors, Inc., 181 F.3d 634, 642 (5th Cir. 1999)).

[154] 738 F.3d 522, 532–34 (2d Cir. 2013) (alternative holding).

[155] 563 U.S. 421 (2011).

Disclosure

97

compensation and interest credits were being added to the notional account each year. The transition rules caused many participants who continued to work for the company to derive no increase in their accumulated retirement savings despite performing several additional years of service after the new plan was instituted. In essence, this meant a catch-up period was required before the cash balance account would actually exceed the value of the frozen pension.[156] This undisclosed suspension of benefit accrual – which is functionally identical to a period of ineligibility for earning additional retirement benefits – conveniently sidestepped controversy and "avoided any significant negative reaction from employees."[157] That, of course, was because employees were left entirely unaware of the true consequences of the change. Workers did not know that if they took a job with comparable pay at another company, and if their new employer provided retirement plan coverage, then they would actually have obtained increased compensation. In substance, CIGNA had temporarily and covertly barred them from active participation.

The distinction between deliberate and inadvertent failures to warn – between breaches of the plan administrator's fiduciary duties of loyalty and care, respectively – could be relevant in determining the availability of relief. As explained earlier, plan reformation may constitute appropriate equitable relief in circumstances where fraud or inequitable conduct causes workers to misunderstand the employer's benefit commitment.[158] An SPD that is carefully crafted to omit or obscure notification of hazards to benefit entitlement fits this mold exactly, and in fact a class-wide remedy of plan reformation was ordered in *Amara* and like cases.[159] Where plan reformation is authorized, the equitable relief is accompanied by an order to pay benefits according to the terms of the plan as so reformed – disregarding or excising the hidden defect.[160]

Where the failure to warn is inadvertent an additional obstacle may hinder monetary remedy. Recall that silence supports equitable estoppel where there is a duty to speak, hence reliance on an SPD's failure to communicate a required

---

[156] *Id.* at 429–31.

[157] Amara v. CIGNA Corp. (*Amara II*), 775 F.3d 510, 530–31 (2d Cir. 2014). *Accord* Osberg v. Foot Locker, Inc., 862 F.3d 198, 202–05 (2d Cir. 2017). *See also* Nolan v. Detroit Edison Co., 991 F.3d 697, 712–15 (6th Cir. 2021) (refusing to dismiss claim brought by retiree, who had been employed as a financial analyst, that benefit accrual suspension following cash balance plan conversion was not described in a manner understandable to the average plan participant).

[158] *See supra* Chapter 3 notes 69–80 and accompanying text.

[159] *Amara II*, 775 F.3d at 531; *Osberg*, 862 F.3d at 213 (class-wide mistake demonstrated by clear and convincing evidence where "'defendants made uniform misrepresentations about an agreement's contents and have undertaken efforts to conceal its effect'", quoting *Amara II*, 775 F.3d at 529).

[160] *See* ERISA § 502(a)(1)(B), 29 U.S.C. § 1132(a)(1)(B) (2018) (claim for benefits includes suit by a participant or beneficiary "to enforce his rights under the terms of the plan, or to clarify his rights to future benefits under the terms of the plan").

Conduct Controls: Welfare and Pension Plans

warning is justified.[161] The difficulty lies in proof of reliance – many participants and beneficiaries impacted by the hidden defect will lack independent evidence that they would have acted differently had the danger been disclosed. If individualized objective proof is demanded, many plan members *actually* deceived by a missing warning will not receive redress for their injuries, and class-wide relief will be unavailable.[162] Such widespread under-enforcement of disclosure standards would undermine career and financial planning, and attainment of ERISA's economic efficiency goal. This suggests that inadvertent failure to warn may be a domain in which the federal courts ought to take a flexible approach to traditional equity norms and remedial limitations.[163] Where circumstances indicate a high probability that an omitted warning was material to a substantial segment of the workforce, that probability should be accepted as a substitute for individualized proof of causation. Such a salience-based categorical substitute for individualized proof of reliance – the elaboration of ERISA estoppel standards crafted to be responsive to statutory policy – would support class-wide relief.

b Acceptable Omissions

If instead of failing to warn of potential pitfalls, the SPD implies that benefits will be available more broadly than plan terms actually authorize, different considerations come into play. *Mattias v. Computer Sciences Corporation* illustrates the problem.[164] *Mattias* involved a plan that provided partial disability benefits. The plan document defined partial disability to require that the employee be unable to perform substantial duties of her regular occupation and actually be employed in her regular occupation on a partial or part-time basis. The SPD used, but did not define, the term "partial disability." The district court recognized that "[t]he issue in this case is how a court should interpret an ERISA plan where the SPD uses words with relatively broad definitions, and the Plan Documents contain a more restricted limiting definition of those words."[165] Observing that there were "two doctrines in tension," the court attempted to reconcile them.

> First, where an SPD and the Plan Documents contradict or conflict with each other, the SPD controls. The policy rationale for this rule is that the ERISA statute contemplates that employees will depend on the SPD, and if the Plan Documents are allowed to supersede, then the SPD is useless.

---

[161] See *supra* Chapter 3 notes 92–94 and accompanying text.

[162] See *supra* Chapter 3 notes 96–99 and accompanying text.

[163] See *supra* Chapter 3 notes 100–102 and accompanying text.

[164] 34 F. Supp. 2d 120 (*Mattias I*), *rev'd on other grounds*, 50 F. Supp. 2d 113 (D.R.I. 1999) (concluding that plaintiff failed to prove significant reliance on or possible prejudice flowing from SPD, as required to recover in First Circuit) (*Mattias II*).

[165] *Mattias I*, 34 F. Supp. 2d at 125.

Disclosure

Second, where an SPD is silent on an issue, the Plan Documents control. The policy rationale for this view is that if silence in the SPD were enough to trump an underlying plan, then SPDs would mushroom in size and complexity until they mirrored the Plan Documents.

At the extremes, these two doctrines work. This Court would have no difficulty applying them if the CSC Summary had made no mention of partial disability coverage or if the CSC Summary included a detailed definition of "partial disability" that conflicted with the CSC Plan. However this case occupies the swath where neither rule controls perfectly and where the two policies are in tension, namely where an SPD uses a term and then the Plan Documents define that term. The [CSC] Summary says that partial disability benefits are available, and the [CSC] Plan defines "partial disability." Using merely common sense, it is not obvious that this situation is either a "conflict" or "silence" on the issue of partial disability benefits.[166]

In light of the language and policy of ERISA, the court rejected the view that a conflict exists only if both the plan and the SPD explicitly define a term and those definitions conflict. Instead, it adopted a common-meaning rule, concluding that "conflict occurs where an SPD uses a term and the Plan Documents define it in a fashion inconsistently with the term's common meaning."[167] Because partial disability is ordinarily understood to mean an incapacitating condition that keeps an employee out of her job, but does not prevent her from working in any job, the court refused to enforce the plan's undisclosed part-time work requirement.[168]

As *Mattias* illustrates, the dichotomy between contradiction and silence is overly simplistic. The court treated the undisclosed part-time work requirement as in conflict with the plain meaning of "partial disability," a term used without definition in the SPD. From that perspective *Mattias* is another inaccurate SPD case. Alternatively, *Mattias* can be seen as a failure-to-warn case. Ordinary understanding of the term "partial disability" in the SPD created a reasonable implication of

---

[166] *Id.* (citations omitted).

[167] *Id.* at 126. The opinion cautions that "There would be no conflict where a word has no common meaning or where it would be unreasonable for a plan member to rely thereon. That would include where an SPD explicitly refers to a definition in the Plan Documents, for example, by noting that the specific term was used as defined by the Plan Documents." *Id.* at 127.

[168] *Id.* Similarly, in Heady v. Dawn Food Products, Inc., No. 3:03CV-26-H, 2003 U.S. Dist. LEXIS 21634 (W.D. Ky. Nov. 25, 2003), benefit eligibility under a long-term disability plan changed after 24 months from inability to perform one or more essential duties of the employee's previous occupation to the inability to perform essential duties of *any* occupation. The SPD included the former, more liberal definition of disability, but failed to indicate that after two years a more stringent test applied. The court noted that "a fine line can separate differences created by an omission and those created by a conflict." *Heady*, at *7. While the SPD technically omitted the stricter eligibility condition, the court recognized that participants had no reason to believe the SPD's definition was incomplete. Accordingly, the defect was characterized as a case of conflict rather than silence, and the court held that the SPD controls. *Id.* at *7–*8.

coverage; not flagging the plan's idiosyncratic part-time work condition hid the circumstances that triggered ineligibility for benefits. From either standpoint, *Mattias* concerns the weight to be accorded impressions generated by the SPD's abbreviated explanation.

Abbreviated explanation is the crux of the matter. To provide workers the tools needed for career and financial planning the SPD must be understandable to the average plan participant, which requires simplification and distillation. The objective of the SPD, as emphasized earlier, is *optimal disclosure*, not full disclosure.[169] Rank and file workers will not research, sift, and analyze an avalanche of detailed technical information – instead they will quite rationally ignore it. Simplification and distillation typically require resort to generalizations unaccompanied by all their attendant qualifications and exceptions. Precision is the casualty of summary exposition. Consequently, it should come as no surprise that an SPD written to facilitate career and financial planning by its intended readers, i.e., average plan participants, will sometimes imply that benefits may be available in circumstances where they are not actually authorized by the plan. Trade-offs between "understandable" and "accurate and comprehensive" are inevitable, as Congress acknowledged.[170] When a plan member complains she was misled to her detriment, how should a court evaluate the plan administrator's compromise?

The trade-off entails a judgment call – an exercise of discretion that tags it as fiduciary action.[171] ERISA's obligations of loyalty and care accordingly set the legal standard.[172] The standard of *review*, however, sets the intensity of judicial oversight of the fiduciary's decision, and so as a practical matter establishes its durability when challenged in court.

Virtually all plans today expressly grant the administrator or fiduciary discretionary authority to determine eligibility for benefits or to construe the terms of the plan.[173] Conferral of discretion ordinarily triggers the limited abuse-of-discretion standard of review of a denial of benefits. Under abuse-of-discretion review the plan administrator's good faith reasonable resolution of the tension between accessible and reliable information – the honest attempt to achieve optimal disclosure – becomes virtually unassailable.[174] Under this approach, the administrator would be given

---

[169] *See supra* Chapter 3 notes 47–51 and accompanying text.

[170] ERISA § 102(a), 29 U.S.C. § 1022(a) (2018).

[171] The statute defines fiduciary to include any person who has or exercises "any discretionary authority or discretionary responsibility in the administration of such plan. ERISA § 3(21)(A), 29 U.S.C. § 1002(21)(A) (2018). Moreover, the SPD regulation provides that the plan administrator, in writing the SPD to be understandable and sufficiently comprehensive, "shall exercise considered judgment and discretion by taking into account such factors as the level of comprehension and education of typical participants in the plan and the complexity of the terms of the plan." 29 C.F.R § 2520.102-2(a) (2022). *See generally* Chapter 4A, *infra*.

[172] ERISA §§ 3(21)(A), 404(a)(1)(A), (B), 29 U.S.C. §§ 1002(21)(A), 1104(a)(1)(A), (B) (2018).

[173] *See Wiedenbeck, supra* Chapter 3 note 120, at 1073–74 & notes 283–84.

[174] Commonly the plan administrator is an executive or managerial employee of the sponsoring employer. *See* ERISA § 408(c)(3), 29 U.S.C. § 1108(c)(3) (2018) (excepting insider's service as

Disclosure

broad latitude to condense and simplify plan terms – freedom to translate into plain English, to generalize, and to omit technical details that apply only in unusual circumstances – without being exposed to liability for not saying enough. Provided that the document describes the "plan's requirements respecting eligibility for participation and benefits; a description of the provisions providing for nonforfeitable pension benefits; [and] circumstances which may result in disqualification, ineligibility, or denial or loss of benefits"[175] the plan sponsor could, under this view, dispense with an extended disclaimer of warranties.

Limited oversight of the administrator's compromises in SPD drafting might allow the SPD to become the understandable balanced abridgment that Congress envisioned. If so, the SPD could actually serve as a basis for the typical worker's career and financial planning, rather than functioning as a lengthy unreadable liability shield written by plan lawyers to deter plaintiffs' lawyers.[176]

---

fiduciary from prohibited transaction definition). Such insider fiduciaries make disclosure determinations under a conflict of interest, such that good faith may be open to question. Yet if the plan expressly confers discretion, the limited abuse-of-discretion scope of review still applies. Metropolitan Life Ins. Co. v. Glenn, 554 U.S. 105 (2008). *See* Wiedenbeck, *supra* Chapter 3 note 120, at 1074–85 (explaining how the allowance of insider fiduciaries combined with a limited scope of review operate to establish a safe space for employer-regarding decisions, a kind of "implicit exculpation" that runs counter to the express prohibition of ERISA § 410(a), 29 U.S.C. § 1110(a)).

[175] ERISA § 102(b), 29 U.S.C. § 1022(b) (2018).

[176] One of the authors has proposed that the combination of abuse-of-discretion review of disclosure decisions and liability for lack of understandability could reclaim ERISA's economic efficiency objective, substantially improving worker career and financial planning. Peter J. Wiedenbeck, *Unbelievable: ERISA's Broken Promise* [ver. 4.0; August 2021] (August 6, 2021). Washington University in St. Louis Legal Studies Research Paper No. 21-08-01, available at SSRN: https://ssrn.com/abstract=3900735. Brendan Maher disagrees, believing that disclosure is not the sort of discretionary determination to which a limited scope of review applies, and he briefly explains why here.

First, the statute specifically provides that SPDs "*shall* be sufficiently accurate and comprehensive to *reasonably apprise . . . participants and beneficiaries* of their rights and obligations under the plan." ERISA § 102(a) (emphasis supplied). The point of notice provisions generally and ERISA's in particular – both in spirit and by its terms – is to *achieve* understanding in the minds of the participants about their entitlements. If, upon examination, average plan participants would *not* have been reasonably so apprised, then section 102(a) has been violated, even if the fiduciary can provide a reasonable account of why he wrote the SPD the way he did. In contrast, when construing *plan* terms, the participants' understanding is legally irrelevant – a contract (or trust instrument) means what it means regardless of whether a party understands it or not. Whatever its other flaws, *Firestone* deference regarding the construing of plan terms does not facially frustrate any statutory right of understanding possessed by participants. Deference in the SPD setting would. E.g., Koehler v. Aetna Health Inc., 683 F.3d 182, 188 (5th Cir. 2012) (quoting §102(a) in order to explain that, in contrast to plan interpretation, "[a]mbiguities in a plan summary are resolved in favor of the beneficiary.")

Second, the argument is discordant with how we think about ERISA generally. Nowhere does ERISA suggest that a fiduciary's obligation to discharge statutory responsibilities is entitled to deferential review merely because a fiduciary has real-world discretion as to the precise manner of discharge. Put differently, plan interpretation and fiduciary "discretion" in

102 *Conduct Controls: Welfare and Pension Plans*

For two reasons this utopian vision has not materialized. First, case law to date does not directly and unambiguously establish that disclosure decisions, given appropriate plan language, are entitled to a limited scope of review under *Firestone*. The more important obstacle lies in the absence of an incentive to make the SPD understandable.[177] Administrators have not been moved to simplify and condense, so there's been no need to justify SPD omissions. Hence the shelter offered by limited judicial review has been neglected. It would quickly become highly salient, and hotly contested, if steps were taken to revive understandability. In that event a cautious – even skeptical – judicial attitude toward imposing liability based on an allegedly incomplete SPD would become the essential bulwark preserving understandability. Relief would still be appropriate in instances (like *Mattias*[178]) where the omission is practically equivalent to an inaccurate SPD or a failure to warn. Otherwise, the proposed focus on optimal disclosure should cause a

connection therewith – and the resulting judicial deference under *Firestone* – constitutes the special case, not the baseline one.

Deference, for example, is not appropriate in informal communications cases, even though they facially involve fiduciary discretion. A fiduciary has numerous ways to satisfactorily respond to a participant's informal inquiry about benefits – but that does not mean that the fiduciary's communications are entitled to deferential review with regard to whether they were misleading (including by omission). *Cf.* Krohn v. Huron Mem'l Hosp., 173 F.3d 542, 547 (6th Cir. 1999) (analyzing informal communication case without considering deference). Either the communications were misleading or they were not; no deference is due when making that inquiry. More broadly, a fiduciary's compliance with ERISA's various statutory commands is not entitled to deferential review merely because there is more than one way to comply; whatever compliance choice the fiduciary makes, the court will determine whether *that* choice, under the circumstances, satisfies the statute's terms. *Cf.* Chao v. Merino, 452 F.3d 174, 182 (2d Cir. 2006) (taking pains to note that "ERISA does not impose a duty to take any particular course of action if another approach seems preferable" while nonetheless ruling, without any deference to the fiduciary's judgment, that she had taken insufficient steps to protect the plan's funds). So too here. *E.g.*, Arnold v. Arrow Transp. Co. of Delaware, 926 F.2d 782, 785 (9th Cir. 1991) (reviewing an SPD dispute under a *de novo* standard and observing generally that "[t]he interpretation of a federal statute, such as ERISA, is a question of law, and we review it *de novo*.")

Third, handing ERISA's often-conflicted administrators yet another legal tool to avoid paying out benefits poses a meaningful risk of participant exploitation. A deferential review standard that would permit if not require widespread judicial indifference to participants honestly confused by SPD language is inconsistent with the protective intent of ERISA's drafters. More specifically, in spite of the explicit command of ERISA § 102(b) (providing that an SPD "shall contain the ... circumstances which may result in disqualification, ineligibility, or denial or loss of benefits"), one fears a deferential standard could obstruct relief even when the SPD is functionally inaccurate and/or fails to warn of conditions that materially reduce or eliminate benefits. In contrast, *de novo* review of whether the SPD in fact reasonably apprised the participants of their rights and obligations generally – and specifically did so with regard to benefit-losing conditions – is more likely to protect workers in the way Congress originally envisioned. Were deferential review in the SPD setting likely to on balance favor workers, one might expect to see Labor urge such a position. It has not done so.

[177] *See supra* Chapter 3 notes 53–54 and accompanying text. For a more detailed analysis, see Wiedenbeck, *supra* Chapter 3 note 103, at 16–18.

[178] *See supra* Chapter 3 notes 164–168 and accompanying text.

Disclosure

good faith attempt to summarize to defeat a plan member's complaint that more should have been said.

C NON-SPD COMMUNICATIONS

Administrators regularly provide more information about the plan than the minimum required by the SPD and ERISA's other disclosure obligations. If participants are given a brief understandable SPD, such voluntary supplementary communications are needed to provide guidance on the application of plan terms to specific situations. If participants are given a lengthy complex liability-shield SPD, the plan sponsor knows that the advantages of the plan will have to be made clear to employees by other means, and non-SPD communications are used to substitute for an understandable SPD. In either case, can the employer be bound by misleading or erroneous informal communications?

Supplying additional information about benefits is discretionary action undertaken in the course of plan administration. Therefore it is fiduciary action, subject to ERISA's obligations of loyalty and care.[179] If the information is inconsistent with the terms of the plan and the discrepancy results from deliberate or negligent misrepresentation, then injured plan members can pursue "appropriate equitable relief" to redress the violation of the fiduciary's statutory duties.[180]

1 Objections to Enforcement

This analysis is compelling, yet courts have shown reluctance to impose liability based on inaccurate non-SPD communications. That hesitance is grounded in ERISA policies. Enforcing informal representations might undercut workers' incentive to consult the SPD for plan-related information. Protecting the plan or its sponsor from unpredictable unintended liabilities is another salient concern. Those policy concerns can manifest themselves when courts apply doctrinal conditions for obtaining equitable relief, such as estoppel's requirement that reliance be "justifiable." Yet despite such objections, decisional law recognizes that relief from some types of mistaken informal messaging is warranted.

The SPD was intended to ensure that employees have on hand a reliable source of understandable information about the plan. If workers have ready access to solid information, perhaps they should be savvy enough to check the veracity of other representations against the SPD. That stance suggests that reliance on any

---

[179] See Varity Corp. v. Howe, 516 U.S. 489, 505 (1996) (holding voluntary "statements about the security of benefits amounted to an act of plan administration"); ERISA §§ 3(21)(A), 404(a)(1), 29 U.S.C. §§ 1002(21)(A), 1104(a)(1) (2018).

[180] ERISA § 502(a)(3), 29 U.S.C. § 1132(a)(3) (2018); see Varity, 516 U.S. at 506, 515 (holding that lying to participants breaches ERISA's duty of loyalty, which may be redressed in a suit for individual relief under ERISA § 502(a)(3)).

communications that conflict with the SPD should be judicially discouraged by treating it as unworthy of protection. Refusing estoppel in those circumstances – in effect, holding reliance in such a case to be unjustified as a matter of law – amounts to imposing a duty of inquiry on participants and beneficiaries. Such a duty of inquiry would reinforce the primacy of the SPD, perhaps spurring better-informed decision making. It might also lead to prompt identification and correction of errors and ambiguities in the employer's representations. Plus, refusing estoppel reassures plan sponsors that an undertaking to provide benefits will generate predictable obligations: incautious remarks will not magnify costs.[181]

In contrast, widespread application of estoppel, the argument goes, would bless unthinking acceptance of any plausible assertion. Applying estoppel in conflicting communication cases would thus both promote litigation and lead to the non-uniform application of plan provisions, as a series of "special deals" would arise from judicial enforcement of ill-considered employer representations.[182]

Starting with *Nachwalter* v. *Christie*,[183] a long line of cases refuses to apply estoppel to permit oral modifications of employee benefit plans. Parol variance claims are properly rejected because the conditions of estoppel cannot be satisfied.[184] If an understandable SPD gives participants ready access to trustworthy plan information, reliance on oral representations that contradict the summary cannot be

---

[181] This rationale is of course limited to negligent as opposed to intentional misinformation, i.e., intelligence failures proceeding from imprudence, not disloyalty.

[182] Numerous cases hold that other writings cannot override the plan summary, but most involve informal assurances of lifetime health benefits juxtaposed against an SPD that reserves to the plan sponsor the unconditional right to amend or terminate the plan. *E.g.*, Gable v. Sweetheart Cup Co., 35 F.3d 851, 857 (4th Cir. 1994) ("ERISA prohibits informal written or oral amendments of employee benefit plans, and references to lifetime benefits contained in non-plan documents cannot override an explicit reservation of the right to modify contained in the plan documents themselves.") (citations omitted); Alday v. Container Corp. of Am., 906 F.2d 660, 665–66 (11th Cir. 1990) (personal benefits summary, letters sent to employees nearing retirement and documents accompanying retirement seminars cannot override unambiguous language of SPD reserving right to terminate plan); Moore v. Metro. Life Ins. Co., 856 F.2d 488, 492 (2d Cir. 1988) (where filmstrips and articles in employee newspapers referred to lifetime benefits without mention of reserved amendment power, the court held that "absent a showing tantamount to proof of fraud, an ERISA welfare plan is not subject to amendment as a result of informal communications between an employer and plan beneficiaries").

[183] 805 F.2d 956, 960 (11th Cir. 1986).

[184] *See, e.g.*, Curcio v. John Hancock Mut. Life Ins. Co., 33 F.3d 226, 235 (3d Cir. 1994) (reasonable reliance required); *In re* Unisys Corp. Retiree Med. Benefit "ERISA" Litig., 58 F.3d 896, 908 (3d Cir. 1995) ("[A] participant's reliance on employer representations regarding benefits may never be 'reasonable' where the participant is in possession of a written document notifying him of the conditional nature of such benefits."); Schmidt v. Sheet Metal Workers' Nat'l Pension Fund, 128 F.3d 541, 546 (7th Cir. 1997) ("[O]ral representations that conflict with the terms of a written plan [in this case, including the SPD] will not be given effect, as the written instrument must control."); *see also* RESTATEMENT (SECOND) OF CONTRACTS § 90 (1) & cmt. b (1979) (reasonableness of promisee's reliance and formality with which promise is made are factors bearing on whether enforcement necessary to prevent injustice).

Disclosure

reasonable or justifiable.[185] (ERISA's writing requirement, in effect, serves as a statute of frauds.) In addition, giving legal effect to such informal assurances could give rise to a series of unauthorized commitments to favored participants which would drain funds from the plan, and in some circumstances could jeopardize the continued benefits of other employees.[186]

The no-estoppel rule originated in cases involving unduly favorable *oral* representations about the plan. Compared to oral assertions, written representations are more permanent and verifiable, and apparently more deliberate. The mode of communication does not convey an implicit caveat respecting dependability, and so workers may be more inclined to credit a writing that contradicts the SPD. Nevertheless, the no-estoppel rule was soon extended to informal *written* communications at odds with the current SPD.[187] Inconsistent writings engendered no

---

[185] Even oral representations that purport to reflect plan amendments (thereby explaining away the SPD inconsistency) should be dismissed because ERISA requires authentic plan changes to be reported to participants in *writing*, via a summary of material modifications (SMM). ERISA §§ 102(a), 104(b)(1), 29 U.S.C. §§ 1022(a), 1024(b)(1) (2018).

[186] Courts have sometimes refused to give effect to informal worker-friendly representations in part out of concern that such changes may render the plan underfunded, jeopardizing payments to other participants and beneficiaries. E.g., *Nachwalter*, 805 F.2d at 960–61; Armistead v. Vernitron Corp., 944 F.2d 1287, 1300 (6th Cir. 1991). That concern is often misplaced or overblown, however. Under a defined contribution pension plan, a participant is entitled to the balance of her account, and disbursements from that account do not affect other participants' account balances.

With respect to defined benefit pension plans, it is true that oral modifications ordinarily would not have been taken into account in determining the actuarial cost of the plan and so would negatively impact funding. A defined benefit plan sponsor cannot disclaim liability for unfunded accrued benefits, however, ERISA §§ 4062(a), (b), 4001(a)(16), (18), 29 U.S.C. §§ 1362(a), (b), 1301(a)(16), (18) (2018), and a solvent sponsor cannot terminate an underfunded plan. ERISA § 4041(a), (b), 29 U.S.C. § 1341(a), (b) (2018) (voluntary "standard" termination of single-employer plan authorized only if plan assets are sufficient to satisfy all benefit liabilities). Consequently, the disbursement of larger benefits to some employees pursuant to an oral modification, even if it creates or increases underfunding, triggers an increase in the employer's cost. Conceivably, the employer might respond to that cost increase by reducing *future* benefit accruals under the plan, but it cannot reduce benefits already earned. ERISA § 204(g)(1), 29 U.S.C. § 1054(g)(1) (2018); *accord* I.R.C. § 411(d)(6) (corresponding tax qualification rule).

Some courts apply estoppel against welfare plans on the ground that actuarial concerns vanish where there is no fund to deplete. E.g., Black v. TIC Inv. Corp., 900 F.2d 112, 115 (7th Cir. 1990) (allowing estoppel against unfunded welfare plan); *Armistead*, 944 F.2d at 1300 (allowing estoppel against insured welfare plan). Yet actuarially unanticipated benefit increases under welfare plans (whether unfunded or insured) lead to the same sort of future cost escalation as under defined benefit pension plans, which might induce the sponsor to trim the program's *prospective* generosity, or even jeopardize its continuance.

[187] E.g., Alday v. Container Corp. of Am., 906 F.2d 660, 665–66 (11th Cir. 1990) (extending *Nachwalter* to contradictory written communications); Moore v. Metro. Life Ins. Co., 856 F.2d 488, 492 (2d Cir. 1988) ("absent a showing tantamount to proof of fraud, an ERISA welfare plan is not subject to amendment as a result of informal communications between an employer and plan beneficiaries").

greater respect from the courts, which have been keen to protect the plan sponsor from increased benefit liability exposure.

Courts should not enforce non-SPD communications if the participant or beneficiary knows or *should know* that the information they contain is mistaken or dangerously incomplete. But what information is reasonably knowable? The arguments against enforcement of informal communications just surveyed are premised on workers having ready resort to superior information. Often, they do not.

2 Circumstances Counseling Enforcement

Too ready invocation of constructive notice will undercut disclosure's objectives. Indeed, refusing to enforce non-SPD communications is open to a fundamental global objection. The now prevalent liability-shield SPD is frequently, as a practical matter, uninformative. Checking representations against the SPD cannot work if the SPD fails to convey understandable information. Rather than a balanced and understandable summary (i.e., the optimal disclosure envisioned by Congress) the SPD has morphed into a bloated, unreadable liability shield. Consequently, plan participants and beneficiaries cannot confirm the veracity of other representations at minimal expense. As a result, informal communications are often the sole means by which plan members can actually learn about their benefit rights and obligations. Where the SPD is not understandable, plan members have no reason to know they should be skeptical of other communications, and no real ability to protect themselves. Foreclosing estoppel in such circumstances does not promote planning, compliance, or collaboration. To the contrary, it exposes workers to confusion and manipulation. The notion that reliance on non-SPD communications is unjustified if the participant or beneficiary has reason to know of inconsistent plan terms should accordingly be tempered by sensitive appraisal of what plan information is realistically accessible. Plan members' claims for relief based on non-SPD communications cannot fairly be repulsed with the observation that they "should have known better," if "knowing better" requires deciphering a lengthy, opaque, liability-shield SPD.

a Plan Clarification

Even supposing the SPD to be understandable, important limitations on its content preclude verification of some informal communications. Statements interpreting an ambiguous plan provision are one example. Interpretation supplements plan terms rather than overriding them. The plan member advised of the interpretation would not detect an inconsistency by checking the advice against the plan or SPD. Such interpretations have been enforced via estoppel.[188] Similarly, communications

---

[188] *E.g.*, Kane v. Aetna Life Ins. Co., 893 F.2d 1283, 1285 (11th Cir. 1990) (distinguishing *Nachwalter*, 805 F.2d 956); Greany v. W. Farm Bureau Life Ins. Co., 973 F.2d 812, 821–22 (9th Cir. 1992); Slice v. Sons of Norway, 34 F.3d 630, 634–35 (8th Cir. 1994); Law v. Ernst &

Disclosure

resolving an ambiguity in an understandable SPD would raise no red flag and would naturally induce reliance.

b Future Status of the Plan

Some communications address matters beyond the scope of the SPD, such as the future status of the plan (e.g., the probability of amendment or termination). In those situations it is literally impossible to verify the statement, and the SPD presents no obstacle to justifiable reliance.[189] In a line of cases beginning with *Berlin v. Michigan Bell Telephone Co.*,[190] the appellate courts have held that material misrepresentations concerning the likelihood of future benefit enhancements breach the administrator's duty of loyalty even though the underlying decision to offer such retirement bonuses is a nonfiduciary business decision.[191] Thus some communications made prior to the ultimate decision to amend the plan, although necessarily predictive and therefore possibly incorrect, may be subject to oversight for fidelity and prudence. *Berlin* involved a severance pay plan that was offered to managers who retired during a window period in order to correct a management surplus.[192] After the close of the window period in late 1980, Michigan Bell discovered that some managers were delaying retirement in the hopes of a second offering. The company advised workers considering retirement not to delay because there were no plans for a second general application of the severance program.[193] After a second offering was announced in mid-1982, managers who retired before its effective date brought suit, contending that Michigan Bell breached its fiduciary duty by intentionally misleading them concerning the

---

Young, 956 F.2d 364, 369–72 (1st Cir. 1992). *See also* Spink v. Lockheed Corp., 125 F.3d 1257, 1261–63 (9th Cir. 1997) (estoppel available where employee relied on oral and written statements that apparently resolved an inconsistency in the provisions of the plan).

[189] Varity Corp. v. Howe, 516 U.S. 489 (1996), involved communications concerning the future of the plan, and supports the principle that communications concerning nonfiduciary acts, such as the likelihood of plan amendment or termination, can be a fiduciary function.

[190] 858 F.2d 1154 (6th Cir. 1988).

[191] E.g., Beach v. Commonwealth Edison Co., 382 F.2d 656 (7th Cir. 2004); Martinez v. Schlumberger, Ltd., 338 F.3d 407 (5th Cir. 2003) (providing an in-depth analysis of the evolution of the case law); Bins v. Exxon Co. U.S.A., 220 F.3d 1042, 1049–50 (9th Cir. 2000) (en banc); McAuley v. IBM Corp., 165 F.3d 1038 (6th Cir. 1999); Hockett v. Sun Co., 109 F.3d 1515 (10th Cir. 1997); Vartanian v. Monsanto Co., 131 F.3d 264, 268 (1st Cir. 1997); Muse v. IBM Corp., 103 F.3d 490 (6th Cir. 1996); Wilson v. Sw. Bell Tel. Co., 55 F.3d 399, 406 (8th Cir. 1995); Mullins v. Pfizer, Inc., 23 F.3d 663, 668–69 (2d Cir. 1994); Fischer v. Phila. Elec. Co., 994 F.2d 130 (3d Cir.) (hereinafter *Fischer I*), *cert. denied*, 510 U.S. 1020 (1993), *appeal after remand*, 96 F.3d 1533 (3d Cir. 1996) (hereinafter *Fischer II*), *cert. denied*, 520 U.S. 1116 (1997); *Berlin*, 858 F.2d at 1163–64. *See also* Barnes v. Lacy, 927 F.2d 539, 544 (11th Cir.).

[192] *Berlin*, 858 F.2d at 1157.

[193] *Id.* at 1158, 1160.

Conduct Controls: Welfare and Pension Plans

future availability of enhanced benefits.[194] The Sixth Circuit held that if the administrator communicates with plan participants after serious consideration is given to providing enhanced benefits, then a material misrepresentation would give rise to liability.[195] The court also indicated, however, that a defendant had no baseline duty to say anything at all about the future availability of enhanced benefits, and suggested that misrepresentations concerning a future offering would not be material and thus not actionable if they occurred prior to giving any serious consideration to implementing such a benefit change.[196]

Later cases tried to define the "serious consideration" inflection point with more particularity. Because "large corporations regularly review their benefit packages as part of an on-going process of cost-monitoring and personnel management," the Third Circuit concluded it would be undesirable to require disclosure of all proposed changes, as "truly material information could easily be missed if the flow of information was too great."[197] Accordingly, the court held that "[s]erious consideration of a change in plan benefits exists when (1) a specific proposal (2) is being discussed for purposes of implementation (3) by senior management with the authority to implement the change."[198] The first element is designed to distinguish "serious consideration" from preliminary efforts such as "gathering information, developing strategies, and analyzing options."[199] The second factor "protects the ability of senior management to take a role in the early phases of the process without automatically triggering a duty of disclosure." And the third ensures that the proposal has some practical likelihood of actually becoming a reality.[200]

In contrast, the Second Circuit has rejected the "bright-line rule that serious consideration ... is a prerequisite to liability for misstatements regarding the availability of future ... benefits."[201] From the premise that a misrepresentation is material if it would induce a reasonable person to rely on it, the court concluded that "[w]hether a plan is under serious consideration is but one factor in the materiality inquiry."[202]

> [T]he employer's false assurance that future enhancements have been ruled out for some specific period can be decisive in inducing an employee to hasten retirement, rather than delay in the hope of receiving enhanced future benefits. This aspect of

---

[194] *Id.*

[195] *Id.* at 1164.

[196] *Id.* at 1164 & n.7. *Accord* Muse v. IBM Corp., 103 F.3d 490, 494 (6th Cir. 1996).

[197] *Fischer II*, 96 F.3d at 1539.

[198] *Id. Accord Hockett*, 109 F.3d at 1523; *McAuley*, 165 F.3d at 1043; *Bins*, 220 F.3d at 1049–50. *See* Mushalla v. Teamsters Local No. 863 Pension Fund, 300 F.3d 391, 398 (3d Cir. 2002) (*Fisher II*'s serious-consideration test applies with equal force to multiemployer plans).

[199] *Fischer II*, 96 F.3d at 1539–40.

[200] *Id.* at 1540.

[201] Ballone v. Eastman Kodak Co., 109 F.3d 117, 123 (2d Cir. 1997).

[202] *Id.* at 123–24.

the assurance can render it material regardless of whether future changes are under consideration at the time the misstatement is made.[203]

Fiduciary liability for misstatements regarding future benefits is compatible with ERISA's policy of promoting worker career and financial planning in that it ensures the sponsor's voluntary disclosures are reliable without undermining the primacy of the SPD. It also finds support in the analytical tools of law and economics.[204] Absent fiduciary liability, which serves as an anti-fraud rule in the ERISA disclosure context, some firms would attract and retain workers with informal prospective promises that they did not intend to keep, thereby paying lower compensation than truthful firms (and effectively misappropriating labor). That behavior arguably will cause workers to discount the promises of all firms unless truthful firms can distinguish themselves to attract better workers. Verification of information about the future of employee benefit programs is difficult for workers because only the sponsor has the necessary information (e.g., profit projections or actuarial cost data).[205] Truthful firms may take steps to give credence to their representations by independent certification or adopting enforceable plan amendments, but these devices entail additional costs. A rule against fraud, properly enforced, functions as an informational warranty and makes it unnecessary for workers to verify information or for sponsors to undertake expensive certification. It decreases the cost of providing truthful prospective information while increasing the cost of falsehood. This cost reallocation to mendacious employers permits sponsors of higher-quality plans to compete effectively in the labor market.[206]

---

[203] *Id.* at 124. *Accord* Wayne v. Pac. Bell, 238 F.3d 1048, 1055 (9th Cir. 1999) ("The fiduciary duty not to deceive plan participants exists at all times, not merely once serious consideration of offering such benefits has begun."); Martinez v. Schlumberger, Ltd., 338 F.3d 407, 428 (5th Cir. 2003) (concluding, after extended analysis of ERISA appellate case law and consideration of the Supreme Court's definition of materiality in the securities fraud context, that *Ballone* represents the better approach). *Contra* Beach v. Commonwealth Edison Co., 382 F.3d 656, 660–61 (7th Cir. 2004) (rejecting *Ballone* and *Martinez* in favor of the serious-consideration test).

[204] *See generally* EASTERBROOK & FISCHEL, *supra* Chapter 3 note 97, at 279–85; Kent Greenfield, *The Unjustified Absence of Federal Fraud Protection in the Labor Market*, 107 YALE L.J. 715, 738–54 (1997) (arguing that fraud protections may be more important to the efficient operation of labor markets than it is for the capital markets).

[205] If disclosures are untrustworthy or incomprehensible, workers would act on the assumption that all plans providing a certain type of benefit offer only some baseline value. If workers do not put a premium on a better plan, it becomes uneconomic for an employer to offer a more costly higher-quality program, and soon only baseline-value plans subsist. This collapse, of course, is characteristic of a "lemons" market. *See* George A. Akerlof, *The Market for "Lemons": Quality Uncertainty and the Market Mechanism*, 84 Q. J. Econ. 488 (1970). Lack of fraud protection in the labor market may trigger such decay. Greenfield, *supra* Chapter 3 note 204, at 743–44, 753.

[206] This rationale also applies to misleading statements about lifetime retiree health insurance (vesting by contract), discussed in connection with the self-contradictory SPD containing imperceptible conflicts, *supra* Chapter 3B2b.

110   *Conduct Controls: Welfare and Pension Plans*

c Conspicuous Fiduciary Advice

Taking a broader view, one can fairly question whether fiduciaries should some-times be liable for faulty communications even if the problem could be detected by reference to the SPD. Guidance from an executive who is reasonably understood to be communicating as a plan fiduciary – an official obligated to act prudently and solely in the interests of participants and beneficiaries – carries its own seal of authenticity and believability. Trusting advice coming from an executive who may be pursuing the employer's business interest is naive and risky. But checking guidance provided by an official who is both well informed and fairly believed to be acting for the exclusive purpose of providing benefits seems wasteful and unnecessary. In such cases of notorious fiduciary advice, reliance appears reasonable without resort to the SPD, and it should arguably be treated as justifiable.[207]

3 *Fiduciary Disclosure's Scope*

The principle that voluntary provision of plan-related information is a fiduciary act is broad but not limitless. Its breadth is exemplified by cases finding that some situations create a duty to speak.

Apart from the statutory disclosure obligations, can the administrator safely stand mute? *Berlin* suggested that the administrator could avoid liability for misleading statements about future benefit enhancements by simply keeping silent.[208] Later appellate decisions indicated otherwise. In *Eddy v. Colonial Life Insurance Co.,*[209] the plaintiff called the insurer to inquire about maintaining coverage when he learned that his employer's group health plan would terminate on the eve of surgery. The district court found that Eddy had not specifically inquired about converting group coverage into an individual policy and found no fault in Colonial Life's failure to tell him that such a right existed.[210] Relying on the common law of trusts, the DC Circuit ruled that "refraining from imparting misinformation is only *part* of the fiduciary's duty. Once Eddy presented his predicament, Colonial Life was required to do more than simply *not misinform*; Colonial Life also had an affirmative obligation to *inform* – to provide complete and correct material information on

---

[207] *See* Varity Corp. v. Howe, 516 U.S. 489, 505 (1996) (holding corporate executives' assurances of the continuance of plan benefits were fiduciary acts where the corporation created the impression that the executives were speaking on behalf of workers interested in the plan). *Varity* can be read to adopt an apparent authority approach to identifying information fiduciaries. *See id.* at 503.

[208] Berlin v. Michigan Bell Telephone Co., 858 F.2d 1154, 1164 (6th Cir. 1988) ("[P]laintiffs are not arguing, nor do we hold, that defendants had any duties, under the circumstances, to say anything at all or to communicate with potential plan participants about the future availability of [early retirement severance benefits].").

[209] 919 F.2d 747 (D.C. Cir. 1990).

[210] *Id.* at 749, 751.

Disclosure

Eddy's status and options."[211] Relying on *Eddy*, the Third Circuit ruled that an ERISA fiduciary who is aware of a beneficiary's situation has a "duty to convey complete and accurate information that [is] material to [that] circumstance," even if asked the wrong question.[212] In each of these cases, an inquiry from the plan participant or beneficiary initiated the obligation.

Potentially more far-reaching is *Shea* v. *Esensten*,[213] which indicates that an inquiry is not necessary to trigger a duty to speak if the fiduciary otherwise has reason to know that silence may be harmful. *Shea* involved a health plan participant who died of heart failure after his primary care physician refused, in the face of an extensive family history of heart disease and existent symptoms, to refer him to a cardiologist.[214] The Eighth Circuit held that the HMO breached its duty of loyalty in failing to disclose that its "doctors were penalized for making too many referrals and could earn a bonus by skimping on specialized care," even though no request for this information had been made.[215] The Eighth Circuit has since given *Shea* a limiting interpretation, asserting that the employer was required to disclose the referral disincentives in the SPD but failed to do so.[216] Other circuits have flatly rejected a duty to disclose in the absence of an inquiry.[217]

---

[211] *Id.* at 751.

[212] Bixler v. Cent. Pa. Teamsters Health & Welfare Fund, 12 F.3d 1292, 1302–03 (3d Cir. 1993). *Accord* Krohn v. Huron Mem'l Hosp., 173 F.3d 542, 548 (6th Cir. 1999); Hamilton v. Allen-Bradley Co., 244 F.3d 819, 827 (11th Cir. 2001). *See Unisys II*, 57 F.3d at 1264 ("[W]hen a plan administrator affirmatively misrepresents the terms of the plan or fails to provide information when it knows that its failure to do so might cause harm, the plan administrator has breached its fiduciary duty to individual plan participants and beneficiaries."); *id.* at 1266 (employer's knowledge that employees were accelerating retirement decisions on the mistaken belief that they would thereby qualify for free lifetime health care created a duty to disabuse them because "the trustees had to know that their silence might cause harm"). *Accord Unisys III*, 242 F.3d at 509–10.

[213] 107 F.3d 625 (8th Cir. 1997).

[214] *Id.* at 626.

[215] *Id.* at 629. *See also Unisys II*, 57 F.3d at 1264 (plan administrator breaches its fiduciary duty if it "fails to provide information when it knows that its failure to do so might cause harm"; but employer had engaged in concerted program of deception); Barker v. Am. Mobil Power Corp., 64 F.3d 1397, 1403 (9th Cir. 1995) (alternative holding or dicta) ("[A] fiduciary has an obligation to convey complete and accurate information material to the beneficiary's circumstance, even when a beneficiary has not specifically asked for the information"). *But see* Ehlmann v. Kaiser Found. Health Plan of Tex., 198 F.3d 552, 556 (5th Cir. 2000) (no duty to disclose HMO incentives to ration care absent inquiry from plan member or "other special circumstances," while expressing skepticism of *Shea*); Horvath v. Keystone Health Plan E., Inc., 333 F.3d 450, 460–63 (3d Cir. 2003) (HMO does not breach fiduciary duties by failing to disclose incentive to ration care absent either a member request for such information or circumstances putting the HMO on notice that the member needed such information to avoid making harmful decisions about health care coverage).

[216] Ince v. Aetna Health Mgmt., Inc., 173 F.3d 672, 676 (8th Cir. 1999) ("*Shea* involved a breach of the plan administrator's duty to publish an accurate description of plan benefits to participants and beneficiaries.").

[217] Martinez v. Schlumberger, Ltd., 338 F.3d 407, 428 (5th Cir. 2003) (employer has no fiduciary duty to affirmatively disclose whether it is considering amending its benefit plan); Pocchia

Conduct Controls: Welfare and Pension Plans

Duties of loyalty and care attach to speaking, and sometime to keeping mum, but still there are limits to liability: (1) not all persons communicating plan-related information are fiduciaries; and (2) ERISA fiduciaries are not subject to strict liability. The Labor Department abides by its long-standing position that a person performing certain "purely ministerial functions ... for an employee benefit plan within a framework of policies, interpretations, rules, practice and procedures made by other persons is not a fiduciary because such person does not have discretionary authority or discretionary control."[218] Among the functions that escape fiduciary classification if purely ministerial are "[p]reparation of employee communications materials"; "[p]reparation of reports," and "[o]rientation of new participant and advising participant of their rights and options under the plan."[219] Lower-level staff implementing plan disclosures may err or exceed their authority, but are not thereby answerable as fiduciaries. And as ERISA conditions liability on personal fault, harms caused by such misinformation does not trigger supervisory liability unless the harm was enabled by the fiduciary-supervisor's breach of duty, such as by imprudent selection, training, or oversight of staff.[220]

D CONCLUSION

Several major themes can be distilled from the voluminous, complex and confusing appellate case law on disclosure obligations. The threshold issue concerns the status of the summary plan description vis-à-vis the underlying plan documents. The SPD is designed to provide participants and beneficiaries with an accessible, reliable source of information about the plan. But because it is a simplified explanation of the principal features of the plan, it is necessarily incomplete and may be inconsistent with the plan documents, which are typically lengthy, complex, and technically worded legal instruments. Where the SPD contradicts the plan documents, the sponsor is held to the advertised terms even if the summary disclaims binding effect, but the courts were initially divided on the question whether the SPD governs as a matter of contract or estoppel. Some courts and commentators took the position that in view of its special role the SPD should be treated as the "deal," and its terms, as far as they go, should be treated as the terms of the plan itself. As such, SPD representations would be enforceable in a suit for benefits without proof of reliance. In CIGNA Inc. v. Amara[221] the Supreme Court rejected that approach, holding that

v. NYNEX Corp., 81 F.3d 275, 278 (2d Cir. 1996) (If prior acts of the fiduciary have not created confusion, "a fiduciary is not required to voluntarily disclose changes in a benefit plan before they are adopted."). The Fifth Circuit suggested that there is also no duty to respond to employee inquiries about possible plan changes. *Martinez*, 338 F.3d at 407 n.171.

[218] 29 C.F.R. § 2509.75-8, Q&A D-2 (2022).

[219] *Id.*

[220] ERISA § 404(a)(1), 29 U.S.C. § 1104(a)(1) (2018).

[221] 563 U.S. 421 (2011).

the summary, as important as it may be, is only that: an explanation of the principal features of the plan. As such, the SPD is not enforceable in a suit for benefits.

A defective SPD nevertheless violates ERISA, and so participants and beneficiaries may bring suit for "appropriate equitable relief" to redress that violation.[222] That relief, the Court advised, can include a monetary award (equitable compensation) if the claimant can show that the violation caused her harm under the standard required to qualify for the equitable remedy sought, which might be reformation, surcharge, or estoppel. While estoppel traditionally demanded a showing of detrimental reliance, the Court observed, that showing was not always necessary for other equitable remedies, such as reformation or surcharge.

After *Amara*, monetary redress for an inaccurate SPD can be sought via estoppel, but insistence on individualized proof of detrimental reliance will likely cause significant under-enforcement of the SPD accuracy standard. Many plan members won't have objective confirmation that inaction (e.g., failure to save or change jobs) proceeded from their understanding of the SPD, and those that do will rely on individual events or circumstances that preclude collective litigation (class action treatment). If the summary is deliberately misleading, however, lower courts have sidestepped reliance by reforming the plan to incorporate the fraudulent or inequitable representations, and ordering benefits paid under the terms of the plan as reformed. Where the error is not the product of fraud or inequitable conduct but rather imprudence, breach of the duty of care in SPD drafting may be eligible for collective relief via surcharge upon a showing of "likely harm" – as opposed to individual detrimental reliance – but the availability and requisites of this remedy remain unsettled. Even the detrimental reliance condition of estoppel, it should be noted, may be susceptible to some relaxation in light of the objectives of disclosure if the courts attend to the historic flexibility of equity and their power to develop a policy-infused federal common law of "ERISA estoppel."

If, instead of contradicting the underlying plan documents, the SPD contradicts itself, the courts generally refuse to impose liability on the view that reliance is unjustified. Caveat emptor makes sense if the contradiction or inconsistency is apparent to the average plan participant. In that case the natural and responsible reaction is to report the problem and request clarification. But most of the cases do not involve glaring inconsistencies: the contradiction may be buried in a 100-page "summary" or it may be discernible only to a lawyer or judge. Attention to the origin of the contradiction, its lack of salience, and the relative costs that the employer and workers would have to incur to avoid the resulting harm, suggests that in such cases of imperceptible conflicts ERISA's policies would be better served by enforcing the plan in accordance with the natural reading of the SPD. Where the hidden SPD contradiction reflects an effort to mislead, plan reformation could be ordered as in the case of a deliberately inaccurate SPD. The case law in this area has mostly

---

[222] ERISA § 502(a)(3), 29 U.S.C. § 1132(a)(3) (2018).

avoided realistic assessment of SPD "contradictions," allowing plan administrators to get away with sharp practices – in some cases arguably endorsing widespread labor theft.

Where the SPD is silent on an issue that the plan documents address, workers may interpret the simplified presentation, viewed in isolation, as the announcement of a general rule that admits no exceptions or qualifications. Here too an important dichotomy comes into play. The SPD is required to contain a description of "circumstances which may result in disqualification, ineligibility, or denial or loss of benefits."[223] If such required notice is missing, some cases refuse to enforce the detrimental condition. That approach incentivizes careful drafting by the employer and reinforces workers' reasons to consult the SPD. In contrast to failure-to-warn cases, many other omissions should be treated as acceptable. To be useful a summary must necessarily generalize and simplify, and the details omitted will frequently impose technical (but important) limitations and qualifications. The SPD obligation presents an inherent trade-off, for if disclosures are made more detailed and complex, so that they are more informative to participants in unusual circumstances, they also become correspondingly longer, more difficult to understand, and therefore less useful to workers generally. To promote *optimal disclosure*, courts could recognize that SPD drafting involves discretionary compromises between understandability and completeness (sufficiently accurate and comprehensive to reasonably apprise). If those disclosure judgment calls are fiduciary decisions reviewable under the abuse-of-discretion standard,[224] then omissions that reflect reasonable efforts to make the SPD useful to workers should be upheld.[225]

Non-SPD (informal) communications present a different set of considerations. Not being required by ERISA, voluntary supplemental disclosures involve discretionary acts of plan administration. Accordingly, non-SPD communications ordinarily trigger fiduciary duties of loyalty and care, the breach of which can be asserted by means of a suit for appropriate equitable relief to redress violations of ERISA. Despite such reviewability courts have been reluctant to provide equitable relief based on informal representations. The justifiability of reliance on non-SPD representations at variance with the SPD may be suspect, inasmuch as the SPD was intended to serve as the primary source of information about plan rights and obligations, and courts have been solicitous of the plan sponsor's interest in avoiding increased benefit obligations caused by unauthorized commitments. Upon an adequate showing of reliance, many courts will prohibit the plan from reneging on an informal communication that clarifies an ambiguous plan provision, but not one that would override clear plan terms. Similarly, reliance on plan-related information that is beyond the scope of the SPD, such as the prospect of plan

---

[223] ERISA § 102(b), 29 U.S.C. § 1022(b) (2018); *see* 29 C.F.R. § 2520.102-3(*l*) (2022).

[224] Brendan Maher's disagreement with this view is set forth in Chapter 3 note 176.

[225] *See supra* text accompanying Chapter 3 notes 172–178.

amendment or termination, may be protected. Moreover, workers have no reason to mistrust communications reasonably understood to be disinterested fiduciary guidance: reliance on such representations seems entirely justified even if they could be checked for consistency with the SPD. The breadth of ERISA's functional definition of fiduciary and the stringency of fiduciary obligations (topics explored in Chapter 4) may even create a duty to speak if the fiduciary has reason to know that silence may be harmful.

4

Fiduciary Obligations

The focus of the statute thus is on the administrative integrity of benefit plans.[1]

Assurance of integrity is the heart and soul of ERISA. Federal fiduciary standards were designed to work in combination with improved disclosure (Chapter 3) and powerful enforcement tools (Chapter 5) to stem misconduct in plan administration.[2] Experience suggests that this convergence of means to the end of controlling mismanagement and abuse is no overreaction, for claims of fiduciary misconduct are presented in most cases litigated under ERISA.

ERISA's fiduciary rules were abstracted from state trust law. In combination with preemption, federal fiduciary standards avoid the conflicts, costs, and complications that would arise from local variations in the law of trusts. But ERISA's fiduciary responsibility provisions serve an interest in addition to, and more important than, uniformity. To tailor administrative requirements to the special circumstances of employee benefit plans, Congress prescribed several departures from conventional trust law.

Three modifications are central to ERISA's mission. First, Congress adopted a broad functional definition of fiduciary so that all benefit plan decision makers – not just asset managers (traditional trustees) – can be called to account. Second, to hold their feet to the fire, ERISA not only specifies a stringent set of fiduciary duties, it also outlaws plan provisions (known as exculpatory clauses) that would relax their force. Third, certain transactions involving insider dealings with the plan are prohibited without regard to fairness or whether loss ensues. This chapter explores

---

[1] Fort Halifax Packing Co. v. Coyne, 482 U.S. 1, 15 (1987).

[2] E.g., S. REP. NO. 93-127, at 27–28, 29 (1973) ("without provisions . . . allowing ready access to both detailed information about the plan and to the courts, and without standards by which a participant can measure the fiduciary's conduct . . . he is not equipped to safeguard either his own rights or the plan assets"), *reprinted in* 1 ERISA LEGISLATIVE HISTORY, *supra* Chapter 1 note 55, at 587, 613–14, 615.

Fiduciary Obligations

each of these departures from traditional state trust law and then takes up the phenomenon of participant-directed investments under defined contribution pension plans – importantly including most 401(k) plans – paying particular attention to the extent to which employee decision making insulates plan fiduciaries from liability for poor investment choices, including losses from substantial holdings of stock in the employer corporation.

A DEFINITION OF FIDUCIARY

General Principles

Liability for misconduct in the affairs of an employee benefit plan is generally limited to fiduciaries.[3] Fiduciaries are also granted standing to enforce the duties of other fiduciaries and to seek equitable relief for violations of the terms of the plan or ERISA.[4] Status as a plan fiduciary is determined under ERISA § 3(21), which provides in part:

> [A] person is a fiduciary with respect to a plan to the extent (i) he exercises any discretionary authority or discretionary control respecting management of such plan or exercises any authority or control respecting management or disposition of its assets, (ii) he renders investment advice for a fee or other compensation, direct or indirect, with respect to any moneys or other property of such plan, or has any authority or responsibility to do so, or (iii) he has any discretionary authority or discretionary responsibility in the administration of such plan. Such term includes any person designated under section 405(c)(1)(B) [of this title.][5]

Several aspects of this definition are noteworthy. Comparing the first part of clause (i) with clause (iii), it is apparent that *discretionary* authority over plan administration, whether or not exercised, is sufficient to ensure fiduciary classification ("exercises" versus "has"). In contrast, any reference to discretion is notably absent from the second part of clause (i), which provides that the exercise of "any authority or control respecting the management or disposition of [plan] assets" also triggers fiduciary status. Finally, payments for investment advice can bring automatic fiduciary classification, even if the ultimate discretionary investment decision lies in other hands, and even if the investment adviser does not handle plan assets.

This definition brings fiduciary duties to bear on those persons whose venality or neglect could injure plan participants. Discretionary authority, large or small, could be abused to the detriment of participants, and so all judgment calls are monitored under the law's most exacting standards. Persons who are not involved in operational decision making cannot ordinarily do much damage, unless they are in a position to

---

[3] ERISA § 409(a), 29 U.S.C. § 1109(a) (2018).
[4] ERISA § 502(a)(2), (3), 29 U.S.C. § 1132(a)(2), (3) (2018).
[5] ERISA § 3(21)(A), 29 U.S.C. § 1002(21)(A) (2018).

Conduct Controls: Welfare and Pension Plans

loot the fund. For that reason, the statute indicates that anyone who handles the money will also be held to the strictest standards of loyalty and care, even in the absence of decision-making authority. Investment advisers who don't make final decisions and don't have access to plan assets would not be subject to fiduciary obligations absent their express inclusion in clause (ii), and, in fact, other paid professional advisers, such as lawyers, accountants, and actuaries, ordinarily are not fiduciaries.[6] The legislative history does not explain this discrepancy, but a Labor Department regulation substantially narrows it.[7]

---

[6] 29 C.F.R. § 2509.75-5, D-1 (2021) (attorney, accountant, actuary, or consultant is not a fiduciary solely by virtue of rendering legal, accounting, actuarial, or consulting services to the plan). The ERISA conference report observes:

"While the ordinary functions of consultants and advisers to employee benefit plans (other than investment advisers) may not be considered as fiduciary functions, it must be recognized that there will be situations where such consultants and advisers may because of their special expertise, in effect, be exercising discretionary authority or control with respect to the management or administration of such plan or some authority or control regarding its assets. In such cases, they are to be regarded as having assumed fiduciary obligations within the meaning of the applicable definition." H.R. REP. NO. 93-1280, at 323 (1974), *reprinted in* 3 ERISA LEGISLATIVE HISTORY, *supra* Chapter 1 note 55, at 4590.

[7] 29 C.F.R. § 2510.3-21(c)(1)(ii)(B) (2021) provides that paid investment advisers who lack discretionary authority will be classified as fiduciaries only if they (1) render advice (2) on a regular basis (3) pursuant to a mutual understanding that (4) their "services will serve as a primary basis for investment decisions with respect to plan assets," and that they will render (5) "individualized investment advice ... based on the particular needs of the plan." Where there is such a special relationship, reliance is to be expected, and the adviser can price his services to account for the increased exposure. Such ongoing individualized investment advice is akin to de facto delegation of discretionary authority, which is the case where other paid professionals can be held liable as fiduciaries. *See supra* Chapter 4 note 6. The foregoing regulation was originally promulgated in 1975 and came to be known as the "five-part test" for determining who is a fiduciary when rendering investment advice.

Critics charged that the five-part test was too restrictive and excluded from ERISA's reach a wide range of self-serving behavior that benefited investment advisers at the expense of participants – in particular the recommending of products with fee structures that favored the adviser but meaningfully undermined the return to the investor. A long-standing effort by federal regulators to tighten this rule was promulgated on April 8, 2016. Referred to in common parlance as DOL's "Fiduciary Rule," regulators "overhaul[ed] ... the investment advice fiduciary definition, together with amendments to six existing exemptions and two new exemptions to the prohibited transaction provision in both ERISA and the Code." Chamber of Com. of United States of Am. v. United States Dep't of Lab., 885 F.3d 360, 366 (5th Cir. 2018). The latter was necessary in part to ensure that monies in IRAs were also subject to tightened regulations.

The Fiduciary Rule, *inter alia*, jettisoned the "regular basis" and "primary basis" requirements, qualifying far more investment professionals who might interact with a plan as fiduciaries subject to ERISA's duties and prohibited transaction rules. It further tied the granting of prohibited transaction exemptions (a prohibition which would otherwise be sweeping, under the new fiduciary definition) to a party functionally agreeing to abide by heightened duties of impartial conduct (essentially duties of loyalty and prudence); to forswear unreasonable compensation; and to make certain disclosures. *Id.* at 366–69.

The Fiduciary Rule was successfully challenged in court and vacated by the Fifth Circuit. *Id.* at 363. After the Rule's promulgation in 2016 and its vacatur by the court of appeal in 2018,

De Facto Fiduciaries

ERISA's functional definition of fiduciary extends not only to those who are authorized to perform the designated task, but also to those who wield power de facto. A person who "exercises any discretionary *authority*" over plan management, or who "exercises any *authority* ... respecting management or disposition of [plan] assets," is a fiduciary. But so is anyone who, absent authority, "exercises any ... discretionary *control*" or "exercises any ... *control*" over plan assets.[8] That is, anyone who actually exercises control, regardless of legitimacy, is a fiduciary.[9]

The courts have repeatedly held such de facto fiduciaries accountable for their conduct. For example, the sponsoring employer is often found to be a de facto fiduciary where, by deliberately failing to provide necessary information (a ministerial duty), the employer prevents a participant from presenting her claim for benefits to an independent fiduciary.[10]

Discretion and Funding

Fiduciary classification under ERISA is founded on functions performed, not on formal designation. It also does not depend on satisfaction of the requirements for creation of a valid trust. The existence of some trust property, a "res," is essential to the creation of a trust,[11] yet some unfunded employee benefit programs are welfare

---

the Obama Administration was replaced by the Trump Administration. The Trump Administration declined to appeal the Fifth Circuit panel's ruling either *en banc* or to the Supreme Court, allowing the ruling vacating the Fiduciary Rule to stand.

Controversy over the five-part test remains. *E.g.*, Am. Sec. Ass'n v. United States Dep't of Lab., 2023 WL 1967573 (M.D. Fla. Feb. 13, 2023) (litigation challenging Department of Labor guidance regarding recommendations to roll assets out of an ERISA-covered plan into an IRA). New regulatory action seems likely. The Biden Administration's Fall 2022 Unified Agenda of Regulatory and Deregulatory Actions included proposed rulemaking by Labor that would modify the five-part test, which in the current Department's view "is not founded in the statutory text of ERISA" and does not "align with retirement investors' reasonable expectations." Introduction to the Unified Agenda of Federal Regulatory and Deregulatory Actions – Fall 2022, 88 Fed. Reg. 10,966, 11,097 (proposed Feb. 22, 2023).

[8] ERISA § 3(21)(A)(i), 29 U.S.C. § 1002(21)(A)(i) (2018) (emphasis added).

[9] *See* Explanation of H.R. 12906, 120 CONG. REC. 3983 (1974) ("Conduct alone may in an appropriate circumstance impose fiduciary obligations"), *reprinted in* 2 ERISA LEGISLATIVE HISTORY, *supra* Chapter 1 note 55, at 3293, 3309.

[10] *E.g.*, Blatt v. Marshall & Lassman, 812 F.2d 810 (2d Cir. 1987) (employer's failure to provide insurer with confirmation of employee's separation from service, delaying pension plan distribution, held to be exercise of actual control over disposition of plan assets); Hamilton v. Allen-Bradley Co., 244 F.3d 819 (11th Cir. 2001) (employer exercised actual control over claim process by failure to timely provide application for long-term disability benefits).

[11] RESTATEMENT (SECOND) OF TRUSTS § 74 (1959); RESTATEMENT (THIRD) OF TRUSTS § 2 & cmt. i (2003).

plans,[12] and their decision makers are ERISA fiduciaries even though there are no plan assets to protect or invest.

Oversight of discretionary decisions is a primary concern of the fiduciary rules, but it is not the exclusive concern. Where a plan is funded, anyone who handles the money is a fiduciary, even absent decision-making responsibility.[13] Unfortunately, courts have sometimes overlooked this prong of the fiduciary definition, holding that "discretion" is the sine qua non of fiduciary status.[14] Judicial confusion over the fiduciary status of directed trustees and other ministerial asset handlers may have its origin in an early and misguided Labor Department pronouncement. Issued in 1975 and still in effect, Interpretive Bulletin 75-8[15] provides, in part, that persons who have no power to make decisions about plan policy, interpretation, practices, or procedures, but who merely perform certain administrative tasks under a framework of rules established by others, are not fiduciaries. Most of the listed tasks involve information processing (such as recordkeeping, communicating, reporting, and initially applying plan rules determining eligibility for participation or benefits) and advisory functions. As to these tasks, the conclusion that purely "ministerial" acts conducted under rules set and overseen by others (i.e., persons who unquestionably have discretion and are fiduciaries) will not trigger fiduciary status is clearly correct. Unfortunately, however, the list of nonfiduciary ministerial tasks includes "[c]ollection of contributions and application of contributions as provided in the plan," which entails handling the money. The proposition that a person with access to plan assets who performs only ministerial duties could loot the fund without being subject to robust fiduciary remedies would surely have startled the Congress that

---

[12] *See supra* Chapter 2C, text accompanying Chapter 2 notes 110–116.

[13] In Chao v. Day, 436 F.3d 234 (D.C. Cir. 2006), an insurance broker misappropriated premium payments from twenty-nine health plans, to which he issued fake insurance policies. In a suit brought by the Secretary of Labor, the defendant argued that he could not be held liable as a fiduciary because he lacked discretion in the use of the funds. The court found no statutory support for this defense: "Because the disposition clause [of ERISA's definition of fiduciary] contains no 'discretion' requirement, it is irrelevant whether Day exercised 'discretion' in his thievery. 'Any authority or control' is enough." *Id.* at 236. *See also* IT Corp. v. Gen. Am. Life Ins. Co., 107 F.3d 1415, 1421–22 (9th Cir. 1997) (check-writing control over plan bank account may trigger fiduciary status despite lack of discretionary authority because "[t]he statute treats control over the cash differently from control over administration"), *cert. denied*, 522 U.S. 1068 (1998); Coldesina v. Estate of Simper, 407 F.3d 1126, 1132 (10th Cir. 2005) ("Discretion is conspicuously omitted from the fiduciary function of controlling plan assets. . . . As other courts have recognized, this distinction evidences Congress's intent to treat control over assets differently than control over management or administration.").

[14] *E.g.*, Maniance v. Commerce Bank, 40 F.3d 264, 267 (8th Cir. 1994) ("discretion is the benchmark for fiduciary status under ERISA"), *cert. denied*, 514 U.S. 1111 (1995). The problem has been particularly pronounced in the case of directed trustees. *See generally* Patricia Wick Hatamyar, *See No Evil? The Role of the Directed Trustee Under ERISA*, 64 Tenn. L. Rev. 1, 41–52 (1996), and cases cited and discussed therein.

[15] 29 C.F.R. § 2509.75-8, D-2 (2021).

Fiduciary Obligations 121

enacted ERISA.[16] As the Supreme Court has observed, "[a] fair contextual reading of the statute makes it abundantly clear that its draftsmen were primarily concerned with the possible misuse of plan assets, and with remedies that would protect the entire plan . . . ."[17]

Multiple Hats

Discretionary authority relating to employee benefits is not alone sufficient to trigger fiduciary classification. It must be discretion of a certain type, namely, that involved in the management or administration of the plan. Judgments respecting the design, establishment, or modification of an employee benefit plan are not fiduciary acts, for they do not implicate program management. This fundamental distinction between design and implementation is often referred to as the difference between "settlor" and "trustee" functions, by analogy to the private trust law counterparts. Long recognized by the lower courts, the Supreme Court affirmed that when a plan sponsor adopts, amends, or terminates an employee benefit plan (either welfare or pension), it is not acting in a fiduciary capacity.[18] Consequently, the obligation to act "solely in the interest of the participants and beneficiaries" does not attach to plan-design decisions, leaving employers free (subject to ERISA's content controls) to structure the program to maximal business advantage. That flexibility to tailor benefit plans to best promote the sponsor's personnel policies is crucial to the maintenance of ERISA's delicate balance between public regulation and private sponsorship.[19]

Under ERISA, settlor functions can be conducted for the sponsor's benefit, but trustee or administrative functions must generally be carried out for the "exclusive purpose of providing benefits to participants and their beneficiaries and defraying reasonable expenses of administering the plan."[20] ERISA, however, permits one person to act in both roles. An individual who is a fiduciary because of certain activities does not thereby become a fiduciary for *all* purposes nor in *all* of her dealings with the plan. Rather, one is a fiduciary only "to the extent" that she has or exercises managerial discretion, handles plan assets, or provides investment advice

---

[16] Federal fiduciary standards were an early and noncontroversial component of legislative proposals for benefit plan regulation. The consensus grew out of spectacular revelations in the mid-1960s of the diversion of more than $4 million from the welfare funds of two small local unions to the unfettered command of the union boss. *See* Senate Comm. on Government Operations, Diversion of Union Welfare-Pension Funds of Allied Trades Council and Teamsters Local 815, S. Rep. No. 89-1348, at 33–39 (1966).

[17] Mass. Mut. Life Ins. Co. v. Russell, 473 U.S. 134, 142 (1985).

[18] Curtiss-Wright Corp. v. Schoonejongen, 514 U.S. 73, 78 (1995) (welfare plan); Lockheed Corp. v. Spink, 517 U.S. 882, 890–91 (1996) (pension plans); Hughes Aircraft Co. v. Jacobson, 525 U.S. 432, 443–44 (1999) (rule applies whether or not employees have contributed to the plan).

[19] *See generally supra* Chapter 1C.

[20] ERISA § 404(a)(1)(A), 29 U.S.C. § 1104(a)(1)(A) (2018).

Conduct Controls: Welfare and Pension Plans

for a fee.[21] Consequently, a sometimes-fiduciary can, at other times, be a plan participant serving her own interest in obtaining benefits. Likewise, a fiduciary may be an employee, officer, or director of the sponsor carrying out plan-design functions or business-management functions that affect benefits (hiring, firing, or transferring employees, for example). Or she may even serve in all three capacities, as fiduciary, participant, and agent of the sponsor.[22]

> [T]he statute does not describe fiduciaries simply as administrators of the plan, or managers or advisers. Instead it defines an administrator, for example, as a fiduciary only "to the extent" that he acts in such a capacity in relation to a plan. 29 U.S.C. § 1002(21)(A). In every case charging breach of ERISA fiduciary duty, then, the threshold question is not whether the actions of some person employed to provide services under a plan adversely affected a plan beneficiary's interest, but whether that person was acting as a fiduciary (that is, was performing a fiduciary function) when taking the action subject to complaint.[23]

Where a fiduciary wears "multiple hats" in her various dealings with the plan, it is sometimes difficult to determine in which capacity a particular action was undertaken. If confusion surrounds the role in which one deals with the plan, the Supreme Court has indicated that the ambiguity should be resolved in favor of fiduciary status, at least in cases where the confusion is deliberately fostered.[24]

Health maintenance organizations (HMOs) and other managed care plans bring cost-containment considerations to bear on the central fiduciary function of determining eligibility for benefits. In *Pegram v. Herdrich*,[25] the Supreme Court was asked to decide whether mixed eligibility and treatment decisions made by HMO doctors are fiduciary acts. Costs are, of course, always relevant to plan design (with plan design being a nonfiduciary "settlor" function). Under a traditional indemnity-based health care plan, costs are restrained by limiting covered conditions or procedures, requiring participants to pay a portion of their health care costs (coinsurance features), and by imposing annual or lifetime caps on coverage. These cost-containment devices are separate from the medical treatment decision. Managed care plans typically employ some or all of these strategies, but they additionally enlist physicians in the cost-containment effort by making benefit eligibility depend upon the necessity of a particular diagnostic or treatment program, a matter of professional judgment, and by providing financial incentives to exercise that judgment conservatively.

---

[21] ERISA § 3(21)(A), 29 U.S.C. § 1002(21)(A) (2018).

[22] *See* ERISA § 408(c)(1), (3), 29 U.S.C. § 1108(c)(1), (3) (2018) (multiple roles not barred by prohibited-transaction rules).

[23] Pegram v. Herdrich, 530 U.S. 211, 225–26 (2000).

[24] *See* Varity Corp. v. Howe, 516 U.S. 489 (1996), discussed *supra* Chapter 3 note 207.

[25] 530 U.S. 211 (2000).

Pegram began as a medical malpractice case in which the patient, Cynthia Herdrich, sued her doctor for failing to properly diagnose and treat appendicitis. The patient initially presented with pain in the midline area of her groin, and when she returned six days later, Dr. Pegram discovered an inflamed mass in her abdomen. Nevertheless, Dr. Pegram did not order an immediate ultrasound at the local hospital, but decided that the patient could wait another eight days to have the procedure performed fifty miles away at a facility run by the for-profit HMO of which Dr. Pegram was a physician–owner. In the meantime, Ms. Herdrich's appendix ruptured, causing peritonitis. Ms. Herdrich won a jury award on her malpractice claims, but the question before the Court was whether treatment decisions made by an HMO acting through its physician–employees are fiduciary acts subject to ERISA.[26]

The *Pegram* Court held *unanimously* that HMO physicians' "mixed" eligibility and treatment decisions are *not* fiduciary acts within the meaning of ERISA.[27] The Court was persuaded that Congress did not intend these decisions to be measured against fiduciary standards, both because such suits would undercut a long-standing congressional policy of promoting HMOs, and because they would boil down to medical malpractice claims of the sort already available under state law.[28] Moreover, recognition of such fiduciary claims might even federalize medical malpractice law by triggering ERISA's preemption provision.[29]

Did *Pegram* portend a more general relaxation of fiduciary oversight in dual status (multiple hat) situations?[30] It did not. While conflicted decision making is endemic to some other plan types that Congress has promoted,[31] *Pegram*'s reasoning has not meaningfully spread beyond its original circumstances. In *Aetna Health Inc. v. Davila*,[32] for example, the Court clarified that a "benefit determination under ERISA ... is generally a fiduciary act," and the "fact that a benefit determination is infused with medical judgments does not alter this result."[33] Thus, the exception in *Pegram* is a narrow one, which applies only "where the underlying negligence also plausibly constitutes medical treatment by a party that can be deemed to be a treating physician or such a physician's employer."[34]

---

[26] *Id.* at 214–15.

[27] *Id.* at 237.

[28] *Id.* at 235–36.

[29] *Id.* at 236–37.

[30] *See* Marks v. Watters, 322 F.3d 316, 324–27 (4th Cir. 2003) (distinguishing *Pegram*; utilization review under preferred provider organization health plan not a mixed eligibility and treatment decision; state law claims for negligent utilization review subject to complete preemption).

[31] E.g., Grindstaff v. Green, 133 F.3d 416 (6th Cir. 1998) (voting of employee stock ownership plan stock by directors to perpetuate their own incumbency not breach of fiduciary duty in light of dual nature of ESOPs as retirement plans and method of corporate finance).

[32] 542 U.S. 200 (2004).

[33] *Id.* at 219.

[34] *Id.* at 221 (quoting from Judge Calabresi's dissent in Cicio v. Does, 321 F.3d 83, 109 (2d Cir. 2003)). Land v. CIGNA Healthcare of Fla., 381 F.3d 1274 (11th Cir. 2004) (medical

Multiple Fiduciaries

Another consequence of ERISA's functional definition of fiduciary is the proliferation of limited-role fiduciaries. Just as one person may deal with the plan in multiple capacities, multiple people may deal with the plan in a fiduciary capacity, with either overlapping or distinct responsibilities. Certain responsibilities are statutorily defined. Foremost is the named fiduciary, who has "authority to control and manage the operation and administration of the plan."[35] The named fiduciary functions as the chief executive officer of the plan, with ultimate authority over operations. The plan may, however, call for multiple named fiduciaries, having either joint or divided responsibilities.[36] For a funded plan, the trustee is the fiduciary who is legal owner of the assets and generally has exclusive authority over investment decision making.[37] The plan administrator is the person designated by the plan (or in default of which, the plan sponsor) with statutory responsibility for satisfying reporting and disclosure requirements. Thus, the administrator is a fiduciary who functions, in effect, as the chief information officer of the plan.[38]

---

malpractice claim preempted because adverse medical necessity determination by HMO approval nurse was benefit decision by ERISA fiduciary; *Pegram* exception for mixed eligibility and treatment decisions does not apply where decision maker is not the treating physician); Mayeaux v. La. Health Serv. & Indem. Co., 376 F.3d 420 (5th Cir. 2004) (ERISA preempts state law claims against health plan administrator based on denial of benefits under plan's experimental therapy exclusion).

[35] ERISA § 402(a)(1), 29 U.S.C. § 1102(a)(1) (2018). ERISA calls for the named fiduciary to be named in the plan instrument or identified by a procedure set forth in the plan. ERISA § 402 (a)(2), 29 U.S.C. § 1102(a)(2) (2018). Since no trust fails for want of a trustee, RESTATEMENT (SECOND) OF TRUSTS § 108 (1959), RESTATEMENT (THIRD) OF TRUSTS § 31 (2007), failure of the plan instrument to provide for a named fiduciary would not invalidate the plan, just as breach of the requirement of a written instrument does not, *see supra* Chapters 2A and 3C.

[36] ERISA §§ 402(a)(1) ("jointly or severally"), 405(c)(1) (plan procedures for allocation responsibilities), 29 U.S.C. §§ 1102(a)(1), 1105(c)(1) (2018).

[37] ERISA § 403(a), 29 U.S.C. § 1103(a) (2018). ERISA recognizes three exceptions to the trustee's exclusive authority to manage and control plan assets. First, the plan may provide the named fiduciary with authority to appoint one or more investment managers to manage plan assets. ERISA §§ 402(b)(3), 403(a)(2), 29 U.S.C. §§ 1102(b)(3), 1103(a)(2) (2018). Second, the plan may provide that trustees' dealings with plan assets will be subject to the direction of a named fiduciary who is not a trustee (the directed trustee). ERISA § 403(a)(1), 29 U.S.C. § 1103(a)(1) (2018). Third, a defined-contribution pension plan may permit a participant to exercise investment control over the assets in his account (a "404(c) plan"). ERISA § 404(c)(1), 29 U.S.C. § 1104(c)(1) (2018); 29 C.F.R. § 2550.404c-1 (2021). Trustees are immunized from liability for the acts or omissions of investment managers, provided that the trustee does not knowingly participate in or try to conceal the investment manager's breach. ERISA § 405(d)(1), 29 U.S.C. § 1105(d)(1) (2018). The potential continuing liability of a directed trustee is analyzed in *Hatamyar, supra* Chapter 4 note 14. Exposure of fiduciaries under a participant-directed 404(c) plan is an ongoing question explored *infra* Chapter 4D.

[38] ERISA §§ 3(16)(A), 101, 104, 105, 29 U.S.C. §§ 1002(16)(A), 1021, 1024, 1025 (2018). *See supra* Chapter 3D.

Fiduciary Obligations

Beyond the roles of named fiduciary, trustee, and administrator, other fiduciaries abound. Recall that any actual involvement in the management or disposition of plan assets – even if only by an underling (agent or employee) who lacks discretionary authority and is answerable to the trustee – suffices to bring about fiduciary classification. And ERISA permits the plan instrument to establish a procedure by which named fiduciaries may allocate fiduciary responsibilities among themselves or delegate their responsibilities to others.[39] Even if a delegation does not conform to ERISA's requirements, the delegate would nevertheless actually "have" or "exercise" discretionary authority respecting some aspects of plan management or operations, and would, to that extent, satisfy ERISA's definition of fiduciary.

Diffuse responsibility raises the question, who is to be held accountable? Speaking broadly, fiduciary liability under ERISA is premised on personal fault, not on notions of joint or vicarious responsibility. An act or omission in breach of duty by one fiduciary does not by itself render a cofiduciary liable. Instead, the cofiduciary is ordinarily liable only if his own breach of duty enabled the other fiduciary to commit the breach, or if, *knowing* that the other's act or omission is a breach, he knowingly participates in, knowingly undertakes to conceal, or fails to make reasonable efforts to remedy the other's breach.[40] In each of these cases the cofiduciary's own misconduct is a proximate cause of the loss that flows from another fiduciary's breach.

Conversely, if such direct responsibility is lacking, then a cofiduciary is ordinarily not held liable for another fiduciary's breach. As noted earlier, ERISA permits the plan instrument to establish a procedure by which named fiduciaries may allocate fiduciary responsibilities (other than asset management) among themselves or designate others to perform them. If a plan provides such a procedure, and if a named fiduciary does not breach her own duties in making or continuing an allocation or delegation of responsibilities thereunder, then ERISA insulates her from liability for the acts or omissions of the person assigned to carry out the tasks.[41] Similarly, the ERISA conference report observes that fiduciaries may sometimes hire agents to perform ministerial acts, in which case "the liability of the trustees (or other fiduciaries) for acts of their agents is to be established in accordance with the

---

[39] ERISA § 405(c), 29 U.S.C. § 1105(c) (2018). Named fiduciaries are not permitted to allocate or delegate asset-management functions, *id.*, but asset management is normally the exclusive province of the trustee rather than the named fiduciary, except in the case where the plan expressly provides that the trustee is subject to proper direction by a named fiduciary who is not a trustee. *See* ERISA § 403(a)(1), 29 U.S.C. § 1103(a)(1) (2018).

[40] ERISA § 405(a), 29 U.S.C. § 1105(a) (2018); H.R.. REP. No. 93-1280, at 299–300 (1974) (Conf. Rep.) (liability for failure to take reasonable steps to remedy a breach requires more than mere knowledge of a cofiduciary's act or omission; it requires actual knowledge that it is a breach), *reprinted in* 3 ERISA LEGISLATIVE HISTORY, *supra* Chapter 1 note 55, at 4566–67.

[41] ERISA § 405(c), 29 U.S.C. § 1105(c) (2018).

Conduct Controls: Welfare and Pension Plans

prudent man rule."[42] In other words, a fiduciary principal must be shown to have been negligent in hiring or supervising the agent to become liable to participants for the agent's acts. In suits to enforce fiduciary obligations, ERISA does *not* adopt a rule of respondeat superior: fiduciaries are not generally subject to imputed or vicarious liability.[43]

There is an important situation in which one fiduciary is accountable for a breach of duty committed by another, even though the first neither participated in nor had knowledge of the other's breach. ERISA permits the allocation or delegation of fiduciary functions (other than asset management) only if the plan expressly allows it and provides a procedure for doing so.[44] If in contravention of those rules a named fiduciary assigns some responsibility to another person, the named fiduciary remains on the hook for any breach committed by his deputy.[45] It seems that Congress sought to deter such informal delegations, even if not imprudent or disloyal, "so the employees may know who is responsible for operating the plan."[46] Thus, the named

---

[42] H.R. Rep. No. 93-1280, at 301 (1974) (Conf. Rep.), *reprinted in* 3 ERISA LEGISLATIVE HISTORY, *supra* Chapter 1 note 55, at 4568. This observation seems to indicate that Congress expected ordinary trust law principles to govern an ERISA fiduciary's liability for an agent's acts. *See* Restatement (Second) of Trusts § 225 (1959); 3 SCOTT ON TRUSTS, *supra* Chapter 3 note 16, §§ 225, 225.1 at 415–16.

[43] *See, e.g.,* Schmidt v. Sheet Metal Workers' Nat'l Pension Fund, 128 F.3d 541, 547–48 (7th Cir. 1997) (fiduciaries not liable for misinformation provided by ministerial agent where fiduciaries exercised due care in hiring, training, and supervising agent), *cert. denied*, 523 U.S. 1073 (1998).

[44] ERISA § 402(b)(2), 29 U.S.C. § 1102(b)(2) (2018).

[45] Fiduciary duties always include the obligation to follow the terms of the plan insofar as they are consistent with ERISA. ERISA § 404(a)(1)(D), 29 U.S.C. § 1104(a)(1)(D) (2018). Consequently, the act of allocating or delegating responsibilities would entail a breach of the named fiduciary's own obligations if it is not authorized by the plan or fails to conform to plan procedures. Under ERISA § 405(c)(2)(A)(i), 29 U.S.C. § 1105(c)(2)(A)(i) (2018), a named fiduciary who violates his own duties in allocating or delegating fiduciary functions is not exempt from liability for the acts of the deputy. Moreover, ERISA § 405(a)(2), 29 U.S.C. § 1105(a)(2) (2018), provides that if a fiduciary's failure to comply with his own duties in carrying out the specific responsibilities that give rise to his fiduciary status enables another fiduciary to commit a breach, then the first is liable for the other's breach. The ERISA conference report observes that "[a]llocation or delegation (and the consequent elimination of liability) can only occur" where the plan expressly provides for it. H.R. Rep. No. 93-1280, at 301 (1974) (Conf. Rep.), *reprinted in* 3 ERISA LEGISLATIVE HISTORY, *supra* Chapter 1 note 55, at 4568.

ERISA's rule of derivative liability based upon improper delegation is consistent with, and apparently derived from, state trust law. A trustee is liable to the beneficiary if he "improperly delegates the administration of the trust to his co-trustee," or if he delegates to an agent, the performance of which the trustee "was under a duty not to delegate." RESTATEMENT (SECOND) OF TRUSTS §§ 224(2)(b), 225(2)(b) (1959); 3 SCOTT ON TRUSTS, *supra* Chapter 3 note 16, §§ 224.2, 225.1 at 405, 416. *See* RESTATEMENT (SECOND) OF TRUSTS, *supra*, §§ 171 (duty not to delegate), 184 (where there are several trustees, each is under a duty to participate in the administration of the trust, to use reasonable care to prevent a cotrustee from committing a breach of trust, or to compel a cotrustee to redress a breach); RESTATEMENT (THIRD) OF TRUSTS §§ 80 & cmts. d–h, 81 (2007).

[46] H.R. Rep. No. 93-1280, at 297 (1974) (Conf. Rep.), *reprinted in* 3 ERISA LEGISLATIVE HISTORY, *supra* Chapter 1 note 55, at 4564.

Fiduciary Obligations

fiduciary is a proper defendant and remains subject to liability unless there is a paper trail showing proper delegation of authority to someone who can be readily identified.

Making significant personal involvement a necessary element of cofiduciary liability is consistent with traditional state trust law.[47] As between multiple fiduciaries, fairness seems to demand such a restriction, because a fiduciary in breach is "personally liable to make good to [the] plan any losses to the plan resulting from" the breach.[48] More importantly, in passing ERISA, Congress sought to promote plan sponsorship, and some such limit on exposure to risks imposed by the actions of other persons is surely necessary to keep monitoring, insurance, and plan-administration costs within acceptable bounds.[49]

B FIDUCIARY DUTIES

In General

ERISA's general standards of fiduciary conduct were derived from trust law. There are four major imperatives: (1) the exclusive benefit rule, which is based on the trust law duty of loyalty;[50] (2) the prudence requirement, which follows the trust law duty

---

[47] RESTATEMENT (SECOND) OF TRUSTS § 224 (1959) provides:
"(1) Except as stated in Subsection (2), a trustee is not liable to the beneficiary for a breach of trust committed by a co-trustee.
(2) A trustee is liable to the beneficiary, if he
(a) participates in a breach of trust committed by his co-trustee; or
(b) improperly delegates the administration of the trust to his co-trustee; or
(c) approves or acquiesces in or conceals a breach of trust committed by his co-trustee; or
(d) by his failure to exercise reasonable care in the administration of the trust has enabled his co-trustee to commit a breach of trust; or
(e) neglects to take proper steps to compel his co-trustee to redress a breach of trust." *Accord* RESTATEMENT (THIRD) OF TRUSTS § 81 cmt. e (2007).
The five instances in which RESTATEMENT (SECOND) OF TRUSTS § 224(2) authorizes cotrustee liability correspond, respectively, to (a) ERISA § 405(a)(1), participation; (b) § 405(c)(2)(A), improper delegation; (c) § 405(a)(1), concealment; (d) § 405(a)(2), enablement; and (e) § 405(a)(3), failure to remedy. Unlike the Restatement, however, in cases of participation, concealment, or failure to remedy, ERISA demands *actual* knowledge, not just reason to know, that the other's conduct constitutes a breach, and that one's own act or omission facilitates injury.
[48] ERISA § 409(a), 29 U.S.C. § 1109(a) (2018).
[49] Rather than performing different functions, multiple fiduciaries may act at different times. Taking an approach similar to the limits on cofiduciary liability, section 409(b) broadly absolves a successor trustee from liability for breaches committed by his predecessor. ERISA § 409(b), 29 U.S.C. § 1109(b) (2018). In contrast, trust law imposes a duty on a successor trustee to examine his predecessor's accounts and take steps to redress any breach. RESTATEMENT (SECOND) OF TRUSTS § 223 (1959).
[50] ERISA § 404(a)(1)(A), 29 U.S.C. § 1104(a)(1)(A) (2018). *See* RESTATEMENT (SECOND) OF TRUSTS § 170(1) (1959); RESTATEMENT (THIRD) OF TRUSTS § 78 (2007). The language of ERISA's exclusive benefit rule is similar to a long-standing qualification criterion (i.e.,

Conduct Controls: Welfare and Pension Plans

of reasonable care;[51] (3) the diversification rule, which under state trust law is a specific application or corollary of the general duty of reasonable care;[52] and (4) a requirement that the fiduciary act in accordance with plan documents, insofar as they are consistent with the requirements of ERISA.[53]

Despite its trust law origins, ERISA's specification of fiduciary duties entails three striking departures from traditional trust administration principles. First, ERISA does not explicitly impose a duty to deal impartially with multiple plan participants and beneficiaries.[54] Second, unlike their trust law counterparts, ERISA's fiduciary duties are *mandatory*; they do not serve merely as default rules that can be overridden by agreement (here, the plan instrument).[55] Third, ERISA's exclusive benefit rule looks to subjective motivation, unlike the trust law duty of loyalty.

Even where ERISA's fiduciary obligations follow state trust law, Congress understood that the traditional duties were being imported into a very different environment and that they might have to evolve differently in their new surroundings. Employee benefit plan administration bears little resemblance to the main function of private trusts, which is to provide a vehicle for ongoing management of intergenerational transfers of family wealth. "The conferees expect that the courts will

condition on obtaining preferential tax treatment) applicable to pension, profit-sharing, and stock bonus plans. I.R.C. § 401(a)(2) (2018) provides that under the trust instrument it must be "impossible, at any time prior to the satisfaction of all liabilities with respect to employees and their beneficiaries under the trust, for any part of the corpus or income to be ... used for, or diverted to, purposes other than the exclusive benefit of his employees or their beneficiaries."

[51] ERISA § 404(a)(1)(B), 29 U.S.C. § 1104(a)(1)(B) (2018). See RESTATEMENT (SECOND) OF TRUSTS § 174 (1959); RESTATEMENT (THIRD) OF TRUSTS § 77 (2007).

[52] ERISA § 404(a)(1)(C), 29 U.S.C. § 1104(a)(1)(C) (2018). In certain circumstances an ESOP, profit-sharing plan, or stock bonus plan is permitted to invest heavily in employer securities or employer real estate notwithstanding the diversification rule (or the prudence requirement, to the extent that it would require diversification). ERISA §§ 404(a)(2), 407(d)(3)-(6), 29 U.S.C. §§ 1104(a)(2), 1107(d)(3)-(6) (2018). In plan years beginning after 2006, defined contribution plan participants must in some cases be allowed to direct the plan to switch their account investments from employer securities to diversified investment options. ERISA § 204(j), 29 U.S.C. § 1054(j) (2018); see I.R.C. § 401(a)(35) (2018). See RESTATEMENT (SECOND) OF TRUSTS § 228 (1959); RESTATEMENT (THIRD) OF TRUSTS § 90(a), (b) (2007).

[53] ERISA § 404(a)(1)(D), 29 U.S.C. § 1104(a)(1)(D) (2018). See RESTATEMENT (THIRD) OF TRUSTS § 76(1) & cmt. B(1) (2007).

[54] See RESTATEMENT (SECOND) OF TRUSTS § 183 (1959) ("When there are two or more beneficiaries of a trust, the trustee is under a duty to deal impartially with them."); id. § 232 ("If a trust is created for beneficiaries in succession, the trustee is under a duty to the successive beneficiaries to act with due regard to their respective interests."); RESTATEMENT (THIRD) OF TRUSTS § 79 (2007).

[55] See RESTATEMENT (SECOND) OF TRUSTS § 164 (1959): "The nature and extent of the duties and powers of the trustee are determined: (a) by the terms of the trust, except as stated in §§ 165–168; and (b) in the absence of any provision in the terms of the trust, by the rules stated in §§ 169–196." Accord RESTATEMENT (THIRD) OF TRUSTS §§ 76, 77 cmt. D, 78(1) (2007). It is significant that the Restatement treats the general fiduciary duties of trustees as a set of default rules that can be modified by the trust agreement, while ERISA sections 404(a)(1)(D) and 410 (a) forbid such modifications. See infra Chapter 4 note 63 and accompanying text.

Fiduciary Obligations

interpret this prudent man rule (and the other fiduciary standards) bearing in mind the special nature and purpose of employee benefit plans."[56] The Supreme Court explained the appropriate analytic approach as follows:

> [W]e recognize that these fiduciary duties draw much of their content from the common law of trusts, the law that governed most benefit plans before ERISA's enactment.
>
> We also recognize, however, that trust law does not tell the entire story. After all, ERISA's standards and procedural protections partly reflect a congressional determination that the common law of trusts did not offer completely satisfactory protection.
>
> Consequently, we believe that the law of trusts often will inform, but will not necessarily determine the outcome of, an effort to interpret ERISA's fiduciary duties. In some instances, trust law will offer only a starting point, after which courts must go on to ask whether, or to what extent, the language of the statute, its structure, or its purposes require departing from common-law trust requirements. And, in doing so, courts may have to take account of competing congressional purposes, such as Congress' desire to offer employees enhanced protection for their benefits, on the one hand, and, on the other, its desire not to create a system that is so complex that administrative costs, or litigation expenses, unduly discourage employers from offering welfare benefit plans in the first place.[57]

Impartiality

Temporal division of property ownership always creates the potential for conflict between current and future claimants. Left unsupervised, the owner of the current interest may be inclined to consume the whole; the common law responded by protecting future interest holders with the doctrine of waste. Where property is held in trust, current and future beneficiaries typically have very different preferences regarding investment policy. The current income beneficiary wants to generate the maximum short-term return, and so favors high-risk investments, while the principal beneficiary prefers maximum security, even though minimizing risk of loss will reduce or eliminate current yield. The duty of loyalty enjoins the trustee to act for the exclusive benefit of the beneficiaries, yet on matters of investment policy beneficiaries' interests inevitably conflict. Trust law handles this dilemma by

---

[56] H.R. Rep. No. 93-1280, at 302 (1974) (Conf. Rep.), *reprinted in* 3 ERISA LEGISLATIVE HISTORY, *supra* Chapter 1 note 55, at 4569. *See* H.R. REP. No. 93-533, at 12, 13 (1973) ("the typical employee benefit plan, covering hundreds or even thousands of participants, is quite different from the testamentary trust both in purpose and in nature," so the "principles of fiduciary conduct are adopted from existing trust law, but with modifications appropriate for employee benefit plans"), *reprinted in* 2 ERISA LEGISLATIVE HISTORY, *supra* Chapter 1 note 55, at 2359, 2360.

[57] Varity Corp. v. Howe, 516 U.S. 489, 496–97 (1996).

imposing a duty of impartiality, which prohibits favoritism and instructs the trustee (in effect) to fairly compromise the beneficiaries' conflicting interests. Similar conflicts arise between current and future retirees under pension trusts, yet ERISA does not explicitly impose a duty to deal impartially with multiple plan participants and beneficiaries.

Some differences of opinion between pension plan participants present classic impartiality questions. Retirees and older workers under a defined contribution plan will tend to favor more secure investments bearing a lower yield, while younger participants ordinarily have a greater risk tolerance and seek higher rates of return. Under specified conditions, it is now possible (and extremely common) to let participants exercise investment control over their own individual accounts, and so make separate decisions in line with their personal risk tolerance.[58] But where a named fiduciary, an investment manager, or the trustee is in charge of investment decision making, the fiduciary must select appropriate risk and return objectives for the fund as a whole, and participants will differ over that collective decision. In such a case, the traditional trust law duty of impartiality is clearly the correct approach, and the federal courts should have little difficulty imposing it despite ERISA's silence. The interpolation of a duty of impartiality would be an appropriate exercise of the courts' power to craft a federal common law of employee benefit plans. Moreover, a duty of impartiality is implicit in the general standard of care, for a prudent person charged with representing conflicting interests would pursue a reasonable accommodation of those interests.[59]

Many cases involving inter-participant conflicts do not present true impartiality issues; they only masquerade as such. These pseudo-impartiality cases are of two types. The first consists of situations where participants' interests conflict but the fiduciary is also a plan participant. As to these, loyalty is usually the real issue.[60]

---

[58] ERISA § 404(c), 29 U.S.C. § 1104(c) (2018); 29 C.F.R. § 2550.404c-1 (2021). These "section 404(c) plans" have become popular, in part because trustees and other fiduciaries are absolved from liability for losses that directly result from the participant's investment choices. *See supra* Chapter 4D.

[59] In Varity Corp. v. Howe, 516 U.S. 489 (1996), after observing that ERISA's "fiduciary duties draw much of their content from the common law of trusts," *id.* at 496, the Court said that recognizing an ERISA "fiduciary obligation, enforceable by beneficiaries seeking relief for themselves, does not necessarily favor payment over nonpayment. The common law of trusts recognizes the need to preserve assets to satisfy future, as well as present, claims and requires a trustee to take impartial account of the interests of all beneficiaries." *Id.* at 514. *See* Morse v. Stanley, 732 F.2d 1139, 1145 (2d Cir. 1984) ("[A] trustee has a duty to deal impartially with beneficiaries. In this case there are working Plan participants and retired beneficiaries and/or their families. The trustee must deal even-handedly among them, doing his best for the entire trust looked at as a whole."). *See* RESTATEMENT (THIRD) OF TRUSTS §§ 79 cmt. b, 90 cmt. c (2007) (duty of impartiality derivative of general duties of prudence and loyalty).

[60] *See, e.g.*, Foltz v. U.S. News & World Rep., Inc., 865 F.2d 364 (D.C. Cir. 1989) (no breach of duty found where plan administered in favor of future rather than past retirees, but the court took no note of the fact that the fiduciaries were themselves members of the favored class).

Fiduciary Obligations

The second type of case that presents conflicts of interest between classes of participants involves interests other than plan benefits. Consider the takeover defense cases, where the issue is whether employer stock held in a pension trust should be tendered for sale at a substantial premium over the current market price for the shares. Retirees and older workers are likely to favor tendering the plan's shares, while younger workers, fearing that the change in ownership will entail corporate restructuring with attendant job losses through downsizing, are likely to oppose the takeover. Employment security (and with it the prospect of future pension accruals) is likely to be much more important to younger participants than is the security of previously accrued pension benefits, while only the latter consideration is relevant to workers who are already out the door. In these instances there is clear-cut difference of opinion among participants, but it's not just about plan benefits – it's also about other important interests (here, continued employment). The trouble with approaching the issue from the perspective of impartiality is that an ERISA fiduciary is not empowered to promote the interests of the participants at large. Far from having a general warrant to do good, a fiduciary must discharge his duties for the exclusive purpose of providing plan benefits and defraying reasonable expenses of administration. Consequently job security, although vitally important to young workers, is simply not a cognizable interest under ERISA. Nor should it be, for in cases of this sort the younger workers opposed to the takeover are, in substance, seeking to trade a portion of their accumulated pension wealth for increased job security, which clearly violates the protective policy of ERISA's anti-alienation rule. A worker cannot directly trade a portion of her accrued pension benefit for a no-cut clause in her contract, and the exclusive benefit rule prohibits her from accomplishing the same result indirectly through fiduciary decision making. The lesson here is that not every dispute between participants should be analyzed as an impartiality question: only the interest in plan benefits is statutorily cognizable.[61] A compromise that takes into account other illegitimate interests necessarily undermines ERISA policies.

Exculpatory Clauses

The settlor of a private trust may, by an express provision in the trust instrument, relax otherwise applicable obligations, including the trustee's stringent duties of loyalty and care.[62] ERISA outlaws such exculpatory provisions, both implicitly, by

---

[61] *E.g.*, Summers v. State St. Bank & Tr. Co., 104 F.3d 105, 108 (7th Cir. 1997) (favoring active over retired participants "would be picking and choosing among beneficiaries, in violation of the traditional duty imposed by trust law of impartiality among beneficiaries," but that principle does not apply to a trade-off between wages and employee stock ownership plan benefits because the "trustee's sole duty is to the participants as participants").

[62] RESTATEMENT (SECOND) OF TRUSTS § 222 (1959); RESTATEMENT (THIRD) OF TRUSTS §§ 77 cmt. d, 78(1) & cmt. c(2), 87 & cmt. d (2007).

the stipulation that the fiduciary must follow plan documents only insofar as they are consistent with ERISA, including ERISA's specification of fiduciary duties, and explicitly, by declaring such indulgences "void as against public policy."[63] Setting high standards of administrative integrity and competence would accomplish little if they could be gutted in the fine print of the plan document.

Instead of barring exculpatory clauses, Congress might have simply demanded prominent notice, leaving it up to employees to decide how much confidence to put in a plan that excuses faithless or foolish management. In taking the matter out of the hands of individual decision makers, the prohibition of exculpatory clauses can be viewed as another instance of ERISA's protective policy. But an alternative explanation is that uniform fiduciary standards may facilitate career and financial planning by reducing information costs.

Disclosure provides access to information, but a rational worker won't use the information if the cost of evaluating it exceeds the benefit likely to be gained from it. Comparing the health care, group life insurance, and retirement plans sponsored by several potential employers is a daunting task. The task is greatly complicated if one must delve beyond the plan terms governing participation and benefits to assess the extent to which the apparent benefit promise is undermined by fiduciary rules that absolve negligent or disloyal decisions. To identify the most valuable plan, workers would have to discount nominal benefits by the probability of nonreceipt through fiduciary misconduct. The cost of ferreting out and computing the effect of such differences may be so high that the rational response to variation in fiduciary standards is simply to ignore it and assume that all plans, whatever their nominal participation and benefit rules, are of average quality. In contrast, limited standardization of benefit plan terms might reduce information costs enough to make it worthwhile for workers to attend to the remaining important differences between plans. If so, plans would become more valuable to employers and employees alike, because differences in plan terms could be used to compete for labor, and better-informed workers would make better career and financial planning decisions. The ban on exculpatory clauses ensures that ERISA imposes *uniform* fiduciary obligations, and thereby standardizes the key unwritten terms of employee benefit plans. That standardization may well be paternalistic, but the information cost perspective suggests that it could actually enhance efficiency.[64] Of course, the validity of the

---

[63] ERISA §§ 404(a)(1)(D), 410(a), 29 U.S.C. §§ 1104(a)(1)(D), 1110(a) (2018). The labor committees of both the Senate and House singled out exculpatory provisions as the reason that "reliance on conventional trust law is often insufficient to adequately protect the interests of plan participants and beneficiaries." S. REP. NO. 93-127, at 29 (1973), *reprinted in* 1 ERISA LEGISLATIVE HISTORY, *supra* Chapter 1 note 55, at 615; H.R. REP. NO. 93-533, at 12 (1973), *reprinted in* 2 ERISA LEGISLATIVE HISTORY, *supra* Chapter 1 note 55, at 2359.

[64] Wiedenbeck, *supra* Chapter 1 note 56, at 570 ("A single set of interstitial rules (contract and trust) governing all plans would limit information costs and increase the efficiency of the labor market."); *id.* at 576 ("By imposing uniform fiduciary obligations and authorizing the development of a federal common law of benefit plans (conduct controls) the unwritten terms of the

Fiduciary Obligations

133

information cost hypothesis is an empirical question that requires further investigation.

Despite its central role in the scheme of fiduciary oversight and the important policy ambiguity underlying it, the ban on exculpatory clauses has received very little judicial attention. Apparently, plan drafters got the message and have shied away from the more blatant attempts to limit fiduciary duties. But the courts have not always recognized covert exculpatory clauses when they encounter them. From one perspective, the question of the proper scope of review of fiduciary plan interpretations concerns the enforceability of a well-disguised exculpatory clause, but the Supreme Court did not approach the question as such.[65]

The Exclusive Benefit Rule

ERISA demands that a fiduciary discharge his duties "solely in the interests of the participants and beneficiaries and for the *exclusive purpose* of providing benefits to participants and their beneficiaries and defraying reasonable expenses of administering the plan."[66] This standard of integrity is the third momentous discrepancy between the obligations of private trustees and employee benefit plan fiduciaries. The exclusive benefit rule looks to the decision maker's purposes, and therefore the duty apparently turns upon subjective motivation. This perspective is reiterated by ERISA's anti-inurement rule, which provides that "the assets of a plan shall never inure to the benefit of any employer and shall be held for the *exclusive purposes* of providing benefits to participants in the plan and their beneficiaries and defraying reasonable expenses of administering the plan."[67] ERISA's acceptance of divided loyalties apparently reflects a concession to the practice of benefit plan management by representatives of the plan sponsor. Congress expressly provided that the prohibited-transaction rules do not bar a fiduciary from also serving as an "officer, employee, agent or other representative of a party in interest," which includes the employer.[68] By permitting a fiduciary to wear multiple hats in his relation to the plan, ERISA accepts the existence of pervasive conflicts of interest, while at the same

---

benefit arrangement are standardized as well [referring to the standardization achieved by the pension plan content controls]."). As suggested by the last-cited source, this information cost perspective may also provide an economic justification for several important pension plan content controls, including the minimum standards governing benefit accrual and vesting. *See infra* Chapter 7B, C.

[65] *See* Firestone Tire & Rubber Co. v. Bruch, 489 U.S. 101 (1989), discussed *infra* Chapter 5B.

[66] ERISA § 404(a)(1)(A), 29 U.S.C. § 1104(a)(1)(A) (2018) (emphasis added).

[67] ERISA § 403(c)(1), 29 U.S.C. § 1103(c)(1) (2018) (emphasis added).

[68] ERISA §§ 408(c)(3), 3(14), 29 U.S.C. §§ 1108(c)(3), 1002(14) (2018). From the perspective of trust law, section 408(c)(3) functions as a statutory exculpatory clause for employee benefit plan fiduciaries, permitting them to proceed under a conflict of interest so long as they seek to advance only the interest in plan benefits of participants and their beneficiaries (i.e., they act in good faith). *See infra* Chapter 4 note 75.

time the exclusive benefit rule purportedly demands that those conflicts never influence decision making.

Several decades ago, Professors Daniel Fischel and John Langbein called the exclusive benefit rule "ERISA's fundamental contradiction" and convincingly demonstrated how it "bedevil[s] a remarkable array of the main issues in modern pension trust administration: takeover cases, social investing, employee stock ownership schemes, asset reversions from terminated plans, and judicial review of benefit denials and other plan decisions."[69] They warned that a "rule favoring employees that overrides the initial understanding between the parties, whether explicit or implicit, will actually harm employees by discouraging plan formation."[70] Their proposed solution was to recognize that the employer is, in important respects, also a beneficiary of the plan,[71] and their analysis suggested that the exclusive benefit rule should be construed to permit the courts to take into account the employer's interests.

The statutory language presents a stumbling block to such an expansive interpretation of the exclusive benefit rule (as Fischel and Langbein acknowledged).[72] Although the employer obviously benefits from the program by deriving advantages such as lower compensation costs or reduced worker turnover, the employer is neither a "participant" nor a "beneficiary" as those terms are used by ERISA to designate the protected class under the exclusive benefit rule.[73] Moreover, the exclusive benefit rule does not permit any action that is designed to promote some interest of participants and beneficiaries (e.g., continued employment); instead it authorizes only actions directed to providing participants with plan benefits. When, on matters of administration, the employer's and employees' interests diverge, the employer is typically seeking either to deny benefits (contain costs) or to use the plan for other purposes (e.g., to finance an acquisition or a takeover defense).

Trust law generally avoids these problems by prohibiting the trustee from entering into any transaction in which she would have a conflict of interest.[74] Such an

---

[69] Daniel Fischel & John H. Langbein, *ERISA's Fundamental Contradiction: The Exclusive Benefit Rule*, 55 U. Chi. L. Rev. 1105, 1107, 1126–57 (1988).

[70] *Id.* at 1158.

[71] *Id.* at 1117 ("it is best for many purposes to conceive of employer and employee as both settlor and beneficiary"), 1118 ("plans are established for the mutual advantage of employer and employee, not for the exclusive benefit of one"), 1158 ("We believe that ERISA permits the courts to be more forth-right in recognizing the employer's interest as beneficiary.").

[72] *Id.* at 1118, 1158 (language of the exclusive benefit rule "appears to preclude recognition of the employer as a beneficiary").

[73] ERISA §§ 3(7), (8), 404(a)(1), 29 U.S.C. §§ 1002(7), (8), 1104(a)(1) (2018). "Beneficiary" means a person designated to receive plan benefits either by the participant or the terms of the plan. *See also* Treas. Reg. § 1.401-1(b)(4) (2021) (definition of beneficiary for purposes of the qualified plan rules).

[74] *See, e.g.*, Restatement (Third) of Trusts § 78(1), (2) & cmt. b (2007); 2A Scott on Trusts, *supra* Chapter 3 note 16, § 170 at 311; George G. Bogert & George T. Bogert, The Law of Trusts and Trustees § 543 at 264, 267–68 (rev. 2d ed. 1993).

Fiduciary Obligations

objective prohibition on divided loyalties forestalls questions of good faith or fairness.[75] In contrast, ERISA's acceptance of nonneutral fiduciaries often makes it impossible to assume that a fiduciary's act proceeds from a purity of motives.[76] In making the fiduciary's "exclusive purpose" the touchstone, ERISA demands assessment of a conflicted decision maker's state of mind. Subjective purpose, of course, is necessarily inferred from objective facts. Because people are assumed to intend the natural consequences of their actions, the extent to which the fiduciary's decision promotes some competing interest is often the most relevant evidence of purpose. Mutually beneficial outcomes are, of course, the hardest case. A decision that promotes the participants' and beneficiaries' interests in plan benefits as well as some conflicting interest creates a strong inference of improper motivation if another decision would have *better* served participants and beneficiaries. On the other hand, if results appear optimal from the standpoint of providing plan benefits, one cannot automatically condemn a decision that also serves the employer's or fiduciary's interest, because an unbiased decision maker would have reached the same conclusion.[77]

The leading takeover defense case, *Donovan v. Bierwirth*,[78] illustrates both the practical difficulty of identifying improper motivation and the approaches taken by the federal courts. In the fall of 1981, LTV Corporation attempted to acquire Grumman Corporation by making a tender offer at a price of $45 per share for 70 percent of Grumman's stock, which, prior to the offer, had been trading for about

---

[75] Where the settlor authorizes the trustee to enter into a transaction in which she has a conflict of interest, the trustee must act in good faith. RESTATEMENT (THIRD) OF TRUSTS § 78 cmt. c(2) (2007) (despite exculpatory clause, "a trustee violates the duty of loyalty to the beneficiaries by acting in bad faith or unfairly"); RESTATEMENT (SECOND) OF TRUSTS §§ 170 cmt. t, 222(2) (1959) ("provision in the trust instrument is not effective to relieve the trustee from liability for breach of trust committed in bad faith"). That is, an exculpatory clause that implicates the duty of loyalty is interpreted to lift the objective prohibition but substitute an inquiry into subjective purpose. Correspondingly, ERISA § 408(c)(3), the authorization of nonneutral fiduciaries, functions as a statutory exculpatory clause and the exclusive benefit rule imposes the good-faith criterion.

[76] Benefit determinations by structurally conflicted fiduciaries are so commonplace in practice that the Supreme Court crafted one opinion expressly addressing (and largely tolerating) such conflict (*see generally* Metro. Life Ins. Co. v. Glenn, 554 U.S. 105 (2008)), and another expressly holding that arbitrary and capricious conduct by a conflicted benefit administrator is insufficient to strip deference (*see generally* Conkright v. Frommert, 559 U.S. 506 (2010)). For a fuller discussion of conflicted benefit determinations, *see infra* Chapter 5B. *See also* Peter J. Wiedenbeck, *Untrustworthy: ERISA's Eroded Fiduciary Law*, 59 WM. & MARY L. REV. 1007, 1074–84 (2018) (analyzing *Glenn* and *Conkright* in laying out how the Court intends in practice to only very modestly police conflicted benefits administrators).

[77] A qualification is in order here. If the optimal result from the standpoint of participants' and beneficiaries' interests in plan benefit could also have been achieved by means of another decision or course of action that would not have benefited the employer or fiduciary, then the fiduciary's selection of the mutually beneficial means necessarily reflects a prohibited purpose.

[78] 680 F.2d 263 (2d Cir.), *cert. denied*, 459 U.S. 1069 (1982). The case is discussed at length by Fischel and Langbein, *supra* Chapter 4 note 69, at 1126–28, 1138–41.

136 — Conduct Controls: Welfare and Pension Plans

$25 per share. Two days after the tender offer was announced, the Grumman board unanimously voted to oppose it and issued a press release stating that the LTV offer was "inadequate, and not in the best interests of Grumman, its shareholders, employees or the United States."[79] At the time of the offer, Grumman's defined benefit pension plan owned 525,000 shares of the company's stock. The trustees of the Grumman pension plan consisted of Grumman's chairman of the board (Bierwirth), the company's chief financial officer, and the treasurer of Grumman Aerospace; the first two were directors, and all of them worked feverishly in their capacity as management employees to defeat the LTV tender offer. When they met as plan trustees, they voted not to sell the plan's Grumman shares to LTV, and then quickly authorized the plan to purchase additional Grumman shares up to the 10 percent limit imposed by ERISA's prohibited-transaction rules.[80] The plan bought about 1,275,000 additional shares for a cost of about $44 million. A few days later Grumman's request for a temporary injunction of LTV's tender offer based on alleged securities and antitrust violations was granted, and the value of the Grumman shares bought by the plan dropped to $32.5 million. The Secretary of Labor (Donovan) brought suit against the plan trustees for breach of fiduciary duties, despite the fact that the Grumman plan participants overwhelmingly supported the trustees' actions.

Judge Friendly's seminal opinion establishes several important points. First, fiduciary action that advances a conflicting interest and does not also promote (or even harm) the participants' interest *in benefits* almost necessitates finding a breach of the exclusive benefit rule. The trustees' decision to purchase additional Grumman shares at a price greatly inflated by the LTV tender offer was of this sort, for it advanced management's interest in blocking the takeover, while exposing the plan to a substantial risk of loss.[81] On the other hand, Judge Friendly agreed with the defendants' argument that fiduciaries do not *necessarily* violate their duties by

---

[79] *Bierwirth*, 680 F.2d at 266.

[80] *See* ERISA § 407(a)(2), 29 U.S.C. § 1107(a)(2) (2018).

[81] Judge Friendly explained:

"[I]n purchasing additional shares when they did, the trustees were buying into what, from their own point of view, was almost certainly a 'no-win' situation. If the LTV offer succeeded, the Plan would be left as a minority stockholder in an LTV-controlled Grumman – a point that seems to have received no consideration. If it failed, as the Plan's purchase of [an] additional 8 percent of the outstanding Grumman stock made more likely, the stock was almost certain to sink to its pre-offer level, as the trustees fully appreciated. Given the trustees' views as to the dim future of an LTV-controlled Grumman, it is thus exceedingly difficult to accept Bierwirth's testimony that the purchase of additional shares was justified from an investment standpoint – or even to conclude that the trustees really believed this. Investment considerations dictated a policy of waiting. If LTV's offer were accepted, the trustees would not want more Grumman shares; if it failed, the shares would be obtainable at prices far below what was paid. Mid-October 1981 was thus the worst possible time for the Plan to buy Grumman stock as an investment. It is almost impossible to believe that the trustees did not realize this and that their motive for purchasing the additional shares was for any purpose other than blocking the LTV offer." *Bierwirth*, 680 F.2d at 275 (footnote omitted).

Fiduciary Obligations

following a course of action that actually benefits *both* the corporation and the participants. The court cautioned, however, that to avoid liability where a decision incidentally benefits the corporation or themselves, the fiduciaries must conclude that the action is "*best* to promote the interests of participants and beneficiaries," and the decision "must be made with an eye single to the interests of the participants and beneficiaries."[82] This is in line with the earlier conclusion that, if results appear optimal from the standpoint of providing plan benefits, one cannot automatically condemn a decision that also serves the employer's or fiduciary's interest. Consistent with the statutory "exclusive purpose" standard, Judge Friendly's formulation confirms that one also cannot automatically approve it.

When a fiduciary asserts that some challenged action was in fact best for participants and beneficiaries, and only incidentally benefited a conflicting interest, how can one determine if the decision was "made with an eye single to the interests of participants and beneficiaries"? How can a court put the subjective loyalty standard into practical effect? *Bierwirth* typifies the judicial response, which is to abandon the exclusive benefit rule and fall back on prudence. In contrast to the exclusive benefits rule's focus on motivation, the prudence rule, being a negligence-based reasonable person standard, is an objective test. Under ERISA case law, the prudence rule has a predominantly procedural cast, for neglect in monitoring, fact gathering, or obtaining expert advice is ordinarily a surer sign of careless decision making than is any particular judgment on the merits.[83] Often a decision that promotes the employer's or fiduciary's interest is arrived at without full information and deliberation, because the illegitimate consideration drives the process. The record in *Bierwirth* revealed numerous failures to investigate facts that were clearly relevant to the trustees' decision not to tender the plan's Grumman stock.[84] But the Friendly opinion goes farther, suggesting that decisions made by interested fiduciaries are subject to more exacting standards of prudence. "[T]hey should have realized that,

---

[82] *Id.* at 271.

[83] *See* ABA Section of Labor and Employment Law, EMPLOYEE BENEFITS LAW 10-63 to 10-69 (4th ed. 2017) ; Beck v. Pace Int'l Union, 427 F.3d 668, 678 (9th Cir. 2005) *rev'd and remanded on other grounds,* 551 U.S. 96 (2007). In principle, of course, a decision made upon full information after adequate deliberation could seem so illogical as to be imprudent. With respect to investment decision making, ERISA does not assess the prudence of a particular investment in isolation; instead, the propriety of the investment is gauged by its role (with respect to risk, return, and liquidity) in the portfolio as a whole. 29 C.F.R. § 2550.404a-1(b)(1), -1(b)(2) (2021). In this, ERISA fiduciary law substantially predated trust law's incorporation of modern portfolio theory. RESTATEMENT (THIRD) OF TRUSTS § 90(a) (2007) (prudence of investment assessed "not in isolation but in the context of the trust portfolio and as part of an overall investment strategy, which should incorporate risk and return objectives reasonably suitable to the trust").

[84] *Bierwirth*, 680 F.2d at 272–74. For later examples of the application of the "eye single" standard by resort to noting procedural shortcomings, *see* Perez v. Bruister, 823 F.3d 250, 261–62 (5th Cir. 2016); Beck v. Pace Int'l Union, 427 F.3d 668, 678 (9th Cir. 2005) *rev'd and remanded on other grounds,* 551 U.S. 96 (2007).

Of course, review for prudence – even applying heightened scrutiny – does not ensure complete integrity of decision making. With adequate investigation, independent advice, and full deliberation, the well-advised fiduciary can avoid prudence violations even as he pursues a mutually beneficial course of action. By going through the motions of reasoned decision making and reaching a determination that appears, in retrospect, to have been designed to best promote participants' interest in benefits, the fiduciary can ensure that his action will be upheld, even if that course was in fact chosen because of the advantages it offers to the fiduciary, the employer, or another interested party. In this situation, the practical impossibility of determining motivations gives the fiduciary freedom to select, from among the alternatives that would yield comparable benefits for participants, the course of action that also promotes another interest. In this limited sense, the subjective loyalty standard of the exclusive benefit rule sometimes permits the fiduciary to promote the joint welfare of the employer and employees.[86] In contrast, a prophylactic ban on conflicts of interest, such as trust law's objective duty of loyalty, would prevent such mutually beneficial decisions even where the employer's gains were not made at the employees' expense.

Interaction between the exclusive benefit rule and procedural prudence is likewise exemplified by politically charged ongoing debates about the propriety of considering environmental, social, or governance (ESG) factors in investment decision making and in exercising shareholder rights, such as voting stock owned by the plan. The "exclusive purpose of providing benefits" demands that fiduciaries not sacrifice investment returns or bear additional investment risk to achieve objectives unrelated to the provision of plan benefits.[87] A union plan investing in firms and projects to increase demand for unionized labor, or an employer plan investing to thwart a hostile takeover, illustrate pursuit of interests that are not cognizable under

---

[85] *Bierwirth*, 680 F.2d at 276. "One way for the trustees to inform themselves would have been to solicit the advice of independent counsel." *Id.* at 272.

[86] The maneuvering room inherent in the exclusive benefit rule is a much more limited freedom than Fischel and Langbein advocate (*supra* Chapter 4 notes 69–71 and accompanying text) – on the employees' side, only the interest in plan benefits is cognizable (not employee welfare writ large), and the workers' interest in benefits cannot be materially sacrificed to advance employer objectives.

[87] Concerning cognizable interests, *see supra* Chapter 4 notes 61, 77, 82 and accompanying text. The Labor Department's investment duty regulation provides in part: "A fiduciary may not subordinate the interests of the participants and beneficiaries in their retirement income or financial benefits under the plan to other objectives, and may not sacrifice investment return or take on additional investment risk to promote benefits or goals unrelated to interests of the participants and beneficiaries in their retirement income or financial benefits under the plan." 29 C.F.R. § 2550.404a-1(c)(1) (2023).

Fiduciary Obligations

ERISA. In contrast, environmental threats like climate change, or corporate governance structures that insulate management from accountability, can influence financial returns and investment risk. To that extent, such considerations are relevant to prudent design and implementation of an appropriate investment policy and portfolio structure.

Whether ESG considerations can properly figure into investment decisions beyond assessment of a portfolio's risk-adjusted financial return is a more difficult issue. Successive presidential administrations since the 1990s have grappled with the question: can a choice between apparently equal alternative investments, evaluated on risk-return characteristics, be made based on other benefits?[88] Does ERISA condone use of a "social good" tiebreaker? (Instead of societal benefits, can a choice between otherwise-equal financial options take into account advantages that the plan sponsor or fiduciary would derive?) Is such a question even coherent? Arguably, throwing additional criteria or considerations into the balance necessarily increases costs of decision making, to the detriment of the interest of participants and beneficiaries in plan benefits. Proxy voting, a component of plan asset management, poses the issue particularly starkly. Expert evaluation entails costs, the benefits of which are often small or uncertain, and perhaps nonfinancial.

C PROHIBITED TRANSACTIONS

Holding nonneutral fiduciaries to a standard of subjective loyalty has the advantage of permitting some actions that benefit the employer or fiduciary without injuring plan participants. But that occasional benefit could come at a formidable cost. If the exclusive benefit and prudence rules were the sole means of policing fiduciary conduct, the result would be frequent fact-intensive inquiries into the decision maker's state of mind. Immense legal expenses and frequent mistakes would follow.[89] ERISA limits these costs by imposing a set of prohibited-transaction rules that outlaw certain conflict-of-interest transactions on the basis of readily identified objective criteria. "Congress enacted § 406 'to bar categorically a transaction that [is] likely to injure the ... plan.'"[90] By cheaply screening out the cases where there is a

---

[88] See generally Prudence and Loyalty in Selecting Plan Investments and Exercising Shareholder Rights, 87 Fed. Reg. 73,822 (Dec. 1, 2022) (extended discussion of ESG issues in the preamble to the 2022 final rule). The current rule permits tiebreaker consideration of ESG matters. 29 C.F.R. § 2550.404a-1(c)(2) (2023).

[89] See S. Rep. No. 93-383, at 95 (1973) (noting that an arm's length standard of dealing requires substantial enforcement efforts, "resulting in sporadic and uncertain effectiveness"), reprinted in 1 ERISA Legislative History, supra Chapter 1 note 55, at 1069, 1163–64.

[90] Lockheed Corp. v. Spink, 517 U.S. 882, 888 (1996) (quoting Comm'r v. Keystone Consol. Indus., Inc., 508 U.S. 152, 160 (1993)). Accord Cutaiar v. Marshall, 590 F.2d 523, 528–30 (3d Cir. 1979) (prohibited-transaction rules apply without regard to good faith or fairness of the transaction; they establish a blanket prohibition, relief from which is available only by use of the statutory exemption procedure).

strong likelihood that the participants' interest will be compromised, the prohibited-transaction rules narrow the operation of the exclusive benefit rule to a range of cases in which the latter rule's high costs may be justified.

Prohibited transactions are of three types: party-in-interest transactions, employer-investment transactions, and fiduciary conflicts. A fiduciary is prohibited from causing the plan to engage in a transaction with a "party in interest" if the fiduciary knows or should know that the transaction involves a direct or indirect sale, exchange, or leasing of property, lending of money or other extension of credit, or furnishing of goods, services, or facilities between the plan and the party in interest. Also prohibited is the transfer of plan assets to or use of plan assets by a party in interest.[91]

A "party in interest," with whom such dealings are forbidden, means any plan fiduciary, regardless of the extent or nature of his fiduciary capacity; the plan's legal counsel; any plan employee or other person providing services to the plan (i.e., independent contractors); an employer of covered employees; a union, any of whose members are covered by the plan; any person who owns, directly or indirectly, a controlling interest in such an employer or union; and any corporation, partnership, trust, or estate that is controlled, directly or indirectly, by any of the foregoing persons (for example, a subsidiary of the employer, or a partnership in which the plan's accountant holds a 50 percent or greater interest in capital or profits).[92] Certain close relatives of an individual who is a party in interest (specifically, the spouse, ancestors, lineal descendants, and spouses of lineal descendants) are also included as parties in interest, as is any person who is an employee, officer, director, or 10 percent or greater shareholder or partner of a plan service provider, employer, union, or of any business, trust, or estate that controls or is controlled by the employer or union, or that is controlled by a plan fiduciary or service provider.[93] In short, Congress defined "party in interest" broadly, "to encompass those [individuals and] entities that a fiduciary might be inclined to favor at the expense of the plan's beneficiaries."[94]

Prohibited employer-investment transactions involve the fiduciary's acquiring or holding employer securities or employer real property if the fiduciary knows or should know that the property in question does not constitute "qualifying employer securities" or "qualifying employer real property," or if the plan's holdings of qualifying employer securities or real property exceed 10 percent of the fair market value of the plan's assets.[95] These prohibitions apply independently of the general fiduciary duty to diversify plan investments; but an exception is provided for certain

---

[91] ERISA § 406(a)(1)(A)–(D), 29 U.S.C. § 1106(a)(1)(A)–(D) (2018).
[92] ERISA § 3(14)(A)–(E), (G), 29 U.S.C. § 1002(14)(A)–(E), (G) (2018).
[93] ERISA § 3(14)(F), (H), (I), 3(15), 29 U.S.C. § 1002(14)(F), (H), (I), 1002(15) (2018).
[94] Harris Tr. & Sav. Bank v. Salomon Smith Barney, Inc., 530 U.S. 238, 242 (2000).
[95] ERISA §§ 406(a)(1)(E), (a)(2), 407(a), 29 U.S.C. §§ 1106(a)(1)(E), (a)(2), 1107(a) (2018). "Qualifying employer security" generally means stock or debt instruments issued by the

Fiduciary Obligations

141

defined contribution pension plans (including profit-sharing plans, stock-bonus plans, and employee stock ownership plans) that explicitly provide for the acquisition and holding of larger amounts of qualifying employer securities or real property.[96]

The third type of prohibited transaction forbids a fiduciary from dealing with the assets of the plan for his own account (i.e., self-dealing), receiving consideration from any party dealing with the plan (i.e., kickbacks), or representing any party in a transaction involving the plan whose interests are adverse to the interests of the plan or the interests of its participants or beneficiaries.[97] Unlike party-in-interest and employer-investment prohibited transactions, fiduciary conflict transactions are barred without regard to whether the fiduciary knows or should know that the dealing in question is forbidden, and more stringent procedural safeguards apply to a request for an administrative exemption from the ban.[98]

Prohibited transactions (as so defined) are banned even if the fiduciary actually acted in good faith and regardless of whether the result of the transaction is fair to plan participants and beneficiaries. In effect, such dealings are conclusively presumed to be undertaken to promote a conflicting interest, and even if no loss ensues, participants can insist that the fiduciary disgorge any profits made through the use of

---

employer or its affiliate, but in the case of indebtedness, special requirements apply to ensure that the price of the instrument is not excessive, that the plan doesn't have too large a stake in employer debt, and that at least half of the debt issue is held by persons independent of the issuing employer. ERISA § 407(d)(1), (d)(5), (e), 29 U.S.C. § 1107(d)(1), (d)(5), (e) (2018). "Qualifying employer real property" generally means realty leased to the employer or its affiliate, but only if there are multiple parcels (a substantial number of which are dispersed geographically), and each parcel and its improvements are suitable for more than one use. ERISA § 407(d)(2), (d)(4), 29 U.S.C. § 1107(d)(2), (d)(4) (2018).

[96] ERISA §§ 404(a)(1)(C), 407(b), (c)(3), 29 U.S.C. §§ 1104(a)(1)(C), 1107(b), (c)(3) (2018). In plan years beginning after 2006, defined contribution plan participants must in some cases be allowed to direct the plan to switch their account investments from employer securities to diversified investment options. ERISA § 204(j)(3), 29 U.S.C. § 1054(j)(3) (2018); see I.R.C. § 401(a)(35) (2018).

[97] ERISA § 406(b), 29 U.S.C. § 1106(b) (2018). For purposes of the ban on self-dealing, a fiduciary's "own interest" is "read broadly in light of Congress' concern with the welfare of plan beneficiaries." Leigh v. Engle, 727 F.2d 113, 126 (7th Cir. 1984) (fiduciary who is an officer of an acquiring corporation who uses plan assets to purchase stock in a corporation that is the target of a takeover attempt by the acquiring corporation has an interest in the outcome of the control contest).

[98] Compare ERISA § 406(a)(1) (introductory clause) ("knows or should know"), 406(a)(2) (same), 29 U.S.C. § 1106(a)(1), (2) (2018), with ERISA § 406(b), 29 U.S.C. § 1106(b) (2018). Formal adjudication is required for the Labor Department to grant an exemption to the fiduciary conflict prohibitions, while informal notice-and-comment procedures are ordinarily all that's required to support a regulatory exemption from the party-in-interest or employer-investment prohibitions. Compare the last two sentences of ERISA § 408(a), 29 U.S.C. § 1108 (a) (2018); in the case of fiduciary conflict transactions, the Secretary of Labor must afford opportunity for a hearing and make "a determination on the record." See 29 C.F.R. § 2570.46 (2021) (affording opportunity for hearing).

plan assets.[99] This approach bears an obvious resemblance to trust law's handling of self-dealing, according to which a trustee who deals with the trust in his personal capacity (e.g., buys trust assets for his own account, sells individually owned property to the trust, borrows from or loans money to the trust) is automatically liable for breach of the duty of loyalty, regardless of good faith or the objective fairness of the transaction (the "no-further-inquiry" rule).[100] In contrast, trust law treats certain (less egregious) conflicts of interests more leniently, in that the trustee is allowed to defend the breach of trust claim by proving that the transaction was fair to the trust's beneficiaries and was undertaken in good faith. ERISA's prohibited-transaction provision, like the trust law self-dealing rule, dispenses with such difficult context-specific factual determinations in favor of a blanket ban, but ERISA's ban is profoundly more encompassing, in a way that surprises the uninitiated. While ERISA's prohibited transactions most certainly include fiduciary acts that constitute self-dealing under traditional trust-law standards, ERISA also refuses to give individualized consideration to dealings with any other person who has a significant connection with the plan. The startling breadth of ERISA's automatic-breach rule is necessitated by the difficulty of administering the subjective loyalty standard (i.e., the exclusive benefit rule) as the primary safeguard of employees' interests.

Exemptions

Left unmodified, the statutory proscriptions would interdict many deals that are fair and commercially reasonable. Recognizing this overbreadth, Congress modulated the prohibitions with a series of narrow statutory exceptions and a procedure for granting regulatory relief. For example, a person providing services to the plan is a party in interest, and the furnishing of services between the plan and a party in interest is designated a prohibited transaction.[101] Consequently, ERISA would bar the provision of *any* services to a plan absent a statutory exception that allows a party in interest to provide "office space, or legal, accounting, or other services necessary for the establishment or operation of the plan, if no more than reasonable compensation is paid therefor."[102] Similarly, all employees of an employer, any of whose workers are covered by the plan, are parties in interest, and the list of prohibited

---

[99] ERISA § 409(a), 29 U.S.C. § 1109(a) (2018).

[100] *See, e.g.*, UNIF. TR. CODE § 802(b) & cmt. (2000); RESTATEMENT (THIRD) OF TRUSTS § 78 cmt. b (2007); RESTATEMENT (SECOND) OF TRUSTS § 170 cmt. b (1959); Bogert & Bogert, *supra* Chapter 4 note 74, § 543, at 218–19, 248; George G. Bogert & George T. Bogert, THE LAW OF TRUSTS AND TRUSTEES § 543 at 264, 267–68 (rev. 2d ed. 1993). John H. Langbein, *Questioning the Trust Law Duty of Loyalty: Sole Interest or Best Interest?*, 114 YALE L.J. 929 (2005) (explaining the origins, scope, and rationale of the rule in the private trust context, and recommending modification).

[101] ERISA §§ 3(14)(B), 406(a)(1)(C), 29 U.S.C. §§ 1002(14)(B), 1106(a)(1)(C) (2018).

[102] ERISA § 408(b)(2), 29 U.S.C. § 1108(b)(2) (2018).

Fiduciary Obligations

transactions includes loans between a plan and a party in interest.[103] This lending ban would outlaw plan loans to participants but for a statutory exception for even-handed plan loans that are adequately secured and bear a reasonable rate of interest.[104] The proliferation of plans permitting individuals to direct the investment of their defined contribution plan savings led Congress in 2006 to grant a statutory exemption from the prohibited-transaction rules for the provision of investment advice to participants and beneficiaries under such self-directed plans, if certain safeguards are met.[105]

Many of the enumerated statutory exceptions are quite specialized and limited; so, to provide flexibility, Congress included a mechanism for granting administrative exemptions from ERISA's prohibited-transaction rules. These exemptions may be either generic (so-called class exemptions) or transaction-specific, and may be subject to such conditions as the Secretary of Labor considers appropriate. An exemption may issue only if all interested persons are notified and given the opportunity to present their views, and only if the Labor Department finds that the exemption is "(1) administratively feasible, (2) in the interests of the plan and of its participants and beneficiaries, and (3) protective of the rights of participants and beneficiaries of such plan."[106] To date, more than thirty class exemptions have been granted, the terms of which must be carefully consulted to determine whether a particular insider transaction is actually prohibited.[107]

Remedies

The prohibited-transaction rules forbid a fiduciary from engaging in the designated transactions. A threatened transgression may be enjoined, and a fiduciary who commits a violation is personally liable to restore any losses to the plan.[108] In contrast, the conduct of a party in interest who deals with the fiduciary is not

---

[103] ERISA §§ 3(14)(C), (H), 406(a)(1)(B), 29 U.S.C. §§ 1002(14)(C), (H), 1106(a)(1)(B) (2018).

[104] ERISA § 408(b)(1), 29 U.S.C. § 1108(b)(1) (2018).

[105] ERISA § 408(b)(14), (g), 29 U.S.C. § 1108(b)(14), (g) (2018); see I.R.C. § 4975(d)(17), (f)(8) (2018).

[106] ERISA § 408(a), 29 U.S.C. § 1108(a) (2018). Where an exemption to the fiduciary conflict prohibitions is sought, the Labor Department is required to provide opportunity for a hearing (formal adjudication procedures), but in other cases (involving party-in-interest or employer-investment transactions, that is), notice-and-comment procedures suffice. *Id.*

[107] Notice of the grant of any administrative exemption is published in the Federal Register, 29 C.F.R. § 2570.48 (2021), and the full text of class exemptions can be obtained electronically at the Department of Labor website, see www.dol.gov/agencies/ebsa/laws-and-regulations/rules-and-regulations/exemptions/class, or through topical reporters. E.g., 6 Pens. & Profit Sharing 2d (RIA) ¶ 93,001.

[108] ERISA §§ 409(a), 502(a)(2), (3), 29 U.S.C. §§ 1109(a), 1132(a)(2), (3) (2018).

144   *Conduct Controls: Welfare and Pension Plans*

expressly outlawed.[109] That omission raised doubts as to whether a nonfiduciary party in interest may be held liable for participating in a prohibited transaction. The Supreme Court has held that ERISA § 502(a)(3) authorizes suit against a nonfiduciary party in interest to a prohibited transaction, provided that the defendant is not a bona fide purchaser of plan assets.[110] Where the plan received value, the party in interest must be shown to have had actual or constructive knowledge that the transaction violated the prohibited-transaction rules.[111] The Court indicated that "appropriate equitable relief" may include rescission of the transaction, restitution of the plan assets, and disgorgement of profits that the party in interest made through use of those assets.

Excise Tax and Civil Penalties

Congress was not content to remedy prohibited transactions; it sought to deter them. To supplement the prohibited-transaction rules, Congress enacted an excise tax counterpart that imposes a nondeductible 15 percent penalty tax on any "disqualified person" who participates in certain prohibited transactions. The tax Code's definition of "disqualified person" is essentially the same as ERISA's definition of a "party in interest."[112] While ERISA's prohibited-transaction rules focus on the fiduciary, the excise tax is directed at deterring the counterparty from entering into the transaction. It does so by making the disqualified person (party in interest) liable for the penalty without regard to intent, knowledge, or fault.[113]

---

[109] H.R. Rep. No. 93-1280, at 306 (1974) (Conf. Rep.), *reprinted in* 3 ERISA Legislative History, *supra* Chapter 1 note 55, at 4277, 4573 ("Under the labor provisions (title I), the fiduciary is the main focus of the prohibited transaction rules.").

[110] Harris Tr. & Sav. Bank v. Salomon Smith Barney, Inc., 530 U.S. 238 (2000).

[111] *Id.* at 251. The Court interpreted ERISA § 502(a)(3) to incorporate trust law remedial principles, including the trust pursuit rule. *Id.* at 249–52. *See* Restatement (Second) of Trusts §§ 284, 291, 294 (1959).

[112] *Compare* ERISA § 3(14), (15), 29 U.S.C. § 1002(14), (15) (2018) (labor title definition of "party in interest"), *with* I.R.C. § 4975(e)(2)–(6) (2018) (excise tax definition of "disqualified person"). The category of disqualified persons subject to the excise tax is narrower than ERISA's definition of "party in interest" in one important respect: employees of the employer, the union, or various affiliated businesses are treated as parties in interest, but only highly compensated employees are classified as disqualified persons. *Compare* ERISA § 3(14)(A), (H), 29 U.S.C. § 1002(14)(A), (H) (2018), *with* I.R.C. § 4975(e)(2)(A), (H) (2018). In addition, a fiduciary acting solely in his fiduciary capacity is not subject to the excise tax. I.R.C. § 4975(a), (b) (2018) ("other than a fiduciary acting only as such").

[113] H.R. Rep. No. 93-1280, at 306 (1974) (Conf. Rep.), *reprinted in* 3 ERISA Legislative History, *supra* Chapter 1 note 55, at 4277, 4573–74. *Accord id.* at 321 ("The first-level tax is imposed automatically without regard to whether the violation was inadvertent."), *reprinted in* 3 ERISA Legislative History, *supra* Chapter 1 note 55, at 4588. Under the labor provisions, a fiduciary will only be liable if he knew or should have known that he engaged in a prohibited transaction. Such a knowledge requirement is not included in the tax provisions. This distinction conforms to the distinction in present law in the private foundation

Fiduciary Obligations 145

The penalty tax is limited in scope to pension plans that have, at some point, qualified for preferential tax treatment.[114] To deter insider abuse of other employee benefit plans, Congress authorized the Secretary of Labor to assess a corresponding 5 percent civil penalty on a party in interest who engages in a prohibited transaction with a plan that is not subject to the excise tax.[115]

An additional civil penalty is potentially applicable in cases of serious insider abuse of an employee benefit plan. The penalty can apply against a fiduciary who violates any of her responsibilities, or against another person who knowingly partici- pates in the fiduciary's violation, whether or not the transgression involves a pro- hibited transaction.[116] The penalty is set at 20 percent of the "applicable recovery amount," which is the amount of damages recovered from the fiduciary or the knowing participant under a settlement agreement with the Labor Department, or by judgment in an enforcement action brought by the Labor Department. The Labor Department's involvement serves a screening function, preventing applica- tion of the penalty where the misdeeds are doubtful or inconsequential. Where the violation involves a prohibited transaction, setoff is allowed for any excise tax (or the cognate civil penalty) imposed on the fiduciary or knowing participant.[117]

D PARTICIPANT-DIRECTED INVESTMENTS

In view of Congress's objective to stamp out mismanagement and abuse of employee benefit funds, one might expect that ERISA's fiduciary duties, reinforced by object- ive prohibited-transaction rules, would apply with special force to investment deci- sion making. While intensive oversight is the norm for defined benefit pension plans and welfare benefit funds,[118] the fiduciaries of many defined contribution pension plans are largely absolved of investment responsibility. That absolution is granted where a plan permits a participant or beneficiary to exercise control over the investment of assets in his own account and the participant or beneficiary actually exercises such control.[119] If the sponsor washes its hands of investment manage- ment, ceding responsibility to plan participants and beneficiaries, then fiduciary

---

provisions (where a foundation's manager generally is subject to a tax on self-dealing if he acted with knowledge, but a disqualified person is subject to tax without proof of knowledge).

[114] I.R.C. § 4975 (2018) (excise tax), *id.* § 275(a)(6) (2018) (deduction disallowed). In addition to qualified or formerly qualified pension plans, the prohibited-transactions excise tax also applies to individual retirement accounts and certain medical and educational savings accounts, *id.* § 4975(e)(1) (2018), but does not apply to governmental or church plans, *id.* § 4975(g) (2018).

[115] ERISA § 502(a)(6), (i), 29 U.S.C. § 1132(a)(6), (i) (2018).

[116] ERISA § 502(*l*), 29 U.S.C. § 1132(*l*) (2018). Under ERISA § 502(a)(6), the Secretary of Labor can sue to collect the penalty.

[117] ERISA § 502(*l*)(4), 29 U.S.C. § 1132(*l*)(4) (2018).

[118] ERISA § 403(b)(4), 29 U.S.C. § 1103(b)(4) (2018), allows the Secretary of Labor to exempt welfare plans from the requirement that plan assets be held in trust by a trustee with exclusive investment management authority, but no such exemption has been granted.

[119] ERISA § 404(c)(1), 29 U.S.C. § 1104(c)(1) (2018).

Conduct Controls: Welfare and Pension Plans

obligations are relaxed on the theory that employer abuse of pension funds is no longer a concern. Instead, the focus in this situation should be on worker autonomy and promoting informed financial decision making.[120] The recent rise to dominance of defined contribution plans,[121] and 401(k) plans in particular, has been accompanied by the proliferation of such participant-directed investments. The proportion of defined contribution plan participants who have some say over their investments rose from approximately 15 percent in 1988 to approximately 88 percent in 2019,[122] while for 401(k) plan participants those percentages rose from approximately 30 percent in 1988 to 98 percent in 2019.[123]

Not surprisingly, given the ubiquity of participant-directed defined contribution plans, the scope of fiduciary immunity in situations where selected investments perform poorly has been challenged. ERISA section 404(c) provides that if a participant or beneficiary is granted and exercises control over assets in his account in the manner provided by Labor Department regulations, then "no person who is otherwise a fiduciary shall be liable under this part for any loss, or by reason of any breach, which results from such participant's or beneficiary's exercise of control."[124] Accordingly, the "it's-his-own-damn-fault" defense applies if (1) regulatory

---

[120] *See generally supra* Chapter 1C. *But see* Susan J. Stabile, *Freedom to Choose Unwisely: Congress' Misguided Decision to Leave 401(k) Plan Participants to Their Own Devices*, 11 Corn. J.L. & Pub. Pol'y 361 (2002) (arguing from a behavioral economics perspective that plan sponsors retain substantial control over participant investment decisions through their ability to manipulate the framing or context of investment choices).

[121] *See generally* Employee Benefits Security Administration, Department of Labor, Private Pension Plan Bulletin Historical Tables and Graphs 1975–2019 (2022) at www.dol.gov/sites/dolgov/files/EBSA/researchers/statistics/retirement-bulletins/private-pension-plan-bulletin-historical-tables-and-graphs.pdf.

[122] *Compare* William E. Even & David A. Macpherson, *The Growth of Participant Direction in Defined Contribution Plans*, Inst. for Study Labor (INZ) Disc. Paper No. 4088, at 2, 23 (Mar. 2009), http://papers.ssrn.com/sol3/papers.cfm?abstract_id=1369834# (setting forth 1988 estimate of participant-directed investments in defined contribution plans) *with* U.S. Dep't of Lab., Emp. Benefits Sec. Admin., Priv. Pension Plan Bull., Abstract of 2019 Form 5500 Annual Reports, 53, Table D5, (2021) (approximately 88 percent of participants in defined contribution plans in 2019 directed at least some investments).

[123] *Compare* William E. Even & David A. Macpherson, *The Growth of Participant Direction in Defined Contribution Plans*, Inst. for Study Labor (INZ) Disc. Paper No. 4088, at 23 (Mar. 2009), http://papers.ssrn.com/sol3/papers.cfm?abstract_id=1369834# (setting forth 1988 estimate of participant-directed investments in 401(k) plans) *with* Employee Benefits Security Administration, Department of Labor, Private Pension Plan Bulletin Historical Tables and Graphs 1975–2019 32, Table E24 (2022) at www.dol.gov/sites/dolgov/files/EBSA/researchers/statistics/retirement-bulletins/private-pension-plan-bulletin-historical-tables-and-graphs.pdf (approximately 98 percent of participants in 401 (k) or similar plans directed at least some investments).

[124] ERISA § 404(c)(1)(A), 29 U.S.C. § 1104(c)(1)(A) (2018). "[U]nder this part" refers to part 4 of ERISA title I, the fiduciary responsibility provisions, including both the general fiduciary duties and the prohibited transaction rules. Notice that the liability shield does not extend to the Code's prohibited transaction excise tax, I.R.C. § 4975. 29 C.F.R. § 2550.404c-1(d)(3) (2018).

Fiduciary Obligations

conditions for the exercise of control are satisfied,[125] and (2) the loss "results from" such an exercise of control.

A regulation first issued in 1992 and amended in 2010 provides detailed guidance on the conditions that must be satisfied for a plan to be considered to give participants the opportunity to exercise independent control over the assets in their accounts, but litigation has called into question the meaning of the causation element (that the loss result from the participant's exercise of control). The relevant regulation defines an "ERISA section 404(c) plan" as a defined contribution plan that provides an opportunity for a participant or beneficiary to exercise control by choosing the manner in which some or all of the assets in his account will be invested from among a "broad range" of investment alternatives.[126] To constitute a broad range of investment alternatives the plan must offer at least three core investments, each of which is diversified and has materially different risk and return characteristics, and which in various combinations allow the participant to adjust the aggregate risk and return characteristics of his portfolio over an appropriate range.[127] Participants must be allowed to give investment instructions as to these three core investment alternatives at least once within any three month period.[128] Importantly, the regulation demands that the plan enable informed autonomous decision making. The participant or beneficiary must be warned that plan fiduciaries may be relieved of liability for losses and be provided with or have the opportunity to obtain sufficient information to make informed decisions with respect to any available investment alternative (not just the three core alternatives that satisfy the broad range requirement).[129] Such information includes a description of available investment alternatives and their general risk and return characteristics, an explanation of transaction fees and the latest available information on annual operating expenses, a prospectus for investments in registered securities, and information concerning the value of shares or units of designated investment alternatives along

---

[125] The fiduciary of a plan that does not satisfy the conditions of the regulation is not entitled to the defense of § 404(c), but that does not mean that he has necessarily breached his fiduciary obligations. The selected plan investment options may still be determined to satisfy the general duties of prudence, loyalty, and diversification. 29 C.F.R. § 2550.404c-1(a)(2) (2021), Jenkins v. Yager, 444 F.3d 916, 924 (7th Cir. 2006) (finding no breach although section 404(c) was not satisfied); Preamble to 29 C.F.R. § 2550.404c, 57 Fed. Reg. 46,906 (Oct. 13, 1992) ("non-complying plans do not necessarily violate ERISA; non-compliance merely results in the plan not being accorded the statutory relief described in section 404(c)").

[126] 29 C.F.R. § 2550.404c-1(b)(1) (2021).

[127] 29 C.F.R. § 2550.404c-1(b)(3) (2021).

[128] 29 C.F.R. § 2550.404c-1(b)(2)(ii)(C) (2021).

[129] 29 C.F.R. § 2550.404c-1(b)(2)(i)(B)(1) (2021). To ensure autonomy the regulation defines "independent control" to bar improper influence by the plan sponsor or fiduciary and to prohibit concealment of material non-public facts regarding the investment (unless disclosure would constitute a violation of law). Id. -1(c)(2).

with their past and current performance, net of expenses, presented in a reasonable and consistent basis.[130]

Additional safeguards come into play if employer stock is offered as an investment alternative: the stock must be publicly traded in sufficient volume to permit prompt execution of transactions; voting and tender rights must be passed through to the account owner; and procedures must be established to maintain confidentiality of information relating to the purchase, holding, and sale of employer stock, and the exercise of voting and tender rights, including the appointment of an independent fiduciary in situations (such as a takeover battle) fraught with potential for undue employer influence over the exercise of shareholder rights.[131]

Liability in Participant-Directed Plans

Where the conditions of the regulation are satisfied and a participant or beneficiary exercises independent control over the assets in her account, "no other person who is a fiduciary with respect to such plan shall be liable for any loss ... that is a direct and necessary result of that participant's or beneficiary's exercise of control."[132]

Assume that the plan provided the information and disclosures required by section 404(c), provided the necessary opportunity for investment instructions, presented at least three core investments that were diversified and offered a materially different combination of risk and return, and so on, but contained other investment options that plaintiffs plausibly alleged were imprudent. Did section 404(c) immunize fiduciaries in such a plan? Put differently: did the fact that the plan contained the required number of sound investment options mean, if a participant *chose* an imprudent alternative option, that any resulting loss was "a direct and necessary result of that participant's ... exercise of control" for which the fiduciary could not be liable?

The Labor Department's answer to the question, from the original 1992 regulation onward, was "no." Under the Department's long-standing view, a fiduciary who acted disloyally or imprudently in selecting a designated investment alternative, or in continuing to make it available, is liable for a loss suffered by participants who selected that investment vehicle, regardless of whether the plan otherwise contained better options the participant was free to choose.[133]

---

[130] 29 C.F.R. § 2550.404c-1(b)(2)(i)(B) (2021). Some of these items must be provided directly by an identified plan fiduciary or his designee, while others need be provided only upon request.

[131] 29 C.F.R. § 2550.404c-1(d)(2)(ii)(E)(4) (2021). There is an affirmative duty to provide participants an explanation of procedures established to preserve the confidentiality of information relating to investments in employer stock. *Id.* -1(b)(2)(i)(B)(3).

[132] 29 C.F.R. § 2550.404c-1(d)(2)(i) (2021).

[133] The Department's original expression of that view was contained in the preamble to the relevant regulation and did not make its way into the text of the regulation until 2010. *Compare* Preamble to 29 C.F.R. § 2550.404c, 57 Fed. Reg. 46,906, 46,924, n.27 (Oct. 13, 1992), *with* 29 C.F.R. § 2550.404c-1(d)(2)(iv) (2021).

Fiduciary Obligations

Some courts rejected Labor's view while others adopted it. The former group included appellate courts that reasoned that section 404(c) *must* have been intended to immunize fiduciaries in these circumstances, for absent a breach by the plan fiduciary there would be no liability in any case and therefore no need for an affirmative defense.[134] Other courts and judges rejected this surplusage[135]

---

[134] Langbecker v. Electronic Data Sys. Corp., 476 F.3d 299, 311 (5th Cir. 2007) (participants' argument "would render the § 404(c) defense applicable only where plan managers breached no fiduciary duty, and thus only where it is unnecessary"); *id.* at 312 ("A plan fiduciary may have violated the duties of selection and monitoring of a plan investment, but § 404(c) recognizes that participants are not helpless victims of every error."); *see* In re Unisys Savs. Plan Litig., 74 F.3d 420, 445 (3d Cir. 1996) (plain language of ERISA § 404(c) suggests that fiduciary breach of duty of prudence and diversification in selecting investment alternative does not bar application of the defense so long as participant's or beneficiary's exercise of control is a substantial contributing factor in bringing about the loss). *See also* Hecker v. Deere & Co., 556 F.3d 575, 589 (7th Cir. 2009) (declining to answer whether the § 404(c) safe harbor applies to the selection of investment options for a plan in all circumstances but finding that it does apply where a broad range of investment options are offered that allowed participants to avoid allegedly excessive fees).

[135] The key to understanding why Labor's reading of 404(c) is not surplusage lies in its relationship to sections 403 and 405, the mandatory trusteeship and co-fiduciary liability provisions of ERISA.

Investment management, including the authority to acquire, hold, or dispose of plan assets, is a trustee function. ERISA section 403(a) makes investment management by the trustee(s) a mandatory, nondelegable duty: "the trustee or trustees shall have *exclusive* authority to manage and control the assets of the plan." ERISA § 403(a), 29 U.S.C. § 1103(a) (2018) (emphasis added). The only exceptions are for (1) plans that call for investment management to be under the direction of a named fiduciary, and (2) plans that allow the named fiduciary to appoint one or more investment managers to whom the authority to manage, acquire and dispose of assets is delegated. ERISA §§ 403(a)(1), (2), 402(c)(3), 29 U.S.C. § 1103(a)(1), (2), 1102(c)(3) (2018). That the duty to make investment decisions is personal and nondelegable is confirmed by ERISA's rules governing co-fiduciary liability. Dovetailing with the exceptions to the trustee's exclusive responsibility for asset management, section 405 provides that a trustee is absolved from liability (1) for following the instructions of a named fiduciary where the plan provides for investment management by a named fiduciary, *compare* ERISA § 403(a)(1), 29 U.S.C. § 1103 (a)(1) (2018), *with* ERISA § 405(b)(3)(B), 29 U.S.C. § 1105(b)(3)(B) (2006), *and* (2) for the acts or omissions of investment managers where the plan provides for delegation of the investment duties to one or more investment managers. *Compare* ERISA § 403(a)(2), 29 U.S.C. § 1103(a)(2) (2018), *with* ERISA § 405(d)(1), 29 U.S.C. § 1105(d)(1) (2018). Most revealing is section 405(c), which generally allows a plan to specify procedures for the delegation of *any* fiduciary responsibility, and correspondingly limits the liability of other fiduciaries for the acts or omissions of a proper delegate. The statute expressly cabins that blanket delegation authority in one respect: delegation is forbidden for "trustee responsibilities," which are defined as any responsibility "to manage or control the assets of the plan". ERISA § 405(c)(1), (3), 29 U.S.C. § 1105(c)(1), (3) (2018).

Because investment management is in general a nondelegable trustee function, in the absence of section 404(c) a trustee who permitted participants to direct the investment of their accounts would commit an *automatic* breach of fiduciary duty. Consequently, the trustee would be personally liable for any losses resulting from that breach, including losses flowing from imprudent investment decisions made by the account owner. ERISA § 409(a), 29 U.S.C. § 1109(a) (2018). Even if the plan expressly called for participant decision making the trustee's exposure would not be limited. *See* ERISA §§ 404(a)(1)(D) (cannot follow plan terms if in

150 Conduct Controls: Welfare and Pension Plans

argument, concluding that plan fiduciaries remain on the hook for the faulty initial selection of an investment option and for the failure to adequately monitor its continuing propriety.[136]

The Supreme Court resolved the issue in *Hughes v. Northwestern. University*,[137] after signaling its intentions several years earlier in *Tibble v. Edison International*.[138] At issue in *Northwestern* were two of Northwestern University's defined contribution plans, in which participants were entitled to "choose[] how to invest [their] funds, subject to an important limitation: [they] may choose only from the menu of options selected by the plan administrators."[139] Plaintiffs alleged that the defendant-fiduciaries had violated their duty of prudence in three ways: (1) defendants "failed to monitor and control the fees they paid for recordkeeping"; (2) defendants offered a number of retail investment options that carried higher fees than those "of otherwise identical" institutional investment options and (3) defendants offered

conflict with ERISA), 410(a) (exculpatory provisions void as against public policy), 29 U.S.C. §§ 1104(a)(1)(D), 1110(a) (2018). Therefore, absent section 404(c), the trustee who allowed participants or beneficiaries to direct the investment of their own accounts would be liable as a co-fiduciary for certain losses caused by their investment decisions. Specifically, the partici-pants granted investment authority would, due to the improper *delegation* of trustee responsi-bilities, be acting as de facto or functional fiduciaries. *See supra* Chapter 4A. Therefore, if such a participant's investment selection is imprudent, or under-diversified, or involves a conflict of interest (e.g., investing in securities of a business that a participant or her spouse owns or controls), then the loss is caused by a breach of fiduciary responsibility, and the trustee would be personally liable for the loss as a co-fiduciary. ERISA § 405(a)(2) 29 U.S.C. § 1105(a) (2) (2018).

The conclusion is that a mere delegation of investment decision making that does not comport with section 404(c) is itself a breach *even if there is no showing of independent fault by the fiduciary (e.g., imprudence) in initially selecting or continuing to make available designated investment alternatives.* Because the trustee would be on the hook for losses attributable to the account owner's mistakes where the menu of investment alternatives was properly constructed, the defense has a real immunizing effect. It follows that section 404(c) cannot be considered surplusage if its operation is limited to that situation. Stated another way, ERISA section 404(c), in combination with section 403(a), provides a third exception to the ban on delegation of investment management, along with a corresponding limitation on trustee liability. *See* Jenkins v. Yager, 444 F.3d 916, 920–21, 924 (7th Cir. 2006). In effect, then, the trustee is solely responsible for investment management except where: (1) the plan assigns that task to a named fiduciary; (2) the plan authorizes delegation to one or more investment managers; or (3) a defined contribution plan permits a participant or beneficiary to exercise control over the assets in his account and such control is actually exercised in accordance with the standards of § 404 (c). In addition, note that the trust instrument may permit multiple trustees to divvy up investment management tasks and in so doing limit their exposure for breaches by a co-trustee. ERISA § 405(b)(1)(B), 29 U.S.C. § 1105(b)(1)(b) (2018).

[136] DiFelice v. U.S. Airways, Inc., 497 F.3d 410, 418 n.3, 423–24 (4th Cir. 2008) ("a fiduciary must initially determine, and continue to monitor, the prudence of *each* investment option available to plan participants"); Franklin v. First Union Corp., 84 F. Supp. 2d 720, 732 (E.D. Va. 2000); *see* Langbecker, 476 F.3d at 320–22 (Reavley, J., dissenting, citing commentators and courts).

[137] Hughes v. Nw. Univ. (*Northwestern*), 142 S. Ct. 737 (2022).

[138] Tibble v. Edison Int'l, 575 U.S. 523 (2015).

[139] *Northwestern*, 142 S. Ct. at 740.

Fiduciary Obligations

"too many investment options – over 400 in total ... and thereby caused participant confusion and poor investment decisions."[140]

The Seventh Circuit had affirmed the district court's dismissal of the plaintiffs' complaint, reasoning that because defendants "had provided an adequate array of choices, including 'the types of funds plaintiffs wanted (low-cost index funds),'" the inclusion of other allegedly imprudent options was not actionable.[141] That the "menu" of investment options presented to participants included some allegedly imprudent choices, in other words, was excused by the inclusion of admittedly prudent ones – because it was plaintiffs, after all, who *chose* the imprudent options that resulted in losses.[142]

In a unanimous opinion, the *Northwestern* Court squarely rejected the Seventh Circuit's reasoning, holding that a plan's inclusion of imprudent investment options was a breach that could not be excused by the fact that a participant could have chosen to invest differently. The Court noted that several years before, in *Tibble*, it had been asked to resolve, for statute of limitations reasons, whether fiduciaries who selected for inclusion in a participant-directed plan a number of imprudent investment options had an ongoing duty to monitor the prudence of those options.[143] In *Tibble*, the Court held that ERISA fiduciaries have "a continuing duty to monitor trust investments and remove imprudent ones" along with a "duty to exercise prudence in selecting investments at the outset."[144] In *Northwestern*, the Court chastised the Seventh Circuit for not following *Tibble*:

> The Seventh Circuit's exclusive focus on investor choice elided [*Tibble's* holding regarding] the duty of prudence ... In the court's view, because petitioners' preferred type of investments were available, they could not complain about the flaws in other options ... Given the Seventh Circuit's repeated reliance on this reasoning, we vacate the judgment below so that the court may reevaluate the allegations as a whole."[145]

---

[140] *Id.*

[141] *Id.* at 742 (describing the panel's reasoning below).

[142] Divane v. Nw. Univ., 953 F.3d 980, 991 (7th Cir. 2020), *vacated and remanded sub nom.* Hughes v. Nw. Univ., 142 S. Ct. 737 (2022) (concluding the inclusion of prudent options "eliminates any claim that plaintiffs were forced to stomach an unappetizing menu.")

[143] *Northwestern*, 142 S. Ct. at 741. If not, then certain of the *Tibble* plaintiffs' claims would have been barred by the statute of limitations. In *Tibble*, the potentially immunizing effect of section 404(c) was not formally at issue. The Ninth Circuit had held that 404(c), following Labor's view, did *not* immunize a fiduciary from the selection of imprudent investment options. The petitioner, for whatever reason, did not seek certiorari on that question. Tibble v. Edison Int'l, 729 F.3d 1110 (9th Cir. 2013), *vacated*, 575 U.S. 523 (2015); Brief for the United States as Amicus Curiae, Tibble v. Edison Int'l, (No. 13-550), 2014 WL 4089204 (U.S.); Petition for a Writ of Certiorari, Tibble v. Edison Int'l, 575 U.S. 523 (No. 13-550), 2013 WL 5864007 (U.S.).

[144] Tibble v. Edison Int'l, 575 U.S. 523, 529 (2015).

[145] *Northwestern*, 142 S. Ct. at 742.

The Supreme Court has thus plainly stated, in two unanimous opinions, that fiduciaries in participant-directed plans bear a duty to prudently select, monitor, and remove investment options.[146] Yet unresolved questions remain. In particular it is unsettled as to precisely what constitutes imprudent conduct with respect to the selection, monitoring, or removal of investment options. That the duty of prudence attaches to such conduct (e.g., menu construction and maintenance) is one thing; mapping out what manner of conduct rises to the level of actionable imprudence is a task that will require judicial development. The Supreme Court, for its part, made clear in *Northwestern* that whether a given fiduciary has acted imprudently will be "context-specific."[147] On that score, the *Northwestern* opinion pointedly closed with an admonition to lower courts to keep in mind that "[a]t times, the circumstances facing an ERISA fiduciary will implicate difficult tradeoffs, and courts must give due regard to the range of reasonable judgments a fiduciary may make based on her experience and expertise."[148]

Employer Stock Investments

Intractable prudence issues frequently arise where stock in the employer corporation is offered as an investment option.[149] To be permissible under an ERISA section 404(c) plan, stock in the employer corporation must satisfy several criteria, including that it be publicly traded in sufficient volume to permit expeditious execution of directions to buy or sell.[150] Even if these conditions are satisfied, facilitating

---

[146] *Northwestern* thus suggests that the proper way to read the various examples set forth in the pertinent Labor regulation is that, for those instances (such as examples 5 and 9) where the fiduciary is described as not liable, that example presumes that the *initial* choice by the plan at issue (namely to make a single stock investment available in example 5, or to offer an open brokerage window in 9), as well as the choice to keep that option in the plan, was otherwise prudent. *See* 29 C.F.R. § 2550.404c-1(f) (2021).

[147] *Northwestern*, 142 S. Ct. at 742. Areas that the Court has flagged for judicial development are the specific form and frequency of monitoring that prudence requires, *Tibble*, 575 U.S. at 530–31, and whether in some circumstances offering a set of investment options that was "too numerous" might be imprudent. *Northwestern*, 142 S. Ct. at 742.

[148] *Northwestern*, 142 S. Ct. at 742.

[149] We note at the outset that our discussion does not address whether facilitating employee ownership of company stock is wise in the first instance. Congress has made clear its view that there is some policy merit in (1) promoting employee ownership and (2) doing so through use of the tax subsidy ostensibly devoted to retirement savings. Numerous scholars have criticized that Congressional conclusion on a variety of grounds, not the least of which is since an employee's *human* capital is already heavily invested in a particular employer, tying one's retirement savings to the employer's prospects is unnecessarily risky. *See generally* Andrew Stumpff Morrison and Norman P. Stein, *Repeal Tax Incentives for Esops*, 125 TAX NOTES 337, 337–340 (2009); Dana Muir & Norman Stein, *Two Hats, One Head, No Heart: The Anatomy of the ERISA Settlor/Fiduciary Distinction*, 93 N.C. L. REV. 459, 528 (2015).

[150] More precisely, the fiduciaries of an ERISA section 404(c) plan have a defense to claims arising out of the acquisition or sale of employer stock only if these criteria are satisfied. Failure to satisfy these criteria would not necessarily defeat status as a 404(c) plan or negate the availability

Fiduciary Obligations 153

undiversified investment in the employer invites imprudent risk taking. Fiduciaries of profit-sharing or stock bonus plans (including employee stock ownership plans, ESOPs) can be released from the duty to diversify and from their obligation of prudence "to the extent that it requires diversification" when they invest in employer stock if the plan explicitly authorizes such investment.[151] Such an "eligible individual account plan" also exempts the fiduciary from the ban on acquiring or holding more than 10 percent of the fair market value of plan assets in employer securities or real property.[152] These eligible individual account plan diversification exceptions apply whether plan fiduciaries or participants make investment decisions.[153] Consequently, many publicly traded corporations offer an employer stock fund as a designated investment alternative in their 401(k) plan (in addition to investments that provide the required "broad range" of investment alternatives).

Predictably, participants invested in company stock sue when its value drops substantially, whether the decline is due to general economic conditions, industry downturns, or firm-specific reverses. Faced with the individual account plan diversification exception, complaints in such "stock drop cases" allege that the investment in employer stock (or, in the case of participant-directed investments, the continued *availability* of the employer stock fund as an investment alternative) was either imprudent (apart from its concentration), or breached the duty of loyalty.

Where the stock is publicly traded (as it will be under an ERISA section 404(c) plan), however, an asserted breach of the duty of care runs into a major stumbling block. While stock in the employer corporation may have a very high risk of loss compared to an equity stake in a more stable company, the market will presumably have taken that risk into account in pricing so that the risk is compensated by the small chance of a very large gain compared to the safer investment. Assuming efficient capital markets, while individual stocks differ in their risk profiles (risk dispersion), for each the risk is fully compensated. Consequently, the stock of a single publicly traded company, even one on the verge of bankruptcy, has a net positive expected return. Hence with proper pricing a single stock investment is in theory always economically sensible, apart from loss aversion. Loss aversion, of course, is the point of diversification, but there is no duty to diversify under the eligible individual account plan exception. Absent an obligation to minimize the risk of large losses, then, a publicly traded stock would always seem to be a prudent investment; prudence, in other words, arguably has no content apart from the duty

---

of the defense as applied to the selection of other investment alternatives. 29 C.F.R. § 2550.404c-1(b)(2)(ii)(B) (2021); *see id.* -1(d)(2)(ii)(E)(4) (disclosure of confidentiality protections).

[151] ERISA §§ 404(a)(2), 407(d)(3), (4), (6), 29 U.S.C. §§ 1104(a)(2), 1107(d)(3), (4), (6) (2018).

[152] ERISA §§ 406(a)(2), 407(a), (b)(1), 29 U.S.C. §§ 1106(a)(2), 1107(a), (b)(1) (2018).

[153] In fact, a 401(k) plan that is not an ESOP ordinarily cannot require participants' elective deferrals be invested in employer stock, but participant-directed investment of elective deferrals in employer stock is permitted. ERISA § 407(b)(2), 29 U.S.C. §§ 1107(b)(2) (2018).

Conduct Controls: Welfare and Pension Plans

to diversify. Nevertheless, Congress seems to have thought that the duty of care has some meaning and independent force as applied to a single investment viewed in isolation, because in the case of an eligible individual account plan it withdrew the prudence requirement "only to the extent that it requires diversification."[154] But while Congress apparently believed that there were some cases in which a fiduciary's reliance upon efficient markets would be imprudent, it offered no hint of what those cases might look like.

The circuit courts of appeal addressed this conundrum by adopting the so-called *Moench* presumption, following the Third Circuit's analysis in *Moench v. Robertson*.[155] *Moench* involved a suit for breach of duty by former ESOP plan participants against members of the plan committee. The defendant-fiduciaries had continued to invest plan monies in the employer bank's stock for a two-year period during which (1) federal bank regulators repeatedly expressed concern about the financial condition of the bank and (2) the stock price plummeted from $18.25 to pennies per share. Defendants, who were corporate directors as well as members of the plan committee, argued that even in that situation investing solely in employer stock was permissible due to the special nature of an ESOP. Because Congress intended the ESOP to be both an employee retirement benefit plan *and* a technique of corporate finance that would encourage employee ownership,[156] the Third Circuit concluded that neither goal should prevail to the exclusion of the other. Only in limited circumstances, the Third Circuit explained, can ESOP fiduciaries "be liable under ERISA for continuing to invest in employer stock according to the plan's direction."[157] To accommodate the ESOP's competing purposes the court of appeals held that an ESOP fiduciary who invests assets in employer stock is entitled to a "presumption" that it acted consistently with ERISA (prudently).[158] The plaintiff may overcome that presumption by introducing evidence that, owing to circumstances that the settlor did not know nor anticipate, continuing to invest in

---

[154] ERISA § 404(a)(2), 29 U.S.C. § 1104(a)(2) (2018).

[155] Moench v. Robertson, 62 F.3d 553 (3d Cir. 1995), *abrogated by* Fifth Third Bancorp v. Dudenhoeffer, 573 U.S. 409 (2014).

[156] *Moench*, 62 F.3d at 569.

[157] *Id.* at 556.

[158] The standard announced by the Third Circuit was taken directly from the rule on "administrative deviation" in the Second Restatement of Trusts, which provides in part:

"The court will direct or permit the trustee to deviate from the terms of the trust if owing to circumstances not known to the settlor and not anticipated by him compliance would defeat or substantially impair the accomplishment of the purposes of the trust; and in such case, if necessary to carry out the purposes of the trust, the court may direct the trustee to do acts which are not authorized or are forbidden by the terms of the trust." RESTATEMENT (SECOND) OF TRUSTS § 167(1) (1959). Further, § 167(2) says that where the trustee reasonably believes there is an emergency he may deviate from the terms of the trust without first obtaining judicial authorization.

Fiduciary Obligations

employer stock would defeat or substantially impair the accomplishment of the plan's purpose to provide workers retirement savings.[159]

The Third Circuit later applied the *Moench* rationale outside the ESOP setting, including with respect to participant-directed defined contribution plans that merely offered employer stock as an option.[160] Others circuits to have considered the issue likewise adopted some version of the *Moench* approach, that is, a "presumption of prudence" in employer stock drop cases.[161] Additional justifications (beyond the idea that employee ownership of employer stock was a special aim Congress wished fiduciaries to promote) in favor of applying the presumption were offered. In cases where the plaintiffs accused a fiduciary of continuing to offer employee stock after *public* information had suggested the stock was overpriced, for example, defense counsel argued that it would be unfair, absent extraordinary circumstances, to in effect declare a fiduciary imprudent for failing to second-guess the market. In cases where the plaintiffs accused a fiduciary of continuing to offer employer stock even though *nonpublic* information (such as fraudulent conduct by company insiders) suggested a price drop was imminent, defense counsel argued that it would be unfair, absent extraordinary circumstances, to declare a fiduciary imprudent for failing to act on insider information when so acting would violate securities laws.

The question of whether or not ERISA required a "presumption of prudence" in employer stock drop cases finally reached the Supreme Court in 2014 in *Fifth Third Bancorp v. Dudenhoeffer*. At issue in *Dudenhoeffer* was a participant-directed plan that both offered company stock as an investment option and supplied the company's matching contribution in the default form of company stock.[162] The plaintiffs alleged that both public and nonpublic information about the value of Fifth Third's stock made it imprudent for the defendant-fiduciaries to continue to hold and buy such stock.[163] The district court, relying on what it understood to be the governing version of the *Moench* presumption, dismissed the case. The Sixth Circuit nonetheless reversed. While it agreed that the defendants *were* entitled to a presumption of prudence, it determined that such was an "evidentiary presumption" that played no role in the pleading stage.[164] The defendants sought certiorari, and "[i]n light of differences among the Courts of Appeals as to the nature of the presumption of

---

[159] *Id.* at 571.

[160] *Edgar v. Avaya, Inc.*, 503 F.3d 340, 343, 347 (3d Cir. 2007), *abrogated by* Fifth Third Bancorp v. Dudenhoeffer, 573 U.S. 409 (2014).

[161] Fifth Third Bancorp v. Dudenhoeffer, 573 U.S. 409, 412 (2014) ("The Courts of Appeals that have considered the question have held that such a presumption [of prudence] does apply.").

[162] *Id.* The plan did give participants the right to put the company match into another investment alternative, that is, the participants were not "stuck" with company stock. *Id.*

[163] *Id.* at 413. The public information related to early reports that "subprime lending, which formed a large part of Fifth Third's business," was about to collapse. *Id.* The nonpublic information was that defendants, as insiders, were aware that "Fifth Third officers had deceived the market by making material misstatements about the company's financial prospects." *Id.*

[164] *Id.* at 414.

156   *Conduct Controls: Welfare and Pension Plans*

prudence applicable to ESOP fiduciaries," the Supreme Court granted the petition.[165]

In a unanimous opinion, the Court held that ERISA nowhere requires a "presumption of prudence" with respect plan fiduciaries purchasing or holding employer stock. That Congress intended to promote employee ownership of company stock – such as through the use of tax incentives, and by relaxing the duty of diversification with respect to plan ownership of employee stock – did not, according to the Court, mean that ESOP fiduciaries were somehow excused from the duty of prudence so long as doing so promoted employee ownership.[166] To the contrary, the Court concluded that a careful review of ERISA's structure and text required the conclusion that plan fiduciaries handling employer stock bear the same duty of prudence as other ERISA fiduciaries – a duty that comes with no "presumption" in favor of prudence.[167]

While the Court disavowed the *Moench* family of formal presumptions, it took pains to explain that other procedural mechanisms were available to weed out meritless stock drop suits. Federal pleading rules require plaintiffs to state a plausible claim for relief, and that requirement has special force in employer stock drop cases. To the extent fiduciaries were alleged to have acted imprudently by failing to appreciate that certain *public* information suggested company stock was overpriced, the Court explained that such an allegation would normally be "implausible." Absent "special circumstances" (on which the Court did not elaborate), a fiduciary's duties would not require him to "outsmart a presumptively efficient market."[168] To the extent fiduciaries were faulted for failing to act on the basis of learning *nonpublic* information about the value of company stock, the Court observed that the duty of prudence categorically does not require a fiduciary to violate the law. Even among lawful actions (e.g., by disclosing negative information or publicly halting new purchases of the employer stock), a prudent fiduciary need assess whether such action would do more harm than good (e.g, by sending a negative signal about the stock's prospects that could tank the value of the plan's existing holdings). The Court accordingly held that "a plaintiff must plausibly allege a [lawful] alternative action that the defendant could have taken" and "that a prudent fiduciary in the same circumstances" would have believed such action was "[not] more likely to harm the fund than to help it."[169] *Dudenhoeffer*, while rejecting the *Moench* presumption, nonetheless poses daunting "plausibility" hurdles upon plaintiffs accusing

---

[165] *Id.* at 414.

[166] *Id.* at 422.

[167] *Id.* at 418–20.

[168] *Id.* at 427 (internal quotation omitted). The Court explained that the lower court's "decision to deny dismissal therefore appears to have been based on an erroneous understanding of the prudence of relying on market prices." *Id.*

[169] *Id.* at 428. In private conversation an academic colleague (Professor Colleen Medill) of the authors once described *Dudenhoeffer* as "rejecting a presumption of prudence in favor of a presumption of efficient markets." That does seem to succinctly state the gist of it.

Fiduciary Obligations

fiduciaries of breaches in connection with offering employee stock as an investment option.[170]

E CONCLUSION

A robust voluntary system of employment-based pension and welfare benefits requires competence and integrity in benefit plan administration. Absent assurance of professionalism workers will lose confidence in the plan; demand for benefit programs will suffer as participants discount employer promises by the anticipated probability of loss through managerial misconduct. Sponsors generally share the interest in faithful plan administration, but the employer's overriding goal is to get

---

[170] As of early 2022, no court of appeals had found that a post-*Dudenhoeffer* plaintiff bringing suit with respect to a publicly traded company has plausibly alleged a breach on the basis of a fiduciary's failure to realize that *publicly* available information suggested an imminent price drop. In contrast (although not involving a participant-directed plan), the Seventh Circuit reversed a motion to dismiss in a fiduciary breach case involving *privately* traded company stock, correctly noting that *Dudenhoeffer*'s "special circumstances" requirement only made sense with respect to stocks traded in liquid markets. Allen v. GreatBanc Tr. Co., 835 F.3d 670, 679 (7th Cir. 2016).

With respect to claims alleging failure of defendant-fiduciaries to respond appropriately to *nonpublic* information, those suits have also proved challenging, given *Dudenhoeffer*'s twin constraints that the untaken responsive action must (1) not conflict with securities laws and (2) not be likely to do more harm than good. *See, e.g.*, Allen v. Wells Fargo & Co., 967 F.3d 767, 773 (8th Cir. 2020) (citing cases and noting that the public disclosure of negative information is rarely a plausible alternative action, "[because] a prudent fiduciary could readily conclude that disclosure would do more harm than good by causing a drop in the stock price") (internal citations and quotations omitted).

With regard to the untaken alternative action "not doing more harm than good," the courts of appeal have disagreed, *inter alia*, over whether the "inevitability" of negative inside information becoming public could make disclosure a plausible alternative course. The Eighth Circuit in *Allen* explicitly rejected that argument, and other circuits have perhaps implicitly done so, *see, e.g.*, Martone v. Robb, 902 F.3d 519, 526–27 (5th Cir. 2018). The Second Circuit, however, concluded otherwise, reasoning that when a "drop in the value of the stock already held by the fund is inevitable . . . it is far more plausible that a prudent fiduciary would prefer to limit the effects of the stock's artificial inflation on the ESOP's beneficiaries through prompt disclosure." Jander v. Ret. Plans Comm. of IBM, 910 F.3d 620, 630 (2d Cir. 2018), *vacated and remanded*, 140 S. Ct. 592 (2020) (internal citations and quotations omitted). *Jander* was vacated and remanded by the Supreme Court for reasons unrelated to any flaw in *that* part of the holding (as discussed in the next paragraph of this note). *Id.* at 592–4. On remand, the Second Circuit "reinstate[d] the judgment entered pursuant to [its] initial opinion." Jander v. Ret. Plans Comm. of IBM, 962 F.3d 85, 86 (2d Cir.), *cert. denied*, 141 S. Ct. 816 (2020).

With regard to the untaken alternative action "not violating securities law," the issue is sufficiently complex that the Court itself declined to wade into the subject without further briefing. Indeed, that specifically is what motivated the Court to vacate and remand *Jander*. Ret. Plans Comm. of IBM v. Jander, 140 S. Ct. 592, 594–95 (2020) (vacating and remanding a Second Circuit decision for the purpose of developing argument on the relevant requirements and constraints the securities laws imposed on an ERISA ESOP fiduciary.)

the most out of its investment, which sometimes requires changing the plan or adapting its application to unforeseen circumstances.

ERISA's fiduciary responsibility provisions mediate between employee protection and employer flexibility. While the central fiduciary duties were imported from state trust law, three modifications strengthen the defenses. First, a sweeping functional definition of fiduciary imposes stringent obligations on anyone with decision-making authority or access to plan assets. Second, ERISA's fiduciary duties are uniform and uncompromising – they cannot be relaxed by including exculpatory provisions in the instrument. In contrast to traditional trust law, fiduciary duties under ERISA are not default rules that may be modified by agreement of the parties. Third, the prohibited transaction rules, with the associated excise tax and civil penalty, deter insider transactions that are rife with potential for abuse.

These exacting employee protections have their limits, however. ERISA demands that every employee benefit plan contain a procedure for amendment, and the courts interpret the definition of fiduciary as excluding acts relating to amendment or termination. Consequently, amendments are not required to be for the exclusive benefit of participants and beneficiaries, leaving the employer free to cut back plan coverage or future benefit accruals as circumstances dictate. Limited flexibility is also provided by allowing employer representatives to serve as fiduciaries and holding them to a standard of subjective loyalty. These concessions permit the fiduciary to enter into a transaction that is advantageous to the employer so long as the employer's gain does not come at the employees' expense.

ERISA's fiduciary rules implicitly protect an interest that is distinct from the immediate concerns of the employer and employees. Only the provision of plan benefits is cognizable under the exclusive benefit rule; job security and other interests of participants and beneficiaries, however urgent, are beyond the pale. This uncompromising objective safeguards the societal interest in employee benefit plans (and taxpayers' investment in qualified retirement plans) by empowering the Labor Department and dissident participants to object to diversion of benefit funds to other purposes, providing another check on opportunistic behavior.

Despite these protections, society's overarching goal of retirement income security clashes with ERISA's tolerance of participant-directed investments and concentrated holdings of employer stock under defined contribution pension plans, including most 401(k) plans. ERISA section 404(c) grants participants freedom to select investments, and if the plan provides the requisite alternatives and information it may absolve plan fiduciaries from liability for losses resulting from workers' choices. In addition, ERISA section 404(a)(2) permits certain profit-sharing and stock bonus plans to make undiversified investments in stock of the employer corporation, and if the stock is publicly traded that decision can be left to employees by offering an employer stock fund as an investment alternative under a participant-directed plan.

Few workers have investment expertise, however, and their freedom to choose unwisely frequently brings them to grief. What originated as a concession to practice in an era when defined benefit plans were the norm and defined contribution plans, where they existed, simply offered a supplemental savings opportunity, has become, in the age of 401(k) plan ascendency, a dominant design feature that imperils the prospect of comfortable retirement. While the case law reflects a judicial willingness to intervene – by finding, for example, that the inclusion of investment options in a plan is a fiduciary act subject to judicial oversight – perhaps the core challenge lies with Congress's unwillingness to more carefully structure what a participant-directed world should look like. The reality is that employees are not, and will never be, expert investors. Allowing investment freedom and promoting actual retirement security are in tension. Expecting courts – including a generation of judges increasingly unwilling to defer to the judgments of federal regulators – to strike the right balance on that score seems a risky bet.

5

Enforcement

ERISA's enforcement mechanisms, like many of ERISA's component parts, have proven to be considerably more complicated than one might hope for a remedial statute. The result is that ERISA enforcement has long been a major focus of litigation. The source of all the controversy is a set of limitations on participants' ability to obtain complete relief for alleged violations of the plan or of ERISA. These limitations – on standing, the scope of judicial review of fiduciary decision making, causes of action, and remedies – are the focus of this chapter.

The rich law and economics literature on efficient breach of contract teaches that limitations on relief and the measure of damages are as important as the underlying substantive law in shaping the behavior of contracting parties. Similarly, ERISA's enforcement regime molds the conduct of employee benefit plan sponsors, participants, and administrators, affecting (consciously or not) the level of compliance with the statutory norms. Employers contend that limitations on relief are, like preemption, crucial to the maintenance of a voluntary system of employment-based pension and welfare benefit delivery. Without them, cost increases would curtail plan sponsorship and workforce coverage, and that change would have profound distributional implications. Disappointed workers, on the other hand, complain that enforcement limitations permit an unintended and unacceptably high level of fiduciary misconduct and systematic employer abuse of benefit programs.[1]

The main battleground on which this war is waged is ERISA § 502, the statute's civil enforcement provision.[2] While the statute authorizes criminal sanctions in three limited circumstances,[3] the sanctions are almost never invoked. Instead, the civil penalties and causes of action established by section 502 are the primary means

---

[1] *See supra* Chapter 1C.

[2] ERISA § 502, 29 U.S.C. § 1132 (2018).

[3] Willful violation of ERISA's reporting and disclosure obligations subjects the offender to imprisonment for up to ten years and a fine of up to $100,000 ($500,000 if the defendant is a corporation or other entity) under ERISA § 501, 29 U.S.C. § 1131 (2018); coercive

Enforcement

of implementing ERISA. The civil penalties, which are directed against various disclosure violations and fiduciary breaches, have been briefly addressed in preceding chapters.[4] Here the focus is on obtaining legal and equitable relief for a violation of the terms of the plan or the requirements of ERISA.

A STANDING

Section 502(a) establishes three basic enforcement actions, apart from civil penalties. First, a plan participant or beneficiary may bring a claim to recover benefits due under the plan or to clarify his rights to future benefits under the plan.[5] Second, the Secretary of Labor or a participant, beneficiary, or fiduciary may bring an action for damages or for equitable relief to enforce ERISA's fiduciary obligations.[6] Third, a participant, beneficiary, or fiduciary may bring an action "(A) to enjoin any act or practice which violates any provision of this title or the terms of the plan, or (B) to obtain appropriate equitable relief (i) to redress such violations or (ii) to enforce any provision of this title or the terms of the plan."[7]

Each entry on the list of civil enforcement actions in section 502(a) begins with a designation of the persons "by" whom the suit may be brought. Courts have generally interpreted the statutory specification of eligible plaintiffs as exhaustive – persons who do not fit within the designated categories lack standing.[8] For the most

interference with protected rights is criminalized under ERISA § 511, 29 U.S.C. § 1141 (2018); and it is a crime for persons previously convicted of certain specified offenses to intentionally violate a ban on carrying out various functions for an employee benefit plan under ERISA § 411(b), 29 U.S.C. § 1111(b) (2018). In addition, three sections of the criminal code create ERISA-related crimes: 18 U.S.C. § 664 (2018) (theft or embezzlement from an employee benefit fund); *id.* § 1027 (false statements or concealment of facts concerning reports or records of employee benefit plans); *id.* § 1954 (offer, acceptance, or solicitation of anything of value to influence employee benefit plan operations).

4 Civil penalties for various disclosure violations are prescribed by ERISA § 502(a)(1)(A), (a)(6), (c), 29 U.S.C. § 1132 (a)(1)(A), (a)(6), (c) (2018). *See supra* Chapter 3. In addition, the Secretary of Labor is authorized to assess civil penalties for certain breaches of fiduciary obligations, ERISA § 502(*l*), (m), 29 U.S.C. § 1132(*l*), (m) (2018). *See supra* Chapter 4.

5 ERISA § 502(a)(1)(B), 29 U.S.C. § 1132(a)(1)(B) (2018).

6 ERISA §§ 409, 502(a)(2), 29 U.S.C. §§ 1109, 1132(a)(2) (2018).

7 ERISA § 502(a)(3), 29 U.S.C. § 1132(a)(3) (2018). In certain circumstances, the Secretary of Labor is given corresponding authority to seek equitable enforcement of ERISA but not to enforce the terms of any particular plan. *Compare id. with* ERISA § 502(a)(5), 29 U.S.C. § 1132(a)(5) (2018). In the case of a tax-qualified pension, profit-sharing, stock bonus, or annuity plan, Labor Department enforcement is authorized only at the request of the Treasury Department, or suit may be brought in a representative capacity upon the written request of a participant, beneficiary, or fiduciary. ERISA § 502(b)(1), 29 U.S.C. § 1132(b)(1) (2018).

8 Leuthner v. Blue Cross & Blue Shield Ne. Pa., 454 F.3d 120, 125–26 (3d Cir. 2006) (holding an argument invalid that claimed a finding of ERISA § 502(a)'s prudential "zone of interest" standing automatically gives a plaintiff statutory standing, which requires a plaintiff be a plan participant or beneficiary, in ERISA cases); Felix v. Lucent Techs., Inc., 387 F.3d 1146, 1160 n.14 (10th Cir. 2004) (§ 502 designation of plaintiffs limits subject matter jurisdiction); Miller v. Rite Aid Corp., 334 F.3d 335, 340 (3d Cir. 2003) ("ERISA § 502(a)(1) ... *restricts* civil

part, this approach works because Congress wisely placed primary responsibility for enforcing ERISA in the hands of the interested private parties, the plan participants, beneficiaries, and fiduciaries. In two respects, however, legislative limitations on standing have proven problematic.

First, participants and beneficiaries in a defined benefit pension plan may have little or no incentive to enforce ERISA's fiduciary obligations.[9] Minimum funding standards and the Pension Benefit Guaranty Corporation (PBGC) termination insurance system largely insulate covered workers from loss of vested pension benefits.[10] This security blunts the incentive for fiduciary oversight, and makes it unwise to rely on participant monitoring in the case of a defined benefit pension plan.[11] Instead, standing should be granted to the real party in interest, the defined

actions [brought] against a plan administrator to actions brought by a 'participant or beneficiary.'" (emphasis added) (quoting Saporito v. Combustion Eng'g Inc., 843 F.2d 666, 670–71 (3d Cir. 1988), *vacated by* 489 U.S. 1049 (1989))). *But see* Vartanian v. Monsanto Co., 14 F.3d 697, 701–02 (1st Cir. 1994) (looking to whether plaintiff is within the zone of interests ERISA was intended to protect, and citing Ass'n Data Processing Serv. Orgs. v. Camp, 397 U.S. 150 (1970), the foundation for the modern prudential test for standing).

[9] *Cf.* Thole v. U.S. Bank N.A, 140 S. Ct. 1615 (2020) (holding that defined benefit plan participants lack constitutional standing to sue for fiduciary breach under §§ 1132(a)(2) and (a)(3) when the harmed plan is not currently underfunded). In *Thole*, the Court's animating rationale was that, because the plan was not underfunded, plaintiffs would receive the entirety of their promised pensions, regardless of whether their suit for breach prevailed or not. *Id.* at 1622. Plaintiffs accordingly had no "concrete stake" in the dispute and thus no Article III standing. *Id.* The Supreme Court reserved the question of whether a defined benefit participant would have Article III standing if he plausibly alleged that the "mismanagement of the plan was so egregious that it substantially increased the risk that the plan and the employer would fail and be unable to pay the participants' future pension benefits," *id.* at 1621, although it hinted that standing might not exist even in that case to the extent the PBGC fully guaranteed a plaintiff's pension. *Id.* at n.2.

[10] Most defined benefit plans are well funded, and the continued applicability of the minimum funding standards will eventually eliminate any shortfall because an underfunded plan cannot be terminated unless the sponsor is in financial distress. ERISA § 4041(b)(1)(D), 29 U.S.C. § 1341(b)(1)(D) (2018) (standard termination is only permitted if plan assets are sufficient to pay all benefit liabilities). Where termination of an underfunded plan is authorized, the PBGC steps in to pay guaranteed benefits. ERISA § 4022, 29 U.S.C. § 1322 (2018). *See generally infra* Chapter 9B.

[11] In contrast, participants in a defined contribution pension plan are not guaranteed any particular level of benefits; they are entitled only to the balance in their accounts. ERISA § 3(34), 29 U.S.C. § 1002(34) (2018) (defined contribution plan is defined as a pension plan that provides "benefits based solely on the amount contributed to the participant's account, and any income, expenses, gains and losses, and any forfeitures of accounts of other participants which may be allocated to such participant's account"). Because defined contribution plan participants are directly harmed by bad investments or theft, they have a strong interest in fiduciary oversight.

Although welfare plans are usually defined benefit arrangements, this incentive problem does not ordinarily arise. Participants normally do not acquire vested rights to welfare benefits, so losses from fiduciary misconduct jeopardize continuation of the plan. Multiemployer welfare benefit funds are found in some industries like trucking and construction. But because employers are permitted to limit their liability to the amount contributed to the fund, and

Enforcement

benefit plan sponsor, because it is the sponsor who will be obliged to make up any losses that might be caused by fiduciary breach.[12] Standing might also be granted to the PBGC, which is secondarily liable for a funding shortfall, as it will have to pay guaranteed benefits if the sponsor cannot.

Second, the meaning of the term "participant" originally caused difficulty for courts ruling on standing. The statute defines participant as "any employee or former employee ... who is or may become eligible to receive a benefit of any type from an employee benefit plan."[13] Eligibility to receive a benefit is generally the central contested issue in a claim for benefits and normally defines the scope of informational rights and fiduciary obligations. Consequently, defining proper plaintiffs by reference to participant status would often force the courts to take a peek at the merits of the claim to resolve the standing question.

It is possible to imagine a sequence of events (e.g., hiring, satisfaction of plan membership conditions, fulfilling service requirements for vesting) that, however unlikely, would permit almost anyone "to become eligible to receive a benefit" from any particular plan. Such a literal reading would make surplus the statutory reference to eligibility, effectively equating participant status with the set of all current and former employees. But that cannot have been intended. In the case of a pension plan it is clear that an employee does not become a participant unless and until he starts earning benefits under the plan,[14] and the subjunctive language, "may become eligible," was apparently intended to indicate that workers whose accrued benefits have not yet vested are nonetheless entitled to statutory protection. For a welfare plan, the subjunctive language indicates that participation begins as soon as "the individual becomes eligible ... for a benefit subject only to occurrence of the contingency for which the benefit is provided."[15] For example, an employee who would be entitled to health care benefits if she or her dependents were injured or

---

because welfare benefits are not guaranteed, participants and beneficiaries of funded welfare plans bear the risk of loss.

[12] To be clear: plan sponsors, if they also serve as plan fiduciaries (as many do), have standing to sue *as fiduciaries*. ERISA § 502, 29 U.S.C. § 1132 (2018). But they are not granted statutory standing merely by virtue of being plan sponsors, even though they are the ones who bear additional funding obligations if the plan is underfunded. Note further that in the case of an *overfunded* plan, the sponsor ordinarily takes the surplus (after paying a tax on the reversion), which creates an interest in preserving it. ERISA §§ 403(o)(1), 4044(d)(1), 29 U.S.C. §§ 1103 (c)(1), 1344(d)(1) (2018). *Accord* I.R.C. § 401(a)(2) (2018). A 20 percent or 50 percent tax on reversions from a qualified defined benefit plan is imposed by I.R.C. § 4980.

[13] ERISA § 3(7), 29 U.S.C. § 1002(7) (2018).

[14] The statute imposes precise minimum standards on the commencement of pension plan participation in ERISA § 202(a)(4), 29 U.S.C. § 1052(a)(4) (2018). *Accord* I.R.C. § 410(a) (4); Treas. Reg. § 1.410(a)-4(b) (as amended in 1980). Note that Department of Treasury regulations prescribed under I.R.C. §§ 410 and 411 are authoritative interpretations of the corresponding provisions of ERISA's labor title. 29 C.F.R. § 2530.200a-2 (2022).

[15] 29 C.F.R. § 2510.3-3(d)(1)(i)(B) (2022).

164   *Conduct Controls: Welfare and Pension Plans*

sick is a current plan participant. Similarly, an employee is a current life insurance plan participant if a death benefit would be due upon their demise.

Dealing with outgoing employees has proven harder. A sponsor may assert that separation from service terminates the right to all benefits under the terms of a plan.[16] Can a former employee contest that reading? It would seem that the former worker has standing if and only if she will prevail on the merits. In *Firestone Tire & Rubber Co.* v. *Bruch*, the Supreme Court majority refused to be quite so literal:

> In our view, the term "participant" is naturally read to mean either "employees in, or reasonably expected to be in, currently covered employment," *Saladino v. I.L.G.W.U. National Retirement Fund*, 754 F.2d 473, 476 (CA2 1985), or former employees who "have . . . a reasonable expectation of returning to covered employment" or who have "a colorable claim" to vested benefits, *Kuntz v. Reese*, 785 F.2d 1410, 1411 (CA9) (*per curiam*), cert. denied, 479 U.S. 916 (1986). In order to establish that he or she "may become eligible" for benefits, a claimant must have a colorable claim that (1) he or she will prevail in a suit for benefits, or that (2) eligibility requirements will be fulfilled in the future. "This view attributes conventional meanings to the statutory language since all employees in covered employment and former employees with a colorable claim to vested benefits 'may become eligible.' A former employee who has neither a reasonable expectation of returning to covered employment nor a colorable claim to vested benefits, however, simply does not fit within the [phrase] 'may become eligible.'" *Saladino v. I.L.G.W.U. National Retirement Fund, supra*, at 476.[17]

Firestone's "colorable claim" gloss allows the adjudication of bona fide eligibility disputes without unnecessary procedural complications, but it does not solve all the problems. Take the example of an employee who alleges that his decision to retire was based on employer misrepresentations constituting a breach of fiduciary duty and who shows that absent the misrepresentation he would have continued working and so qualified for greater benefits. The First Circuit held that the "receipt of payment cannot be used to deprive him of 'participant' status and hence, standing to sue under ERISA" provided that the true facts were not available to the employee until after he received all of his vested benefits.[18]

In response to a similar fiduciary misrepresentation claim, the Third Circuit put the matter this way:

> A plan administrator's alleged ERISA violation should not be the means by which the plan is able to insulate itself from suits arising from the alleged violation. We will not read ERISA so myopically. As the Sixth Circuit observed, "ERISA should

---

[16] *See id.* § 2510.3-3(d)(2)(i)(A) (2022) (welfare plan participation ends "on the earliest date on which the individual – [i]s ineligible to receive any benefit under the plan even if the contingency for which the benefit is provided should occur").

[17] Firestone Tire & Rubber Co. v. Bruch, 489 U.S. 101, 117–18 (1989).

[18] Vartanian v. Monsanto Co., 14 F.3d 697, 703 (1st Cir. 1994).

Enforcement

not be construed to permit the fiduciary to circumvent his ERISA-imposed fiduciary duty in this manner." [citation omitted] Therefore, in the proper case, we may find that a plaintiff has statutory standing if the plaintiff can in good faith plead that she was an ERISA plan participant or beneficiary and that she still would be but for the alleged malfeasance of a plan fiduciary.[19]

The circuits are split on the issue, but the majority have embraced this "but for" extension of participant status.[20]

The approach of testing participant status at the time of the alleged violation was adopted by the Ninth Circuit for retaliatory discharge claims. In *McBride* v. *PLM International, Inc.*, the plaintiff alleged that he was discharged in violation of ERISA § 510 for his vociferous objections to the proposed termination of the employer's pension plans.[21] After he was fired, McBride, along with all other participants, received a lump-sum distribution of his benefits and the plan was terminated. Consequently, at the time McBride brought suit he was a former employee who had received all benefits due under the plan and who, even if reinstated, had no "reasonable expectation of returning to covered employment" because the plans had been terminated. Relying on ERISA's protective policy, the court concluded that an "employer cannot be allowed to evade section [510] accountability simply by terminating the plan and distributing the benefits."[22] To prevent that injustice, the court held that standing to assert section 510 claims must be determined at the time of the alleged ERISA violation, rather than the usual approach of judging standing as of the time of filing suit.[23] An extended dissent charged that this special whistleblower exception was unfaithful to the statutory language as well as both Supreme Court (i.e., *Firestone*) and Ninth Circuit precedent.[24]

In the misrepresentation and retaliatory discharge contexts the "but for" test grants standing to a former employee who asserts that his separation from service was caused by an ERISA violation. Does a former employee have standing if separation from service was unrelated to the claimed violation of plan terms or ERISA? Suppose an individual takes distribution of her entire account balance in the company's defined contribution pension plan following separation from service, then later discovers that the plan fiduciaries might have breached their duties of loyalty or care in making investments or selecting available investment options. May

---

[19] Leuthner v. Blue Cross & Blue Shield Ne. Pa., 454 F.3d 120, 129 (3d Cir. 2006) (quoting Swinney v. GMC, 46 F.3d 512, 518–19 (6th Cir. 1995)).
[20] The circuits' positions are cataloged in *Leuthner*, 454 F.3d at 128–29, and Chastain v. AT & T, 558 F.3d 1177, 1183 (10th Cir. 2009). *Compare* Raymond v. Mobil Oil Co., 983 F.2d 1528, 1532–37 (10th Cir. 1993) (standing to bring a constructive discharge claim denied, relying on *Firestone*), *with* Christopher v. Mobil Oil Co., 950 F.2d 1209, 1220–21 (5th Cir.) (standing to challenge the same actions granted), *cert. denied*, 506 U.S. 820 (1992).
[21] 179 F.3d 737, 741 (9th Cir. 1999).
[22] *Id.* at 742.
[23] *Id.* at 743.
[24] *Id.* at 746–53 (Beezer, J., dissenting).

166 *Conduct Controls: Welfare and Pension Plans*

such a former employee bring suit for the additional amount that would have been in her account absent the breach, or does cashing out of a defined contribution plan extinguish participant status? Standing originally presented a barrier to such suits.[25] Since 2007 a series of appellate decisions have coalesced around the view that a former employee who seeks payment of the additional amount that her account would have contained if it were unimpaired by fiduciary misconduct is asserting a colorable claim to benefits, and is therefore a proper plaintiff.[26]

Welfare benefits are not required to vest under ERISA, and so the references in *Firestone* to a "colorable claim to vested benefits" might call into question the power to adjudicate welfare plan eligibility disputes. No policy consideration supports such a distinction, and the "vested" language has not proved a stumbling block to standing in claims involving welfare plans.[27] Whether the assignee of a welfare plan participant or beneficiary has standing to sue has been challenged, however. Unlike pension benefits, welfare benefits are assignable.[28] A health care provider, for example, may accept an assignment of the patient's plan benefits instead of insisting on payment when services are rendered. If the claim for benefits is denied, can the doctor or hospital bring suit? Although assignees are not specifically listed in the statute, the courts generally hold that an assignee has derivative standing to bring an action under section 502 in place of the assignor participant or beneficiary.[29]

---

[25] *See* 34 Pens. & Ben. Rep. (BNA) 115–17 (2007) (synopsis of conflicting district court decisions issued during 2006 involving former employee standing).

[26] *E.g.*, Vaughn v. Bay Env't. Mgmt. Inc., 544 F.3d 1008 (9th Cir. 2008); Lanfear v. Home Depot, Inc., 536 F.3d 1217 (11th Cir. 2008); Evans v. Akers, 534 F.3d 65 (1st Cir. 2008); Wangberger v. Janus Cap. Grp., Inc., 529 F.3d 207 (4th Cir. 2008); Bridges v. Am. Elec. Power Co., 498 F.3d 442 (6th Cir. 2007); Graden v. Conexant Sys. Inc., 496 F.3d 291 (3d Cir. 2007); Harzewski v. Guidant Corp., 489 F.3d 799 (7th Cir. 2007). The Supreme Court cited *Harzewski* with apparent approval in LaRue v. DeWolff Boberg & Assocs., 552 U.S. 248, 256 n.6 (2008), which may account for the rapid alignment of appellate court approaches. *See also* Bilello v. JPMorgan Chase Ret. Plan, 592 F. Supp. 2d 654, 662–67 (S.D.N.Y. 2009) (a former employee who cashed out of a cash balance defined benefit plan has standing to pursue a claim for additional benefits based on a theory that plan amendment reducing benefit accruals were ineffective due to lack of required prior notice).

[27] *See* Andre v. Salem Tech. Servs. Corp., 797 F. Supp. 1416, 1420, 1422–23 (N.D. Ill. 1992) ("vested" in the context of welfare plans should be taken to mean "fixed in time during the employment relationship"; alternatively, former employees who incurred covered expenses are "eligible to receive a benefit" within the meaning of ERISA).

[28] *See* ERISA § 206(d)(1), 29 U.S.C. § 1056(d)(1) (2018) (antialienation rule limited to pension plans).

[29] Bristol SL Holdings, Inc. v. Cigna Health & Life Ins. Co., 22 F.4th 1086, 1091 (9th Cir. 2022) (collecting cases and noting that courts have "consistently recognized derivative standing when based on the valid assignment of ERISA health and welfare benefits by participants and beneficiaries") (internal citations omitted). *But see* Simon v. Value Behav. Health, Inc., 208 F.3d 1073, 1080 (9th Cir.), *amended*, 234 F.3d 428 (9th Cir. 2000), and *overruled on other grounds by* Odom v. Microsoft Corp., 486 F.3d 541 (9th Cir. 2007) (denial of derivative standing to an attorney-litigant, Stephen Simon, who had aggregated, via assignment, hundreds of ERISA benefit claims that he then brought against some 1600 payer defendants). The *Bristol* court wrote several paragraphs cabining the reach of *Simon* by explaining that *Simon* involved

Moreover, a valid assignment amounts to the participant's designation of a person entitled to collect plan benefits, and therefore seems to fit the statutory definition of "beneficiary."[30]

B SCOPE OF REVIEW

ERISA enforcement actions invariably challenge a plan official's decision making. When called to account, the decision maker may argue that his official status or presumed expertise entitles the decision to a presumption of correctness, or to some special weight in court. The intensity of judicial scrutiny will often determine the outcome on judicial review, and yet the statute is silent on the question of the appropriate scope of review.

Although elsewhere the Supreme Court has invoked ERISA's "comprehensive" nature in refusing to supplement the statute,[31] neither it (nor the courts of appeal) have been reluctant to create law with respect to the scope of review of benefit claims. In particular, the federal courts have constructed a regime where, practically speaking, federal judges can only review a plan's benefit determinations for abuse of discretion. Indeed, even a judicial conclusion that an administrator has abused its discretion warrants only a remand to the administrator for a second bite at the apple (rather than the immediate imposition of judicial judgment). Moreover, this judicial deference to plan administrators is due even where (as is frequently the case) the administrator labors under a conflict of interest. Nor can a claimant simply sidestep a conflicted administrator and head directly to court; a litigant must have "exhausted" the plan's review procedures before a suit can be heard. None of these rules (whatever their policy wisdom) appear anywhere in the statute.

Plan Interpretations

In ERISA's early years most lower courts applied the abuse-of-discretion standard to fiduciary decision making, as that limited scope of review had been applied to suits for benefits brought against trustees of collectively bargained plans under the Taft-Hartley Act. In 1989, the Supreme Court rejected that approach in *Firestone Tire &*

---

an unusual and acute risk of the "commodification" of benefit claims not present in *Bristol* or most assignment contexts. *Id.* at 1090–91. Yet the Ninth Circuit nonetheless acknowledged that "there are certain limits to . . . derivative standing for assignees bringing ERISA claims." *Id. Cf.* Gables Ins. Recovery, Inc. v. Blue Cross & Blue Shield of Fla., Inc., 813 F.3d 1333, 1339–40 (11th Cir. 2015) (doubting the persuasive value of a series of anti-assignment decisions involving plaintiff Stephen Simon but nonetheless explaining that the court's instant holding in favor of assignment did not resolve the question of whether "*all* assignees" had standing to sue) (emphasis in original).

[30] ERISA § 3(8), 29 U.S.C. § 1002(8) (2018).
[31] Great–West Life & Annuity Ins. Co. v. Knudson, 534 U.S. 204, 209 (2002).

Rubber Co. v. Bruch.[32] Turning to the trust-law origins of ERISA, the Court noted that a deferential standard of review is appropriate where a trustee is granted discretionary powers, but that a trustee's interpretation of the terms of the trust is ordinarily reviewed by the courts de novo.[33] De novo review of plan interpretations, the Court observed, is also consistent with the contract-law basis of suits for benefits prior to ERISA.[34] Accordingly, the *Firestone* Court held "that a denial of benefits challenged under § 1132(a)(1)(B) [ERISA § 502(a)(1)(B)] is to be reviewed under a de novo standard unless the benefit plan gives the administrator or fiduciary discretionary authority to determine eligibility for benefits or to construe the terms of the plan."[35]

Employers retain the power to amend their benefit plans,[36] and if the plan does not cover unionized workers they can typically do so unilaterally. Not surprisingly, sponsors responded to *Firestone* by inserting in their plans an express grant of fiduciary discretion to interpret plan terms and determine benefit eligibility, although some question remains as to how clear a grant of discretionary authority must be to work a relaxation of the scope of review.[37] Therefore, notwithstanding the Court's conclusion that de novo review is the general or default mode of judicial oversight for benefit claim denials, as a practical matter the abuse-of-discretion standard is now overwhelmingly dominant.[38] And the Court's devotion to discretion is robust. In *Conkright* v. *Frommert*, the Court held that even in the aftermath of a finding that an administrator had acted arbitrarily and capriciously, a court was obligated to remand the matter to the administrator for a second chance to exercise discretion.[39]

Firestone concerns the standard of review applicable to benefit claim denials based on plan interpretations, and the Court expressed "no view as to the appropriate standard of review" in other areas.[40] Two vitally important questions that have vexed the lower courts concern the proper scope of review to be applied to fiduciary

---

[32] 489 U.S. 101, 109 (1989) (a comparison of the statutes "shows that the *wholesale* importation of the arbitrary and capricious standard into ERISA is unwarranted") (emphasis in original).

[33] *Id.* at 111–12.

[34] *Id.* at 112–13.

[35] *Id.* at 115.

[36] ERISA § 402(b)(3), 29 U.S.C. § 1102(b)(3) (2018).

[37] *See infra* Chapter 5 note 43.

[38] That development has been sharply criticized but not on the policy ground on which it is most vulnerable. *See, e.g.*, Jay Conison, *Suits for Benefits Under ERISA*, 54 U. Pitt. L. Rev. 1 (1992). A limited scope of review works, in effect, a relaxation of fiduciary duties, and is therefore inconsistent with the command of ERISA § 410(a) that "any provision in an agreement or instrument that purports to relieve a fiduciary from responsibility or liability for any responsibility, obligation or duty imposed under this part shall be void as against public policy." 29 U.S.C. § 1110(a) (2018).

[39] 559 U.S. 506, 509–12 (2010).

[40] *Firestone*, 489 U.S. at 108.

Enforcement

findings of fact and to claims determinations made by a fiduciary who is allegedly acting under a conflict of interest.

Factfinding

Although *Firestone* involved a question of plan interpretation, the Court conditioned its approval of de novo review on the absence of an express grant of discretion to construe plan terms *or to determine eligibility for benefits*.[41] Since eligibility for benefits commonly turns upon disputed issues of fact, the implicit approval of discretionary power to determine eligibility suggests that the Court would adopt the same approach to review of factfinding (i.e., de novo review if the plan is silent, but only limited oversight if discretion is expressly conferred). After *Firestone*, of course, plan provisions expressly limiting judicial scrutiny – for example, by providing that the fiduciary's determination on eligibility questions shall be "final" or "unreviewable" or "conclusive" – are the norm.[42]

In the aftermath of *Firestone*, the circuits split on the proper scope of review to be applied to findings of fact. Hewing close to the line marked by the Supreme Court, in the absence of an explicit reservation of discretionary authority most appellate courts undertake searching de novo review.[43] Nevertheless, important differences

---

[41] *Id.* at 115.

[42] See, for example, the model pension plans published in Michael J. Canan, Qualified Retirement Plans 705 (2007) (profit-sharing plan administrator granted "sole discretion, to interpret or construe the Plan and to determine all questions that may arise hereunder"); *id.* at 862 (same, money purchase pension plan); *id.* at 1031 (same, defined benefit plan); *id.* at 1260 (same, 401(k) plan). *Accord* CCH Pension Plan Guide – Plans and Clauses ¶¶ 30,047 (model defined benefit plan, with an explanatory note on *Firestone*), 30,133 (model money purchase pension plan), 31,133 (model profit-sharing plan). Model group health plans also commonly include an express grant of discretion. E.g., Michael J. Canan & William D. Mitchell, Employee Fringe and Welfare Benefit Plans 591 (1997) (discretion to interpret the plan, with instruction that the exercise of discretion is to be reviewed under the arbitrary and capricious standard).

[43] E.g., Kinstler v. First Reliance Standard Life Ins. Co., 181 F.3d 243, 249–51 (2d Cir. 2000) (discussing circuit split); Pierre v. Conn Gen. Life Ins. Co., 502 U.S. 973, 973 (1991) (White, J., dissenting).

Those appellate courts that apply de novo review absent a grant of discretionary authority differ among themselves on how explicit the conferral of discretion must be to trigger the more deferential abuse-of-discretion standard. E.g., *Kinstler*, at 251–52 (submission of "satisfactory proof" insufficient to relax standard of review); Sandy v. Reliance Standard Life Ins. Co., 222 F.3d 1202, 1204 n. 2 (9th Cir. 2000) (same; reviewing circuit split and noting "awkward position of construing the effect of identical language in plan documents of the same insurer differently from the Sixth Circuit"). Even if the fiduciary has clearly been given factfinding discretion, some circuits hold that de novo review applies if the claim denial is not actually based on an exercise of discretion. E.g., Gilbertson v. Allied Signal, Inc., 328 F.3d 625, 631 (10th Cir. 2003) (automatic denial under Labor Department regulations because of passage of time).

from plan interpretation may justify restricted oversight of factfinding even without explicit plan instructions. Factfinding, after all, whether by lower courts or administrative agencies, has traditionally been accorded substantial deference, and the weighing of competing versions of events, especially when credibility is an issue, may be thought an inherently discretionary function.[44] Concerns about caseload may also support restricted judicial scrutiny; second-guessing a multitude of routine fact determinations could swamp the courts.

Expertise is another policy concern that may justify a limited scope of review. A decision maker possessed of specialized knowledge or experience is comparatively better qualified than a court to make decisions involving that specialized subject matter. Because a specialist will often evaluate information differently than a generalist judge, de novo review (i.e., substituted judgment) may forfeit the value of this expertise. Alternatively, the expert might seek to have the decision sustained by educating the reviewing court as to the validity of the expert's evaluation, effectively replicating any relevant specialized knowledge, but then de novo review entails duplication, delay, and inefficiency. By giving specialized decision makers some slack, a limited scope of review (like the abuse-of-discretion test) promotes an efficient, expert resolution of the issue. Plan fiduciaries making eligibility determinations are repeatedly presented with similar fact patterns or types of evidence (e.g., medical records under a health plan, or wage and hour reports under a pension plan), so expertise may be an important value in fiduciary decision making.[45] Post-*Firestone*, however, factfinding expertise has generally received little attention in the ERISA context, because (1) the ubiquitous adoption of plan amendments expressly conferring discretion mooted the issue, and (2) in reality many claims administrators have no meaningful "expertise" that a court does not.

---

[44] *Cf.* Black & Decker Disability Plan v. Nord, 538 U.S. 822, 825 (2003) (ERISA disability plan administrators not obliged to accord special weight to opinions of claimant's treating physicians vis-à-vis views of plan consultants).

[45] Expertise forms a primary justification for the limited scope of judicial review of factfinding in administrative law. *See generally,* BERNARD SCHWARTZ, ADMINISTRATIVE LAW §§ 10.1, 10.5–10.6 (3d ed. 1991) (limited judicial review of agency factfinding explained by considerations of relative expertise – i.e., comparative competence of the agency and reviewing court – and efficiency). Similar considerations may apply to judicial review of a benefit plan administrator's factual determinations where the administrator has special knowledge or experience, although the likelihood that actual administrators have actual expertise worth crediting is overstated, given the realities of who administrators are. *Contra* Luby v. Teamsters Health, Welfare & Pension Tr. Funds, 944 F.2d 1176, 1183 (3d Cir. 1991) ("Plan administrators are not governmental agencies who are frequently granted deferential review because of their acknowledged expertise. Administrators may be laypersons appointed under the plan, sometimes without any legal, accounting, or other training preparing them for their responsible position, often without any experience in or understanding of the complex problems arising under ERISA, and, as this case demonstrates, little knowledge of the rules of evidence or legal procedures to assist them in factfinding.").

Conflicted Decision Making

Where a plan specifically confers discretion in construing its terms or in determining eligibility for benefits, *Firestone* ordinarily demands deferential abuse-of-discretion review. But does that relaxed standard apply where the decision maker is subject to a conflict of interest? In its parting observation in *Firestone*, the Court noted that "Of course, if a benefit plan gives discretion to an administrator or fiduciary who is operating under a conflict of interest, that conflict must be weighed as a 'facto[r] in determining whether there is an abuse of discretion.'"[46]

Consider a plan that is funded by the purchase of insurance, with the insurer making final decisions on benefit eligibility. The insurer is acting as fiduciary, yet because claims are paid out of the insurer's own assets, benefit grants adversely impact the insurer's profitability. The same sort of direct financial impact is present where a welfare plan is self-insured and claims decisions are made by an employee of the sponsor. As a result of the multiple-hat problem,[47] such inherent or "structural" conflicts of interest are pervasive facts of life in benefit claims decisions.

Thanks to the absence of guidance in the *Firestone* dicta, the question of the impact of such structural conflicts on the intensity of judicial review of benefit claim denials long bedeviled and divided the lower courts.[48] Nearly two decades after *Firestone*, the Supreme Court took up the conflict of interest problem in *Metropolitan Life Insurance Company v. Glenn.*[49] *Glenn* holds that a conflict of interest necessarily exists when an entity both determines employee eligibility for benefits and pays those benefits out of its own pocket.[50] As suggested in *Firestone*, courts should consider this conflict of interest as a factor in determining whether a plan administrator's denial of benefits constitutes an abuse of discretion, but the existence of the conflict does not trigger a higher standard of review (such as de novo review).[51] The Court refused to specify a detailed set of instructions on the impact of

---

[46] *Firestone*, 489 U.S. at 115 (quoting RESTATEMENT (SECOND) OF TRUSTS § 187, cmt. d (1959)).

[47] *See supra* Chapter 4A.

[48] *See* Kathryn J. Kennedy, *Judicial Standard of Review in ERISA Benefit Claim Cases*, 50 AM. U. L. REV. 1083, 1146–62 (2001); *see generally* John H. Langbein, *Trust Law as Regulatory Law, The UNUM/Provident Scandal and Judicial Review of Benefit Denials under ERISA*, 101 NW. U. L. REV. 1315 (2007).

[49] 554 U.S. 105, 108 (2008).

[50] *Id.*

[51] *Id.* at 115–16. Before *Glenn*, several circuits adopted a heightened or modified standard of review in conflict of interest cases, but once the *Glenn* decision was rendered, courts abandoned the heightened standard. Doyle v. Liberty Life Assurance Co., 542 F.3d 1352, 1358–60 (11th Cir. 2008); Champion v. Black & Decker (U.S.) Inc., 550 F.3d 353, 355 (4th Cir. 2008).

Pre-*Glenn* the Second Circuit applied de novo review, empowering the reviewing court to substitute its judgment on eligibility for benefits, but only if the plaintiff produced evidence that a structural conflict actually infected decision making. Sullivan v. LTV Aerospace & Def. Co., 82 F.3d 1251, 1255–56 (2d Cir. 1996). *Glenn* prompted the Second Circuit to abandon its de novo review in favor of treating a conflict of interest as a distinct factor. McCauley v. First

172   *Conduct Controls: Welfare and Pension Plans*

this factor, holding instead that the weight to be given the conflict should be based on the circumstances of the particular case.[52] *Glenn* also disavowed special procedural or evidentiary mechanisms, like shifting the burden of proof, that some circuits had imposed to smoke out whether a structural conflict actually affected the decision.[53]

While *Glenn* embraces an indefinite totality-of-the-circumstances approach, the Court's opinion offers a few clues on the influence of a conflict on the overall assessment of factors. First, the conflict should be given little weight if there are mechanisms in place to promote fair and correct benefit determinations.

> [The conflict] should prove less important (perhaps to the vanishing point) where the administrator has taken active steps to reduce potential bias and to promote accuracy, for example, by walling off claims administrators from those interested in firm finances, or by imposing management checks that penalize inaccurate decisionmaking irrespective of whom the inaccuracy benefits.[54]

This discount for structural safeguards seemed intended to induce insurers and sponsors of large self-insured plans to institute such internal controls.[55]

But the absence of internal safeguards does not doom fiduciaries. Before *Glenn* some circuits had applied law and economic reasoning to disregard structural conflicts on the ground that market forces provide adequate countervailing incentives for fair decision making.[56] MetLife deployed this reasoning to assert that there

---

Unum Life Ins. Co., 551 F.3d 126, 137–38 (2d Cir. 2008) (finding that the plan administrator abused its discretion in denying plaintiff's claim).

[52] *Glenn*, 554 U.S. at 116–19. The Court relied on trust law to support the conclusion that a conflict of interest does not trigger a higher standard of review: "Trust law continues to apply a deferential standard of review to the discretionary decisionmaking of a conflicted trustee, while at the same time requiring the reviewing judge to take account of the conflict when determining whether the trustee, substantively or procedurally, has abused his discretion." *Id.* at 115. In dissent, Justices Scalia and Thomas took ERISA's trust law origins much farther – they would look to trust law for concrete guidelines on the content of abuse of discretion review. Applying trust law, they would find that a conflict is relevant only to the question whether the trustee abused his discretion by acting with an improper motive, and that it is wholly irrelevant (not a factor to be considered) to the question whether the trustee's decision was reasonable. *Id.* at 127–34 (Scalia, J. dissenting).

[53] *Glenn* prompted the Eleventh Circuit to abandon its burden shifting approach and consider a conflict of interest as an additional factor to be weighed. *Doyle*, 542 F.3d at 1358–60.

[54] *Glenn*, 554 U.S. at 117.

[55] Justice Kennedy agreed with the Court's legal analysis, including the combination-of-factors method of review, but concluded that the case should have been remanded because, "so far as one can tell, the Court of Appeals made no effort to assess whether MetLife employed structural safeguards to avoid conflicts of interest, safeguards the Court says can cause the importance of the conflict to vanish." 554 U.S. at 126 (Kennedy, J., concurring in part and dissenting in part).

[56] E.g., Mers v. Marriott Int'l Grp. Accidental Death & Dismemberment Plan, 144 F.3d 1014, 1020 (7th Cir. 1998) ("We presume that a fiduciary is acting neutrally unless a claimant shows by providing specific evidence of actual bias that there is a significant conflict. The existence of a potential conflict is not enough." (citations omitted)); Perlman v. Swiss Bank Corp.

Enforcement

was no cognizable conflict of interest in *Glenn*. The Court rejected that defense because "ERISA imposes higher-than-marketplace quality standards on insurers."[57] Yet the Court acknowledged that an approach that finds "the *existence* of a conflict can nonetheless take account of the circumstances to which MetLife points so far as it treats those, or similar, circumstances as diminishing the *significance* or *severity* of the conflict in individual cases."[58] Thus, under the totality-of-the-circumstances approach countervailing market forces are relevant, but their strength depends upon case-specific facts.[59]

A final (and more speculative) clue to the handling of a structural conflict might lie in *Glenn's* administrative law analogy. In addition to its reliance on ERISA's trust-law origins,[60] the Court drew support from certain cases examining the lawfulness of bureaucratic action.[61] Abuse-of-discretion review is of course best known and most fully developed in the context of judicial oversight of administrative decisions. It is a fundamental tenet of administrative law that reliance on an irrelevant or improper consideration is an abuse of discretion.[62] A fiduciary's consideration of his own or his employer's interest – or, for that matter, anything other than participants' interest

---

Comprehensive Disability Prot. Plan, 195 F.3d 975, 981 (7th Cir. 1999); Rud v. Liberty Life Assurance Co., 438 F.3d 772, 776–77 (7th Cir. 2006); Wright v. R. R. Donnelley & Sons Co. Grp. Benefits Plan, 402 F.3d 67, 75, n.5 (1st Cir. 2005) (following the market forces rationale, while recognizing that other circuits are unpersuaded). The reasoning in this line of cases was that the amount involved in an individual benefit claim is too small to affect a large employer or insurer, and that the employer has an interest in maintaining a reputation for fair dealing with its employees. Similarly, Judge Easterbrook discounted an insurer–fiduciary's conflict on the ground that group insurance policies are experience-rated, with the employer agreeing to reimburse the insurer for benefit payments or pay higher premiums for future years' coverage, so that the insurer does not ultimately bear the cost of approved claims. *Perlman*, 195 F.3d at 981.

A leading ERISA scholar extensively criticized the Seventh Circuit decisions in an article that the *Glenn* court cited to illustrate the principle that a conflict of interest takes on greater significance where an insurance company has a history of biased benefit claims administration. Langbein, *supra* Chapter 5 note 48, cited at *Glenn*, 554 U.S. at 114, 117.

[57] 554 U.S. at 115.

[58] *Id.*; *see* Denmark v. Liberty Life Assurance Co., 566 F.3d 1, 9 (1st Cir. 2009) (in the wake of *Glenn* "the market forces rationale no longer allows a reviewing court to disregard a structural conflict without further analysis").

[59] One way to read *Frommert*, however, is as a sub-rosa cutback of *Glenn* in practice, that is, as a general signal from the Court that it will only be in the rarest of circumstances where the possibility of true conflict will be sufficiently high so as to justify setting aside an administrator's decision. *See* Peter J. Wiedenbeck, *Untrustworthy. ERISA's Eroded Fiduciary Law*, 59 Wm. & Mary L. Rev. 1007, 1084–5 (2018) (explaining how *Frommert's* emphasis on circumscribing judicial review for reasons of cost-containment and predictability – even in cases where the administrator unquestionably acted capriciously – suggests the Court will be unlikely to approve *Glenn*-inspired judicial interventions absent a very high likelihood that an asserted conflict specifically infected a challenged decision).

[60] *See supra* Chapter 5 text accompanying note 53.

[61] *Glenn*, 554 U.S. at 116–19.

[62] E.g., Motor Vehicle Mfrs. Ass'n v. State Farm Mut. Auto. Ins. Co., 463 U.S. 29, 43 (1983) ("Normally, an agency rule would be arbitrary and capricious if the agency has relied on factors

174   *Conduct Controls: Welfare and Pension Plans*

in plan benefits – is unmistakably out-of-bounds under ERISA, and so an abuse of discretion.[63] Yet supposing that the outcome in a close case is influenced in part by a desire to control the insurer's or plan sponsor's costs, the fiduciary's claim denial surely will not disclose that fact. Therefore, where a benefit claim is rejected by a conflicted administrator, the real issue is whether there is sufficient circumstantial evidence of a possible violation of the exclusive benefit rule to set the decision aside. As a practical matter, considering the conflict of interest as a factor when conducting abuse-of-discretion review might mean (as in administrative law) that the reviewing court should look to evidence that is outside the decision file compiled by the fiduciary (the usual "record" on review) to uncover improprieties, or draw adverse inferences from procedural irregularities.[64] The fiduciary's contemporaneous explanation of the claim denial, if incomplete or unconvincing in light of the record evidence (physicians' reports concerning disability, for example), would similarly raise or reinforce suspicions.[65] The administrative law analogy, while suggestive, opens up other nettlesome questions, like whether a reviewing court that finds a benefit denial to have been an abuse of discretion should simply remand the claim to the fiduciary under instructions to decide again, this time giving no weight to cost considerations. *Frommert* is in accord with that view.[66]

---

which Congress has not intended it to consider, entirely failed to consider an important aspect of the problem, offered an explanation for its decision that runs counter to the evidence before the agency, or is so implausible that it could not be ascribed to a difference in view or the product of agency expertise."). The administrative law analogy to the problem discussed here is "hard look" review (also known as review for reasoned decision making) under the abuse-of-discretion standard. *See generally*, RICHARD J. PIERCE, JR., ADMINISTRATIVE LAW TREATISE §§ 7.4, 11.4 (4th ed. 2002); ERNEST GELLHORN & RONALD M. LEVIN, ADMINISTRATIVE LAW AND PROCESS IN A NUTSHELL 102–07, 116–19 (5th ed. 2006).

[63] Recall that a potentially compromising position does not automatically transgress the fiduciary's duty, for ERISA's exclusive benefit rule demands only subjective loyalty. *See supra* Chapter 4B.

[64] *E.g.*, Denmark v. Liberty Life Assurance Co., 566 F.3d 1, 10 (1st Cir. 2009) ("The majority opinion in *Glenn* fairly can be read as contemplating some discovery on the issue of whether a structural conflict has morphed into an actual conflict."); Burke v. Pitney Bowes Inc. Long-Term Disability Plan, 544 F.3d 1016, 1028 (9th Cir. 2008) ("the district court may 'consider evidence outside the administrative record to decide the nature, extent, and effect on the decision-making process of any conflict of interest" (quoting Abatie v. Alta Health & Life Ins. Co., 458 F.3d 955, 970 (9th Cir. 2006))).

[65] *E.g.*, Pinto v. Reliance Standard Life Ins. Co., 214 F.3d 377, 393–94 (3d Cir. 2000), *overruled by* Metro. Life Ins. v. Glenn, 554 U.S. 105, 108 (2008) (in case of structural conflict the court looks to process by which result was achieved, and may draw negative inference from unexplained inconsistent treatment of apparently similar facts, and unexplained selectivity in use of expert evidence; district court may take evidence regarding conflict of interest). While *Pinto's* holding that the existence of a conflict *changed* the standard of review (and was thus overruled by *Glenn*) the approach the Pinto court took to determine whether a conflict improperly affected the administrator's determination is consistent with *Glenn*.

[66] Conkright v. Frommert, 559 U.S. 506, 521–22 (2010) (holding that remand to the administrator, even after he has acted arbitrarily and capriciously, is appropriate absent bad faith or some \ to believe administrator will not act "honestly or fairly").

"Administrative" Exhaustion

The above constraints on review – judicial interpolations all – carry even more practical force when combined with another gloss: the courts of appeals' collective conclusion that ERISA conditions access to court on a claimant having "exhausted" whatever procedures the plan provides regarding internal review of benefit claims.[67] This requirement is often referred to by courts as "administrative exhaustion," notwithstanding that internal review of a claim by a fiduciary "bears little or no resemblance to genuine administrative review."[68] Recall that ERISA is a remedial statute, with one of its express purposes being to provide participants with "ready access to the Federal courts."[69] That it has been construed by the federal bench as requiring deference,

---

[67] See Kathryn J. Kennedy, *The Perilous and Ever-Changing Procedural Rules of Pursuing an ERISA Claims Case*, 70 UMKC L. REV. 329, 358–59 n.158 (2001) (collecting decisions holding the administrative-exhaustion requirement in benefit-denial cases). While the Supreme Court has not yet explicitly held that participants need exhaust their internal review options before having access to court, it has spoken of this requirement approvingly. See LaRue v. DeWolff, Boberg & Assocs., Inc., 552 U.S. 248, 258–59 (2008) (Roberts, C.J., concurring) (observing that among ERISA's "safeguards for plan administrators ... is the requirement, recognized by almost all the Courts of Appeals, ... that a participant [must] exhaust the administrative remedies mandated by ERISA ... before filing suit under § 502(a)(1)(B).").

Even prior to the passage of the ACA, federal regulators had enacted regulations imposing some constraints on internal review procedures for health and disability benefit claims, e.g., expeditious review, the right to bring a section 502(a) claim after arbitration, and limits on the number of levels of internal appeal. See generally Employee Retirement Income Security Act of 1974; Rules and Regulations for Administration and Enforcement, Claims Procedure, 65 Fed. Reg. 70,246 (Nov. 21, 2000). These pre-ACA regulations were subsequently codified at 29 C.F.R. § 2560.503–1 (2001). The ACA imposed even further limits on claims review. See infra Chapter 5 notes 70–73.

[68] Brendan S. Maher, *Creating a Paternalistic Market for Legal Rules Affecting the Benefit Promise*, 2009 WIS. L. REV. 657, 674, n.56 (2009). See also Donald T. Bogan, *Reply to Judge Easterbrook: The Unsupported Delegation of Conflict Adjudication in ERISA Benefit Claims under the Guise of Judicial Deference*, 57 OKLA. L. REV. 21, 27 (2004); MARK D. DEBOFSKY, *The Paradox of the Misuse of Administrative Law in ERISA Benefit Claims*, 37 J. MARSHALL L. REV. 727, 729–31 (2004).

[69] ERISA § 2(b), 29 U.S.C. § 1001(b) (2018). At time of press, the federal courts of appeal were wrestling with how to apply the Supreme Court's much-criticized arbitration jurisprudence to the ERISA setting. See, e.g., Smith v. Bd. of Directors of Triad Mfg., Inc., 13 F.4th 613, 620-21 (7th Cir. 2021) (explaining that while ERISA claims are "generally arbitrable," that general rule is subject to, inter alia, the "effective vindication" exception); and Harrison v. Envision Mgmt. Holding, Inc. Bd. of Directors, 59 F.4th 1090, 1107 (10th Cir. 2023) (finding specific arbitration provision in ESOP unenforceable because it prevented the plaintiff from effectively vindicating ERISA's statutory remedies). Binding arbitration closes rather than opens courtroom doors, and is thus in policy tension with ERISA's central promise of federal court access. While the Supreme Court has not yet ruled on the arbitrability of ERISA claims (or any exceptions thereto), the Court's strongly pro-arbitration jurisprudence, its past willingness to use judicial glosses like exhaustion and deference to keep ERISA claims away from judges, and its insistence on the importance of following plan terms to contain costs, e.g., Heimeshoff v. Hartford Life & Acc. Ins. Co., 571 U.S. 99, 108 (2013), suggest how that question will be resolved.

tolerance of conflicted administrators, and exhaustion – each and all of which *curtail* access to judicial decision making – has not been lost on commentators.[70]

Review under the ACA

Although the vitality of the Affordable Care Act has (whether meritoriously or not) been in question since virtually the day it was enacted, it attempted to address the difficult question of whether a plan administrator's determination regarding health care claims was objectively fair in three ways. First, it provided participants with recourse to a truly independent "administrative review" option.[71] Participants unsatisfied with the result of an internal benefit determination could seek independent external review. Second, it imposed additional requirements about how internal reviews needed to be done.[72] Third, it provided that, to the extent an administrator did not abide by internal review rules, the administrator would lose *Firestone* deference with respect to any subsequent judicial review of that determination.[73] These rules were thought to strike a desirable balance between providing an inexpensive but fair and expeditious administrative review option without overly restricting judicial review.[74] Whether they will survive, or materialize in some part to the pension setting, is an interesting but open question.

C CAUSES OF ACTION

ERISA authorizes three private civil enforcement actions that are commonly used.[75] First, a plan participant or beneficiary may bring a claim to recover benefits due under the plan or to clarify his rights to future benefits under the plan. Second, the Secretary of Labor or a participant, beneficiary, or fiduciary may bring an action for damages or for equitable relief to enforce ERISA's fiduciary obligations. Third, a participant, beneficiary, or fiduciary may bring an action "(A) to enjoin any act or practice which violates any provision of this subchapter or the terms of the plan, or (B) to obtain other appropriate equitable relief (i) to redress such violations or (ii) to enforce any provisions of this subchapter or the terms of the plan."[76]

The Supreme Court has stressed that ERISA's "carefully integrated civil enforcement provisions" form an "interlocking, interrelated and interdependent remedial

---

[70] *See, e.g.*, Brendan S. Maher, *The Affordable Care Act, Remedy, and Litigation Reform*, 63 AM. U. L. REV. 649, 658–59, n.48 (2014).

[71] *Id.* at 668–70 (discussing ACA reforms to claims process).

[72] 29 C.F.R. § 2590.715-2719(b) (2022) (internal claims and appeals rules).

[73] 29 C.F.R. § 2590.715-2719(b)(2)(F)(1) (2022). *See also* Maher, *supra* Chapter 5 note 70, at 699 (explaining the regulations).

[74] Maher, *supra* Chapter 5 note 70, at 678–700. *See also* 29 C.F.R. 2560.503-1(c), (d) (2022) (constraining use of arbitral procedures by group health and disability plans and explicitly authorizing claimants to challenge any adverse determination under section 502(a) of ERISA).

[75] ERISA § 502(a), 29 USC 1132(a) (2018).

[76] ERISA § 502(a)(3), 29 U.S.C. § 1132(a)(3) (2018).

Enforcement

scheme" that "provide[s] strong evidence that Congress did *not* intend to authorize other remedies that it simply forgot to incorporate expressly."[77] Consequently, the Court has rejected arguments that the statutory enforcement scheme should be supplemented with implied private rights of action. "We are reluctant to tamper with an enforcement scheme crafted with such evident care as the one in ERISA."[78] Because it was intended to be comprehensive, ERISA's enforcement mechanism has exceptional preemptive force, superseding related state law causes of action.

> In sum, the detailed provisions of § 502(a) set forth a comprehensive civil enforcement scheme that represents a careful balancing of the need for prompt and fair claims settlement procedures against the public interest in encouraging the formation of employee benefit plans. The policy choices reflected in the inclusion of certain remedies and the exclusion of others under the federal scheme would be completely undermined if ERISA-plan participants and beneficiaries were free to obtain remedies under state law that Congress rejected in ERISA.[79]

Accordingly, the actions authorized by ERISA § 502(a) provide the *exclusive* means for vindicating private rights under employee benefit plans.

The scope of two of the three private enforcement actions is clear: the claim for benefits, ERISA § 502(a)(1), amounts to a federal law contract claim, while ERISA § 502(a)(2) authorizes plan-based relief for breach of fiduciary obligations.[80] The third claim, for equitable enforcement of ERISA or the terms of the plan, ERISA § 502(a)(3), is the most expansive, and has been the foundation for novel theories of liability.

Fraud and Misrepresentation

Curiously, ERISA calls into question the existence and extent of fraud liability for misrepresentations involving employee benefit plans. The statute by its terms contains no federal antifraud rule; it limits the federal courts' authority to apply traditional legal remedies,[81] and it expressly preempts state law, including common-law actions for fraud and deceit.[82] Yet ERISA's disclosure provisions are designed to promote better career and financial planning by giving workers access to important information about plan terms and finances. To increase efficiency through improved decision making, the information disseminated must be correct. Participants who have been misled by inaccurate or incomplete SPDs have sought

---

[77] Mass. Mut. Life Ins. Co. v. Russell, 473 U.S. 134, 146 (1985) (emphasis in original).

[78] *Id.* at 147.

[79] Pilot Life Ins. Co. v. Dedeaux, 481 U.S. 41, 54 (1987). *Accord* Ingersoll-Rand Co. v. McClendon, 498 U.S. 133, 144 (1990).

[80] *See infra* Chapter 5 note 114.

[81] *See infra* Chapter 5D.

[82] ERISA § 514(a), (c), 29 U.S.C. § 1144(a), (c) (2018) (preemption includes state decisional law).

178   *Conduct Controls: Welfare and Pension Plans*

relief by bringing estoppel claims under section 502(a)(3).[83] That provision is also the authority for *individual* relief against a fiduciary who, whether through disloyalty or neglect, misrepresents material facts relating to an employee benefit plan.[84]

Participation in a Fiduciary Breach

Section 502(a)(2), by virtue of its cross-reference to section 409, allows enforcement of ERISA's fiduciary responsibility provisions against fiduciaries alone. In contrast, ERISA's equitable enforcement provision, section 502(a)(3), authorizes equitable relief to redress statutory violations without restricting permissible defendants. For a time, reliance on section 502(a)(3) as the source of nonfiduciary liability for knowing participation in a breach of fiduciary obligations was scotched by *Mertens v. Hewitt Associates*:[85]

> [W]hile ERISA contains various provisions that can be read as imposing obligations upon nonfiduciaries, including actuaries, no provision explicitly requires them to avoid participation (knowing or unknowing) in a fiduciary's breach of fiduciary duty. It is unlikely, moreover, that this was an oversight, since ERISA *does* explicitly impose "knowing participation" liability on cofiduciaries. That limitation appears all the more deliberate in light of the fact that "knowing participation" liability on the part of *both* cotrustees *and* third persons was well established under the common law of trusts.[86]

Although these observations were dicta, after *Mertens* the lower courts dutifully rejected claims against third parties allegedly involved in a breach of fiduciary duties imposed by section 404.[87]

Claims against nonfiduciaries for participation in a prohibited transaction, however, continued to be treated by the courts of appeals as authorized by ERISA § 502 (a)(3).[88] Inasmuch as the prohibited-transaction rules, like the general fiduciary duties, impose obligations only on fiduciaries, the distinction is not very convin-

---

[83]   *See supra* Chapter 3B.

[84]   *See supra* Chapter 3D.

[85]   508 U.S. 248, 254 (1993).

[86]   *Id.* at 253–54 (dictum) (citations and footnote omitted).

[87]   *E.g.*, Reich v. Rowe, 20 F.3d 25, 30–33 (1st Cir. 1994) ("judicial remedies for nonfiduciary participation in a fiduciary breach fall within the line of cases where Congress deliberately omitted a potential cause of action rather than the cases where Congress has invited the courts to engage in interstitial lawmaking"); Reich v. Cont'l Cas. Co., 33 F.3d 754, 757 (7th Cir. 1994), *cert. denied*, 513 U.S. 1152 (1995); Reich v. Compton, 57 F.3d 270, 284 (3d Cir. 1995); Reich v. Stangl, 73 F.3d 1027, 1034 (10th Cir.), *cert. denied*, 519 U.S. 807 (1996).

[88]   *E.g.*, *Compton*, 57 F.3d at 287 (imposing liability on a nonfiduciary involved in a prohibited transaction even though he was *not* a party in interest); Landwehr v. DuPree, 72 F.3d 726, 734 (9th Cir. 1995); *Stangl*, 73 F.3d at 1032; LeBlanc v. Cahill, 153 F.3d 134, 152–53 (4th Cir. 1998); Herman v. S.C. Nat'l Bank, 140 F.3d 1413, 1421–22 (11th Cir. 1998).

cing.[89] In *Harris Trust & Savings Bank* v. *Salomon Smith Barney, Inc.*, the Supreme Court held that a nonfiduciary party in interest who knowingly participates in a prohibited transaction can be called to account under section 502(a)(3).[90] Although the duty to avoid prohibited transactions is imposed by section 406 on the fiduciary, not on the party in interest with whom the fiduciary deals, the Court concluded that section 502(a)(3), which does not restrict the range of possible defendants, *itself* imposes an obligation on persons dealing with a fiduciary to refrain from knowingly participating in a violation of ERISA.[91] The Court's reasoning, moreover, was not limited to parties in interest involved in prohibited transactions. The analysis seems to extend with equal force to any person who knows or should know that he is engaging in a transaction that is a breach of fiduciary duty or otherwise violates ERISA.[92]

Wrongful Discharge and Retaliation

Section 510 protects participants and beneficiaries from dismissal and other adverse employment actions taken to discourage or prevent them from gaining or asserting rights under an employee benefit plan.[93] In many respects it is the linchpin of the whole matrix of federal pension and welfare benefit protections. Most American workers are employees at will. In this environment, assurances of benefit program integrity (conduct controls) and mandatory minimum standards (content controls) by themselves have little meaning, for the employer can dissuade workers from asserting benefit rights by holding the paycheck hostage.[94] The federal cause of action for wrongful discharge or retaliation, however, is not independently enforceable; wrongful discharge or retaliation can only be vindicated under section 502.[95]

---

[89] *Compare* ERISA § 406, 29 U.S.C. § 1106 (2018), *with* ERISA § 404(a)(1), 29 U.S.C. § 1104(a)(1) (2018).

[90] 530 U.S. 238, 241 (2000).

[91] *Id.* at 245–49.

[92] *Id.* at 248–51. The *Harris Trust* rationale would apparently also allow suit to be brought under ERISA § 502(a)(3) to recover plan assets from a transferee who was *not* a purchaser for value, even if the transferee had no reason to know of the fiduciary's breach. The Supreme Court suggested that section 502(a)(3) would authorize recovery of a gratuitous transfer of plan assets from an innocent recipient. *Id.* at 251 & n.3. This position reflects the traditional trust pursuit rule, under which property transferred in breach of trust may be recovered from any recipient other than a bona fide purchaser. *See* RESTATEMENT (SECOND) OF TRUSTS §§ 289, 292 (1959); 4 SCOTT ON TRUSTS, *supra* Chapter 3 note 16, §§ 289, 292.

[93] ERISA § 510, 29 U.S.C. § 1140 (2018).

[94] ERISA § 510 is one of a number of statutes that make limited inroads on the employment-at-will doctrine in order to safeguard employees in the exercise of federal employment rights. Other examples include the noninterference provisions of the Fair Labor Standards Act, 29 U.S.C. § 215(a)(3) (2018), and the Occupational Safety and Health Act, 29 U.S.C. 660(c) (2018). Similarly, a variety of federal and state "whistleblower" statutes protect employees from retaliation for reporting certain illegal employer conduct.

[95] ERISA § 510, 29 U.S.C. § 1140 (2018) (final sentence).

As a result, relief for a violation of section 510 is limited to equitable remedies under section 502(a)(3), such as an injunction ordering reinstatement.

Two elements are necessary to support an action under ERISA § 510. The worker must have suffered some type of adverse employment action, and that detriment must have been imposed for an improper purpose. Each component of the claim presents important interpretive issues. Section 510 makes it unlawful to "discharge, fine, suspend, expel, discipline, or discriminate against a participant or beneficiary." Clearly, "discriminate against" is a catchall provision, intended to outlaw unfavorable changes in the terms and conditions of employment not otherwise specifically enumerated, including, for example, demotion, transfer, or loss of seniority. Could a change in the employee benefit plan itself constitute such discrimination? If health care costs become too high, does an employer "discriminate against" participants for exercising their rights (overutilization, to the employer's way of thinking) when it amends the plan to reduce benefits? Several courts have held that section 510 does not extend to detrimental alterations of pension and welfare plans.[96]

A showing of specific intent to retaliate or interfere with protected rights is the second element of a cause of action under ERISA § 510. Direct evidence of an unlawful purpose (e.g., a supervisor's statement that the worker is being fired or demoted for claiming benefits) is rarely available. Accordingly, unlawful intent must be shown by circumstantial evidence, and courts applying section 510 have looked to cases under Title VII of the Civil Rights Act for guidance in allocating the burden of producing evidence of discriminatory intent. Using the Title VII approach, the plaintiff must make out a prima facie case of unlawful interference by showing that he has rights protected by ERISA, that he was qualified for his position, and that the circumstances of the adverse employment action give rise to an inference of discrimination. If the prima facie case is established, then the burden shifts to the defendant to articulate some legitimate, nondiscriminatory reason for the adverse action. If the employer offers such a reason, the plaintiff must be given an opportunity to prove that the asserted reason was not the true basis for the adverse action, but was rather a pretext for unlawful interference.[97]

Section 510 bars both retaliation for "exercising any right to which [the participant or beneficiary] is entitled" and "interfering with the attainment of any right to which such participant *may become* entitled." The scope of the latter prohibition is

---

[96] *E.g.*, Coomer v. Bethesda Hosp., Inc., 370 F.3d 499, 509 (6th Cir. 2004); McGath v. Auto-Body N. Shore, Inc., 7 F.3d 665, 668 (7th Cir. 1993); Haberern v. Kaupp Vascular Surgeons Ltd. Defined Benefit Pension Plan & Tr. Agreement, 24 F.3d 1491, 1502–04 (3d Cir. 1994). *See also* McGann v. H & H Music Co., 946 F.2d 401, 407–08 (5th Cir. 1991) (questioning whether a change in plan terms can constitute illegal discrimination under section 510), *cert. denied sub nom.* Greenberg v. H & H Music Co., 506 U.S. 981 (1992). *See infra* text accompanying Chapter 5 note 104.

[97] *E.g.*, Cole v. Permanente Med. Grp., Inc., 609 F. App'x 445 (9th Cir. 2015); Ritter v. Hughes Aircraft Co., 58 F.3d 454, 457 (9th Cir. 1995); Dister v. Cont'l Grp., Inc., 859 F.2d 1108, 1111–15 (2d Cir. 1988).

Enforcement

unclear. At its core, it was intended to prohibit employee dismissals to avoid vesting, and many cases so hold. For example, in *Gavalik v. Continental Can Co.*,[98] the defendant was found to have systematically reduced its workforce by laying off employees whose pensions were close to vesting and ultimately paid $415 million to settle the class action.[99] Yet the indefinite and future-sounding language of section 510 is susceptible to an interpretation that would go far beyond vesting, to protect much more inchoate rights – for example, the right to accrue future benefits.

Inter-Modal Rail Employees Association v. *Atchison, Topeka and Santa Fe Railway Co.* presented the question of whether the subjunctive language of section 510 (i.e., "any right to which such participant may become entitled under the plan") refers only to rights capable of vesting.[100] The case involved unionized employees of a Santa Fe subsidiary who were terminated en masse when the railway decided to contract out the rail-to-truck cargo transfer work previously performed by the subsidiary. Many of the workers were kept on by the successful bidder, but that company provided less-generous pension and welfare benefits than the Santa Fe subsidiary. The workers brought suit under section 510, claiming that their termination was motivated by the railway's desire to reduce benefit costs by preventing the workers from claiming the higher pension and welfare benefits provided under the subsidiary's benefit plans.

The Ninth Circuit held that section 510 prohibits acts intended to prevent a pension from vesting, but does not authorize a cause of action for interference with welfare benefits because ERISA does not require vesting under welfare plans. The Supreme Court reversed, holding that section 510 also protects certain rights under welfare plans even though they are not subject to vesting. The Court based its conclusion on the plain meaning of the statutory language, which applies to any "employee benefit plan," not just pension plans, and to "any right," not just nonforfeitable rights.[101] The employer argued that its acknowledged right to amend or terminate a welfare plan is incompatible with a broad reading of section 510 – after all, there's no need to sack employees to control benefit costs if the sponsor remains free to sack (amend or terminate) the plan. The Court disagreed, noting that ERISA requires that a plan provide a procedure for amendment, and that "[t]he formal amendment process would be undermined if § 510 did not apply because employers could 'informally' amend their plans one participant at a time."[102] Accordingly, when the employer wants to reduce benefit costs it must own up to the fact and do so explicitly by invoking the plan amendment process.

This process-oriented analysis supports the view that a detrimental plan amendment cannot constitute forbidden "discrimination" within the meaning of section

---

[98] 812 F.2d 834 (3d Cir. 1987).
[99] 18 Pens. Rep. (BNA) 8 (1991).
[100] 520 U.S. 510, 511(1991); ERISA § 510, 29 U.S.C. § 1140 (2018).
[101] *Id.* at 514–15.
[102] *Id.* at 516.

510.[103] If the noninterference provision forces benefit cutbacks out in the open and ensures that appropriate safeguards apply, then an employer's use of the plan amendment process cannot be a violation.[104] In each case, worker understanding of the change would be the touchstone of validity: if the employer leads participants to reasonably understand that a change has been made, the company cannot later disavow it, nor can an actual change in employment practices work a secret amendment.

As a last resort, the employer in *Inter-Modal Rail* argued that if section 510 applies to welfare plans, it "only protects the employee's right to cross the 'threshold of eligibility' for welfare benefits."[105] An employee who is eligible to receive benefits, the argument goes, has already attained her rights ("become entitled") under the plan, and section 510 has spent its force. The Supreme Court remanded the case for consideration of that question, leaving unresolved the scope of welfare plan rights protected by section 510. For two reasons the proffered distinction between initial eligibility (plan membership) and the ongoing right to earn benefits (benefit accrual) does not sit well with the Court's focus on the plain meaning of the statute. First, section 510 protects "any right," not just plan membership and vesting. Second, section 510 never applies at all until a worker becomes a "participant," at which point the "threshold of eligibility" for a welfare plan has already been crossed.[106] More importantly, the proposition that section 510 protects the integrity of the plan amendment process, preventing covert cutbacks, compels the conclusion that its strictures extend beyond satisfaction of membership conditions.

D REMEDIES

In addition to specifying the forms that civil enforcement actions must take and the persons withstanding to institute them, section 502(a) also limits the relief available under ERISA. These limits have been a major focus of litigation since the statute's enactment. In effect, the Court announced that ERISA does not provide complete relief to injured workers and was never intended to, despite ERISA's declaration of policy to "protect . . . the interests of participants in employee benefit plans and their beneficiaries, . . . by providing for appropriate remedies, sanctions, and ready access to the Federal courts."[107] "Appropriate" remedies are defined by reference to ERISA's distributive norms and the reality that employers are not required to provide

[103] *But see* Heath v. Varity Corp., 71 F.3d 256, 258–59 (7th Cir. 1995) (explaining that plan amendments improperly targeting one employee by name would likely violate ERISA).
[104] Nor is there a violation of the duty of loyalty, because the amendment of an employee benefit plan is not a fiduciary act. Curtiss-Wright Corp. v. Schoonejongen, 514 U.S. 73, 78 (1995) (welfare plan); Lockheed Corp. v. Spink, 517 U.S. 882, 891 (1996) (pension plan). *See supra* text accompanying Chapter 4 notes 18–24.
[105] *Inter-Modal Rail*, 520 U.S. at 516.
[106] ERISA § 3(7), 29 U.S.C. § 1002(7) (2018); 29 C.F.R. § 2510.3-3(d)(1)(i)(B) (2022).
[107] ERISA § 2(b), 29 U.S.C. § 1001(b) (2018).

Enforcement 183

welfare or pension benefits to their workers.[108] Nevertheless, the balance struck in the Ninety-Third Congress is open to revision.

Tort-Like Damages

In addition to financial hardship, wrongful delay or denial of benefits can cause emotional distress, and in the case of medical care, even permanent injury or death. Tort-like consequential damages (such as awards for pain and suffering, for lost earning capacity, or for wrongful death) are not recoverable in employee benefits cases, nor are punitive damages. The claim for benefits sounds in contract, and so has never been conceived as authorizing the imposition of tort-like "extracontractual" damages.[109] In *Massachusetts Mutual Life Insurance Co. v. Russell*[110] the Court refused to recognize an implied private right of action for emotional distress or punitive damages based on improper processing of benefit claims. The Court was "reluctant to tamper with an enforcement scheme crafted with such evident care as the one in ERISA" because, "[i]n contrast to the repeatedly emphasized purpose to protect contractually defined benefits, there is a stark absence – in the statute itself and in its legislative history – of any reference to an intention to authorize the recovery of extracontractual damages."[111]

The Court later extended this principle, holding that a state tort action for bad-faith insurance claims handling is incompatible with section 502's remedial scheme and therefore preempted, even though the case involved an insured plan and ERISA exempts state laws regulating insurance from preemption.[112] The Court set aside an award of emotional distress and punitive damages, finding that Congress clearly expressed an intent that the civil enforcement provisions of ERISA § 502(a) be exclusive.[113]

Accepting that section 502(a) establishes a civil enforcement mechanism that is not to be supplemented by either federal common law or state law, section 502(a) expressly authorizes suit in cases of fiduciary misconduct. A corrupt or incompetent denial of benefits (in contrast to a merely mistaken one) implicates fiduciary liability. (Eligibility decisions, or the factual determinations on which they depend, are fiduciary functions because they are discretionary.) For two reasons, a participant or beneficiary cannot recover tort-type damages where the denial of benefits is a breach of fiduciary duty. First, section 502(a)(2), by virtue of its reliance on section

---

[108] See supra Chapter 1C.
[109] See Mass. Mut. Life Ins. Co. v. Russell, 473 U.S. 134, 144 (1985) (the claim for benefits, ERISA § 502(a)(1)(B), "says nothing about the recovery of extracontractual damages, or about the possible consequences of delay in the plan administrators' processing of a disputed claim").
[110] Id. at 145–48.
[111] Id. at 147, 148.
[112] Pilot Life Ins. Co. v. Dedeaux, 481 U.S. 41, 57 (1987).
[113] Id. at 52, 57.

184   *Conduct Controls: Welfare and Pension Plans*

409, safeguards plan assets. While it clearly authorizes monetary awards *to the plan*, it does not offer a remedy for collateral injuries sustained by individual participants and beneficiaries as a result of a fiduciary breach.[114] Second, remedies under section 502(a)(3), which can run in favor of particular individuals rather than to the plan as a whole,[115] are limited to "appropriate equitable relief," which means, according to the Court in *Mertens v. Hewitt Associates*, remedies "*typically* available in equity (such as injunction, mandamus and restitution, but not compensatory damages)."[116] Therefore, although wrongful denial of benefits may be a breach of fiduciary duty and may cause serious harm, including emotional distress, permanent physical impairment, disease, or even death, ERISA offers no redress for such injuries.

Equitable Relief

While the competition is stiff, section 502(a)(3) of ERISA might be the statute's most infamous provision. The section authorizes courts to grant "appropriate equitable relief" to wronged parties, and the Court has spent over twenty-five years charting out what precisely that means.

The seminal case on the subject is *Mertens*. In that opinion, the Court declared that Congress's use of the word "equitable" was as much a limit on as a grant of judicial power. Equitable relief, the Court concluded, simply meant such relief as would have been available at equity in the old days of the divided bench.[117] In contrast, legal relief – of which the classic form is compensatory damages – was *verboten* under section (a)(3).[118] Nor could the force of the Court's conclusion be evaded by noting that equity courts sometimes awarded legal relief. To read (a)(3) as permitting the awarding of legal relief merely because equity courts themselves often did so would render Congress's use of the word equitable "superfluous."[119] Accordingly, the Court stressed that only "those categories of relief that were

---

[114] LaRue v. DeWolff, Boberg & Assocs., 552 U.S. 248, 256 (2008) (holding "that although § 502 (a)(2) does not provide a remedy for individual injuries distinct from plan injuries, that provision does authorize recovery for fiduciary breaches that impair the value of plan assets in a participant's individual account."); *Russell*, 473 U.S. at 142, 144.

[115] Varity Corp. v. Howe, 516 U.S. 489, 507–15 (1996) (rejecting the argument, based on *Russell*, that fiduciary obligations are enforceable only under ERISA §§ 502(a)(2) and 409).

[116] 508 U.S. 248, 256 (1993) (emphasis in original).

[117] The Court's resurrection of the old law-equity divide to interpret a statute enacted in 1974 has been sharply and repeatedly criticized from the get go. *See generally* John Langbein, *What ERISA Means by "Equitable": The Supreme Court's Trail of Error in* Russell, Mertens, *and* Great West, 103 COLUM. L. REV. 1317, 1321 (2003).

[118] "'Equitable' relief must mean *something* less than *all* relief," *Mertens*, 508 U.S. at 258 n.8 (emphasis in original).

[119] *Id.* at 257–58.

typically available in equity (such as injunction, mandamus, and restitution, but not compensatory damages)" were authorized by 502(a)(3).[120]

Monetary recoveries could sometimes be had in equity via an order of restitution, but because restitution is a remedy with both legal and equitable antecedents, the Court issued multiple decisions grappling with the contours of permissible restitutionary (and related) relief in cases where a plan was attempting to recoup money from a beneficiary.[121]

Great-West Life & Annuity Insurance Co. v. Knudson presented the question whether restitution is "appropriate equitable relief" under section 502(a)(3).[122] The case involved a suit to enforce the reimbursement provision of a health care plan, which gave the plan the right to receive the amount of any medical benefits paid by the plan that the beneficiary recovers from a third party. The respondent, who became quadriplegic as a result of an automobile accident, had about $411,000 of her medical expenses covered by the plan. The negotiated settlement of her tort suit allocated almost the entire $650,000 settlement to a trust for future medical expenses and to attorneys' fees. Less than $14,000 was designated as attributable to past medical expenses subject to the plan's reimbursement rights.[123] The petitioner, the plan's stop-loss insurer and assignee of the plan's reimbursement rights, brought suit in federal court under ERISA § 502(a)(3) seeking reimbursement of the full amount of covered medical expenses.[124] The Supreme Court held that section 502(a)(3) authorizes restitution only if the relief sought corresponds to the form of restitution traditionally available in equity.[125] Such equitable restitution transfers (via a constructive trust or equitable lien) particular property or identifiable proceeds in the defendant's possession to a plaintiff who is judged the equitable owner of those specific funds. Legal restitution, in contrast, imposes personal liability to pay for benefits conferred by the plaintiff, benefits that cannot be traced to identifiable funds in the defendant's hands (for example, where the benefit was services

---

[120] *Id.* at 256 (emphasis in original). Scholars quickly criticized the Court's three purported exemplars of equity. Restitution, for example, can be *either* equitable or legal, as the Court subsequently admitted in Great West Life & Annuity Ins. Co. v. Knudson, 534 U.S. 204, 212 (2002) (explaining that "not all relief falling under the rubric of restitution is available in equity"). And mandamus, while it can function like an injunction, is one of the historic prerogative or extraordinary writs at *common law. See, e.g.,* James Pfander, *Marbury, Original Jurisdiction, and Supreme Court's Supervisory Powers,* 101 COLUM. L. REV. 1515, 1523–32 (2001); James E. Pfander & Jacob P. Wentzel, *The Common Law Origins of Ex Parte Young,* 72 STAN. L. REV. 1269, 1292–1305 (2020).

[121] *Id.;* Harris Tr. & Sav. Bank v. Salomon Smith Barney, Inc., 530 U.S. 238, 253 (2000). Distinct from section 502(a)(3), the Secure Act 2.0 of 2022 added some additional statutory constraints with regard to potential plan recoupment of pension overpayments. ERISA § 206(h), 29 U.S.C.A. § 1056(h) (West Supp. 2023).

[122] 534 U.S. 204, 209–10 (2002).

[123] *Id.* at 207–08.

[124] *Id.* at 208.

[125] *Id.* at 218.

performed by plaintiff, or where money or property obtained from plaintiff has been dissipated).[126] Because the proceeds of the tort settlement in *Knudson* were not paid to the plan beneficiary, the suit did not seek the recovery of specific property, and as a claim for legal restitution it was not authorized by ERISA's equitable relief provision.[127]

In 2006, the Court revisited the issue whether a suit to enforce the reimbursement provision of a health care plan seeks "appropriate equitable relief" under section 502 (a)(3). *Sereboff* v. *Mid Atlantic Medical Services, Inc.*[128] involved facts very similar to *Knudson*, except that the proceeds of the tort settlement from which the fiduciary sought reimbursement were distributed to the plan beneficiaries on whom the plan imposed the reimbursement obligation. Consequently, the administrator's action sought recovery via the imposition of "a constructive trust or equitable lien on a specifically identified fund, not from the Sereboffs' assets generally, as would be the case with a contract action at law."[129] The settlement fund, however, was created after Sereboff became a participant subject to the reimbursement provision, and the Sereboffs argued that equitable restitution required that the funds sought be traceable to an asset in existence at the time the contract was made.[130] The Court distinguished equitable restitution from an equitable lien by agreement and relied on prior case law to hold that "the fund over which a lien is asserted need not be in existence when the contract containing the lien provision is executed."[131] Accordingly, the plan administrator's action sought equitable relief under section 502(a)(3), the enforcement of an equitable lien by agreement, even if that relief would not be classified as equitable restitution.

In *Montanile* the Court revisited the recoupment question yet again. The petitioner beneficiary had been injured in a car accident and obtained a settlement from the third-party tortfeasor. The respondent welfare plan had paid for the petitioner's medical costs, and thereafter sought recoupment of those monies pursuant to the plan's reimbursement provision. But the monies had allegedly been spent, and the beneficiary argued that equity could not reach dissipated funds. The Court agreed. "[A]t equity, a plaintiff ordinarily could not enforce any type of equitable lien ... [against] ... the defendant's general assets ... because those assets were not part of the specific thing to which the lien attached."[132]

Yet *Mertens* implicated more than recoupment cases. The Court's admonition in *Mertens* that it viewed injunction, mandamus, or restitution as the classic forms of

---

[126] *Id.* at 213–14.
[127] *Id.* at 214.
[128] 547 U.S. 356 (2006).
[129] *Id.* at 363.
[130] *Id.* at 366.
[131] *Id.*
[132] Montanile v. Bd. Trs. Nat'l Elevator Indus. Health Benefit Plan, 577 U.S. 136, 146 (2016). The case was remanded to determine the degree to which the funds in questions were actually dissipated. *Id.* at 151.

Enforcement

equitable relief led the lower federal courts to construe the reach of 502(a)(3) extremely narrowly – a fact which attracted criticism from judges and scholars alike.[133] The landscape shifted somewhat in 2011, when the Court revisited – outside the recoupment setting – the (a)(3) question in *CIGNA Corp. v. Amara*.[134] *Amara* involved a dispute over disclosures made to beneficiaries in connection with the amending of a pension plan, and what relief the beneficiaries were entitled to.

Although the *Amara* court hewed to the *Mertens* conception that (a)(3) relief was limited to relief typically available in equity, it took a considerably broader view of what that included. More specifically, the Court explained that the remedies of surcharge, reformation, and estoppel were typically available in equity – at least against fiduciaries.[135] Surcharge permits an award of monetary relief against a breaching fiduciary to prevent unjust enrichment or make good a loss; reformation judicially amends the plan (and permits payment therefrom) so as to be consistent with misled party's justifiable expectations regarding what the plan supposedly provided; and estoppel holds the speaker to his word or otherwise aims to treat the victim as if the misrepresentation had been true. There is little dispute that those three remedies reach far more fact patterns, and provide more relief, than do or would injunction, mandamus, and restitution. Since *Amara*, a series of decisions in the federal courts of appeals have acknowledged the expansion of the (a)(3) remedy – although there has been disagreement about *how* expansive *Amara* permits courts to be.[136]

---

[133] *See, e.g.*, Callery v. U.S. Life Ins. Co. in City of N.Y., 392 F.3d 401, 404–09 (10th Cir. 2004), *cert. denied*, 546 U.S. 812 (2005), Amschwand v. Spherion Corp., 505 F.3d 342, 345–47 (5th Cir. 2007), *overruled by* Gearlds v. Entergy Servs., Inc., 709 F.3d 448, 452–53 (5th Cir. 2013); *see also* Langbein, *supra* Chapter 5 note 117, at 1362 (criticizing the Supreme Court's treatment of ERISA in *Mertens*).

[134] 563 U.S. 421, 425 (2011).

[135] In *Mertens*, the defendants were not fiduciaries; a fact the Court in *Amara* explicitly noted. *Id.* at 442. It is uncertain whether *Amara*'s observations and holdings are entirely confined to suits against fiduciary defendants. Some of these observations – such as equity not tolerating a right without a remedy, *id.* at 440 – seem to apply outside of the fiduciary defendant context. *Id.* at 440–42.

[136] For example, the "Supreme Court [in *Amara*] did not... explicitly state whether reformation pursuant to ERISA sounds in trust or contract law. There is a meaningful difference between reformation in trust law and reformation in contract law. In the law of trust, the court's analysis focuses mainly on the settlor's intent. In contrast, in the law of contract, the court considers the intent and actions of both parties." Pearce v. Chrysler Grp. LLC Pension Plan, 893 F.3d 339, 346–47 (6th Cir. 2018) (internal citations and quotations omitted). The Second Circuit takes a contract approach, Amara v. CIGNA Corp. (Amara V), 775 F.3d 510, 524 (2d Cir. 2014), whereas the Ninth Circuit takes a trust approach, Skinner v. Northrop Grumman Retirement Plan B, 673 F.3d 1162, 1165–67 (2012). The Sixth Circuit declined to decide the issue. *Pearce*, 893 F.3d at 347. For a broad discussion of the equitable remedies of surcharge, reformation, and estoppel, and in particular how they operate in disclosure settings, *see supra* Chapter 3B1.

188   *Conduct Controls: Welfare and Pension Plans*

One area in which *Amara* has so far had little effect is with respect to claims based upon interference with ERISA-protected rights under section 510. There, the finicky line between legal and equitable restitution continues to have tremendous practical importance. While a court can clearly order reinstatement of an unlawfully terminated employee, it is a disputed question as to whether it can award back pay. Payment of lost wages does not return a specific item in which a plaintiff owned an interest (equitable restitution); instead, back pay looks more like ordinary contract damages, and thus forbidden legal relief. For that reason, courts have often held that back pay awards are beyond the remedial power of the federal courts in section 510 cases.[137] Some courts, however, have reasoned that backpay may be available when accompanied by reinstatement. The theory is that reinstatement, as an equitable remedy, allows courts to award backpay that is "incidental to and intertwined with" the reinstatement.[138]

Policy: ERISA's Remedial Balance

LaRue v. *DeWolff, Boberg & Associates* illustrates the interaction of ERISA's remedial mechanisms.[139] There a 401(k) plan participant sued the fiduciary under section 502(a)(3) for failure to follow his investment directions, seeking compensation for the additional value his account would have had if his instructions had been properly executed. As the additional value had never been realized by the fiduciary, there was no misappropriated fund to serve as a basis for equitable restitution. In premerger equity courts, profits that a trust beneficiary would have made but for a breach of trust were recoverable (a remedy known as surcharge).[140] The Fourth Circuit "rejected the notion that whether a particular form of relief is 'equitable' depends on the identity of the parties" (i.e., whether the defendant is a breaching

---

[137] *See, e.g.*, Millsap v. McDonnell Douglas Corp., 368 F.3d 1246, 1253–54 (10th Cir. 2004). *See also* Dana M. Muir, *ERISA Remedies: Chimera or Congressional Compromise*, 81 Iowa L. Rev. 1, 37–38 (1995) (analyzing and expressing concern over the limits of ERISA remedies in 510 cases); Peter K. Stris & Victor O'Connell, *ERISA & Equity*, 29 ABA J. Lab. & Emp. L. 125, 140–43 (2013) (examining caselaw on section 510 remedies, including back pay).

[138] *Cf.* Tull v. United States, 481 U.S. 412, 424 (1987) ("A court in equity was empowered to provide monetary awards that were incidental to or intertwined with injunctive relief.") *Millsap* recognized such a possibility but rejected it because of the *Millsap* facts. 368 F.3d at 1255–56 (10th Cir. 2004) (acknowledging the argument that a "backpay claim is equitable because it is a monetary award incidental to or intertwined with reinstatement" is consistent with Supreme Court precedent but rejecting it on the facts); Michaelis v. Deluxe Fin. Servs., Inc., 446 F. Supp. 2d 1227, 1231 (D. Kan. 2006) (same).

The Supreme Court has never decided whether back pay is available in section 510 cases. The closest it came was a footnote in *Knudson*, in which it disputed the accuracy and relevance of the dissent's assertion that the Court had held that backpay was a form of acceptable equitable relief in Title VII cases. Great West Life & Annuity Ins. Co. v. Knudson, 534 U.S. 204, 218 n.4 (2002).

[139] 552 U.S. 248, 250–51, 256 (2008).

[140] Restatement (Second) of Trusts §§ 205(c), (i), 211 (1959).

Enforcement

fiduciary) and dismissed the claim as seeking money damages.[141] Under a defined benefit plan, lost profits attributable to a fiduciary breach affect funding, potentially impacting all participants, and therefore a claim for plan-based relief lies under sections 502(a)(2) and 409. In contrast, fiduciary mistakes under participant-directed defined contribution plans often impact only one individual, which presents the question whether restoring a single participant's account to the balance it should have attained is authorized by sections 502(a)(2) and 409 as make-whole relief "to the plan." In *LaRue*, the Fourth Circuit also concluded that such particularized recovery is not within the ambit of section 502(a)(2).[142]

The Supreme Court unanimously reversed the Fourth Circuit decision in *LaRue*, holding that "although § 502(a)(2) does not provide a remedy for individual injuries distinct from plan injuries, that provision does authorize recovery for fiduciary breaches that impair the value of plan assets in a participant's individual account."[143] A concurring opinion explored a third possibility, that LaRue might have framed his complaint as a claim for benefits under section 502(a)(1)(B), in which case the remedy sought (lost profits) would conform nicely to a cause of action that corresponds to breach of contract. If such a claim for benefits is cognizable, the concurring justices suggested that it might preclude a claim for breach of fiduciary duty under sections 502(a)(2) and 409; otherwise, artful drafting might circumvent important limitations on a claim for benefits, including the requirement of exhaustion of administrative remedies and a limited scope of review.[144]

ERISA's civil enforcement section has been interpreted to provide a comprehensive specification of the persons entitled to bring suit, the causes of action that are available to them, and the relief that can be granted. The statute's broad preemption

---

[141] LaRue v. DeWolff, Boberg & Assocs., 450 F.3d 570, 577–78 (4th Cir. 2006), *vacated*, 552 U.S. 248 (2008).

[142] *Id.* at 574.

[143] *LaRue*, 552 U.S. 248, 256 (2008). The Court declined to address the question of the availability of the surcharge remedy as appropriate equitable relief under section 502(a)(3) despite having granted cert on the issue. *Id.* at 252. It would issue a holding three years later on surcharge in *Amara*. CIGNA Corp. v. Amara, 563 U.S. 421, 442 (2011).

[144] *LaRue*, 552 U.S. at 257–60 (Roberts, C.J., concurring). Whether redress for a fiduciary breach like that alleged in *LaRue* could actually be obtained via a suit for benefits under section 502(a)(1)(B) is an open question (as Chief Justice Roberts conceded). *Id.* Typically, an action to recover benefits due is brought against the plan or the person who controls administration of the plan. ABA SECTION OF LABOR AND EMPLOYMENT LAW, EMPLOYEE BENEFITS LAW 12-18 (4th ed. 2017). A defined contribution plan, however, ordinarily has no assets that are not allocated to individual accounts, which makes enforcement of a money judgment against the plan problematic, as it threatens to deprive other participants of their benefits. This obstacle might be avoided by holding that a fiduciary who is alleged to have caused a shortfall in a defined contribution plan account is a proper defendant and may be held personally liable for breach of fiduciary duty in a suit brought by the participant under section 502(a)(1)(B) to "enforce his rights under the terms of the plan, …." *See* ERISA § 502(d)(2), 29 U.S.C. § 1132 (d)(2) (2018) (money judgments against a plan are enforceable only against the plan as an entity or against a person held liable in their individual capacity).

of state law ensures that injured claimants have nowhere else to turn.[145] Yet the conclusion that section 502(a) is the exclusive means of vindicating workers' benefit rights means that many glaring injuries go uncompensated: participants and beneficiaries can recover benefits wrongly withheld, but not consequential damages. An erroneous denial of health care benefits can cause permanent injury or death, attended by mental anguish, pain, suffering, and loss of income, for both the patient and dependent family members, but none of these injuries are redressable under ERISA. As currently interpreted, only two straightforward monetary remedies are authorized: the suit for benefits (section 502(a)(1)(B)) and plan-based relief for breach of fiduciary duty (sections 502(a)(2) and 409).[146] The catchall enforcement provision, section 502(a)(3), authorizes only "appropriate equitable relief." As explained above, the Supreme Court has read that phrase to sharply limit the circumstances in which monetary relief is available. While *Amara* expanded the remedies available under (a)(3) to include remedies (surcharge, reformation, and estoppel) that more commonly involve a monetary award,[147] it is still the case that a plaintiff must demonstrate that the remedy she claims justifies monetary relief was "typically available in equity" in the circumstances at bar.[148]

The Supreme Court asserts that this limitation on monetary remedies is the product of a deliberate congressional compromise between competing

---

[145] ERISA § 514, 29 U.S.C. § 1144, discussed *infra* Chapter 6. The preemptive force of ERISA is at its greatest under section 502(a) – it so completely displaces state law actions to enforce rights under employee benefit plans that any such action is removable to federal court, even if the complaint makes no reference to federal law. Metro. Life Ins. Co. v. Taylor, 481 U.S. 58, 60–62 (1987) (complete preemption exception to well-pleaded complaint rule applies to actions to enforce employee benefit plans because ERISA section 502(a) was modeled on section 301 of the Labor-Management Relations Act of 1947).

[146] Plan-based relief under section 502(a)(2) need not inure to the benefit of *all* plan participants and beneficiaries. That provision also "authorize[s] recovery for fiduciary breaches that impair the value of plan assets in participant's individual account" under a defined contribution plan. *LaRue*, 552 U.S. at 256.

[147] *See, e.g.*, Kenseth v. Dean Health Plan, Inc., 722 F.3d 869, 882 (7th Cir. 2013) (holding that, whether through surcharge or otherwise, a plaintiff "may seek make-whole money damages as an equitable remedy under section 1132(a)(3) if she can in fact demonstrate that [the defending fiduciary] breached its fiduciary duty to her and that the breach caused her damages"); Gearlds v. Entergy Servs., Inc., 709 F.3d 448, 450–52 (5th Cir. 2013) (explaining that the circuit's prior ruling in Amschwand v. Spherion Corp., 505 F.3d 342 (5th Cir.2007) that (a)(3) did not permit "make whole" monetary relief, such as surcharge, was implicitly overruled by *Amara*; McCravy v. Metropolitan Life Ins. Co., 690 F.3d 176, 182–83 (4th Cir. 2012) (explaining that *Amara* makes clear that surcharge and estoppel may justify monetary awards needed to make a misled insured whole, beyond the restitutionary remedy of the return of premiums).

[148] This is no small hurdle. While restitution was clearly available at equity, for example, the Supreme Court has made clear that the *circumstances* in which equitable restitution (as opposed to legal restitution) apply are highly dependent upon the satisfaction of exacting technical requirements, the substance of which can require a searching examination of primary and secondary authorities from the "days of the divided bench." Montanile v. Bd. of Trustees of Nat. Elevator Indus. Health Benefit Plan, 577 U.S. 136, 142 (2016).

Enforcement

objectives.[149] As noted above, the Court says section 502(a) "represents a careful balancing of the need for prompt and fair claims settlement procedures against the public interest in encouraging the formation of employee benefit plans."[150] The fear is that the large and unpredictable damage awards characteristic of tort-type relief might discourage employer sponsorship, with the result that full compensation would come at the cost of restricted coverage. Congress, in short, decided to promote widespread worker access to benefits at the expense of the injured few.

E CONCLUSION

In the main, courts have applied ERISA's enforcement apparatus narrowly, insisting on strict adherence to the statutory wording. That interpretive approach is premised on the assumption that Congress supplied a meticulously crafted, comprehensive response to statutory and plan transgressions. Wish as one might for a studied balance between competing interests, the reality is that ERISA's compliance kit is really quite haphazard and incomplete. The defects become apparent upon examination of the primary limitations on participants' ability to obtain complete relief for violations of the plan or ERISA.

Congress wisely placed primary enforcement responsibility in the hands of interested private parties, relying most importantly on plan participants. While generally sound, that decision is marred by two defects. First, defined benefit plan participants have little incentive to monitor and enforce fiduciary obligations because the sponsor's liability to correct underfunding, backstopped by the PBGC insurance system, largely insulates workers from losses resulting from fiduciary misconduct. Neither the plan sponsor nor the PBGC – the real stakeholders – were given standing to sue, however. Second, the statute's definition of participant, "any employee or former employee ... who is or may become eligible to receive a benefit," provides little guidance with respect to former employees who lose coverage upon separation from service. Where an outgoing employee alleges that his departure was occasioned by a violation of ERISA, or that the defined contribution

---

[149] Varity Corp. v. Howe, 516 U.S. 489, 511–12 (1996) (ERISA § 502(a)(2) reflects special congressional concern with asset management, but that is not inconsistent with an intent to make individual relief for breach of fiduciary duty available under section 502(a)(3), which was designed to serve as a catchall safety net); see Great-West Life & Annuity Ins. Co. v. Knudson, 534 U.S. 204, 221 (2002) ("We will not attempt to adjust the 'carefully crafted and detailed enforcement scheme' embodied in the text that Congress has adopted." (quoting Mertens, 508 U.S. at 254)). Both scholars and dissenting Justices have challenged that conclusion. See, e.g., Knudson, 534 U.S. at 234 (Ginsburg, J., dissenting) ("in my view Congress cannot plausibly be said to have 'carefully crafted' such confusion"); Aetna Health Inc. v. Davila, 542 U.S. 200, 223 (2004) (Ginsburg, J., concurring) ("fresh consideration of the availability of consequential damages under § 502(a)(3) is plainly in order" (citing with approval John Langbein, supra Chapter 5, note 117)); Brendan S. Maher, The Benefits of Opt-In Federalism, 52 B.C. L. Rev. 1733, 1762–64 (2011).

[150] Pilot Life Ins. Co. v. Dedeaux, 481 U.S. 41, 54 (1987).

account balance distributed to him was insufficient due to a fiduciary breach, the courts now generally allow the suit to go forward.

Every employee benefit plan must have a claims procedure, including a mechanism for review of benefit denials by the appropriate fiduciary (plan-level appeal). A disappointed claimant can seek relief in court, yet the statute is silent on the intensity of judicial scrutiny of the fiduciary's decision. Where the plan gives the fiduciary discretion to determine benefit eligibility or interpret the plan, those questions are decided using a deferential scope of review. Even where the claim is denied by a fiduciary acting under a conflict of interest, divided loyalty does not trigger de novo or some other heightened standard of review. The Supreme Court insists that the conflict is merely to be weighed as one factor in an overall abuse-of-discretion calculus, without recourse to special procedural, evidentiary, or burden-of-proof rules. While the presence of a conflict is only one factor, it may cast many others in a different light; in the presence of a conflict, slipshod investigation by the fiduciary or selectively crediting some types of evidence over others may take on a new meaning, supporting an inference of improper purpose.[151] The lower courts have been assigned the task of ferreting out the effects of a conflict (if any), while balancing *Glenn*'s admonition to consider circumstances with *Frommert*'s insistence the judiciary be careful not to overly supplant fiduciary discretion.

There are a couple of curious omissions from the private civil enforcement actions authorized by section 502(a) of ERISA. Despite the centrality of disclosure and fiduciary duties, the statue does not expressly authorize fraud claims, nor does it clearly allow claims against a nonfiduciary who knowingly participates in a breach. Civil penalties that may be imposed for specified disclosure violations are not an adequate substitute for fraud liability (see Chapter 3). Nor can fiduciary liability offer complete relief if a nonfiduciary who knowingly participates in the breach escapes with plan assets. Judicial decisions have largely mended these holes, but they reinforce skepticism as to ERISA's "carefully integrated civil enforcement provisions."

Remedial limitations are the final piece of the enforcement puzzle. Despite the serious physical, emotional, and financial harm that may ensue from an improper denial of benefits, tort-like damages (such as awards for pain and suffering, lost earning capacity, or wrongful death) are not recoverable in employee benefits cases, nor are punitive damages. While this resolution of the tension between protecting workers and promoting widespread voluntary plan sponsorship predates the tort reform movement, it can still be fairly characterized as reflecting a deliberate congressional compromise. Of less certain provenance is section 502(a)(3), which authorizes "appropriate equitable relief" to redress violations of ERISA or the terms of the plan. ERISA's origins lie in law of trusts, trusts are a creature of equity, and equity offered ample measures of monetary relief to redress fiduciary misconduct. *Amara* is more cognizant of that reality than was *Mertens*.[152]

---

[151] *E.g.*, Demer v. IBM Corp. LTD Plan, 835 F.3d 893, 905 (9th Cir. 2016).

[152] *See supra* Chapter 3B1, discussing *Amara* and the three remedies of surcharge, estoppel, and reformation at length.

6

Preemption

[Many consider] the crowning achievement of this legislation [to be] the reservation to Federal authority the sole power to regulate the field of employee benefits. With the preemption of the field we round out the protection afforded participants by eliminating the threat of conflicting and inconsistent State and local regulation.[1]

Courts, however, have struggled to define the boundaries of the statute's purported "crowning achievement."[2] Indeed, given the bewildering contours of ERISA preemption,[3] a reader might be forgiven for wondering whether the inclusion of the chapter-opening quote above is in service of irony rather than elucidation. The answer is a little of both. When enacted, the statute's intendedly broad preemptive footprint was sincerely hailed by supporters as the mark of an efficient, engaged Congress. ERISA, after all, was enacted in the 1970s, perhaps the last decade of New Deal thinking about the role of the federal government – an era when a piece of legislation's sweeping invocation of federal power was touted as a feature rather than a bug. One need look no further than the reaction to the Affordable Care Act – a

---

[1] 120 CONG. REC. 29,197 (1974), reprinted in 3 ERISA LEGISLATIVE HISTORY, supra Chapter 1 note 55, at 4656, 4670 (remarks of Rep. Dent). Accord 120 CONG. REC. 29,933 (1974) (Congress "intended to preempt the field for Federal regulations, thus eliminating the threat of conflicting or inconsistent State and local regulation of employee benefit plans"), reprinted in 3 ERISA LEGISLATIVE HISTORY, supra Chapter 1 note 55, at 4746 (remarks of Sen. Williams). See generally James A. Wooten, A Legislative and Political History of ERISA Preemption (pts. 1–4), in 14 J. PENSION BENEFITS 31 (2006), 14 J. PENSION BENEFITS 5 (2007), 15 J. PENSION BENEFITS 15 (2008), 22 J. PENSION BENEFITS 3 (2014).

[2] See infra Chapter 6 note 6.

[3] Marking the boundaries of ERISA preemption has proven highly challenging despite legislative ambitions, as this chapter will demonstrate. In hindsight, Congressman Dent's observation may seem ironic.

194   *Conduct Controls: Welfare and Pension Plans*

much less invasive exercise of federal power than ERISA – to see how times have changed.[4]

As surely as times have changed, the text of ERISA's preemptive provisions has not. The latter part is unfortunate, as no observer from any quarter has commended the work the statutory text itself does, which is very little. As the Supreme Court put it:

> Section 514(a) marks for pre-emption "all state laws insofar as they . . . relate to any employee benefit plan" covered by ERISA, and one might be excused for wondering, at first blush, whether the words of limitation ("insofar as they . . . relate") do much limiting. If "relate to" were taken to extend to the furthest stretch of its indeterminacy, then for all practical purposes pre-emption would never run its course, for "really, universally, relations stop nowhere."[5]

The result has been voluminous litigation in the lower courts in search for extra-textual limits on preemption.[6] It's accordingly not the ambition of this chapter to make sense of the welter of lower court ERISA preemption decisions. Instead, this chapter outlines the general framework of preemption analysis, describes the evolution of the Supreme Court's approach in ERISA cases, and distinguishes areas that are settled from those that are in flux.

The courts are not blameless in this messy state of affairs. As we will suggest below, the Supreme Court perhaps began with the wrong premise about what the language of Section 514(a) was intended by drafters to accomplish. Subsequent pronouncements of the Court have not openly recast the interpretative task, despite an explicit call to do so from Justices Scalia and Ginsburg. Instead, the Court has taken a series of incremental steps that have served to chisel the precedential meaning of its earlier decisions into something more sensible.

* * *

A brief word about preemption generally. There are four typically recognized categories of statutory preemption: express, conflict, obstacle, and field. Congress may, by explicit statutory language, reserve exclusive federal control over a specified subject (express preemption). Where the federal statute is silent as to its preemptive

---

[4] *E.g.*, Alicia Ouellette, *Health Reform and the Supreme Court: The ACA Survives the Battle of the Broccoli and Fortifies Itself against Future Fatal Attack*, 76 ALB. L. REV. 87, 91–92 (2013) ("On the same day the President signed [the ACA] into law, the Attorney General from Florida and a dozen other states filed a lawsuit challenging its constitutionality . . . . Eventually, twenty-six states joined in the Florida suit and another lawsuit filed by the NFIB and two individual plaintiffs."); CNN.COM, *Health Care Reform Anger Takes a Nasty, Violent Turn*, (March 26, 2010 8:25 a.m. EDT) www.cnn.com/2010/POLITICS/03/25/congress.threats/index.html.

[5] N.Y. State Conf. of Blue Cross & Blue Shield Plans v. Travelers Ins. Co., 514 U.S. 645, 655 (1995) (citations omitted).

[6] D.C. v. Greater Wash. Bd. of Trade, 506 U.S. 125, 135 n.3 (1992) (Stevens, J., dissenting). The Supreme Court itself issued over twenty ERISA preemption opinions between 1981 and 2022.

Preemption

force, any state law that directly conflicts with a provision of the national legislation must fall (conflict preemption). In still other cases, where compliance with the commands of both sovereigns is technically possible, additional state-imposed requirements, either substantive or procedural, might impair the accomplishment of national goals. In those circumstances, the courts may find state prerogatives to be implicitly constrained. Put slightly differently, attention to the structure and purposes of the federal statute may indicate that a more burdensome or nonuniform rule, while not contradicting Congress's language, would nonetheless undercut its objectives. This implied preemption is of two types, although the division is not a sharp one. Where uniformity or cost concerns loom large, a specific state law requirement may pose an obstacle to the federal goal, and so it is displaced by implication (obstacle preemption). Alternatively, the subject matter or comprehensiveness of the federal statute may support the inference that Congress intended it to stand as the sole legislative word on the subject, without supplementation by complementary state laws (field preemption).[7]

The Supreme Court succinctly summarized the relationships between these four categories of statutory preemption in an early ERISA case:

Where the pre-emptive effect of federal enactments is not explicit, "courts sustain a local regulation 'unless it conflicts with federal law or would frustrate the federal scheme, or unless the courts discern from the totality of the circumstances that Congress sought to occupy the field to the exclusion of the States.'"[8]

A THE ARCHITECTURE OF EXPRESS PREEMPTION

Preemption under ERISA usually turns on three statutory provisions, each constraining the last. The first, the "relate to" provision, is set forth in Section 514(a). It provides that ERISA "shall supersede any and all State laws insofar as they may now or hereafter relate to any employee benefit plan ..." A state law that relates to employee benefit plans is preempted, unless it "regulates insurance, banking, or securities." The provision that provides this protection against preemption, section 514(b)(2)(A), is commonly referred to as ERISA's "savings clause," for obvious reasons. Finally, the statute includes a third provision, section 514(b)(2)(B), which is intended to prevent states from "deeming" a plan to be an insurer (or engaging in

---

[7] See generally Viet D. Dinh, Reassessing the Law of Preemption, 88 GEO. L.J. 2085, 2105–06 (2000).

[8] Metro. Life Ins. Co. v. Mass., 471 U.S. 724, 747–48 (1985) (quoting Allis-Chalmers Corp. v. Lueck, 471 U.S. 202, 209 (1985), and Malone v. White Motor Corp., 435 U.S. 497, 504 (1978)).

insurance activity) such that the state's saved insurance laws could directly regulate the plan.[9]

The statute's three-step approach is stated simply enough. Yet the interpretative and conceptual challenges present themselves in the very first sentence of section 514. We start there.

B THE PUZZLE OF ERISA'S "RELATE TO" CLAUSE

"[W]e have virtually taken it for granted that state laws which are 'specifically designed to affect employee benefit plans' are pre-empted under § 514(a)."[10]

Section 514(a) states that ERISA supersedes "any and all state laws insofar as they may now or hereafter relate to any employee benefit plan" that is subject to federal regulation.[11] The inherent ambiguity of what the phrase "relate to" includes (and what it does not) was an immediate problem for the Court. Before delving into that particular struggle, let us take a step back and ask: what would ERISA preemption look like in the *absence* of section 514(a)? Thinking this through is useful because it can show us what a rational drafter may have hoped to accomplish by inserting 514(a) as written into the statute.

Let us consider in particular what the absence of 514(a) would mean with respect to *field* preemption: it would likely mean that field preemption would arise with respect to pension plan regulation but *not* with respect to welfare plan regulation. (Conflict and obstacle preemption would still arise with respect to both.) The reason is that field preemption is implied only when the substantive content of the federal regulation is so significant that by force of its footprint it "occupies the field" and thus justifies judicial exclusion of state regulation. In the case of ERISA's regulation of pension plans, the substantive regulation is sufficiently expansive and detailed as to warrant that conclusion. In the case of ERISA's regulation of welfare plans, it is not. Put differently, if ERISA lacked section 514(a), the federal bench may very well have read implied field preemption into the statute with respect to pension plan regulation. There is no chance it would have done so with respect to welfare plan regulation.

A brief recapitulation of the different ways the statute treats pension and welfare plans is instructive. While all employee benefit plans, both welfare and pension, are subject to various conduct controls (including reporting and disclosure obligations, fiduciary responsibility rules, and the federal enforcement mechanism), pension

---

[9] Section 514(b) includes other exceptions. But it is the two cited provisions, along with 514(a), that are primarily responsible for ERISA's preemption power in practice, as well as the confusion about its boundaries.

[10] Mackey v. Lanier Collection Agency & Serv., Inc., 486 U.S. 825, 829 (1988); Ingersoll-Rand Co. v. McClendon, 498 U.S. 133, 140 (1990).

[11] ERISA § 514(a), 29 U.S.C. § 1144(a) (2018).

Preemption 197

plans are also subject to extremely detailed content regulation (including minimum standards governing participation, benefit accrual, vesting and spousal protection, and, in the case of defined benefit plans, advance funding and termination insurance requirements). Pension content regulation is limited to specified subjects, but the limits were intended to promote sponsorship by maintaining flexibility. In unregulated areas, such as setting coverage and benefit levels, employers can tailor the plan to fit their own budget and personnel priorities, and even in highly regulated areas like vesting, employers are allowed to exceed the statutory minimum standards. State laws that would encroach on employers' freedom in plan design would increase costs and curtail coverage. Consequently, limited federal subject-matter regulation is not compatible with state controls in other areas, for Congress was not simply concerned with preventing specified abuses; it also sought to expand the availability of private pensions. The combination of detailed regulation of some subjects and the deliberate preservation of employer control over others shows that pension plan regulation is a delicate balance that would be upset by state intervention. In short, pension plan regulation is "so pervasive as to make reasonable the inference that Congress left no room for the States to supplement it."[12] As the Supreme Court observed in one of its first forays into ERISA, Congress "meant to establish pension plan regulation as exclusively a federal concern."[13]

In contrast to its detailed and deliberate regulation of pension arrangements, ERISA is largely silent about the content of welfare benefit programs, and in the absence of express preemption it is not obvious that that forbearance betokens a preference for laissez-faire. Moreover, far from any desire to promote welfare plans, history shows that Congress included them in ERISA in 1974 to achieve the limited objective of curbing fiduciary abuse of welfare benefit funds, especially looting by union officials. The bill's fiduciary responsibility rules were the hook that brought in welfare plans, with reporting and disclosure and the federal enforcement regime conceived as a means to that end. Disclosure was expected to deter abuses, but should they occur, it would alert workers and arm them with the information they would need to enforce their rights. Mandated benefit laws and state regulation of welfare plan content are not inconsistent with this narrow focus on effective fiduciary monitoring.

In light of Congress's limited objective, in the absence of section 514(a), state supplementation of ERISA's conduct controls might even have been acceptable. For instance, a state might enact more detailed disclosure rules, or forbid agents, employees, or persons related to the sponsor from serving as plan fiduciaries, or authorize punitive damages as a remedy for willful breach. Not only do such more

---

[12] Rice v. Santa Fe Elevator Corp., 331 U.S. 218, 230 (1947), *quoted in* Com. of Pa. v. Nelson, 350 U.S. 497, 502 (1956).

[13] Alessi v. Raybestos-Manhattan, Inc., 451 U.S. 504, 523 (1981) (quoted language actually refers to section 514(a), ERISA's express preemption provision).

exacting requirements not contradict ERISA, they positively promote Congress's goal of eradicating welfare fund abuses. Laws of this sort present no obstacle to attaining the national objective, and so there seems to be no call for implied preemption (either obstacle or field) of state welfare plan regulation. Had Congress kept silent on ERISA's preemptive effect, it appears that the slender federal interest in welfare plans would have supported only conflict rather than field preemption.

But Congress did not stay silent. And while the legislative history of ERISA's preemption provision is sparse, it does have something to say about the scope of express preemption. At a minimum, section 514(a) was meant to exclude state regulation directed to the operation or content of both welfare and pension plans. That Congress meant at least to legislate field preemption is shown by the change from prior versions of the bill, which would have set aside those state laws that "relate to the reporting and disclosure responsibilities, and fiduciary responsibilities" or "to subject matters regulated by this Act or the Welfare and Pension Plans Disclosure Act."[14] Under these narrower approaches, states would not have been allowed to impose more burdensome conduct controls, nor regulate pension plan content in areas that ERISA addresses – but nothing would stop mandated benefits or other content regulation of welfare plans. Instead, ERISA's draftsmen settled on the broader "relate to any employee benefit plan" language present in the enacted version of 514(a).

Given that, a coherent explanation for why Congress might have included 514(a) as written emerges: it was a command that courts apply field preemption with respect to both pension plan and welfare plan regulation. With respect to pension plan regulation, 514(a) would serve to avoid any doubt that field preemption was the objective; as the precise amount of regulation needed to "occupy a field" is not clear, 514(a) is a rational way to forestall any potential judicial reluctance to imply field preemption. With respect to welfare plan regulation, 514(a) would serve to create field preemption where judges would not have done so otherwise. Whatever Congress may have actually intended (if anything),[15] the foregoing explanation is a

---

[14] H.R. 2, 93d Cong. § 514(a) (as passed by the House, Mar. 6, 1974), *reprinted in* 3 ERISA LEGISLATIVE HISTORY, *supra* Chapter 1 note 55, at 3898, 4057–58; H.R. 2, 93d Cong. § 699 (a) (as passed by the Senate, Mar. 4, 1974), *reprinted in* 3 ERISA LEGISLATIVE HISTORY, *supra* Chapter 1 note 55, at 3599, 3820. Jacob Javits, the Senate cosponsor and long-time Republican advocate of comprehensive pension reform legislation, observed that earlier versions of the bill "defined the perimeters of preemption in relation to the areas regulated by the bill." In contrast, he explained that the broad preemption language of the conference bill would close the door to state laws that "deal with some particular aspect of private welfare or pension benefit plans not clearly connected to the Federal regulatory scheme." 120 Cong. Rec. 29,942 (1974) (remarks of Sen. Javits), *reprinted in* 3 ERISA LEGISLATIVE HISTORY, *supra* Chapter 1 note 55, at 4770–71.

[15] The sudden emergence of the broad preemptive language from the conference committee makes it difficult to discern, at least from the legislative history, Congress's true motivations. *See generally* Wooten, *supra* Chapter 6 note 1, at 31. But whatever the reality, the point is that

Preemption

conceptually coherent response to the question of what a federal legislature might have hoped to achieve in the first instance by inserting 514(a) into the statute, viz., *explicit* field preemption. Nor does this account limit the role that obstacle and conflict preemption might play in rounding out preemption analysis.

All that said, there is certainly another way to read 514(a), which is that Congress had no message to send with respect to field preemption at all, and simply left to courts the work of fleshing out what "relate to" meant, by using the normal tools of statutory construction and purposive analysis. Indeed, *that* is what the Supreme Court originally thought its task was, and it has written opinions trying to give content to "relate to" ever since. But an astute observer might wonder if the best way to predict how the Court is going to resolve "relate to" questions is to first ask what a traditional field preemption analysis might find preempted, and then ask whether the state law offends the more narrow prohibitions of conflict and obstacle preemption. State law that failed either inquiry would be preempted.

C GENERAL STATE LAWS

"That phrase [superseding state laws that 'relate to' a plan] gives rise to some confusion where . . . it is asserted to apply to a state law ostensibly regulating a matter quite different from pension plans."[16]

Given, *inter alia*, the drafting history that resulted in 514(a)'s language being broadened (discussed *supra* in Chapter 6B), the Court concluded early on that "§ 514(a) [cannot] be interpreted to pre-empt only state law dealing with the subject matters covered by ERISA – reporting, disclosure, fiduciary responsibility, and the like."[17] By dispensing with limitations on regulatory subject matter, Congress took over "sole power to regulate the field of employee benefits."[18] In the absence of federal action, such field preemption protects from state interference "conduct that Congress intended to be unregulated."[19] That is, Congress reserved to private decision making all aspects of employee benefit plans not addressed by federal regulation.

In the first years after ERISA's enactment the Court speculated about Congress intending a kind of super-preemption, one that went far beyond field preemption

---

there is a conceptually coherent reading of the statute's preemptive provisions that is quite different from the one the Court began with (and at least facially abides by to this day).

[16] *Alessi*, 451 U.S. at 523–24.

[17] Shaw v. Delta Air Lines, Inc., 463 U.S. 85, 98 (1983).

[18] *See supra* text accompanying Chapter 6 note 1 (remarks of Rep. Dent). *Accord* Alessi v. Raybestos-Manhattan, Inc., 451 U.S. 504, 523 (1981) (Congress "meant to establish pension plan regulation as exclusively a federal concern"); N.Y. State Conf. of Blue Cross & Blue Shield Plans v. Travelers Ins. Co., 514 U.S. 645, 656 (1995) (same for welfare plans).

[19] Metro. Life Ins. Co. v. Mass., 471 U.S. 724, 749 (1985) (referring to field preemption implied under the National Labor Relations Act).

Conduct Controls: Welfare and Pension Plans

and resembled benefit plan immunity to state law. ERISA, for example, contains a savings clause that excepts from preemption "any generally applicable criminal law of a state."[20] Presumably, this stipulation was included to ensure that criminal sanctions would apply to larceny or embezzlement from an employee benefit fund. But "generally applicable criminal laws" like larceny and embezzlement are *not* laws directed at regulating pension or welfare plans, and so would not be displaced if Congress meant only to occupy the field. The Supreme Court said in 1983:

> To interpret § 514(a) to pre-empt only state law specifically designed to affect employee benefit plans would be to ignore the remainder of § 514. It would have been unnecessary to exempt generally applicable state criminal statutes from pre-emption in § 514(b), for example, if § 514(a) applied only to state law dealing specifically with ERISA plans.[21]

Despite its allure, this negative inference proves too much. If a statutory savings clause is necessary to preserve generally applicable state criminal laws from express preemption, then it would seem that generally applicable state laws in other areas must fall (on the principle that *expressio unis est exclusio alterius*). Besides general criminal laws, ERISA § 514 as originally enacted expressly saved only state laws regulating insurance, banking, and securities. Nevertheless, the Supreme Court has repeatedly found that some generally applicable state laws in other fields escape preemption, including garnishment, health care regulation, prevailing wage laws, hospital gross receipts taxes, and pharmacy benefit manager regulation.[22] Certainly, the Court has also held that other sorts of generally applicable state laws are preempted.[23] Sometimes the result is presented as an application of express preemption, but that is difficult to reconcile with the decisions that let other general state laws stand. The discussion that follows explores this perplexing state of affairs.

Viewed through the lens of the Court's early approach to ERISA preemption, the division between acceptable and superseded state laws is indistinct and unfocused. Attention to case outcomes, however, shows that the state laws that the Court has set aside fall into three well-defined categories.[24] That pattern of preemption largely supports the following two propositions: (1) section 514(a), ERISA's express

---

[20] ERISA § 514(b)(4), 29 U.S.C. § 1144(b)(4) (2018).

[21] *Shaw*, 463 U.S. at 98.

[22] Mackey v. Lanier Collection Agency & Serv., Inc., 486 U.S. 825 (1988) (garnishment); N.Y. State Conf. of Blue Cross & Blue Shield Plans v. Travelers Ins. Co., 514 U.S. 645 (1995) (health care regulation); Cal. Div. of Lab. Standards Enf't v. Dillingham Constr., N.A., Inc., 519 U.S. 316 (1997) (prevailing wage law); De Buono v. NYSA-ILA Med. & Clinical Servs. Fund, 520 U.S. 806, 814–15 (1997) (hospital gross receipts tax); Rutledge v. Pharm. Care Mgmt. Ass'n, 141 S. Ct. 474 (2020) (pharmacy benefit manager regulation).

[23] *E.g.*, *Shaw*, 463 U.S. 85 (anti-discrimination law); Boggs v. Boggs, 520 U.S. 833 (1997) (community property law).

[24] The three categories are discussed *infra* Chapter 6, *Categories of Preempted Laws*.

Preemption

preemption clause, works only field preemption; and (2) general state laws are ousted only if they run afoul of traditional conflict or obstacle preemption analysis.[25]

Early Approach to Preemption

Working from the "deliberately expansive" language of section 514(a),[26] the Supreme Court, in its first fifteen years of ERISA preemption jurisprudence, emphasized that Congress had enacted an express preemption clause that was "conspicuous for its breadth"[27] and concluded that a state law must give way "even if the law is not specifically designed to affect such plans, or the effect is only indirect, and even if the law is consistent with ERISA's substantive requirements."[28] With one important exception, in those early years the Court held preempted *every* state law it encountered that had an impact on pension or welfare plans.[29]

"A law 'relates to' an employee benefit plan, in the normal sense of the phrase, if it has a connection with or reference to such a plan."[30] This early interpretation of ERISA's preemption clause became a mantra in subsequent decisions, and one that is still repeated today. Taken to require a two-part inquiry,[31] experience has shown that the first part is indeterminate and the second has been whittled down to encompass only the most obvious offenders. The Court has not disavowed this formulation, but the trend of recent decisions is to downplay express preemption.

We shall begin with the "reference to a plan" prong, as it is more easily understandable than its partner. Under this prong, the Court has preempted three laws: "a law that 'impos[ed] requirements by reference to [ERISA] covered programs,' a law that specifically exempted ERISA plans from an otherwise generally applicable garnishment provision, and a common-law cause of action premised on the existence of an ERISA plan."[32]

---

[25] The three categories of preempted laws identified below – regarding benefits, plan administration, and remedies, *see infra* Chapter 6 notes 43–45 and accompanying text – can all be understood as the application of the two stated propositions to a given subject.

[26] Pilot Life Ins. Co. v. Dedeaux, 481 U.S. 41, 46 (1987).

[27] FMC Corp. v. Holliday, 498 U.S. 52, 58 (1990).

[28] D.C. v. Greater Wash. Bd. of Trade, 506 U.S. 125, 130 (1992) (internal cites and quotation marks omitted).

[29] The exception was Georgia's general garnishment law as applied to a participant's interests in a vacation pay plan. *Mackey*, 486 U.S. 825. In addition, in two other cases the Court found that state laws relating to employee benefits survived preemption because they did not affect an employee benefit "plan." Fort Halifax Packing Co. v. Coyne, 482 U.S. 1 (1987) (state may require nondiscretionary lump-sum severance payments in the event of plant closing because one-time contingent obligation does not entail the establishment or maintenance of a plan); Mass. v. Morash, 490 U.S. 107 (1989) (practice of compensating discharged employees for unused vacation time subject to state's wage-payment statute because not a welfare plan).

[30] Shaw v. Delta Air Lines, Inc., 463 U.S. 85, 96–97 (1983).

[31] Cal. Div. of Lab. Standards Enf't v. Dillingham Constr., N.A., Inc., 519 U.S. 316, 324 (1997).

[32] *Id.*

The first of these three cases shows that the "reference" standard, although easily applied, sometimes yields outcomes that seem impossible to justify. The law at issue in *District of Columbia v. Greater Washington Board of Trade* was a District of Columbia statute requiring employers who provide health insurance to their employees to provide equivalent health insurance coverage to injured employees receiving workers' compensation benefits.[33] Because the statute "specifically refers to welfare benefit plans regulated by ERISA," the Court found it preempted "on that basis alone."[34] The precedent provided by two prior "reference" cases was the only support offered for the result. In dissent, Justice Stevens emphasized that the purpose of the District's law was to compute "workers' compensation benefits on the basis of the entire remuneration of injured employees when a portion of the remuneration is provided by an employee benefit plan."[35] "Nothing in ERISA," he explained, "suggests an intent to supersede the State's efforts to enact fair and complete remedies for work-related injuries; it is difficult to imagine how a State could measure an injured worker's health benefits without referring to the specific health benefit that the worker receives."[36] Attending to the policies of the state and federal laws led Justice Stevens to conclude that "a state law's mere reference to an ERISA plan is an insufficient reason for concluding that it is pre-empted."[37]

By striking down state laws that do not interfere with federal objectives, mechanistic application of the "reference" standard sometimes causes overbroad preemption. This realization is no doubt what moved the Court subsequently to trim the preemptive reach of the "reference" prong. In *Dillingham Construction*, the Court held that a mere "reference to" an employee benefit plan was not enough; the state law must also either act "immediately and exclusively upon ERISA plans" or be a law for whom "the existence of ERISA plans is essential to the law's operation." What this means in plain English is that any state law that addresses subjects *other* than employee benefit plans will avoid preemption under the "reference" analysis. Only state laws that cannot meet that standard – that is, only state laws whose raison d'être is benefit plan regulation and whose enactment is therefore nothing more than brazen defiance of ERISA's dominion – will run afoul of the "reference" prong.

In the other prong of the query, "[c]onnection with" is a phrase, that, on its own, accomplishes little more than the "relate to" language it was summoned to define. "For the same reasons that infinite relations cannot be the measure of pre-emption,

---

[33] *Greater Wash.*, 506 U.S. at 126–27, 128. From a long-term perspective, this case can be seen as the high-water mark of the Court's expansive interpretation of ERISA preemption.

[34] *Id.* at 130.

[35] *Id.* at 133.

[36] *Id.* at 137–38.

[37] *Id.* at 137.

Preemption 203

neither can infinite connections."[38] Congress could not have meant to suspend every state law that has *any* effect, however minimal or indirect, on an employee benefit plan or its constituents (i.e., sponsors, fiduciaries, participants, and beneficiaries). Yet while a line between acceptable and unacceptable effects must be drawn, formulations like "relate to" and "connection with" offer no principled basis on which to draw it. From the start, the Court noted that "[s]ome state actions may affect employee benefit plans in too tenuous, remote, or peripheral a manner to warrant finding that the law 'relates to' the plan."[39] But "too tenuous, remote, or peripheral" is merely a characterization – a conclusory label, not a standard for decision – and subsequent cases do little to give it content.[40]

By resting its early decisions on the interpretation of section 514(a), the Supreme Court indicated that express preemption bars some, but not all, general state laws that affect a plan. Under this approach, however, the statutory text offers no clear-cut stopping point. Consequently, the Court is forced to grapple with the uncertain extent of laws that "relate to [a] plan" on a case-by-case basis. In its first preemption case the Court observed, "That phrase gives rise to some confusion where ... it is asserted to apply to a state law ostensibly regulating a matter quite different from pension plans."[41] Years later the Court admitted that its "prior attempt to construe the phrase 'relate to' does not give us much help drawing the line here."[42] None of the opinions posit a determinate test for whether a generally applicable state law has a sufficiently close relationship to an employee benefit plan to trigger preemption. Instead, results are often justified by analogy to the few prior data points offered by earlier decisions.

Categories of Preempted Laws

Putting aside *Greater Washington Board of Trade*, all of the state laws that the Court has held superseded fall into three categories, roughly summarized as benefits, plan

---

[38] N.Y. State Conf. of Blue Cross & Blue Shield Plans v. Travelers Ins. Co., 514 U.S. 645, 656 (1995).

[39] Shaw v. Delta Air Lines, Inc., 463 U.S. 85, 100 n.21. (1983). After announcing this limitation, the Court immediately observed that "[t]he present litigation plainly does not present a borderline question, and we express no views about where it would be appropriate to draw the line." *Id.*

[40] *See Greater Wash.*, 506 U.S. at 130 n.1 (suggesting that "many laws of general applicability," such as general garnishment laws, are too tenuous, remote, or peripheral to warrant preemption); *Travelers*, 514 U.S. at 661 (health care quality control and hospital workplace regulation too tenuous for preemption); Cal. Div. of Lab. Standards Enf't v. Dillingham Constr., N.A., Inc., 519 U.S. 316, 330 (1997) (apprenticeship training standards and wages paid on public works projects "quite remote from the areas with which ERISA is expressly concerned"). *But see* Mackey v. Lanier Collection Agency & Serv., Inc., 486 U.S. 825, 842 (1988) (Kennedy, J., dissenting) (general garnishment laws not tenuous, remote, or peripheral).

[41] Alessi v. Raybestos-Manhattan, Inc., 451 U.S. 504, 523–24 (1981).

[42] *Travelers*, 514 U.S. at 655.

204   *Conduct Controls: Welfare and Pension Plans*

administration, and remedies. The Court has not taken particular care to specify which type of preemption has supported each holding, sometimes adverting to express and conflict preemption in the same breath. Whatever the basis for the preemptive holding, however, the preempted categories are instructive. First, state laws that affect the type or amount of benefits provided under a pension or welfare plan are uniformly set aside.[43] Second, laws that affect the uniform administration of plans likewise fall.[44] Third, laws that provide additional remedies for conduct violating ERISA are also preempted.[45]

In the first category, laws mandating that a plan provide benefits of a certain type or amount interfere with a central design feature that Congress intended to reserve to the plan sponsor to promote flexibility and maximize voluntary plan sponsorship. The policy of laissez-faire is strongest in matters touching upon workforce coverage (participation rules) and the type and amount of benefits to be provided by the plan. Consequently, mandated benefit rules (and, likely, mandated coverage rules) cannot stand.[46] This, of course, is a result that follows automatically from field preemption, which would be inferred in the case of pension plans, and which is confirmed and extended to the case of welfare plans by ERISA's express preemption provision. As the Court has repeatedly observed, "we have virtually taken it for granted that state laws which are 'specifically designed to affect employee benefit plans' are pre-empted under § 514(a)."[47]

---

[43] *Alessi*, 451 U.S. at 504 (law prohibiting integration of workers compensation and pension benefits); *Shaw*, 463 U.S. at 85 (state anti-discrimination law requiring provision of pregnancy benefits); FMC Corp. v. Holliday, 498 U.S. 52 (1990) (law prohibiting subrogation of health care plan from recovery based on motor vehicle tort claim). *See also* Metro. Life Ins. Co. v. Mass., 471 U.S. 724 (1985) (law mandating inclusion of minimum mental health benefits in health insurance policies purchased by employee health care plans relates to a plan within the meaning of section 514(a), but preemption avoided by insurance savings clause).

[44] Boggs v. Boggs, 520 U.S. 833 (1997) (community property law permitting deceased nonparticipant spouse to devise an interest in the survivor's pension); Egelhoff v. Egelhoff, 532 U.S. 141 (2001) (nonprobate transfer law providing automatic revocation on divorce of spousal beneficiary designation).

[45] Pilot Life Ins. Co. v. Dedeaux, 481 U.S. 41, 46 (1987) (common-law action seeking emotional distress and punitive damages for bad-faith insurance claims processing); Ingersoll-Rand Co. v. McClendon, 498 U.S. 133 (1990) (common-law wrongful discharge claim seeking compensation for mental anguish and punitive damages based on firing to prevent pension vesting).

[46] In holding that a gross receipts tax on hospitals could be applied without preemption to facilities run by an ERISA health care plan, the Supreme Court emphasized that "[t]his is not a case in which New York has forbidden a method of calculating pension benefits that federal law permits, or required employers to provide certain benefits." De Buono v. NYSA-ILA Med. & Clinical Servs. Fund, 520 U.S. 806, 814–15 (1997) (footnotes omitted).

[47] Mackey v. Lanier Collection Agency & Servs., Inc., 486 U.S. 825, 829 (1988); Ingersoll-Rand Co. v. McClendon, 498 U.S. 133, 140 (1990). *See supra* text accompanying Chapter 6 notes 10–19.

Preemption of the second category can be approximately described as laws interfering with the "uniform administrative practice" of a plan.[48] The first examples of such laws were those affecting the identification of plan beneficiaries. Those laws were most certainly not "specifically designed to affect employee benefit plans"; instead they were laws of general application. *Boggs v. Boggs*[49] held Louisiana community property law preempted insofar as it allowed a nonparticipant spouse to make a testamentary transfer of an interest in the undistributed pension benefits of the surviving participant spouse. Louisiana's community property regime did not deal with subject matters regulated by ERISA (e.g., funding, vesting, fiduciary obligations), nor was it directed at welfare or pension plans, so it hardly seemed a candidate for field preemption.[50] In its prospects for withstanding preemption, community property seemed to have everything going for it. The Court acknowledged that it "is more than a property regime[, it] is a commitment to the equality of husband and wife" that "implement[s] policies and values lying within the traditional domain of the States."[51] Yet when applied to confer a devisable interest on a nonparticipant spouse, it frustrates ERISA's purposes because it diverts funds destined to provide retirement income for the participant and any later spouse.[52] Moreover, the transfer of an interest by will or intestacy fails to satisfy the requirements of a qualified domestic relations order (QDRO), the sole ERISA-endorsed mechanism for granting a nonbeneficiary access to accumulated pension savings.[53] Accordingly, *Boggs* represents a straightforward application of obstacle preemption.[54]

Another instance of preemption of state laws affecting identification of plan beneficiaries involved the state of Washington's nonprobate transfer law. *Egelhoff v. Egelhoff*[55] held preempted a statute providing for automatic revocation on divorce of a spousal beneficiary designation. Although the statute explicitly referred to employee benefit plans, it needn't have, as it applied generally to a wide range of will substitutes (such as contractual payable-on-death clauses and revocable inter vivos trusts). The Supreme Court found the law to be expressly preempted by

---

[48] N.Y. State Conf. of Blue Cross & Blue Shield Plans v. Travelers Ins. Co., 514 U.S. 645, 660 (1995).

[49] 520 U.S. 833 (1997).

[50] The Court found it unnecessary to consider the applicability of field preemption. *Id.* at 841.

[51] *Id.* at 840.

[52] *Id.* at 852 ("it would be inimical to ERISA's purposes to permit testamentary recipients to acquire a competing interest in undistributed pension benefits, which are intended to provide a stream of income to participants and their beneficiaries"). *Accord* Ablamis v. Roper, 937 F.2d 1450 (9th Cir. 1991).

[53] *Boggs*, 520 U.S. at 843–44, 848–51.

[54] The *Boggs* Court referred to its decision as an application of conflict preemption, but it used the term "conflict" broadly, to include not only contradictory commands, but also state laws that frustrate ERISA's objects. *Id.* at 841.

[55] 532 U.S. 141 (2001).

206   *Conduct Controls: Welfare and Pension Plans*

ERISA, not because it made reference to employee benefit plans, but because it had an "impermissible connection with ERISA plans."[56]

> The statute binds ERISA plan administrators to a particular choice of rules for determining beneficiary status. The administrators must pay benefits to the beneficiaries chosen by state law, rather than to those identified in the plan documents. The statute thus implicates an area of core ERISA concern. In particular, it runs counter to ERISA's commands that a plan shall "specify the basis on which payments are made to and from the plan," and that the fiduciary shall administer the plan "in accordance with the documents and instruments governing the plan," making payments to a "beneficiary" who is "designated by a participant, or by the terms of [the] plan." In other words, unlike generally applicable laws regulating "areas where ERISA has nothing to say," which we have upheld notwithstanding their incidental effect on ERISA plans, this statute governs the payment of benefits, a central matter of plan administration.[57]

While resting its decision on express preemption, this analysis suggests that laws affecting beneficiary designation actually contradict ERISA, so that conflict preemption is also called for. Alternatively, the identification of plan beneficiaries may be such a "core ERISA concern" that it (like the type and amount of benefits or the extent of workforce coverage) must yield to field preemption.

A recent Supreme Court decision on preemption, *Gobeille*, also falls in this second category.[58] At issue in *Gobeille* was a Vermont law which required all health care payers in the state to gather certain information about monies expended paying for health care. The Vermont law was intended not to regulate what plans were doing *qua* plans, or to assess, for example, whether plan fiduciaries were fulfilling

---

[56] *Id.* at 147.

[57] *Id.* at 147–48 (footnotes and citations omitted).

[58] Gobeille v. Liberty Mut. Ins. Co., 577 U.S. 312 (2016). There is a contrarian view that *Gobeille* was wrongly decided. Under this account, the regulation of plans was entirely incidental: Vermont was gathering health care cost information from any and all parties that possessed it, and plans were one of those parties. No benefit choice a plan made was either substantively interfered with or made more costly by Vermont's law. In this way, the Vermont law was little different than a state law concerning garnishment or health care surcharges – both of which the Court had previously held could reach plans without running afoul of preemption. *Compare id.*, *with* Mackey v. Lanier Collection Agency & Serv., Inc., 486 U.S. 825 (1988), *and* N.Y. State Conf. of Blue Cross & Blue Shield Plans v. Travelers Ins. Co., 514 U.S. 645 (1995). That Vermont's law involved handing over information (and thus could be facially described as a state "reporting" requirement) no more implicated the field of benefit regulation than garnishment or health care surcharge laws implicated the field of benefit regulation merely because they involved the plan handing over money (and thus could facially be described as a state requirement concerning the use of plan monies). It cannot be that any state law seeking information from a plan interferes with ERISA's reporting requirements, or no state could, for example, require a plan that acquired real property to make a filing with the Registry of Deeds. Nor was there any evidence that the Vermont law would so acutely burden plans as to somehow interfere with Congressional objectives. *Gobeille* is thus an example of where a more transparent approach to field preemption would have likely yielded a different result.

Preemption 207

their duties to their beneficiaries. The aim of the law was simply to gather information from any and all entities that possessed information the state wanted to collect so that it could understand the cost and utilization of medical care within its borders. The Court, in holding the law preempted, concluded that a law obligating a self-insured plan to provide such information would disrupt the uniform reporting requirements that had been a central aspect of the business of plan administration since ERISA was enacted.[59] Like the rules governing identification of beneficiaries, the rules governing what information a plan must collect and yield were part of the core matters Congress claimed for itself when it enacted ERISA.

The third category of state laws that the Supreme Court has found superseded consists of laws providing additional remedies for conduct violating ERISA. Common-law tort actions for bad-faith breach of contract in insurance claims processing, and for wrongful discharge to prevent pension vesting, fall under this ban.[60] Such state law claims support awards of compensatory damages for nonpecuniary injuries (such as emotional distress) or even punitive damages, remedies that are not authorized by ERISA's civil enforcement provision. In several cases the Court has held that that omission was quite deliberate: "The policy choices reflected in the inclusion of certain remedies and the exclusion of others under the federal scheme would be completely undermined if ERISA-plan participants and beneficiaries were free to obtain remedies under state law that Congress rejected in ERISA."[61] In other words, under ERISA, as elsewhere, the nature of the remedy defines the extent of the right. Such supplemental remedies would upset the balance of considerations employers face in deciding whether to sponsor a plan.[62] ERISA's legislative history also persuaded the Court that Congress intended section 502(a), the civil enforcement provision, to have uniquely "powerful preemptive force."[63] Supplemental state remedies, therefore, would present an obstacle to the

---

[59] Congress amended ERISA in the aftermath of *Gobeille*, as explained *infra* Chapter 11 notes 168–69 and accompanying text.

[60] Pilot Life Ins. Co. v. Dedeaux, 481 U.S. 41, 46 (1987); Ingersoll-Rand Co. v. McClendon, 498 U.S. 133 (1990).

[61] *Ingersoll-Rand*, 498 U.S. at 144 (quoting Mass. Mut. Life Ins. Co. v. Russell, 473 U.S. 134, 146 (1985), discussed *supra* Chapter 5D).

  Conversely, the existence of long-standing state law remedies for medical malpractice was one factor that persuaded the Court that mixed eligibility and treatment decisions by HMO physicians are not fiduciary acts subject to ERISA's fiduciary duty and enforcement provisions. Pegram v. Herdrich, 530 U.S. 211, 235–36 (2000), *see supra* Chapter 4 notes 25–34 and accompanying text.

[62] "Any such provision [allowing additional state law remedies] patently violates ERISA's policy of inducing employers to offer benefits by assuring a predictable set of liabilities, under uniform standards of primary conduct and a uniform regime of ultimate remedial orders and awards when a violation has occurred." Rush Prudential HMO, Inc. v. Moran, 536 U.S. 355, 379 (2002).

[63] *Ingersoll-Rand*, 498 U.S. at 144. Aetna Health Inc. v. Davila, 542 U.S. 200, 209 (2004) ("any state law cause of action that duplicates, supplements, or supplants the ERISA civil enforcement remedy conflicts with the clear congressional intent to make the ERISA remedy exclusive

208   *Conduct Controls: Welfare and Pension Plans*

full accomplishment of ERISA's policies. In *Ingersoll-Rand*, as in *Boggs*, the Supreme Court referred to its decision as an application of conflict preemption. But here too, the conflict is with ERISA's underlying objectives; it does not entail a direct contradiction of commands.[64]

The Purposive Approach

Each of the three categories of state laws that the Supreme Court has held preempted – laws affecting the type or amount of benefits, laws affecting the uniform administrative practice of plans, and laws supplementing ERISA's remedies – offend ERISA's fundamental policies. Notwithstanding the Court's rough reliance on express preemption, application of conventional principles of field preemption and obstacle preemption is sufficient to explain these decisions. Perhaps despairing of its efforts to capture the elusive plain meaning of "relate to," in 1997 the Court announced a new context-sensitive and policy-oriented interpretation of section 514(a):

> [T]o determine whether a state law has the forbidden connection, we look both to "the objectives of the ERISA statute as a guide to the scope of the state law that Congress understood would survive," as well as to the nature of the effect of the state law on ERISA plans.[65]

This standard makes express preemption turn on a purposive inquiry that seems to embody the approach of field and obstacle preemption. Even more forthrightly, Justice Scalia observed:

> I think it would greatly assist our function of clarifying the law if we simply acknowledged that our first take on this statute was wrong; that the "relate to" clause of the pre-emption provision is meant, not to set forth a *test* for pre-emption, but rather to identify the field in which ordinary *field pre-emption* applies – namely, the field of laws regulating "employee benefit plan[s].... ." I think it accurately describes our current ERISA jurisprudence to say that we apply ordinary field preemption, and, of course, ordinary conflict pre-emption. Nothing more mysterious than that; and except as establishing that, "relates to" is irrelevant.[66]

---

and is therefore preempted"). The Court has gone so far as to hold that a law arguably saved from express preemption because it regulates insurance nevertheless falls to implied preemption where it would supplement ERISA's remedial scheme. *Davila*, 542 U.S. at 217–18. *But see* UNUM Life Ins. Co. of Am. v. Ward, 526 U.S. 358, 376 n.7 (1999) (noting Solicitor General's disavowal of the argument that remedial conflict requires preemption of a law that would otherwise be protected by the insurance saving clause).

[64] *Ingersoll-Rand*, 498 U.S. at 142–45; Boggs v. Boggs, 520 U.S. 833, 843–44 (1997).

[65] Cal. Div. of Lab. Standards Enf't v. Dillingham Constr., N.A., Inc., 519 U.S. 316, 325 (1997) (quoting N.Y. State Conf. of Blue Cross & Blue Shield Plans v. Travelers Ins. Co., 514 U.S. 645, 656, 658–69 (1995)). *Accord* Egelhoff v. Egelhoff, 532 U.S. 141, 147 (2001).

[66] *Dillingham*, 519 U.S. at 336 (citations omitted) (Scalia, J. concurring). Concurring in a subsequent decision, Justice Scalia, joined by Justice Ginsburg, observed, "if [section 514(a)]

Here the term "conflict pre-emption" is used to include conflict with the underlying policy of the federal statute (i.e., it subsumes obstacle preemption). Accordingly, Justice Scalia is prepared to construe ERISA's preemption clause to legislate field preemption only; outside the field of laws regulating employee benefit plans, he would uphold general state laws, except insofar as they actually conflict with federal regulation or create an obstacle to the accomplishment of ERISA's policies.

There is great explanatory force in the proposition that generally applicable state laws (meaning laws not addressed to regulation of employee benefits) are superseded only if they conflict with ERISA or present an obstacle to the achievement of its goals, not because they run afoul of express preemption. Under this view all generally applicable state laws survive express preemption without needing the protection of a savings clause (express or implied) because they simply fail to "relate to" a plan. If their application would undermine ERISA's purposes, however, the federal interest must prevail. This approach cannot reduce preemption issues to a simple algorithm because ERISA's purposes sometimes conflict. Yet by focusing debate on the right question – the proper balance of ERISA's competing policies – it should yield more coherent results.

Thinking about what the Court has done from this perspective suggests a much more modest role for express preemption than the Court's pronouncements assert. The limited function of ERISA § 514(a) is confirmed by a series of cases in which the Court has refused to set aside general state laws that impose substantial costs on employee benefit plans. The case that led the retreat from the extremist implications of express preemption is *New York State Conference of Blue Cross & Blue Shield Plans v. Travelers Insurance Company*.[67] The case challenged the enforceability of statutory surcharges on in-patient hospital care imposed on patients whose bills were paid by a variety of providers other than Blue Cross/Blue Shield (the "Blues"), including commercial insurers and HMOs. The object of the New York law was to make insuring with the Blues relatively more attractive, in order to offset cost disadvantages stemming from the Blues' practice of open enrollment. Despite this deliberate effort to influence the purchasing choices of health plan administrators, the Court upheld the charges.

> An indirect economic influence, ... does not bind plan administrators to any particular choice and thus function as a regulation of an ERISA plan itself; commercial insurers and HMO's may still offer more attractive packages than the Blues. Nor does the indirect influence of the surcharges preclude uniform administrative practice or the provision of a uniform interstate benefit package if a plan

---

is interpreted to be anything other than a reference to our established jurisprudence concerning conflict and field pre-emption [it] has no discernible content that would not pick up every ripple in the pond, producing a result 'that no sensible person could have intended.'" *Egelhoff*, 532 U.S. at 153.

[67] 514 U.S. 645 (1995).

Conduct Controls: Welfare and Pension Plans

wishes to provide one. It simply bears on the costs of benefits and the relative costs of competing insurance to provide them.[68]

Pointing to hospitals' long-standing practice of providing indigent care through cross-subsidies imposed by means of charge differentials for commercial insurers, the Court saw nothing about ERISA that suggested a purpose to bar such practices when imposed by state law.[69] If state laws having indirect effects on plan costs were preempted, quality standards for hospital services and basic regulation of workplace conditions would fall, but the Court found no indication that Congress intended to displace general health care regulation.[70] Therefore the Court concluded that indirect economic effects flowing from the application of general state laws do not call for preemption, at least if the effects are not so acute "as to force an ERISA plan to adopt a certain scheme of substantive coverage or effectively restrict its choice of insurers, ..."[71]

Subsequent cases reaffirm that indirect influences, in the form of economic incentives created to serve legitimate state ends, don't trigger preemption.[72] Qualitatively, such influences may, by virtue of their indirectness, have only a "tenuous, remote, or peripheral connection with covered plans,"[73] but quantitatively their impact can be substantial. Tension exists between the Court's acceptance of such influences and the notion that Congress intended to give sponsors wide latitude in structuring benefit programs to maximize their advantage.[74] Costs figure prominently in plan design, so substantial cost increases, even if indirect, will sway the employer's decisions. The following section investigates this apparent contradiction.

---

[68] *Id.* at 659–60.

[69] *Id.* at 660.

[70] *Id.* at 660–61, 664–65.

[71] *Id.* at 668.

[72] Cal. Div. of Labor Standards Enforcement v. Dillingham Constr., N.A., Inc., 519 U.S. 316, 332, 333 (1997) (prevailing wage law's economic incentive for ERISA apprenticeship program to comply with state qualification requirements acceptable absent showing that inducement is "tantamount to a compulsion"); De Buono v. NYSA-ILA Med. & Clinical Servs. Fund, 520 U.S. 806, 814–15 (1997) (discussing a state gross receipts tax on medical centers applicable to facilities operated directly by ERISA health care plans). The tax in *De Buono* fell on the plan directly, but nonetheless represented an indirect economic influence because, like the quality control standards and workplace safety regulation discussed in New York State Conference of Blue Cross & Blue Shield Plans v. Travelers Insurance Co., it was a general law that increased the costs of covered services, whether provided by an ERISA plan or otherwise. *De Buono*, 520 U.S. at 816; *Travelers*, 514 U.S. at 661.

[73] *Travelers*, 514 U.S. at 661; *Dillingham*, 519 U.S. at 334. The "tenuous, remote, or peripheral" limitation on express preemption was announced in dicta in Shaw v. Delta Air Lines, Inc., and repeated in subsequent cases. 463 U.S. 85, 100 n.21 (1983). *See supra* Chapter 6 notes 29–30 and accompanying text.

[74] *See supra* Chapter 1C.

D COSTS AND PREEMPTION POLICY

"Congress pre-empted state laws relating to *plans*, rather than simply to *benefits*."[75]
"In sum, cost uniformity was almost certainly not an object of pre-emption[.]"[76]

Federal preemption obviously achieves uniformity in the regulation of employee benefit plans. The Supreme Court has suggested that interstate administrative uniformity, with its tendency to minimize costs, was *the* central object of preemption.[77] Nevertheless, an exclusive focus on uniformity is misleadingly incomplete; ERISA, after all, does not except uniform state laws from preemption. Freedom of contract (laissez-faire) more accurately captures the central objective of preemption. Freedom of contract preserves a system of voluntary plan sponsorship and prevents the states from upsetting the balance Congress struck between the quantity and quality of employer-provided welfare and pension benefits. That balance is cost-driven, of course, but not all costs are created equal. Since its retreat from the "uncritical literalism" of its early approach to preemption,[78] the Court has indicated that state laws that affect the cost of certain goods or services generally are *not* displaced when those goods or services are financed or provided through an employee benefit plan.

Employee benefit plans are not immune from indirect costs imposed generally in the legitimate exercise of a state's police power, even if interstate differentials in the cost of plan benefits are the result. In contrast, state laws that obligate a change in the plan's day-to-day operations – such as having to identify a different beneficiary or having to gather and report information beyond what ERISA requires – are preempted not because that increases costs, but rather because those laws intrude on the autonomy Congress reserved to the plan sponsor, preventing the sponsor from using the same benefit package and plan operating manual in every state.

Uniformity versus Laissez-Faire

An employer-initiated severance pay arrangement generally constitutes a welfare plan (or, under some circumstances, a pension plan). Nevertheless, in *Fort Halifax Packing Co. v. Coyne*, the Supreme Court found that a Maine law requiring one-time severance payments in the event of a plant closing was not preempted by ERISA because the statute "neither establishes, nor requires an employer to maintain, an employee welfare benefit 'plan.'"[79] The Court equated an ERISA plan with

---

[75] Fort Halifax Packing Co. v. Coyne, 482 U.S. 1, 11 (1987).
[76] *Travelers*, 514 U.S. at 662.
[77] *See Fort Halifax*, 482 U.S. at 11.
[78] *Travelers*, 514 U.S. at 656.
[79] 482 U.S. at 6.

Conduct Controls: Welfare and Pension Plans

an "ongoing administrative program for processing claims and paying benefits."[80] That criterion, the Court explained, is supported by the policy of preemption. Conforming a benefit program to a patchwork of state regulation would forfeit the advantages of uniform administrative practice, and the resulting cost increases "might lead those employers with existing plans to reduce benefits, and those without such plans to refrain from adopting them."[81] In contrast, a contingent, one-time obligation to make nondiscretionary, lump-sum payments of the sort imposed by the Maine law entails no such inefficiency.[82]

State conduct controls (such as additional reporting requirements, higher fiduciary standards, or specified procedures for claim processing) may interfere with uniform administration, and so must be set aside.[83] "Pre-emption ensures that the administrative practices of a benefit plan will be governed by only a single set of regulations."[84] But the *Fort Halifax* Court used the term "administrative practices" capaciously, to include the funding, computation, and payment of benefits, and so state laws that mandate certain types or levels of benefits likewise disrupt uniform administrative practices. The justices worried that differing state laws would force a plan "to make certain benefits available in some States but not in others."[85] For that reason, the Court explained, ERISA preempted a Hawaii law mandating employer provision of specified health insurance benefits.[86] Similarly, the Court noted that it struck down a New Jersey statute that prohibited offsetting worker compensation payments against pension benefits in *Alessi v. Raybestos-Manhattan, Inc.*[87], because the statute "force[d] the employer either to structure all its benefit payments in accordance with New Jersey law, or to adopt different payment formulae for

---

[80] *Id.* at 12.

[81] *Id.* at 11.

[82] *Id.* at 12. The Court also observed that the Maine plant-closing law "not only fails to implicate the concerns of ERISA's pre-emption provision, it fails to implicate the regulatory concerns of ERISA itself." *Id.* at 15. Looking to the legislative history of ERISA's fiduciary-responsibility rules, the Court concluded that "[t]he focus of the statute thus is on the administrative integrity of benefit plans – which presumes that some type of administrative activity is taking place." *Id. Fort Halifax* was examined earlier (Chapter 2A), where it was seen that discretionary decision making and asset handling have emerged as criteria for the kinds of administrative activity it takes to make a plan. Close attention to the definition of fiduciary (Chapter 4A) reveals that those two functions (i.e., managerial discretion and custody of assets) invariably trigger fiduciary obligations, and so it seems that the essence of a plan is the presence of a fiduciary.

[83] *Fort Halifax*, 482 U.S. at 9 ("A plan would be required to keep certain records in some States but not in others; . . . to process claims in a certain way in some States but not in others; and to comply with certain fiduciary standards in some States but not in others.").

[84] *Id.* at 11.

[85] *Id.* at 9.

[86] *Id.* at 12–13 (discussing Standard Oil Co. v. Agsalud, 633 F.2d 760 (9th Cir. 1980), *summarily aff'd*, 454 U.S. 801 (1981)). By later amendment, Congress saved the Hawaii law. ERISA § 514 (b)(5), 29 U.S.C. § 1144(b)(5) (2018).

[87] 451 U.S. 504, 526 (1981).

Preemption

employees inside and outside the State."[88] Thus, from this view of preemption policy, state content controls are just as pernicious as conduct controls.

Uniformity, however, is only part of the concern underlying ERISA preemption, and perhaps not the most important part. As the Court noted, benefits mandated by one state could be extended to participants in other states to achieve uniformity. Similarly, a plan could comply with the most restrictive state procedural standards (conduct controls). If states impose conflicting procedural protections, the problem could be sidestepped by including a choice-of-law provision in the plan document. Approaches such as these would ensure nationwide operational uniformity, but it would come at the price of increased expense and reduced employer flexibility.[89]

Increased cost and reduced flexibility "might lead those employers with existing plans to reduce benefits, and those without such plans to refrain from adopting them."[90] State imposition of more demanding standards, while ensuring first-rate coverage for some workers, would cause a larger proportion of the US labor force to receive smaller benefits, or none at all. Federal preemption prevents the states from upsetting the balance Congress struck between the quantity and quality of employee benefit plan coverage.[91] ERISA leaves unregulated some subjects, such as workforce coverage and benefit levels,[92] and imposes only minimum standards even in fields that are intensively controlled, such as pension funding and vesting. Thus, federal law preserves an important residue of freedom of contract. Under a system of voluntary plan sponsorship, additional state regulation would shift the equilibrium,

---

[88] *Fort Halifax*, 482 U.S. at 10.

[89] In addition, the choice-of-law solution would only eliminate conflicts for plan employers, not employees.

"Although selection of one state's law meets the employer's cost-based need for uniform administrative procedures, it is not enough from the worker's perspective. Even though any one plan could be interpreted and administered in accordance with the law of a single state, one worker may need to evaluate numerous alternative plans associated with different employment opportunities. Those plans may select different governing laws (corresponding to the differing locations of corporate headquarters, for example), making the precise contours of competing benefit offers dependent on the idiosyncrasies of several states' contract and trust law. Under these circumstances, fully informed evaluation of competing job offers is probably uneconomic – the cost of identifying the vagaries of alternative legal regimes would likely exceed the benefit of a marginally more valuable compensation package. A single set of interstitial rules (contract and trust) governing all plans would limit information costs and increase the efficiency of the labor market." Wiedenbeck, *supra* Chapter 1 note 56, at 569–70 (footnote omitted).

[90] Fort Halifax, 482 U.S. at 11.

[91] Referring to the cost consequences of restricting the integration of pension plans with Social Security, the House Ways and Means Committee observed: "Employees, as a whole, might be injured rather than aided if such cost increases resulted in slowing down the growth or perhaps even eliminated private retirement plans." H.R. REP. NO. 93-807, at 69 (1974), *reprinted in* 2 ERISA LEGISLATIVE HISTORY, *supra* Chapter 1 note 55, at 3189.

[92] For a discussion of how the Affordable Care Act impacts employer obligations with respect to certain group health plans, *see infra* Chapter 11.

214 *Conduct Controls: Welfare and Pension Plans*

reducing the availability of employee benefits. By prohibiting state intrusion, pre-emption reserves that policy decision for Congress.

The Relevance of Costs

A commitment to freedom of contract bars the states from imposing more onerous and costly requirements. But how far does this cost-containment principle extend? A plan may incur higher costs because of state regulatory action that is not directed at employee benefit plans as such. Is state public health legislation preempted because increased life expectancy triggers higher costs for defined benefit pension plans? Employee benefit plans are designed to provide insurance or financing for morbidity (health and disability plans) and mortality (pension and life insurance plans) losses. It cannot be the case that states are barred from addressing public health and safety concerns because of their laws' incidental effects on benefit costs under ERISA plans. Cognizance of this implication seems to be what put the brakes on the Supreme Court's early expansive interpretation of section 514(a).[93]

Perhaps cost control is the fundamental objective of ERISA preemption, but the objective is limited to containing *plan* costs – that is, barring state coverage and benefit mandates, and containing the cost of benefit delivery (i.e., plan adminis-tration). Employment and health laws, which vary from state to state, also lead to interstate differentials in costs faced by a large employer providing a uniform nationwide package of benefits. Such "cost uniformity was almost certainly not an object of pre-emption," the Court has explained.[94] That is, laws affecting the cost of freely contracted benefits, whether by altering insured risks or changing the cost of covered services, were not expected to fall to ERISA preemption. A natural calamity like a serious epidemic can substantially affect costs incurred by a health care plan (or even a defined benefit pension plan), but so can local health and welfare regulation, like a state immunization program, hospital quality-of-care standards, wage and hour legislation, or pharmacy purchasing regulation.[95] Possible cost effects should not undermine such unremarkable exercises of state police power. Instead, state action of these sorts should, like an epidemic, be treated as just another

---

[93] *See* N.Y. State Conf. of Blue Cross & Blue Shield Plans v. Travelers Ins. Co., 514 U.S. 645, 661 (1995) (noting that hospital quality standards and basic employment regulation increase costs, but "to read the pre-emption provision as displacing all state laws affecting costs and charges on the theory that they indirectly relate to ERISA plans that ... cover such services would effectively read the limiting language in § 514(a) out of the statute"). *See supra* Chapter 6B.

[94] *Travelers*, 514 U.S. at 662.

[95] While upholding an Alabama law regulating the price pharmacy benefit managers (which are often used by plans) could charge pharmacies, a unanimous Court explained: "Crucially, not every state law that affects an ERISA plan or causes some disuniformity in plan administration has an impermissible connection with an ERISA plan. That is especially so if a law merely affects costs." Rutledge v. Pharm. Care Mgmt. Ass'n, 141 S. Ct. 474, 480 (2020).

component of the financial risk that the plan sponsor assumes when promising to provide benefits dependent on health or longevity. The indirect cost consequences of general laws designed to serve legitimate state ends are both ubiquitous and indistinguishable from other risks that normally inhere in plan sponsorship. General state laws speak to a wider audience than employers and plan participants, and that broader constituency offers some assurance that those laws are supported by public policy justifications independent of ERISA's concerns and are not designed to alter the congressional balance between benefit plan quantity and quality.

A pair of preemption decisions provides vivid confirmation that the distinction between acceptable and unacceptable costs is not a matter of magnitude. *Mackey v. Lanier Collection Agency & Services, Inc.*[96] held that Georgia's general garnishment statute could be applied to collect money owed by a welfare plan participant from benefits due the participant under the plan, even though application of the law would subject the plan to substantial legal and administrative costs.

> Petitioners are required to confirm the identity of each of the 23 plan participants who owe money to respondent, calculate the participant's maximum entitlement from the fund for the period between the service date and the reply date of the summons of garnishment, determine the amount that each participant owes to respondent, and make payments into state court of the lesser of the amount owed to respondent and the participant's entitlement. Petitioners must also make decisions concerning the validity and priority of garnishments and, if necessary, bear the costs of litigating these issues. Further, as trustees of a multiemployer plan covering participants in several States, petitioners are potentially subject to multiple garnishment orders under varying or conflicting state laws.[97]

On the other hand, in *Egelhoff v. Egelhoff*,[98] the Court concluded that ERISA preempts a Washington statute calling for automatic revocation of a spousal beneficiary designation upon divorce, even though the statute functioned only as a default rule that could be overridden by including specific language in the plan. Consequently, the statute's interference with nationally uniform plan administration (i.e., making the administrator pay benefits to the person specified by state law instead of the beneficiary identified in accordance with plan documents) could be avoided at minimal cost.

Thus, while high administrative costs did not trigger preemption in *Mackey*, a law that imposed very little cost was preempted in *Egelhoff*. The difference, of course, is that *Mackey* involved a general state law that could stand because garnishment of welfare benefits does not undermine ERISA's objectives, while the divorce revocation statute in *Egelhoff* was directed at plan beneficiary designation and so fell to field preemption, and arguably conflict preemption as well. Put differently, high

---

[96] 486 U.S. 825, 837–38, 841 (1988).
[97] *Id.* at 842 (Kennedy, J., dissenting).
[98] 532 U.S. 141, 143 (2001).

costs do not necessarily determine the fate of a general state law, while low costs cannot save a state law that regulates plan content or operations. That said, the Court *has* noted that otherwise general state laws that impose "acute, albeit indirect, economic effects" that are so burdensome as to "force an ERISA plan to adopt a certain scheme of substantive coverage or effectively restrict its choice of insurers" would be preempted.[99] Admittedly, since first articulating that potentiality in *Travelers*, the Court has never found preemption on that ground. But the Court's continued acknowledgment of that unlikely possibility[100] suggests even general state laws are not categorically free from preemption scrutiny by the Court.

E THE ROLE OF FEDERAL COMMON LAW

"It is also intended that a body of Federal substantive law will be developed by the courts to deal with issues involving rights and obligations under private welfare and pension plans."[101]

Express preemption clears the field of employee benefit plan regulation, leaving matters not addressed by ERISA open to private ordering (freedom of contract). Occasionally, however, preemption sweeps away state laws that actually facilitate private ordering. Consider state killer laws, which revoke beneficiary designations naming a person who murders the property owner. Such laws are designed to carry out the owner's probable intent in a situation that was not foreseen, and presumably killer laws do so in the overwhelming majority of cases. Yet under *Egelhoff*, the revocation of a participant's beneficiary designation by operation of such a state law, and the designation by law of a substitute taker, would be preempted. This scenario was presented to the Supreme Court as an argument weighing against preemption of the divorce revocation law sub judice. Conveniently avoiding the problem, the Court responded that such slayer "statutes are not before us, so we do not decide the issue."[102] It noted, however, that the principle underlying such statutes has a long history and has been adopted almost everywhere, and that near uniformity may mitigate such statutes' interference with ERISA.[103]

The intimation that a sufficiently broad consensus among the states may save from preemption a law regulating plan terms misapprehends the relevant question. Perhaps such a near universal principle should apply to employee benefit plans, but not as a matter of *state* law. To apply a state killer statute would violate the "reservation to Federal authority [of] the sole power to regulate the field of employee

---

[99] Gobeille v. Liberty Mut. Ins. Co., 577 U.S. 312, 320, (2016) (citing *Travelers*).

[100] Rutledge v. Pharm. Care Mgmt. Ass'n, 141 S. Ct. 474, 480 (2020).

[101] *See* 3 ERISA Legislative History, *supra* Chapter 1 note 55, at 4771.

[102] *Egelhoff*, 532 U.S. at 152.

[103] *Id.*

Preemption

benefit plans."[104] That reservation was not to *congressional* authority specifically, but to federal authority generally, and Congress contemplated that the federal courts would exercise interstitial lawmaking power under ERISA. Accordingly, the proper approach might be for the courts to adopt a nationally uniform killer disqualification rule as a matter of the federal common law of employee benefit plans. That such federal common law might very well mirror the collective judgment of the states would not be surprising.

The appropriate scope of judicial lawmaking under ERISA is an important and still unresolved question. Clearly, congressional silence is not enough to justify judicial intervention, for the absence of legislative standards was often by conscious forbearance, intended to preserve a large area of freedom of contract. That flexibility, in turn, was designed to promote broad sponsorship. That goal may offer the best guideline for the federal courts' exercise of their common-law powers. If the proposed rule could adversely affect sponsorship by increasing plan costs or reducing employer flexibility, then it should be left to the free play of economic forces – off limits, that is, for the courts. If, instead, the rule responds to unforeseen circumstances by filling a gap in the plan contract, then common-law development may be warranted.[105]

Kennedy v. *Plan Administrator for DuPont Savings and Investment Plan*,[106] illustrates these competing concerns. The case presented the question whether to enforce an ex-spouse's waiver of pension benefits where the participant died without having changed a pre-divorce beneficiary designation naming the former spouse as successor. The Court suggested that such a waiver might in certain circumstances be given effect as a matter of federal common law,[107] but it held that where the plan required distribution to the beneficiary designated in accordance with the method specified by the plan the waiver must be disregarded. The interest in simple, low-cost plan administration dissuaded the Court from looking beyond the plan's beneficiary designation rules.[108] Noting that *Boggs* and *Egelhoff* held state laws affecting the identification of plan beneficiaries preempted, the unanimous Court

---

[104] 120 Cong. Rec. 29, 197 (1974), *reprinted in* 3 ERISA Legislative History, *supra* Chapter 1 note 56, at 4656, 4670.

[105] *See, e.g.*, PM Grp. Life Ins. Co. v. W. Growers Assurance Tr., 953 F.2d 543, 546–48 (9th Cir. 1992) (exemplifying the development of common-law rules under ERISA where self-insured health care plans of each parent covered an infant's hospital expenses, but the plans contained incompatible coordination-of-benefits provisions resulting in the Court's adoption of a rule to determine which plan bears primary liability).

[106] 555 U.S. 285, 288 (2009), discussed *infra* Chapter 8B.

[107] *Id.* at 299 n.10, 299–300. The waiver had been incorporated in a divorce decree but that was "only happenstance" – "recognizing a waiver in a divorce decree would not be giving effect to state law". *Id.* at 299. In principle a court could apply "federal [common] law to a document that might also have independent significance under state law." *Id.*

[108] *Id.* at 301. Despite countervailing equitable considerations, ERISA's policy of promoting voluntary sponsorship supports carrying out the plan's directive to pay the person whose name is on file. The prospect of increased cost, uncertainty, and delay "are good and sufficient

218 Conduct Controls: Welfare and Pension Plans

declared: "What goes for inconsistent state laws goes for a federal common law of waiver that might obscure a plan administrator's duty to act 'in accordance with the documents and instruments.'"[109]

F THE INSURANCE SAVINGS CLAUSE

Additional considerations come into play when ERISA collides with a state law regulating insurance, banking, or securities. Section 514(b)(2), ERISA's insurance savings clause, provides in part that "nothing in this subchapter shall be construed to exempt or relieve any person from any law of any State which regulates insurance, banking, or securities."[110] This reservation of state authority is not an "unqualified deferral to state law"; rather, the savings clause "leaves room for complementary or dual federal and state regulation" in these fields.[111]

Complementary state regulation, however, is permissible only insofar as it applies to independent insurance companies and insurance contracts. Although a self-funded pension or welfare plan functions as an insurer, in the sense that the plan pools and underwrites risk, ERISA's "deemer clause" provides that "[n]either an employee benefit plan ... nor any trust established under such a plan, shall be deemed to be an insurance company or other insurer, ... or to be engaged in the business of insurance" for purposes of state laws regulating insurance.[112] Consequently, pension and welfare plans that provide benefits through the purchase of insurance are subject to indirect state insurance regulation (by operation of the savings clause), while self-insured benefit plans are not (by operation of the deemer clause).[113] The Supreme Court explained:

> We read the deemer clause to exempt self-funded ERISA plans from state laws that "regulat[e] insurance" within the meaning of the saving clause. By forbidding States to deem employee benefit plans "to be an insurance company or other

reasons for holding the line, just as we have done in cases of state laws that might blur the bright-line requirement to follow plan documents in distributing benefits." *Id.* at 302.

[109] *Id.* at 303.

[110] ERISA § 514(b)(2)(A), 29 U.S.C. § 1144(b)(2)(A) (2018).

[111] John Hancock Mut. Life Ins. Co. v. Harris Tr. & Sav. Bank, 510 U.S. 86, 98 (1993).

[112] ERISA § 514(b)(2)(B), 29 U.S.C. § 1144(b)(2)(B) (2018).

[113] Metro. Life Ins. Co. v. Mass., 471 U.S. 724, 747 (1985) ("We are aware that our decision results in a distinction between insured and uninsured plans, leaving the former open to indirect regulation while the latter are not. By so doing we merely give life to a distinction created by Congress in the 'deemer clause,' a distinction Congress is aware of and one it has chosen not to alter."). A benefit plan is treated as self-insured and exempt from state regulation even if it limits its risk by purchasing stop-loss insurance, although the stop-loss policy would be subject to state regulation. *See* Russell Korobkin, *The Battle over Self-Insured Health Plans, or "One Good Loophole Deserves Another,"* 5 YALE J. HEALTH POL'Y L. & ETHICS 89, 117–18 (2005) ("If states are unhappy that [health plans] use stop-loss insurance to make self-insuring a relatively more attractive option than purchasing state-regulated third-party insurance, their best response is to regulate stop-loss insurers in a way that undermines that advantage.").

insurer ... or to be engaged in the business of insurance," the deemer clause relieves plans from state laws "purporting to regulate insurance." As a result, self-funded ERISA plans are exempt from state regulation insofar as that regulation "relate[s] to" the plans. State laws directed toward the plans are pre-empted because they relate to an employee benefit plan but are not "saved" because they do not regulate insurance. State laws that directly regulate insurance are "saved" but do not reach self-funded employee benefit plans because the plans may not be deemed to be insurance companies, other insurers, or engaged in the business of insurance for purposes of such state laws. On the other hand, employee benefit plans that are insured are subject to indirect state insurance regulation. An insurance company that insures a plan remains an insurer for purposes of state laws "purporting to regulate insurance" after application of the deemer clause. The insurance company is therefore not relieved from state insurance regulation. The ERISA plan is consequently bound by state insurance regulations insofar as they apply to the plan's insurer.[114]

The distinction between insured and self-insured plans leads to dramatic differences in the applicability of state law. Express (read field) preemption ordinarily bars deliberate state regulation of employee benefit plans, including laws requiring that a plan provide specified benefits or cover certain workers (content regulation) and laws regulating the administration of an employee benefit plan (conduct regulation). But where the plan provides benefits through the purchase of insurance, the savings clause lets stand state laws requiring that certain benefits be included in the policy,[115] as well as laws regulating the insurance claims process.[116]

Notwithstanding the savings clause, some state laws that regulate insurance may still be preempted. The savings clause "leaves room for complementary or dual federal and state regulation," but ERISA still "calls for federal supremacy when the two regimes cannot be harmonized or accommodated."[117] The Court "discern[ed] no solid basis for believing that Congress, when it designed ERISA, intended fundamentally to alter traditional preemption analysis. State law governing insurance generally is not displaced, but 'where [that] law stands as an obstacle to the

---

[114] FMC Corp. v. Holliday, 498 U.S. 52, 61 (1990).

[115] *Metro. Life*, 471 U.S. at 740–41 (mandatory minimum mental health coverage); see *Holliday*, 498 U.S. at 60–61 (anti-subrogation law preempted as applied to self-funded plan, but would be saved if benefits were insured).

[116] UNUM Life Ins. Co. of Am. v. Ward, 526 U.S. 358, 368–73 (1999) (California decisional law prohibiting an insurer from denying claim as untimely unless the insurer was prejudiced by delay applied to claims under disability insurance policy purchased to provide welfare plan benefits); Rush Prudential HMO Inc. v. Moran, 536 U.S. 355, 372–73 (2002) (required opportunity for independent review of medical necessity under Illinois HMO Act applies to benefits provided by HMO under contract with health care plan); Ky. Ass'n of Health Plans, Inc. v. Miller, 538 U.S. 329, 341–42 (2003) (Kentucky's "any willing provider" statute, by limiting HMOs' ability to restrict physician access, is a law that regulates insurance).

[117] John Hancock Mut. Life Ins. Co. v. Harris Tr. & Sav. Bank, 510 U.S. 86, 98 (1993).

220 *Conduct Controls: Welfare and Pension Plans*

accomplishment of the full purposes and objectives of Congress,' federal preemption occurs."[118] The Court has suggested that a state insurance law cause of action or remedy might present such an obstacle, because Congress intended ERISA's civil enforcement scheme to provide the exclusive means of relief.[119] Moreover, in recent decisions involving state laws regulating insurance claims handling, after finding the laws in question to be protected by the savings clause, the Court proceeded to consider (and reject) arguments that the laws undermined ERISA's objectives.[120]

The scope of the savings clause turns upon the meaning of a "law ... which regulates insurance," a phrase Congress left undefined. In its initial encounters with the savings clause, the Court looked for guidance to criteria identified by case law interpreting the McCarran-Ferguson Act's reference to the "business of insurance."[121] In 2003, the Court disavowed that approach in *Kentucky Association of Health Plans v. Miller* and made a "clean break from the McCarran-Ferguson factors," holding that "for a state law to be deemed a 'law ... which regulates insurance' under [the savings clause], it must satisfy two requirements. First, the state law must be specifically directed toward entities engaged in insurance. Second, ... the state law must substantially affect the risk pooling arrangement between the insurer and the insured."[122]

The first prong of *Miller* is reasonably self-explanatory, whereas prong two of the *Miller* test requires some explication. More specifically, the *Miller* Court's use of the term "risk pooling arrangement"[123] caused some initial confusion, because of uncertainty about what the term "risk pooling" encompasses (and thus what states may permissibly regulate under *Miller*).[124] Strictly speaking, insurance arrangements deal with more than risk pooling alone; they also involve risk pricing and risk transfer, for example. Courts of appeal have nonetheless often read *Miller* to save laws that substantially limit or alter any part of the insurance deal, regardless of

---

[118] *Id.* at 99 (quoting Silkwood v. Kerr-McGee Corp., 464 U.S. 238, 248 (1984)).

[119] Aetna Health Inc. v. Davila, 542 U.S. 200, 217–18 (2004); Pilot Life Ins. Co. v. Dedeaux, 481 U.S. 41, 51–57 (1987) (arguably dicta, in that the Court had concluded that the Mississippi cause of action for bad-faith breach of contract is not a law that regulates insurance). *But see UNUM Life,* 526 U.S. at 376 n.7 (noting, but not addressing, Solicitor General's argument questioning *Pilot Life's* obstacle preemption analysis).

[120] *UNUM Life,* 526 U.S. at 377 ("notice-prejudice rule complements rather than contradicts ERISA['s]" claims-handling rules); *Rush,* 536 U.S. at 375–80, 384–86.

[121] *Metro. Life,* 471 U.S. at 742–44; *Pilot Life,* 481 U.S. at 48–51; *UNUM Life,* 526 U.S. at 373–75; *Rush,* 536 U.S. at 373–75.

[122] 538 U.S. 329, 341–42.

[123] *Ky. Ass'n of Health Plans,* 538 U.S. at 341–42.

[124] Beverly Cohen, *Saving the Savings Clause: Advocating a Broader Reading of the Miller Test to Enable States to Protect ERISA Health Plan Members by Regulating Insurance,* 18 GEO. MASON L. REV. 125, 139–42 (2010) (describing lower court confusion).

Preemption

whether those laws are heartland examples of what an actuary might consider risk pooling regulation.[125] For example, in *Fontaine v. Metropolitan Life*, Met Life argued that Illinois' law prohibiting the use of discretionary clauses in health insurance policies was not saved, because a law barring discretionary clauses does not regulate risk pooling insofar as it does not "determine whether a class of risks is covered, does not extend coverage to a class of previously excluded risks, and does not mandate new claim review procedures."[126] The Seventh Circuit rejected Met Life's argument as an attempt to "narrow artificially" what the Supreme Court meant to save from preemption in *Miller*, finding the Illinois discretionary clause law saved because there was no question it changed the very deals insureds and insurers could strike.[127] That rationale deliberately and precisely mapped onto *Miller*, where the Supreme Court explained that Kentucky's any-willing-provider law was saved by virtue of it "alter[ing] the scope of permissible bargains between insurers and insureds" such that the law "substantially affect[ed] the type of risk pooling arrangements that insurers may offer."[128] Decisions that find *Miller*'s second prong not satisfied are thus often (but not always) rooted in the conclusion that the state law in question either does not alter permissible insurance bargains or has only incidental effects, rather than because the court has adopted a narrow definition of risk pooling.[129]

---

[125] *Cf.* Standard Ins. Co. v. Morrison, 537 F.Supp.2d 1142, 1151 (D.Mont. 2008) (explaining that it is unlikely "the [*Miller*] Court intended lower courts to interpret 'risk pooling' as an insurance industry actuary would" and instead intended the term to be interpreted more broadly).

[126] Fontaine v. Metro. Life Ins. Co., 800 F.3d 883, 888 (7th Cir. 2015).

[127] *Id.* at 888. *See also* Standard Ins. Co. v. Morrison, 584 F.3d 837, 844–45 (9th Cir. 2009) (state law barring discretionary clauses saved); American Council of Life Insurers v. Ross, 558 F.3d 600, 607 (6th Cir. 2009) (state law barring discretionary clauses saved); Benefit Recovery, Inc. v. Donelon, 521 F.3d 326, 331 (5th Cir. 2008) (state law limiting subrogation rights of health insurers in favor of insureds saved). *But see* Hancock v. Metro. Life Ins. Co., 590 F.3d 1141, 1149 (10th Cir. 2009) (state law limiting – rather than banning outright – the way in which a discretionary clause can appear in an insurance contract not saved).

[128] Kentucky Ass'n of Health Plans, Inc. v. Miller, 538 U.S. 329, 338–39 (2003). Kentucky's any-willing-provider law in essence required health insurers to allow any geographically proximate provider who accepted the health insurer's terms and conditions to be a participating provider. That thus necessarily affected the possible deals (in terms of providers covered) an insured could offer insureds.

[129] *E.g.*, Sgro v. Danone Waters of North America, Inc., 532 F.3d 940, 944 (9th Cir. 2008) (state law requiring reimbursement for copying medical records not preempted because it did not "substantially" affect risk deal). *But see* N. Cypress Med. Ctr. Operating Co. v. Cigna Healthcare, 781 F.3d 182, 199 (5th Cir. 2015). In N. *Cypress*, the Fifth Circuit held Texas law governing the prompt payment of insurance claims to health care providers to be pre-empted because the law (1) did not alter directly bargains between insureds and insurers, (2) did not have any (indirect) substantial effect on those bargains, *and* (3) targeted a type or risk – payment risk – different than the underlying risks *Miller* intended to save state regulation of. *Id.* at 198–99 (noting that, *inter alia*, the Texas law at issue impermissibly targeted payment risk rather than the "risk of occurrence of injury or loss for which the insurer contractually agrees to compensate the insured.") *See also* Provident Life & Acc. Ins. Co. v. Sharpless, 364 F.3d 634,

G CONCLUSION

ERISA's express preemption clause, section 514(a), is "conspicuous for its breadth,"[130] and for many years the Supreme Court approached preemption questions by construing section 514(a) in such a way as to distinguish between those state laws that bear too closely on employee benefit plans and those that have only a "tenuous, remote or peripheral" connection, with the former being preempted because they "relate to [a] plan," and the latter not. But attributing everything to the reach of express preemption runs into the difficulty that the Court's metric of relatedness is at best difficult to discern, and at worst indeterminate. Since 1995 the Justices have struggled to reign in ERISA preemption, yet the Court has not repudiated its earlier holdings, nor yet disavowed its earlier reasoning.

Attention to case outcomes and the conceptual underpinnings of preemption leads to a much more coherent explanation. ERISA's express preemption clause can be construed to mandate field preemption not only for pension plans, which the statute intensively regulates, but for welfare plans as well, even though the federal law leaves them largely unregulated. As such, any state law designed to regulate the content or conduct of any employee benefit plan, whether pension or welfare, falls prey to express preemption, even if it concerns an issue on which ERISA is silent. In legislating field preemption, Congress intended to promote sponsorship by preserving freedom of contract on matters that it did not address.

The validity of general state laws that incidentally affect an employee benefit plan is best understood without reference to express preemption. Laws aimed at achieving state goals in areas such as health care regulation, employment training, taxation, and the like, clearly lie outside the field of benefit plan regulation. Therefore, if section 514(a) is interpreted as legislating field preemption, express preemption leaves such laws untouched.

Although express preemption can be construed to leave general state laws undisturbed, in some situations the application of those laws to employee benefit plans may undermine the accomplishment of ERISA's purposes. Accordingly, legitimate state regulation in other fields may be superseded by the application of general principles of conflict and obstacle preemption. Proper application of obstacle preemption, of course, demands close attention to ERISA's policies. Cost containment promotes plan sponsorship and forms the principal justification for express (field) preemption. Nevertheless, the indirect cost that a general state law may impose on an employee benefit plan or its sponsor is *not* a factor that can be taken into account in applying *obstacle* preemption. For the simple reason that regulation always

---

640 (5th Cir. 2004) (Louisiana law barring rescission based on innocent misrepresentation was preempted because that law addressed "legal risk" rather than "coverage risk").

[130] FMC Corp. v. Holliday, 498 U.S. 52, 58 (1990).

imposes costs, financial impact alone is not enough to invalidate an otherwise-legitimate general state law.

Simply stated, the conclusion is that ERISA's express preemption clause accomplishes only field preemption, and that decisions holding generally applicable state laws superseded are best understood as applications of conflict or obstacle preemption. This methodology does not make preemption issues formulaic, because obstacle preemption requires careful attention to statutory objectives and ERISA's purposes sometimes conflict. Yet by focusing debate on the right question – the impact of the state law in question on the proper balance of ERISA's competing policies – this approach should yield more coherent results. Attention to those policies should have the added advantage of revealing when an offending state law is symptomatic of a real need that should be met by the interstitial elaboration of federal common law. Congress intended to preserve wide latitude for private ordering (laissez-faire) within the domain of employee benefits, and so judicial lawmaking that facilitates rather than restricts private ordering is fully justified.

PART III

Content Controls: Pension Plans

We have seen that ERISA incorporates two very different approaches to the regulation of employee benefits. As discussed in Part II, the administration of all employee benefit plans is subject to federal oversight to promote informed participation, ensure compliance with plan terms, and to protect the interests of participants and beneficiaries. The specification of welfare plan terms is generally left to market forces, although since ERISA's enactment group health plan terms have been constrained in several respects.[1] In contrast, the substance of a pension promise is intensively regulated along many important dimensions. Thus, ERISA monitors only the administration or *conduct* of most welfare plans, while pension plans are subject to both *conduct* and *content* regulation.

---

[1] Since ERISA's passage Congress has made inroads on the general principle of welfare plan laissez-faire by imposing several important content requirements on certain group health care plans. The Consolidated Omnibus Budget Reconciliation Act of 1985 (COBRA) added Part 6 to ERISA Title I, which provides that a group health plan of an employer that normally employs twenty or more employees must offer employees and beneficiaries who would lose health insurance coverage as a result of certain changes in employment or family status the opportunity to purchase continuation coverage at group rates for a period of eighteen or thirty-six months. ERISA §§ 601–609, 29 U.S.C. §§ 1161–1169 (2018); *see* I.R.C. §§ 4980B (2018) (excise tax imposed for failure to satisfy corresponding continuation coverage requirements). In 1996, Part 7 of ERISA Title I was enacted to increase health insurance portability by prohibiting group health plans from imposing certain health-status-based eligibility rules and strictly limiting preexisting condition coverage exclusions. ERISA §§ 701–703, 731–734, 29 U.S.C. §§ 1181–1183, 1191–1191c (2018); *see* I.R.C. §§ 4980D, 9801–9803, 9831–9834 (2018) (excise tax imposed for failure to satisfy corresponding portability requirements). The Patient Protection and Affordable Care Act, enacted in 2010, prohibits group health plans from imposing lifetime or annual dollar limits on essential health benefits, bars rescission of coverage except in cases of fraud or misrepresentation, requires coverage of certain preventative health services, and makes coverage available to the plan participant's children until age twenty-six, among other reforms. ERISA § 715, 29 U.S.C. § 1185d (2018); 29 C.F.R. §§ 2590.715-2711, -2712, -2713, -2714; *see* I.R.C. §§ 4980D, 9815 (2018) (corresponding excise tax). These health plan content controls are explored *infra* Chapter 11.

226   *Content Controls: Pension Plans*

ERISA's pension plan content controls constrain the terms of most deferred compensation programs in three broad areas. First, the accumulation of pension savings is influenced by rules governing eligibility for plan participation, the rate at which benefits accrue under defined benefit plans, and when benefits vest (Chapter 7). Second, the distribution of pension benefits can be made only to certain persons and at certain times (Chapter 8). Third, pension claims are converted from unsecured contract rights (that are implicitly contingent on the long-term financial health of the sponsor) into property rights by the requirement that defined benefit plans be funded and insured (Chapter 9). These pension plan content controls are generally applicable, but an exception to all of them is made for top-hat plans.[2]

The pattern of substantive pension regulation deserves special notice. To preserve a system of voluntary plan sponsorship, Congress trod lightly. Most matters were left unregulated, including the central design issues of a pension plan, namely, the extent of workforce coverage and the level of benefits. Where it chose to regulate, Congress restricted but did not eliminate freedom of contract. Instead of mandating particular plan features, it set minimum standards for certain key terms, leaving sponsors the flexibility to exceed the baseline.[3] Legislative intervention was not directed to ensuring a particular level of retirement income. Instead, reliability is the principle that animates ERISA's pension content controls. The employer may craft the program to cover as many or as few workers as desired, at any benefit level it chooses,[4] but once a pension promise is made, the statute backs it up by restricting plan terms that would undercut the commitment. Traditionally, those restrictions have been understood as paternalistic protection of the interests of plan participants and beneficiaries. But it isn't necessarily so. By limiting the variability of the more arcane plan terms, ERISA standardizes ancillary features of the pension contract. Standardization reduces information costs, and so may actually improve worker career and financial planning.[5]

---

[2] ERISA §§ 201(2), 301(a)(3), 401(a)(1), 4021(b)(6), 29 U.S.C. §§ 1051(2), 1081(a)(3), 1101(a) (1), 1321(b)(6) (2018). *See supra* Chapter 2D.

[3] *See supra* Chapter 1C.

[4] Tax law nondiscrimination standards, however, deny preferential tax treatment for deferred compensation if, in actual operation, either the membership of the plan or the contributions or benefits that it provides unduly favor highly compensated employees. I.R.C. §§ 401(a)(3), (a) (4), (a)(5), (*l*), 410(b), 414(q) (2018). Qualified defined benefit plans are also required to cover at least fifty employees or, if fewer, 40 percent of all employees (but never fewer than two employees, except in cases where the employer has only one employee). *Id.* § 401(a)(26). All employees of certain commonly controlled or functionally related businesses are taken into account in applying these tax-law nondiscrimination and minimum coverage rules. *Id.* § 414 (b), (c), (m), (n). These tax rules are examined in depth in Chapter 10B.

[5] *See supra* Chapter 1C.

7

Accumulation

Three sets of rules bear on an employee's accumulation of pension rights. ERISA imposes minimum standards governing (1) participation (also known as plan membership or coverage), (2) benefit accrual (the earning of benefits by the performance of services), and (3) vesting (the attainment of a nonforfeitable right to future benefits). A worker must be a plan member to earn pension rights, but that alone is not enough to ensure that benefits will ultimately be paid. Pension plans may (and commonly do) make the payment of earned benefits contingent upon the satisfaction of prescribed conditions, like working a specified minimum number of years for the employer, failing which the pension is forfeited. (That is, accrued benefits may be subject to defeasance by conditions subsequent.) Once all such conditions are satisfied, the pension is said to "vest," or become nonforfeitable. At that point, the participant is entitled to the *eventual* distribution of her accrued benefit – not immediately, but at the time and in the manner specified by the distribution rules of the plan and ERISA.[1] Accordingly, participation, accrual, and vesting are all necessary to establish a worker's right to pension benefits.

Imposing vesting standards was a principal means to achieving ERISA's central goal of increasing retirement income security. Previously, pre-retirement vesting was not generally required. A plan could lawfully hold a worker's pension hostage until the moment the worker reached retirement age, so that an employee who quit or was fired on the brink of retirement could lose pension savings accumulated over many years of faithful service. Finding that unconscionable, Congress determined to limit the duration of forfeiture conditions. ERISA provides that once a participant completes a reasonable period of service (today, seven years or less), the participant's pension rights become irrevocable. We shall see that ERISA's participation and benefit accrual rules are a byproduct of the central decision to limit forfeitures, in that the rules function in part to prevent evasion of the vesting standards.

[1] *See infra* Chapter 8.

A PARTICIPATION

Age and Service Conditions

Pension plan coverage, like sponsorship itself, is voluntary. The decision to offer a plan does not obligate the employer to cover all employees or any particular group of employees. ERISA's regulation of pension plan participation is limited to banning the use of certain age and service conditions on plan membership. In general, a plan cannot impose minimum age and service requirements that are more demanding than reaching age twenty-one and completing one year of service; alternatively, two years of service can be required, but only if participants are at all times fully vested.[2] ERISA also outlaws all maximum age conditions (that is, provisions excluding from membership workers who are older than a specified age).[3] Even when an employee who is older than twenty-one completes a year of service, she can still be excluded from participation on other grounds (such as pay rate, work situs, or job classification) because ERISA leaves all other eligibility criteria unregulated.[4]

A year of service, for purposes of the prohibited eligibility conditions, means a twelve-month period in which the employee has at least 1,000 hours of service, with the first such period beginning on the date of initial employment.[5] All years of service must be counted for purposes of determining eligibility to participate unless the employee incurs a "break in service," defined as a twelve-month period during which the employee has 500 or fewer hours of service.[6] A plan that uses the two-year, 100 percent vested entry rule may provide that an employee who has not yet satisfied the two-year service condition and who has a break in service loses credit for

---

[2] ERISA § 202(a)(1), 29 U.S.C. § 1052(a)(1) (2018); see I.R.C. § 410(a)(1) (2018). Tax-exempt educational institutions may impose a minimum age condition of twenty-six rather than twenty-one if participants are immediately fully vested, but this extended age condition cannot be combined with the two-year service condition. ERISA § 202(a)(1)(B)(ii), 29 U.S.C. § 1052 (a)(1)(B)(ii) (2018); see I.R.C. § 410(a)(1)(B)(ii) (2018).

[3] ERISA § 202(a)(2), 29 U.S.C. § 1052(a)(2) (2018); see I.R.C. § 410(a)(2) (2018).

[4] For example, the First Circuit found:

"Despite Plaintiffs' attempt to hitch their claim to ERISA's minimum participation standards limiting the use of age- or length-of-service-related conditions of participation, their true complaint remains that the GTE ERISA plans use arbitrary criteria to establish an employee's threshold eligibility for plan participation – a complaint that has nothing to do with ERISA's minimum participation standards. Indeed, Plaintiffs identify no statutory provision that prohibits the use of such arbitrary eligibility criteria." Edes v. Verizon Comms., Inc., 417 F.3d 133, 143 (1st Cir. 2005).

[5] ERISA § 202(a)(3), 29 U.S.C. § 1052(a)(3) (2018); see I.R.C. § 410(a)(3) (2018). An "hour of service" was left for regulatory definition. Service may be credited by counting actual hours of work and paid leave, where employment records are adequate to support the determination. Alternatively, hours of service may be credited using various hour equivalencies (based on working time, employment period, or earnings) or the elapsed-time method. 29 C.F.R. §§ 2530.200b-2, -3 (2022); Treas. Reg. § 1.410(a)-7 (1980).

[6] ERISA §§ 202(b)(1), 203(b)(3)(A), 29 U.S.C. §§ 1052(b)(1), 1053(b)(3)(A) (2018); see I.R.C. §§ 410(a)(5)(A) 411(a)(6)(A) (2018).

Accumulation 229

service before the break, thereby delaying participation until two years of service are completed *after* the break.[7] In addition, any plan may provide that an employee who incurs a break in service after becoming a participant loses credit for his pre-break service *until* completing a year of service after the break.[8] Under this rule, pre-break service is only temporarily disregarded; upon completing a year of post-break service, all pre-break service must again be taken into account, with the result that the employee is retroactively entitled to plan membership as of the start of the first year of service after the break. A third break-in-service rule permits a plan to permanently disregard all years of service before a break if an employee who is not vested (to any extent) incurs the greater of: (1) five consecutive one-year breaks in service; or (2) a number of consecutive one-year breaks in service that equals or exceeds the number of his pre-break years of service.[9]

The impact of the service-break rules is softened where absence from work is occasioned by the birth or adoption of a child. In that case, the period of the maternity or paternity leave is counted as hours of service, up to a maximum of 501 hours, but solely for purposes of avoiding a break in service, *not* for purposes of determining contributions or benefits earned under the plan.[10]

---

[7] ERISA § 202(b)(2), 29 U.S.C. § 1052(b)(2) (2018); *see* I.R.C. § 410(a)(5)(B) (2018).
[8] ERISA § 202(b)(3), 29 U.S.C. § 1052(b)(3) (2018); *see* I.R.C. § 410(a)(5)(C) (2018).
[9] ERISA § 202(b)(4), 29 U.S.C. § 1052(b)(4) (2018); *see* I.R.C. § 410(a)(5)(D) (2018). Consider an employee in a defined contribution plan that requires one year of service for participation and uses three-year cliff vesting. If after completing two years of service this worker (then an active participant having no nonforfeitable rights) incurs five consecutive one-year service breaks, following which she is rehired or resumes full-time employment, she could be required to complete another qualifying year before admission to participation, and that admission would not be retroactive because the two pre-break service years can be ignored entirely. This delayed entry rule may be applied only to employees who have not acquired any nonforfeitable right to an accrued benefit derived from employer contributions. Therefore under current vesting schedules it ordinarily applies only to employees with fewer than three years of service under a defined contribution plan, or fewer than five years of service under a defined benefit plan. *Compare* ERISA § 202(b)(4)(C), 29 U.S.C. § 1052(b)(4)(C) (2018) *with id.* § 203(a)(2), 29 U.S.C. § 1053(a)(2). *Accord* I.R.C. §§ 410(a)(5)(D)(iii), 411(a)(2) (2018).
  As originally enacted this break-in-service rule permitted a plan to permanently disregard all years of service before a break whenever a non-vested employee incurred a number of consecutive one-year breaks in service at least equal to the number of his pre-break years of service. To reduce its disparate impact on women, who frequently leave the labor force for a period of child-rearing, the Retirement Equity Act of 1984 tightened this rule by making it applicable only if the service break is at least five years long. As a result of subsequent tightening of ERISA's vesting schedules a participant with five years of service generally will be at least partially vested, making the rule inapplicable. Hence, the statutory language providing that more than five consecutive one-year service breaks could sometimes be necessary to trigger the rule has become irrelevant.
[10] ERISA § 202(b)(5), 29 U.S.C. § 1052(b)(5) (2018); *see* I.R.C. § 410(a)(5)(E) (2018). *Cf.* ERISA § 204(b)(4)(A), 29 U.S.C. § 1054(b)(4)(A) (2018) (parenthetical clause excludes maternity/paternity leave period for purposes of determining accrued benefits); *see* I.R.C. § 411(b)(4)(A) (2018) (same).

230 *Content Controls: Pension Plans*

ERISA does *not* demand immediate admission to the plan once all permissible eligibility requirements have been satisfied. Instead, participation must commence no later than the beginning of the next plan year or, if earlier, a date that is six months after satisfying the age and service requirements. This rule accords sponsors the administrative advantage of bringing all new members into the plan on fixed semiannual entry dates (namely, the first day of the plan year and the date that is six months later), while limiting the maximum waiting period to six months.[11]

All the prohibited age and service conditions rules (including the rules governing service credit, breaks in service, and time of entry) prescribe minimum standards. The plan sponsor is free to specify more liberal membership criteria by not imposing any age or service criteria, by imposing lower requirements, or by declining to utilize the break-in-service rules. Indeed, the minimum standard (age twenty-one with one year of service) is so exacting, and the recordkeeping necessary to implement service conditions so burdensome, that one might wonder if employers would be better off simply dropping service conditions on plan membership. Because three years of service can be required for vesting, benefits won't have to be paid to short-term employees even if they are allowed to participate, and the resulting forfeitures can be used to reduce future employer contributions.

Nevertheless, pension plans still overwhelmingly contain minimum age and service conditions, highly restricted though they are. There are several advantages in doing so. First, service conditions avoid the plan administration costs (record-keeping and accounting) that would be entailed in tracking, over a prolonged period, small accrued benefits earned by numerous short-term employees. Second, some benefit costs are saved for those employees who do stay long enough to vest because they will not have earned any deferred compensation for work performed in the year or two it took them to become participants. Third (and most important), employees excluded from participation by minimum age or service conditions do not have to be taken into account in applying the tax law's tests for discrimination in plan coverage, making it more likely that the plan will qualify for preferential tax treatment.[12]

---

[11] ERISA § 202(a)(4), 29 U.S.C. § 1052(a)(4) (2018); Treas. Reg. § 1.410(a)-4(b) (as amended in 1980); Rev. Rul. 80-360, 1980-2 C.B. 142; *see* I.R.C. § 410(a)(4) (2018). Observe, however, that an employee who has a vested benefit when he separates from service and who incurs a break in service is entitled to reenter the plan retroactively as of the date he returns to work, provided he completes a year of service after returning to work. An additional waiting period is *not* permissible. Treas. Reg. § 1.401(a)-4(b)(1) (as amended in 1980) (final sentence); *id.* -4(b) (2), Examples (3) and (4); Rev. Rul. 80-360, Plan 4, *supra*.

[12] I.R.C. § 410(b)(4)(A) (2018). Because pay rates typically rise as age and experience increase, a smaller proportion of employees who are young or recently hired will be highly compensated, compared to the workforce as a whole. If employees who are under age twenty-one or who have less than a year of service had to be taken into account in testing for coverage nondiscrimination, many plans that exclude such workers from membership would find that they are in jeopardy of disqualification. Therefore, as a practical matter, ERISA's permission to impose

Accumulation 231

ERISA's prohibited age and service condition rules are a compromise. They are based on the belief that "it is desirable to have as many employees as possible covered by private pension plans and to begin such coverage as early as possible, since an employee's ultimate pension benefits usually depend to a considerable extent on the number of his years of participation in the plan."[13] But that preference for early coverage was tempered by a concern for employer costs, especially the administrative burden of covering transient employees.[14] In attempting to induce early coverage of workers who would prefer additional cash compensation, ERISA's participation standards betray an element of a forced savings program.[15]

The ban on extended service conditions also functions to prevent evasion of the vesting rules. Vesting is tied to years of service; currently, a participant will have a nonforfeitable right to his entire accrued benefit after at most seven years of service. If minimum-service conditions on plan membership were not controlled, a sponsor wanting to avoid paying benefits to short-service workers could do so by simply holding them out of the plan for an extended period, rather than by admitting them but forfeiting their benefits in the event of early departure. Being fully vested under a plan that delays entry for fifteen years is little different from being a participant whose nominal accrued benefit remains forfeitable for fifteen years.

Expanding Coverage

ERISA's "minimum participation standards" are inaptly named. They do not grant any employee the right to plan participation. A worker who has satisfied permissible age and service conditions can be barred from admission for virtually any reason other than insufficient age or service, including factors such as job classification, work location, salaried or hourly pay status. Nor is a plan prohibited from using membership criteria that may be closely correlated with age or service. Moreover, a year of service is defined to allow the ongoing exclusion of long-term part-time employees, those working less than half-time year after year. For all of these reasons, the prohibited age and service conditions do not require or even strongly encourage widespread plan participation.

---

limited age and service conditions would be largely illusory without a corresponding concession in coverage nondiscrimination testing.

[13] H.R. Rep. No. 93-807, at 43–44 (1974), *reprinted in* 2 ERISA Legislative History, *supra* Chapter 1 note 55, at 3115, 3163–64; H.R. Rep. No. 93-779, at 42–43 (1974), *reprinted in* 2 ERISA Legislative History, *supra* Chapter 1 note 55, at 2584, 2631–32.

[14] H.R. Rep. No. 93-807, at 44 (1974), *reprinted in* 2 ERISA Legislative History, *supra* Chapter 1 note 55, at 3115, 3164; H.R. Rep. No. 93-779, at 43 (1974), *reprinted in* 2 ERISA Legislative History, *supra* Chapter 1 note 55, at 2584, 2632.

[15] Wiedenbeck, *supra* Chapter 1 note 56, at 574–75 (footnotes omitted). The anti-alienation requirement (discussed *infra* Chapter 8B) is the other principal forced savings component of ERISA.

Retirement plan participation among all workers in private industry stood at 52 percent in 2022 (62 percent for full-time workers, but only 20 percent for part-time workers).[16] The private industry participation rate has hovered around 50 percent (often just under) for many years. ERISA did not increase pension plan coverage. That is not surprising, because ERISA was about improving pension plan quality and reliability, not about increasing coverage.[17] In fact, Congress expected many employers to respond to the cost increases imposed by comprehensive pension reform by terminating their plans.[18]

The job of encouraging broad private retirement plan coverage was left to the qualified plan tax subsidy and particularly the nondiscrimination requirements. For reasons explored later, the tax subsidy hasn't materially increased overall private plan coverage.[19] Increasing coverage to enhance retirement readiness is among the most urgent pension policy questions of our time.[20] To date, attempts to move the needle have been limited and cautious. Measures to decrease barriers to coverage within the cost constraints imposed by a system of voluntary plan sponsorship have taken center stage.

High plan administration costs – costs which are largely independent of the number of covered workers – are often cited as an important deterrent to plan sponsorship by small employers. Low-census plans also typically pay higher asset management expenses, yielding lower net return on investments. Covering the workforces of numerous small employers under one plan might make offering retirement benefits economically feasible for small employers. Traditionally, workers of unrelated employers could be covered under a multiple employer plan (MEP) only if the companies were part of some bona fide group or association of employers (such as a trade association) sharing a common economic or representational interest unrelated to the provision of benefits.[21] In an effort to expand

---

[16] BUREAU OF LABOR STATISTICS, U.S. DEPARTMENT OF LABOR, NATIONAL COMPENSATION SURVEY: EMPLOYEE BENEFITS IN THE UNITED STATES, MARCH 2022, Private Industry Workers by Work and Bargaining Status, Table 1, at www.bls.gov/ebs/publica tions/september-2022-landing-page-employee-benefits-in-the-united-states-march-2022.htm.

[17] *See infra* Chapter 7 note 98 and accompanying text. *Accord* Remarks of Daniel Halperin, *in* Panel Discussion, *Some New Ideas and Some New Bottles: Tax and Minimum Standards, in* Symposium, *ERISA at 40: What Were They Thinking?*, 6 DREXEL L. REV. 385, 399 (2014) (observing that greater retirement plan coverage was not the focus of ERISA, instead, "The focus was saying, 'You can promise whatever you want, but if you promise it, you got to deliver it.'").

[18] Data on pension plan terminations in the wake of ERISA's enactment is summarized in Peter J. Wiedenbeck, *"Ninety-Five Percent of [Them] Will Not Be Missed": Recovering the Tax Shelter Limitation Aspect of ERISA*, 6 DREXEL L. REV. 515, 530–32 (2014).

[19] *See generally infra* Chapter 10B.

[20] Halperin, *supra* Chapter 7 note 17 ("I would say that the major issue today is coverage and the major issue has been coverage forever. And we haven't made a heck of a lot of progress.").

[21] ERISA requires that an employee benefit plan be "established or maintained by an employer or an employee organization," ERISA § 3(1), (2)(A), 29 U.S.C. § 1002(1), (2)(A) (2018), and the term employer is defined as any person acting directly as an employer or indirectly in the

Accumulation 233

coverage by exploiting economies of scale, the Labor Department in 2019 adopted a rule authorizing "association retirement plans," which are MEPs with a relaxed common interest requirement.[22] In late 2019 Congress went further, dispensing with the common interest requirement altogether by authorizing "pooled employer plans": defined contribution plans maintained by a "pooled plan provider," an independent business operating for profit.[23] At this writing it is too early to tell whether pooled employer plans will reduce costs and expand defined contribution plan coverage to many more small firm employees, but a preliminary empirical study of MEP cost and investment performance is not encouraging.[24]

In 2019 Congress also took an initial tentative step toward increasing pension participation by long-term part-time workers. An employee who has at least 500 hours of service in three consecutive twelve-month periods (beginning after 2020) cannot be excluded from 401(k) plan participation on the basis of insufficient service despite not having completed a year of service. And effective for plan years after 2024, only two consecutive twelve-month periods with 500 hours of service are required, and the rule is extended to 403(b) plans, a tax-favored retirement savings program that can be provided for employees of tax-exempt charitable organizations and public schools.[25] Part-time workers who satisfy this reduced service requirement must be permitted to direct a portion of their pay toward retirement savings under these elective contribution programs. They are *not* required to be taken into account for purposes of qualified plan nondiscrimination testing, however, nor is the employer required to make matching or non-elective contributions on their behalf,

---

interest of an employer in relation to a plan, including a group or association of employers so acting, *id.* § 3(5), 29 U.S.C. § 1002(5). *See generally* Natalya Shnitser, *Are Two Employers Better Than One? An Empirical Assessment of Multiple-Employer Retirement Plans*, 45 J. Corp. L. 743 (2020).

[22] Definition of "Employer" Under Section 3(5) of ERISA – Association Retirement Plans and Other Multiple-Employer Plans, 84 Fed. Reg. 37,508, to be codified at 29 C.F.R. § 2510.3-55.

[23] Setting Every Community Up for Retirement Enhancement Act of 2019, Pub. L. No. 116-94, Div. O, § 101 [hereinafter SECURE Act], adding ERISA § 3(2)(C) (exception to common interest requirement), (43) (definition of pooled employer plan), (44) (definition of pooled plan provider), 29 U.S.C.A. § 1002(2)(C), (43), (44) (West Supp. 2020) and I.R.C. § 413(e) (West Supp. 2020), *see* H.R. Rep. 116-63, Part 1, at 32–43 (2019). Legislation enacted in late 2022 extends this authorization to multiple employer 403(b) plans. SECURE 2.0 Act of 2022, Pub. L. No. 117-328, Div. T, § 106, 136 Stat. 4459, ____ (2023), adding I.R.C. § 403(b)(15) (West Supp. 2023) and amending ERISA § 3(43)(A), 29 U.S.C. § 1102(43)(A) (West Supp. 2023).

[24] *See* Shnitser, *supra* Chapter 7 note 21; *see also* Michael Doran, *The False Promise of Portman-Cardin Pension Reform*, 163 Tax Notes 1673 (2019) (situating 2019 pension legislation as latest iteration of a series of reforms that primarily benefited the financial services industry and high-income families); Michael Doran, *The Great American Retirement Fraud*, 30 Elder L.J. 265 (2022).

[25] ERISA § 202(c), 29 U.S.C. § 1052(c) (West Supp. 2023); I.R.C. § 401(k)(2)(D), (k)(15) (West Supp. 2023). SECURE Act § 112(b), 133 Stat., 2534, 3154, provides that periods before 2021 shall not be taken into account in service counting.

as it would for other participants.[26] Hence retirement savings for such persistent part-time workers can be financed exclusively by the workers' own voluntary reductions of take-home pay, even though other plan participants benefit from additional employer contributions to their accounts. As a result, the utilization of this 401(k) and 403(b) plan elective contribution option by part-time workers is projected to be low.[27]

Frustration with this stubbornly low workforce participation rate spurred the development of state-based initiatives to broaden retirement savings. Several states, including California, Oregon, Illinois, Connecticut, and Maryland, require employers that do not offer retirement plans to make specified automatic payroll deductions, with the funds transferred into individual retirement accounts for their employees.[28] Such state-mandated auto-IRA programs have been challenged as incompatible with ERISA, but proponents assert that state-run programs escape preemption because they do not constitute an "employee benefit plan" within the meaning of the statute.[29] Such state auto-IRA programs require no employer contributions and allow workers to opt out; their efficacy in inducing retirement savings is thus far unclear.[30]

---

[26] I.R.C. §§ 401(k)(15)(B), 403(b)(12)(D), 416(g)(4)(H) (West Supp. 2023). These exceptions reduce the employer's cost of allowing participation by long-term part-time workers, limiting the burden of coverage to the incremental costs of additional recordkeeping (e.g., service tracking) and plan administration expenses.

[27] See Doran, *The False Promise of Portman-Cardin Pension Reform, supra* Chapter 7 note 24, at 1680; Kathryn L. Moore, *Closing the Retirement Savings Gap: Are State Automatic Enrollment IRAs the Answer?*, 24 GEO. MASON L. REV. 35 (2016).

[28] For an overview of state-sponsored auto-IRA programs, see AARP, State Facilitated Retirement Savings Interactive Map, at www.aarp.org/ppi/state-retirement-plans/savings-plans/; Kathryn L. Moore, *State Automatic Enrollment IRAs after the Trump Election: Are They Preempted by ERISA?*, 27 ELDER L.J. 51, 54–60 (2019); Kathryn L. Moore, *A Closer Look at the IRAs in State Automatic Enrollment IRA Programs*, 23 CONN. INS. L.J. 217 (2016); *Moore, supra* Chapter 7 note 27; JOHN SCOTT, HOW STATES ARE WORKING TO ADDRESS THE RETIREMENT SAVINGS CHALLENGE (2016), www.pewtrusts.org/en/research-and-analysis/reports/2016/06/how-states-are-working-to-address-the-retirement-savings-challenge; Richard H. Thaler, *State I.R.A. Plans Are Ready, If Congress Doesn't Interfere*, N.Y. TIMES (Mar. 3, 2017).

[29] Howard Jarvis Taxpayers Ass'n v. Cal. Secure Choice Ret. Savings Program, 443 F. Supp.3d 1152 (E.D. Cal. 2020) (holding CalSavers plan not preempted), *aff'd*, 997 F.3d 848 (9th Cir. 2021), *cert. denied*, 142 SCt. 1204 (2022); *see* ERISA §§ 3(1)-(3), 514(a), 29 U.S.C. §§ 1002(1)-(3), 1144(a) (2018); 29 C.F.R. § 2510.3-2(d) (2022) (voluntary IRA program not a pension plan).

In late 2016 the Labor Department adopted a rule to facilitate state auto-IRA programs for private-sector workers. Savings Arrangements Established by States for Non-Governmental Employees, 81 Fed. Reg. 59,464 (Aug. 30, 2016) (to be codified at 29 C.F.R. § 2510). Following the 2016 election the rule was quickly disapproved by Congress under the Congressional Review Act. H.J. Res. 66, Pub. L. No. 115-35, 131 Stat. 848 (2017). *See generally* Moore, *State Automatic Enrollment IRAs after the Trump Election: Are They Preempted by ERISA?, supra* Chapter 7 note 28.

[30] See John Chambers et al., *Do State-Sponsored Retirement Plans Boost Retirement Saving?*, 112 AM. ECON. ASS'N PAPERS & PROC. 142 (2022) (reporting initial participation rates and

Several initiatives to encourage greater pension plan participation were enacted by the SECURE 2.0 Act of 2022.[31] Foremost among these is a general requirement that newly established plans allowing elective contributions (here meaning 401(k) plans and 403(b) plans) include an automatic enrollment feature.[32] By default the plan must provide automatic salary reduction contributions of at least 3 percent of compensation and not more than 10 percent, and call for automatic escalation of the contribution rate by one percentage point following each completed year of participation, up to a maximum of 10 percent but not more than 15 percent.[33] Employees must be permitted to elect out (and to promptly withdraw the initial contribution) and to elect a different contribution rate, including overriding the automatic escalation of contribution rates. If they fail to make an affirmative choice their contributions must be invested according to the Labor Department rules on qualified default investment alternatives, under which contributions are most commonly invested in an age-appropriate target date fund.[34]

In addition to inertia, Congress sought to alleviate two other important inhibitors of voluntary participation in elective contribution plans. First, some employees who are eligible to contribute to a 401(k) plan or similar elective contribution program cannot afford to defer part of their pay because it is needed to meet their student loan obligations. To "assist employees who may not be able to save for retirement because they are overwhelmed with student debt, and thus are missing out on available matching contributions under retirement plans,"[35] starting in 2024 plans may treat student loan payments as elective deferrals that qualify the employee to receive employer matching contributions.[36] Such treatment is not mandated, but could be attractive to firms as a device to recruit recent graduates.

---

account balances under OregonSaves). As explained in Chapter 10A, low income individuals obtain little if any financial benefit from income tax deferral through an IRA, and pressing current consumption needs often preclude saving.

[31] Pub. L. No. 117-328, Div. T, 136 Stat. 4459, ____ (2023),

[32] I.R.C. §§ 414(w), 414A (2018 & West Supp. 2023). The requirement is an additional condition on favorable tax treatment of the deferred compensation, rather than an ERISA labor law mandate, but virtually all pension plans other than top hat plans and excess benefit plans are designed to qualify for favorable tax treatment. Exceptions are provided for governmental and church plans, for certain new businesses, and for businesses that normally employ ten or fewer employees. *Id.* § 414A(c). The auto-enrollment requirement is effective for plan years beginning after 2024. SECURE 2.0 Act of 2022, Pub. L. No. 117-328, Div. T, § 102(c), 136 Stat. 4459, ____ (2023).

[33] I.R.C. § 414A(b)(3) (West Supp. 2023).

[34] *Id.* § 414A(b)(1), (2), (4); 29 C.F.R. § 2550.404c-5 (2022).

[35] H.R. Rep. No. 117-283, at 78 (2022).

[36] I.R.C. §§ 401(m)(4)(A)(iii), (m)(4)(D), (m)(13), 403(b)(12)(A), 408(p)(2)(F), 457(b) (West Supp. 2023). Equal treatment rules apply: matching of student loan payments must be available to all employees eligible to receive matching contributions on account of elective deferrals; the match rate must be the same for elective deferrals and student loan payments; and matching contributions based on student loan payments must vest in the same manner as those based on elective deferrals. *Id.* § 401(m)(13).

236 *Content Controls: Pension Plans*

Second, low-income employees who are eligible to defer part of their pay may be deterred by the inaccessibility of retirement savings.[37] The prospect of pressing immediate financial needs – such as living expenses during a period of layoff, or unexpected health care or automobile repair costs – may cause low-income workers to prioritize readily accessible precautionary saving. To lower this barrier, Congress authorized pension-linked emergency savings accounts.[38] Employers may amend individual account plans to incorporate short-term savings accounts for nonhighly compensated employees, and can automatically opt employees into these accounts (at no more than 3 percent of their salary) with participant contributions capped at a maximum of $2,500.[39] If the pension plan to which the emergency saving account is linked calls for employer matching contributions, then participant contributions to the emergency saving account must be matched at the regular match rate by employer contributions to the pension plan.[40] Participant contributions in excess of the $2,500 limit can be directed into a designated Roth account under the pension plan.[41] No minimum balance may be imposed on the emergency savings account and employees must be permitted to withdraw from the account for personal or family emergencies at least once per month (four times per year without incurring withdrawal fees).[42] The account is accorded favorable Roth-style tax treatment (i.e., contributions nondeductible but earnings exempt from tax).[43] Upon termination of employment the emergency savings account balance can be transferred into the participant's designated Roth account under the pension plan if the employee so elects; otherwise balance must be distributed to employee.[44]

---

[37] See the discussion of early distributions and plan loans *infra* Chapter 10C.

[38] See SECURE 2.0 Act of 2022, Pub. L. No. 117-328, Div. T, § 127, 136 Stat. 4459, ____ (2023), which adds ERISA § 3(45) defining pension-linked emergency saving account, establishes operating rules (including notice and disclosure requirements) in new part 8 to subtitle B of ERISA title I and new I.R.C. § 402A(e). The amendments apply to plan years beginning after 2023. SECURE 2.0 Act of 2022, § 127(g). Extensive amendments were required because: (1) a short-term savings program would not otherwise satisfy the definition of either a pension or a welfare plan, see ERISA §§ 3(1)–(3), 4(a), 29 U.S.C. §§ 1002(1)–(3), 1003(a) (2018); and (2) short-term savings would otherwise receive unfavorable tax treatment under the Code, see I.R.C. § 72(t)(2)(J) (West Supp. 2023).

[39] ERISA § 801(b)(1)(B), (d)(1)(A)(i), (d)(2)(A), 29 U.S.C.A. § 1193(b)(1)(B), (d)(1)(A)(i), (d)(2)(A) (West Supp. 2023); I.R.C. § 402A(e)(2)(A)(ii), (e)(3)(A)(i), (e)(4)(A) (West Supp. 2023).

[40] ERISA § 801(e)(4)(A), 29 U.S.C.A. § 1193(e)(4)(A) (West Supp. 2023); I.R.C. § 402A(e)(6)(A) (West Supp. 2023).

[41] ERISA § 801(d)(1)(B)(i), 29 U.S.C.A. § 1193(d)(1)(B)(i) (West Supp. 2023); I.R.C. § 402A(e) (3)(B)(i) (West Supp. 2023).

[42] ERISA § 801(c)(1), 29 U.S.C.A. § 1193(c)(1) (West Supp. 2023); I.R.C. § 402A(e)(7)(A) (West Supp. 2023).

[43] I.R.C. § 402A(e)(1)(A)(i), (e)(7)(B) (West Supp. 2023). *See generally infra* Chapter 10A.

[44] ERISA § 801(e), 29 U.S.C.A. § 1193(e) (West Supp. 2023); I.R.C. § 402A(e)(8)(A) (West Supp. 2023).

B BENEFIT ACCRUAL

Pension plan participation is significant primarily because it brings with it the opportunity to earn (or "accrue") benefits under the plan.[45] Participation is a necessary condition for accruing pension benefits, and most participants in active service accrue increased benefits based on that service. Importantly, however, participant status alone is not sufficient to ensure current benefit accrual. In addition to participation, plans may, and commonly do, condition benefit increases on some sort of current-year service requirement. A defined benefit plan is not required to take a participant's service into account for purposes of determining accrued benefits if the employee has less than 1,000 hours of service during the accrual computation period (a calendar year, plan year, or other consecutive twelve-month period designated by the plan).[46] An employee who has at least 1000 hours of service during the accrual computation period must receive some credit for benefit accrual purposes, but if the employee's service is less than that required by the plan to qualify as a full year of participation, then the plan may grant only a fractional year of participation (the fraction being at least equal to the ratio of the employee's service to that required for full credit).[47] A defined contribution plan may go even further and provide that a participant whose employment terminates before the last day of the plan year will not share in the allocation of employer contributions or forfeitures for the year, even if she has more than 1,000 hours of service.[48]

A participant's accrued benefit is the total amount of deferred compensation that has been earned to date. Under a defined contribution plan, the accrued benefit at any time is simply the current balance in the participant's individual account and therefore reflects contributions and forfeitures allocated to the account as well as an appropriate share of plan income, expenses, gains, and losses.[49] Under a defined benefit plan, the accrued benefit must be specified by the plan and is expressed in the form of an annual benefit (annuity payment) commencing at normal retirement age.[50] Normal retirement age is defined as either the time a participant attains the

---

[45] *See* 29 C.F.R. § 2530.204-1(b)(1) (2022) (service before an employee first becomes a participant need not be taken into account in determining accrued benefits under a defined benefit plan).

[46] ERISA § 204(b)(4)(C), 29 U.S.C. § 1054(b)(4)(C) (2018); 29 C.F.R. § 2530.204-2(c)(1), -1(b)(1) (2022); *see* I.R.C. § 411(b)(4)(C) (2018).

[47] ERISA § 204(b)(4)(B), 29 U.S.C. § 1054(b)(4)(D) (2018); 29 C.F.R. §§ 2530.204-2(c)(1), 2530.200b-1(a) (2022); *see* I.R.C. § 411(b)(4)(B) (2018).

[48] 29 C.F.R. § 2530.200b-1(b) (2022) (final four sentences). *But cf.* Treas. Reg. § 1.410(b)-6(f) (as amended in 2006) (outgoing employee who fails to accrue a benefit because of such a last-day requirement must be taken into account in coverage nondiscrimination testing if she has more than 500 hours of service).

[49] ERISA § 3(23), (34), 29 U.S.C. § 1002(23), (34) (2018); *see* I.R.C. §§ 411(a)(7)(A)(ii), 414(i) (2018).

[50] ERISA § 3(23), (24), (35), 29 U.S.C. § 1002(23), (24), (35) (2018); *see* I.R.C. §§ 411(a)(7)(A)(i), (a)(8), 414(j) (2018). An exception is made for cash balance plans (a type of defined benefit

Content Controls: Pension Plans

normal retirement age specified by the plan or, if earlier, the later of attaining age sixty-five or the fifth anniversary of commencing plan participation.[51] This deference to the plan is circumscribed by a regulation providing that the normal retirement age specified by the plan must be "an age that is not earlier than the earliest age that is reasonably representative of the typical retirement age for the industry in which the covered workforce is employed."[52] A normal retirement age under the plan of at least age sixty-two (or age fifty in the case of a plan substantially all of the participants in which are qualified public safety employees such as police, firefighters, and emergency medical services personnel) is automatically acceptable, but earlier ages require factual support.[53]

Consistent with the policy of maintaining a voluntary pension system, ERISA does not specify the amount of contributions or benefits to be provided under a plan. But while the employer is free to set the level of pension contributions or benefits, ERISA regulates the *rate* at which contributions or benefits are earned from year to year. Limitations on the rate of accrual serve two purposes: preventing age discrimination and preventing evasion of the vesting requirements by backloading benefits under a defined benefit plan.

Age Discrimination

Congress amended ERISA, the Age Discrimination in Employment Act (ADEA), and the qualified plan provisions of the tax Code in 1986 to outlaw age discrimination in the accrual of pension benefits. In the case of a defined contribution plan, allocations of contributions or forfeitures to an employee's account may not be cut

---

plan that mimics a money purchase pension plan) and certain other hybrid defined benefit plans under which the accrued benefit may be calculated as the accumulated balance of a hypothetical account maintained for the participant. ERISA §§ 203(f), 204(c)(3), 29 U.S.C. §§ 1053(f), 1054(c)(3) (2018); see I.R.C. § 411(a)(13), (c)(3) (2018). *See infra* Chapter 7 note 63 (describing circuit split over whether cash balance plans could calculate benefits in this manner before the 2006 enactment of ERISA § 203(f)).

[51] ERISA § 3(24), 29 U.S.C. § 1002(24) (2018); see I.R.C. § 411(a)(8) (2018).

[52] Treas. Reg. § 1.401(a)-1(b)(2)(i) (as amended in 2007); *see generally* Distributions from a Pension Plan upon Attainment of Normal Retirement Age, 72 Fed. Reg. 28604 (May 22, 2007) (explanatory preamble). The requirement that the plan's definition of normal retirement age must specify an "age" was relaxed by 2014 statutory amendments that allow certain existing plans to continue to apply a partially service-based definition to workers who participated in the plan on or before January 1, 2017. That grandfather rule is available only to plans that defined normal retirement age as the earlier of a permitted age or the completion of at least thirty years of service. ERISA § 204(k), 29 U.S.C. § 1054(k) (2018); I.R.C. § 411(f) (2018).

[53] Treas. Reg. § 1.401(a)-1(b)(2)(ii)-(v) (as amended in 2007); I.R.C. § 72(t)(10)(B) (2018). The IRS has proposed adding more safe harbors for governmental plans that would allow such plans to use age-plus-service definitions of normal retirement age. For example, age sixty plus five years of service, age fifty-five with ten years of service, or combined years of age and service of eighty or more, would be acceptable. The proposed rule would also expand safe harbors for qualified public safety employees. Applicability of Normal Retirement Age Regulations to Governmental Pension Plans, 81 Fed. Reg. 4599 (Jan. 27, 2016).

Accumulation

off, nor may the rate of allocation be reduced, on account of the attainment of any age.[54] Similarly, a defined benefit plan cannot cease benefit accrual or reduce the rate of accrual based on the employee's age.[55] Benefit accrual can be stopped on grounds that are not age-based, such as an overall limitation on the amount of accrued benefits or a limitation on the number of years of service or years of participation that the plan takes into account in determining accrued benefits.[56] But while service-based limitations on *additional* accrual are permissible, a defined benefit plan cannot reduce previously accrued benefits on account of increasing service.[57]

There has been a trend since the 1990s of large employers substituting cash balance plans for their traditional defined benefit pension plans. A cash balance plan is a defined benefit plan that mimics a defined contribution plan – specifically, a money purchase pension plan. Active plan participants earn annual pay credits (for example, 5 percent of compensation) and interest credits according to a specified rate or index (for example, prime plus 1 percent); at retirement, each participant is entitled to a benefit defined as the cumulative total of her prior pay and interest credits.[58] Younger workers have more time before retirement during which they accrue interest credits under a cash balance plan, while the traditional defined benefit plans that the new cash balance plans replaced typically favored older workers with a higher rate of benefit accrual.[59] This difference triggered a spate of

---

[54] ERISA § 204(b)(2), 29 U.S.C. § 1054(b)(2) (2018); ADEA § 4(i)(1), 29 U.S.C. § 623(i)(1) (2018); *see* I.R.C. § 411(b)(2) (2018).

[55] ERISA § 204(b)(1)(H), (b)(5), 29 U.S.C. § 1054(b)(1)(H) (2018); ADEA § 4(i)(1), (i)(10), 29 U.S.C. § 623(i)(1), (i)(10) (2018); *see* I.R.C. § 411(b)(1)(H), (b)(5) (2018); Treas. Reg. § 1.411 (b)(5)-1 (as amended 2015).

[56] ERISA § 204(b)(1)(H)(ii), 29 U.S.C. § 1054(b)(1)(H)(ii) (2018); *see* I.R.C. § 411(b)(1)(H)(ii) (2018). Despite the absence of a corresponding affirmative authorization in ERISA or the Code, the same principle apparently applies to defined contribution plans. That is, contributions may be cut off because the participant's account balance exceeds a specified level or because of a limitation on the number of years for which contributions will be made (i.e., where the plan specifies a maximum number years of active participation). ADEA § 4(i)(2), (9), 29 U.S.C. § 623(i)(2), (9) (2018).

[57] ERISA § 204(b)(1)(G), 29 U.S.C. § 1054(b)(1)(G) (2018); *see* I.R.C. § 411(b)(1)(G) (2018).

[58] Cash balance plan benefits are defined without reference to actual trust fund investment results, so that benefits are not based solely on contributions to an individual account, with adjustment for income, gain, losses, and expenses allocated to that account. Because participants are insulated from the risks and rewards of investment performance, technically the arrangement is not an individual account (i.e., defined contribution) plan. Instead, cash balance plans are defined benefit plans. ERISA § 3(34), (35), 29 U.S.C. § 1002(34), (35) (2018); *see* I.R.C. § 414(i), (j) (2018). As such, they are subject to ERISA's minimum standards on benefit accrual and actuarial funding, as well as the PBGC insurance program and restrictions on termination.

[59] The benefit formula under a traditional defined benefit plan is typically tied to final average or highest average compensation. For example, under a unit credit plan, the annuity at normal retirement age might be specified as 1.5 percent of final average compensation multiplied by the participant's years of service. Because compensation levels in most occupations systematically increase with increasing job tenure, under such a formula a larger proportion of the final

ERISA age discrimination litigation. The Seventh Circuit, in an opinion by Judge Easterbrook, ruled that the age discrimination rule for defined benefit plans, including the cash balance plan at issue, has the same meaning as the rule for defined contribution plans, and that differences attributable to the time value of money are not age discrimination. "[R]emoving a feature that gave extra benefits to the old does not discriminate against them. Replacing a plan that discriminates against the young with one that is age-neutral does not discriminate against the old."[60] Although district courts had differed over whether cash balance plans violate ERISA's age discrimination ban,[61] other Courts of Appeal soon followed the Seventh Circuit's analysis in *Cooper*.[62] Prospectively, the Pension Protection Act of 2006 amended ERISA to ensure that new cash balance plans providing age-neutral pay and interest credits are not discriminatory and to grant a safe harbor for conversions of traditional defined benefit plans into cash balance plans.[63]

---

retirement benefit is earned in the later years of service, as the compensation factor increases each year. This "backloading" of the rate at which a defined benefit pension is earned is permissible under ERISA's minimum standards on benefit accrual (discussed immediately below), because in testing for excessive backloading, those standards ignore future compensation increases.

[60] Cooper v. IBM Pers. Pension Plan, 457 F.3d 636, 642 (7th Cir. 2006). In reaching its decision, the court concluded that the term "benefit accrual," used in the defined benefit plan age discrimination rule, ERISA § 204(b)(1)(H)(i), refers to the annual addition to pension rights, and so has a meaning different from "accrued benefit," as defined in ERISA § 3(23), which refers to the participant's accumulated pension entitlement. *Cooper*, 457 F.3d at 641.

[61] *Compare* Hirt v. Equitable Ret. Plan for Emps., Managers and Agents, 441 F. Supp. 2d 516 (S.D.N.Y. 2006) (no age discrimination), *and* Laurent v. PriceWaterhouseCoopers LLP, 448 F. Supp. 2d 537, 553–54 (S.D.N.Y. 2006) (same), *and* Drutis v. Quebecor World (USA) Inc., 459 F. Supp. 2d 580 (E.D. Ky. 2006) (same), *with* Richards v. FleetBoston Fin. Corp., 427 F. Supp. 2d 150 (D. Conn. 2006) (refusing to dismiss age discrimination claims), *and In re* J.P. Morgan Chase Cash Balance Litig., 460 F. Supp. 2d 479 (S.D.N.Y. 2006) (same), *and In re* Citigroup Pension Plan ERISA Litig., 470 F. Supp. 2d 323 (S.D.N.Y. 2006) (same).

[62] Register v. PNC Fin. Servs. Group, Inc., 477 F.3d 56, 68–69 (3d Cir. 2007); Drutis v. Rand McNally & Co., 499 F.3d 608 (6th Cir. 2007); Hirt v. Equitable Ret. Plan for Emps., Managers and Agents, 533 F.3d 102 (2d Cir. 2008); Hurlic v. Southern California Gas Co., 539 F.3d 1024 (9th Cir. 2008); Tomlinson v. El Paso Corp., 653 F.3d 1281, 1288 (10th Cir. 2011).

[63] ERISA § 204(b)(5), 29 U.S.C. § 1054(b)(5) (2018); ADEA § 4(i)(10), 29 U.S.C. § 623(i)(10) (2018); *see* I.R.C. § 411(b)(5) (2018); Treas. Reg. § 1.411(b)(5)-1 (as amended 2015). The rules are generally effective for periods beginning after June 29, 2005, *id.* § 1.411(b)(5)-1(f)(1), but the statute provides that the amendments are not to be construed to create an inference as to the meaning of the age discrimination rules as in effect before that date. Pension Protection Act of 2006, Pub. L. No. 109-280, § 706(d), (e)(1), 120 Stat. 780, 991 (2006). *See generally* Staff of the Joint Comm. on Taxation, 109th Cong., JCX-38-06, Technical Explanation of H.R. 4, The "Pension Protection Act of 2006," As Passed by the House on July 28, 2006, And As Considered by the Senate on August 3, 2006, at 150–58 (explaining special rules for cash balance plans).

A lingering unresolved question is whether a cash balance plan was permitted, prior to 2006, to define normal retirement age as five years of service regardless of age. Under such a definition the plan would pay a participant who separated from service and elected an immediate single sum distribution the current balance of thier hypothetical account. This

Voluntary early retirement incentives remain lawful, and Congress provided a safe harbor for subsidized early retirement benefits and Social Security bridge payments under defined benefit plans.[64] Therefore, an employer may use increased benefits to induce early retirement (the carrot), but an age-based cutback in the ability to earn additional retirement income (the stick) is not an acceptable tool of personnel management. These rules presumably increase total labor costs for older workers; they are an instance of ERISA's incorporation of covert distributive norms.[65]

Backloaded Accrual under Defined Benefit Plans

The age discrimination rules prevent *decreases* in the rate of pension accrual as a worker gets older. For defined benefit plans, ERISA also bars excessive *increases* in the rate that benefits are earned over the course of a worker's career. Functionally, patrolling increases in the rate of benefit accrual backstops the vesting rules. Vesting requires that a participant's right to deferred compensation become irrevocable once she completes a reasonable period of service, often five years. Vesting applies to a

definition avoided the so-called whipsaw calculation, under which a departing participant's single sum distribution was determined by compounding the hypothetical account balance on separation from service by the plan's promised interest credits to age sixty-five (for example) and discounting the result to present value using a prescribed (and generally lower) interest rate. The Seventh Circuit found that such a service-based definition of normal retirement age was acceptable, while the Second Circuit concluded that it violated ERISA. *Compare* Fry v. Exelon Corp. Cash Balance Pension Plan, 571 F.3d 644 (7th Cir. 2009) (per Easterbrook, J.) *with* Laurent v. PricewaterhouseCoopers LLP, 794 F.3d 272, 283–85 (2d Cir. 2015), *appeal following remand*, 945 F.3d 739 (2019) (authorizing reformation of plan terms to comply with ERISA). *See* STAFF OF THE JOINT COMM. ON TAXATION, 109TH CONG., *supra*, at 152–54, 156–57 (explaining whipsaw calculation of single sum distributions under cash balance plans, that in the future it will not be required to compute the present value of accrued benefits, but stipulating that no inference is intended concerning whether whipsaw calculation of pre-2006 single sum distributions is mandatory).

[64] ADEA § 4(f)(2)(B)(ii), (l)(1)(A)(ii), 29 U.S.C. § 623(f)(2)(B)(ii), (l)(1)(A)(ii) (2018); ERISA § 204(b)(1)(G), (b)(1)(H)(v), 29 U.S.C. § 1054(b)(1)(G), (b)(1)(H)(v) (2018); *see* I.R.C. § 411(b) (1)(G), (b)(1)(H)(iv) (2018). Subsidized early retirement occurs where benefit payments commence before the normal retirement age (NRA) specified in the plan (hence, early retirement) and the amount of benefits is not reduced to the level (i.e., actuarial equivalence to the pension payable at NRA) that would fully offset the longer payment period (the subsidy). Social Security bridge payments are additional pension benefits paid temporarily to early retirees to substitute for Social Security benefits until the retirees are old enough to receive either reduced or unreduced old-age benefits. (The earliest that individuals may claim reduced Social Security old-age benefits is age sixty-two; unreduced benefits are payable at full retirement age, which is increasing gradually from sixty-five, for persons born in 1937 or earlier, to sixty-seven, for those born in 1960 or later.) The Older Workers Benefit Protection Act of 1990 amended the cited ADEA provisions to counteract a restrictive interpretation announced by the Supreme Court in Public Employees Retirement System v. Betts, 492 U.S. 158 (1989).

[65] The termination insurance program of ERISA Title IV is also rife with distributional implications. *See infra* Chapter 9B.

242 *Content Controls: Pension Plans*

participant's accrued benefit, which is the total pension accumulation *earned to date*. Left unregulated, a defined benefit plan could defeat the vesting rules by defining a participant's accrued benefit to require prolonged service before significant pension obligations arise. For instance, a plan might promise (and the employer might tout) a generous retirement annuity but stipulate in fine print that the promised benefit is earned at the rate of one dollar per year for each of the first twenty-nine years of service, with the balance earned in the thirtieth year of service. Such delay or "backloading" of benefit accrual, if allowed, would cause a long-term employee who separates from service prior to normal retirement age (NRA) to have a fully vested right to a trivial amount of benefits. The minimum standards on benefit accrual do not allow this end run around the vesting rules.

The anti-backloading rules apply only to defined benefit plans; age-based or service-based increases in contributions under defined contribution plans are permissible. (The policy implications of this distinction will be explored shortly.) Backloading has no impact on participants whose employment continues until the plan's NRA, hence the concern of the accrual rules is with the benefit entitlement of participants who separate from service before that time. ERISA does not require that a participant's accrued benefit at any time be given by applying the plan's formula for the normal retirement benefit to the participant's years of participation at the time in question. Instead, ERISA allows the accrued benefit of a participant who separates from service before retirement age to be defined by the terms of the plan, subject only to the anti-backloading rules. The rules prohibit substantial increases in the rate at which the promised retirement benefit is earned over a member's years of participation.

To provide flexibility, a plan need only satisfy one of three alternative anti-backloading tests. The tests establish a floor on the portion of the normal retirement benefit that must be earned with each year of plan participation. That floor (like so many of ERISA's pension content controls) sets a *minimum* standard: any amount of frontloading is permissible.[66]

ERISA's alternative accrual rate standards are known as the 3 percent rule, the $133^{1/3}$ percent rule, and the fractional rule. Under the 3 percent rule, a participant's accrued benefit on separation from service must be no less than the product of (1) the number of years of plan participation (up to a maximum of $33^{1/3}$), and (2) 3 percent of the normal retirement benefit to which the participant would have been entitled if participation had begun at the plan's earliest possible entry date and continued to the earlier of age sixty-five or the plan's NRA.[67] An important feature of

---

[66] Where benefits are frontloaded, the rate of accrual eventually decreases. The decrease will not violate the age discrimination rules if it is based on increasing years of service rather than age.

[67] ERISA § 204(b)(1)(A), 29 U.S.C. § 1054(b)(1)(A) (2018); *see* I.R.C. § 411(b)(1)(A) (2018). If plan benefits depend on compensation, the compensation taken into account under the 3 percent rule is the highest average computation over a period of at most ten consecutive years (even if the promised retirement benefit is a function of compensation over some longer

Accumulation

the 3 percent rule is that all plan participants accrue benefits (expressed as a percentage of compensation) at a uniform annual rate, regardless of when their membership began.

The $133\frac{1}{3}$ percent rule is satisfied if no participant (actual or hypothetical) can experience a greater than one-third increase in the annual rate of benefit accrual between a given year of plan participation and any later year.[68] That is, the rate of accrual for any future year of participation cannot exceed $133\frac{1}{3}$ percent of the rate for any prior year. This approach permits some upward variation in accrual rates over a particular worker's career, and so sanctions a modest amount of backloading.

The fractional rule requires that the accrued benefit of a participant who separates from service before normal retirement age must be at least equal to the product of (1) the normal retirement benefit to which the participant would be entitled under the terms of the plan had he continued to work for the employer until NRA, assuming that such employment would not change the amount of compensation taken into account under the plan's benefit formula, and (2) the ratio of the departing employee's actual number of years of plan participation on separation from service to the total number of years he would have participated in the plan had he continued working to NRA.[69]

Carollo v. Cement & Concrete Workers District Council Pension Plan[70] illustrates the impact of the benefit accrual rules. The plan in *Carollo* provided for pension accrual at the rate of 2 percent of career average compensation for the first twenty-four years of service, but participants who worked for twenty-five years without an extended break in service had their pension benefits recalculated for all previous years of service at 2 percent of final average compensation. For each year of service beyond twenty-five, however, the benefit accrued at the rate of 1.66 percent of final average compensation. The defendant argued that the plan complied with the anti-backloading rules because the rate of accrual actually *decreased* with increasing service. Taking its cue from a Treasury Regulation, the court ruled that a plan may not circumvent the prohibition on benefit accrual rate increases by changing the base used in the calculation.[71] The retroactive switch from career average to final average compensation caused an immediate large jump in total accrued benefits in the twenty-fifth year of service that exceeded the limited backloading permitted by

---

period, such as career average compensation). Treas. Reg. § 1.411(b)-1(b)(1)(ii)(A) (as amended in 2014).

[68] ERISA § 204(b)(1)(B), 29 U.S.C. § 1054(b)(1)(B) (2018); *see* I.R.C. § 411(b)(1)(B) (2018).

[69] ERISA § 204(b)(1)(C), 29 U.S.C. § 1054(b)(1)(C) (2018); *see* I.R.C. § 411(b)(1)(C) (2018). If plan benefits are based on average compensation, no more than the last ten consecutive years may be taken into account when determining the projected normal retirement benefit under the fractional accrual rule. Treas. Reg. § 1.411(b)-1(b)(3)(ii)(A), -1(b)(3)(iii), Example (2) (as amended in 2014).

[70] 964 F. Supp. 677 (E.D.N.Y. 1997).

[71] *Id.* at 681–83. Treas. Reg. § 1.411(b)-1(b)(2)(ii)(F) (as amended in 2014).

244   *Content Controls: Pension Plans*

the $133^{\frac{1}{3}}$ percent rule. Therefore, the plan failed to satisfy ERISA's benefit accrual minimum standards.[72]

The anti-backloading rules work a compromise between protecting defined benefit plan participants from forfeitures and preserving a substantial range of employer autonomy in plan design. That design flexibility is achieved by allowing the plan to set the year-by-year accumulation of retirement benefits (via its definition of accrued benefit), subject to three alternative minimum standards that prevent excessive delay in earning the promised pension. The anti-backloading rules demand that each participant obtain the right to a significant share of the promised pension during the early years of plan participation, so that a worker is not left empty-handed in the event of separation from service before attaining normal retirement age. Unfortunately, that limited objective neglects another important ERISA policy: promoting informed financial decision making.

The disconnect between the benefit formula applicable to retirement at the plan's specified normal retirement age and the participant's current accrued benefit creates fertile ground for confusion under a traditional pension plan. In the event of separation from service before normal retirement age, the participant's entitlement is his accrued benefit. The accrued benefit will be some fraction of the normal retirement benefit, but under ERISA's benefit accrual (anti-backloading) rules the fraction can sometimes be shockingly small.

Consider, for example, a plan that promises an annuity at age sixty-five equal to 1.5 percent of the participant's final average compensation for each year of participation up to a maximum of thirty years of credited service. (This is an example of a unit-credit plan, under which the benefit formula explicitly depends on years of participation or service.) A thirty-five-year-old who separates from service with ten years of participation would likely anticipate a pension at age sixty-five equal to 15 percent of his final average compensation (ten years credited at 1.5 percent per year), but instead of receiving one-third of the maximum attainable benefit he may find that he will get one-quarter or less.[73] Or consider a flat benefit plan that

---

[72] Revenue Ruling 78-252, 1978-1 C.B. 123, provides an excellent example of the application of the anti-backloading rules. The ruling involves a defined benefit plan that promises a normal retirement benefit at age sixty-five of 2.4 percent of the participant's average compensation for each year of participation, offset by 2 percent of the participant's Social Security primary insurance benefit for each of the first twenty-five years of participation. The ruling shows that *if the plan defines the accrued benefit at any time as the amount given by applying the benefit formula to the participant's years of participation at that time*, none of the three alternative benefit accrual rules is satisfied.

[73] Under the fractional accrual method the participant is entitled only to a fraction of the benefit he would get if he continued working to age sixty-five (i.e., 45 percent of final average compensation) given by the ratio of his years of participation on separation from service (ten) to the number of years of plan participation he would have if he were to continue at the job until age sixty-five (40), or 11.25 percent (25 percent of 45 percent). ERISA § 204(b)(1)(C), 29 U.S.C. § 1054(b)(1)(C) (2018); *see* I.R.C. § 411(b)(1)(C) (corresponding qualification condition). The permissible accrued benefit under the 133⅓-rule of ERISA § 204(b)(1)(B) could be

Accumulation

promises each participant with at least ten years of service an annuity at age sixty-five equal to 40 percent of final average compensation. A worker hired at age fifty who separates from service at age sixty-two might anticipate a full 40 percent come age sixty-five, but she would be entitled to only 32 percent under the fractional (or pro rata) accrual method (= 40 percent × 12/15), and as little as 14.4 percent under the 3 percent rule.[74] As these examples illustrate, the technical definition of accrued benefit translates the plan's specified maximum benefit, payable to an employee who works for the company until normal retirement age, into the actual pension to be paid to a worker who leaves the job earlier, and the results are frequently counterintuitive. The apparently generous maximum benefit may be touted in recruiting materials and workforce communications, even if it's inapplicable to most employees. In this era of declining job tenures, the definition of accrued benefit controls what most participants will receive, but that definition is typically buried in the plan's fine print.

Amendments Affecting Accrual

The final component of ERISA's regulation of benefit accrual prohibits certain amendments that would alter a pension plan's accrual provisions. First, a participant's accrued benefit may not be decreased by plan amendment.[75] This rule, known as the accrued benefit anti-cutback (or anti-reduction) rule, applies to both defined benefit and defined contribution plans. It functions as an adjunct to the vesting rules by protecting an employee's previously earned pension rights from forfeiture. Retroactive reductions in accrued benefits would often violate ERISA's vesting rules,[76] but the accrued benefit anti-cutback rule is broader, as it protects even nonvested participants from pension cutbacks.[77] Only retirement-type benefits

---

even smaller, perhaps 9.65 percent. *See* Peter J. Wiedenbeck & Russell K. Osgood, Cases and Materials on Employee Benefits 303–10 (2d ed. 2013).

[74] ERISA § 204(b)(1)(A), 29 U.S.C. § 1054(b)(1)(A) (2018). The maximum feasible benefit under the plan (40 percent of final average compensation) multiplied by 3 percent per year of participation yields 14.4 percent (= 40 percent × 3 percent per year × 12 years).

[75] ERISA § 204(g)(1), 29 U.S.C. § 1054(g)(1) (2018); *see* I.R.C. § 411(d)(6)(A) (2018).

[76] The term "nonforfeitable," as used in ERISA's vesting rules, generally means a claim to a pension benefit that is unconditional and legally enforceable against the plan. ERISA § 3(19), 29 U.S.C. § 1002(19) (2018). Previously earned benefits that could be reduced by plan amendment would be subject to a condition subsequent, which would render workers' pension claims forfeitable.

[77] Congress permits a few limited exceptions to the anti-reduction rule. Although safeguarding the amount of previously earned retirement benefits is fundamental to retirement security, in exigent circumstances deferred compensation earned in a preceding plan year may be reduced if funding the additional accrued benefits would impose substantial business hardship, provided that stringent conditions are satisfied. ERISA §§ 204(g)(1), 302(d)(2), 29 U.S.C. §§ 1054 (g)(1), 1082(d)(2) (2018); *see* I.R.C. §§ 411(d)(6)(A), 412(d)(2) (2018). Such funding-based benefit cutbacks can be made only to benefits earned in the plan year immediately preceding adoption of the amendment, or the preceding two plan years in the case of a multiemployer

246 Content Controls: Pension Plans

are protected; medical benefits, life insurance, and other ancillary benefits that are provided under some pension plans are not.[78]

Retirement benefits, however, are strongly protected, as illustrated by *Central Laborers' Pension Fund* v. *Heinz*.[79] The case presented the question whether a plan amendment expanding the categories of post-retirement employment that would trigger suspension of payment of previously accrued early retirement benefits violates the anti-cutback rule. A unanimous Supreme Court held that it does, noting that "an amendment placing materially greater restrictions on the receipt of the benefit 'reduces' the benefit just as surely as a decrease in the size of the monthly benefit payment."[80]

> [The participant] was being reasonable if he relied on [plan terms that allowed him to supplement retirement income with certain permissible employment] in planning his retirement. The 1998 amendment undercut any such reliance, paying retirement income only if he accepted a substantial curtailment of his opportunity to do the kind of work he knew. We simply do not see how, in any practical sense, this change of terms could not be viewed as shrinking the value of Heinz's pension rights and reducing his promised benefits.[81]

plan. Benefit reductions are also authorized where an underfunded multiemployer pension plan terminates as a result of mass withdrawals. ERISA §§ 204(g)(1), 4281, 29 U.S.C. §§ 1054(g)(1), 1441 (2018); *see* I.R.C. § 411(d)(6)(A) (2018).

The Multiemployer Pension Reform Act of 2014 also authorizes, in narrow circumstances and subject to special procedures, more general benefit reductions, including reductions of benefits that are already in pay status. Such reductions are permitted only where that action is necessary to avoid insolvency of an ongoing but critically underfunded multiemployer pension plan. ERISA § 305(e)(9), 29 U.S.C. § 1085(e)(9) (2018); *see* I.R.C. § 432(e)(9) (2018).

[78] Treas. Reg. § 1.411(a)-7(a)(1) (as amended in 2000); *id.* § 1.411(d)-3(b)(3)(i), -3(g)(2) (as amended in 2009); *id.* § 1.411(d)-4, Q&A-1(d) (as amended in 2012). *See* Arndt v. Sec. Bank S.S.B. Emps.' Pension Plan, 182 F.3d 538 (7th Cir. 1999) (increases in pension benefits payable at NRA based on grant of imputed service credit for period of disability is a disability benefit rather than an early retirement benefit or retirement-type subsidy, and so may be eliminated by plan amendment).

Ancillary benefits such as life insurance or disability benefits reflect the inclusion of welfare-type benefits under a pension plan. The anti-reduction rule does not apply to welfare plans. ERISA § 201(1), 29 U.S.C. § 1051(1) (2018). Limiting the scope of the anti-reduction rule to retirement-type benefits ensures that the inclusion of welfare benefits under a pension plan does not enhance the protection afforded those benefits. This limitation is consistent with ERISA's stipulation that a pension plan exists only "to the extent that" the program either provides retirement income to employees or results in a deferral of income to the termination of covered employment. ERISA § 3(2)(A), 29 U.S.C. § 1002(2)(A) (2018).

Certain plant shutdown benefits (early retirement pensions contingent on plant closure) are protected by the anti-cutback rule. Treas. Reg. § 1.411(d)-3(b)(1)(ii), -3(b)(4), Example 2 (as amended in 2009). *See* Bellas v. CBS, Inc., 221 F.3d 517 (3d Cir. 2000); Ameri R. Giannotti, Comment, *ERISA's Anticutback Rule and Contingent Early Retirement Benefits*, 68 U. CHI. L. REV. 1341 (2001).

[79] 541 U.S. 739 (2004).

[80] *Id.* at 744 (quoting from the lower court opinion, 303 F.3d 802, 805 (7th Cir. 2002)).

[81] *Id.* at 744–45. Treas. Reg. § 1.411(d)-3(a)(3)(i) (as amended in 2009), was amended to incorporate the holding in *Heinz*. T.D. 9280, 2006-38 I.R.B. 450.

Accumulation 247

Protecting the amount of previously earned retirement benefits is clearly fundamental to retirement security. Although imposing a new condition on pension receipt does not reduce the nominal dollar amount of the annuity, it nevertheless decreases benefits by lowering the probability of payment or increasing the burden to qualify.

Heinz indicates that any plan change which impairs the value of pension benefits violates the anti-cutback rule. But is reduction of actuarial present value necessary to trigger ERISA § 204(g)? What is the status of an amendment that restricts access to early retirement benefits or eliminates an alternative form of distribution while keeping in place some actuarially equivalent pattern of benefit payments? Arguably, the statutory definition of accrued benefit is exclusively quantitative, a measure of the amount of deferred compensation earned under the plan by service to date.[82]

The Retirement Equity Act of 1982 expanded the scope of the anti-cutback rule, declaring that an amendment which has the effect of eliminating or reducing an early retirement benefit or retirement-type subsidy or eliminating an optional form of benefit will generally be treated as a prohibited reduction of accrued benefits.[83] Consequently, a defined benefit plan early retirement option, whether subsidized or not, must continue to be made available with respect to benefits previously accrued,[84] and a lump-sum distribution alternative (under either a defined contribution or a defined benefit plan) must likewise abide.

---

[82] *See supra* Chapter 7 notes 49–50 and accompanying text.

[83] ERISA § 204(g)(2), 29 U.S.C. § 1054(g)(2) (2018); *see* I.R.C. § 411(d)(6)(B) (2018). Optional forms of distribution which are redundant, or which are burdensome to plan administration and of de minimis value to participants, may be retroactively eliminated by plan amendment, however. ERISA § 204(g)(2), 29 U.S.C. § 1054(g)(2) (penultimate sentence); *see* I.R.C. § 411 (d)(6)(B) (same); Treas. Reg. § 1.411(d)-3(c) to -3(g) (as amended in 2009).

    To prevent evasion of the anti-cutback rule and ensure that benefits are definitely determinable, regulations outlaw plan terms that grant the employer, a fiduciary, or another person discretion to approve payment of benefits in a particular form. Treas. Reg. § 1.411(d)-4, Q&A-4, Q&A-5 (as amended in 2012).

    Technically, early retirement benefits and most early retirement subsidies under a defined benefit plan do not satisfy the statutory definition of accrued benefit, which focuses on an annuity commencing at normal retirement age. Nor do alternate forms of distribution under a defined contribution plan fall within that definition, which looks only to the balance of the employee's account (hence the sole concern is quantitative, not qualitative). *See* ERISA § 3 (23), 29 U.S.C. § 1002(23); *see* I.R.C. § 411(a)(7); Treas. Reg. § 1.411(a)-7(a) (as amended in 2000) (subsidized early retirement benefit not taken into account as accrued benefit unless subsidized early retirement benefit is the normal retirement benefit). For this reason, the impairment of early retirement benefits, retirement-type subsidies, or optional forms of benefits is "treated as" reducing accrued benefits, and regulations reflect the expanded scope of the anti-cutback rule by referring to the protected features generally as "section 411(d)(6) protected benefits" rather than as accrued benefits. Treas. Reg. § 1.411(d)-3(a)(1), -3(b)(1)(i), -3(g)(14), (15) (as amended in 2009); *id.* §1.411(d)-4, Q&A-1 (as amended in 2012).

[84] If at the time of the plan amendment a participant has not satisfied eligibility conditions attached to an early retirement benefit, retirement-type subsidy, or optional form of benefit, but the participant later satisfies the pre-amendment conditions, she must be entitled to the benefit,

Distribution timing options are important to participants because of the pension anti-alienation rule.[85] Because accrued benefits are nontransferable, a worker who doesn't like the normal form of distribution provided by the plan ordinarily cannot sell his interest and use the proceeds to arrange a payment stream better suited to his circumstances.[86] Defined contribution plans, however, commonly permit a single-sum distribution of all or a portion of the participant's account balance. If such a plan is qualified, a participant can arrange a tax-free rollover of a single-sum distribution into an individual retirement account (IRA), and as owner of the IRA, she can thereafter largely control the timing of distributions.[87] In recognition of this flexibility, defined contribution plans may be amended to eliminate a particular form of distribution if affected participants have ready access to a single-sum distribution.[88]

From a policy perspective, the anti-cutback rule mediates between a pension plan sponsor's general freedom to adjust or discontinue the program at any time and ensuring that plan participants and beneficiaries can safely rely on promised retirement income. Recall that the settlor function doctrine allows the employer to attend solely to its own interests in setting the terms of an employee benefit plan, paying no heed to the needs or interests of employees and their beneficiaries.[89] Nor do ERISA's fiduciary obligations apply to the modification of a plan because "without exception, 'plan sponsors who alter the terms of a plan do not fall into the category of fiduciaries.'"[90] ERISA requires that every employee benefit plan be amendable,[91] and to the extent of that amendment authority the plan sponsor's apparent obligations are latently revocable. But in the case of a pension plan, the plan sponsor's

---

subsidy, or distribution option as applied to benefits earned by services performed prior to the applicable amendment date. Treas. Reg. § 1.411(d)-3(b) (as amended in 2009).

[85] ERISA § 206(d)(1), 29 U.S.C. § 1056(d)(1) (2018); *see* I.R.C. § 401(a)(13)(A) (2018). *See generally infra* Chapter 8B.

[86] *See* S. Rep. No. 98-575, at 27 (1984) ("The committee also believes that valuable rights of participants should not be lost through the elimination of benefit options because options of equal actuarial value may not be of equal value to people whose particular circumstances are not taken into account in determining actuarial equivalence.").

[87] I.R.C. §§ 402(c), 408(a)(6), (d) (2018).

[88] ERISA § 204(g)(5), 29 U.S.C. § 1054(g)(5) (2018); *see* I.R.C. § 411(d)(6)(E) (2018); *see also* Treas. Reg. § 1.411(d)-4, Q&A-2(e) (as amended in 2012). A similar rule allows the transfer in a plan merger of a participant's account balance from one defined contribution plan to another, even though the transferee plan doesn't provide all the same forms of distribution, provided that the participant consents to the transfer after receiving notice of its consequences, and the transferee plan allows single-sum distributions. ERISA § 204(g)(4), 29 U.S.C. § 1054(g)(4) (2018); *see* I.R.C. § 411(d)(6)(D) (2018); *see* STAFF OF THE JOINT COMM. ON TAXATION, 108TH CONG., GENERAL EXPLANATION OF TAX LEGISLATION ENACTED IN THE 107TH CONGRESS, at 130–33 (Comm. Print 2003).

[89] *See supra* Chapter 4A. *See generally* Dana Muir & Norman Stein, *Two Hats, One Head, No Heart: The Anatomy of the ERISA Settlor/Fiduciary Distinction*, 93 N.C. L. REV. 459 (2015).

[90] Hughes Aircraft Co. v. Jacobson, 525 U.S. 432, 445 (1999) (quoting Lockheed Corp. v. Spink, 517 U.S. 882, 890 (1996)).

[91] ERISA § 402(b)(3), 29 U.S.C. § 1102(b)(3) (2018).

Accumulation

reserved amendment authority is limited by the anti-cutback rule. In rendering pension claims based on past service irrevocable, the anti-cutback rule protects workers' reliance and effectively converts conditional offers of deferred compensation into robust property rights.[92]

Inadvertent overpayments of pension benefits can similarly threaten reliance interests of participants and beneficiaries, but different rights and obligations apply. A worker who has unwittingly received excess distributions may be called upon to repay the excess; if he is continuing to receive annuity distributions he may find future payments drastically reduced by the plan's efforts to recoup the excess. Fiduciaries are obligated to collect and prudently manage plan assets, and in the case of a defined benefit plan failure to recover unauthorized excess distributions impairs funding and could jeopardize the benefits of other participants. Where the overpayment is large, efforts to protect the plan can impose severe hardship, potentially impoverishing retirees in extreme old age. Where the recipient lacked reason to know of the error and the money has been spent, insisting upon the plan's rights may be heartless. Failing to do so, however, could jeopardize the plan's favorable tax treatment. Traditionally, fiduciaries faced with this dilemma often felt that the Code and ERISA left them powerless to achieve a reasonable accommodation of competing interests. In 2022 Congress acted to allow the responsible fiduciary to exercise discretion not to seek recovery of all or part of an inadvertent benefit overpayment, and if recovery is sought, to impose limits and conditions on the manner and amount of recoupment of such overpayments.[93]

Nothing in the accrual rules explored thus far prevents an employer from *prospectively* amending a plan to reduce contributions or benefits to be earned in the future. ERISA § 204(h), however, provides that an amendment that significantly reduces the rate of future benefit accrual under a defined benefit or money purchase pension plan cannot take effect unless each participant is given reasonable advance written notice of the amendment.[94] Under ERISA's generally applicable reporting and disclosure rules, the plan administrator is required to provide participants notice of material modifications in a plan within 210 days after the close of the plan year in which the change is adopted.[95] Not only is earlier notice demanded of accrual rate reductions, but the sanction for failure to give timely notice is much more serious:

---

[92] *See generally* Peter J. Wiedenbeck, *Untrustworthy: ERISA's Eroded Fiduciary Law*, 59 Wm. & Mary L. Rev, 1007, 1037–51 (2018).

[93] ERISA § 206(h), 29 U.S.C. § 1056(h) (West Supp. 2023); I.R.C. § 414(aa) (West Supp. 2023); *see* H.R. Rep. No 117-283, at 101–07 (2022).

[94] ERISA § 204(h), 29 U.S.C. § 1054(h) (2018). Alternate payees (family law creditors entitled to plan payment under a qualified domestic relations order) and unions representing plan participants must also be provided advance notice of the change. The plan amendment can be ignored only in cases of egregious failure to give the required advance notice, ERISA § 204 (h)(6), 29 U.S.C. § 1054(h)(6) (2018). I.R.C. § 4980F (2018) imposes an excise tax penalty for late notice. *See* Treas. Reg. § 54.4980F-1 (2019).

[95] ERISA § 104(b)(1), 29 U.S.C. § 1024(b)(1) (2018). *See supra* Chapter 3A.

250 *Content Controls: Pension Plans*

the amendment does not take effect. The *advance* notice required of accrual rate reductions gives affected employees a chance to object to their employer, seek alternative employment, or take other steps to protect their interests.[96] Consistent with a focus on information costs, the rule was apparently designed to promote better retirement planning.[97]

C VESTING

"Primarily, [ERISA] was a consumer protection bill. Vesting was its main focus."[98]

Statutory Standards

ERISA's vesting rules draw a fundamental distinction between employee- and employer-financed pension rights. The accrued benefit derived from employee contributions must be nonforfeitable (fully vested) at all times; to the extent that a pension is paid for with the employee's money, the employer is not permitted to hold it hostage.[99] The accrued benefit derived from employer contributions,

---

[96] *See* Frommert v. Conkright, 433 F.3d 254, 269 (2d Cir. 2006) ("employees [rehired after plan amendment reducing future benefit accruals was adequately disclosed], unlike their predecessors who lacked such information, had the opportunity to make an informed decision about taking or leaving the terms of the deal offered to them under the Plan"); Davidson v. Canteen Corp., 957 F.2d 1404, 1409 (7th Cir. 1992) (Wisdom, J.) ("amendment of a retirement plan to deprive some of the plan's participants of a benefit they were promised, when advance notice of that amendment would have allowed them to prevent injury from the amendment, is exactly what § 204(h) clearly outlaws").

[97] Reductions in the rate that future contributions will be allocated to a participant's account under a profit-sharing or stock bonus plan are not subject to the section 204(h) advance notice requirement. In contrast to a money purchase pension plan (a defined contribution plan that is subject to section 204(h) and ERISA's funding rules), the amount contributed from year to year under a profit-sharing or stock bonus plan need not be specified in the plan; it can be left to the discretion of the employer. Where contributions are wholly discretionary, the possibility of an allocation rate reduction does less harm to a participant's ability to plan for retirement, because the participant could not prudently count on getting anything more anyway.

[98] Cummings, *supra* Chapter 1 note 54, at 881.

[99] ERISA § 203(a)(1), 29 U.S.C. § 1053(a)(1) (2018); *see* I.R.C. § 411(a)(1) (2018). Although intuitively appealing, this distinction between employee- and employer-financed benefits is in fact highly artificial because the definition of employee contributions is largely formalistic. *See* I.R.C. § 414(h)(1) (2018). While common at the time ERISA was enacted, plans calling for after-tax employee contributions have become less prevalent as a result of subsequent tax law developments, particularly the advent of 401(k) plans. *See infra* Chapter 10B. In the unusual case where a plan is funded by both employer and employee contributions, the distinct status of the two types of contributions under the vesting rules requires a method for distinguishing the portions of a participant's accrued benefit that are derived from employee and employer contributions. These tracing or allocation rules are supplied by ERISA § 204(c), 29 U.S.C. § 1054(c) (2018) and I.R.C. § 411(c) (2018).

Accumulation

however, can be made subject to forfeiture for violation of any conditions the employer chooses to impose, but only for a limited period of time.[100] Once the participant completes a reasonable period of service, his pension saving must be secure, regardless of whether he continues to work for the plan sponsor, although distribution of the vested benefit may be deferred until retirement age.

ERISA prescribes alternative generally applicable minimum vesting schedules for accrued benefits derived from employer contributions. A defined benefit plan may comply with either the five-year cliff or the three-to-seven-year graded vesting schedule. Under the five-year cliff schedule, the entire employer-financed accrued benefit of a participant with less than five years of service may be subject to forfeiture, but once the participant completes five years of service, her pension rights must be fully vested at all times thereafter. Under the three-to-seven-year graded schedule, a participant with three years of service must have a nonforfeitable right to at least 20 percent of the accrued benefit derived from employer contributions, and her vested percentage must increase by 20 percent with each succeeding year of service, so that a participant with seven or more years of service is fully vested.[101] Defined contribution plans must provide more rapid vesting, satisfying either a three-year cliff or a two-to-six-year graded schedule (again, at 20 percent per year).[102]

The vesting schedules apply to the participant's entire accrued benefit derived from employer contributions, regardless of when it was earned. Once a participant satisfies the cliff schedule, for example, all prior employer contributions (in the case of a defined contribution plan) or accruals (in the case of a defined benefit plan) become vested – even increases occurring within the last three or five years, respectively – and all subsequent contributions or benefits are secure from the moment they are earned.[103]

---

[100] A forfeiture of accrued benefits derived from employer contributions, when that forfeiture is triggered by the withdrawal of employee contributions, is subject to special restrictions so as not to undercut the protection afforded employee contributions. ERISA §§ 203(a)(3)(D), 206(c), 29 U.S.C. §§ 1053(a)(3)(D), 1056(c) (2018); see I.R.C. §§ 401(a)(19), 411(a)(3)(D) (2018).

[101] ERISA § 203(a)(2)(A), 29 U.S.C. § 1053(a)(2)(A) (2018); see I.R.C. § 411(a)(2)(A) (2018). ERISA originally permitted ten-year cliff vesting and graded vesting over a five- to fifteen-year period and authorized a third alternative, the "Rule of 45," which called for incremental vesting under a schedule that took into account both age and years of service. That alternative was repealed by the Tax Reform Act of 1986, which greatly accelerated vesting under the cliff and graded schedules.

[102] ERISA § 203(a)(2)(B), 29 U.S.C. § 1053(a)(2)(B) (2018); see I.R.C. § 411(a)(2)(B) (2018). Matching contributions under defined contribution plans became subject to three-year cliff and two-to-six-year graded schedules in 2001; amendments in 2006 made those schedules the general rules for defined contribution plans.

[103] ERISA originally authorized an exception to this once-and-for-all aspect of vesting: a profit-sharing, stock bonus, or money purchase pension plan was permitted to employ class-year vesting, under which an employee's right to employer contributions made in a particular plan year became nonforfeitable only if the employee performed services for the employer for five plan years thereafter. ERISA § 203(c)(3), 29 U.S.C. § 1053(c)(3) (1982) (repealed 1986); see

Content Controls: Pension Plans

As is typical of ERISA's pension content controls, these alternative statutory vesting schedules are just minimum standards: a plan may call for more rapid vesting, or even provide that all accrued benefits are immediately nonforfeitable.[104] In addition, upon reaching normal retirement age, a participant must be fully vested, even if at that time he does not have sufficient service to vest under the applicable schedule.[105]

Vesting turns upon years of service. Service counting and break-in-service rules are used that closely correspond to those used to specify permissible minimum-service conditions.[106] For vesting purposes, however, years of service before age eighteen or before the employer established the plan may be disregarded.[107] Service before a particular employee became a participant cannot be ignored, however, so a plan that imposes a one-year minimum-service condition on membership must count that pre-participation service toward vesting.

ERISA bars certain changes in a pension plan's vesting schedule. A plan amendment is not permitted to reduce any employee's vested percentage, even if the employee would not have to be vested under the statutory minimum standards.[108] For example, a plan that provides full vesting after two years of service might be amended to substitute five-year cliff vesting, but that amendment cannot be applied to the previously accrued benefits of participants who have between two and five years of service, because that would subject them to a risk of loss benefits that had become nonforfeitable under the prior terms of the plan. Amendments that delay vesting without reducing current nonforfeitable rights are permitted, but any participant having at least three years of service (counting all years, and disregarding the

---

I.R.C. § 411(d)(4) (1982) (repealed 1986). Under this rolling vesting schedule, a worker who separated from service before normal retirement age would lose employer contributions made over the preceding five years even if he had been employed for decades. Class-year vesting was repealed in 1986. *See* Treas. Reg. § 1.411(d)-5 (1988).

[104] ERISA § 203(d), 29 U.S.C. § 1053(d) (2018). The tax-law qualification requirements do not contain a parallel declaration, but the tax Code's vesting requirements are interpreted as minimum standards despite that oversight.

Immediate vesting is encouraged by the rule allowing plans to impose a two-year service condition on membership, provided that accrued benefits are at all times fully vested. ERISA § 202(a)(1)(B)(i), 29 U.S.C. § 1052(a)(1)(B)(i) (2018); *see* I.R.C. § 410(a)(1)(B)(i) (2018). *See supra* Chapter 7A.

[105] ERISA § 203(a), 29 U.S.C. § 1053(a) (2018) (first sentence); *see* I.R.C. § 411(a) (2018) (first sentence).

[106] ERISA § 203(b)(2), (3), 29 U.S.C. § 1053(b)(2), (3) (2018); *see* I.R.C. § 411(a)(5), (6) (2018). *See supra* Chapter 7 notes 5–10 and accompanying text.

[107] ERISA § 203(b)(1), 29 U.S.C. § 1053(b)(1) (2018); *see* I.R.C. § 411(a)(4) (2018).

[108] ERISA § 203(c)(1)(A), 29 U.S.C. § 1053(c)(1)(A) (2018); *see* I.R.C. § 411(a)(10)(A) (2018); Treas. Reg. § 1.411(a)-8(a) (as amended in 2006). This vesting anti-cutback rule complements the accrued benefit anti-cutback rule, ERISA § 204(g), 29 U.S.C. § 1054(g) (2018), discussed *supra* text accompanying Chapter 7 notes 75–92. Section 204(g) outlaws plan amendments that reduce previously earned pension rights, while section 203(c)(1)(A) prohibits amendments that do not directly reduce previously earned rights but expose those rights to increased risk of loss.

Accumulation

break-in-service rules) must be given sixty days to elect to continue to have the old vesting schedule apply.[109] So, for example, if a plan is amended to switch from a five-year cliff to three-to-seven-year graded vesting, each participant with at least three years of service must be given the choice to remain on the cliff schedule, which employees who expect to leave with between five and seven years of service would wish to do.

In a few tightly circumscribed situations, forfeiture of employer-financed pension benefits is permitted in spite of the vesting rules.[110] Most important, rights may be made contingent upon survival to retirement age, because pensions are designed to provide a source of income to meet retirement living expenses. Accordingly, a plan may call for forfeiture on death of the participant – even a fully vested participant – provided that the deceased leaves no spouse entitled to a survivor annuity under ERISA's spousal protection rules.[111]

Apart from the few very limited statutory exceptions, all contingencies must vanish within a time frame that satisfies ERISA's minimum vesting rules. The term "nonforfeitable," as used in ERISA, means nonforfeitable for *any* reason, other than the express statutory exceptions (like death without a spouse entitled to survivor benefits).[112] Even if a plan calls for forfeiture in circumstances that are unrelated to length of service – such as forfeiture in the event of dismissal for cause, or forfeiture upon violation of a noncompetition agreement – pension rights cannot be revoked once a participant has accumulated enough years of service to be fully vested. Prior to ERISA, many plans granted benefits to participants whose employment terminated before retirement age, provided they had completed a specified (often lengthy) period of service. Some of these plans also provided that a participant who committed various sorts of malfeasance would lose all benefits regardless of length of service (so-called bad boy forfeiture). Different forfeiture conditions, that is, would operate over different periods; commonly, forfeiture for inadequate service was time limited, while bad boy forfeiture was not. In response to ERISA, some of these plans were amended to bring forfeiture for inadequate service within one statutory vesting schedule, while forfeiture for malfeasance was subject to another.

---

[109] ERISA § 203(c)(1)(B), 29 U.S.C. § 1053(c)(1)(B) (2018); *see* I.R.C. § 411(a)(10)(B) (2018); Temp. Treas. Reg. § 1.411(a)-8T(b) (1988). The election period must begin no later than the date the vesting amendment is adopted and continue for at least sixty days after the later of (1) the date the amendment is adopted, (2) the date the amendment becomes effective, or (3) the date the participant is given written notice of the amendment. *Id.* § 1.411(a)-8T(b)(2).
[110] Accrued benefits financed by employee contributions cannot be forfeited in these circumstances. The exceptions listed in each of subparagraphs (A) through (E) of ERISA § 203(a)(3), 29 U.S.C. § 1053(a)(3) (2018), apply only to a "right to an accrued benefit derived from employer contributions." *Accord* I.R.C. § 411(a)(3)(A)–(G) (2018).
[111] ERISA § 203(a)(3)(A), 29 U.S.C. § 1053(a)(3)(A) (2018); *see* I.R.C. § 411(a)(3)(A) (2018). On the spousal protection rules generally, see *infra* Chapter 8C.
[112] ERISA § 3(19), 29 U.S.C. § 1002(19) (2018); *see* Treas. Reg. § 1.411(a)-4(a) (as amended in 2009) & Temp. Treas. Reg. §1.411(a)-4T(a) (1988).

Content Controls: Pension Plans

Participants challenged this situation, arguing that the same statutory vesting schedule must apply to *all* causes of forfeiture.[113] The statutory minimum standards are expressed as alternatives and the inclusive "or" would support multiple vesting schedules. On the other hand, because "nonforfeitable" means unconditional, a participant has a "nonforfeitable right" only when *all* contingencies terminate, which suggests that the *combined* preclusive effect of all contingencies must fit within *one* of ERISA's alternative minimum standards. The cases conform to the latter view: a pension plan may specify multiple causes of forfeiture and may even provide that those conditions operate over different periods, but all such contingencies must terminate within a time frame that satisfies the same statutory schedule.[114] For example, a defined benefit plan could vest benefits at the rate of 25 percent per year of service beginning with the participant's second year of service, but also require forfeiture of all employer-derived accrued benefits if a participant is dismissed for cause before completing five years of service. Here, both forfeiture conditions – inadequate tenure and dismissal for cause – fit within the five-year cliff standard. (Of course, vesting at 25 percent per year starting with the second year of service is more generous than necessary; it also satisfies the three-to-seven-year graded schedule.) In contrast, the plan would violate ERISA if its general schedule vested benefits at the rate of 20 percent per year of service (again starting with the second year) and, in addition, called for complete forfeiture on dismissal for cause within five years. In this case, service-based vesting would only satisfy the three-to-seven-year graded schedule (the vested percentage does not reach 100 percent until the sixth year of service, beyond the five-year cliff), while the bad boy forfeiture would only satisfy the five-year cliff schedule (complete forfeiture after three or four years of service contravenes the partial vesting requirement of the three-to-seven-year graded schedule).

Where a plan imposes multiple forfeiture conditions that do not all comply with the same statutory schedule, a court must revise the plan to conform to ERISA's requirements. But what principles apply to determine whether cliff or graded vesting should be made generally applicable? The cases seem to take the statutory standard to which the plan's general vesting provision (that is, forfeiture for inadequate service) conforms and apply it to bad boy forfeiture, but the opinions offer no

---

[113] A regulation first issued in 1975 expressly permits the forfeiture of accrued benefits in excess of the minimum amount that ERISA requires to be nonforfeitable. The regulation includes an example showing that a plan may contain multiple vesting schedules applicable to different causes of forfeiture, but in the example, each of the plan's forfeiture conditions complies with the *same* statutory vesting schedule (cliff vesting). Treas. Reg. § 1.411(a)-4(a), -4(c) Example (1) (as amended in 2009). *Accord* Lojek v. Thomas, 716 F.2d 675, 680 (9th Cir. 1983); Hepple v. Roberts & Dybdahl, Inc., 622 F.2d 962 (8th Cir. 1980).

[114] *E.g.*, Hummell v. S. E. Rykoff & Co., 634 F.2d 446, 450–51 (9th Cir. 1980); Nedrow v. McFarlane & Hays Co. Profit Sharing Plan & Trust, 476 F. Supp. 934, 937 (E.D. Mich. 1979). *See* Rev. Rul. 85-31, 1985-1 C.B. 153, 154.

Accumulation

persuasive reason for doing so.[115] The policy of promoting sponsorship by maintaining employer flexibility suggests an inquiry into the relative importance to a particular employer of discouraging malfeasance (indicating that the plan's bad boy clause should not be cribbed) versus encouraging longer job tenure. In contrast, an emphasis on employee expectations and the goal of promoting retirement planning counsels review of the summary plan description to determine whether one or the other vesting schedule was given prominence. If each is adequately disclosed, perhaps preference should be given to the schedule used by the plan's general vesting provision, as many workers will have taken the plan's length-of-service requirements into account in making decisions about changing jobs and saving for retirement.

Enforcement

A plan failing to comply with the vesting standards can be brought into line by participant action. Participants and beneficiaries have standing to sue for equitable relief to redress violations of ERISA, and that relief could include an injunction ordering the payment of benefits improperly forfeited (restitution).[116]

Suppose that the plan's terms comply with the minimum vesting standards, but workers are laid off shortly before they would vest. Section 510 prohibits intentional interference with vesting, making it unlawful for an employer to discharge or otherwise penalize a participant "for the purpose of interfering with the attainment of any right to which such participant may become entitled under the plan" or ERISA.[117] While the full reach of this protection has yet to be resolved, dismissals to prevent vesting were a core concern.[118] Section 510 liability requires proof of specific intent to interfere with the attainment of vested rights, but that intent need

---

[115] E.g., *Hummell*, 634 F.2d at 452; *Nedrow*, 476 F. Supp. at 937–38.

[116] See generally supra Chapter 5D. A former employee whose benefits are forfeited in violation of ERISA has a colorable claim to vested benefits and thus has standing to sue under the Supreme Court's interpretation of "participant." Firestone Tire & Rubber Co. v. Bruch, 489 U.S. 101, 117–18 (1989), discussed *supra* Chapter 5A.

[117] ERISA § 510, 29 U.S.C. § 1140 (2018). Section 510 is enforced via section 502, generally by a suit for injunction or other appropriate equitable relief. See generally supra Chapter 5C.

[118] "A further protection for employees is the prohibition against discharge, or other discriminatory conduct toward participants and beneficiaries which is designed to interfere with attainment of vested benefits or other rights under the bill, or to discourage the exercise of any rights afforded by the legislation." 120 Cong. Rec. 29,933 (1974) (remarks by Sen. Williams, a cosponsor of ERISA, explaining the conference report), *reprinted in* 3 ERISA Legislative History, *supra* Chapter 1 note 55, at 4745. Whether section 510 extends beyond vesting, barring actions intended to prevent welfare plan participants or vested pension plan participants from earning additional benefits, remains unclear. See the discussion of Inter-Modal Rail Employees Ass'n v. Atchison, Topeka & Santa Fe Railway, 520 U.S. 510 (1997), *supra* text accompanying Chapter 5 notes 100–106.

Content Controls: Pension Plans

not be directed against specific individuals; ERISA is violated if an employer acts to minimize pension claims in deciding which plants to close.[119]

Instead of terminating employees to prevent vesting, suppose that the employer terminates the plan. Does ERISA provide relief if a plan is amended or terminated to prevent participants from vesting? Several courts have concluded that section 510 was only meant to bar adverse employment actions (to "discharge, fine, suspend, expel, discipline" a worker), and that its catchall ban on "discriminat[ion] against a participant" does not embrace detrimental alteration of plan terms.[120] Nor does ERISA demand early vesting upon plan termination. The tax Code, however, expressly requires that *qualified* plans provide for the immediate vesting of the accrued benefits of all affected employees in the event of a partial or complete termination of the plan, and a partial termination may include "the exclusion, by reason of a plan amendment, of a group of employees who have previously been covered by the plan."[121] Nearly all retirement savings programs are intended to qualify for preferential tax treatment, so pension plans generally contain a clause calling for vesting on complete or partial termination. Even though such a clause has its genesis in the tax law, ERISA gives participants and beneficiaries a private right of action to enforce their rights under the terms of the plan.[122] As a result, many of the disputes over whether a partial termination has occurred have triggered litigation between excluded participants and the plan. The IRS has issued no regulation defining partial termination or indicating how large the group of

---

[119] *See generally* Dana M. Muir, *Plant Closings and ERISA's Noninterference Provision*, 36 B.C. L. REV. 201 (1995). *But see* Nemeth v. Clark Equip. Co., 677 F. Supp. 899, 909 (W.D. Mich. 1987) (section 510 not violated where pensions accounted for only 20 percent of higher costs of plant selected for closing because it would have been shut down even if pension costs had been ignored); Lorraine Schmall & Nathan Ihnes, *Failure of Equity: Discriminatory Plant Closing as an Irremediable Injury under ERISA*, 55 CATH. U.L. REV. 81 (2005) (back pay remedy may be unavailable).

[120] *See supra* Chapter 5 note 95 and accompanying text. The Supreme Court has observed that section 510 reinforces the formal amendment process by ensuring that employers cannot "'informally' amend their plans one participant at a time." *Inter-Modal Rail*, 520 U.S. at 516, discussed *supra* text accompanying Chapter 5 notes 89–95. However, the Court did not go so far as to say that a plan amendment motivated by the purpose of preventing vesting would be valid. While the act of amending the plan is indisputably a settlor rather than fiduciary function, section 510 by its terms bars any "person" (not just fiduciaries) from interfering with the exercise of a beneficiary's plan rights. ERISA § 510, 29 U.S.C. § 1140 (2018).

[121] I.R.C. § 411(d)(3) (2018); Treas. Reg. § 1.411(d)-2(b)(1) (as amended in 2019). The tax Code's vesting-on-termination rule predates ERISA. (Its predecessor was enacted in 1962 as I.R.C. § 401(a)(7) (repealed 1974).) It was enacted to prevent abuse of the tax subsidy and, presumably for that reason, the rule was not extended to nonqualified plans under ERISA. The anti-abuse policy is suggested by the fact that benefits are required to vest only "to the extent funded." On plan termination, a sponsor is generally permitted to claim a reversion of any excess funds in the pension trust. *See infra* Chapter 9C. Congress apparently decided that the employer has no legitimate claim to a tax-subsidized reversion where the overfunding is the product of forfeiture of nonvested benefits on termination. *But see* Matz v. Household Int'l Tax Reduction Inv. Plan, 774 F.3d 1141, 1143 (7th Cir. 2014) (questioning this rationale). *See infra* Chapter 7 note 123.

[122] ERISA § 502(a)(1)(B), (a)(3), 29 U.S.C. § 1132(a)(1)(B), (a)(3) (2018).

Accumulation

excluded workers must be to support a finding of partial termination. The courts repeatedly struggled with the issue and with whether all excluded employees should be considered for this purpose, or only those who are not fully vested and so would lose benefits absent the partial termination finding. An illuminating 2004 opinion by Judge Posner collects the authorities and concludes, first, that a 20 percent reduction in plan participation is the appropriate rule of thumb for determining whether a partial termination occurred; second, that in computing the fraction of participants excluded by plan amendment, both vested and nonvested participants should be taken into account in both the numerator and the denominator; third, that a 20 percent exclusion establishes only a rebuttable presumption of partial termination; and fourth, that the purpose of I.R.C. $\S$ 411(d)(3) is to prevent the employer from obtaining a windfall at the expense of participants who are not fully vested, and so deviations from the 20 percent guideline should be based on the presence or absence of such a predatory motive.[123]

Vesting Policy

ERISA's vesting rules have been notably successful, but the security they offer has come at a price. Because pension sponsorship is voluntary, employers can make a trade-off between coverage and vesting, and they will do so if the reduction of forfeitures makes pension coverage too costly.[124] That response would have clear-cut distributional effects. Long-term employees in high-turnover jobs – the loyal or lucky few who would have qualified for pensions under plans with prolonged forfeiture periods – will lose out because their employers cannot afford to pay benefits to their many transient coworkers.[125] Instead of cutting back coverage, employers could accommodate vesting cost increases by reducing benefits (prospectively) or limiting benefit increases. In that event, the pensions of vested shorter-term

[123] Matz v. Household Int'l Tax Reduction Inv. Plan, 388 F.3d 570 (7th Cir. 2004). *See* Rev. Rul. 2007-43, 2007-2 C.B. 45 (IRS follows 20 percent presumption of *Matz*). On appeal after remand the Seventh Circuit affirmed the district court's application of the approach announced in its 2004 opinion, but expressed doubt about its prior conclusion that vesting on partial termination is designed to prevent the employer from obtaining a tax windfall. Judge Posner questioned that rationale, noting that a reversion is taxable income to the employer and also triggers a 20- or 50-percent excise tax. Matz v. Household Int'l Tax Reduction Inv. Plan, 774 F.3d 1141, 1143 (7th Cir. 2014). While the excise tax on reversions was indeed intended to recapture undeserved tax benefits, it was first enacted in 1986. STAFF OF THE JOINT COMM. ON TAXATION, 100TH CONG., GENERAL EXPLANATION OF THE TAX REFORM ACT OF 1986, 750, 751 (1987). That was twelve years after ERISA extended the long-standing termination vesting rule to partial terminations, and therefore does not undercut the inference that I.R.C. $\S$ 411(d)(3) was directed to preventing tax abuse.

[124] *See supra* Chapter 1C. Recall that the overall private labor force pension plan coverage rate has hovered around 50 percent since ERISA was enacted. *See supra* Chapter 7 notes 16–18 and accompanying text.

[125] *See* Daniel I. Halperin, *Special Tax Treatment for Employer-Based Retirement Programs: Is It "Still" Viable as a Means of Increasing Retirement Income?*, 49 TAX L. REV. 1, 16–21 (1993).

workers would come out of the savings of their long-tenure colleagues.[126] ERISA, in other words, favors smaller pensions for many short-term workers over larger pensions for the few who make a career-long commitment.

Limiting employers' ability to use contingent deferred compensation to encourage loyalty and longevity of service seems to have reduced average job tenures.[127] Labor mobility increases the economy's responsiveness to changes, both in production technology and demand for goods and services.[128] But labor mobility may also decrease firms' willingness to invest in training, for it reduces their ability to recoup their investment, as workers shop their new skills for higher pay elsewhere.

By restricting forfeitures, ERISA limits freedom of contract. In assessing the wisdom of that infringement of private autonomy, it is good to remember that mandatory vesting has both distributional and efficiency implications (as outlined above). Clearly, favoring the many over the few was the politically astute course of action once forfeitures became a subject of widespread public concern. Broader pension recipiency, however, is not necessarily inconsistent with collective welfare maximization.

---

[126] Congress was acutely aware of the cost implications of mandatory vesting. To reduce the risk that employers would resort to undesirable cost containment strategies, ERISA § 207, 29 U.S.C. § 1057 (2006) (repealed 2006), authorized the Secretary of Labor to grant variances, for periods of up to seven years, from ERISA's benefit accrual and/or vesting rules. Such variances could only be granted to plans in effect on January 1, 1974, and only if the Labor Department found that ERISA's accrual or vesting rules would increase costs to such an extent that it created a substantial risk of discontinuance of the plan or of a substantial reduction in benefit levels or other compensation. *See* Wiedenbeck *supra* Chapter 7 note 18, at 530–32 (post-enactment oversight hearings and agency studies on plan terminations).

Concerns about the cost of vesting were expressed early and often during the development of pension reform proposals. *See, e.g.,* S. Rep. No. 93-127, at 12–13, 73–79, *reprinted in* 1 ERISA LEGISLATIVE HISTORY, *supra* Chapter 1 note 55, at 598–99, 659–65 (actuarial study of likely cost of mandatory vesting); 118 CONG. REC. 16,919–20 (1972) (remarks of Sen. Taft asserting that immediate vesting would trigger a 50 percent reduction in benefit levels); Richard M. Nixon, Private Pension Plans, H.R. DOC. No. 92-182, at 3 (1971) (if "set at too early a point, so that too many younger workers were vested, [required vesting] could create a considerable burden for employers and reduce the level of benefits for retiring workers"); PRESIDENT'S COMM. ON CORPORATE PENSION FUNDS AND OTHER PRIVATE RETIREMENT AND WELFARE PROGRAMS, PUBLIC POLICY AND PRIVATE PENSION PROGRAMS 44–46 (1965) (hereinafter PRESIDENT'S COMMITTEE REPORT).

[127] Vincenzo Andrietti & Vincent A. Hildebrand, *Evaluating Pension Portability Reforms: The Tax Reform Act of 1986 as a Natural Experiment,* 54 ECON. INQUIRY 1402 (2016) (finding that the dramatic acceleration of vesting required by 1986 legislation had a positive and significant effect on voluntary job mobility); Douglas A. Wolf & Frank Levy, *Pension Coverage, Pension Vesting, and the Distribution of Job Tenures, in* RETIREMENT & ECONOMIC BEHAVIOR 23, 25–28 (H. Aaron & G. Burtless eds., Brookings Inst., Washington, D.C.) (1984).

[128] *See* S. REP. No. 93-383, at 14 (1973), *reprinted in* 1 ERISA LEGISLATIVE HISTORY, *supra* Chapter 1 note 55, at 1063, 1082 (Finance Committee report observes that "failure to vest more rapidly is charged with interfering with the mobility of labor, to the detriment of the economy").

Accumulation 259

ERISA's minimum vesting standards, like the anti-backloading benefit accrual rules, mask a major policy ambiguity between worker protection and worker empowerment. The often-expressed concern over workers' loss of "anticipated retirement benefits owing to the lack of vesting" is equivocal on this point.[129] Absent vesting, pension receipt could be mistakenly anticipated either because workers underestimate their risk of forfeiture or because they base their expectations on readily accessible but incomplete information. Most of the vesting rules are, in fact, consonant with both the protective and the information cost rationales.[130]

Conceptually, ERISA's accrual and vesting rules may draw support from either a worker protective policy or information cost concerns, but politically, these interventions in the market for deferred compensation originate in a preference for broader distribution of pension benefits. Much of the public pressure for vesting requirements grew out of the fact that contingencies were often downplayed, with the result that workers came to understand their pension coverage as representing a right to deferred wages, as opposed to *conditional* deferred wages (or a lottery ticket). As such, forfeitures were seen as an unfair refusal to pay earned compensation.[131] Effective disclosure might have eradicated this misapprehension,[132] but Congress

[129] ERISA § 2(a), 29 U.S.C. § 1001(a) (2018).

[130] The vesting amendment rules may be an illuminating exception. Recall that a plan cannot be amended to reduce any participant's current nonforfeitable accrued benefit (even a participant who would not yet have vested under ERISA's minimum standards); and that any participant with at least three years of service must be allowed to continue on the plan's former vesting schedule if she chooses, even if the new schedule conforms to ERISA and does not curtail her vested rights. Since the difference in timing between one acceptable vesting schedule and another is slight, these rules do not seem necessary to protect workers from misjudging the long-term risk of forfeiture. The rules do, however, make it safe to rely on near-term decisions founded on the plan's existing provisions, thereby facilitating career and financial planning.

[131] *See ERISA at 40: What Were They Thinking?*, 6 DREXEL L. REV. 265, 285–86 (2014) (remarks by Frank Cummings and Daniel Halperin on publicizing forfeiture horror stories to generate support for pension reform bills); Michael S. Gordon, *Overview: Why Was ERISA Enacted?*, in S. SPEC. COMM. ON AGING, 98TH CONG., THE EMPLOYEE RETIREMENT INCOME SECURITY ACT OF 1974: THE FIRST DECADE 8, 15–17 (Comm. Print 1984) (1958 disclosure legislation unleashed torrent of mail from constituents complaining of failure to qualify for pension, and 1971 Senate Labor Subcommittee hearings publicized series of late-career forfeiture horror stories); H.R. REP. NO. 93-533, at 6 (1973) ("In its final analysis, the issue basically resolves itself into whether workers, after many years of labor, whose jobs terminate voluntarily or otherwise, should be denied benefits that have been placed for them in a fund for retirement purposes."), *reprinted in* 2 ERISA LEGISLATIVE HISTORY, *supra* Chapter 1 note 55, at 2348, 2353, S. REP. NO. 99-313, at 590 (1986) ("[I]t is arguable that an employee who ... accepts a reduced current compensation package in exchange for qualified plan benefits should not have receipt of plan benefits made contingent on an overly lengthy deferred vesting schedule.").

[132] During debate on ERISA, Representative Erlenborn, Republican House manager of the bill, observed:

"[I]f people do have this sort of meaningful information made available to them, I think some of the unwarranted expectations that gave rise to the horror stories that people were not getting what they anticipated will be a thing of the past, because many of them are based on what people anticipated getting that they never were entitled to, because they did not honestly

chose instead to ratify it. Its goal was to promote greater access to private pensions to supplement Social Security.

Under a regime of voluntary plan sponsorship, mandatory vesting may not achieve broader distribution because higher costs may trigger terminations. But employers do not bear the full cost of employee pensions. Most pension plans, both before ERISA's enactment and since, have been designed to satisfy the Internal Revenue Code's definition of a qualified pension, profit-sharing, stock bonus, or annuity plan, in order to obtain preferential tax treatment (specifically, tax-deferred accumulation). The result is a large public subsidy for pension savings. With the net revenue loss attributable to qualified plan savings now on the order of $300 billion annually (excluding individual retirement accounts), there is a strong societal stake in employment-based retirement savings programs.[133] In enacting ERISA, Congress declared that pension plans "substantially affect the revenue of the United States because they are afforded preferential Federal tax treatment," and that it is "desirable in the interests of employees and their beneficiaries [and] for the protection of the revenue of the United States ... that minimum standards be provided assuring the *equitable character* of such plans."[134] Public money comes with strings attached, and the participation, benefit accrual, and vesting rules work together to insist that short-service employees get a reasonable share of subsidized retirement savings.[135]

know what was in their pension plan; they did not honestly know what their rights would be." 120 Cong. Rec. 4284 (1974), *reprinted in* 2 ERISA Legislative History, *supra* Chapter 1 note 55, at 3386–87.

[133] *See supra* Chapter 1D and Chapter 1 notes 84–85; Staff of the Joint Comm. on Taxation, 117th Cong., Estimates of Federal Tax Expenditures for Fiscal Years 2022–2026, at 42 (2022) (estimate for FY 2022).

[134] ERISA § 2(a), 29 U.S.C. § 1001(a) (2018) (emphasis added).

[135] President's Committee Report, *supra* Chapter 7 note 126, at 39, 42 (observing that vesting is required as "a matter of equity and fair treatment"; it was recommended in 1965 as condition of favorable tax treatment because "[t]he Committee is convinced that a vesting requirement is necessary if private pension plans are to serve the broad social purpose justifying their favored status"). Vesting was proposed as a condition of receiving favorable tax treatment along with the original version of the tax law nondiscrimination rules in 1942, but it was not enacted at that time. *Revenue Revision of 1942: Hearings before the H. Comm. on Ways and Means*, 77th Cong. 2405–09 (1942) (statement of Randolph Paul, special tax adviser to the Secretary of the Treasury).
Using public money to induce broader pension distribution is, of course, the motif of the qualified retirement plan provisions of the Internal Revenue Code. A new variation on that theme was adopted with the tremendous acceleration of vesting required by the 1986 amendments. The goal of this faster vesting was to increase the retirement security of women, minorities, and lower-income workers. These historically disadvantaged groups had shorter average job tenures and were therefore more likely to lose their retirement benefits under ERISA's original lengthy vesting schedules. S. Rep. No. 99-313, at 590 (1986).

D CONCLUSION

Entitlement to a pension requires that a worker become a plan member, earn deferred compensation by performing service under the plan, and satisfy any conditions necessary to avoid forfeiture of benefits. These three components of pension accumulation – participation, benefit accrual, and vesting – share a close functional and policy relationship.

Functionally, the decision to restrict the duration of forfeiture conditions necessitated legal intervention with respect to participation and benefit accrual as well. Banning forfeiture after ten years of service would be illusory if plans could require fifteen years of service to qualify for membership, for example. Alternatively, consider a defined benefit plan that grants prompt membership and immediate vesting, but under which the promised retirement annuity is earned disproportionately in the final year or two before normal retirement age. Left unregulated, such "backloading" of benefit accrual would give a long-term employee who separates from service before normal retirement age vested rights in a trivial amount of benefits. Either of these stratagems would defeat the pension expectation that ERISA's vesting rules were intended to protect.

Policy-wise, ERISA's accumulation rules shape both the distribution and quality of pensions. Tight limits on age and service conditions encourage early plan entry of otherwise eligible workers. Early membership, combined with fairly even year-by-year benefit accrual and rapid vesting, provides a longer accumulation period and potentially higher benefits, but may also force the employer to provide more contributions or benefits to employees who work for the firm for only a few years (albeit long enough to vest). Instead of bestowing pensions on those few workers who make a career-long commitment to the firm, ERISA's accumulation rules incorporate a preference for broader distribution of retirement savings. This covert distributive norm comes at a price: young and recently hired workers generally value retirement savings less than their senior coworkers, while on the employer side, the utility of a pension plan as a workforce bonding mechanism (an inducement to long and loyal service) is restricted. Given our system of voluntary employment-based pension plans, where these cost increases prove material, the employer is free to respond by terminating the plan, decreasing future benefit accruals, or restricting coverage based on criteria other than age or service. Yet because our pension system is tax subsidized (and thus only semi-private), in many instances increased costs will be met by the public subsidy – the preferential tax treatment of qualified retirement savings (discussed in Chapter 10).

The benefit accrual and vesting rules assure that any employer's pension promise meets a baseline standard of quality. This limited regulation of pension plan content may be seen as either paternalistic worker protection or efficiency-enhancing worker empowerment. Restrictions on backloading and forfeitures protect workers who casually rely on the employer's pension promise without attending to the details.

By outlawing pension limitations that are often overlooked or misunderstood, participants are given the right to receive what they consider their due.

Instead of aligning the content of the pension promise with workers' mistaken (over-) estimation of its value, effective disclosure of accrual rates and forfeiture risks could, in principle, alter workers' assessment of the promise (by downward adjustment) to make it congruent with their pension's actual expected value. Whether disclosure can be "effective" is another matter, however. The time and expense involved in understanding plan terms and assessing individual risks (determining expected value) would often exceed the advantage that could be gained by comparing pension plans associated with alternative employment opportunities. Reining in abstruse outlier plan terms could be used as a mechanism to limit information costs and thereby allow workers to inexpensively assess salient differences that remain. From this information cost perspective, reducing variation in accrual rates and forfeiture risks empowers workers to compare retirement plan alternatives and make better career and financial planning decisions.

8

Distribution

Once an employee has become a participant, has earned benefits, and has worked long enough to vest, the employer cannot cancel that employee's pension (see *supra* Chapter 7 on the rules governing accumulation). A vested participant does not normally have an immediate right to the money, however, nor can she direct its payment to someone else. Pension plans are designed to provide workers with a secure source of retirement income, not to facilitate general purpose savings. Therefore, access to pension savings is restricted, either by the terms of the plan or by ERISA itself.

ERISA's rules governing pension plan distributions are a curious mix of not-altogether-coherent policies. The rules address three issues. First, the timing of distributions is restricted. Second, the anti-alienation rule generally limits the recipients of distributions to the participant and her beneficiaries. And third, the participant's spouse is, in effect, designated primary beneficiary.

A TIMING

Despite its central goal of increasing the security of *retirement* income, ERISA has little to say about the timing of plan distributions. Instead, the task of discouraging pre-retirement (in-service) distributions, as well as excessive deferral (intergenerational transfers), is left almost entirely to the tax law.

Early Distributions

Private pensions supplement Social Security old-age benefits to help maintain workers' standard of living after retirement. To replace lost wage or salary income, pensions must be available upon retirement. Defined benefit plans have traditionally provided distribution in the form of a life annuity commencing at a specified retirement age. Defined contribution plans, in contrast, commonly permit distribution in the form of a lump-sum payment upon separation from service. Separation from service may occur long before permanent withdrawal from the labor force. Such pre-retirement distributions create a risk that pension benefits will be used for more immediate goals, like increasing current consumption or sending children to college. Nevertheless, ERISA does not restrict pre-retirement pension plan distributions.

Instead, the task of restricting early distributions is left entirely to the tax law. Qualified pension plans have always been directed to retirement savings and generally are prohibited from allowing in-service distributions or providing nonretirement benefits.[1] Profit-sharing and stock bonus plans, in contrast, need not be devoted exclusively to retirement saving, but may provide short term deferred compensation by making available in-service distributions after as little as two years of participation, or in the event of the employee's financial hardship.[2] Such liberal access to distributions creates the risk that qualified plan savings will be dissipated before retirement. Congress has tried to avoid that result by imposing an additional 10 percent income tax on early distributions from qualified plans that are not preserved as retirement savings by being promptly contributed to another qualified plan or an individual retirement account (IRA).[3]

---

[1] Treas. Reg. § 1.401-1(b)(1)(i) (as amended in 2020). Statutory amendments were enacted in 2006 to facilitate phased retirement programs, under which employees are allowed to reduce their work schedules and receive a portion of their accrued pension benefits during a period of transition between full-time employment and complete retirement. I.R.C. § 401(a)(36) (Supp. 2021) (qualified pension plan may permit in-service distributions to employees aged 59½ or older); ERISA § 3(2)(A), 29 U.S.C. § 1002(2)(A) (2018) (final sentence) (in-service distributions to employees aged sixty-two or older satisfy ERISA's definition of pension plan). *See* Prop. Treas. Reg. § 1.401(a)-3, 69 Fed. Reg. 65108 (Nov. 10, 2004) (proposed rule would allow qualified pension plan to distribute phased retirement benefits to an employee who, being at least 59½ years old, voluntarily reduces his customary work schedule by at least 20 percent).

[2] A profit-sharing plan is "primarily a plan of deferred compensation," Treas. Reg. § 1.401-1(b) (1)(ii) (as amended in 2020), while a pension plan, in the tax Code's parlance, must be meant "to provide for the livelihood of the employees or their beneficiaries after the retirement of such employees," *id.* § 1.401-1(a)(2)(i). Rev. Rul. 54-231, 1954-1 C.B. 150 ("fixed number of years" means two or more); Rev. Rul. 68-24, 1968-1 C.B. 150 (same); Rev. Rul. 71-224, 1971-1 C.B. 124 (financial hardship, if objectively defined, is permissible grounds for distribution of vested interest in an employee's profit-sharing account).

[3] I.R.C. §§ 72(t), 402(c) (2018). The early distribution penalty tax generally applies to distributions made before the employee attains age 59½, but does not apply to distributions made following separation from service after age fifty-five, to distributions on account of disability, to distributions to a beneficiary after the death of the employee, or to annuity-type distributions, regardless of when they commence, paid over the life or life expectancy of the employee (or over the joint lives or life expectancies of the employee and his designated beneficiary). Distributions to cover extraordinary medical expenses are also exempt. An early distribution that would otherwise trigger the tax becomes nontaxable if contributed to another qualified plan or IRA within sixty days of receipt because the tax applies only to the amount of a distribution that is *includible* in gross income, and such a "rollover" renders a distribution

Late Distributions

To ensure that pension plan savings are available to finance retirement, ERISA requires that, *absent the participant's consent*, the plan must provide that distributions commence within sixty days after the close of the plan year in which either (1) the participant attains the earlier of age sixty-five or the plan's normal retirement age (NRA), or, if later, (2) the participant separates from service. If plan participation commenced within ten years of the relevant date (whichever applies), distributions need not begin earlier than sixty days after the close of the plan year in which the tenth anniversary of initial participation falls.[4] This rule is meant to ensure access to benefits as soon as the participant is likely to need retirement income, upon separation from service at an advanced age. Where separation from service occurs earlier, payment can generally be deferred until the plan's NRA (but not later than age sixty-five), which is the time when the participant was told that his pension would be available. If the plan allows for payment of early retirement benefits, however, a vested participant who has enough service to qualify for early retirement benefits, but who separates from service before the earliest age for payment, must be permitted to start taking distribution once he satisfies the age requirement. The amount payable to such a former employee is the benefit to which he would be entitled at NRA (i.e., his accrued benefit), actuarially reduced for early commencement.[5] A former employee is not entitled to any early retirement subsidy that the plan may offer because the purpose of such a subsidy is to induce separation from service.

B ANTI-ALIENATION

Standing alone, constraints on early distributions are insufficient to prevent premature dissipation of retirement savings. Instead of waiting for distributions to commence, a participant determined to use his pension for other purposes could sell his interest immediately. Similarly, the short-sighted participant could run up his personal debts, leaving his creditors to collect from his pension accumulation. To prevent such indirect plundering of retirement savings, ERISA generally requires that pension benefits be nontransferable.[6]

According to the Supreme Court, ERISA's "anti-alienation provision can 'be seen to bespeak a pension law protective policy of special intensity: Retirement funds

---

excludible from gross income. *Compare* I.R.C. § 72(t)(1) (2018), *with id.* § 402(c)(1). See the discussion of the early distribution penalty tax and rollovers *infra* Chapter 10C.

[4] ERISA § 206(a), 29 U.S.C. § 1056(a) (2018); *see* I.R.C. § 401(a)(14) (2018).

[5] ERISA § 206(a), 29 U.S.C. § 1056(a) (2018) (final sentence); *see* I.R.C. § 401(a)(14) (2018) (final sentence); Treas. Reg. § 1.401(a)-14(c) (1976).

[6] ERISA § 206(d)(1), 29 U.S.C. § 1056(d)(1) (2018); *see* I.R.C. § 401(a)(13)(A) (2018).

shall remain inviolate until retirement.'"[7] The goal is to "safeguard a stream of [retirement] income for pensioners" and their dependents by putting it beyond their own reach, and beyond the reach of their creditors.[8] By making retirement savings inaccessible, ERISA's so-called spendthrift clause works as a pre-commitment device that tends to bind the worker to a particular use of the fund.[9] In so limiting participants' freedom of choice, the value of pension accruals is impaired for many workers, relative to cash, because they have more immediate and higher-priority uses for their compensation.[10] Mandatory spendthrift protection, of course, reflects a congressional judgment that those priorities are often misguided.

Inalienability serves the employer's interest as well, by ensuring that pension savings will be available to provide an incentive for retirement. Consequently, pension trusts commonly included spendthrift restraints long before ERISA demanded it. Uncertainty and variation in state spendthrift trust law, however, made it difficult for workers to gauge the accessibility of pension savings offered under plans of different employers. ERISA's anti-alienation requirement, by mandating uniform efficacious spendthrift protection for all pensions, reduces those information costs. Hence the anti-alienation rule promotes improved worker career and financial planning. Thus, while it is central to the protective policy, anti-alienation also serves ERISA's goal of increasing efficiency through better-informed decision making.[11]

Congress has authorized a few narrow exceptions to the anti-alienation requirement. Once distributions have begun, a voluntary revocable assignment of not more than 10 percent of any benefit payment is permissible.[12] The grant of an interest in benefits to secure repayment of a loan from the plan, provided that the loan meets

---

[7] Boggs v. Boggs, 520 U.S. 833, 851 (1997) (quoting JOHN LANGBEIN & BRUCE WOLK, PENSION AND EMPLOYEE BENEFIT LAW 547 (2d ed. 1995)). Or, as the committee reports explained, the anti-alienation rule is meant to "ensure that the employee's accrued benefits are actually available for retirement purposes." H.R. REP. No. 93-779, at 66 (1974), *reprinted in* 2 ERISA LEGISLATIVE HISTORY, *supra* Chapter 1 note 55, at 2584, 2655; H.R. REP. No. 93-807, at 68 (1974), *reprinted in* 2 ERISA LEGISLATIVE HISTORY, *supra* Chapter 1 note 55, at 3115, 3188.

[8] Guidry v. Sheet Metal Workers Nat'l Pension Fund, 493 U.S. 365, 376 (1990).

[9] *See generally* Richard H. Thaler & H.M. Shefrin, *An Economic Theory of Self Control, in* QUASI RATIONAL ECONOMICS 77, 81–84 (Richard H. Thaler ed., 1991); Hersh M. Shefrin & Richard H. Thaler, *The Behavioral Life-Cycle Hypothesis, in id.* at 91, 95–96, 103–07.

[10] This impairment of value, in turn, increases the need to subsidize pensions, which is accomplished via the preferential tax treatment accorded qualified pension, profit-sharing, and stock bonus plans. *See infra* Chapter 10B.

[11] Wiedenbeck, *supra* Chapter 1 note 56, at 575. *See supra* Chapter 1C.

[12] Curiously, the tax Code's qualification criteria permit limited, voluntary revocable assignments only if the participant or beneficiary is already receiving benefits under the plan, while ERISA's corresponding exception is not restricted to benefits that are already in pay status. *Compare* ERISA § 206(d)(2), 29 U.S.C. § 1056(d)(2) (2018), *with* I.R.C. § 401(a)(13)(A) (2018). *See* Treas. Reg. § 1.401(a)-13(d)(1) (as amended in 1988) (exception extends to assignments by beneficiaries, although the tax Code mentions only participants; 10 percent limit applies to the total of all assignments, multiple assignments of 10 percent each impermissible).

Distribution

certain tests to prevent favoritism, is also allowed.[13] The plan loan exception undercuts the policy of the anti-alienation rule: if loan proceeds are used for nonretirement purposes and are not repaid, enforcement of the security interest will extinguish the participant's pension. For that reason, the tax Code discourages most plan loans other than small, short-term loans.[14]

Involuntary assignments (i.e., enforcement of creditors' claims against a participant's or beneficiary's interest in the pension plan) are generally barred as well.[15] And ERISA's restraint on alienation is even effective in bankruptcy proceedings. A debtor's interest in an ERISA-regulated pension plan is excluded from the bankruptcy code's definition of property of the estate, so that retirement savings continue to be shielded from creditors, even as virtually all other property interests are marshaled for creditors' benefit.[16]

The startling force of the anti-alienation rule is illustrated by *Guidry* v. *Sheet Metal Workers National Pension Fund*.[17] Guidry, who was both the chief executive officer of a union local and a trustee of the local's pension fund, pleaded guilty to embezzling more than $377,000 from the union and later stipulated to the entry of a judgment of $275,000 in favor of the union. While serving his prison sentence, Guidry brought suit against two union pension plans in which he was a participant, claiming that they were wrongfully refusing to pay benefits. The plans countered

[13] ERISA § 206(d)(2), 29 U.S.C. § 1056(d)(2) (2018); *see* I.R.C. § 401(a)(13)(A) (2018). A security interest in plan benefits is valid only if it backs a plan loan that is made in accordance with specific provisions in the plan, is available to all participants or beneficiaries on a reasonably equivalent basis in amounts that do not favor highly compensated employees, and is adequately secured and bears a reasonable rate of interest. I.R.C. § 4975(d)(1) (2018). These anti-favoritism criteria apply whether or not the plan loan is made to a "disqualified person" (designated insiders and related parties who are subject to the penalty tax on prohibited transactions). Treas. Reg. § 1.401(a)-13(d)(2)(iii) (as amended in 1988).

[14] I.R.C. § 72(p) (2018). The discouragement takes the form of taxing the proceeds of plan loans as distributions. (Under general tax principles, ordinary loan proceeds are not income.) As deemed distributions, the loan proceeds might also trigger the additional 10 percent tax on early withdrawals, I.R.C. § 72(t) (2018). To avoid taxation, the total amount of plan loans must not exceed the *lesser* of (1) $50,000 (but with amounts repaid within the prior year treated as outstanding and counted against this limit) or (2) one-half of the present value of the participant's vested accrued benefit (or $10,000, if greater). In addition, the loan must be subject to level amortization with payments at least quarterly, and, except in the case of a loan to purchase a principal residence, must be for a term of not more than five years. I.R.C. § 72(p) (2) (2018).

[15] The IRS takes the position that federal tax levies and judgments can be enforced against pension plan benefits notwithstanding the anti-alienation rule, Treas. Reg. § 1.401(a)-13(b)(2) (as amended in 1988), presumably on the authority of ERISA's federal law savings clause, ERISA § 514(d), 29 U.S.C. § 1144(d) (2018). *See* I.R.C. § 72(t)(2)(A)(vii) (2018) (levy excepted from additional tax on early distributions). *But see* Guidry v. Sheet Metal Workers Nat'l Pension Fund, 493 U.S. 365, 375–76 (1990) (Taft-Hartley Act's remedial provisions do not override ERISA's anti-alienation rule despite the federal law savings clause), discussed *infra* text accompanying Chapter 8 notes 17–19.

[16] 11 U.S.C. § 541(c)(2) (2018); Patterson v. Shumate, 504 U.S. 753 (1992).

[17] 493 U.S. 365 (1990).

268 *Content Controls: Pension Plans*

that Guidry's accrued benefits should be paid to the union under a constructive trust. The Supreme Court held that the Taft-Hartley Act's general authorization of "appropriate equitable relief" to remedy violations of an officer's duties to the union does not override ERISA's anti-alienation provision. The Court refused to approve any generalized equitable exception to the anti-alienation rule based on employee wrongdoing, observing:

> Section 206(d) reflects a considered congressional policy choice, a decision to safeguard a stream of income for pensioners (and their dependents, who may be, and perhaps usually are, blameless), even if that decision prevents others from securing relief for the wrongs done them. If exceptions to this policy are to be made, it is for Congress to undertake that task.[18]

While he was a convicted felon, Guidry was found not to have violated any duty owed *to the pension plans*, and so the case did not present an internal conflict between ERISA's remedies for fiduciary breach and its anti-alienation provision. The Court declined to resolve that conflict,[19] and a circuit split quickly developed on this issue.[20] In 1997, Congress accepted the Court's invitation to legislate exceptions to the anti-alienation policy, declaring that an order offsetting a participant's pension benefits against an amount the participant owes the plan is enforceable if the liability arises from conviction of a crime involving the plan, a judgment for breach of an ERISA fiduciary obligation, or a settlement agreement with the Labor Department or the Pension Benefit Guaranty Corporation (PBGC) involving alleged violations of fiduciary obligations. But where the pension being offset is subject to the spousal survivor annuity rules, Congress protected the spouse's interest. If the spouse is not also liable for the harm done to the plan and has not voluntarily consented to the setoff, then a portion of the wrongdoer's accrued benefits sufficient to provide the spouse with ERISA's minimum required survivor annuity protection must be preserved.[21]

In contrast to ERISA's laissez-faire attitude toward distribution timing, the statute takes a hard line on indirect access to pensions. The anti-alienation rule prevents participants and beneficiaries from transferring undistributed pension accumulations, and so bars anticipation by sale or execution by creditors. Taken together, these rules prohibit participants and their beneficiaries from doing indirectly what the plan could lawfully have allowed them to do directly (i.e., by authorizing in-service or early distributions). Still, where a plan does not, in fact, permit

---

[18] *Id.* at 376 (footnote omitted).

[19] *Id.* at 373.

[20] *Compare* Herberger v. Shanbaum, 897 F.2d 801 (5th Cir. 1990) (offset of breaching fiduciary's pension barred), *with* Coar v. Kamizir, 990 F.2d 1413 (3d Cir. 1993) (offset permitted).

[21] ERISA § 206(d)(4), (d)(5), 29 U.S.C. § 1056(d)(4), (d)(5) (2018); *see* I.R.C. § 401(a)(13)(C), (a)(13)(D) (2018). ERISA's spousal survivor annuity requirements are discussed *infra* Chapter 8C.

Distribution

pre-retirement distributions (defined benefit plans commonly forbid them), the anti-alienation rule reinforces the employer's design control, increasing the utility of the plan as an instrument of personnel policy, perhaps thereby encouraging sponsorship. In backstopping the plan's distribution rules, the stringent national anti-alienation rule is commonly viewed as another of ERISA's worker protection devices. This protection, however, is of an unusual sort. Anti-alienation does not safeguard against *employer* abuses, such as misrepresentation, forfeiture, or insolvency (compare ERISA's disclosure, vesting, and funding rules). Instead, anti-alienation protects workers from their *own* improvidence.[22]

Qualified Domestic Relations Orders

The anti-alienation rule makes pension plans a sort of federal law spendthrift trust.[23] State spendthrift trust law recognizes a number of public policy exceptions: certain categories of creditors' claims may be enforced against a protected beneficial interest, notwithstanding a restraint on alienation.[24] Foremost among these favored claims are claims for support by the spouse or children of the beneficiary.[25] Whether federal courts would adopt a comparable family law creditor exception to ERISA's anti-alienation rule was a hotly contested issue during ERISA's first decade. In the Retirement Equity Act of 1984, Congress stepped in to resolve the controversy, creating an express statutory exception for family law creditors whose claims satisfied certain requirements.[26] The conditions that must be met to make family law claims enforceable against a pension plan are set forth in the definition of a "qualified domestic relations order," or QDRO. At the same time, however, Congress amended ERISA's preemption provision to make clear that support claims not meeting the strict definition of a QDRO are unenforceable against pension plans.[27]

[22] It also simplifies planning by clarifying exactly where a worker stands in terms of access to her pension savings – like it or not, wherever you live and whatever the plan has to say about transferability, you can't get the money until all distribution conditions are satisfied. *See supra* Chapter 8 note 11 and accompanying text.

[23] RESTATEMENT (SECOND) OF TRUSTS § 152(2) (1959) provides: "A trust in which by the terms of the trust or by statute a valid restraint on the voluntary and involuntary transfer of the interest of the beneficiary is imposed is a spendthrift trust."

[24] RESTATEMENT (SECOND) OF TRUSTS § 157 (1959); 2A SCOTT ON TRUSTS, *supra* Chapter 3 note 16, § 157.

[25] RESTATEMENT (SECOND) OF TRUSTS § 157(a) (1959); 2A SCOTT ON TRUSTS, *supra* Chapter 3 note 16, § 157.1.

[26] ERISA § 206(d)(3), 29 U.S.C. § 1056(d)(3) (2018), enacted by Pub. L. No. 98-397, § 104 (1984). The corresponding tax-law qualification requirements appear as I.R.C. §§ 401(a)(13) (B), 414(p) (2018).

[27] ERISA § 514(b)(7), 29 U.S.C. § 1144(b)(7) (2018). *See* S. REP. NO. 98-575, at 19 (1984) ("conforming changes to the ERISA preemption provision are necessary to ensure that only those orders that are excepted [by the QDRO rules] from the spendthrift provisions are not preempted by ERISA"; domestic relations order not a prohibited alienation of benefits "if and only if" it is a QDRO). *Accord* I.R.C. § 401(a)(13)(B) (2018) (anti-alienation rule "shall apply"

To be "qualified," a domestic relations order must recognize the participant's liability to a spouse, former spouse, child, or other dependent of a participant for the payment of child support, alimony, or marital property, and it must also authorize such an "alternate payee" to collect from the plan.[28] In addition, the order must meet a number of statutory criteria that are designed to protect pension plans from increased costs, so that enforcing one participant's family support obligations will not impair the interests of other participants and their beneficiaries. There are two components to this endeavor. First, ERISA demands a certain degree of specificity and clarity in order to minimize compliance costs and avoid having the plan become enmeshed in litigation. Second, family law creditors' claims must not increase the plan's liability to pay benefits.

To be a QDRO, the order must "clearly specif[y]" (1) the name and address of the participant and each payee covered by the order, (2) the amount or percentage of the participant's benefits to be paid to each alternate payee, or the manner for determining the amount or percentage, (3) the number of payments or periods to which the order applies, and (4) the plans to which the order applies.[29] The purpose is to enable the plan administrator to act on the order alone, without having to look behind the document to resolve ambiguities or supply missing information, and without being sued by rival claimants. Where an order lacks the necessary information, but the plan administrator has independent knowledge of the missing facts, the courts disagree on whether the order is a QDRO. Some adopt a lenient attitude suggested by the legislative history, while others, fearing that controversies over the existence and extent of such subjective knowledge would embroil the plan in litigation, are more strict.[30]

---

to a domestic relations order unless it is determined to be a QDRO). *See* Ablamis v. Roper, 937 F.2d 1450, 1458 (9th Cir. 1991) (rejecting argument that ERISA's anti-alienation provision is simply inapplicable to allocations or transfers between spouses); Boggs v. Boggs, 520 U.S. 833, 851 (1997).

[28] ERISA § 206(d)(3)(B), (K), 29 U.S.C. § 1056(d)(3)(B), (K) (2018); *see* I.R.C. § 414(p)(1), (8) (2018). *See* Hawkins v. Comm'r, 86 F.3d 982, 989–91 (10th Cir. 1996) (where marital property settlement agreement incorporated in divorce decree stated that the wife was to receive $1 million from the husband's pension plan, order was sufficient to recognize right to receive plan benefits, even though the wife not referred to as alternate payee and agreement did not mimic statutory language).

[29] ERISA § 206(d)(3)(C), 29 U.S.C. § 1056(d)(3)(C) (2018); *see* I.R.C. § 414(p)(2) (2018).

[30] *Compare Hawkins*, 86 F.3d at 991–93 (QDRO specificity requirement must be enforced because required by plain meaning and to avoid embroiling plan in costly litigation), *with* Metro. Life Ins. Co. v. Wheaton, 42 F.3d 1080, 1085 (7th Cir. 1994) (strict compliance with QDRO specificity requirements not necessary). This difference of opinion is reviewed in Stewart v. Thorpe Holding Co. Profit Sharing Plan, 207 F.3d 1143 (9th Cir. 2000). See S. Rep. No. 98-575, at 20 (1984) (order with incorrect address should be treated as QDRO if administrator has independent knowledge of current address); EBSA, QDROs: The Division of Retirement Benefits Through Qualified Domestic Relations Orders 18–19 (2014), www.dol.gov/sites/dolgov/files/EBSA/about-ebsa/our-activities/resource-center/publications/qdros.pdf (if order "incomplete only with respect to factual identifying information within the plan administrator's knowledge or easily obtained through a

Distribution

ERISA forbids plan compliance with a domestic relations order that would force the plan to pay increased benefits or that would require the plan to provide any type or form of benefit or any option not otherwise available under the plan.[31] Nor may effect be given to an order that would require the payment of benefits to a family law claimant if the benefits are required to be paid under a prior QDRO to another alternate payee (a first-in-time rule).[32] These rules shield the plan from any obligation to provide different or increased benefits to family law creditors.[33] So, for

> simple communication with the alternate payee or the participant" administrator should not reject order as defective).

[31] ERISA § 206(d)(3)(D), 29 U.S.C. § 1056(d)(3)(D) (2018); *see* I.R.C. § 414(p)(3) (2018). The tax Code does not apply its version of these plan protection rules, nor the clear-statement rule (*supra* Chapter 8 note 29 and accompanying text), to qualified government plans or qualified church plans. I.R.C. § 414(p)(11), (p)(1)(A)(i). Government and church plans, of course, are exempt from ERISA. ERISA § 4(b), 29 U.S.C. § 1003(b).

[32] ERISA § 206(d)(3)(D), 29 U.S.C. § 1056(d)(3)(D) (2018); *see* I.R.C. § 414(p)(3) (2018). Similarly, procedural rules protect the plan from inconsistent liability. Payments to the participant are suspended during the period in which the status of a domestic relations order as a QDRO is being determined; if the matter cannot be resolved within eighteen months, the withheld amounts are then paid to the participant, and any later determination that the order is a QDRO is given only prospective effect. ERISA § 206(d)(3)(H), 29 U.S.C. § 1056(d)(3)(H) (2018); *see* I.R.C. § 414(p)(7) (2018).

[33] The prospect of inconsistent or increased benefit liabilities can arise where an otherwise proper domestic relations order (DRO) is not presented to the plan until after the retirement of the participant. If a divorced participant remarries and later retires the pension would normally be payable in the form of a qualified joint and survivor annuity (QJSA) with the new spouse (*see infra* Chapter 8C). If the former spouse presents a DRO after retirement and commencement of QJSA payments (based on the life expectancies of the participant and the new spouse), it could not be honored without either decreasing payments from a QJSA that is already in the distribution phase or increasing plan benefits. Several decisions hold that survivor benefits vest in the participant's current spouse upon retirement; a DRO presented after the participant's retirement cannot grant survivor benefits to a former spouse. Hopkins v. AT&T Global Info. Sols. Co., 105 F.3d 153 (4th Cir. 1997) (state court order to collect alimony and granting former wife survivor benefits not QDRO because not entered until after participant's retirement, at which time surviving spouse benefits vested in second wife); Rivers v. Cent. & S.W. Corp., 186 F.3d 681 (5th Cir. 1999) (first wife's community property claim, presented years after participant retired with QJSA and died, not QDRO because benefits vested in second wife on date of retirement); Langston v. Wilson McShane Corp., 828 N.W.2d 109 (Minn. 2013). It appears, however, that QJSA survivor benefits for a subsequent spouse can be overridden by a DRO *filed with the plan* before retirement, so long as it is thereafter found to satisfy the QDRO criteria (determined to be "qualified"). *See* Vorris J. Blankenship, *Divorce, QDRO, Retirement, Death: Not Necessarily in That Order,* 163 Tax Notes 707, 710–11 (Apr. 29, 2019).

> Can a family law creditor obtain access to a participant's pension following the *pre-retirement death* of the participant? This question remains unsettled. *Compare* Samaroo v. Samaroo, 193 F.3d 185 (3d Cir. 1999) (divorced participant's defined benefit pension forfeited on death without surviving spouse; divorce decree did not give former wife survivor benefits, and post-death amendment purporting to confer survivorship rights not QDRO because it would increase plan benefits) *with* Files v. ExxonMobil Pension Plan, 428 F.3d 478 (3d Cir. 2005) (finding that property settlement agreement awarding former spouse 50 percent separate interest in pension could be recognized as QDRO after participant's death and rejecting argument that participant's pension was forfeited upon death; unlike *Samaroo,* DRO did not attempt to grant former spouse survivor annuity rights after participant's death); Patton

example, the divorced spouse of a forty-year-old participant cannot immediately collect all or a portion of the participant's accrued benefits if the plan does not permit lump-sum distributions at that time. If the plan does allow such distributions, a QDRO may call for immediate payment to the spouse, even if the participant elects payment in the form of an annuity. That is, a QDRO may be drafted to award the alternate payee a separate interest in a specified portion of the participant's benefits, with the alternate payee treated like a participant with respect to that interest, including having the right to select among alternative investments and having the right to choose the form and timing of distributions from among the options (if any) available to participants under the plan. (This is known as the separate interest approach.) Alternatively, a QDRO may be drafted to give the alternate payee a specified share of payments made under the form of distribution applicable to the debtor–participant, with the alternate payee receiving benefit payments only when the participant receives payments. (This method of division is known as the shared payment approach.)[34]

The prohibition on departures from the plan's ordinary distribution rules is subject to one important exception involving the time for commencement of distributions. Where a plan makes no provision for in-service distributions, the continued employment of the debtor–participant would normally bar distribution to alternate payees, even if a spouse or child has a pressing need for immediate support payments. To prevent this hardship, a special rule permits access by alternate payees on the later of (1) the date the participant attains age fifty, or (2) the earliest date on which the participant could begin receiving benefits if the participant separated from service.[35]

The QDRO rules reflect an accommodation between family law and pension policy. A homemaker who expects retirement support from an employee-spouse's

---

v. Denver Post Corp., 326 F.3d 1148, 1153–54 (10th Cir. 2003) (upholding nunc pro tunc DRO issued eleven years after a divorce decree pertaining to benefits from a plan not known about at the time of the divorce, and declining to infer that the plan must have been notified of the interest prior to the death of the participant); Yale-New Haven Hosp. v. Nicholls, 788 F.3d 79 (2d Cir. 2015); Hogan v. Raytheon Co., 302 F.3d 854, 857 (8th Cir. 2002) (permitting posthumous qualification of a DRO because during husband–participant's life, plan was provided with a copy of divorce decree awarding ex-wife fifty percent of husband–participant's present retirement funds, and DRO obtained subsequent to husband–participant's death designating ex-wife as alternate payee for purposes of survivorship benefits was done within the eighteen month period permitted to secure a QDRO); Trustees of the Dirs. Guild of Am. – Producer Pension Benefits Plans v. Tise, 234 F.3d 415 (9th Cir. 2000) (if, before participant's death, plan has notice of state court order requiring payment of child support from pension, order may be modified after death to fulfill QDRO requirements, despite impact on nonspouse death beneficiary).

[34] The shared payment and separate interest approaches are explained in EBSA *supra* Chapter 8 note 30, at 29–31, 36–40.

[35] ERISA § 206(d)(3)(E), 29 U.S.C. § 1056(d)(3)(E) (2018); *see* I.R.C. § 414(p)(4) (2018). For illustrations of the operation of this special timing rule, see EBSA, *supra* Chapter 8 note 30, at 41–42.

Distribution

pension may be impoverished by a late-life divorce. In such situations, giving the ex-spouse access to the participant's pension is a logical extension of Congress's recognition that two people may be relying on the participant's retirement income. ERISA generally gives a spouse the right to receive a survivor annuity in the event of the participant's death;[36] similar protections would be appropriate where the marriage ends in divorce. Yet this retirement security concern is obviously not the principal impetus for the QDRO rules. Children and other non-spouse dependents can be granted an interest in pension benefits as alternate payees. For a spouse, pension access may provide the wherewithal to finance a marital property settlement rather than providing support, much less retirement support. And we have just seen that where distributions are conditioned on separation from service, access may be granted even if the participant is still employed. In this field, pension policy takes a back seat to enforcement of family law obligations. That is apparent, as well, from the fact that retirement income protection is available under a QDRO, but is neither required nor automatically included as a default rule. A former spouse can be granted survivorship rights in the participant's pension (with the consequence that any subsequent spouse of the participant will be denied that protection), but only "to the extent provided" in the QDRO.[37]

Overriding a Beneficiary Designation

Upon the death of the participant, any remaining benefits go to her beneficiaries.[38] The beneficiary is "the person designated by a participant, or by the terms of an employee benefit plan," as entitled to plan benefits.[39] Pension plan survivor benefits amount to a death-time donative transfer from the participant. Under state wills and succession laws, a property owner's beneficiary designation is revoked by operation of law in some circumstances. Typically, divorce cuts off all gifts under a will in favor of a spouse,[40] and an intentional killer is barred from taking the victim's property as heir or devisee.[41] Similar beneficiary disqualification issues can arise with respect to

---

[36] *See infra* Chapter 8C on the spousal protection rules.

[37] ERISA § 206(d)(3)(F), 29 U.S.C. § 1056(d)(3)(F) (2018); *see* I.R.C. § 414(p)(5) (2018).

[38] Recall, however, that a plan may call for forfeiture on the death of the participant if the spousal protection rules do not apply. ERISA § 203(a)(3)(A), 29 U.S.C. § 1053(a)(3)(A) (2018); *see* I.R.C. § 411(a)(3)(A) (2018). Defined benefit plans often call for forfeiture in the event the participant dies without a surviving spouse, but defined contribution plans rarely contain such a provision.

[39] ERISA § 3(8), 29 U.S.C. § 1002(8) (2018). *See also* Treas. Reg. § 1.401-1(b)(4) (as amended in 2020) (for purposes of the definition of qualified pension, profit-sharing, and stock bonus plans, the beneficiaries of the employee include "the estate of the employee, dependents of the employee, persons who are the natural objects of the employee's bounty, and any persons designated by the employee to share in the benefits of the plan after the death of the employee").

[40] *See, e.g.*, UNIF. PROBATE CODE §§ 1-201(18), 2-804 (amended 2019).

[41] *See, e.g.*, UNIF. PROBATE CODE §§ 1-201(18), 2-803 (amended 2019).

274 *Content Controls: Pension Plans*

pensions, but they are complicated by ERISA's anti-alienation and preemption provisions.

Divorce is the most common issue. Almost invariably, pension plan beneficiary designations can be changed by the participant, and while spousal consent to the change is often required, that is not an obstacle following divorce.[42] Where the participant designates a spouse as beneficiary, the parties are later divorced, and the participant subsequently dies without having changed the beneficiary designation, what inference should be drawn from the participant's inaction? Was the failure to change the beneficiary designation an oversight, or does it evidence a continuing desire to benefit the former spouse? State laws calling for revocation of bequests to a former spouse proceed from the view that in this situation failure to change the will was probably inadvertent, so that a default rule of revocation on divorce is most likely to effectuate the owner's desires. The same considerations apply to pension plan beneficiary designations, but ERISA makes no provision for revocation on divorce. Nor is there any indication that this omission was deliberate; Congress simply never considered the issue.

The states have, however. In many jurisdictions nonprobate transfer laws call for revocation on divorce of spousal beneficiary designations made in a wide variety of contracts, including life insurance, annuity contracts, bank accounts, payable-on-death instructions, and employee benefit plans.[43] Application of such a state law to a pension plan beneficiary designation works a transfer of succession rights from the former spouse, causing alienation of benefits in contravention of the literal terms of ERISA's spendthrift clause. Beyond their specific conflict with the anti-alienation rule, state divorce revocation laws seem to run afoul of ERISA's statutory preemption provision, for by altering the pension beneficiary, they apparently "relate to [an] employee benefit plan."[44]

The Supreme Court faced this issue in *Egelhoff* v. *Egelhoff*.[45] There, the decedent had named his wife, Donna Rae Egelhoff, as beneficiary under both his employer-provided life insurance and pension plans. The participant died due to an automobile accident less than three months after the couple divorced, not having changed his beneficiary designation under either plan. The decedent's children from a prior marriage challenged Donna Rae's entitlement to benefits, relying on a Washington statute that revokes transfers to a former spouse under a "payable-on-death provision of a life insurance policy, employee benefit plan, annuity or similar

---

[42] *See* ERISA § 205(c)(2), 29 U.S.C. § 1055(c)(2) (2018); I.R.C. § 417(a)(2) (2018). *See generally infra* Chapter 8C.

[43] *See, e.g.,* Unif. Probate Code § 1-201(18) (1990) (instrument subject to divorce revocation rules includes "deed, will, trust, insurance or annuity policy, account with POD designation, security registered in beneficiary form (TOD), pension, profit-sharing, retirement, or similar benefit plan").

[44] ERISA § 514(a), 29 U.S.C. § 1144(a) (2018).

[45] 532 U.S. 141 (2001).

Distribution 275

contract, or individual retirement account."[46] Nonprobate transfers to which the statute applies are redirected as though the former spouse died on the date of divorce.[47] Applying that rule, the children claimed the life insurance proceeds as heirs and asserted survivors' rights in the pension under a plan provision appointing default beneficiaries in the absence of an effective beneficiary designation by the participant.[48] The former wife, of course, argued that ERISA prevents application of the state divorce revocation statute, and that, as the participant's designated beneficiary, she was entitled to benefits under the terms of the plans.

The Court held that Washington's nonprobate transfer law ran afoul of ERISA. The divorce revocation rule was preempted because it "directly conflicts with ERISA's requirements that plans be administered, and benefits paid, in accordance with plan documents."[49] Here, the plan documents included the deceased participant's written beneficiary designation. The Washington statute prevented uniform plan administration because administrators could not simply make payment to the beneficiary whose name was on file. Instead, they would have to familiarize themselves with state law and investigate the marital status of beneficiaries to determine whether a beneficiary designation remained valid. In cases where the participant worked in one state and resided in another, with the former spouse perhaps living in a third, reliance on state law would present choice-of-law issues and potentially conflicting legal obligations.[50] This sort of nonuniformity is unacceptable because increased plan-administration costs ultimately reduce net benefits to employees,

---

[46] WASH. REV. CODE § 11.07.010(5)(a) (1994). In 2002 in response to *Egelhoff* the quoted language was qualified by appending "unless otherwise provided by controlling federal law". 2002 Wash. Sess. Laws. 51; S.B. 6242, 57th Leg., Reg. Sess. (Wash. 2002).

[47] WASH. REV. CODE § 11.07.010(2)(a) (1994).

[48] *Egelhoff*, 532 U.S. at 145. In the court below, the children also argued that they were entitled to pension benefits apart from the divorce revocation statute, because the participant's ex-wife had voluntarily waived her right to pension benefits in a property settlement incorporated in the divorce decree. Egelhoff v. Egelhoff, 989 P.2d 80, 83–84 (Wash. 1999). The Supreme Court did not take up this question. The enforceability of such a waiver is discussed *infra*, Chapter 8 notes 56–63 and accompanying text.

[49] *Egelhoff*, 532 U.S. at 150. *See* ERISA §§ 402(b)(4), 404(a)(1)(D), 29 U.S.C. §§ 1102(b)(4), 1104(a)(1)(D) (2018). The Court did not address whether Washington's divorce revocation law conflicts with ERISA's anti-alienation rule, perhaps because that ground of decision was only relevant to the pension plan. Benefits under the life insurance program (a welfare plan) were not subject to transfer restrictions. ERISA §§ 201(1), 206(d)(1), 29 U.S.C. §§ 1051(1), 1056(d) (1) (2018). Moreover, even though application of the divorce revocation statute would work a transfer of pension benefits, it is far from clear that this is the sort of transfer against which ERISA's anti-alienation rule is directed. The transfer is not a voluntary disposition (sale or gift, for example) of the participant's interest, nor does it give creditors access to the fund. Consequently, the divorce revocation law does not undercut the goal of ensuring that pensions will be available to provide retirement income to participants and their beneficiaries. Instead, it simply supplies an answer to the question, who is the participant's intended beneficiary?

[50] *Egelhoff*, 532 U.S. at 148–49. State law is actually highly uniform in calling for automatic revocation of gifts under a will in favor of a spouse upon divorce and in providing for disposition of the property as if the ex-spouse had died on the date of divorce. But while wills law is consistent on this point, the same cannot be said for the treatment of nonprobate transfers.

276   *Content Controls: Pension Plans*

thereby imposing "precisely the burden that ERISA preemption was intended to avoid."[51]

Preemption of state divorce revocation laws clears the way for uniform plan administration. Yet from the standpoint of effectuating the average participant's intent, the Washington statute seems to achieve the preferable result. The Court could have secured the benefits of uniformity *and* better served participants' interests by holding the Washington statute preempted and simultaneously adopting the same approach as a matter of federal common law. Congress expected the judiciary to develop interstitial rules to implement ERISA,[52] and the effectiveness of spousal beneficiary designations following divorce seems to call for just that sort of limited lawmaking. None of the opinions in *Egelhoff* consider the possibility that preemption could go hand-in-hand with creation of a federal common-law rule. That oversight is unfortunate, for it offers the solution to a conundrum that troubled both the majority and the dissent, namely, that state slayer laws might also be preempted. The prospect of federal courts ordering an award of survivor benefits to a named beneficiary who murdered the plan participant is clearly unpalatable. In dissent, Justice Breyer asserted that state killer laws are virtually indistinguishable from the Washington divorce revocation statute, so that they too would fall prey to the Court's ERISA preemption analysis.[53] The Court majority sidestepped the issue, but suggested that the longer history and greater uniformity of state killer laws might save them from preemption.[54] A better solution would vindicate ERISA's uniformity interest by holding state killer laws preempted, while announcing a federal common-law rule barring an intentional killer from taking his victim's welfare or pension plan benefits.[55]

---

[51] *Egelhoff*, 532 U.S. at 150 (quoting Fort Halifax Packing Co. v. Coyne, 482 U.S. 1, 29 (1987)). In addition to cost containment, preemption preserves employer flexibility in setting plan terms (freedom of contract). *See supra* Chapter 6C. An employee benefit plan could be drafted to provide a specific default taker in the event of divorce. A plan might specify, for example, that in the event of divorce, benefits will be paid to secondary beneficiaries designated by the participant. Looking to state law takes the matter of divorce revocation out of the hands of the plan sponsor (or, in the case of a collectively bargained plan, the sponsor and the union). The *Egelhoff* opinion did not address this concern, which (unlike uniformity) weighs against creation of a federal common-law rule of divorce revocation.

[52] 120 CONG. REC. 29,942 (1974) (remarks of Sen. Javits) ("A body of Federal substantive law will be developed by the courts to deal with issues involving rights and obligations under private welfare and pension plans."). *See* Pilot Life Ins. Co. v. Dedeaux, 481 U.S. 41, 56 (1987); Firestone Tire & Rubber Co. v. Bruch, 489 U.S. 101, 110–11 (1989).

[53] *Egelhoff*, 532 U.S. at 159–60 (Breyer, J., dissenting). As with divorce revocation, killer laws work an automatic substitution of beneficiaries by operation of law, and they may be rationalized as an attempt to identify the individuals who would have been the intended beneficiaries had the circumstances been foreseen.

[54] *Egelhoff*, 532 U.S. at 152. Disqualification of an intentional killer under state law is almost universal, either by statute or judicial decision (typically by the application of constructive trust principles to prevent unjust enrichment), although there is some variation in the details.

[55] The Supreme Court has not yet settled this issue. *Compare* Laborers' Pension Fund v. Miscevic, 880 F.3d 927, 934 (7th Cir. 2018) (holding that ERISA does not preempt the

Egelhoff holds that ERISA supersedes state divorce revocation laws, and the Court did not announce a federal common-law rule of automatic revocation on divorce. That still leaves one important question unanswered. Where an ex-spouse renounces her claim to the pension as part of a separation agreement or divorce settlement, and the participant later dies without having changed his beneficiary designation, should such a voluntary waiver (as distinguished from revocation by operation of law) be given effect? Such a waiver, even if incorporated in the divorce decree, is not a QDRO because it does not give the former spouse a right to benefits; instead it disclaims any such right.[56]

The divorce waiver problem arises when a participant who has named a spouse as plan beneficiary fails to change that designation after divorce. The divorce revocation issue presented in *Egelhoff* arose in the same way. In a waiver case, however, the court is not faced with mere inaction. Instead of uncertainty as to the intended beneficiary, the inference that the participant's failure to name a substitute taker was inadvertent seems unmistakable. The participant, after all, negotiated the waiver of rights in plan benefits as part of the divorce settlement, and presumably the ex-spouse agreed to the waiver in return for other concessions, such as higher maintenance payments or a larger share of the participant's other assets.[57] In these circumstances, declining to enforce a divorce waiver that is voluntary and sufficiently specific seems unjust. Yet there is a downside to doing the right thing. Resort to extrinsic documents and the application of context-dependent standards to determine their validity (such as a federal common-law rule on enforceable waivers) muddies the water. By complicating the task of determining the appropriate payee, distributions would be delayed and plan-administration expenses would escalate.

Illinois slayer statute based on *Egelhoff* dicta distinguishing slayer laws from state nonprobate transfer laws) *with* Ahmed v. Ahmed, 158 Ohio App. 3d 527, 536, 817 N.E.2d 424, 431 (2004) (concluding that ERISA preempts Ohio's slayer statute based on Egelhoff analysis, emphasizing lack of uniformity of state slayer laws).

The frequency of homicide is quite low compared to divorce, so the additional administrative burden imposed by a federal common-law rule (compared to simply paying the beneficiary whose name is on file) would be insignificant. Moreover, general equitable principles (unclean hands defense), together with a concern for public respect for the courts and the legal system, support slayer disqualification. Pre-*Egelhoff* decisions seemed to point in that direction. *See* New Orleans Elec. Pension Fund v. Newman, 784 F. Supp. 1233, 1236 (E.D. La. 1992) (Louisiana killer statute not preempted; alternatively, killer not entitled to benefits under federal law); I.R.S. Priv. Ltr. Rul. 90-08-079 (Nov. 30, 1989) (principles embodied in state killer statute constitute an implied exception to anti-alienation and spousal survivor annuity rules). Guidry v. Sheet Metal Workers National Pension Fund, 493 U.S. 365, 376 (1990) (discussed *supra* text accompanying Chapter 8 notes 17–19), in which the Supreme Court refused to create an equitable exception to the anti-alienation rule, is distinguishable in this respect, for there the Court based its decision in part on concern for the needs of the participant's "blameless" beneficiaries.

[56] ERISA § 206(d)(3)(B)(i)(I), 29 U.S.C. § 1056(d)(3)(B)(i)(I) (2018); *see* I.R.C. § 414(p)(1)(A)(i) (2018); Kennedy v. Plan Adm'r for DuPont Sav. & Inv. Plan, 129 S. Ct. 865, 873 (2009).

[57] *See* McGowan v. NJR Serv. Corp., 423 F.3d 241, 253 (3d Cir. 2005) (Becker, J., concurring), *cert. denied*, 549 U.S. 1174 (2007).

278   *Content Controls: Pension Plans*

Those costs could be avoided by ignoring the equities and emphasizing instead the fiduciary obligation to follow plan documents, namely, the unchanged pre-divorce beneficiary designation. Given this value-laden trade-off, it is hardly surprising that a circuit split developed over whether a waiver of beneficiary status in the context of a divorce settlement can be given effect under ERISA.[58]

The Supreme Court opted for certainty in *Kennedy v. Plan Administrator for DuPont Savings and Investment Plan.*[59] William Kennedy, a pension plan participant, had properly designated his wife Liv as beneficiary. When they divorced, the decree provided that Liv relinquished all rights under any retirement, pension, or similar benefit plan associated with William's employment, but William failed to change his beneficiary designation after the divorce. The Court concluded that a waiver which does not attempt to direct pension plan benefits to another taker is not an assignment or alienation and so "escape[s] ... inevitable nullity under the express terms of the anti-alienation clause."[60] Nevertheless, the Court unanimously held that the administrator properly paid plan benefits to the participant's ex-wife because, even though Liv had apparently agreed to the waiver incorporated in the divorce decree, the plan documents provided for payment to the designated beneficiary. The fiduciary duty to act in accordance with the documents and instruments governing the plan overrides a waiver that might otherwise be effective under federal common law, allowing the plan administrator "to look at the plan documents and records conforming to them to get clear distribution instructions, without going to court."[61]

> The point is that by giving a plan participant a clear set of instructions for making his own instructions clear, ERISA forecloses any justification for enquiries into nice expressions of intent, in favor of the virtues of adhering to an uncomplicated rule: "simple administration, avoid[ing] double liability, and ensur[ing] that beneficiaries get what's coming quickly, without the folderol essential under less-certain rules."[62]

Still, there are equities to consider, and so prompt payment of the designated beneficiary might not be the end of the matter. *Kennedy* explicitly left open the issue whether *after distribution* the participant's estate could bring an action to

---

[58] E.g., Manning v. Hayes, 212 F.3d 866 (5th Cir. 2000) (enforcing divorce waiver); Hill v. AT&T Corp., 125 F.3d 646, 648 (8th Cir. 1997) (same); Estate of Altobelli v. IBM, 77 F.3d 78 (4th Cir. 1996) (same); Metro. Life Ins. Co. v. Hanslip, 939 F.2d 904 (10th Cir. 1991) (same); Fox Valley & Vicinity Const. Workers Pension Fund v. Brown, 897 F.2d 275, 279–80 (7th Cir. 1990) (same). *Contra* McGowan v. NJR Serv. Corp., 423 F.3d 241 (3d Cir. 2005) (waiver ineffective), *cert. denied*, 549 U.S. 1174 (2007); Krishna v. Colgate Palmolive Co., 7 F.3d 11 (2d Cir. 1993) (same); McMillan v. Parrott, 913 F.2d 310 (6th Cir. 1990) (same).

[59] 555 U.S. 285 (2009); *see supra* Chapter 6D.

[60] *Kennedy*, 555 U.S. at 292–93 (waiver not assignment), 299 (quotation).

[61] *Id.* at 301.

[62] *Id.* (quoting Fox Valley & Vicinity Const. Workers Pension Fund v. Brown, 897 F.2d 275, 283 (7th Cir. 1990) (Easterbrook, J., dissenting)).

Distribution

recover benefits paid to the ex-spouse.[63] Because the plan and its fiduciaries would not be parties, such a suit could vindicate the waiver without embroiling the plan in litigation that would inflate plan-administration expenses to the long-run disadvantage of other participants. Lower courts have followed that approach.[64]

C SPOUSAL RIGHTS

Survivor Protection

To prevent the impoverishment of surviving spouses, ERISA requires most plans to make distributions in the form of a qualified joint and survivor annuity (QJSA), unless the participant is unmarried or the spouse consents to some other form of distribution. Under a QJSA, payments are made during the joint lives of the participant and his or her spouse, and continue for the life of the survivor. The surviving spouse's annuity must be equal to at least half of (and cannot exceed) the amount paid periodically while both are living, and the combined value of the joint and survivor annuity must be actuarially equivalent to the participant's accrued benefit.[65] ERISA also provides the participant's spouse with qualified pre-retirement survivor annuity (QPSA) protection.[66] The surviving spouse must be entitled to receive QPSA distributions for the period beginning on the participant's death, if the participant dies after having attained the earliest retirement age permitted under the plan, or for the period beginning with the month in which the participant would have reached the plan's earliest retirement age, if the participant dies earlier.[67] The amount of the surviving spouse's annuity is set by QJSA rules and depends on whether the participant died before or after attaining the earliest retirement age.[68]

---

[63] *Id.* at 875 n.10.

[64] Estate of Kensinger v. URL Pharma, Inc., 674 F.3d 131, 137 (3d Cir. 2012) (holding ERISA does not preempt post-distribution suits against plan beneficiaries; such actions do not implicate any concern of expeditious payment or undermine any core objective of ERISA); Andochick v. Byrd, 709 F.3d 296, 301 (4th Cir. 2013) (same); *see* Metlife Life & Annuity Co. of Conn. v. Akpele, 886 F.3d 998, 1008 (11th Cir. 2018) (finding that the suit preceded plan distribution).

[65] ERISA §§ 205(a)(1), (d), 3(23), 29 U.S.C. §§ 1055(a)(1), (d), 1002(23) (2018); *see* I.R.C. §§ 401(a)(11)(A)(i), 417(b), 411(a)(7) (2018).

[66] ERISA § 205(a)(2), (e), 29 U.S.C. § 1055(a)(2), (e) (2018); *see* I.R.C. §§ 401(a)(11)(A)(ii), 417 (c) (2018); Treas. Reg. § 1.401(a)-20, Q&A-13 (as amended in 2006) (forfeiture on death not permissible with respect to QPSA or spousal survivor rights under profit-sharing or stock bonus plan).

[67] ERISA § 205(e)(1)(A)(i), (e)(1)(B), 29 U.S.C. § 1055(e)(1)(A)(i), (e)(1)(B) (2018); *see* I.R.C. § 417(c)(1)(A)(i), (c)(1)(B) (2018).

[68] ERISA § 205(e)(1)(A), 29 U.S.C. § 1055(e)(1)(A) (2018); *see* I.R.C. § 417(c)(1)(A) (2018). If the QJSA/QPSA requirement applies to a defined contribution plan (as it does to a money purchase pension plan, for example) and the participant dies before distributions commence, then the surviving spouse need only be provided with a life annuity equal in value to half of the participant's vested account balance. Thus it is permissible for a defined contribution plan to

The spousal survivor annuity protections have a very broad scope. They apply to all defined benefit plans and to defined contribution plans that are subject to ERISA's minimum funding standards (meaning money purchase pension plans, in general). Profit-sharing and stock bonus plans, which are the types of defined contribution plans that are not subject to the minimum funding standards, must also provide QJSA and QPSA protection unless the plan provides that the participant's vested account balance is payable in full on the death of the participant to the surviving spouse. This survivorship right substitutes for life annuity protection, but only imperfectly so. That is because a profit-sharing or stock bonus plan participant could take complete distribution of the account during life and invest the funds in other property (including a rollover IRA) in which the spouse has no beneficial interest or survivorship rights.[69]

Even if the normal form of distribution under a profit-sharing or stock bonus plan is a lump-sum payout to the surviving spouse, any participant who elects distribution in the form of a life annuity must get a QPSA or QJSA unless the survivor protections are waived, with spousal consent, under the rules described below.[70] Moreover, the survivor annuity distribution requirements apply to all vested benefits, whether they are derived from employer or employee contributions.[71] Consequently, even in-service withdrawals of prior voluntary employee contributions to a money purchase pension plan must be paid as a QJSA unless the survivor protections are properly waived with spousal consent.[72]

Plans are permitted to impose a one-year marriage requirement as a precondition to spousal protections (including both the survivor annuities and the substitute right of survivorship, whichever applies), and a marriage after the annuity starting date does not entitle the spouse to QJSA protection.[73] On the other hand, divorce after

---

require forfeiture on death of up to half of a married participant's vested account balance. ERISA § 205(e)(2), 29 U.S.C. § 1055(e)(2) (2018); *see* I.R.C. § 417(c)(2) (2018).

[69] IRAs are not, in general, subject to either ERISA or the tax-law version of the spousal protection rules. *See* Treas. Reg. § 1.408-2(b)(8) (as amended in 2007) (providing that the beneficiary of an IRA may include the estate of the IRA owner and "any person designated by the individual to share in the benefits of the account after the death of the individual"). Moreover, IRAs are exempt from state community property laws. I.R.C. § 408(g) (2018). Other investment assets purchased with funds distributed from a profit-sharing or stock bonus account would be subject to state succession laws if still owned by the participant at death, but the protections accorded the surviving spouse (e.g., inheritance or elective share rights) are less robust than the QJSA/QPSA regime.

[70] ERISA § 205(b)(1), 29 U.S.C. § 1055(b)(1) (2018); *see* I.R.C. § 401(a)(11)(B) (2018).

[71] Treas. Reg. § 1.401(a)-20, Q&A-11, Q&A-12 (as amended in 2006).

[72] Treas. Reg. § 1.401(a)-20, Q&A-9, Example (as amended in 2006). A participant could, however, without spousal consent, rifle a profit-sharing or stock bonus account via in-service distributions, leaving very little in the account that is subject to the spouse's right of survivorship. *See* ERISA § 205(b)(1)(C), 29 U.S.C. § 1055(b)(1)(C) (2018); *see also* I.R.C. § 401(a)(11)(B)(iii) (2018).

[73] ERISA § 205(b)(4), (f), 29 U.S.C. § 1055(b)(4), (f) (2018); *see* I.R.C. §§ 401(a)(11)(D), 417(d) (2018).

Distribution 281

the QJSA starting date does not cut off the former spouse's right to receive the survivor annuity, unless a QDRO provides otherwise.[74] Nor may a plan terminate annuity payments (whether QJSA or QPSA) to a surviving spouse because the spouse remarries after the participant's death.[75]

Recognizing that workers should not be forced to pay the price of unnecessary spousal protection – for example, if the nonparticipant spouse is independently wealthy, or where each spouse has earned a sufficient pension of his own – Congress requires that participants be permitted to waive the QJSA and QPSA forms of distribution.[76] In addition, a participant who waives the plan's QJSA or QPSA protections must be allowed to elect a qualified optional survivor annuity (QOSA) to provide an intermediate alternative level of the survivor annuity.[77] ERISA requires that participants be given a written explanation of the effect of a waiver, and of the substitution of a QOSA, and conditions the validity of the waiver on spousal consent.[78] The explanation facilitates retirement planning, as does the choice of an alternative survivor annuity level (i.e., the QOSA), while the consent requirement protects the nonparticipant spouse – from the participant.

To promote careful consideration, the required explanation of the consequences of waiving QJSA distribution must be provided within a reasonable time before the annuity starting date, and any election to waive the survivor annuity must generally be made within the 180-day period preceding the annuity starting date.[79] That is, the explanation and waiver must come once distributions (including lump-sum and

---

[74] Treas. Reg. § 1.401(a)-20, Q&A-25(b)(3) (as amended in 2006); S. REP. NO. 98-575, at 15–16 (1984).

[75] Treas. Reg. § 1.401(a)-20, Q&A-25(b)(1) (as amended in 2006); *id.* § 1.401(a)-11(b)(2), -11(g) (2)(ii) (as amended in 2003).

[76] ERISA § 205(c), 29 U.S.C. § 1055(c) (2018); *see* I.R.C. § 417(a) (2018).

[77] ERISA § 205(c)(1)(A), (d)(2), 29 U.S.C. § 1055(c)(1)(A), (d)(2) (2018); *see* I.R.C. § 417(a)(1) (A), (g) (2018). A QOSA is defined as a joint and survivor annuity that is actuarially equivalent to a single life annuity for the life of the participant, but if the plan's QJSA survivor annuity is 75 percent or more of the annuity during the participant's life (remember that it must be at least 50 percent and not more than 100 percent), then the survivor annuity payment under the QOSA is set lower, at 50 percent of annual payment during the participant's life. Alternatively, if the survivor payment level under the plan's QJSA is less than 75 percent, then the survivor annuity payment under the QOSA is set higher, at 75 percent of annual payment during the participant's life.

[78] ERISA § 205(c), 29 U.S.C. § 1055(c) (2018); *see* I.R.C. § 417(a) (2018). A waiver contained in a prenuptial agreement is ineffective because the consent is not given by a "spouse." Treas. Reg. § 1.401(a)-20, Q&A-28 (as amended in 2006); *e.g.*, Hagwood v. Newton, 282 F.3d 285 (4th Cir. 2002). Where the participant bears no cost from survivor protection, there is nothing to be gained by waiver, and so the sponsor is allowed to dispense with the explanation and waiver requirements, provided that the plan does not allow participants to either waive the spousal survivor annuities or substitute a nonspouse beneficiary. ERISA § 205(c)(5), 29 U.S.C. § 1055(c)(5) (2018); *see* I.R.C. § 417(a)(5) (2018); Treas. Reg. § 1.401(a)-20, Q&A-37, -38 (as amended in 2006).

[79] ERISA § 205(c)(1)(A)(i), (c)(3)(A), (c)(7)(A), 29 U.S.C. § 1055(c)(1)(A)(i), (c)(3)(A), (c)(7)(A) (2018); *see* I.R.C. § 417(a)(1)(A)(i), (a)(3)(A), (a)(6)(A) (2018). An exception allows the explanation to be provided after the annuity starting date, but in this event, the period for waiving the

Content Controls: Pension Plans

in-service distributions[80]) are about to commence – when the mind is focused on retirement support needs, rather than years earlier when retirement may be only a dim and unreal prospect. Moreover, the election must remain revocable throughout that 180-day period.[81]

Aligning information with receptivity is more difficult in the case of the QPSA, for there is no single identifiable time at which workers and their spouses are likely to focus on the financial consequences of an unexpected death. In this case, Congress requires that an explanation of the QPSA, and the method and consequences of waiving it, must generally be supplied within the period between the start of the plan year in which the participant attains age thirty-two and the close of the plan year before the participant turns thirty-five, or, if later, within a reasonable period after the worker becomes a participant.[82] The period for waiving the QPSA, or revoking a prior waiver, must ordinarily commence the first day of the plan year in which the participant attains age thirty-five and continue to the date of the participant's death.[83]

A participant's waiver of QJSA or QPSA protection is ineffective unless accompanied by the spouse's consent. That consent must be in writing, acknowledge the effect of the waiver, and be witnessed by a plan administrator or notary. In addition,

---

QJSA is extended until thirty days after the explanation is provided. ERISA § 205(c)(8)(A), 29 U.S.C. § 1055(c)(8)(A) (2018); *see* I.R.C. § 417(a)(7)(A) (2018).

[80] ERISA § 205(h)(2), 29 U.S.C. § 1055(h)(2) (2018); *see* I.R.C. § 417(f)(2) (2018); Treas. Reg. § 1.401(a)-20, Q&A-9 (as amended in 2006).

[81] ERISA § 205(c)(1)(A)(iii), (c)(7)(A), 29 U.S.C. § 1055(c)(1)(A)(iii), (c)(7)(A) (2018); *see* I.R.C. § 417(a)(1)(A)(iii), (a)(6)(A) (2018).

[82] ERISA § 205(c)(3)(B), 29 U.S.C. § 1055(c)(3)(B) (2018); *see* I.R.C. § 417(a)(3)(B) (2018). The regulations specify that in the case of an employee who becomes a participant at age thirty-five or older, a "reasonable period" for providing the explanation means a period of one year before and after becoming a participant. Treas. Reg. § 1.401(a)-20, Q&A-35(c) (as amended in 2006). If a participant separates from service before age thirty-five, the QPSA waiver explanation must be provided within the period of one year before and after separation from service. ERISA § 205(c)(3)(B)(ii), 29 U.S.C. § 1055(c)(3)(B)(ii) (2018) (final sentence); *see* I.R.C. § 417(a)(3) (B)(ii) (2018) (final sentence); Treas. Reg. § 1.401(a)-20, Q&A-35(b) (as amended in 2006).

[83] ERISA § 205(c)(7)(B), 29 U.S.C. § 1055(c)(7)(B) (2018); *see* I.R.C. § 417(a)(6)(B) (2018). If a participant separates from service before the QPSA waiver period would ordinarily begin (i.e., the first day of the plan year in which the participant attains age thirty-five), the period must start earlier, on separation from service. ERISA § 205(c)(7), 29 U.S.C. § 1055(c)(7) (2018) (final sentence); *see* I.R.C. § 417(a)(6) (2018) (final sentence). These statutory rules suggest that the QPSA is not waivable before the year in which the participant turns thirty-five, with the result that the survivor annuity is automatically provided to spouses of workers who die before their mid-thirties. However, the regulations authorize pre-age-thirty-five waivers, provided that the participant is given a written explanation, the spouse consents, and the early waiver becomes ineffective upon the beginning of the plan year in which the participant's thirty-fifth birthday occurs. If there is no new waiver after the statutory election period commences, the spouse must receive a QPSA upon the participant's death. Treas. Reg. § 1.401(a)-20, Q&A-33(b) (as amended in 2006). *But see* S. REP. No. 98-575, at 15 (1984) ("Of course, the preretirement survivor benefit coverage may become automatic prior to the time that the participant is entitled to decline such coverage.").

Distribution 283

the spouse's consent must specify the specific non-spouse beneficiary and, in the case of a QJSA waiver, specify the particular optional form of benefit payment (such as an annuity for the life of the participant only). Unless the consent expressly permits future changes without further consent of the spouse, the participant cannot later designate another beneficiary or form of distribution.[84] Any such spousal consent binds only the spouse who gives it, not any later husband or wife of the participant,[85] but a plan may provide that consent, once given, is irrevocable.[86] As the consent is necessary to validate the participant's waiver, it must apparently be obtained within the permitted waiver period and at a time when the parties are married.[87] Comparable spousal consent is required to use the participant's accrued benefit as security for plan loans because repayment of a loan by setoff would deplete spousal survivor benefits.[88] These consent requirements empower the spouse with a veto over the participant's decision to waive ERISA's survivor protections so that retirement planning takes into account the support needs of *both* parties.[89]

ERISA's distribution requirements attempt to ensure that the participant's decision making takes into account the retirement income needs of his or her spouse.[90] In effect, a spouse automatically becomes the participant's primary beneficiary with

---

[84] ERISA § 205(c)(2)(A), 29 U.S.C. § 1055(c)(2)(A) (2018); *see* I.R.C. § 417(a)(2)(A) (2018); Treas. Reg. § 1.401(a)-20, Q&A-31 (as amended in 2006). Where QPSA is properly waived the participant may subsequently change the optional form of pre-retirement benefit, but not the nonspouse beneficiary, without obtaining spousal consent. *Id.*

[85] ERISA § 205(c)(2), 29 U.S.C. § 1055(c)(2) (2018) (final sentence); *see* I.R.C. § 417(a)(2) (2018) (final sentence).

[86] Treas. Reg. § 1.401(a)-20, Q&A-30 (as amended in 2006).

[87] Treas. Reg. § 1.401(a)-20, Q&A-28 (as amended in 2006) (consent contained in premarital agreement ineffective even if within the applicable election period for waiver); Hurwitz v. Sher, 982 F.2d 778 (2d Cir. 1992).

[88] ERISA § 205(c)(4), 29 U.S.C. § 1055(c)(4) (2018); *see* I.R.C. § 417(a)(4) (2018); Treas. Reg. § 1.401(a)-20, Q&A-24 (as amended in 2006).

[89] As originally enacted, ERISA made the QJSA the default form of distribution for married participants, but permitted the participant acting alone to select another mode of payment. The danger this unilateral decision making posed for dependent spouses (impoverishment caused by the participant's neglect, selfishness, or malice) was noted by some congresswomen during the 1974 legislative debates, but it was another ten years before the fix was made. *See* 120 Cong. Rec. 4317, 4445 (Feb. 26, 27, 1974) (remarks of Rep. Schroeder) ("While the legislation under consideration does mandate survivorship benefits to be automatic unless they are explicitly waived, I would support a plan whereby both the worker and spouse are required to waive their rights to these benefits. Since it is the spouse who is directly affected, he or she should participate directly in the process of waiver."), *reprinted in* 2 ERISA Legislative History, *supra* Chapter 1 note 55, at 3475, 3497; 120 Cong. Rec. 4773 (Feb. 28, 1974) (remarks of Rep. Chisholm), *reprinted in* 3 ERISA Legislative History, *supra* Chapter 1 note 55, at 3572.

[90] *But see supra* Chapter 8 note 69 and accompanying text. In addition, if the present value of participant's nonforfeitable accrued benefit is $5,000 or less ($7,000 or less for distributions made after 2023) a plan may require distribution without the participant's consent; spousal consent is likewise unnecessary provided that such an involuntary cash-out is made before the QPSA or QPSA starting date. ERISA §§ 203(e), 205(g), 29 U.S.C. §§ 1053(e),1055(g), (2018); *see* I.R.C. §§ 411(a)(11), 417(e). The limit on mandatory cash-outs increases to $7,000 for

284 Content Controls: Pension Plans

a prescribed minimum interest in the pension. (Apart from the spouse, ERISA does not insist that anyone be granted an interest in the participant's pension, nor does it require that a beneficiary be given an interest of any particular value.) This statutory spousal beneficiary designation can be changed only with the spouse's consent, which empowers the spouse to look out for himself or herself.

Community Property

If instead of surviving, the worker's spouse is the first to die, what becomes of the spouse's priority? Can a nonparticipant spouse obtain property rights in a pension and transfer those rights on death by bequest or inheritance? In *Boggs* v. *Boggs*,[91] the Supreme Court determined that ERISA's spousal protection scheme is exclusive, and that greater rights afforded by state community property laws present an obstacle to the accomplishment of ERISA's objectives and so must give way under conflict preemption analysis.

In *Boggs*, the participant and his first wife were longtime residents of Louisiana, a community property state. The wife died in 1979, before her husband retired, and left a will transferring ownership of most of her property to the couple's three sons. The participant husband soon remarried. When he retired in 1985 he began receiving monthly annuity distributions under the defined benefit pension plan maintained by Bell South, his employer, as well as a large lump-sum distribution from a defined contribution plan and ninety-six shares of AT&T stock from the Bell South ESOP. Upon the participant's death in 1989, his second wife began receiving QJSA spousal survivor annuity payments. After their father's death, however, the sons asserted claims based on their mother's will to a portion of the annuity payments (including undistributed amounts and payments already made, both before and after the participant's death), to part of the lump-sum distribution, and to some of AT&T stock.[92]

The Court explained that the sons' claim to a share of the survivor annuity conflicted with the spousal protections accorded by ERISA § 205:

> ERISA's solicitude for the economic security of surviving spouses would be undermined by allowing a predeceasing spouse's heirs and legatees to have a community property interest in the survivor's annuity. Even a plan participant cannot defeat a nonparticipant surviving spouse's statutory entitlement to an annuity. It would be odd, to say the least, if Congress permitted a predeceasing nonparticipant spouse to do so. Nothing in the language of ERISA supports concluding that Congress made

distributions made after 2023. SECURE 2.0 Act of 2022, Pub. L. No. 117–328, Div. T, § 304(a), 136 Stat. 4459, ___ (2023).

[91] 520 U.S. 833 (1997). *See supra* Chapter 6 notes 49–54 and accompanying text.

[92] *Boggs*, 520 U.S. at 836–37. The participant had rolled the lump sum distribution over into an individual retirement account from which he took no withdrawals during life, and at death he also still owned the AT&T shares distributed from the ESOP.

Distribution 285

such an inexplicable decision. Testamentary transfers could reduce a surviving spouse's guaranteed annuity below the minimum set by ERISA (defined as 50% of the annuity payable during the joint lives of the participant and spouse).[93]

Accordingly, ERISA preempts state law rights to a share of the spousal survivor annuity.

The Court also concluded that ERISA precludes a testamentary transfer by a nonparticipant spouse of a community property interest in undistributed pension plan benefits, even if there is no subsequent spouse entitled to survivor protection. Recognizing such a transfer would reduce pension distributions to the participant or beneficiaries. Such a bequest would violate ERISA in two ways. First, while ERISA is designed to protect the interests of plan participants and beneficiaries, the legatee of a predeceased nonparticipant spouse is neither a participant nor a beneficiary, because "beneficiary" is defined as a person designated either by the participant or by the terms of the plan.[94] Second, the testamentary transfer of the predeceased spouse's community property interest is prohibited by the anti-alienation rule.[95] The Court observed that "it would be inimical to ERISA's purposes to permit testamentary recipients to acquire a competing interest in undistributed pension benefits."[96] The majority concluded that Congress meant to favor the retirement support needs of the living participant over the property rights of the deceased spouse.[97] In sum, spousal pension rights under ERISA are not about mandating gender equity, but about promoting retirement support.

D CONCLUSION

When it comes to pension plan distributions, ERISA's anti-abuse and worker-protective impulses have less force than on matters involving fiduciary conduct and pension accumulation (Chapters 4 and 7). In this area, Congress legislated against the background of long-standing tax-law rules, adding as a new motif the imposition of restraints on the participant.

---

[93] *Id.* at 843–44. The Court also noted that under state wills law the recipient of a bequest that would deprive the surviving spouse of the support required by ERISA might not even be a family member.

[94] *Id.* at 848–51. *See* ERISA § 3(8), 29 U.S.C. § 1002(8) (2018).

[95] *Boggs*, 520 U.S. at 851–52. *See* ERISA § 206(d)(1), 29 U.S.C. § 1056(d)(1) (2018).

[96] *Boggs*, 520 U.S. at 852.

[97] *Id.* at 854 ("Congress has decided to favor the living over the dead and we must respect its policy"). In a questionable extension of this reasoning, the Ninth Circuit ruled that where a former spouse, who is entitled under a divorce decree to a portion of the participant's pension as community property, dies before pension payments commence, her interest is extinguished. Instead of finding that the ex-spouse's judicially confirmed community property interest passes to her heirs, the court concluded that *Boggs* and *Egelhoff* require that the participant be reinstated in the entire pension. Branco v. UFCW-N. Cal. Employers Joint Pension Plan, 279 F.3d 1154 (9th Cir. 2002). *See* Eller v. Bolton, 168 Md. App. 96, 895 A.2d 382 (Md. Ct. Spec. App. 2006) (distinguishing *Branco*).

Generally, pension distributions must commence promptly once the participant reaches the plan's normal retirement age (or age sixty-five, if earlier), unless the participant is still working for the plan sponsor, in which case the start date can be delayed until separation from service. Additional delay is possible if the participant consents, which necessitated tax-law intervention to discourage "excessive" deferral, so as to avoid publicly subsidized intergenerational wealth transfers. Similarly, the task of restricting early distributions has been left to the tax law, which provides carrots and sticks (tax-deferred rollover treatment and early distribution penalties) in an effort to prevent pension savings from being dissipated before retirement. The historic flexibility of the qualified retirement plan distribution rules is the source of many of the continuing challenges of pension policy, such as whether rollovers should be mandatory for distributions made before age fifty-five, and whether distributions should be required to be made as life annuities rather than lump-sum payouts. These questions are explored in Chapter 10.

In contrast to its acquiescence in the tax law's distribution timing rules, ERISA has much to say about permissible pension plan distributees. The basic commands are two: retirement savings are nontransferable, and the participant's spouse is functionally granted a co-ownership interest.

Pensions receive automatic spendthrift protection by federal law. ERISA's anti-alienation rule prevents the participant from gaining access to his retirement savings by sale or encumbrance. This barrier is necessary to give effect to plan terms governing the timing and form or distributions, for without it, a participant could accomplish indirectly what the plan attempts to forbid. If pension rights were transferable, a defined benefit plan requiring distribution in the form of a life annuity commencing at age sixty-five could, for example, be converted by sale into a lump sum of cash at age forty-seven. Anti-alienation in this context is generally understood as paternalism (forced saving), but it may also serve the employer's interest in assuring that financial arrangements made to induce older workers to exit the workforce are not undermined. The pension anti-alienation rule is remark-ably robust; it routinely withstands bankruptcy and most crime victims' restitution claims. The statute yields, however, to family law creditors who may obtain access to a participant's pension under a qualified domestic relations order, even if their claim relates to current support needs (as opposed to retirement income) or adjusts property rights. To shield other participants from adverse effects, a qualified domes-tic relations order must not increase the plan's benefit liability, and ERISA estab-lishes a process to minimize administrative costs.

Beyond restraining the participant (and his creditors) from obtaining access to retirement savings during working years, ERISA also restricts the participant's ability to unilaterally determine succession to his pension. Originally, plans were allowed to forfeit all employer-financed benefits upon death of the participant, regardless of length of service. The Retirement Equity Act of 1984 generally limited forfeiture on death to instances where the participant leaves no surviving spouse, granted the spouse an interest in the participant's pension, and protected that interest by giving the spouse a say over changes in the participant's successor. Defined benefit and money purchase pension plans must provide minimum survivor annuity protection to the participant's spouse as the default form of distribution, while profit-sharing and stock bonus plans must either provide such spousal survivor annuities or give the spouse the right to take the participant's entire vested account balance on death. The participant acting alone cannot designate a non-spouse beneficiary or otherwise dispense with these spousal protections. Such changes are effective only if the spouse gives written consent after full disclosure. Recognizing that married individuals without pension savings of their own frequently count on their spouse's plan for retirement support, ERISA protects the nonparticipant spouse from short-sighted or malevolent decisions by the participant.

Succession questions frequently arise for unmarried participants, particularly because defined contribution plans typically do not call for forfeiture on death. Apart from a qualified domestic relations order, ERISA supersedes any state law that would identify takers or work a substitution of pension plan beneficiaries, including state inheritance, wills, and community property regimes. Preemption even applies to laws that would correct a divorced participant's inadvertent failure to change a beneficiary designation in favor of the former spouse. Despite sometimes inequitable results, preemption in such circumstances at least yields an easily administered rule (i.e., pay the person whose name is on file with the plan), which avoids the complication and expense that state law variation could inject. Yet sometimes there is no need to economize on justice in determining a successor. Federal courts could effectuate prevalent preferences uniformly and at minimal cost by coupling preemption of state law with announcement of interstitial federal common-law rules governing succession to welfare and pension plan benefits. But, as the Supreme Court warned in 2009, federal common law will not be allowed to displace *plan* rules that serve the goal of uniform, low-cost administration.

9

Security[1]

"The Congress finds ... that owing to the inadequacy of current minimum standards, the soundness and stability of plans with respect to adequate funds to pay promised benefits may be endangered; that owing to the termination of plans before requisite funds have been accumulated, employees and their beneficiaries have been deprived of anticipated benefits; and that it is therefore desirable in the interests of employees and their beneficiaries, for the protection of the revenue of the United States, and to provide for the free flow of commerce, that minimum standards be provided assuring the equitable character of such plans and their financial soundness.. ..

It is hereby further declared to be the policy of this Act to protect interstate commerce, the Federal taxing power, and the interests of participants in private pension plans and their beneficiaries by improving the equitable character and the soundness of such plans by requiring them to vest the accrued benefits of employees with significant periods of service, to meet minimum standards of funding, and by requiring plan termination insurance."[2]

To increase the security of the pension promise, ERISA requires systematic advance funding of future benefits. Instead of mandating a particular funding schedule, however, Congress imposed only a minimum funding obligation, leaving employers

---

[1] **Scope Note:** The explanation in this chapter is limited to single-employer defined benefit plans. The funding, insurance, and withdrawal liability rules governing multiemployer plans are beyond the scope of this book.

    Also excluded from coverage are special relaxed minimum funding rules available to certain cooperatives and multiple-employer plans maintained by tax-exempt charitable organizations ("CSEC plans"). *See* ERISA §§ 210(f), 302(a)(2)(D), 306, 29 U.S.C. §§ 1060(f), 1082(a)(2) (D), 1085a (2018); I.R.C. §§ 412(a)(2)(D), 414(y), 433 (2018). Such CSEC plans are subject to the PBGC termination insurance system but are charged reduced rate premiums. ERISA § 4006(a)(3)(A)(vii), (a)(8)(E), 29 U.S.C.A. § 1306(a)(3)(A)(vii), (a)(8)(E) (West Supp. 2020).

[2] ERISA § 2(a), (c), 29 U.S.C. § 1001(a), (c) (2018).

the flexibility to contribute larger amounts, subject to certain upper limits set by tax-law deductibility rules.[3] Moreover, until 2008, ERISA tolerated considerable flexibility in the determination of the annual minimum funding obligation.

Congress chose not to insist upon immediate full funding of all accrued benefits under defined benefit plans, and so employees are exposed to the risk that the plan may be terminated before sufficient assets have been accumulated to pay all promised benefits. The termination insurance system of ERISA Title IV, administered by the Pension Benefit Guaranty Corporation (PBGC), was instituted to limit, but not eliminate, this risk. Because participants in defined benefit plans bear a residual risk of loss to the extent that unfunded uninsured benefits prove uncollectible (i.e., in cases of employer insolvency), information concerning the funded status of the plan is pertinent to their situation, as it is to the PBGC and firm creditors. To facilitate planning and self-protection, ERISA requires that certain disclosures be made to these interested parties.

During the 1980s and 1990s, many plans became substantially *overfunded*. That raised the question whether (or to what extent) the employer, who is obligated to correct underfunding, should be granted a reciprocal right of access to excess assets. Under ERISA, plan assets must generally be held in trust and cannot revert to the employer absent plan termination, although the reclamation of erroneous contributions is permitted in limited circumstances. An unintended consequence of those benefit security rules was to create pressure to terminate overfunded plans to obtain the surplus. That incentive, together with the complexity and cost of compliance with the funding rules, may have contributed to the recent pronounced trend away from defined benefit plan sponsorship.[4] This phenomenon illustrates once again that there is a delicate balance between quality-control regulation and voluntary plan sponsorship.

A MINIMUM FUNDING STANDARDS[5]

As a practical matter, a full funding requirement would have largely halted the practice of granting past-service credit. Past-service credit refers to benefits created retroactively for service before the plan was instituted, or subsequent retroactive

---

[3] *See* I.R.C. §§ 404(a)(1), (a)(7), (o), 412, 430 (2018); *see generally infra* Chapter 10C. Contributions in excess of the maximum deductible amount may be carried forward for deduction in subsequent years. *Id.* § 404(a)(1)(E). But concerns about excessive prefunding led Congress in 1987 to strongly discourage excess contributions by imposing an excise tax of 10 percent of the amount of nondeductible contributions to a qualified plan. *Id.* § 4972.

[4] *See generally*, JOHN BROADBENT ET AL., THE SHIFT FROM DEFINED BENEFIT TO DEFINED CONTRIBUTION PENSION PLANS – IMPLICATIONS FOR ASSET ALLOCATION AND RISK MANAGEMENT 17–21 (2006), at www.bis.org/publ/wgpapers/cgfs27broadbent3.pdf.

[5] Portions of the discussion in this section are adapted from PETER J. WIEDENBECK & RUSSELL K. OSGOOD, CASES AND MATERIALS ON EMPLOYEE BENEFITS 389–96, 443–46 (1996), and is reprinted with permission of West, a Thomson Reuters business.

benefit enhancements. Immediate funding of the large liability created by such retroactive benefit grants would often impose a crushing cash flow burden. And because defined benefit plans are commonly instituted once a business has achieved the stability and profitability necessary to provide for its founders' retirement, discouraging past-service credits might curtail the growth of private plan coverage. Apparently, Congress thought it wiser public policy to allocate and control the risk of loss associated with unfunded past-service liabilities than to prohibit such benefit commitments.

Congress acted to limit the risk of plan default by strengthening minimum funding standards. Naturally, the key element of the new regime was the requirement that unfunded past-service liabilities be systematically retired. ERISA originally required that outstanding past-service liabilities be amortized over a forty-year period, while past-service liabilities created or increased after the law took effect were to be funded over at most thirty years. Since enactment, ERISA has been repeatedly amended to tighten the minimum funding rules. Underfunding caused by grants of past-service credit in plan years beginning after 2007 must generally be eliminated by level annual installment payments over seven years.[6]

The minimum funding standards only *limit* the risk of plan default. Long-term amortization of past-service benefits concedes an extended period during which plan assets will, in the event of termination, be insufficient to pay promised benefits. Congress enacted the termination insurance system of ERISA Title IV and associated employer liability rules to *allocate* rather than eliminate the remaining risk of underfunding (*see infra* Chapter 9B).

Funding Overview

ERISA's minimum funding standards apply to most pension plans other than profit-sharing and stock bonus plans. Governmental and church plans are exempt, as are plans that do not call for employer contributions and certain plans funded exclusively with the purchase of individual or group insurance or annuity contracts.[7] It is important to note that there is an exception for wholly unfunded plans promising

---

[6] ERISA §§ 302(a), 303(a)(1)(B), (c), (d), 29 U.S.C. §§ 1082(a), 1083(a)(1)(B), (c), (d) (2018); *see* I.R.C. §§ 412(a), 430(a)(1)(B), (c), (d) (2018).

[7] ERISA § 301(a), 29 U.S.C. § 1081(a) (2018). ERISA's funding rules apply only to pension plans, *see* ERISA § 301(a)(1), 29 U.S.C. § 1081(a)(1) (2018) (welfare plans exempt), and are primarily concerned with the actuarial problems involved in the advance funding of defined benefit pensions. One type of defined contribution plan, the money purchase pension plan, is covered to ensure that promised contributions are made when due. ERISA § 302(a)(2)(B), 29 U.S.C. § 1082(a)(2)(B) (2018); *see* I.R.C. § 412(a)(2)(B) (2018). Profit-sharing and stock bonus plans are not subject to the funding rules, ERISA § 301(a)(8), 29 U.S.C. § 1081(a)(8) (2018), apparently because contributions under such plans may be discretionary, in which case there is no contribution obligation to enforce.

Security

deferred compensation to "a select group of management or highly compensated employees" (commonly called "top hat plans").[8]

For plan years beginning before 2008, the employer's funding obligation is determined with reference to the plan's actuarial funding method. Actuarial funding methods are akin to depreciation methods, which estimate a cost of producing income (the decline in value of structures or of equipment that wears out) and allocate the cost over the multiple taxable years that compose the expected life of the property. Advance funding of a defined benefit pension presents a similar problem. One must *estimate* both the *total cost* and *total period* over which benefits will be earned. The annual funding obligation follows from a rule for allocating that total cost among taxable years within that total period. The plan's actuarial funding method supplies the allocation rule. For example, assume that a plan provides each participant a benefit of $X per year at age sixty-five. The cost of an immediate single life annuity of $X is readily determinable; call this cost $Y. For funding purposes, the question is, what savings pattern should the plan follow to generate the $Y through yearly contributions during the participant's period of service? The savings pattern is the plan's actuarial cost method. As with any timing rule, consistency is critical, so a change in the plan's actuarial method requires the Treasury's consent, just as change in a taxpayer's method of accounting (or method of depreciation) does.[9]

Most defined benefit plans do not promise a fixed-dollar benefit. Instead, they determine retirement benefits by a formula that takes into account each participant's compensation, years of service, and retirement age. Accordingly, each participant's pension can only be estimated, and to do this, the sponsor must make some assumptions as to duration of service, future compensation increases, retirement age (especially if the plan provides subsidized early retirement benefits), and, if the plan calls for forfeiture on death, mortality rates. If the plan provides ancillary benefits, such as disability income or life insurance, probability estimates for these eventualities are needed as well. The probability estimates for such contingencies are called actuarial assumptions. Actuarial assumptions must be reasonable and periodically revised in light of actual experience[10] (just as the useful life and salvage value estimates used to compute traditional depreciation allowances were required to be reasonable).

There is one major conceptual difference between actuarial funding and depreciation: depreciation allocates a past expenditure, while actuarial funding

---

[8] ERISA § 301(a)(3), 29 U.S.C. § 1081(a)(3) (2018). *See supra* Chapter 2D. Excess benefit plans (whether funded or not) are also exempt from the minimum funding rules, but by definition, such plans cover only highly compensated employees. ERISA §§ 3(36), 4(b)(5), 301(a)(9), 29 U.S.C. §§ 1002(36), 1003(b)(5), 1081(a)(9) (2018).

[9] ERISA § 302(d), 29 U.S.C. § 1082(d) (2018). *Compare* ERISA § 302(c)(5)(A), 29 U.S.C. § 1082(c)(5)(A) (2000) (repealed 2006), *and* I.R.C. § 412(c)(5)(A) (2000) (repealed 2006), *with* I.R.C. § 446(e) (2018).

[10] ERISA § 303(h)(1), 29 U.S.C. § 1083(h)(1) (2018); *see* I.R.C. § 430(h)(1) (2018).

accumulates for a future expenditure. Returning to the earlier example, the cost of an $X single life annuity may be $Y at age sixty-five, but the employer does not need to contribute $Y. Instead, it must save enough so that the combination of contributions and fund earnings will total $Y. That is, to determine required contributions, the $Y future cost must be discounted by the anticipated rate of fund earnings. This "interest rate" actuarial assumption has a major impact on funding obligations.

Prior to 2008, ERISA allowed plan sponsors to compute their minimum funding obligation according to the actuarial funding method selected by the plan, and the statute expressly authorized six acceptable actuarial methods.[11] The acceptable methods could yield very different cost calculations. Under some methods, the plan's annual benefit cost depended on the plan's liability for benefits actually earned during the year, while other methods computed projected total benefits and allocated that career aggregate cost in level amounts or as a level percentage of pay over the participant's period of service. Past-service benefits were also financed differently under the various actuarial methods, with some breaking out the cost of retroactive benefits as a distinct supplemental liability that is amortized over a fixed period of up to thirty years, while other methods funded the liability over the projected future period of service of the participants who were granted past-service benefits.[12] In addition, under any given actuarial method, the sponsor's funding obligation could vary dramatically according to the actuary's assumptions concerning the fund's investment performance (the interest rate assumption), the likelihood of forfeiture as a result of death (mortality assumption), the probability of lump-sum distributions or early retirement benefits, and other factors. While ERISA required that actuarial methods be consistently applied, with actuarial assumptions reasonable and subject to revision in light of actual experience,[13] ERISA's original approach to advance funding gave actuaries (and so, indirectly, plan sponsors) very wide latitude.

The Pension Protection Act of 2006 imposed a much stricter approach to defined benefit plan funding. In support of the new legislation, the Treasury explained:

> One reason for this problem [widespread underfunding and a rash of plan terminations causing large claims against the PBGC] is the byzantine and often ineffectual set of funding rules under current law. They are needlessly complex and often fail

---

[11] ERISA § 3(31), 29 U.S.C. § 1002(31) (2018); ERISA § 302(a), (b), (c)(1), 29 U.S.C. § 1082(a), (b), (c)(1) (2000) (repealed 2006); see I.R.C. § 412(a), (b), (c)(1) (2000) (repealed 2006). ERISA § 3(31) declares that "[t]he terminal funding cost method and the current funding (pay-as-you-go) cost method are not acceptable actuarial cost methods." Pay-as-you-go involves no advance funding, while terminal funding merely sets aside the cost of promised benefits when the worker retires. These techniques expose workers to a prolonged risk of employer default and are therefore incompatible with the goal of increasing the security of the pension promise.

[12] See generally DAN M. MCGILL & DONALD S. GRUBBS, JR., FUNDAMENTALS OF PRIVATE PENSIONS 239–327 (6th ed. 1989).

[13] ERISA § 302(c)(3), (c)(5), 29 U.S.C. § 1082(c)(3), (c)(5) (2000) (repealed 2006); see I.R.C. § 412(c)(3), (c)(5) (2000) (repealed 2006).

Security

to ensure that many pension plans become and remain adequately funded. Current rules give employers too much discretion in setting their funding targets and provide insufficient opportunity for plans to become well funded. Current rules also do not provide enough incentive to be well funded because there are few significant consequences that arise from a plan being poorly funded, especially for a plan sponsor in poor financial health.[14]

Responding to these concerns, Congress made sweeping changes in pension funding. As explained below, freedom of choice in actuarial methods was eliminated; underfunding triggered by grants of past-service benefits must now be rapidly retired; interest rate and mortality assumptions are prescribed by the Treasury. In return for stricter minimum funding obligations, the 2006 legislation encouraged plan sponsors to exceed the minimum by relaxing the tax Code's limits on the deductibility of advance funding contributions.[15]

Since 2008, defined benefit pension plans have been required to compute their minimum funding obligation with reference to two components: the funding target and the target normal cost.[16] The funding target is "the present value of all benefits accrued or earned under the plan as of the beginning of the plan year," and the target normal cost is "the present value of all benefits which are expected to accrue or to be earned under the plan during the plan year."[17] Consequently, the funding rules are geared to the plan's legal liability for benefits actually earned through the current year, rather than being tied to a share of the plan's projected future benefit obligation. Moreover, where the plan's benefit formula is based on compensation (e.g., a unit credit formula using a highest average or final average compensation multiplier), "if any benefit attributable to services performed in a preceding year is increased by reason of any increase in compensation during the current plan year, the increase in such benefit shall be treated as having accrued during the current plan year," thereby increasing the target normal cost and the minimum required contribution.[18]

Where, as of the start of the plan year, the value of plan assets is less than the funding target (the present value of all previously accrued benefits), the resulting

[14] U.S. Dep't of the Treasury, General Explanations of the Administration's Fiscal Year 2007 Revenue Proposals, 76 (Feb. 2006) (hereinafter Treasury General Explanations).

[15] I.R.C. § 404(a)(1)(A), (o) (2018). The "cushion amount" allows sponsors to deduct contributions that render a plan substantially overfunded relative to existing benefit liabilities (determined on a plan termination basis). In order to control the cost of the qualified plan tax subsidy, prior law strongly discouraged such overfunding by means of a full funding limit on deductions and the excise (penalty) tax on nondeductible contributions. I.R.C. §§ 404(a)(1)(A) (final sentence), 412(c)(7), 4972 (2000) (amended 2006). Treasury General Explanations, *supra* Chapter 9 note 14, at 78–79.

[16] ERISA §§ 302(a), 303(a), 29 U.S.C. §§ 1082(a), 1083(a) (2018); *see* I.R.C. §§ 412(a), 430 (a) (2018).

[17] ERISA § 303(d)(1), (b), 29 U.S.C. § 1083(d)(1), (b) (2018); *see* I.R.C. § 430(d)(1), (b) (2018).

[18] ERISA § 303(b), 29 U.S.C. § 1083(b) (2018); *see* I.R.C. § 430(b) (2018).

294   *Content Controls: Pension Plans*

funding shortfall must be amortized in level annual installments over the next seven years.[19] This rule applies regardless of whether the shortfall is traceable to a drop in the value of plan assets or an increase in plan liabilities. Accordingly, retroactive benefit enhancements (past-service benefits) must be funded over seven years, not the thirty-year amortization period ERISA originally authorized.[20]

Actuarial Assumptions

Experience showed that plan sponsors in financial difficulty often minimized their minimum funding obligation by adopting overly optimistic assumptions regarding investment performance (such as interest rate assumptions based on returns to equity, causing a high discount rate to be used in determining the present value of liabilities), while downplaying the magnitude of expected benefits. The Pension Protection Act of 2006 required that the interest rate used in determining the funding target be based on the yield of investment-grade corporate bonds having periods of maturity that correspond to the timing of expected benefit payments under the plan. The mortality tables used by the plan are similarly prescribed.[21] In line with prior law, other actuarial assumptions must each be reasonable, "taking into account the experience of the plan and reasonable expectations," and such assumptions must, "in combination, offer the actuary's best estimate of anticipated experience under the plan."[22]

The reasonableness of actuarial assumptions is ordinarily based upon the experience under the plan "unless it is established that past experience is not likely to recur and thus is not a good indication of future experience."[23] Assumptions that are mutually inconsistent or that conflict with the benefit structure of the plan are unreasonable.[24] For a new plan, where experience is no guide, actuarial

---

[19] ERISA § 303(a)(1)(B), (c), 29 U.S.C. § 1083(a)(1)(B), (c) (2018); *see* I.R.C. § 430(a)(1)(B), (c) (2018).

[20] Prior to 2008, the minimum funding standard only required that new grants of past-service benefits be funded over either thirty years or the future career of affected participants. ERISA § 302(b)(2)(B)(iii), 29 U.S.C. § 1082(b)(2)(B)(iii) (2000) (repealed 2006); *see* I.R.C. § 412(b)(2) (B)(iii) (2000) (repealed 2006). Accordingly, retroactive liberalization of the plan's benefit formula could cause a plan that is terminated within a few years after the grant of past-service benefits to have far greater benefit liabilities than it has accumulated assets with which to pay them. Because of the extended period allowed for funding past-service benefits, such a plan might have complied with ERISA's minimum funding rules at all times. ERISA's original funding rules tolerated this situation so as not to discourage the grant of past-service benefits. The 2006 amendments strike a new balance between promoting and securing retroactive benefit grants. TREASURY GENERAL EXPLANATIONS, *supra* Chapter 9 note 14, at 78.

[21] ERISA § 303(h)(2), (h)(3), 29 U.S.C.A. § 1083(h)(2), (h)(3) (2018); *see* I.R.C. § 430(h)(2), (h) (3) (2018).

[22] ERISA § 303(h)(1), 29 U.S.C. § 1083(h)(1) (2018); *see* I.R.C. § 430(h)(1) (2018).

[23] Prop. Treas. Reg. § 1.412(b)-1(h)(1), 47 Fed. Reg. 54,093, 54,098 (Dec. 1, 1982).

[24] *See id.* 1(h)(3), (4). In *Rhoades,* McKee & Boer v. United States, 43 F.3d 1071 (6th Cir. 1995), the court found unreasonable (1) an assumption of retirement at age sixty where the participant would have to work until age sixty-three to qualify for an increase in plan benefits, and (2) the

Security   295

assumptions must be based on "reasonable expectations." The IRS has suggested that assumptions would be evaluated in light of experience "[a]fter a plan has been in effect for a period of five years or so."[25]

Actuarial assumptions must not only be reasonable, in combination they must also "offer the actuary's best estimate of anticipated experience under the plan."[26] The IRS has argued that this condition obligates the plan's actuary to "neutrally pick the most likely result" from within the range of reasonable actuarial assumptions.[27] The courts of appeals have generally rejected this substantive interpretation of the best-estimate test on the ground that it is inconsistent with the latitude in professional judgment that Congress intended to give actuaries, and because it would render the reasonableness test superfluous.[28] Instead, several appellate courts have concluded that the best-estimate test imposes only a procedural hurdle: the plan must show that the assumptions selected reflect the independent professional judgment of the actuary.[29] The weakness of the procedural approach lies in the fact that the absence of overt pressure does not guarantee independence; the actuary is unlikely to be ignorant of the sponsor's financial needs, and nothing prevents a sponsor from "shopping around" for a complaisant actuary.

Additional constraints on actuarial assumptions come into play if a plan with more than 500 participants is significantly underfunded. To account for the greater likelihood that a plan maintained by a financially weak sponsor will be called upon to pay benefits on an accelerated schedule, for such at-risk plans all employees who will be eligible to elect benefits during the current and ten succeeding plan years

---

     use of a female mortality table for a male participant where "the only explanation . . . seems to be an effort to increase contribution levels." *Rhoades, McKee*, 43 F.3d at 1076 (quoting from the district court's opinion).

[25] Rev. Rul. 63-11, 1963-1 C.B. 94, 96. In *Wachtell*, Lipton, Rosen & Katz v. Commissioner, 26 F.3d 291 (2d Cir. 1994), the IRS argued that the actuary should have based the interest rate assumption more on the first two years of plan experience than on long-term statistical averages. The Second Circuit disagreed. There was expert actuarial testimony that experience in the early years of a plan is not given much weight, and the IRS had previously announced that a change would not be required "unless there has been a consistent pattern of substantial gains over a period of years from sources which would be likely to recur in the future." *Wachtell*, 26 F.3d at 296 (quoting Rev. Rul. 63-11). *But see* Jerome Mirza & Assocs. v. United States, 882 F.2d 229 (7th Cir. 1989) (actuary's use of 5 percent interest rate based on long-term returns on large pension fund equity investments was unreasonable where newly established plan that invested in certificates of deposit would quickly be fully funded, at a time when long term certificates of deposit paid about 12 percent interest).

[26] ERISA § 303(h)(1), 29 U.S.C. § 1083(h)(1) (2018); I.R.C. § 430(h)(1) (2018).

[27] Vinson & Elkins v. Comm'r, 7 F.3d 1235, 1238 (5th Cir. 1993).

[28] *Vinson & Elkins*, 7 F.3d at 1238; *Wachtell, Lipton*, 26 F.3d at 296; Citrus Valley Estates, Inc. v. Comm'r, 49 F.3d 1410, 1414–15 (9th Cir. 1995); *Rhoades, McKee*, 43 F.3d at 1075.

[29] *Vinson & Elkins*, 7 F.3d at 1238 ("One goal of such an inquiry would be to determine whether assumptions truly came from the plan actuary or whether they were instead chosen by plan management for tax planning or cash flow purposes."). *Accord Wachtell*, 26 F.3d 291; *Citrus Valley*, 49 F.3d 1410; *Rhoades, McKee*, 43 F.3d 1071.

must be assumed to retire at the earliest possible retirement date under the plan and to elect the retirement benefit that would result in the highest present value of benefits.[30] If the plan has been in at-risk status for two of the four preceding years, the plan's funding target and target normal cost are also increased by a "loading factor" to "reflect the additional administrative cost of purchasing a group annuity if the plan were to terminate."[31]

Relief Provisions

The Treasury is allowed to waive (meaning defer, not excuse) compliance with the minimum funding standard if the employer is unable to satisfy it without *temporary* substantial business hardship (substantial business hardship, in the case of a multi-employer plan) and if enforcement would be adverse to the interests of plan participants in the aggregate.[32] Waiver offers the possibility of deferral of the entire minimum contribution for the year, excepting only the amount required to amortize previously waived minimum funding obligations. The employer must notify each affected labor organization, participant, and beneficiary (and any alternate payee under a qualified domestic relations order) of the waiver application, and the IRS must consider any relevant information submitted by these affected parties.[33] If the requested waiver would cause the plan's funding shortfall to reach $1 million or more, certain PBGC protective measures come into play, including the right to comment on the request and the possible grant of a security interest.[34]

Another relief mechanism is available in certain extraordinary cases, where the minimum funding standards would cause temporary substantial business hardship

---

[30] ERISA § 303(i), 29 U.S.C.A. § 1083(i) (2018); *see* I.R.C. § 430(i) (2018).

[31] ERISA § 303(i), 29 U.S.C. § 1083(i) (2018); *see* I.R.C. § 430(i) (2018). *See also* TREASURY GENERAL EXPLANATIONS, *supra* Chapter 9 note 14, at 77, 83.

[32] ERISA § 302(c), 29 U.S.C. § 1082(c) (2018); *see* I.R.C. § 412(c) (2018). In determining whether the substantial business hardship condition is satisfied, the IRS considers (among other factors) (1) whether the employer is operating at a loss; (2) whether there is substantial unemployment or underemployment in the business and industry concerned; (3) whether profits and sales in the industry are depressed or declining; and (4) whether it is reasonable to expect that the plan will be continued only if the waiver is granted. *See* Rev. Proc. 2004-15, § 2.03(2), (4), 2004-1 C.B. 490 (specified facts concerning the employer's financial condition and the nature and extent of business hardship must be submitted with request for waiver). All members of the employer's controlled group (under the commonly controlled business and affiliated service group rules) are treated as a single employer in making this hardship evaluation. ERISA § 302(c)(5)(B), 29 U.S.C. § 1082(c)(5)(B) (2018); *see* I.R.C. § 412(c)(5)(B) (2018).

[33] ERISA §§ 302(c)(6), 4001(a)(21), 29 U.S.C. §§ 1082(c)(6), 1301(a)(21) (2018); *see* I.R.C. § 412(c)(6) (2018). Although these parties have a right to comment, their ability to comment effectively is seriously hampered by the fact that the waiver application is treated as confidential return information. ERISA § 302(c)(4)(B), 29 U.S.C. § 1082(c)(4)(B) (2018); *see* I.R.C. § 412 (c)(4)(B) (2018); McGarry v. Sec'y of the Treasury, 853 F.2d 981 (D.C. Cir. 1988).

[34] ERISA § 302(c)(4), 29 U.S.C. § 1082(c)(4) (2018); *see* I.R.C. § 412(c)(4) (2018).

Security 297

and a waiver is unavailable or inadequate. If the IRS is notified and finds that these conditions are satisfied, it may approve a plan amendment that retroactively reduces participants' accrued benefits, notwithstanding ERISA's anti-cutback rule.[35] An amendment adopted within two and one-half months after the close of a plan year may reduce benefits that have accrued since the start of that year, but only to the extent required by the circumstances.[36]

If either of these relief methods has been employed, the plan generally cannot be amended to increase plan liabilities, whether by increasing benefits, changing benefit accrual, or accelerating benefit vesting, for as long as the waiver is in effect, or for twelve months after adoption of an amendment that reduces accrued bene-fits.[37] A comparable ban on liability-increasing amendments applies to any under-funded plan insured by the PBGC for as long as the sponsor is subject to bankruptcy administration.[38] Significantly underfunded plans are subject to additional restric-tions. Plans less than 80 percent funded generally may not be amended to increase benefit liabilities, and if funding falls below 60 percent, further benefit accruals must cease (i.e., benefits are frozen). Lump-sum and other accelerated distribution options, which deplete funds and increase risks for other participants, may also be restricted for plans that are less than 80 percent funded or whose sponsor is subject to bankruptcy or insolvency proceedings.[39]

Enforcement

Minimum funding contributions are ordinarily due eight and a half months after the close of the plan year.[40] Underfunded single-employer plans must make quar-terly installments of 25 percent of the lesser of 90 percent of the required minimum contribution for the year or 100 percent of the required minimum contribution for the prior year. Interest is also due on such contributions or installments, computed from the valuation date of the plan (generally the first day of the plan year to which the contribution relates), and the interest rate is increased by five percentage points on past-due installments.[41] For a single-employer plan, the sponsor and all members

[35] *See supra* Chapter 7 notes 62–68 and accompanying text.
[36] ERISA §§ 204(g)(1), 302(d)(2), 29 U.S.C. §§ 1054(g)(1), 1082(d)(2) (2018); *see* I.R.C. §§ 411 (d)(6)(A), 412(d)(2) (2018).
[37] ERISA § 302(c)(7), 29 U.S.C. § 1082(c)(7) (2018); *see* I.R.C. § 412(c)(7) (2018). Such a liability-increasing amendment is nevertheless allowed if it is required for qualification, if it merely repeals a prior benefit cutback, or if the IRS finds that it is reasonable and provides only a de minimis increase in plan liabilities.
[38] ERISA § 204(i), 29 U.S.C. § 1054(i) (2018); *see* I.R.C. § 401(a)(33) (2018).
[39] ERISA § 206(g), 29 U.S.C. § 1056(g) (2018); *see* I.R.C. §§ 401(a)(29), 436 (2018). *See also* TREASURY GENERAL EXPLANATIONS, *supra* Chapter 9 note 14, at 79–80.
[40] ERISA § 303(j), 29 U.S.C. § 1083(j) (2018); *see* I.R.C. § 430(j) (2018). In response to the Coronavirus pandemic, Congress extended the date for single-employer plan minimum funding contributions (including required installments) that would otherwise fall due in 2020 until January 1, 2021. CARES Act, Pub. L. No. 116-136, § 3608 (Mar. 27, 2020).
[41] ERISA § 303(j), 29 U.S.C. § 1083(j) (2018); *see* I.R.C. § 430(j) (2018).

of its controlled group bear joint and several liability for the annual minimum contribution and any required installments.[42] Moreover, if the aggregate amount of past-due minimum contributions (including required installments and interest) exceeds $1 million, then an underfunded insured single-employer plan is given a lien against all property rights of the sponsor and all members of its controlled group.[43] The lien, which is perfected and enforced by the PBGC, continues until the close of the first plan year in which the unpaid balance of required payments falls below $1 million.

Although the IRS generally interprets and administers the minimum funding requirements, any plan participant, beneficiary, or fiduciary may seek an injunction enforcing ERISA's minimum funding standards.[44] The Secretary of Labor may also seek enforcement, but if the plan is qualified, the Labor Department can sue only if requested to do so by the Treasury or by the written request of one or more participants, beneficiaries, or fiduciaries.[45] In addition, if the amount of missed contributions exceeds $1 million, the PBGC may bring suit.[46]

To put extra teeth in the rules, ERISA's funding requirements are replicated in the qualified plan provisions of the Internal Revenue Code.[47] Noncompliance with the tax-law version triggers a nondeductible annual tax on the employer equal to 10 percent of the amount of unpaid required minimum contributions, which rises to 100 percent if the shortfall is not timely corrected.[48]

Disclosure of Funded Status

Participants in a defined benefit pension plan bear a residual risk of loss to the extent that their benefits are unfunded and uninsured. In the four largest underfunded plan terminations that had occurred as of 2005, only two-thirds of the shortfall was covered by PBGC, with the remainder, some $6 billion, representing a loss to plan participants.[49] Information concerning the funded status of the plan could facilitate financial planning and self-protection. Therefore, ERISA imposes requirements concerning disclosure of funding information to participants and beneficiaries.[50]

---

[42] ERISA § 302(b)(2), (d)(3), 29 U.S.C. § 1082(b)(2), (d)(3) (2018); see I.R.C. § 412(b)(2), (d)(3) (2018). For this purpose, "controlled group" means the composite employer used by the tax law to test for discrimination under the qualified retirement plans. See infra Chapter 10B.

[43] ERISA § 303(k), 29 U.S.C. § 1083(k) (2018); see I.R.C. § 430(k) (2018).

[44] ERISA § 502(a)(3), 29 U.S.C. § 1132(a)(3) (2018).

[45] ERISA § 502(a)(5), (b), 29 U.S.C. § 1132(a)(5), (b) (2018).

[46] ERISA § 4003(e), 29 U.S.C. § 1303(e) (2018).

[47] I.R.C. §§ 412, 430, 436 (2018).

[48] Id. § 4971.

[49] PBGC, The Impact of Pension Reform Proposals on Claims Against the Pension Insurance Program, Losses to Participants, and Contributions 6 (2005), www.pbgc.gov/documents/impact_of_reform_proposals_1005.pdf.

[50] ERISA § 101(a)(2), (f), 29 U.S.C. § 1021(a)(2), (f) (2018). See supra Chapter 3A. Participants and beneficiaries must also be promptly notified if, as a result of severe underfunding, benefit

B PBGC TERMINATION INSURANCE[51]

ERISA's minimum funding rules have been repeatedly tightened since 1974, but they still concede an extended period during which plan assets will, in the event of termination, be insufficient to pay promised benefits. Without intervention, participants would bear that risk of loss because plan sponsors have traditionally disclaimed liability for unfunded benefits. Congress intervened by instituting a mandatory termination insurance system for defined benefit plans under ERISA Title IV. That system shifts most risk of loss from participants to the universe of defined benefit plan sponsors generally, including financially healthy sponsors of fully funded plans. ERISA's *reallocation* of the risk of underfunding works a wholesale conversion of workers' expectancies into entitlements.

The termination insurance system of ERISA Title IV applies only to defined benefit pension plans, and it contains the familiar exceptions for governmental and church plans, plans that do not provide for post-ERISA employer contributions, and plans established and maintained outside the United States for nonresident aliens.[52] Also excepted from termination insurance coverage are unfunded plans providing deferred compensation to a select group of management or highly compensated employees (i.e., top hat plans), excess benefit plans (whether funded or not), and plans established and maintained exclusively for substantial owners.[53] In terms of both access to information and bargaining power, substantial owners and highly paid employees are in a better position than the rank-and-file to protect themselves from the risk of underfunding, and Congress left them to their own devices. Finally, Title IV contains an unusual exception for a plan of a "professional service employer," which has not at any time since the date of enactment of ERISA had more than twenty-five active participants.[54]

The termination insurance program is administered by the PBGC, a government corporation within the Department of Labor.[55] To accomplish its mission of

---

accruals are frozen or the plan becomes subject to restrictions on plant shutdown benefits or lump-sum distributions. ERISA §§ 101(j), 502(a)(6), (c)(4), 29 U.S.C. §§ 1021(j), 1132(a)(6), (c)(4) (2018).

[51] The discussion in this section is adapted from Peter J. Wiedenbeck & Russell K. Osgood, Cases and Materials on Employee Benefits 787–832 (1996), and is reprinted with permission of West, a Thomson Reuters business. This section addresses the termination insurance program for single-employer plans only. The rules governing insurance of multiemployer pension plan benefits and the withdrawal liability imposed upon an employer's dissociation from a multiemployer plan are beyond the scope of this monograph.

[52] ERISA § 4021(a), (b)(1)–(5), (7), 29 U.S.C. § 1321(a), (b)(1)–(5), (7) (2018).

[53] ERISA §§ 4021(b)(6), (8), (9), 4022(b)(5)(A), 29 U.S.C. §§ 1321(b)(6), (8), (9), 1322(b)(5)(A) (2018). "Substantial owner" is defined to mean sole proprietors, partners who own a greater than 10 percent stake in capital or profits, and shareholders who own greater than 10 percent in value of either the voting stock or all stock of the corporation. ERISA § 4021(d), 29 U.S.C. § 1321(d) (2018).

[54] ERISA § 4021(b)(13), (c)(2), (c)(3), 29 U.S.C. § 1321(b)(13), (c)(2), (c)(3) (2018).

[55] ERISA § 4002(a), 29 U.S.C. § 1302(a) (2018).

300 *Content Controls: Pension Plans*

ensuring uninterrupted payment of benefits, the PBGC charges plan sponsors annual premiums.[56] Its obligations are *not* backed by the full faith and credit of the United States.[57]

Guaranteed Benefits

With certain exceptions, the PBGC guarantees the payment "of all nonforfeitable benefits (other than benefits becoming nonforfeitable solely on account of the termination of a plan) under a single-employer plan which terminates at a time when this title applies to it."[58] For purposes of Title IV, a "nonforfeitable benefit" means

> a benefit for which a participant has satisfied the conditions for entitlement under the plan or the requirements of this Act (other than submission of a formal application, retirement, completion of a required waiting period, or death in the case of a benefit which returns all or a portion of a participant's accumulated mandatory employee contribution upon the participant's death), whether or not the benefit may subsequently be reduced or suspended by a plan amendment, an occurrence of any condition, or operation of this Act or the Internal Revenue Code of 1986 ... .[59]

Under this definition, added in response to the Supreme Court's first decision involving ERISA,[60] the right to a disability pension is not guaranteed unless the injury or other disability occurred before the date of plan termination.[61] Moreover, the PBGC imposes the condition that only *pension* benefits are guaranteed, meaning:

> a benefit payable as an annuity, or one or more payments related thereto, to a participant who permanently leaves or has permanently left covered employment, or to a surviving beneficiary, which payments by themselves or in combination with Social Security, Railroad Retirement, or workmen's compensation benefits provide a substantially level income to the recipient.[62]

Although single-sum payments are generally excluded, if the plan provides a life annuity alternative, the PBGC guarantees that alternative, and it will also pay out *as*

[56] ERISA §§ 4005(b)(1), 4007(a), (e), 29 U.S.C. §§ 1305(b)(1), 1307(a), (e) (2018).
[57] ERISA § 4002(g)(2), 29 U.S.C. § 1302(g)(2) (2018).
[58] ERISA § 4022(a), 29 U.S.C. § 1322(a) (2018).
[59] ERISA § 4001(a)(8), 29 U.S.C. § 1301(a)(8) (2018).
[60] Nachman Corp. v. PBGC, 446 U.S. 359 (1980) (rejecting sponsor's argument that Title I definition of "nonforfeitable," ERISA § 3(19), 29 U.S.C. § 1002(19) (2018), controls scope of PBGC's guarantee).
[61] 29 C.F.R. §§ 4022.3(a), 4022.4(a)(1), (3), 4022.6(a) (2022). The latter regulation also requires that, to be insured, a disability pension must be payable "on account of the total and permanent disability of a participant which is expected to last for the life of the participant."
[62] 29 C.F.R. §§ 4022.2, 4022.3(a) (2022).

an annuity the value of a single-sum benefit provided under the plan on the death of a participant.[63]

Early retirement benefits are guaranteed to participants who have satisfied any applicable age or service conditions before plan termination, even if not yet retired.[64] If the plan offers subsidized early retirement, the full benefit is guaranteed, even though the employer subsidy might be viewed as financing a holiday (early exit from the labor force) rather than old age support. Plant shutdown benefits that are in pay status when a plan terminates are also guaranteed even though the pension may commence many years before the plan's normal retirement age, but the guarantee is phased in ratably over a five-year period following the effective date of the plant shutdown or other unpredictable contingent event.[65]

Benefits that vest on termination (under I.R.C. § 411(d)(3)) are *not* guaranteed, nor are benefits that accrue after a plan becomes disqualified.[66] There are two other important limits on the guarantee. First, there is a maximum guaranteed amount (which is conceptually akin to a coverage limit in a property or liability insurance policy). The actuarial value of guaranteed benefits cannot exceed the value of a life annuity, commencing at age sixty-five, paying $750 per month in 1974 dollars, indexed for inflation ($6,750 monthly in 2023).[67] The guaranteed benefit also cannot exceed the participant's average monthly gross income from the employer during her highest-paid five consecutive calendar-year period.[68] Second, for benefits that have been in effect less than five years (either because the plan was instituted or benefits were increased within that period), the guarantee is not fully effective; instead, it is phased in at the rate of 20 percent per year.[69] But in the case of a majority owner (determined using the tax Code's constructive ownership rules), the

---

[63] *Id.* § 4022.7(a), (c)(1).

[64] 29 C.F.R. §§ 4022.2, 4022.3, 4022.4(a)(3) (2022). An early retirement pension is paid as an annuity, and only formal application and retirement stand in the way of entitlement for an active participant who has satisfied all applicable age and service conditions. Consequently, in this situation the early retirement pension satisfies the definition of "nonforfeitable benefit" quoted earlier. *See supra* text accompanying Chapter 9 note 59.

[65] ERISA § 4022(b)(1), (7), (8), 29 U.S.C. § 1322(b)(1), (7), (8) (2018); 29 C.F.R. §§ 4022.2, 4022.3, 4022.4(a)(1), 4022.27 (2022). The five-year phase-in applies to plant closings or other unpredictable contingent events occurring after July 26, 2005. It responds to a moral hazard problem revealed by findings that a large share of claims against the PBGC were generated by plant shutdowns occurring shortly before plan termination. *See* RICHARD A. IPPOLITO, THE ECONOMICS OF PENSION INSURANCE 75–80 (1989) (special early benefits accounted for nearly 25 percent of the claims in a sample of large plan terminations). ERISA was also amended in 2006 to bar payment of plant shutdown benefits by substantially underfunded plans. ERISA § 206(g), 29 U.S.C. § 1056(g) (2018); *see* I.R.C. §§ 401(a)(29), 436(b) (2018) (corresponding qualification condition).

[66] ERISA § 4022(a) (parenthetical clause), (b)(6), 29 U.S.C. § 1322(a), (b)(6) (2018).

[67] ERISA § 4022(b)(3)(B), 29 U.S.C. § 1322(b)(3)(B) (2018); 29 C.F.R. § 4022.22(a) (2022); PBGC, Maximum Monthly Guarantee Tables, www.pbgc.gov/wr/benefits/guaranteed-bene fits/maximum-guarantee.

[68] ERISA § 4022(b)(3)(A), 29 U.S.C. § 1322(b)(3)(A) (2018); 29 C.F.R. § 4022.22(a) (2022).

[69] ERISA § 4022(b)(1), (7), 29 U.S.C. § 1322(b)(1), (7) (2018); 29 C.F.R. § 4022.25 (2022).

amount of new benefits that would otherwise be guaranteed (taking into account the general five-year phase-in, if applicable) is further limited by a ten-year pro rata phase-in.[70]

The allocation of the assets of a terminating insured single-employer plan is governed by ERISA. Following the technique of bankruptcy law, benefit claims are assigned to six different priority categories. Plan assets are used to pay all accrued benefits assigned to priority Category 1 in full before any payment is made toward Category 2 benefits, and so on down the ladder (with a reversion possible if all six categories are paid in full).[71] Within a category, assets are generally allocated in proportion to the present value of each participant's accrued benefits assigned that priority.[72] Thus, if an underfunded plan runs out of assets in priority Category 3, all accrued benefits assigned to the top two categories will be paid in full, no payment will be made to satisfy benefits in Categories 4, 5, and 6, and Category 3 claims will generally be paid pro rata.

ERISA's asset allocation priority schedule is drawn more with a view to protecting participants' expectations than for the purpose of reducing moral hazard and protecting the PBGC. Available funding is devoted first to certain favored categories of benefits, whether guaranteed or not. The top three categories clearly evidence the anxiety to preserve reliance interests; they cover (1) voluntary employee contributions; (2) mandatory employee contributions; and (3) benefits that were in pay status – or, in the event of retirement, could have been in pay status – three years before the date of plan termination. The fourth category covers all other guaranteed benefits, but includes, in addition, benefits payable to majority owners that are not guaranteed because of the ten-year phase-in. Amounts that exceed the dollar cap on guaranteed benefits can be funded under Category 3 (as benefits that were or could have been in pay status three years before termination) before any allocation is made toward Category 4, which includes the guaranteed benefits of most active workers.[73] To that extent, more guaranteed benefits are left unfunded, resulting in higher insured losses. Category 5 covers all other nonforfeitable benefits under the plan (e.g., benefits that are not guaranteed because they vest on termination); any other

---

[70] ERISA § 4022(b)(5), 29 U.S.C.A. § 1322(b)(5) (2018).

[71] ERISA § 4044(a), (d), 29 U.S.C. § 1344(a), (d) (2018). The possibility of a reversion is discussed more fully *infra* Chapter 9C, concerning overfunded defined benefit plan termination.

[72] ERISA § 4044(b)(2), (b)(3), 29 U.S.C. § 1344(b)(2), (b)(3) (2018). If plan assets run out in Category 5, a special rule provides for allocation first to the amount of Category 5 benefits the participants would be entitled to under the plan as in effect five years before termination, with any remaining assets allocated according to successive plan amendments within that five-year period. ERISA § 4044(b)(4), 29 U.S.C. § 1344(b)(4) (2018). In addition, the plan is permitted to establish priority subcategories based on age, service, or disability, or a combination thereof, except in priority categories 1 and 2. ERISA § 4044(b)(7), 29 U.S.C. § 1344(b)(7) (2018); 29 C.F.R. § 4044.17(a) (2022).

[73] 29 C.F.R. § 4044.13(a) (2022) (final sentence).

benefits fall in Category 6 (e.g., disability benefits where the disability occurs after termination).

The right to terminate an underfunded plan is severely restricted so that the sponsor remains subject to ongoing funding obligations. Underfunded plans may be terminated in a "distress termination," which requires that the sponsor and each member of its controlled group be (1) in liquidation proceedings under bankruptcy or insolvency law; (2) unable to pay its debts and continue in business if the plan continues; or (3) subject to unreasonably burdensome pension costs solely as a result of a decline in the covered workforce.[74] In addition, the PBGC may initiate termination when necessary to protect the interests of plan participants or the insurance program, and *must* terminate any plan that has insufficient assets to pay current benefits.[75] Accordingly, a sponsor can shed its funding obligation only if it and all related businesses are in dire financial straits.

If an underfunded plan is terminated, whether by the PBGC or in a distress termination, the sponsor is liable to the PBGC for "the total amount of the unfunded benefit liabilities (as of the termination date) to all participants and beneficiaries under the plan" together with interest from the termination date.[76] The sponsor's liability extends to *all* benefits, even those not guaranteed by the PBGC. As originally enacted, ERISA made the sponsor of an underfunded plan liable to the PBGC for the amount of unfunded guaranteed benefits,[77] but until 1986 that reimbursement liability was capped at 30 percent of the sponsor's net worth.[78] To prevent evasion, liability to the PBGC extends beyond the contributing sponsor; all businesses under common control with the plan sponsor bear joint and several liability for the funding shortfall.[79] Nor can the financially healthy members

---

[74] ERISA § 4041(a)(1), (c)(1)(C), (c)(2)(B), 29 U.S.C. § 1341(a)(1), (c)(1)(C), (c)(2)(B) (2018). *See In re* Kaiser Aluminum Corp., 456 F.3d 328 (3d Cir. 2006) (where a sponsor seeks distress termination of multiple plans, determination whether sponsor will be unable to pay its debts and continue in business is made considering the aggregate financial burden of all plans sought to be terminated, not on a plan-by-plan basis).

[75] ERISA § 4042(a), 29 U.S.C. § 1342(a) (2018).

[76] ERISA § 4062(b)(1)(A), 29 U.S.C. § 1362(b)(1)(A) (2018). *See* United Steelworkers of Am. v. United Eng'g, Inc., 52 F.3d 1386 (6th Cir. 1995) (ERISA preempts suit brought by employees and union directly against the employer for nonguaranteed benefits; workers must look to PBGC enforcement of PBGC's claim as the sole source of recovery).

[77] Note that the PBGC is designated a "guarantor," not an insurer. Under the law of suretyship, a guarantor who is called upon to pay a debt is subrogated to all the creditor's rights and remedies against the principal debtor. The PBGC's claim for reimbursement of unfunded guaranteed benefits corresponds to the surety's right of subrogation.

[78] ERISA § 4062(b), 88 Stat. 829, 1029 (pre-1986 version).

[79] ERISA § 4062(a), 29 U.S.C. § 1362(a) (2018). Common control is currently defined by reference to the commonly controlled business rules in the Internal Revenue Code's qualified plan provisions. ERISA § 4001(a)(13), (14), 29 U.S.C. § 1301(a)(13), (14) (2018); *see* I.R.C. § 414(b), (c) (2018). The control group liability principle was established early in the administration of the termination insurance program. The original version of ERISA § 4062 made "the employer who maintained a plan" liable to reimburse the PBGC for payment of guaranteed benefits, but Title IV's expansive definition of employer, ERISA § 4001(b)(1), 29 U.S.C. §

304 Content Controls: Pension Plans

of a controlled group shed their liability by arranging a strategic pre-termination disaffiliation. If, for example, the cash-strapped sponsor of an underfunded plan is sold off with the expectation that the plan will later have to be terminated, the seller (and related businesses) may remain liable for the underfunding. ERISA was amended in 1986 to provide such continuing liability if a principal purpose behind the disaffiliation was to evade liability and the plan is ultimately terminated within five years after the sale.[80] Even without statutory authority, some courts reached the same result by ruling that the circumstance of the transaction, analyzed under substance-over-form principles, showed that disaffiliation amounted to constructive termination.[81]

To reduce pre-termination funding erosion, Congress tightened requirements for obtaining a waiver of the minimum funding obligation and barred benefit increases for as long as a waiver is in effect.[82] Plant shutdown and other unpredictable contingent event benefits still do not need to be advance funded, but once the contingency that triggers entitlement occurs, the benefits must be rapidly funded (using a seven-year amortization schedule).[83] Distributions that commence within

---

1301(b)(1) (2018), was held to impose joint and several liability on all commonly controlled businesses. PBGC v. Ouimet Corp., 630 F.2d 4, 12 (1st Cir. 1980), *appeal after remand*, 711 F.2d 1085 (applying family attribution rules to determine group membership and allocating entire liability to solvent affiliates of bankrupt sponsor).

[80] ERISA § 4069(a), 29 U.S.C. § 1369(a) (2018). In PBGC v. White Consolidated Industries, 998 F.2d 1192 (3d Cir. 1993), the seller agreed to make substantial contributions to several underfunded pension plans for five years after sale of the sponsoring unprofitable subsidiaries, allegedly to avoid predecessor liability by preventing termination of the plans within five years. The Third Circuit held that the five-year limit on predecessor liability does not begin to run until the company that transferred the pension plan stops making substantial post-transfer contributions. *White Consol. Indus.*, 998 F.2d at 1198–2000; Blaw Knox Ret. Plan v. White Consol. Indus., 998 F.2d 1185, 1192 (3d Cir. 1993) (same facts). *See also* Raytech Corp. v. PBGC, 241 B.R. 790 (Bankr. D. Conn. 1999) (successor liability for minimum funding contributions imposed on recipient of fraudulent conveyance).

[81] E.g., In re Consol. Litig. Concerning Int'l Harvester's Disposition of Wisc. Steel, 681 F. Supp. 512 (N.D. Ill. 1988) (disaffiliation a constructive termination where the buyer does not have a reasonable chance of paying for unfunded pension benefits and seller intended to evade pension funding obligations). *But see White Consol. Indus.*, 998 F.2d at 1201 (constructive termination theory of *International Harvester* does not apply to transactions after January 1, 1986, to which predecessor liability rule of ERISA § 4069 applies); *White Consol. Indus.*, 215 F.3d at 419 n.15 (dicta expressing uncertainty whether "the tax policy considerations at the heart of the sham transfer doctrine translate neatly when used to disregard a sale transaction for purposes of imposing pension liability").

[82] ERISA § 302(c), 29 U.S.C. § 1082(c) (2018); *see* I.R.C. § 412(c) (2018). Waivers can be granted to a single-employer plan in no more than three of any fifteen years; the waived funding deficiency must be amortized over five years; to qualify for a waiver the employer and all members of its controlled group must be experiencing temporary substantial business hardship; the IRS must consult the PBGC on the waiver application; and the grant of a waiver may be conditioned on the employer's granting security for repayment.

[83] Underfunding triggered by a plant closing or other unpredictable contingent event must generally be amortized over seven years, along with funding shortfalls attributable to all other events. ERISA § 303(a), (c), (d)(1), 29 U.S.C. § 1083(a), (c), (d)(1) (2018); *see* I.R.C. § 430(a),

Security   305

three years before plan termination can be recovered from the recipient to the extent that pre-termination distributions exceed, by more than a specified amount, the present value of the benefits that would have been guaranteed had payments been made as a life annuity.[84]

PBGC Monitoring and Enforcement

ERISA grants the PBGC three major types of liens against the property of the sponsor of an underfunded plan. First, a lien arises for the amount that plan assets at termination prove insufficient to pay all benefit liabilities, whether guaranteed or not. The PBGC's lien, however, is limited to 30 percent of the collective net worth of all members of the contributing sponsor's controlled group.[85] Second, the PBGC is given a lien for the amount of delinquent minimum funding contributions as soon as they exceed \$1 million.[86] The third type of PBGC lien comes into play when the IRS requires security as a condition of granting a minimum funding waiver.[87]

For a number of reasons, the PBGC's liens often fail to work in bankruptcy. The liens for plan asset insufficiency and delinquent minimum funding contributions must be perfected in the same manner as a federal tax lien in order to be effective against later judgment or secured creditors or against the bankruptcy trustee. But once the sponsor files for bankruptcy, the automatic stay prevents the PBGC from taking the steps necessary to perfect the liens. Moreover, if bankruptcy proceedings result in liquidation rather than reorganization of the sponsor, the PBGC's liens are denied secured status even if perfected pre-petition; instead, the PBGC's claims must settle for the seventh priority status accorded tax claims.[88]

Typically, the PBGC's liens are not perfected in time to be effective in bankruptcy. Lacking secured status, the PBGC has asserted that the claims underlying its liens are entitled to one or another priority in bankruptcy. In general, however, the

---

(c), (d)(1) (2018). In addition, plans are required to include a provision that bars the payment of unpredictable contingent event benefits if such benefits would cause the plan's funding level to fall below 60 percent in the year in which the triggering event occurs. ERISA § 206(g), 29 U.S.C. § 1056(g) (2018); *see* I.R.C. §§ 401(a)(29), 436(a), (b) (2018). Recognizing that plant closings within a few years of plan termination can dramatically inflate underfunding, Congress first imposed accelerated funding requirements on unpredictable contingent event benefits in 1994. ERISA § 302(d)(1)(B), (d)(5)(A), 29 U.S.C. § 1082(d)(1)(B), (d)(5)(A) (2000) (repealed 2006); *see* I.R.C. § 412(*l*)(1)(B), (*l*)(5)(A) (2000) (repealed 2006).

[84] ERISA § 4045, 29 U.S.C. § 1345 (2018).
[85] ERISA § 4068, 29 U.S.C. § 1368 (2018).
[86] ERISA § 303(k), 29 U.S.C. § 1083(k) (2018); *see* I.R.C. § 430(k) (2018).
[87] ERISA § 302(c)(4), 29 U.S.C. § 1082(c)(4) (2018); *see* I.R.C. § 412(c)(4) (2018).
[88] *See generally* Daniel L. Keating, *Chapter 11's New Ten-Ton Monster: The PBGC and Bankruptcy*, 77 Minn. L. Rev. 803, 825–40 (1993); Daniel L. Keating, Bankruptcy and Employment Law §§ 4.3–4.8 (1995).

courts have held that claims for benefits that accrued prior to bankruptcy filing are not entitled to priority.[89]

Proposals have been advanced to grant the PBGC super-priority in bankruptcy or to completely prohibit underfunded plan termination except in cases where the sponsor will be liquidated rather than reorganized in bankruptcy.[90] But current law is clear: to be able to enforce employer liability, the PBGC must perfect its liens prior to bankruptcy filing. The lien for plan asset insufficiency does not even arise until plan termination, so to protect its interest the PBGC would have to terminate the plan prior to bankruptcy filing. (Recall that ERISA allows the PBGC to initiate termination if the plan has failed to meet its minimum funding standard or if plan continuation is expected to unreasonably increase the possible long-run loss to the PBGC.[91])

Both pre-petition plan termination and lien perfection call for vigilant monitoring, which requires access to information. ERISA requires the plan administrator or contributing sponsor to notify the PBGC of the occurrence of certain situations, called reportable events, that may indicate possible risk to the financial status of the plan or a threat to the PBGC insurance program.[92] Such notification is due within thirty days after the administrator or contributing sponsor knows or has reason to know that a reportable event has occurred. This reporting requirement is designed to give the PBGC the opportunity to act promptly to protect participants and the insurance system by (for example) perfecting or enforcing liens or involuntarily terminating plans. In addition, if the aggregate unfunded vested benefit liabilities of a privately held sponsor and the other members of its controlled group exceed $50 million and the vested benefits are less than 90 percent funded, then thirty-day *advance* notification is required of certain reportable events.[93]

C OVERFUNDED PLAN TERMINATION

The sponsor of an overfunded single-employer plan may voluntarily discontinue the program at any time, provided that certain procedures are followed. Where plan

---

[89] KEATING, BANKRUPTCY AND EMPLOYMENT LAW, *supra* Chapter 9 note 88, § 4.4; PBGC v. CF & I Fabricators of Utah, Inc., 150 F.3d 1293 (10th Cir. 1998) (lien for delinquent minimum funding contributions not entitled to tax priority; administrative priority available only to the extent unpaid contributions attributable to post-petition services). The Bankruptcy Code gives fifth priority to up to $10,000 (adjusted for inflation to $13,650 in 2020) per employee of unsecured claims for employee benefits based on services rendered within 180 days before bankruptcy filing, but the amount is reduced by the priority for unpaid wages and payments on behalf of employees to other benefit plans. 11 U.S.C. §§ 104(a), 507(a)(4), (5) (2018).

[90] Daniel L. Keating, *Pension Insurance, Bankruptcy and Moral Hazard*, WISC. L. REV. 65, 100 (1991); KEATING, BANKRUPTCY AND EMPLOYMENT LAW, *supra* Chapter 9 note 86, §§ 4.9–4.10.

[91] ERISA § 4042, 29 U.S.C. § 1342 (2018).

[92] ERISA § 4043, 29 U.S.C. § 1343 (2018).

[93] ERISA § 4043(b), 29 U.S.C. § 1343(b) (2018).

assets will be sufficient to pay all benefit liabilities, the transaction is known as a standard termination, which is accomplished in several steps.[94]

First, the plan administrator must provide each affected party with a written "notice of intent to terminate" not less than sixty nor more than ninety days before the proposed termination date.[95] The affected parties entitled to receive notice are each participant, each beneficiary of a deceased participant, each alternate payee under a qualified domestic relations order (QDRO), and every union representing participants.[96] Second, within 180 days after the proposed termination date, the administrator must send a "notice of plan benefits" to each participant, to the beneficiaries of each deceased participant, and to alternate payees under any QDRO. The notice of plan benefits reports the amount and form of benefits to which the specific participant or beneficiary is entitled and the personal data (e.g., age, years of service, compensation history) and actuarial data (e.g., mortality table and interest rate if benefits will or may be paid in a lump sum) on which those benefits are based.[97] Third, after providing the notice of plan benefits, and within 180 days after the proposed termination date, the administrator must send the PBGC a completed PBGC Form 500, the "standard termination notice," which includes the certification of an enrolled actuary showing that the projected amount of plan assets, as of the proposed date of final distribution, will be sufficient to cover the actuarial present value at that date of all benefit liabilities accrued to the proposed termination date.[98] Fourth, a "notice of annuity information," reporting the names and addresses of insurers from whom the plan administrator will purchase annuity contracts, must be provided no later than forty-five days before the distribution date to affected parties (other than those who will be forced to take a lump sum because of the small value of their benefits).[99] The PBGC has sixty days after receiving the standard termination notice (Form 500) to review the information provided for completeness, to ascertain that proper notices were issued to all persons entitled thereto, and, most important, to ensure that the plan assets will be sufficient

---

[94] ERISA § 4041(a), (b), 29 U.S.C. § 1341(a), (b) (2018); 29 C.F.R. § 4041.21 (2022). The PBGC publication, "Standard Termination Filing Instructions," www.pbgc.gov/sites/default/files/legacy/docs/500-instructions.pdf, contains a complete explanation of the steps involved in a standard termination.

[95] ERISA § 4041(a)(2), (b)(1)(A), 29 U.S.C. § 1341(a)(2), (b)(1)(A) (2018); 29 C.F.R. § 4041.23 (2022).

[96] ERISA § 4001(a)(21), 29 U.S.C. § 1301(a)(21) (2018). If an affected party has designated in writing someone else to receive notice, the administrator must follow that instruction. *Id.* The notice of intent to terminate need not be provided to the PBGC in the case of a standard termination, ERISA § 4041(a)(2), 29 U.S.C. § 1341(a)(2) (2018).

[97] ERISA § 4041(b)(1)(B), (b)(2)(B), 29 U.S.C. § 1341(b)(1)(B), (b)(2)(B) (2018); 29 C.F.R. §§ 4041.24, 4041.25(a) (2022).

[98] ERISA § 4041(b)(1)(B), (b)(2)(A), 29 U.S.C. § 1341(b)(1)(B), (b)(2)(A) (2018); 29 C.F.R. §§ 4021.24(a), 4041.25(a) (2022); PBGC Form 500, Standard Termination Notice.

[99] 29 C.F.R. §§ 4041.23(b)(5), 4041.27 (2022); ERISA § 4041(a)(2), 29 U.S.C. § 1341(a)(2) (2018).

308   *Content Controls: Pension Plans*

to satisfy all benefit liabilities.[100] If the PBGC finds a problem, it issues a notice of noncompliance, which halts the termination.

If no notice of noncompliance is received, the plan administrator proceeds to make a final distribution of plan assets.[101] Satisfaction of benefit liabilities is accomplished in three ways. The plan administrator provides for most participants and beneficiaries by purchasing irrevocable commitments from an insurance company to pay all promised benefits, with the insurer issuing nontransferable group or individual annuity contracts to participants. This purchase of annuity contracts allows the plan to go out of existence while assuring retirees uninterrupted pension payment and providing a source of payment for the accrued benefits of workers who have not yet qualified (by satisfying age, retirement, or other conditions) for the commencement of distributions according to the terms of the plan. The annuities so provided are not guaranteed by the PBGC, and the notice of intent to terminate must warn participants and beneficiaries of this fact.[102] The selection of the annuity provider, however, is a fiduciary act that must be carried out prudently and "solely in the interest of the participants and beneficiaries."[103]

To provide for participants who cannot be located, ERISA permits the plan administrator to transfer the participant's benefit to the PBGC, which runs a clearinghouse to search for missing participants.[104] Alternatively, if the plan so provides, the administrator can simply pay a participant the actuarial present value of his accrued benefit in cash, provided that its value does not exceed $5,000.[105] The deadline for making these distributions is the later of (1) 180 days after expiration of the PBGC's sixty-day review period or (2) 120 days after receipt of a favorable IRS

---

[100] ERISA § 4041(b)(2)(C), (d)(1), 29 U.S.C. § 1341(b)(2)(C) (d)(1) (2018); 29 C.F.R. § 4041.31 (a) (2022). The sixty-day review period may be extended with the consent of the plan administrator. ERISA § 4041(b)(2)(C)(ii), 29 U.S.C. § 1341(b)(2)(C)(ii) (2018); 29 C.F.R. § 4041.26 (a)(2) (2022).

[101] ERISA § 4041(b)(2)(D), 29 U.S.C. § 1341(b)(2)(D) (2018); 29 C.F.R. § 4041.28 (2022).

[102] 29 C.F.R. § 4041.23(b)(9) (2022); ERISA § 502(a)(9), 29 U.S.C. § 1132(a)(9) (2018).

[103] ERISA § 404(a)(1), 29 U.S.C. § 1104(a)(1) (2018); 29 C.F.R. § 4041.28(c)(3) (2022). ERISA's civil enforcement provision, moreover, expressly provides that participants and beneficiaries who receive annuities in satisfaction of their interests under a plan retain standing to enforce fiduciary duties involved in the selection of the annuity provider. ERISA § 502(a)(9), 29 U.S.C. § 1132(a)(9) (2018).

[104] ERISA §§ 4041(b)(3)(A)(ii), 4050, 29 U.S.C. §§ 1341(b)(3)(A)(ii), 1350 (2018). The PBGC's missing participant pension search program is now an online resource, www.pbgc.gov/prac/ missing-p-single-employer.

[105] The immediate cash-out can be involuntary (i.e., made without consent of the participant and his spouse) and is permissible even if, under the terms of the plan, the participant's benefits would not otherwise be distributable for many years. ERISA §§ 203(e)(1), 205(g), 29 U.S.C. §§ 1053(e)(1), 1055(g) (2018); see I.R.C. §§ 417(e), 411(a)(11) (2018). Such cash-outs undermine retirement income security because the money is likely to be spent, rather than saved for retirement, but Congress compromised security in favor of avoiding the administrative cost of preserving de minimis benefits. The limit on involuntary cash-outs rises to $7,000 for distributions made after 2023. SECURE 2.0 Act of 2022, Pub. L. No. 117-328, Div. T, § 304, 136 Stat. 4459, __ (2023).

Security   309

determination letter, provided that the plan administrator submits a valid request for an IRS determination letter by the time she files the Form 500 with the PBGC.[106] The administrator has thirty days after finishing benefit distributions to certify to the PBGC that the close-out process has been properly completed.[107]

An overfunded plan will have assets left after making arrangements for the payment of all benefit liabilities. In the unusual case of a contributory defined benefit plan, a share of the overfunding must be distributed to participants, with the share determined by the percentage of the participants' accrued benefits that were financed by mandatory employee contributions.[108] Overfunding that is not so attributed to mandatory employee contributions may be distributed to the employer, but only if the plan provides for such a reversion and it does not violate any provision of law.[109] Moreover, plan amendments that would authorize or increase such a reversion cannot be made on the eve of termination; they are effective only if they have been in effect for at least five full calendar years.[110]

ERISA's anti-inurement, exclusive benefit, and prohibited-transaction rules (and their tax-law counterparts) prevent an employer from withdrawing excess assets from an ongoing pension plan.[111] That prohibition led overfunded plan sponsors to devise techniques by which they could formally terminate the plan to reclaim its excess assets, yet continue the accrual of benefits for active participants without interruption. In a termination/reestablishment transaction, the employer establishes a new defined benefit plan covering the same group of employees and using the

---

[106] 29 C.F.R. § 4041.28(a)(1) (2022). The employer will ordinarily request an IRS determination that the plan is qualified at the time of termination to ensure that participants will receive favorable tax treatment (continued tax deferral) of distributions. If the plan is qualified, no tax is due on receipt of an annuity contract (later distributions under the contract are taxed under the annuity rules), and a cash-out distribution may be eligible for tax-free rollover to an IRA. I.R.C. § 402(a), (c)(1) (2018); Treas. Reg. § 1.402(a)-1(a)(2) (as amended in 2019).

[107] ERISA § 4041(b)(3)(B), 29 U.S.C. § 1341(b)(3)(B) (2018); 29 C.F.R. § 4041.29 (2022); PBGC Form 501.

[108] ERISA § 4044(d)(3), 29 U.S.C. § 1344(d)(3) (2018). Voluntary employee contributions are not taken into account in this computation because, pursuant to ERISA § 204(c)(4), 29 U.S.C. § 1054(c)(4) (2018), and I.R.C. § 411(d)(5) (2018), voluntary employee contributions made under a defined benefit plan are treated as constituting a separate defined contribution plan.

[109] ERISA §§ 403(c)(1) (exception to anti-inurement rule), 4044(d)(1), 29 U.S.C. §§ 1103(c)(1), 1344(d)(1) (2018). These provisions were derived from the qualified plan exclusive benefit rule, which dates from 1938. The tax Code conditions qualification on proof that

"it is impossible, at any time prior to the satisfaction of all liabilities with respect to employees and their beneficiaries under the trust, for any part of the [trust] corpus or income to be (within the taxable year or thereafter) used for, or diverted to, purposes other than for the exclusive benefit of his employees or their beneficiaries ... ." I.R.C. § 401(a)(2) (2018).

[110] ERISA § 4044(d)(2), 29 U.S.C. § 1344(d)(2) (2018).

[111] The exclusive benefit rule, the anti-inurement rule, and the prohibited-transaction rule all expressly except transfers on plan termination that are authorized by section 4044, which permits reversions under the conditions described above. ERISA §§ 403(c)(1), 404(a)(1), 408 (b)(9), 29 U.S.C. §§ 1103(c)(1), 1104(a)(1), 1108(b)(9) (2018); see I.R.C. §§ 401(a)(2), 4975 (d)(12) (2018).

same benefit formula as the terminated plan. In a spin-off termination, the employer splits an overfunded plan into two, one covering active employees and another covering retirees. The plan covering active employees satisfies the minimum funding standards and continues in operation, but all excess assets are assigned to the plan for retirees, which is terminated to claim the reversion. When these techniques were approved in the early 1980s by the agencies charged with ERISA enforcement,[112] there was a rapid and dramatic increase in overfunded plan terminations.[113]

To quell the rash of overfunded plan terminations, Congress took two steps. First, all plans involved in a spin-off termination are disqualified unless a proportionate part of the excess assets is allocated to each resulting plan; the entire surplus can no longer be allocated to the plan covering retirees (a plan destined for termination).[114] Second, to recapture tax benefits, a special 20 percent excise tax is imposed on employer reversions from qualified plans.[115] To discourage employers from simply terminating an overfunded defined benefit plan without making any provision for workers to obtain additional pension benefits, the excise tax is raised from 20 percent to 50 percent of the reversion unless the employer establishes a qualified replacement plan (which may be either defined benefit or defined contribution) covering at least 95 percent of the active participants in the terminated plan who continue as employees, and transfers 25 percent of the excess assets (reduced by certain benefit increases made under the terminating plan) to the replacement plan. Alternatively, the additional 30 percent exaction can be avoided without establishing a new plan, provided that 20 percent of the excess assets are used to provide a pro rata increase in accrued benefits under the terminating plan.[116] ERISA expressly obligates the fiduciary of the terminating plan and the fiduciary of the qualified replacement plan (if any) to follow the excise tax requirements, thereby subjecting the fiduciary's conduct to ERISA's civil enforcement mechanism.[117]

Since 1991 Congress has repeatedly re-authorized a "temporary" inroad on the principle that there can be no reversion prior to plan termination. A portion of the excess assets of a substantially overfunded defined benefit plan may be transferred to

---

[112] Rev. Rul. 83-52, 1983-1 C.B. 156; U.S. Department of Treasury, U.S. Department of Labor, Pension Benefit Guaranty Corporation, *Joint Implementation Guidelines for Terminations of Defined Benefit Pension Plans, reprinted in* 23 TAX NOTES 1088 (1984).

[113] For an outstanding account of the history of these developments and the policy issues involved, see Norman P. Stein, *Reversions from Pension Plans: History, Policies and Prospects*, 44 TAX L. REV. 259 (1989).

[114] I.R.C. § 414(*l*)(2) (2018). *See* S. REP. NO. 100-445, at 443–45 (1988). In addition, the *Joint Implementation Guidelines, supra* Chapter 9 note 112, required advance notice to all employees covered under a plan that will be split in two under a spin-off termination. These special notice requirements are now prescribed by 29 C.F.R. §§ 4041.23(c), 4041.24(f), 4041.27(a)(2) (2022).

[115] I.R.C. § 4980(a) (2018).

[116] *Id.* § 4980(d) (2018).

[117] ERISA § 404(d), 29 U.S.C. § 1104(d) (2018).

Security 311

a special account used to pay retiree health benefits or provide limited amounts of retiree group-term life insurance coverage.[118] Such a diversion of overfunding amounts to a prohibited reversion from an ongoing pension plan followed by a contribution of the reversion to a welfare plan providing retiree health or life insurance benefits. Nevertheless, the pension plan is not disqualified, and the employer is excused from paying taxes on the transferred amounts. This flexibility to redirect excess pension savings to meet retiree health care or life insurance needs illustrates once again the delicate balance between ERISA's promotional and protective urges, this time in the context of a trade-off between pension and welfare benefits.

D CONCLUSION

The defined benefit plan funding, insurance, and termination rules dramatically illustrate the tensions and trade-offs between ERISA's principal policies (*supra* Chapter 1C), particularly the delicate balance between the statute's worker protection and pension promotion impulses. Faced with public outcry over defeated worker expectations from terminated underfunded plans,[119] Congress might have simply mandated periodic, simplified disclosure of the plan's funded status and the sponsor's financial condition, leaving it to workers to determine how much risk they were willing to bear and to take steps to protect themselves (e.g., by seeking alternative employment or bargaining for better funding). Instead, Congress required systematic advance funding of accrued benefits, insisted that employers stand behind their pension promises by outlawing disclaimer of liability for unfunded benefits, and instituted a mandatory government-run insurance program to guarantee most pensions in the event that an underfunded plan is terminated and the sponsor is unable to make good the shortfall.

---

[118] I.R.C. § 420(b)(4) (West Supp. 2023) (expires Dec. 31, 2032). *See* ERISA § 408(b)(13), 29 U.S.C.A. § 1108(b)(13) (West Supp. 2023) (exception to prohibited-transaction rule). Transfers are permitted only if the retiree group health plan or group-term life insurance plan contains a maintenance-of-effort commitment: the employer must continue to provide comparable-cost coverage for five or seven years, depending on the extent of the pension plan's overfunding. I.R.C. § 420(c)(3). Transfers made after August 17, 2006, may be used to finance estimated retiree health benefits for a period of up to ten years. *Id.* § 420(f). Any assets so transferred are not counted toward satisfaction of the pension plan's minimum funding obligation. ERISA § 303(*l*), 29 U.S.C. § 1083(*l*) (2018); *see* I.R.C. § 430(*l*) (2018). Administrators must give advance notice of such transfers of excess pension assets to retiree health benefits accounts. *See* ERISA §§ 101(e), 502(a)(1)(A), (c)(1), 29 U.S.C. §§ 1021(e), 1132(a)(1)(A), (c)(1) (2018).

[119] *See* James A. Wooten, *"The Most Glorious Story of Failure in the Business": The Studebaker-Packard Corporation and the Origins of ERISA*, 49 Buff. L. Rev. 683 (2001); Michael S. Gordon, *Overview: Why Was ERISA Enacted?, in* S. Spec. Comm. on Aging, 98th Cong., The Employee Retirement Income Security Act of 1974: The First Decade 1, 8, 11 (Comm. Print 1984).

Content Controls: Pension Plans

Those substantive defined benefit plan quality controls were tempered by the recognition of cost constraints inherent in a system of voluntary plan sponsorship. Immediate full funding was deemed too onerous, for it would have deterred employers from granting past-service benefits and discouraged the formation or expansion of defined benefit plans. The compromise, long-term amortization of past-service benefits, concedes an extended period of underfunding, during which the PBGC termination insurance program protects participants. To contain insurance costs and limit moral hazard, not all benefits are guaranteed, which leaves participants exposed to a residual risk of loss from underfunding, and leaves a role for disclosure rules (notice of underfunding and of limits on the PBGC insurance) so workers can respond.

Since ERISA's enactment, PBGC losses have led Congress to repeatedly tighten the funding and insurance rules. PBGC insurance premiums have been hiked repeatedly and made more risk-based (reducing the cross-subsidy to workers in failing industries), and financially healthy sponsors have been barred from terminating underfunded plans. To reduce the risk of insured losses, past-service liability amortization periods have been reduced from forty to thirty, to eighteen, and now seven years, discretion in setting actuarial assumptions has been restricted, and the flexibility ERISA originally preserved in the selection of a single employer plan's actuarial funding method was eliminated by the 2006 amendments.

These restrictions on employer autonomy have started to pinch – since the 1990s there has been an accelerating trend away from defined benefit plans, as sponsors prohibit new entrants or freeze benefit accrual under existing plans, convert their defined benefit plans to cash balance or other hybrid plans, or terminate their defined benefit plans and substitute 401(k) or other less costly defined contribution programs. As the walls close in, employers may be voting with their feet, fleeing the defined benefit pension system. The number of active participants in single-employer defined benefit plans fell from 20.1 million in 1975 to less than 7.3 million in 2020.[120] But that exodus carries with it a fundamental realignment of risks and responsibilities: in a defined contribution universe, workers typically have to make savings and investment decisions for themselves, conserve their resources in retirement, suffer the consequences of their own mistakes, and bear the burden of financial and economic calamities over which they have no control. Retirement is a whole new world out there, and it's not for the faint-hearted.[121]

---

[120] EBSA, Private Pension Plan Bulletin Historical Tables and Graphs 1975–2020, Table E7 (2022).
[121] See generally Edward A. Zelinsky, The Origins of the Ownership Society (2007).

PART IV

Tax Controls: Qualified Retirement Savings

10

Taxes and Retirement Saving

ERISA erected a "comprehensive and reticulated"[1] structure of pension regulation, including both conduct and content controls, upon a foundation laid by the
Internal Revenue Code's preexisting (albeit embryonic) criteria for granting favorable tax treatment to qualified pension, profit-sharing, stock bonus, and annuity
plans.[2] Indeed, that favorable tax treatment was largely responsible for the rapid
growth of the private pension system in the latter half of the twentieth century, and
many of the problems that ERISA addressed had emerged because of the rudi-
mentary nature of prior tax-law requirements. Aside from the PBGC termination
insurance system, Congress replicated all of ERISA's pension content controls in
the Internal Revenue Code, imposing them as additional conditions on attaining
qualified plan status.[3] This duplication supplements ERISA's enforcement

---

[1] Nachman Corp. v. PBGC, 446 U.S. 359, 361 (1980).

[2] With respect to conduct controls, ERISA's fiduciary duties have antecedents in the requirement that the assets of a qualified pension, profit-sharing, or stock bonus plan be held "for the
exclusive benefit of [the employer's] employees or their beneficiaries," I.R.C. § 401(a)(2)
(2018). That qualification condition, together with the long-standing requirement that a
qualified plan must be a "definite written program or arrangement which is communicated
to employees," Treas. Reg. § 1.401-2(a)(2) (as amended in 1976), indirectly afforded plan
participants some protection under state contract law. With respect to content controls, before
ERISA the IRS sometimes insisted that qualified plans provide pre-retirement vesting to
prevent a higher rate of turnover among rank and file employees from causing forfeitures that
would skew the amount of deferred compensation actually paid so as to discriminate in favor of
highly compensated employees. S. Rep. No. 93-383, at 44–45 (1973), *reprinted in* 1 ERISA
Legislative History, *supra* Chapter 1 note 55, at 1069, 1112–13; Rev. Rul. 71-263, 1971-1
C.B. 125; *see* Rev. Rul. 68-302, 1968-1 C.B. 163; Rev. Rul. 73-299, 1973-2 C.B. 137.

[3] Specifically, the pension content controls imposed by parts 2 and 3 of ERISA Title I (including
the participation, benefit accrual, vesting, anti-alienation, spousal protection, and minimum
funding standards) were also incorporated in the qualified plan provisions by ERISA Title II.
In addition, the prohibited-transaction rules of ERISA §§ 406–408, 29 U.S.C. §§ 1104–1108
(2018), were reproduced in I.R.C. § 4975 (2018).

316   *Tax Controls: Qualified Retirement Savings*

regime, bolstering it with a powerful tax-based incentive to comply that is backed by regular expert monitoring (IRS audits).[4]

The special tax treatment accorded qualified deferred compensation implicates traditional tax policy concerns about equity, efficiency, and administrability, and those norms have far-reaching implications that extend well beyond ERISA's principal policies (*see* Chapter 1C). Consequently, the Code imposes tax controls on qualified plans that are distinct from and apply in addition to those qualification criteria that reiterate ERISA's pension content controls. The favorable tax treatment of qualified plans provides an inducement to saving, and the tax controls seek to structure the incentive so that it induces retirement savings that would not otherwise occur. The tax controls, in other words, are an effort to properly target and control the tax subsidy.

This chapter begins with an examination of the standard treatment of deferred compensation (so-called nonqualified deferred compensation) under the federal income tax, and compares that approach with the taxation of amounts deferred under qualified pension, profit-sharing, stock bonus, and annuity plans (qualified deferred compensation). Section A also explores the relationship between such qualified retirement plans and other tax-favored savings arrangements, including traditional and Roth Individual Retirement Accounts (IRAs). The study then takes up the qualified plan rules that have no ERISA counterparts – in the terminology used here, these are the "tax controls." Section B is devoted to the nondiscrimination rules, which are the central mechanism for channeling public assistance into additional savings. Their efficacy, it will be shown, is highly sensitive to workforce composition, income tax rates, and the availability of other tax-sheltered savings opportunities.[5] Section C turns to a set of tax controls that limit the amount of the tax subsidy: caps on qualified plan savings, advance funding limits, and distribution timing constraints. Section D explores a number of proposals that would reform or replace the nondiscrimination rules, including some observations on the future of the (semi-) private pension system.

---

[4] Historically, overlapping labor- and tax-law jurisdictions are more accurately ascribed to political considerations than to the functional advantage of increased compliance through tax enforcement. In a colossal political miscalculation, the Senate Finance Committee derailed comprehensive pension legislation in 1972 at the behest of business groups and the Nixon Administration. The resulting public outcry gave momentum to the reform movement and assured the cooperation of the tax-writing committees in the Ninety-Third Congress. Michael S. Gordon, *Overview: Why Was ERISA Enacted?* in S. Spec. Comm. on Aging, 98th Cong., The Employee Retirement Income Security Act of 1974: The First Decade 1, 23–25 (Comm. Print 1984).

[5] A number of proposals that would reform or replace the nondiscrimination rules are explored in Part D, in conjunction with observations on the future of the (semi-) private pension system.

A TAXATION OF DEFERRED COMPENSATION

Nonqualified Deferred Compensation

General tax timing principles provide that income is taxable in the year to which it is properly attributable under the taxpayer's method of accounting.[6] Except for the owners of some unincorporated businesses, nearly all individuals use the cash receipts and disbursements method of accounting (also known as the cash method or cash-basis accounting), according to which items of income are reported for the taxable year in which they are actually or constructively received.[7] Constructive receipt occurs when income, although not actually reduced to the taxpayer's possession, is credited to his account, set apart for him, or otherwise made available so that he may draw upon it at any time, or so that he could have drawn upon it during the taxable year if notice of intention to withdraw had been given. Income is not constructively received if the taxpayer's control of its receipt is subject to substantial limitations or restrictions.[8]

Therefore under the cash method, *unfunded* deferred compensation is *ordinarily* not taxable until the amount is actually paid, even though a legal right to payment has been earned by the performance of services. The qualifications – "unfunded" and "ordinarily" – are hugely important, however.

Other rules come into play if a deferred compensation obligation is advance-funded rather than simply being left to be paid out of the employer's general assets when the time comes. If property is transferred as compensation for services, such in-kind compensation is taxable to the person who performed the services (whether employee or independent contractor) in the first taxable year in which the transferee's rights in the property first become transferable or not subject to a substantial risk of forfeiture.[9] Where in-kind compensation comes with significant strings attached,

---

[6] I.R.C. §§ 446(a), 451(a) (2018).

[7] Treas. Reg. § 1.451-1(a) (as amended in 1993).

[8] Treas. Reg. § 1.451-2(a) (as amended in 1979).

[9] I.R.C. § 83(a) (2018). "Transferable" in this context has a special meaning and does not refer to the mere existence of the power of alienation. Instead, property is transferable only if a transferee's rights in such property are not subject to a substantial risk of forfeiture. *Id.* § 83 (c)(2). Hence "transferable" refers to the ability to transfer free of the risk of loss. Accordingly, the critical event under section 83(a) – the moment when the property first becomes transferable or not subject to a substantial risk of forfeiture – is the earliest time when the risk of loss is actually eliminated or could be lifted simply by transferring the property. Hence actual or constructive elimination of the substantial risk of forfeiture triggers section 83(a).

Even if the property is received by a spouse, child, or another beneficiary, the income is taxed of the person who performed the services. *Id.* In this context, section 83 merely codifies the assignment-of-income doctrine, the general principle that income from services is taxable to the person who earns it, regardless of who actually receives it. Lucas v. Earl, 281 U.S. 111 (1930); Helvering v. Eubank, 311 U.S. 122 (1940) (labor income is taxed to the service provider whether the right to collect the income is assigned before or after services are performed).

Tax Controls: Qualified Retirement Savings

this rule takes a wait-and-see approach to taxation, deferring inclusion in gross income until it becomes reasonably clear that contingencies will be resolved in the worker's favor, so that the recipient will get to keep the property. The amount included in gross income is the unrestricted fair market value of the property at the time the property first becomes transferable or not subject to a substantial risk of forfeiture (whichever occurs earlier) reduced by any amount paid for the property.[10] A condition that requires the future performance of substantial services constitutes a substantial risk of forfeiture.[11] If employer stock or other property is transferred to an employee outright (i.e., unconditionally) as current in-kind compensation, then there is no risk of loss that would defer taxation, and the worker must include in gross income the value of the property on receipt, less the amount paid for it, if any. On the other hand, if company stock is transferred to an employee subject to the condition that the shares be returned to the employer if the employee separates from service within six years after receiving the stock, then the value of the shares would never be taxed to an employee who fails to satisfy the employment condition, while a worker who stays on long enough would not include the stock in income until six years have passed, and would report its value as income at that later time.[12]

---

[10] I.R.C. § 83(a) (2018). Temporary restrictions on transfer, such as prohibitions on assignment or the imposition of a formula price (so-called lapse restrictions), are ignored in determining the amount of income from in-kind compensation. *Id.* § 83(a)(1) (parenthetical clause); Treas. Reg. § 1.83-1(a)(1)(i) (as amended in 2003), *id.* § 1.83-3(h), -3(i) (as amended in 2014). In order to prevent abuse, this rule deliberately disregards the fact that such restrictions may depress value and so, in principle, limit the extent of enrichment. Prior to the enactment of section 83, cooperatively imposed formal restrictions had been used to obtain unjustified tax deferral. *See* Sakol v. Comm'r, 574 F.2d 694 (2d Cir. 1978) (rejecting constitutional challenge to temporary overtaxation mandated by inclusion of unrestricted fair market value). Permanent formula price constraints (so-called nonlapse restrictions) are taken into account in determining the amount included in gross income. Treas. Reg. § 1.83-3(h) (as amended in 2014); *id.* § 1.83-5(a) (1978).

[11] I.R.C. § 83(c)(1) (2018). Contingencies that do not depend, directly or indirectly, upon the future performance (or refraining from performance) of substantial services can constitute a substantial risk of forfeiture only if the condition is related to the purpose of the transfer. For the risk to be substantial there must be a substantial possibility that the forfeiture condition will be triggered and it must be likely that the forfeiture condition will be enforced, as determined by a realistic evaluation of all the facts and circumstances. *See* Treas. Reg. § 1.83-3(c) (as amended in 2014). A requirement that property be retransferred to the employer if the employee is discharged for cause or for committing a crime is not a substantial risk of forfeiture, while loss upon accepting employment with a competitor is not "ordinarily" considered to represent a substantial risk, but may do so if the particular facts (such as the age and skill level of the employee and his or her alternative employment opportunities) indicate that there is a realistic possibility that the eventuality will come to pass. *Id.* -3(c)(2).

[12] Dividends paid while the stock remains subject to the substantial risk of forfeiture would be taxed to the employee, but as additional compensation (ordinary income), rather than as dividends (which may be eligible for reduced tax rates under section 1(h)). Treas. Reg. § 1.83-1(a)(1) (as amended in 2003) (penultimate sentence).

The conclusion in the text implicitly assumes that the employee(s) awarded the contingent stock are not disproportionately older workers who would be close to retirement age upon

"Property," for purposes of I.R.C. § 83, consists of real and personal property of all sorts "other than either money or an unfunded and unsecured promise to pay money or property in the future," and it specifically includes "a beneficial interest in assets (including money) which are transferred or set aside from the claims of creditors of the transferor, for example, in a trust or escrow account."[13] This definition determines the scope of the rules governing taxation of in-kind compensation and is the source of a fundamental distinction in tax treatment between "funded" and "unfunded" deferred compensation. Because a mere "unsecured promise to pay money or property in the future" is not subject to section 83, the general rules of cash-basis accounting apply and such earned but unsecured deferred compensation is not income until it is received. In contrast, if the promise to pay in the future is backed by a transfer of money or property in trust, the beneficiary's interest in the trust (which constitutes an equitable ownership interest in the underlying assets) is subject to section 83, and the person who performed the

---

satisfaction of the six-year service condition. If that assumption is incorrect, then the arrangement arguably constitutes a pension plan under ERISA § 3(2)(A), 29 U.S.C. § 1002(2)(A) (2018), because it would operate to provide retirement income to employees as a result of surrounding circumstances. Due to the risk of forfeiture, an employee receiving such a stock award could not prudently consume its value during the interim, resulting in preservation of the asset throughout the forfeiture period, at the close of which the stock's value is available to finance retirement needs. *See supra* Chapter 2C. If such contingent stock awards were classified as a pension plan, then the six-year employment condition would violate ERISA's minimum vesting standards, ERISA § 203(a)(2)(B), 29 U.S.C. § 1053(a)(2)(B); *see supra* Chapter 7C, unless the stock awards were limited to a select group of management or highly compensated employees, ERISA § 201(2), 29 U.S.C. § 1051(2); *see supra* Chapter 2D. Early elimination of the risk of loss by operation of law (i.e., under ERISA's vesting rules) would correspondingly trigger earlier taxation under I.R.C. § 83. Earlier vesting, however, would to that extent undermine long-term saving (employees awarded stock could sell and consume the proceeds well before retirement), perhaps calling into question the classification of arrangement as an ERISA pension plan. This situation, in other words, presents a possible circularity problem.

A special rule enacted in 2017 provides that stock received upon the exercise of a stock option or settlement of a restricted stock unit may qualify for up to five years of tax deferral beyond the date when inclusion would ordinarily be required by section 83(a) if stock options or restricted stock units are granted to 80 percent or more of the employees of the corporation and none of the corporation's stock is publicly traded. I.R.C. § 83(i) (2018); *see* H.R. Rep. No. 115-466 at 494–503 (2017) (Conf. Rep.); IRS Notice 2018-97, 2018-52 I.R.B. 1062. All members of a controlled group of corporations are treated as one corporation for purposes of the qualified equity grant rules, I.R.C. § 83(i)(5), so if any stock of a group member is readily tradeable on an established securities market additional deferral is not available.

[13] Treas. Reg. § 1.83-3(e) (as amended in 2014). The exclusion from the definition of property of a legally binding but unsecured promise to pay ("an unfunded and unsecured promise to pay money or property in the future") preserves cash-basis accounting. A contractual right to future payment is income under the accrual method as soon as it has been earned by performance; not so under the cash method because there is no constructive receipt until the time for payment falls due. If a general creditor's contractual right to future payment were deemed property so as to trigger inclusion as in-kind compensation, section 83 would in effect require accrual method accounting for deferred payment obligations, swallowing up the cash method.

services will be taxed as soon as the beneficiary's interest is substantially vested. That could be immediately on contribution to the trust if the interest is unconditional, or at some later time when conditions are satisfied and the risk of loss is eliminated. Significantly, section 83 can trigger taxation of such "funded" deferred compensation far in advance of actual distribution. If, however, the employee's interest in deferred compensation remains forfeitable until the time specified for payment – for example, if payment at age sixty-five is conditioned on continued employment until that time – then section 83(a) delays taxation until distribution (just as cash-basis accounting would if the promise of future payment were unfunded).

Section 83 may call for the taxation of funded deferred compensation in advance of receipt, but "funded" and "unfunded" must be understood as loose references to the key classification, "an unfunded and unsecured promise to pay money or property in the future" – as references, that is, to whether a payment obligation is "property" within the meaning of section 83. In fact, use of the terms *funded* and *unfunded* to differentiate the respective spheres in which the in-kind compensation regime and cash-basis accounting hold sway is something of a misnomer because *security* for payment has proven to be the critical consideration. An arrangement known as a "rabbi trust" was developed in the 1980s to provide a source of funds to pay promised deferred compensation without triggering taxation in advance of receipt.[14] Under a rabbi trust, the employer makes contributions to the trust as services are performed, and the trustee invests the assets and distributes deferred compensation at the times specified in the plan (typically upon a participant's retirement, death or disability), but the trust instrument expressly provides that if the employer becomes insolvent the trustee shall cease making distributions and all trust assets will thenceforth be held for the benefit of the employer's general creditors.[15] The IRS ruled that neither the creation of the trust nor the employer's

---

[14] The arrangement is so named because the first IRS letter ruling analyzing the tax consequences of such a funding vehicle involved a trust established by a congregation for the benefit of its rabbi. I.R.S. Priv. Ltr. Rul. 81-13-107 (Dec. 31, 1980). The rabbi trust device quickly became very popular (for the reason explained *infra* Chapter 10 note 15), and the IRS was inundated with requests for private rulings. Eventually the IRS responded by issuing model rabbi trust language that taxpayers may adopt with assurance that employees will not be taxed prior to distribution of the deferred compensation. Rev. Proc. 92-64, 1992-2 C.B. 422.

[15] As the insolvency contingency indicates, a rabbi trust does not protect plan participants from the employer's creditors. Where the unthinkable happens – the employer becomes insolvent – disappointed executives sometimes try to jump the queue, claiming that their interests should be interpreted as secured or entitled to priority over general creditors, or asserting entitlement to relief under state law. Such complaints generally come to naught. *See, e.g.,* Loffredo v. Daimler AG, 500 F. App'x 491 (6th Cir. 2012); In re Lehman Bros. Inc., No. 08-01420 (SCC) SIPA, 2020 WL 3264058 (Bankr. S.D.N.Y. June 15, 2020) (reviewing more than ten-year battle over $270 million in executive deferred compensation).

Instead of security from creditors, the advantage of a rabbi trust lies in the security it provides in the event of a change of control of the sponsoring employer. Participating employees are typically incumbent management whose positions may be in jeopardy following a hostile takeover or other change in control. A new corporate leadership team may be reluctant to give

Taxes and Retirement Saving

contribution of assets constituted a transfer of property subject to section 83. Because there was no constructive receipt, the IRS further concluded that taxation would be deferred until distribution. The rabbi trust rulings demonstrated that insulation from the payer's creditors is the key element of "property" for purposes of section 83, and that absent such protection, the time for taxation of deferred compensation is given by the principles of cash-method accounting.[16]

A remarkable feature of the rabbi trust rulings is that the IRS expressly conditioned its conclusions concerning the tax consequences of the arrangement on the labor-law status of the program under ERISA Title I.[17] Specifically, the tax results (inapplicability of section 83 and delayed inclusion under the cash method) are contingent on the deferred compensation program qualifying as a "top hat" plan: an unfunded plan "maintained by an employer primarily for the purpose of providing deferred compensation to a select group of management or highly compensated employees." While never fully elaborated, the IRS apparently reasons that

full effect to deferred compensation programs designed by and for ousted executives, possibly at the expense of shareholders. A rabbi trust may provide that following a change of control, the trust instrument cannot be amended, nor can the trustee be removed without the consent of the plan participants, and may provide for court appointment or participant involvement in the selection of any successor trustee. By triggering more robust insulation from new management, plan participants may avoid the expense and delay of litigation to enforce their rights to deferred compensation. A rabbi trust, in other words, protects incumbent management from a change of heart following a shift in employer ownership or control.

[16] The section 83 regulations state that an "unfunded and unsecured promise to pay money or property in the future" is not property, and clearly indicate that a promise to pay that is both funded *and* secured is classified as property. Treas. Reg. § 1.83-3(e) (as amended in 2014). The regulatory definition is silent (perhaps deliberately noncommittal) about the status of a promise that is funded but unsecured, as in the case of a rabbi trust, where, as a practical matter, the promise of future payment is advance funded (assets are segregated and invested to provide means of payment), but the assets remain at risk in the event of insolvency (unsecured). As a matter of interpretation, the rabbi trust rulings resolve this ambiguous case, and in concluding that section 83 does not apply, the IRS implicitly rules that "property" status turns only upon security from the employer's general creditors.

The rabbi trust rulings are also conditioned upon the fact that participants' rights to deferred compensation under the plan and trust were expressly declared to be nontransferable. *See, e.g.,* I.R.S. Priv. Ltr. Rul. 92-28-026 (Apr. 13, 1992) (participant's interest under plan and trust may not be anticipated, assigned, mortgaged, pledged, or encumbered); Rev. Proc. 92-64, § 5.02, text Section 13(b), 1992-2 C.B. 422, 427 (required anti-alienation language of model rabbi trust). Presumably this anti-alienation condition is imposed to avoid application of the cash equivalence doctrine, under which receipt of a promissory note or other transferable promise to pay is treated in certain cases as the receipt of cash and taxed immediately. *Compare* Cowden v. Comm'r, 289 F.2d 20, 24 (5th Cir. 1961) (conditions for application of cash equivalence doctrine), *with* Williams v. Comm'r, 28 T.C. 1000 (1957), *acq.,* 1958-1 C.B. 6 (no income on receipt of note where maker was without funds and repeated attempts to sell note were unsuccessful).

[17] E.g., I.R.S. Priv. Ltr. Rul. 92-28-026 (Apr. 13, 1992) (conclusions introduced with proviso "that the creation of the Trust does not cause the Plan to be other than 'unfunded' for purposes of Title I of ERISA"); Rev. Proc. 92-65, § 3.01(d), 1992-2 C.B. 428 (to obtain favorable letter ruling on constructive receipt "the plan must state that it is the intention of the parties that the arrangements be unfunded for tax purposes and for purposes of Title I of ERISA").

(1) ERISA creates property for purposes of I.R.C. § 83 by insulating employee benefit plan assets from the employer's creditors, and (2) section 83 demands taxation in advance of distribution because mandatory pension vesting extinguishes any substantial risk of forfeiture.[18] Top hat plans are excused from ERISA's general asset protection rules, however.[19] Therefore, in the case of a top hat plan, federal law would not override the rabbi trust insolvency condition, and the exposure of top hat plan assets to general creditors sidesteps section 83. Top hat plan treatment requires both that the deferred compensation arrangement be "unfunded" and limited to a "select group of management or highly compensated employees."[20] Taking its lead from the IRS, the Labor Department interprets unfunded to mean unsecured from the employer's creditors, so the mere segregation of assets (holding in trust) does not cause a rabbi trust to be funded.[21] If the program's coverage extends beyond a select group of management or highly compensated employees, however, the Labor Department takes the position that the top hat plan exemption is unavailing.[22] In that case ERISA's protections would trigger taxation in advance of receipt.[23]

[18] See ERISA § 403(c)(1), 29 U.S.C. § 1103(c)(1) (2018) ("[T]he assets of a plan shall never inure to the benefit of any employer and shall be held for the exclusive purpose of providing benefits to participants in the plan and their beneficiaries and defraying reasonable expenses of administering the plan."); ERISA § 203(a), 29 U.S.C. § 1053(a) (2018) (mandatory pension plan vesting).

[19] ERISA § 401(a)(1), 29 U.S.C. § 1101(a)(1) (2018). See generally Peter Wiedenbeck & Norman Stein, The Executive Compensation Threat to Retirement, 26 FLA. TAX REV. ___ (2022).

[20] ERISA §§ 201(2), 401(a)(1), 29 U.S.C. §§ 1051(2), 1101(a)(1) (2018).

[21] ERISA Advisory Op. 92-13A (U.S. Dep't of Labor 1992).

[22] There are no regulations interpreting the top hat plan exemption. ERISA Advisory Op. 90-14A, n.1 (U.S. Dep't of Labor 1990) announced:

"It is the Department's position that the term 'primarily', as used in the phrase 'primarily for the purpose of providing deferred compensation for a select group of management or highly compensated employees' in sections 201(2), 301(a)(3) and 401(a)(1), refers to the purpose of the plan (i.e., the benefits provided) and not the participant composition of the plan. Therefore, a plan which extends coverage beyond 'a select group of management or highly compensated employees' would not constitute a 'top hat' plan for purposes of Parts 2, 3 and 4 of Title I of ERISA."

Under this interpretation, the coverage of any employee who is not "management" or "highly compensated" makes the program ineligible for the top hat plan exemption. Some cases hold otherwise. E.g., Demery v. Extebank Deferred Compensation Plan (B), 216 F.3d 283, 289 (2d Cir. 2000) (reading "primarily" to modify "select group," so top hat plan members may include "very small number" who are not management or highly compensated employees).

The Labor Department defines management or highly compensated employees function-ally, as those individuals who "by virtue of their position or compensation level, have the ability to affect or substantially influence, through negotiation or otherwise, the design and operation of their deferred compensation plan, taking into consideration any risks attendant thereto, and, therefore, would not need the substantive rights and protections of Title I." ERISA Advisory Op. 90-14A, supra. A number of judicial decisions treat bargaining power as an important consideration. See generally Wiedenbeck & Stein, supra Chapter 10 note 19.

[23] See supra Chapter 10 note 18 and accompanying text. Moreover, ERISA can sometimes force early taxation of deferred compensation even without a rabbi trust. A promise of specified

In practice, the coverage of nonqualified deferred compensation programs is carefully circumscribed and regularly monitored to avoid that result.

The rules governing the timing of the employee's inclusion of nonqualified deferred compensation also control the timing of the employer's deduction. Regardless of the employer's usual method of accounting, I.R.C. § 404(a)(5) suspends the employer's deduction until the employee includes the deferred compensation in gross income. This matching principle is necessary to achieve approximate tax neutrality between current and deferred compensation.[24] If the employer and the employee have access to the same investment opportunities and are subject to the same tax rate, then the matching rule ensures that the employee will have the same amount available after taxes whether he receives $X in current compensation and invests the after-tax amount for some period, or instead leaves the $X in the employers' hands under an agreement that the employer will invest the deferred compensation on behalf of the employee and pay the full amount accumulated to the employee at the end of the period. If the employer's tax rate is lower than the employee's, there will be an advantage in deferred compensation,[25] while tax considerations favor current compensation if the employee's tax rate is lower. The tax rates that took effect in 2018 – when the corporate income tax rate was reduced to 21 percent and the top rate on individual income was set at 37 percent – introduced a supercharged incentive to pay nonqualified deferred compensation.

---

future benefits may trigger ERISA's mandatory pension plan funding obligations if it extends beyond a select group of management or highly compensated employees. ERISA §§ 301(a)(3), 302(a), 29 U.S.C. §§ 1081(a)(3), 1082(a) (2018). Such advance funding, combined with insulation from the employer's creditors, would cause the transfer of property that brings I.R.C. § 83 into play. If, however, the program is in the nature of a profit-sharing plan or stock bonus plan (i.e., a defined contribution plan that is not a money purchase pension plan), then ERISA's advance funding rules and the resulting unfavorable tax consequences would not apply. ERISA § 301(a)(8), 29 U.S.C. § 1081(a)(8) (2018).

[24] Judge Halpern, concurring in Albertson's Inc. v. Commissioner, 95 T.C. 415 (1990), aff'd, 42 F.3d 537 (9th Cir. 1994), explained:

"To allow an accrual method employer to deduct interest [credited to executive deferred compensation accounts] in advance of inclusion by employees would frustrate the matching principle apparent in the statute. It can be said that the effect of that matching principle is that the employer is being taxed in substitution for not currently taxing the employee. If the employer were allowed an interest deduction, then the present discounted value of the tax burden on the employer would not be equivalent (i.e., would be less than) an immediate tax on the employee (assuming, of course, equal tax rates)." 95 T.C. at 432 (footnotes omitted).

[25] The tax-exempt employer (zero tax rate) presents a particularly acute case favoring deferral, which led to special rules governing nonqualified deferred compensation programs sponsored by state and local governments, charitable organizations, and other tax-exempt employers. See I.R.C. § 457 (2018). Deferred compensation arrangements of foreign corporations and of partnerships having foreign persons or tax-exempt organizations as partners also present considerable potential for abuse (deferral by the employee without surrogate taxation of the employer), which led Congress in 2008 to restrict deferral in such instances. I.R.C § 457A (2018).

Participants can profit handily by having their investment return taxed at the corporation's rate.[26]

Congress reexamined constructive receipt and its relation to section 83 in 2004, and it concluded that aggressive tax planners had gone too far. The result, section 409A, imposes additional limits on nonqualified deferred compensation plans. The limits are of two sorts. First, the participant's control over distribution timing is cabined: (1) the election to defer must generally be made before the start of the taxable year in which the services are performed, (2) the plan must provide that deferred amounts cannot be distributed earlier than six specified times (separation from service, disability, death, a time specified when the compensation is deferred, change of ownership or control of the corporate payer, or an unforeseeable emergency), and (3) subsequent elections to further delay payment must generally be made at least twelve months before the payment is due and in some cases (distributions tied to separation from service, change of control, or a date fixed by the plan) must call for at least five years of additional deferral.[27] Second, certain rabbi trusts that offer de facto creditor protection, including offshore trusts and trusts that restrict assets to payment of benefits if the employer's financial health deteriorates, are treated as funded. Failure to comply with these requirements triggers taxation of the deferred compensation as soon as it is not subject to a substantial risk of forfeiture, regardless of whether any assets have been set aside to finance future payment. This will often require deferred amounts to be included in gross income far in advance of actual payment.[28] Moreover, if the plan fails to comply with the new distribution timing rules, then interest is charged from the time the compensation is earned, and a 20 percent penalty tax is imposed.[29] Where they apply, the section 409A interest and penalty exaction biases the tax system against deferred compensation.[30] Thus, Congress has constructed a tax regime that distinguishes between "good" nonqualified deferred compensation, meaning arrangements that comply with section 409A and therefore get the benefit of tax neutrality (with deferred amounts taxed to the employee only upon distribution), and "bad" nonqualified deferred compensation, meaning arrangements that run afoul of section 409A and so are taxed more heavily than current compensation (with deferred amounts taxed upon substantial vesting, which might be long before distribution).

---

[26] *See* Michael Doran, *Deferred Compensation Unbound*, 167 TAX NOTES FED. 1589 (June 1, 2020).

[27] I.R.C. § 409A(a)(2)-(4) (2018).

[28] I.R.C. § 409A(a)(1)(A), (b)(1) (2018).

[29] I.R.C. § 409A(a)(1)(B) (2018).

[30] Michael Doran, *Executive Compensation Reform and the Limits of Tax Policy*, Tax Policy Center Discussion Paper No. 18 (Nov. 2004), *available at* www.taxpolicycenter.org/publica tions/executive-compensation-reform-and-limits-tax-policy; *see* Michael Doran, *The Puzzle of Non-Qualified Retirement Pay*, 70 TAX L. REV. 181, 209–11 (2017) (distribution terms of nonqualified plans driven by need to comply with § 409A to avoid adverse tax consequences).

Qualified Retirement Plans

Neutrality between current and nonqualified deferred compensation remains a central objective of tax policy, despite modest infringement by section 409A and occasional disparities between the top corporate and individual income tax rates. In contrast, deliberately favorable tax treatment is accorded compensation deferred through a qualified pension, profit-sharing, stock bonus, or annuity plan (qualified retirement plans).[31] There are three major components of the preferential income tax treatment of such qualified deferred compensation.[32] First, the employer receives a current deduction (subject to certain limits) for amounts actually contributed to the plan.[33] Second, the trust that holds the plan assets is generally exempt from taxation on its investment income.[34] Third, any amount contributed on behalf of an individual employee is not included in gross income until actually distributed by the plan; upon distribution, trust or annuity earnings are taxable to the recipient as well.[35] In some circumstances, distributions may be eligible for further tax

---

[31] Qualified deferred compensation is advance funded and the assets must be protected from the employer's creditors. I.R.C. § 401(a)(1), (a)(2) (2018); *id.* § 404(a)(2) (funding of qualified annuity plans). Hence contributions to the trust or amounts paid toward the purchase of annuities involve a transfer of property within the meaning of section 83. Nevertheless, a special exception removes qualified retirement plans from the operation of that provision. I.R.C. § 83(e)(2) (2018).

[32] In addition to favorable income tax treatment, contributions to and distributions from qualified retirement plans are generally exempt from the federal payroll taxes, including Social Security and unemployment taxes. I.R.C. § 3121(a)(5) (2018) (exclusion from taxable wages under FICA, the Federal Insurance Contributions Act, which finances Social Security and Medicare Hospital Insurance program), *id.* § 3306(b)(5) (exclusion from taxable wages under FUTA, the Federal Unemployment Tax Act). These exemptions confer a substantial benefit, as the combined employer and employee shares of the FICA tax amount to 15.3 percent of wages, §§ 3101(a), (b)(1), 3111(a), (b), while the employer's FUTA tax rate is 6 percent of the first $7,000 of annual wages, §§ 3301, 3306(b)(1). These payroll tax exemptions do *not* apply to elective or salary reduction contributions made under a 401(k) plan or a 403(b) tax-sheltered annuity, however. *Id.* §§ 3121(a)(5)(D), (v)(1), 3306(b)(5)(D), (r)(1). Note that the payroll tax exemptions have the greatest value with respect to qualified deferred compensation earned by moderately paid workers. Due to the limit on wages subject to Social Security taxes, § 3121(a)(1), and the $7,000 limit on taxable wages under FUTA, compensation in excess of the Social Security contribution and benefit base ($160,200 in 2023) is subject only to the Medicare Hospital Insurance (HI) tax. The HI tax rate is 1.45 percent of wages, imposed on both the employer and the employee (2.9 percent total), with a surtax on the employee of 0.9 percent of wages in excess of $200,000, or $250,000 in the case of a joint return, § 3101(h)(2).

[33] I.R.C. § 404(a)(1)-(3) (2018).

[34] I.R.C. § 501(a) (2018).

[35] I.R.C. §§ 83(e)(2), 402(a), 403(a)(1) (2018). Moreover, even though distributions are in large part attributable to accumulated investment income, they are exempt from the 3.8 percent tax on net investment income, I.R.C. § 1411(c)(5) (2018).

Distributions are subject to state or local income taxation (if any) only by the state in which the recipient resides, not by the state where the deferred compensation was earned. 4 U.S.C. § 114 (2018); *see* H.R. REP No. 104-389 (1995). Thus, a pension earned over a thirty-year career of work in New York, for example, would be subject to no state income tax burden if the

deferral if they are directly transferred to or promptly reinvested in another qualified plan or an individual retirement account (so-called rollovers).[36] Even absent a rollover, if securities of the employer corporation are distributed, the net appreciation in the value of the securities that accrued during the plan's ownership may not be taxable until the employee later sells the stock or other securities.[37] Observe that these rules grant the employer a deduction upon contribution even though the employee does not simultaneously report income, nor is the investment income taxed until distributed to the employee. The resulting deferred taxation of both compensation and earnings thereon is the source of the qualified plan tax preference. Because the deferral may extend over decades, its value is immense. Assuming constant tax rates, deferral is equivalent to exempting from tax the investment's yield during the period of deferral.[38] In 2020 the value of assets held in qualified trusts was approximately \$11.9 trillion[39]; assuming a (conservative) average 6 percent return and 24 percent tax rate, the tax subsidy for qualified plan savings is worth about \$171 billion *annually*. That figure omits the tax benefits accorded individual retirement accounts, which held total assets of about \$10.9 trillion as of year-end 2019, most of which was attributable to rollovers from qualified plans.[40]

> employee retires and moves to Florida or another state that does not impose a personal income tax. The federal ban on source-state taxation of pension income applies not only to qualified retirement savings programs, but also to nonqualified deferred compensation arrangements if the distributions are to be made in substantially equal installments over the life (or life expectancy) of the recipient or over a period of not less than ten years. 4 U.S.C. § 114(b)(1) (I)(i) (2018).

[36] I.R.C. §§ 402(c), (e)(6), 401(a)(31), 403(a)(4), (5) (2018).

[37] I.R.C. § 402(e)(4) (2018). Continued tax deferral is granted to net appreciation of employer securities attributable to employee after-tax contributions, presumably on the theory that the transition from indirect employee ownership (through a qualified plan) to direct ownership (post-distribution) is not a sufficient change to warrant gain recognition. In addition, however, appreciation on employer securities is also excluded if the securities are attributable to pre-tax employer contributions, but only if the securities are distributed as part of a lump-sum distribution. The deferral accorded appreciation in securities bought with employer contributions is not a product of general tax principles, but apparently persists as a residue of the favorable tax treatment formerly accorded lump-sum distributions from qualified plans.

[38] For proof of this assertion see *infra* Chapter 10 note 48.

[39] EMPLOYEE BENEFIT SECURITY ADMINISTRATION, U.S. DEPARTMENT OF LABOR, PRIVATE PENSION PLAN BULLETIN: ABSTRACT OF 2020 FORM 5500 ANNUAL REPORTS, at 2 (2022), www.dol.gov/sites/dolgov/files/EBSA/researchers/statistics/retirement-bulletins/private-pension-plan-bulletins-abstract-2020.pdf.

[40] Investment Company Institute (ICI), Report on the US Retirement Market, Second Quarter 2022, at www.ici.org/research/stats/retirement. Anqi Chen & Alicia H. Munnell, *Who Contributes to Individual Retirement Accounts?*, Center for Retirement Research Issue Brief No. 17-8, https://crr.bc.edu/who-contributes-to-individual-retirement-accounts/, at 3 & Chart 2 (Apr. 2017) (rollovers accounted for more than 85 percent of IRA asset inflows in 2014); ICI, *The Role of IRAs in U.S. Households' Saving for Retirement*, 2021, 28 ICI RESEARCH PERSPECTIVE No. 1, at 12 (Jan. 2022) (among traditional IRAs that received qualified plan assets, median percentage of IRA balance attributable to rollover or transfer from employer-sponsored retirement plan was 80 percent in 2021); Craig Copeland, *EBRI IRA Database: IRA Balances, Contributions, Rollovers, Withdrawals, and Asset Allocation, 2016 Update*, EBRI

Taxes and Retirement Saving

The operational tax rules applied to qualified deferred compensation are straightforward (as the description in the preceding paragraph suggests), but they come into play only if the deferred compensation is paid under a program that satisfies the definition of a qualified plan. The general definition of a qualified plan is extraordinarily long and complex; it imposes hundreds of conditions that must be satisfied to obtain favorable tax treatment. Some of this length and complexity is attributable to the fact that Congress reproduced most of ERISA's pension plan content controls (specifically, the rules governing pension accumulation and distribution) in the tax definition of a qualified retirement plan.[41] But the definition also contains many conditions not found in ERISA. These independent tax-law criteria (examined in Chapter 10B and 10C, below) attempt to properly target and contain the retirement savings tax subsidy.

Individual Retirement Accounts

Approximately half of the US labor force is covered under any form of employer-sponsored retirement savings program, and that number has remained essentially unchanged since the early 1970s.[42] Is tax-subsidized retirement saving out of reach for people who happen to work for companies that do not sponsor any sort of qualified plan? In enacting ERISA, Congress sought to make the opportunity for tax-favored retirement savings available to all workers by creating another tax-advantaged savings vehicle, the individual retirement account (IRA).[43] Under the

ISSUE BRIEF No. 456, at 20 (Aug. 13, 2018) ("the amount of dollars moved to IRAs through rollovers was more than 16 times the amount contributed directly to IRAs" in 2016); James J. Choi, *Contributions to Defined Contribution Pension Plans*, 7 ANN. REV. FIN. ECON. 161 (2015) ("The vast majority of IRA balances are the result of rollovers from the DC plans of former employers.").

[41] *See supra* Chapters 7–8. The prospect of losing favorable tax treatment provides a powerful incentive for sponsors to keep their plans in compliance with the pension accumulation and distribution rules, including restrictions on age and service conditions and the minimum standards governing benefit accrual, vesting, anti-alienation, and spousal protection. While private parties lack standing to enforce the tax law, the duplication of these rules in the Code and ERISA assures that violations can still be redressed via ERISA's civil enforcement regime. *See supra* Chapter 5.

ERISA's minimum funding standards, discussed in Chapter 9A, are also duplicated in the Code, but not primarily as qualification conditions. Instead of disqualification, failure to satisfy the minimum funding standards triggers excise tax penalties. I.R.C. § 4971 (2018). But see *id.* § 401(a)(33) (certain benefit increases taking effect while plan sponsor is in bankruptcy cause disqualification).

[42] BUREAU OF LABOR STATISTICS, U.S. DEPARTMENT OF LABOR, NATIONAL COMPENSATION SURVEY: EMPLOYEE BENEFITS IN THE UNITED STATES, MARCH 2022, Table 1. Retirement benefits by occupational group, private industry workers, March 2022 www.bls.gov/ebs/publications/september-2022-landing-page-employee-benefits-in-the-united-states-march-2022.htm (overall participation rate for all workers in private industry in 2022 was 52 percent). *See supra* Chapter 7A.

[43] An IRA proposal was first advanced by the Nixon Administration to promote tax equity, but also in part to head off more comprehensive pension reform legislation. *See* Richard Nixon, Message from the President Concerning Private Pension Plans (Dec. 8, 1971), *reprinted in*

current version of the IRA rules, an individual with earned income is allowed to make tax-deductible contributions in 2023 of up to $6,500 annually ($7,500 if the taxpayer is fifty years of age or older) to an IRA.[44] If the taxpayer or the taxpayer's spouse is an active participant in an employer plan at any time during the taxable year, and if the taxpayer's adjusted gross income (computed with certain modifications) exceeds a specified threshold, then the maximum allowable contribution deduction is reduced.[45] This income phase-out permits low- and moderate-income workers to make tax-deductible IRA contributions even if they participate in a qualified plan, but high-income plan participants cannot supplement their qualified retirement plan savings in this manner. In addition to the contribution deduction, the IRA itself is exempt from tax, so that contributions and investment earnings are not subject to income tax until distributed.[46] Consequently, amounts saved in an IRA receive the same sort of long-term tax deferral as employer contributions to a qualified retirement plan.

An alternative form of IRA, the "Roth IRA," became available in 1998. Contributions to a Roth IRA are not deductible, but the account is tax-exempt, and qualified distributions are entirely excluded from gross income.[47] Thus, the principal difference between the traditional and the Roth IRA lies in the income tax treatment of contributions and distributions, which are reversed. Under a traditional IRA, both contributions and investment earnings go untaxed until distribution, while under a Roth IRA, contributions are tax-paid, but investment earnings get tax forgiveness. If certain conditions are satisfied, these two regimes are financially equivalent: tax deferral until distribution (the result of deductible contributions to a traditional IRA) has the same yield as immediate taxation of the amount invested (no deduction for Roth IRA contributions) combined with exempting from tax the income produced by the investment.[48] For example, assume that a taxpayer, whose

---

PUBLIC PAPERS OF THE PRESIDENTS OF THE UNITED STATES: RICHARD NIXON, 1971, entry 384, at 1168 (1972); Michael S. Gordon, *Overview: Why Was ERISA Enacted?*, in S. SPEC. COMM. ON AGING, 98TH CONG., THE EMPLOYEE RETIREMENT INCOME SECURITY ACT OF 1974: THE FIRST DECADE, at 18; JAMES A. WOOTEN, THE EMPLOYEE RETIREMENT INCOME SECURITY ACT OF 1974, at 169–77 (2004).

[44] I.R.C. § 219(a), (b) (2018); IRS Notice 2022-55, 2022-45 I.R.B. 443, 444. The deductible contribution limits are inflation indexed. I.R.C. § 219(b)(5)(C) (West Supp. 2023).

[45] I.R.C. § 219(g) (2018). For 2023, the IRA deduction phase-out starts at a modified AGI of $73,000 for a single individual, or $116,000 for married individuals filing a joint return. IRS Notice 2022-55, 2022-45 I.R.B. 443 444.

[46] I.R.C. § 408(e)(1), (d)(1) (2018).

[47] I.R.C. §§ 408(e)(1), 408A(a), (c)(1), (d)(1) (2018).

[48] Assume t is the taxpayer's marginal income tax rate and r is the annual rate of investment return, and let n represent the period (number of years) of the investment. Then a $1 contribution to a traditional IRA will grow to $(1 + r)^n$, and the entire balance will be taxed on distribution, yielding $(1 - t)(1 + r)^n$ after taxes. For a Roth IRA, because the contribution is nondeductible, the initial after-tax investment would be only $(1 - t)$; this amount would grow by a factor of $(1 + r)^n$, and no further taxes would be due upon distribution, which again yields $(1 - t)(1 + r)^n$ after taxes. Emil M. Sunley, Jr., *Employee Benefits and Transfer Payments*, in

marginal income tax rate is 35 percent, contributes $1,000 to a traditional IRA, where it earns 6 percent (compounded annually) for twelve years, at which time the entire balance of the account is distributed. The $1,000 IRA account balance will grow to $2,012.20 in that time (= $1,000 × $(1.06)^{12}$), and the 35 percent tax on the full amount distributed (contribution plus earnings) will leave $1,307.93 (= 65 percent of $2,012.20) after tax. Alternatively, if the contribution is not deductible, the taxpayer will have only $650 to invest after tax, which, at a 6 percent annual rate of return, will grow to $1,307.93 in twelve years (= $650 × $(1.06)^{12}$), and no further tax would be due on a qualified distribution from a Roth IRA. In contrast, outside of an IRA the $1,000 would be taxed initially, as would the annual 6 percent return, so that the $650 invested would grow at an after-tax rate of only 3.9 percent (= 65 percent × 6 percent) producing at the end of twelve years a total of only $1,028.73 (= $650 × $(1.039)^{12}$).

Immediate deduction and yield exemption are equivalent only if: (1) the taxpayer's marginal tax rate remains constant over the life of the account; (2) the contribution deduction produces immediate tax savings at that marginal rate (i.e., the deduction is neither limited nor deferred, and does not push the taxpayer into a lower rate bracket); and (3) investment opportunities at the assumed rate of return are not limited. The graduated rate structure of the federal income tax can cause an individual's tax rate to change due to a change in annual income. Consequently, the traditional IRA may be the better choice for a taxpayer who expects to have a substantially lower annual income during retirement. In contrast, taxpayers who expect Congress to hike income tax rates are better served by paying tax sooner under a Roth IRA.

A number of technical differences can have an important bearing on the choice between traditional and Roth IRAs. The contribution limits for each form of account are coordinated,[49] and each has an income phase-out. Because the dollar amount of the maximum annual contribution is the same for traditional and Roth IRAs (generally, $5,000, inflation adjusted), but Roth accounts are funded with after-tax dollars, a taxpayer who can afford to make the maximum contribution to a Roth IRA despite the current tax burden can accumulate a larger amount.[50] The income

---

COMPREHENSIVE INCOME TAXATION 75, 77 n 5 (Joseph A. Pechman ed. 1977); Michael J. Graetz, *Implementing a Progressive Consumption Tax*, 92 HARV. L. REV. 1575, 1597–1623 (1979); DAVID F. BRADFORD & U.S. TREASURY TAX POLICY STAFF, BLUEPRINTS FOR BASIC TAX REFORM 107–11, 115–17 (2d ed. 1984).

[49] I.R.C. §§ 219(b), 408A(c)(2) (2018).

[50] Assuming, as in the preceding example, that the taxpayer is subject to a 35 percent marginal rate and that invested IRA funds will yield a 6 percent compound annual return for twelve years, then a $5,000 contribution to a traditional IRA will produce $6,940 after taxes (= $5,000 × $(1.06)^{12}$ × 65 percent), while a $5,000 Roth IRA contribution will produce $10,061 (= $5,000 × $(1.06)^{12}$). Of course, this is because a $5,000 pre-tax traditional IRA contribution is equivalent to an after-tax Roth IRA contribution of only $3,250 (= $5,000 × 65 percent) for a taxpayer subject to the 35 percent marginal rate; or, stated differently, a $5,000 Roth contribution is equivalent to a traditional IRA contribution of $7,692 (= $5,000/65 percent).

phase-out limits deductible contributions to a traditional IRA if the taxpayer or his spouse is an active participant in a qualified plan, but nondeductible contributions to a traditional IRA may nevertheless be made up to the general limit.[51] In contrast, the contribution phase-out on allowable contributions to a Roth IRA applies generally. The income threshold that triggers the phase-out is substantially higher for Roth than for traditional IRAs, so upper-income taxpayers covered by an employer plan can contribute to a Roth IRA even though they cannot make any deductible contributions to a traditional IRA.[52] In addition, Roth IRAs are not subject to the rule that requires distributions from traditional IRAs to commence in the calendar year following the year in which the taxpayer reaches age seventy-three (or seventy-five in the case of individuals attaining age seventy-four after 2032).[53]

The choice between a traditional and a Roth IRA is not irrevocable. A taxpayer who qualifies under both sets of rules may contribute to either or both a traditional

---

[51] I.R.C. §§ 219(g), 408(o) (2018). Nondeductible contributions to a traditional IRA offer only deferral of the income tax on investment earnings, which is clearly inferior to the tax exemption of investment earnings that is accorded qualified distributions from a Roth IRA. Nevertheless, nondeductible contributions to traditional IRAs can apparently be used as a means to avoid the income phase-out on contributions to Roth IRAs. High income individuals make "back door" Roth IRA contributions in a two-step process, by (1) making designated nondeductible contributions to a traditional IRA, which are not subject to an income-based limit, and thereafter (2) arranging a rollover from the traditional IRA into a Roth IRA. Direct contributions to a Roth IRA are subject to an income phase-out, but rollover contributions are not. *Compare* § 408A(c)(3) *with id.* (c)(5)(B) (West Supp. 2020). The conference report on the Tax Cuts and Jobs Act acknowledges the practice, H.R. Rep. No. 115-466, at 289 n.268 (2017) (Conf. Rep.), but a prompt rollover or conversion to a Roth IRA might be vulnerable under the step transaction doctrine. *See* Stephanie Cumings, *Backdoor Roth IRAs May Be OK, but Timing Issue Remains*, 160 TAX NOTES FED. 1472 (2018); Mazzei v. Commissioner, 150 T.C. 138 (2018) (applying substance-over-form principles to tax avoidance scheme employing Roth IRA); *but see* Benenson v. Commissioner, 887 F.3d 511 (1st Cir. 2018) (refusing to apply substance-over-form).

   The rollover into a Roth IRA requires inclusion in gross income of amounts not previously taxed, § 408A(d)(3), but if the taxpayer's traditional IRA is merely a temporary conduit for nondeductible contributions, the untaxed investment earnings transferred in the rollover will be small. If the taxpayer has one or more traditional IRAs containing substantial pre-tax contributions or earnings, then the back door Roth IRA contribution becomes less attractive, because rules governing the allocation of traditional IRA distributions between pre-tax and after-tax amounts would cause much of the amount rolled into the Roth IRA to be currently includible in gross income. *See* § 408(d)(2) (all traditional IRAs treated as one IRA; all distributions during a taxable year treated as one distribution); IRS Notice 87-16, Part III, 1987-1 C.B. 446, 451–53 (taxpayer cannot designate distribution as being from nondeductible contributions; distributions allocated pro-rata between taxable and nontaxable components).

[52] I.R.C. §§ 219(g)(3)(B), 408A(c)(3)(B) (2018).

[53] I.R.C. § 408A(c)(4) (West Supp. 2020). Prior to 2020 contributions to a traditional IRA were not permitted after attainment of age 70½ but no such age limit applied to Roth IRA contributions. That disparity was eliminated by repealing the age limit for traditional IRAs. I.R.C. § 219(d)(1) (2018) (repealed by Pub. L. No. 116-94, Div. O, § 107(a), 133 Stat. 2534, 3148 (2019)).

Taxes and Retirement Saving

and a Roth IRA in a given tax year, subject to a combined annual contribution limit.[54] Moreover, the owner of a traditional IRA can generally make a qualified rollover contribution to a Roth IRA regardless of the annual contribution limit simply by paying tax on the amount distributed from the traditional IRA and contributing the distribution (or any desired portion thereof) to a Roth IRA within sixty days.[55] Indeed, a traditional IRA may simply be converted to a Roth IRA by including in gross income amounts not previously taxed.[56]

The general equivalence between deferred inclusion (à la qualified plans and traditional IRAs) and yield exemption (à la Roth IRAs) is illustrated by Congress' decision to permit Roth-style accounts to be included under certain qualified plans. Some types of defined contribution plans are funded in whole or in part by employees, who make elective salary-reduction contributions to their individual accounts. Under a 401(k) plan, for example, each eligible employee may choose whether to receive a portion of his compensation in cash or direct that it be contributed to his retirement savings account, and if the plan satisfies the definition of a qualified cash-or-deferred arrangement (CODA), the employee's elective deferral is generally treated as an excludible (i.e., pre-tax) employer contribution.[57] Similar elective deferrals are authorized under 403(b) plans (sometimes called tax-sheltered annuities), a special qualified retirement savings program that can be provided for employees of tax-exempt charitable organizations and public schools.[58] Elective deferrals under 401(k) and 403(b) plans, together with any matching or nonelective employer contributions, historically received the same tax deferral treatment accorded other qualified retirement plans: contributions are excluded from the employee's gross income (even though currently deductible by a taxable employer), fund earnings accumulate tax-free, and contributions and earnings are taxed only when actually distributed to the employee.[59] Since 2006, however, 401(k) and 403(b) plans have been allowed to offer employees the option to direct their

---

[54] I.R.C. § 408A(c)(2) (2018).

[55] I.R.C. § 408A(c)(5) (West Supp. 2020) (qualified rollover contribution exempt from annual contribution limit), *id.* § 408A(d)(3)(A), (B) (2018) (rollover to Roth IRA conditioned on taxation of traditional IRA distribution), *id.* § 408A(e) (definition of qualified rollover contribution), *id.* § 408(d)(3) (sixty-day time limit). The utilization (manipulation?) of these rules to avoid the income phase-out on allowable Roth IRA contributions (so-called back door Roth IRA contributions), is explained *supra* Chapter 10 note 51.

[56] I.R.C. § 408A(d)(3)(C) (2018) (account conversion treated as rollover). Although Roth IRAs are projected to lose revenue in the long run relative to traditional IRAs, rollovers and conversions from traditional IRAs accelerate taxable distributions and therefore increase tax revenues during the limited ten-year forecasting period Congress uses for budget purposes.

[57] I.R.C. §§ 401(k), 402(e)(3) (2018).

[58] I.R.C. §§ 403(b)(1), 402(e)(3) (2018). TIAA (Teachers Insurance and Annuity Association), which administers retirement plans for about 15,000 colleges, universities, schools, research centers, and other nonprofit institutions, is a leading 403(b) plan provider.

[59] *See supra* Chapter 10 notes 31–37 and accompanying text.

elective deferrals into a separate "designated Roth account."[60] Contributions to such an account are includible in the employee's income, but qualified distributions are entirely tax-free (just as under a Roth IRA) so that instead of tax deferral, the designated Roth account exempts the yield on elective (after-tax) contributions.[61] Authorization of elective Roth treatment was broadened to include matching contributions and nonelective contributions in 2022.[62] Because designated Roth accounts are tax prepaid, participants who anticipate a tax increase can hedge that portion of their retirement savings.[63]

Congress has replicated the Roth IRA mechanism (nondeductible contributions and tax-exempt earnings) in other tax-favored savings vehicles. These include savings for education via a Coverdell education savings account or a qualified tuition program (often known as a "529 plan"),[64] and the "ABLE account," which offers

---

[60] I.R.C. § 402A (2018). Designated Roth accounts are also permitted for elective deferrals under eligible deferred compensation plans maintained by state or local governments. *Id.* §§ 402A(e) (1)(C), 457(b). Such eligible deferred compensation plans for state or local public employees are exempt from ERISA as governmental plans, and they are not qualified pension, profit-sharing, or annuity plans (i.e., they do not satisfy the conditions imposed by section 401 or sections 403(a) and 404(a)(2)). Yet if the conditions imposed by section 457(b) are satisfied, the Code grants such plans the same favorable tax treatment accorded qualified plan savings.

[61] I.R.C. §§ 402A(a)(1), (d), 408A(d) (2018); Treas. Reg. § 1.402A-1 (as amended in 2016). To be a qualified distribution, the designated Roth account must, in general, have been held for a minimum of five taxable years. I.R.C. § 402A(d)(2)(B) (2018).

[62] I.R.C. § 402A(c)(1) (West Supp. 2023).

[63] Rollovers *from* a designated Roth account can be made only to another designated Roth account of the same individual, or to a Roth IRA. I.R.C. § 402A(c)(3) (2018). (The rollover of after-tax contributions to another designated Roth account must be accomplished via a direct trustee-to-trustee transfer, however, not by a distribution to the participant and transfer into another plan within sixty days. *Id.* §§ 402A(c)(3)(A) ("otherwise allowable"), 402(c)(2).) As part of a qualified plan, designated Roth accounts were originally subject to the required minimum distribution (RMD) rules, which generally force distributions to commence during the employee's life. I.R.C. § 401(a)(9) (West Supp. 2023); *see infra* Chapter 10C. In contrast, Roth IRAs are exempt from that aspect of the RMD rules. *Id.* § 408A(c)(4) (West Supp. 2020). Because distributions from a designated Roth account can be rolled over into a Roth IRA, apparently such a rollover could be utilized to sidestep application of RMD obligations to retirement savings accumulated in a designated Roth account. For taxable years beginning after 2023 Congress eliminated the requirement that distributions from a designated Roth account commence during the employee's life. I.R.C. § 402A(d)(5) (West Supp. 2023).

Rollovers *into* a designated Roth account can come from the employee's designated Roth account in another plan, as indicated in the prior paragraph. But in addition, taxable in-plan rollovers are permitted, by means of which pre-tax employer contributions and earnings credited to a participant under the plan can be moved into the participant's designated Roth account. I.R.C. § 402A(c)(4). Such transfers, often referred to as in-plan Roth conversions, require the participant to include the amount transferred in gross income, just as in the case of a conversion of a traditional IRA into a Roth IRA. Such transfers are not subject to the additional tax on early distributions, and a plan may allow them even if the amount transferred would not otherwise be distributable. § 402A(c)(4)(A)(ii), (c)(4)(E)(i).

[64] I.R.C. § 530(a), (d)(2)(A) (2018) (Coverdell educational savings account earnings and distributions), *id.* § 529(a), (c)(1), (c)(3)(B)(ii) (529 plan earnings and distributions). Distributions not

Taxes and Retirement Saving

a means of financing certain disability-related expenses of individuals who became blind or severely disabled before attaining age twenty-six.[65]

B TARGETING THE TAX SUBSIDY

The favorable tax treatment of qualified plans provides an inducement to saving. That favorable tax treatment is granted only if the plan satisfies certain conditions designed to structure the incentive so that it induces retirement savings that would not otherwise occur. These tax controls, in other words, are an effort to properly target the tax subsidy and confine its magnitude. The tax controls fall into four broad categories: nondiscrimination rules, caps on qualified plan savings, advance funding limits, and distribution timing constraints. This section explores nondiscrimination in depth. Chapter 10C offers an overview of the remaining tax controls, which operate in combination to limit the amount of the tax subsidy.

Before doing so, however, it is useful to examine overall objectives with some care. Why do we want to encourage savings? Savings for what purpose(s)? Savings by whom? Answers to these questions will illuminate the function of the tax controls, and disagreement on these matters goes far toward explaining the contradictions and instability of the pension tax rules.

The overall personal saving rate in the United States, as a percentage of disposable income, underwent a fairly steady decline from about 10 percent in the early 1980s to a low of about 2.1 percent in 2005, and thereafter recovered somewhat, standing at about 4.0 percent in January 2023.[66] Because savings are the source of investment

---

devoted to eligible educational expenses are taxed to the recipient to the extent of earnings, and a penalty is imposed by increasing the rate of tax on the includible amount by 10 percent unless an exception applies. Penalty exceptions are provided for distributions made on account of the death, disability, or receipt of a scholarship by the beneficiary. *Id.* §§ 530(d)(4), 529(c)(6). The similarity between Roth-style savings mechanisms is highlighted by a new rule allowing the beneficiary of a section 529 plan account that has been open for more than fifteen years to direct, within specified limits, that rollover distributions be made from her 529 plan account into her Roth IRA. I.R.C. § 529(c)(3)(E) (West Supp. 2023) (applicable to distributions made after 2023).

[65] I.R.C. § 529A(b)(1), (e)(1)-(3) (2018). The "Achieving a Better Life Experience [ABLE] Act of 2014" sought to: "(1) encourage and assist individuals and families in saving private funds for the purpose of supporting individuals with disabilities to maintain their health, independence, and quality of life; and (2) provide secure funding for disability-related expenses of beneficiaries with disabilities that will supplement, but not supplant, benefits provided through private insurance, [Supplemental Security Income, and Medicaid]." Pub. L. No. 113-295, Div. B, § 101. To achieve the latter goal, a nontax provision of the legislation requires amounts in ABLE accounts to be disregarded in determining eligibility for means-tested federal programs, except that for purposes of the supplemental security income program (1) distributions for housing expenses, and (2) amounts in an ABLE account exceeding $100,000, are taken into account. *Id.* § 103.

[66] Federal Reserve Bank of St. Louis, Federal Reserve Economic Data (FRED), Personal Savings Rate, at https://fred.stlouisfed.org/series/PSAVERT (graph of monthly personal saving as a percentage of disposable personal income, 1959–present, as reported by Bureau of Economic Analysis, U.S. Department of Commerce, National Income and Product Accounts Table 2.1: Personal Income and Its Disposition).

Tax Controls: Qualified Retirement Savings

capital which fuels higher productivity and real wages, a low saving rate signals danger for long-term economic growth. For that reason, many analysts and politicians advocate measures to encourage savings generally, particularly measures that would move the federal tax system from a realized income tax toward a consumption tax. This macroeconomic concern has seen expression in recent years in a relaxation of various limits on tax-subsidized retirement savings, in the emergence of tax-favored educational savings (such as 529 plans), and in calls for all-purpose Roth-IRA-like tax-advantaged savings accounts.[67]

Instead of encouraging savings generally, the traditional and still dominant justification for the special tax treatment accorded qualified plans is to induce greater *retirement* savings. Social Security old-age benefits provide a baseline level of retirement income, but for a large majority of retirees, Social Security alone is inadequate to maintain their pre-retirement standard of living. Most workers need to supplement Social Security with pensions or private savings to avoid painful cutbacks in their personal budgets and cramped lifestyles in retirement. Without another source of support, even low-wage workers, who receive Social Security benefits that constitute a larger share of their pre-retirement wages than other workers, will experience a significant drop in their standard of living upon retirement. Most experts estimate that retirees typically need to replace about 70 to 80 percent of their pre-retirement earnings to maintain their standard of living.[68]

---

[67] Tax recommendations repeatedly put forward by President George W. Bush would have expanded Roth-style tax-free savings opportunities in individual accounts of two types. A proposed Retirement Savings Account (RSA) would allow contributions of up to $5,000 per year regardless of income or coverage under a qualified retirement plan. As with a Roth IRA, RSA contributions would be nondeductible (after-tax), but earnings would accumulate tax-free, and qualified distributions would be excluded from gross income. As proposed, the RSA would have substituted for all current forms of IRAs, other than rollover IRAs created solely to receive qualified plan distributions. In addition, it was proposed that individuals be allowed to contribute up to $2,000 annually to a Lifetime Savings Account (LSA), another Roth-style personal account that could be used to save for any purpose. Hence the LSA would not be limited to saving for retirement, health care, or education (for which tax-favored accounts are currently available), but could also be used to save for the purchase of a car or a home or for precautionary purposes. LSA contributions would be allowed whether or not the contributor has earned income and regardless of his total income. The annual contribution limit would apply to all accounts held in a particular individual's name, rather than to the contributor, so that an affluent middle-aged couple could put $4,000 (total) into their own LSAs and also contribute $2,000 to accounts for each of their children (or grandchildren, etc.). U.S. DEPARTMENT OF THE TREASURY, GENERAL EXPLANATIONS OF THE ADMINISTRATION'S FISCAL YEAR 2009 REVENUE PROPOSALS 9–10 (2008), https://home.treasury.gov/system/files/131/General-Explanations-FY2009.pdf.

[68] The measure of pre-retirement earnings used to compute replacement rates (the denominator of the fraction) is not standardized. Depending on the purpose of the computation, some measure of final pre-retirement earnings or of career average earnings may be used, and such differences can yield dramatic variations in numerical results. *See* Andrew G. Biggs & Glenn R. Stringstead, *Alternate Measures of Replacement Rates for Social Security Benefits and Retirement Income*, 68 SOC. SEC. BULL. 1 (2008); Johannes Binswanger & Daniel Schunk, *What Is an Adequate Standard of Living during Retirement?* 11 J. PENS. ECON. 203 (2018)

Taxes and Retirement Saving

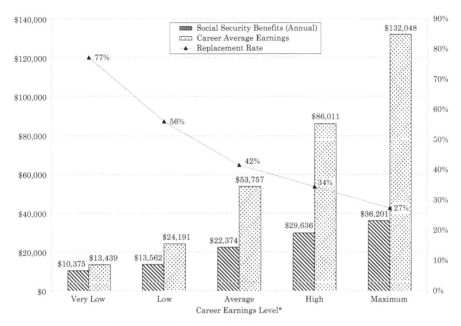

FIGURE 10.1 Social Security benefits and replacement rates: Retirement at age 66 in 2020
* Career earnings levels represent 25 percent, 45 percent, 100 percent, and 160 percent of average wage; maximum reflects annual earnings equal to the taxable wage base.
Source: MICHAEL CLINGMAN ET AL., SOCIAL SECURITY ADMINISTRATION, OFFICE OF THE CHIEF ACTUARY, REPLACEMENT RATES FOR HYPOTHETICAL RETIRED WORKERS, Actuarial Note No. 2020.9, Table C (April 2020).

As Figure 10.1 illustrates, Social Security alone cannot fill the bill. The "Low" earnings level depicted in the figure is roughly comparable to a career of full-time minimum wage work; the "Very Low" earnings level corresponds to a low-paid worker with substantial gaps in labor force participation. These workers get relatively more from Social Security because the program contains a redistributive component (the benefit schedule is progressive or bottom-weighted), but the low earner still falls far short of the 80 percent benchmark. Moreover, the replacement rates shown are computed as a proportion of career average compensation, which arguably overstates Social Security's importance to workers in the upper half of the earnings distribution. Because real wages of skilled workers tend to increase with age and experience, Social Security replacement rates would be lower if computed with reference to immediate pre-retirement earnings (such as average compensation over the final five years of work). Presumably, retirees' sense of whether they have

(survey of prospective preferred levels of old-age spending finds that adequate levels of retirement spending exceed 80 percent of working life spending for a majority of respondents and that minimum acceptable replacement rates depend strongly on income).

experienced a drop in living standards upon retirement is formed with reference to their immediate pre-retirement earnings.

Retirees at virtually every income level need to supplement Social Security to preserve their accustomed lifestyles, but why do they need *public* assistance (the tax subsidy) to do so? Rather than relying on individuals to supplement Social Security with private savings (or suffer the consequences of their failure to do so), the tax-law encourages accumulation through qualified plans which, by virtue of their preferential tax treatment, represent public–private hybrid saving. This elaborate hybrid (or semi-private) retirement savings system is best understood as an effort to counteract a bias in favor of current consumption.

As an incentive, the qualified plan tax subsidy is justified only insofar as it induces retirement savings that would not otherwise occur. To the extent that public monies benefit people who would save adequately on their own, the subsidy amounts to wasted revenue. Low- and moderate-income workers are less able to save on their own (lower disposable income). In addition, they are less likely to prioritize retirement saving because access to those savings is more restricted, often rendering those funds unavailable for more urgent objectives, like saving for education, home ownership, or to build a reserve against illness or unemployment (so-called precautionary saving). Rank-and-file workers are not only less able to save and less focused on retirement, they are less likely to be induced to save by the prospect of tax relief. Recall that the qualified plan subsidy is cast in the form of tax deferral (or equivalently, tax exemption of the investment return). At present, however, the lowest-income 40 percent of US households pay virtually zero federal income tax.[69] In contrast, high-income individuals have the ability to save on their own, and because they are subject to high marginal tax rates, they would receive the greatest benefit from a tax allowance that grants deferral (or exemption of investment returns) based on individual savings decisions. This is the challenge to which the tax controls, and particularly the nondiscrimination rules, are addressed: granting tax deferral for retirement savings on an *individual* basis would do very little to increase saving by low- and middle-income workers, while it would give a windfall to the highly paid, who would simply shift their other savings into the tax-advantaged form. Giving all taxpayers, regardless of income, access to IRAs, for example, is likely to induce: (1) no additional savings by low-income taxpayers; (2) portfolio rearrangement by high-income savers to take advantage of the tax reduction (such behavior is known as tax arbitrage); and (3) some new savings by moderate-income individuals

---

[69] When the US population is ranked by an expanded definition of cash income, the lowest and second-lowest quintiles have average effective federal individual income tax rates of -5.6 percent and -1.3 percent, respectively. Urban-Brookings Tax Policy Center, Table T15–0037, Effective Federal Tax Rates – All Tax Units, By Expanded Cash Income Percentile, 2019, www.taxpolicycenter.org/model-estimates/baseline-share-federal-taxes-febru ary-2020/t20-0037-average-effective-federal-tax. The negative effective tax rates are due to the earned income tax credit and the refundable portion of the child tax credit.

Taxes and Retirement Saving

for whom the tax benefit increases their return enough to make saving more attractive than otherwise-preferred consumption alternatives.

Nondiscrimination and Redistribution

These considerations indicate that deferred taxation of amounts devoted to retirement saving, if extended on the basis of individual savings decisions, would generate a wasteful – even perverse – distribution of public assistance. The qualified plan nondiscrimination rules, first enacted in 1942, seek to avoid that result by conditioning favorable tax treatment of deferred compensation on the dual requirements that (1) the program's coverage does not unduly favor highly compensated employees, and (2) the "contributions or benefits provided under the plan [expressed as a proportion of compensation] do not discriminate in favor of highly compensated employees."[70] A leading Treasury tax policy official told Congress that the qualified plan nondiscrimination rules mean that the "reduction in taxes is designed to induce high-income taxpayers to save for retirement in such a manner that there will also be benefits for rank-and-file employees who are not only less able to save, but also less likely to be induced to do so by reason of tax relief."[71] Professors Fischel and Langbein explained:

> Despite the strongly voluntary or consensual basis of the private pension system, various features of pension regulation are designed to interfere with individual autonomy in pension saving. For example, the anti-discrimination norm – the bedrock principle of pension taxation – conditions access to tax-advantaged pension saving for a firm's better paid workers upon extensive participation of the firm's lower paid workers. The rationale is to create incentives for management to induce lower paid workers to engage in higher levels of pension saving than they would if allowed unfettered choice. Whether this strategy is very successful is open to question, but it exemplifies the idea that some employees should be protected against their inclination to save too little for retirement.[72]

To understand the operation and assess the effectiveness of the nondiscrimination rules, it is helpful to illustrate their application to a simple fact pattern. Assume that a hypothetical employer's workforce is composed of three employees, X, Y, and Z, and that each is forty-five years old. X, an executive, is a highly compensated employee (HCE) who earns a salary of $200,000 and is subject to the 28 percent marginal income tax rate; Y and Z are nonhighly compensated employees (NHCEs), and each earns $80,000 and is taxed at the 15 percent rate. Suppose that instead of a

---

[70] I.R.C. §§ 401(a)(3)-(5), 410(b) (quotation from § 401(a)(4)).

[71] *National Pension Policies: Private Pension Plans: Hearings before the Subcomm. on Retirement Income and Employment of the House Select Comm. on Aging*, 95th Cong. 228, 230 (1978) (statement of Daniel I. Halperin, Tax Legislative Counsel, U.S. Department of the Treasury).

[72] Daniel Fischel & John H. Langbein, *ERISA's Fundamental Contradiction: The Exclusive Benefit Rule*, 55 U. Chi. L. Rev. 1105, 1122–23 (1988) (footnotes omitted).

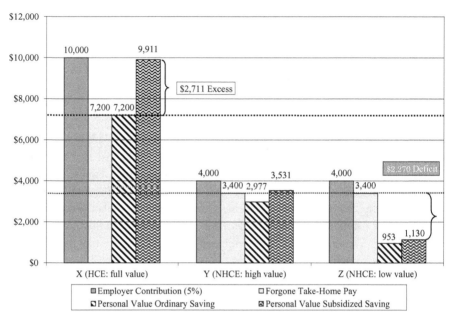

FIGURE 10.2 Nondiscrimination and redistribution*
* Assumptions: (1) all amounts saved, whether individually or in an employer-sponsored retirement fund, earn 6.0 percent compound annual return for twenty years; (2) each employee's tax rate remains constant for the twenty-year duration of the retirement account; (3) X would save more than 5 percent of her compensation in investments that do not receive preferential income tax treatment (hence X's personal discount rate is her after-tax rate of return, 72 percent of 6.0 percent); (4) Y values deferred compensation by applying a personal (internal) discount rate that is 5.8 percent; (5) Z values deferred compensation by applying a personal (internal) discount rate of 12.0 percent.

raise, the employer allows each employee to independently elect whether the employer will contribute an amount equal to 5 percent of the employee's salary to a retirement account (to be invested and the accumulated balance distributed to the employee at age sixty-five), or pay the 5 percent to the employee currently as additional cash compensation. Finally, assume that X, the executive, already saves a substantial portion of her after-tax income for retirement, but Y and Z do not: Y would save if he could get a somewhat higher return on his money than the market now offers, while Z confronts urgent immediate consumption needs (such as family medical and educational expenses) and so strongly dis-prefers saving. Figure 10.2 illustrates how these workers are likely to exercise their choice between retirement saving and additional salary.

For each worker, the first column represents the employer's current outlay (5 percent of salary), whether contributed to a retirement account or paid in cash. The second column is the after-tax value of the employer's payment, and so reflects the amount of consumption the worker would forgo (less take-home pay) in

Taxes and Retirement Saving

selecting a retirement account contribution. The third column, labeled "Personal Value Ordinary Saving," shows each employee's individual assessment (personal valuation) of the saving alternative under the normal income tax rules. By assumption, X would save at least this amount of her after-tax income on her own, and so for X, the present value of the savings option is equal to her forgone take-home pay (in other words, X's personal discount rate is just equal to her after-tax rate of return, 72 percent of 6.0 percent, or 4.32 percent). By comparison, Y slightly prefers current consumption, and Z strongly favors immediate needs, as reflected in their lower personal valuations of saving compared to additional take-home pay (assumed personal discount rates of 5.8 percent and 12.0 percent, respectively). The final column, labeled "Personal Value Subsidized Saving," displays the value of tax-deferred saving (as under traditional IRA treatment) for each employee, which is higher than for ordinary saving because of the additional accumulation that tax deferral facilitates.[73]

The results shown in Figure 10.2 confirm the qualitative predictions made earlier. If the tax-advantaged savings opportunity is made available on an individual basis, then the highly compensated employee, who would have saved anyway, obtains a large benefit by deferring a substantial tax obligation (high marginal rate) for an extended period. X can get $2,711 more after taxes just by rearranging her investments to make use of the tax-deferred savings vehicle. Rather than increasing savings, that arbitrage opportunity might actually *reduce* savings by X and other high-income individuals who have the wherewithal to save because, thanks to the tax concession, they need to put less aside to meet future goals. Z, the middle-income worker with pressing obligations, will not be persuaded to save by tax deferral alone because at his tax rate the incremental return to saving is just too small to make a difference. Y, however, would be moved to save by the tax allowance because it increases his return enough to counteract his impatience and make it worthwhile to postpone consumption.

Figure 10.2 also demonstrates the logic of the nondiscrimination rules. Instead of granting tax deferral on an individual basis, consider a system that conditions the benefit for the highly compensated employee on proportional saving by the rank-and-file workers. Z's personal circumstances are such that he will not consent to reducing his current consumption by $3,400 in favor of savings that are worth only $1,130 to him. But observe that the tax advantage to X is large enough that it would

---

[73] The amount shown is each employee's individual assessment of the present after-tax value of tax-preferred saving. It is computed by taking the future value of the account (using a compound 6 percent tax-free rate of return), reducing that amount by the tax due on distribution, and discounting that after-tax accumulation by the employee's personal discount rate. For X that discount rate is simply her after-tax rate of return on savings, 4.32 percent (= 6.0 percent × 72 percent); the personal discount rate of Y and Z (assumed to be 5.8 percent and 12.0 percent, respectively) exceeds each taxpayer's 5.1 percent (= 6.0 percent × 85 percent) after-tax rate of return.

be worthwhile for X to bribe Z to participate in order to satisfy the nondiscrimination condition. Moreover, because qualified retirement plans are employer-mediated programs, X does not have to take the step of personally making a side payment to induce Z's acquiescence. Instead, the employer can accomplish the transfer by reducing X's current compensation by more than the $10,000 retirement contribution made on behalf of X, while at the same time contributing $4,000 for Z without reducing Z's current compensation by the full amount. On the facts illustrated, Z will accept the $4,000 retirement contribution if his salary is reduced by no more than $1,329 (equivalent to $1,130 of foregone consumption at Z's 15 percent rate), which means that the employer would have to increase Z's total compensation by $2,671 ($2,270 after tax) to satisfy the nondiscrimination requirement. The employer recoups this added cost from X, who should be willing to trade any amount less than $13,765 of her (pre-tax) salary for the $10,000 retirement contribution. The $3,765 compensation savings that can be extracted from X (equivalent to $2,711 after tax at X's 28 percent rate) is of course more than sufficient to fund the $2,671 compensation increase necessary to bribe Z to participate. The exact disposition of this extra tax subsidy, together with a small amount of compensation that could be extracted from Y (who would trade $4,154 in salary for the $4,000 qualified plan contribution), is indeterminate. Relative bargaining power will determine its division between the employer and the employees (X, in particular), and some amount will have to be captured by the employer to compensate it for the additional costs it will incur in administering the plan.

By conditioning favorable tax treatment on broad participation, the nondiscrimination rules can, in the right circumstances, effect a hidden transfer (or covert redistribution) of the tax subsidy from high-income, high-preference employees to lower-paid workers who are reluctant savers. Nondiscrimination thus tends to redirect public monies from windfall tax savings by highly paid workers into retirement savings that would not otherwise occur, and so operates to better target the tax subsidy.

Unfortunately, the complex system that has evolved is riddled with defects and limitations. For although the nondiscrimination rules are the central mechanism for channeling public assistance into additional retirement savings, their efficacy is highly sensitive to employee preferences, workforce composition, income tax rates, and the availability of other tax-sheltered savings opportunities. Many of these limitations are apparent upon further consideration of the example in Figure 10.2.

First consider employee preferences: if Y were in financial straits nearly as tight as Z (high personal discount rate due to current consumption needs), then the compensation savings that could be extracted from X ($3,765 maximum) would be insufficient to fund the compensation increases necessary to persuade both Y and Z to participate. Therefore, the nondiscrimination condition could not be satisfied without increasing employer costs. Assuming that the employer operates in a competitive industry where that is not feasible, it will not sponsor a plan, and the rank-and-file workers will not have retirement savings.

Workforce composition – meaning the number, pay levels, and ages of employees – is another crucial set of factors. Hiring a third person at a salary of $80,000 would sink the plan if that new worker's propensity to save were closer to Z's than Y's. On the other hand, the addition of a second HCE-saver like X would generate a great deal of additional tax savings that would not have to be redistributed to satisfy the nondiscrimination rules if Y and Z remain the only NHCEs; and in that case, the tax subsidy would entail a lot of wasted revenue (shared, in some fashion, between the HCEs and the company). Similarly, the original three-person workforce would be awash in wasted subsidy if X were instead paid $240,000 and taxed in the 33 percent bracket.[74] Tax savings available for redistribution depend not only on the HCE-saver's contribution and tax rate, but also on the duration of saving. The facts on which Figure 10.2 is based assume that the amount contributed for each employee would remain in the account for twenty years until distribution. If, instead, X is only eight years away from retirement, the tax advantage in qualified plan savings would not be sufficient to cover the additional compensation cost required to secure Z's participation.

Because the amount of subsidy is based on the value of tax deferral, legislative income tax rate changes can dramatically affect the attractiveness of qualified plan saving. This underappreciated link can sometimes cause tax and pension policies to work at cross purposes. Consider the Tax Reform Act of 1986, which broadened the base of the individual income tax and in return drastically lowered income tax rates, with the top bracket rate falling from 50 to 28 percent. That statute made the coverage and amount nondiscrimination rules more demanding and tightened the vesting rules; these changes generally increase the cost of maintaining a qualified plan by forcing more benefits to be provided to low-paid, low-preference employees. Yet at the same time that Congress insisted on greater redistribution, it drastically reduced the tax rate and thus the value of deferral for high-income savers, thereby cutting the subsidy available to meet those increased costs! The unforeseen but predictable result was a marked decline in the attractiveness of instituting or expanding qualified retirement savings programs. For any particular employer, the exact impact of tax rate reductions depends, of course, on the factors described above, namely individual savings preferences and workforce composition (number, pay levels, and ages of employees). As seen above, a workforce that includes a lot of highly paid savers can generate much more tax subsidy than needed to satisfy the nondiscrimination rules; any subsidy in excess of the amount that must be shifted to low-paid, reluctant savers either benefits high-paid workers who would save on their own or is captured by the employer (through reduced compensation). From the

---

[74] Assuming the same facts on which Figure 10.2 is based, except for X's higher salary and tax rate, then the $12,000 contribution (5 percent of $240,000) would be worth $17,497 in salary to X, $5,497 more than the employer contribution. Of that excess, only $2,671 is needed to buy Z's cooperation.

perspective of nondiscrimination policy, this excess subsidy is wasted revenue, and in this instance, lowering tax rates reduces waste and improves the effectiveness of redistribution. Another employer whose workforce includes few highly paid savers and is composed predominately of low-paid workers with urgent consumption needs (non-savers), may find that a tax rate reduction makes qualified plan sponsorship uneconomic, because the reduced subsidy means that the potential compensation cost savings that might be extracted from high-paid workers is now insufficient to induce enough participation from low-paid workers to satisfy the nondiscrimination rules. In this case, the post-tax-cut subsidy may simply be too small to pay the compensation increases needed to bribe enough low-paid workers into the plan.[75]

The lesson is that enriching the subsidy by increasing tax rates, while it will make plan sponsorship more attractive across-the-board and induce some employers to institute a plan who previously could not afford to offer one, will not necessarily trigger additional redistribution under preexisting plans. Instead of being shifted to low-income non-savers, the additional subsidy associated with established programs – programs that met nondiscrimination standards under the stingier prior regime – might simply be pocketed by the employer or its highly paid workers. Conversely, while curtailing the subsidy by reducing tax rates might reduce wasted revenue and increase the efficiency of redistribution in some cases, under a system of voluntary sponsorship that step might cause some employers to discontinue existing programs and deter other employers from instituting new plans. Despite their maddening complexity, the nondiscrimination rules accomplish only haphazard and imperfect redistribution. Nor do they apply universally: governmental plans are now entirely exempt from the anti-discrimination imperative, and the coverage nondiscrimination standard is relaxed for church plans.[76]

---

[75] See generally Daniel I. Halperin, *Special Tax Treatment for Employer-Based Retirement Programs: Is It "Still" Viable as a Means of Increasing Retirement Income?*, 49 TAX L. REV. 1 (1993). See Peter J. Brady, *Pension Nondiscrimination Rules and the Incentive to Cross Subsidize Employees*, 6 J. PEN. ECON. & FIN. 127 (2007), which uses a simulation analysis to model the impact of nondiscrimination rules on 401(k) plans, and finds that only firms with a relatively low ratio of NHCEs to HCEs (less than about 4 to 6) would have an economic incentive to sponsor a plan.

[76] I.R.C. §§ 401(a)(5)(G), 414(d), (e), 410(c) (2018). The nondiscrimination exemption covers plans of federal, state, and local governments and their agencies and instrumentalities. It also covers plans maintained by an Indian tribal government or an agency or instrumentality thereof for employees performing noncommercial essential governmental functions. The complete exemption of state and local governmental plans from nondiscrimination obligations was enacted in 1997 (previously, governmental plans were subject to the relaxed pre-ERISA requirements applied to church plans), and the legislation also retroactively excused prior discrimination by such plans. Taxpayer Relief Act of 1997, Pub. L. No. 105-34, § 1505(a)(1), (d)(2), 111 Stat. 788, 1063–64. The only explanation Congress offered was an unelaborated nod to "the unique circumstances of governmental plans and the complexity of compliance." STAFF OF THE JOINT COMM. ON TAXATION, 105TH CONG., GENERAL EXPLANATION OF TAX LEGISLATION ENACTED IN 1997, at 436 (Comm. Print 1997).

Discrimination in Coverage

The central coverage nondiscrimination rule, known as the ratio percentage test, requires that the percentage of nonhighly compensated employees (NHCEs) who "benefit" under a qualified plan must be at least 70 percent of the percentage of highly compensated employees (HCEs) benefiting under the plan.[77] (The regulations rephrase this test by requiring that the plan's "ratio percentage," defined as the percentage of NHCEs who benefit divided by the percentage of HCEs who benefit, must equal or exceed 70 percent, rounded to the nearest hundredth of a percentage point.[78])

Generally speaking, an employee is treated as "benefiting" under the plan for a given year if she receives an allocation of employer contributions or forfeitures to her account under a defined contribution plan for the year, or she receives an increase in the dollar amount of her accrued benefit under a defined benefit plan.[79] Thus, an employee is deemed to "benefit," and so is counted in the numerator of either the HCE or NHCE fraction, if she earns an increase in retirement savings based upon current service. Such workers are sometimes referred to as "active participants." If a firm has ten HCEs and fifty NHCEs, for example, and eight of the HCEs receive an employer contribution under a profit-sharing plan for the year, then the ratio percentage test is satisfied if at least twenty-eight NHCEs also get a contribution (twenty-eight of fifty NHCEs, or 56 percent, divided by eight of ten HCEs, or 80 percent, gives a plan ratio percentage of 70.00 percent).

A plan that fails the ratio percentage test standing alone still has two alternatives for establishing coverage nondiscrimination.[80] First, under a technique known as plan aggregation, the employer may designate two or more pension, profit-sharing, stock bonus, or annuity plans that use the same plan year as being part of a larger

---

Nondiscrimination is not the only tax qualification condition that does not apply, or that is applied with reduced force, to governmental and church plans. Recall that governmental and church are excluded from ERISA's labor-law requirements. ERISA § 4(b), 29 U.S.C. § 1003(b) (2018); *see supra* Chapter 2D. Correspondingly, such plans are generally exempt from the tax qualification rules that parallel ERISA Title I requirements, including the vesting, benefit accrual, anti-alienation, and spousal protection rules. I.R.C. §§ 401(a) (final sentence), 410(c), 411(e), 414(d), (e) (2018).

[77] I.R.C. §§ 401(a)(3), 410(b)(1)(B) (2018).

[78] Treas. Reg. §§ 1.410(b)-2(b)(2), 1.410(b)-9 (as amended in 1994).

[79] Treas. Reg. § 1.410(b)-3(a)(1) (as amended in 2004), § 1.401(a)(4)-2(c)(2)(ii) (as amended in 2007).

[80] A special rule provides that a plan of an employer that has no NHCEs at any time during the plan year is treated as satisfying the coverage nondiscrimination test even though it benefits only one or more HCEs. I.R.C. § 410(b)(6)(F) (2018); Treas. Reg. 1.410(b)-2(b)(5) (as amended in 1994). The tax subsidy is obviously wasted in this unusual situation. The concession does, however, forestall an unseemly but predictable response in such circumstances – the employer might otherwise create a make-work job for one half-time minimum wage employee (perhaps a child of the CEO) and grant that superfluous worker plan membership in order to satisfy the ratio percentage test.

344 Tax Controls: Qualified Retirement Savings

program for nondiscrimination testing. If the combined coverage of the two plans is adequate *and* the contributions or benefits provided under the composite program do not discriminate in favor of highly compensated employees, then each of the plans is treated as satisfying the nondiscrimination tests.[81] Returning to the example of a firm with ten HCEs and fifty NHCEs, assume that eight of the HCEs and none of the NHCEs receive an employer contribution under a profit-sharing plan, while twenty-eight of the NHCEs are active participants in a money purchase pension plan under which they receive annual contributions of 5 percent of compensation. Clearly, the coverage of the money purchase pension plan for the rank-and-file is nondiscriminatory (as is any plan that covers no HCE), but the profit-sharing plan tested alone is just as clearly discriminatory, as it covers no NHCE and has a ratio percentage of zero. If the plans' combined coverage is tested, however, the ratio percentage is satisfactory. Provided that the money purchase and profit-sharing plans use the same plan year, elective plan aggregation permits such composite coverage testing, but the programs must also provide nondiscriminatory contributions or benefits when evaluated on a composite basis. If the contribution rate under the profit-sharing plan does not exceed 5 percent of compensation, then the plans would satisfy the amount nondiscrimination standard when tested together.[82]

The second alternative to separate application of the ratio percentage test is the average benefit test, which has two components: (1) the nondiscriminatory classification test; and (2) a numerical group-average benefit comparison.[83] The first element, the nondiscriminatory classification test, requires that the employees who benefit must be identified categorically under a reasonable classification based on objective business criteria, such as job category, geographic location, salaried

---

[81] I.R.C. § 410(b)(6)(B) (2018); Treas. Reg. 1.410(b)-7(d) (as amended in 2004). This plan aggregation permission is an exception to the general rule that each pension, profit-sharing, stock bonus, or annuity plan must independently satisfy all components of the definition of a qualified plan (hundreds of conditions) to be eligible for favorable tax treatment. *See* I.R.C. § 401(a).

[82] In some cases the composite program could satisfy the amount nondiscrimination standard even if the rate of contribution under the profit-sharing plan were somewhat greater than 5 percent of compensation. A higher contribution rate under the HCE-dominated plan might be acceptable under the rules permitting integration with Social Security, in particular by utilization of the technique known as imputation of permitted disparity. *See infra* text accompanying Chapter 10 notes 162–165.

Elective plan aggregation requires that the combined plan satisfy both the quantitative and qualitative components of section 401(a)(4). Treas. Reg. § 1.410(b)-7(d)(1) (as amended in 2004); *id.* § 1.401(a)(4)-1(c)(4)(i), -1(b)(3). Therefore, in addition to passing the amount nondiscrimination test, the benefits, rights and features provided under the composite program must ordinarily pass a test for nondiscriminatory availability. *Id.* § 1.401(a)(4)-4. *See infra* text accompanying Chapter 10 notes 128–131.

[83] I.R.C. § 410(b)(1)(C), (b)(2) (2018); Treas. Reg. §§ 1.410(b)-2(b)(3) (as amended in 1994). Somewhat confusingly, both the overall test and the second component thereof (the numerical group average benefit comparison) are commonly known as the average benefit percentage test.

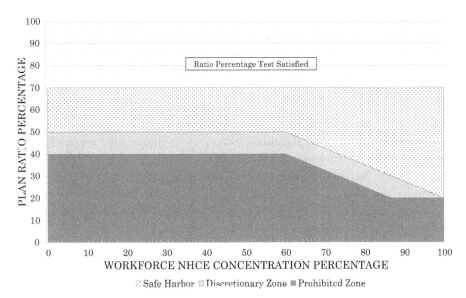

FIGURE 10.3 Nondiscriminatory classification test results by workforce composition

versus hourly pay, etc. In addition, the group of employees so identified must yield a ratio percentage that falls within a specified acceptable range. A ratio percentage of at least 50 percent is always acceptable. (Recall that there is no need to resort to the average benefit test if the plan's ratio percentage is 70 percent or greater.) The safe harbor is expanded to permit a ratio percentage below 50 percent if the proportion of rank-and-file employees in the workforce (known as the nonhighly compensated employee concentration percentage) exceeds 60 percent of all employees. In addition, a somewhat lower ratio percentage (but never more than ten points below the safe harbor) is permissible if, based on a discretionary assessment of all the facts and circumstances, including the nature and importance of the underlying business reason for the classification, the IRS finds that the classification is not discriminatory. Figure 10.3 displays the acceptable ratio percentages under the nondiscriminatory classification test as a function of the employer's NHCE concentration percentage.[84]

The nondiscriminatory classification test is only a gateway to the second and distinctive component of the average benefit test, which is a numerical group-average benefit comparison, generally known as the average benefit percentage test. The average benefit percentage test requires that "the average benefit percentage for employees who are not highly compensated employees is at least 70 percent of the

---

[84] The ratio percentage ranges falling within the safe harbor and discretionary zones are prescribed by formulae and a table in Treas. Reg. § 1.410(b)-4(c)(4) (1991). Figure 10.3 presents those data in graphical form.

average benefit percentage for highly compensated employees."[85] The benefit percentage for each employee is the total employer-provided contribution or benefit under *all* qualified plans for the year, expressed as a percentage of the employee's compensation.[86] The average benefit percentage of each group (HCEs and NHCEs) is the average of the benefit percentages of each member of the group; in computing these group averages *employees are included whether or not they participate in any plan.*[87] Thus an employee who does not benefit from any qualified plan has a benefit percentage of zero, which reduces the average benefit percentage of the group to which he belongs.

The average benefit percentage test substitutes an intergroup benefit rate comparison for the coverage rate comparison of the ratio percentage test. The benefit rates compared are *global* rates – amounts earned under all qualified pension and profit-sharing plans (whether of the defined contribution or defined benefit sort) are aggregated to compute the per-employee total amount of employer-funded deferred compensation. By looking beyond the amounts earned under the plan in question, the test recognizes that the tax subsidy associated with savings by the highly compensated can be shifted to rank-and-file employees as effectively by establishing another plan for their benefit as by including them in the plan that covers – and is tailored to the preferences of – managerial and professional personnel. This broader comparison implements the central policy of the antidiscrimination norm while increasing employer flexibility.[88]

The employer's increased flexibility can be observed by noting the options available when a plan fails the ratio percentage test. The eligibility rules of the plan could be modified to increase the coverage rate for nonhighly compensated employees, or they could be changed to restrict the coverage of highly compensated employees. These are the obvious means of compliance with the ratio percentage test. The average benefit test offers two additional alternatives: (1) the plan could be amended to provide nonhighly compensated participants a higher rate of contributions or benefits than highly compensated members receive; or (2) the employer could establish (or increase contributions or benefits under) another plan with coverage favoring the rank-and-file. These options involve no adjustment in the coverage of the plan that fails the ratio percentage test.

The average benefit test also increases employer flexibility by allowing a trade-off between coverage and benefits. The employer is permitted to cover a proportion of rank-and-file employees that is less than 70 percent of the highly compensated

---

[85] I.R.C. § 410(b)(2)(A)(ii) (2018).

[86] I.R.C. § 410(b)(2)(C) (2018). Instead of computing benefit percentages on the basis of contributions or benefits for the plan year, the employer may elect to use a period composed of the plan year and the one or two preceding years. *Id.*

[87] I.R.C. § 410(b)(2)(B) (2018).

[88] Recall that preserving employer autonomy (maintaining a voluntary employment-based pension system) is a central policy of ERISA. *See supra* Chapter 1C.

Taxes and Retirement Saving 347

coverage rate on the condition that the amount of contributions or benefits flowing to the rank-and-file does not fall below the amount that would be allowed by the ratio percentage test (assuming a plan that grants each active participant an amount of contributions or benefits that is a fixed proportion of compensation). But observe that the trade-off works both ways: an employer that covers an overall proportion (under all qualified plans, that is) of NHCEs that is greater than 70 percent of the HCE coverage rate may give the rank-and-file workers a lower rate of contributions or benefits (as a proportion of compensation) because broader coverage at a lower amount can still satisfy the group-average benefit comparison. This insight suggests that the average benefit test functions as a liberalized version of plan aggregation: the employer is permitted to validate the coverage of a plan with membership tilted in favor of HCEs by taking into account NHCEs covered under other plans, and if specified conditions are met, it may do so even if the plans tested as a single program would not satisfy the amount nondiscrimination test.[89]

In one respect, the average benefit test is not as tolerant as plan aggregation. The nondiscriminatory classification test imposes a threshold condition tied to the ratio percentage of a single plan: coverage may be skewed in favor of the HCEs (a ratio percentage of at least 50 percent always satisfies the nondiscriminatory classification test), but if the disparity between coverage rates of the highly paid and the rank-and-file is too great (a ratio percentage below 20 percent is always disqualifying), then the group-average benefit comparison is unavailable. Consequently, when considered in isolation a management plan that does not have some substantial coverage of rank-and-file employees cannot pass the average benefit test. Compare the following situations:

1. Company X maintains Plan X, a defined contribution plan that covers all HCEs, and only HCEs, with the employer contributing 10 percent of compensation, and in addition Company X also maintains Plan X*, which covers 70 percent of its NHCEs (and no HCEs) at a 10 percent contribution rate;

2. Company Y, which employs a similar workforce, maintains Plan Y, a defined contribution plan that covers all HCEs, and only HCEs, with the employer contributing 10 percent of compensation, and in addition

---

[89] Recall that if plan aggregation is elected for purposes of coverage testing, the programs must also be treated as a single plan for purposes of testing for discrimination in contributions or benefits. I.R.C. §§ 410(b)(6)(B), 401(a)(4) (2018). *See supra* Chapter 10 notes 81–82 and accompanying text. Not so under the average benefit test: while section 410(b)(2) takes into account contributions or benefits provided under other plans of the same employer to validate the coverage of the HCE-dominated plan, each plan is otherwise tested separately, including under Code section 401(a)(4). The average benefit test is more expansive than plan aggregation in a second way as well: multiple plans can be tested under the average benefit test even if they do not share the same plan year. *Compare* Treas. Reg. § 1.410(b)-5(d)(3) (as amended in 1993), and § 1.410(b)-7(e)(1) (as amended in 2004), *with* § 1.410(b)-7(d)(5).

Company Y maintains Plan Y*, which covers all of its NHCEs (and no HCEs) at a 7 percent contribution rate;

3. Company Z, which employs a similar workforce, maintains Plan Z, a defined contribution plan that covers all HCEs and half of its NHCEs with the employer contributing 10 percent of compensation, and in addition Company Z maintains Plan Z*, which covers the rest of its NHCEs (and no HCEs) at a 4 percent contribution rate.

The ratio percentage of Plan X is zero; likewise for Plan Y. Although the average benefit percentage for the group of NHCEs of each company is exactly 70 percent of the average benefit percentage for the group of HCEs, neither Plan X nor Plan Y can pass the section 410(b) coverage test standing alone. In contrast, Plan Z passes the average benefit test of section 410(b)(2): it has enough rank-and-file coverage to satisfy the threshold nondiscriminatory classification test (a ratio percentage of 50 percent always falls within the safe harbor), and the average contribution percentage of the group of NHCEs (i.e., (10 percent + 4 percent)/2) is 70 percent of the average contribution percentage for the group of HCEs. Given that each of the three companies saves 10 percent for every HCE and on average puts aside 7 percent for NHCEs, these results seem curiously inconsistent.[90]

Observe, however, that if Plan X uses the same plan year as Plan X*, then elective plan aggregation can be invoked to test the combined program as a single plan (Plan X/X*), which has a ratio percentage of 70 percent and satisfies the uniformity principle for nondiscrimination in contributions. Plan Y and Plan Y* do not provide uniform contribution rates, yet Company Y is providing its NHCEs the same average level of contributions as both Company X and Company Z do for their NHCEs. Is Plan Y inevitably disqualified? Not necessarily, but not because of the average benefit test. If Plan Y uses the same plan year as Plan Y*, then elective plan aggregation, working in combination with the general test for nondiscrimination in contributions, including rules authorizing operational integration with Social Security, might possibly save the day. Under plan aggregation the combined program (Plan Y/Y*) has a ratio percentage of 100 percent, but it must also satisfy all the

---

[90] The statutory language imposing the nondiscriminatory classification test was carried forward from prior law, and came with historical baggage that apparently convinced the Treasury that substantial NHCE participation in the HCE-dominated plan must be required. S. Rep. No. 99-313, at 578, 579–80 (1986) (expressing dissatisfaction with Rev. Rul. 83–58, 1983–1 C.B. 95, and directing its revocation); see PRESIDENT'S TAX PROPOSALS TO THE CONGRESS FOR FAIRNESS, GROWTH, AND SIMPLICITY 375 (1985) (criticizing laxity of prior nondiscriminatory classification rulings). Other justifications have been suggested, including (1) avoiding the appearance that plans which benefit only highly paid executives receive preferential tax treatment, and (2) preventing qualification of a plan that provides a very high level of benefits (as a percentage of compensation) to one or a few favored NHCEs while the rest of the rank-and-file get nothing. See infra Chapter 10 note 93. The best explanation may be that the average benefit test was not fully thought through.

requirements for nondiscrimination in contributions or benefits.[91] While the amount of Company Y's qualified plan contributions disproportionately favors HCEs, the general test for amount nondiscrimination can be conducted using deemed allocation rates, which are defined to take into account the employer's contribution toward Social Security retirement benefits. That technique, known as "imputation of permitted disparity," might generate a set of deemed allocation rates that passes muster.[92]

The traditional approach to identifying discrimination entails a two-step process applied separately to each plan, first checking plan coverage and then making sure that the percentage of pay saved under that particular plan does not favor the highly paid. The central insight of the average benefit percentage test is that the traditional approach is unnecessarily restrictive. The objective of the antidiscrimination principle is to shift the tax subsidy into additional retirement saving for low-paid workers. That goal can be achieved under one plan, but it might be achieved as well or better under multiple plans tailored to the needs and preferences of different segments of the workforce. By computing employee benefit percentages with reference to the employer-provided contribution or benefit under all qualified plans maintained by the employer, the average benefit percentage test allows consolidated nondiscrimination testing (to a point). Consolidated testing enables the employer to take the subsidy captured from highly paid savers under one plan and pay it out under another plan geared to rank-and-file employees. The nondiscriminatory classification test, however, limits the consolidated approach to situations where the workforce segmentation in plan coverage is not too closely correlated with compensation level. A second perplexing feature of the average benefit percentage test is its limited role as an alternative coverage standard (substituting for the ratio percentage test): although it represents an amalgam of the traditional coverage and amount nondiscrimination tests, the average benefit percentage test is not allowed to substitute for both. Instead, if a plan's coverage is accepted under the average benefit test despite membership that favors HCEs, the plan must still independently pass the amount nondiscrimination test, notwithstanding the fact that the average benefit percentage test functions as a consolidated workforce-wide amount nondiscrimination test.[93] The average benefit percentage test was an innovation that first appeared

---

[91] I.R.C. § 410(b)(6)(B) (2018); Treas. Reg. §§ 1.410(b)-7(d), 1.401(a)(4)-1(c)(4)(i) (as amended in 2004).

[92] The general approach to testing for discrimination in the amount of contributions or benefits (the rate group testing methodology) is explained *infra* text accompanying Chapter 10 notes 139–149. Social Security integration using imputation of permitted disparity (deemed allocation rates) under the general test is discussed *infra* text accompanying Chapter 10 notes 162–165.

[93] Applying the nondiscriminatory classification test as an adjunct to the average benefit percentage test prevents qualification of a plan that provides a very high level of benefits (as a percentage of compensation) to one or a few favored NHCEs while the rest of the rank-and-file get nothing. Correspondingly, applying the general amount nondiscrimination test (rate

350   Tax Controls: Qualified Retirement Savings

in the conference committee report to the Tax Reform Act of 1986 with little explanation, and so these mysterious limitations on the scope of the test might be artifacts of a hasty origin.[94]

Definitions: Employee, Highly Compensated Employee

Nondiscrimination testing is a game of numbers. Computation of coverage rates or average benefit percentages demands clear answers to the questions (1) whether an individual must be taken into account as an employee, and if so, (2) whether she is to be categorized as a highly compensated employee (HCE) or a nonhighly compensated employee (NHCE).

The scope of the term employee is crucial to accomplishing redistribution: if the coverage nondiscrimination requirement were applied only to the employees of a single legal entity, it could be evaded simply by segregating the workforce between two commonly controlled businesses, one of which employs the highly paid executive and professional staff and sponsors a generous retirement plan, while the other hires the rank-and-file and makes no provision for retirement savings. Such a loophole would render the coverage rules a nullity. To prevent this, ERISA amended the Code's qualified plan rules to provide that all employees of a controlled group of businesses (regardless of whether the firms are incorporated) must be treated as employed by a single employer.[95] A controlled group means a parent-subsidiary group, a brother-sister group, or a combined group (brother-sister firms

> group testing) to a plan that relies on the nondiscriminatory classification test and the average benefit percentage test to validate coverage prevents a single HCE from earning benefits that are significantly greater in proportion to compensation than the benefits provided to any NHCE. In each instance, the limited role that current law accords the average benefit percentage test (looking behind group averages) prevents a situation from developing that appears grossly unfair. From the standpoint of redistribution policy only the first scenario is troublesome: while broad distribution of retirement savings among NHCEs who wouldn't save on their own is clearly desirable, it should not matter that the source of the redistributed funds is concentrated among a few HCE-savers.

[94] H.R. Rep. No. 99-841, at II-412 to II-417 (1986) (Conf. Rep.). Circumstantial evidence suggests a couple of possible sources for the average benefit percentage test. In an article published in 1985, one of the authors observed that separate coverage and amount testing could be dispensed with by treating nonparticipants as receiving zero contributions or benefits and computing the average amount of contributions or benefits provided for the group of highly compensated employees with similar averages computed for one or more lower compensation ranges. Peter J. Wiedenbeck, *Nondiscrimination in Employee Benefits: False Starts and Future Trends*, 52 Tenn. L. Rev. 167, 256–57 (1985). That academic insight was not developed into a detailed proposal, but a copy of the article was sent to the Joint Committee on Taxation during the gestation of the 1986 Act. In addition, combined coverage and amount testing was foreshadowed by the special nondiscrimination standard applicable to 401(k) plans, the actual deferral percentage test (discussed below).

[95] I.R.C. §§ 414(b), (c), 1563(a), (f)(5) (2018). *See* Peter J. Wiedenbeck, *"Ninety-Five Percent of [Them] Will Not Be Missed": Recovering the Tax Shelter Limitation Aspect of ERISA*, 6 Drexel L. Rev. 515, 527–28 (2014).

Taxes and Retirement Saving

having one or more subsidiaries). In general, a parent-subsidiary group consists of firms linked by 80 percent ownership ties.[96] A brother-sister group consists of two or more firms if at least 80 percent of each is owned by a group of five or fewer individuals, estates, or trusts, but only if their common ownership exceeds 50 percent, determined by adding each owner's smallest percentage interest in either company (the common ownership or overlap percentage).[97] Constructive ownership (attribution) rules are applied in determining whether these ownership tests are met.[98]

In the 1970s, individual members of some professional service firms began to incorporate, substituting their newly formed professional corporations as partners in the partnership. Each separate professional corporation could then sponsor a plan covering its own workforce (typically consisting of its sole owner-employee), while the professional partnership, which employed the associates and support staff, provided little if any qualified plan savings. Ordinarily none of the separately incorporated professionals held a controlling stake in the partnership (greater than 50 percent share of capital or profits), so the controlled group rule did not apply. Congress responded by demanding that all employees of an "affiliated service group" be treated as employed by a single employer, where affiliated service group means two or more business organizations that are functionally integrated and share ties of ownership (even if common control is lacking).[99] Finally, a company that pays another organization, such as a temporary staffing firm, for the use of its employees must treat such workers as its own employees if they perform services on a substantially full-time basis for a year or longer under the primary direction of the payer company.[100] This "leased employee" rule, in combination with the workforce aggregation required for affiliated service groups and commonly controlled businesses, creates a broad functional definition of employee for purposes of nondiscrimination testing, which is largely immune from manipulation.

Sometimes, however, the workforce aggregation rules sweep too broadly. Consider a conglomerate or holding company that controls businesses in two or more industries that produce different goods or services. If generous pension coverage is typical in one industry but not in the other, then application of the coverage nondiscrimination rules on an enterprise-wide basis would competitively disadvantage one line of business or the other. Management would be put to the choice of

---

[96] I.R.C. § 1563(a)(1) (2018).

[97] I.R.C. § 1563(f)(5)(A) (2018); Treas. Reg. § 1.414(c)-2(c) (as amended in 1994).

[98] I.R.C. § 1563(d), (e), (f) (2018). For example, in applying the definition of brother-sister corporations, stock actually owned by the minor child of an individual must be treated as owned by the individual. Ordinarily, stock owned by an individual's spouse is likewise mandatorily attributed to the individual.

[99] I.R.C. § 414(m) (2018). *See* Lloyd M. Garland, M.D., F.A.C.S., P.A. v. Comm'r, 73 T.C. 5 (1979); H.R. Rep. No. 96-1278, at 34–35 (1980) (affiliated service group rule enacted to require workforce aggregation in situations like *Garland*).

[100] I.R.C. § 414(n) (2018).

either sponsoring no plan, which would handicap them in recruiting and retaining talent in the industry in which pension coverage is the norm, or covering everyone, which would raise labor costs in the industry that does not typically offer retirement savings (because pension costs could not be recouped from workers who strongly prefer current cash compensation). While the nondiscrimination rules are intended to redistribute compensation within a firm's workforce, no such cross-subsidy is required between independently owned firms operating in different industries. To alleviate this competitive disadvantage and reduce the influence of the qualified plan rules on ownership structure (thereby promoting economic neutrality), in certain situations an aggregated workforce can be disaggregated along industry lines. If the employer operates two or more qualified separate lines of business (QSLOBs), the nondiscrimination rules can sometimes be applied independently to the workforce of each line of business.[101] Treasury regulations implementing the QSLOB rules are unusually complex and burdensome, even by tax-law standards, no doubt in an effort to guard against the reemergence of coverage abuses.[102] In any event, from the standpoint of economic substance, QSLOB workforce disaggregation is seriously under-inclusive, as many functionally distinct businesses cannot qualify.[103]

The controlled group, affiliated service group, and leased employee workforce aggregation rules mark the outer boundary of the set of workers that must be taken into account in nondiscrimination testing. The coverage rules, however, allow certain limited categories of employees to be excluded from consideration (treated as not employed). Consequently, exclusion of these workers from plan membership will not weigh against qualification even if the excluded workers disproportionately fall into the category of nonhighly compensated employees.

There are several important categories of excludible employees. First, as noted in the discussion of workforce disaggregation, in testing the coverage of a plan that benefits employees of a qualified separate line of business (QSLOB) the employees

---

[101] I.R.C. §§ 410(b)(5), 414(r) (2018). A workforce that is combined under the affiliated service group rule cannot be broken apart under the QSLOB provision. *Id.* § 414(r)(8); Treas. Reg. § 1.414(r)-2(b)(3)(iv) (as amended in 1994).

[102] To keep matters straight, the Treasury took the unusual and extremely helpful step of issuing a flowchart to clarify relationships between the components of the section 414(r) regulations, which span some forty-six pages in the Code of Federal Regulations. Treas. Reg. § 1.414(r)-0(c) (as amended in 1994).

[103] The two most serious limitations on the availability of QSLOB testing are both statutory. Workforce disaggregation is not available if a line of business has fewer than fifty nonexcludible employees, however functionally distinct it may be. I.R.C. § 414(r)(2) (2018). Still more problematic, the coverage of a plan may be tested separately with respect to the employees of a QSLOB only if the plan also satisfies a modified version of the nondiscriminatory classification test as applied to the aggregated workforce. I.R.C. § 410(b)(5)(B) (2018); Treas. Reg. § 1.414(r)-8(b) (as amended in 1994). Consequently, an enterprise with operations in two different industries may not be able to rely on QSLOB testing to validate the coverage of a plan that is limited to workers in one line of business if the ratio of NHCEs to HCEs working in the other line of business is much larger.

of all other QSLOBs can be ignored.[104] Second, nonresident alien employees are excludible if they receive no earned income from the employer that constitutes income from sources within the United States, or if a treaty exempts their US-source compensation from taxation by the United States.[105] Third, employees covered under a bona fide collective bargaining agreement are excludible in testing plans covering other segments of the workforce provided there is evidence that retirement benefits were the subject of good faith bargaining.[106] Consequently, unionized workers are allowed to trade off retirement savings for higher pay despite the overall aim of discrimination testing, which is to counteract just such a preference for current consumption.[107]

If a plan imposes permissible minimum age and service eligibility conditions and excludes all employees who have not satisfied those conditions from benefiting under the plan, then employees who fail to meet those entry conditions can also be ignored in applying the coverage nondiscrimination tests.[108] Because young and recently hired workers typically fall in the NHCE category, plan qualification often turns upon the license to treat these employees as excludible. Where two or more

[104] I.R.C. §§ 410(b)(5), 414(r) (2018); Treas. Reg. § 1.410(b)-6(e) (as amended in 2006). The QSLOB exclusion does not apply for purposes of the threshold requirement of I.R.C. § 410(b) (5)(B) (2018), that the plan must satisfy a relaxed, nondiscriminatory classification test on an employer-wide basis.

[105] I.R.C. § 410(b)(3)(C) (2018); Treas. Reg. § 1.410(b)-6(c) (as amended in 2006). The treaty rule applies only if all employees so situated are actually excluded from membership. *Id.* Protection would be lost, for example, if a highly paid, nonresident alien employee were covered by the plan but low-paid foreign workers were not.

[106] I.R.C. §§ 410(b)(3)(A), 7701(a)(46) (2018); Treas. Reg. § 1.410(b)-6(d) (as amended in 2006). The requirement that the collective bargaining agreement be bona fide prevents an employer from setting up a company union to "represent" low-paid workers who decline retirement plan coverage in order to make those NHCEs excludible in testing the coverage of a plan that is limited to managerial and professional personnel. In addition, the exclusion of employees covered by collective bargaining vanishes if more than 2 percent of the employees covered by the agreement are highly compensated employees who perform any of various designated professional services. Treas. Reg. § 1.410(b)-6(d)(2)(iii)(B) (as amended in 2006), § 1.410(b)-9 (as amended in 2004).

[107] Data reveal that the overall pension plan coverage rate for unionized workers is actually higher than for the nonunionized segment of the labor force, which might suggest that collective decision making offsets any individual propensity to over-discount the value of retirement savings. BUREAU OF LABOR STATISTICS, U.S. DEPARTMENT OF LABOR, NATIONAL COMPENSATION SURVEY: EMPLOYEE BENEFITS IN THE UNITED STATES, MARCH 2022, Table 1, Retirement Benefits of Private Industry Workers by Age and Bargaining Status (2022), at www.bls.gov/ebs/publications/september-2022-landing-page-employee-benefits-in-the-united-states-march-2022.htm (in 2022 84 percent of union workers in private industry participated in a retirement plan compared to 49 percent of nonunion workers; overall participation rate for all workers in private industry was 52 percent). The aggregate data, however, are not adjusted to correct for selection issues (e.g., that unions are concentrated in large firms, in particular industries, nor for differences in pay or skill levels between union members and other workers).

[108] I.R.C. § 410(b)(4) (2018); Treas. Reg. § 1.410(b)-6(b) (as amended in 2006). ERISA's rules concerning permissible age and service conditions are explained *supra* Chapter 7A.

Tax Controls: Qualified Retirement Savings

plans that use different minimum age and service conditions are considered together in testing coverage – as with elective plan aggregation or in computing employee benefit percentages under the average benefit percentage test – only those employees who fail to satisfy *all* of the different sets of age and service conditions are excludible.[109] Just as incoming employees (those who have not yet satisfied minimum age and service conditions) may be excluded, a limited category of outgoing workers is also excludible. If an employee terminates employment during the year with no more than 500 hours of service and does not receive a benefit for that final year solely because the plan requires that a participant be employed on the last day of the plan year or complete a minimum period of service within the year, then that departing worker can be ignored provided that the exclusion is applied to all employees so situated.[110]

Once the workforce aggregation and excludible employee rules are applied, all the individuals who must be taken into account in testing for coverage discrimination have been identified. Each member of that universe of employees must then be assigned to one of two mutually exclusive categories, highly compensated employee (HCE), or nonhighly compensated employee (NHCE). The qualified plan rules generally classify an employee as highly compensated if she was a 5 percent owner at any time during the current or preceding year or if her compensation from the employer for the preceding year exceeded $80,000, indexed for inflation ($150,000 in 2023).[111] A company with many workers earning more than that compensation threshold may elect to limit the compensation-based HCE category to the group composed of the highest-paid 20 percent of all employees.[112] The 5 percent owner category includes any employee who owns, directly or via application of constructive ownership rules, 5 percent or more of the outstanding stock of a corporation or stock possessing 5 percent or more of the total combined voting power of all stock of the corporation, or any person who owns

---

[109] I.R.C. § 410(b)(2)(D) (2018) (average benefit percentage test); Treas. Reg. § 1.410(b)-6(b)(2) (as amended in 2006). If a plan applies age and service conditions that are less restrictive than ERISA would allow (typically, age twenty-one and one year of service), then the employer is allowed to treat the arrangement as two plans, one covering employees who have attained age twenty-one and completed one year of service, and the other covering those employees who have not. These deemed separate plans are tested independently for coverage discrimination. In testing the plan covering employees who satisfy the age twenty-one and one year of service condition, all employees who do not meet that age and service standard are excludible even if they are actually covered by the plan. In testing the plan covering workers who have not attained age twenty-one or completed a year of service, all employees who have met that standard are excludible, as are all employees who have not met any less exacting age and service conditions imposed by the plan. Treas. Reg. § 1.410(b)-6(b)(3) (as amended in 2006), § 1.410 (b)-7(c)(3) (as amended in 2004).
[110] Treas. Reg. § 1.410(b)-6(f) (as amended in 2006).
[111] I.R.C. § 414(q)(1) (2018); IRS Notice 2022-55, 2022-45 I.R.B. 443.
[112] I.R.C. § 414(q)(1)(B)(ii), (q)(3), (q)(5) (2018).

Taxes and Retirement Saving

more than 5 percent of the capital or profits interest in an unincorporated employer (sole proprietor or partner).[113]

The 5 percent owner category applies regardless of pay level. Owners might decline current compensation and shift their remuneration into the form of dividends or retained earnings (i.e., appreciation in the value of their ownership interest in the business), but they are still the high-income workers who are the source of the subsidy and present the greatest risk of abuse. Assume, for example, that the HCE definition did not include the 5 percent owner rule, and the business owners set their stated compensation at $149,000 in 2023. In that event, the plan could cover *only* the owners and it would be treated as nondiscriminatory, because by definition any plan that covers no HCE satisfies the ratio percentage test. In applying the HCE definition to employees of a controlled group or an affiliated service group, the 5 percent owner category applies to any employee who has that status with respect to any component member of the group of businesses. So, for example, an individual who is a 5 percent owner of the stock of a subsidiary corporation is tagged as an HCE along with any employees having a 5 percent or greater stake in the parent.[114]

Minimum Coverage Requirement

The ban on favoritism imposed by the coverage nondiscrimination tests is a relative standard, meaning that the proportion of NHCEs who must benefit under the plan is fixed by reference to the rate of coverage of HCEs. In addition, a defined benefit plan is required to cover an absolute minimum number of workers, regardless of their compensation level. To be qualified, a defined benefit plan must benefit the lesser of fifty employees or 40 percent of all employees, except that if the company employs only two, three, or four employees, then the required minimum coverage is two.[115] On its face, this minimum body count requirement does not seem related to the antidiscrimination norm, but it is. The core purpose of the rule is to put a stop to small defined benefit plans, especially single-member plans. By relying on plan aggregation to satisfy the nondiscrimination standards, businesses could establish individual defined benefit plans for each executive or professional employee with features that were distinct from the program covering the rank-and-file (such as different funding levels or distribution options, for example). Although combined coverage testing under the plan aggregation rule is conditioned on combined testing for amount nondiscrimination,[116] Congress was concerned that subtle discrimination could escape detection due to the complexity and flexibility inherent in combined testing, and that the IRS did not have the resources to strictly scrutinize

---

[113] I.R.C. §§ 414(q)(2), 416(i)(1)(B), 318 (2018).
[114] Treas. Reg. § 1.414(q)-1T, Q&A-8 (as amended in 1994).
[115] I.R.C. § 401(a)(26) (2018). If there is only one employee, a plan covering that employee is satisfactory. *Id.*
[116] I.R.C. § 410(b)(6)(B) (2018).

356 *Tax Controls: Qualified Retirement Savings*

many plans covering a very small number of employees.[117] To stop to this abuse, elective plan aggregation *cannot* be used to satisfy the minimum coverage requirement, and the Treasury is authorized to treat separate benefit structures included under one plan as separate plans, each of which must independently satisfy the minimum coverage rule.[118]

The minimum coverage requirement applies to a defined benefit plan even if it is the only qualified plan of the employer and even if it contains only a single benefit structure.[119] Given its antidiscrimination origin, this seems curiously over-inclusive. Where there is only one plan, there can be no problem with discrimination eluding detection because of the complexity of comparability analysis. Yet in this instance, there may be an independent justification for the minimum coverage requirement. The administrative cost of issuing determination letters, plan audits, and enforcement is largely independent of the number of participants; such fixed monitoring costs are high, which suggests that there may be a governmental interest in discouraging the proliferation of small plans. The social advantage of increased retirement savings for a handful of low-paid workers might be more than offset by the public burden of administering the system, which burden is not taken into account in the employer's decision whether to sponsor a plan. Under an expanded cost-benefit analysis, in other words, the redistribution achieved by small-membership qualified plans may be insufficient to justify the governmental costs of administering the system. While plausible, this administrative cost justification for a minimum participation rule seems never to have been presented to or relied upon by Congress, and several features of the existing rule do not mesh well with this explanation.[120]

Sanctions for Deficient Coverage

As definitional criteria for qualified retirement plan status, failure to satisfy the coverage nondiscrimination rule or the minimum coverage requirement brings with them unfavorable tax consequences. Disqualification renders trust earnings

---

[117] S. REP. No. 99-313, at 586–88 (1986).

[118] I.R.C. § 401(a)(26)(H) (2018); Treas. Reg. §§ 1.401(a)(26)-2(d)(1)(iii), -3 (1991).

[119] A plan that benefits no HCE and which is not aggregated with any other plan of the employer in order to satisfy nondiscrimination standards is exempted by rule from the minimum coverage requirement. Treas. Reg. § 1.401(a)(26)-1(b)(1) (as amended in 1993).

[120] Most notably, the administrative cost justification standing alone would not support the exemption of defined contribution plans. Administrative costs are generally much lower for defined contribution plans because actuarial computations are not required for purposes of funding and discrimination testing; but this consideration indicates that a lower minimum coverage requirement might be justified for defined contribution plans, not that they should be exempt. (Prior to its amendment in 1996, section 401(a)(26) applied to both defined contribution and defined benefit plans.) Nor do administrative cost concerns support the 40 percent alternative to the fifty-employee minimum. The 40 percent alternative not only permits a small employer to have a low-membership plan, but it also tolerates concurrent sponsorship of multiple low-membership plans.

Taxes and Retirement Saving

taxable[121] and ordinarily entails taxation of employees in advance of distribution because general tax timing rules require inclusion by the person performing services as soon as her compensation is freed of any substantial risk of forfeiture.[122] Generally, the amount taxable is the amount attributable to contributions made in years in which the plan is not qualified, not the full value of the employee's interest under the plan.[123] Accordingly, a participant whose interest is substantially vested pays tax on his share of contributions made in the employee's taxable year that ends with or within the plan year of disqualification, while a substantially nonvested participant pays no tax at that time (if she becomes substantially vested in a subsequent year, she will then be liable for tax on the portion of her interest in the trust attributable to contributions made in disqualified years).[124]

The timing of the employer's deduction for contributions made in a year in which the plan is disqualified is controlled by the time at which amounts become includible in the employees' income.[125] ERISA requires rapid vesting, and the Code demands immediate vesting for most 401(k) plan contributions, and so most participants are likely to be substantially vested in their interests and immediately taxable on contributions made when the plan is disqualified. Under the matching rule, this means that the employer's deduction would not be delayed, and to that extent the employer suffers no direct adverse tax effects from disqualification.

These observations show that the immediate adverse tax consequences of disqualification typically fall on employees, not on the employer, and the consequences are not limited to the executives whose actions or inattention caused the problem. The usual tax consequences of disqualification, in other words, are not well focused on the parties responsible. To better target the sanction, the usual impact of disqualification is modified where the fault lies in a violation of the

---

[121] Upon disqualification, the trust loses its status as a tax-exempt organization under I.R.C. § 501 (a) (2018).

[122] I.R.C. § 83(a), (c)(2) (2018); *see supra* text accompanying Chapter 10 notes 9–23. *See* I.R.C. §§ 402(a), 403(a)(1) (2018) (tax deferral until distribution conditioned upon meeting definition of qualified trust or qualified annuity plan).

[123] I.R.C. §§ 402(b)(1), 403(c) (2018); Treas. Reg. §§ 1.402(b)-1(a), (b), 1.403(c)-1 (as amended in 2007).

[124] The amount of contributions made on behalf of a participant is easily determined under a defined contribution plan, but the absence of separate accounts presents a formidable obstacle to implementing contribution-based taxation in the case of a disqualified defined benefit plan. To alleviate this difficulty, the employer is given a strong incentive to amend the plan to set up separate accounts: failing to do so results in complete disallowance of any deduction for the contribution. I.R.C. § 404(a)(5) (2018); Treas. Reg. § 1.404(a)-12(b)(3) (as amended in 1978). If the employer fails to establish separate accounts, an allocation of contributions must somehow still be made in order to tax the employees. The regulations provide for allocation of a defined benefit plan contribution under a specified formula "or under any other method utilizing recognized actuarial principles which are consistent with the provisions of the plan under which such contributions are made and the method adopted by the employer for funding benefits under the plan." Treas. Reg. § 1.402(b)-1(a)(2) (as amended in 2007).

[125] I.R.C. § 404(a)(5) (2018), discussed *supra* text accompanying Chapter 10 notes 24–25.

Tax Controls: Qualified Retirement Savings

coverage nondiscrimination rule or the minimum coverage requirement. In such cases, HCEs are required to include as income their entire vested accrued benefit under the plan, even if it is largely or entirely attributable to contributions made in years when the plan was qualified![126] On the other hand, workers who have always been nonhighly compensated are not taxed *at all* if the *sole* reason for disqualification is a violation of the coverage rules.[127] Thus, innocent NHCEs are sometimes exempted from immediate adverse tax consequences, while HCEs are in for extraordinary tax hurt. In this instance, Congress armed the IRS with a big stick to focus the minds of the actors who are in the best position to influence compensation policy.

Discrimination in Contributions or Benefits

To be qualified, every plan that satisfies the coverage nondiscrimination test must also show that "the contributions or benefits provided under the plan do not discriminate in favor of highly compensated employees."[128] That standard contains both qualitative and quantitative elements.[129]

The qualitative component demands that each significant benefit, right, or feature provided under the plan be made available in a nondiscriminatory fashion. The objective here is equal access or opportunity; disparity between actual utilization rates of HCEs and NHCEs is not per se disqualifying. A principal concern is with optional forms of distribution. Assume that a plan provides that a participant's accrued benefit will ordinarily be distributed as a life annuity commencing at normal retirement age, but allows participants who meet certain eligibility conditions to elect an actuarially equivalent lump-sum distribution instead. Here, there is no favoritism in the value conferred (due to the actuarial equivalence of the two payment methods), but if the eligibility conditions imposed on the lump-sum alternative are correlated with compensation level, then access to the optional form of distribution might unduly favor HCEs. For instance, if lump-sum distribution can be selected only by employees who have a specified minimum net worth, or who work in certain job categories, occupations, or geographic locations (e.g., head office personnel only), then in operation the condition, although neutral on its face, might restrict eligibility

---

[126] I.R.C. § 402(b)(4)(A), (C) (2018).

[127] I.R.C. § 402(b)(4)(B) (2018).

[128] I.R.C. § 401(a)(4) (2018).

[129] A third element adds a temporal component to review for discrimination in contributions or benefits. The tests for qualitative and quantitative favoritism, although performed annually on the basis of the actual operation of the plan, take into account only the impact of the terms of the plan as currently in effect. That is, the tests for qualitative and quantitative favoritism are static and would not capture favoritism accomplished by means of changes in plan terms over time. Therefore, a temporal or dynamic element is required to prevent abuse. Treas. Reg. § 1.401(a)(4)-5 (1993), *see infra* Chapter 10 note 134.

Taxes and Retirement Saving

in a way that affords greater choice to HCEs.[130] The IRS has consistently interpreted the nondiscrimination rules to forbid such qualitative favoritism and has consistently applied the rules by assessing the impact of specified eligibility conditions in operation, based on the facts and circumstances of the particular workforce.[131]

The quantitative component, often referred to as the amount nondiscrimination test, is satisfied if the amount of contributions or benefits provided under the plan, expressed as a share of each employee's compensation, does not favor HCEs. Hence, a qualified plan may provide retirement savings that represent a fixed or uniform proportion of each employee's compensation (up to a specified compensation cap[132]) even if the dollar amount saved for highly paid workers is ten times larger than for some low-paid employees.

Regulations adopted in 1993 implement the amount nondiscrimination requirement. After fifty years, the Treasury elaborated the pithy statutory command that contributions or benefits not discriminate with detailed regulations under section 401(a)(4) (filling 100 pages of the Code of Federal Regulations). Most of this frightful complexity can be safely left to experts and actuaries, but the resolution of two central interpretive problems deserves attention.

Clearly, a defined contribution plan is most readily tested for discrimination in the amount of contributions, while it is natural to test a defined benefit plan for disparities in the amount of benefits. Now consider a plan that provides benefits that are a larger proportion of compensation for HCEs than for other employees. For example, the normal retirement benefit for an HCE might be 40 percent of final average compensation, while the NHCE benefit is only 35 percent. If the HCEs are younger than the NHCEs, however, their benefits will be funded over a longer period, and therefore the contributions necessary to fund benefits for the HCEs might not be disproportionate to compensation. Does such a plan violate the

---

[130] E.g., Rev. Rul. 85-59, 1985-1 C.B. 135, declared obsolete, Rev. Rul. 93-87, 1993-2 C.B. 124 (because ruling position now specifically covered by regulations).

[131] Treas. Reg. § 1.401(a)(4)-4 (as amended in 2004) now governs the determination whether plan benefits, rights, or features are made available in a nondiscriminatory manner. The regulation applies to all optional forms of benefit (distribution alternatives), ancillary benefits (nonretirement benefits such as life or health insurance, or plant shutdown benefits), and any other right or feature that can reasonably be expected to have meaningful value to employees, such as plan loans or the right to direct investments. Id. -4(e). The regulation provides that each benefit, right, or feature must satisfy both a current availability and an effective availability requirement. The current availability test is largely mechanical and seems intended to function as an objective filter (or under-inclusive screening test). In contrast, effective availability calls for an overall judgment that in actual operation "[b]ased on all the relevant facts and circumstances the group of employees to whom the benefit, right, or feature is effectively available must not substantially favor HCEs." Id. -4(c)(1).

[132] I.R.C. § 401(a)(17) (2018). The $200,000 cap on compensation that may be taken into account under a qualified plan is adjusted for inflation and stands at $330,000 in 2023. As explained later, the compensation cap is the link between the amount nondiscrimination rule and limits on the maximum amount of contributions or benefits that may be provided under a qualified plan. See infra Chapter 10 note 208 and accompanying text.

amount nondiscrimination requirement? Must a defined benefit plan be tested only for discrimination in benefits, and a defined contribution plan tested only for discrimination in contributions, or can benefits be converted into equivalent contributions (and vice versa) for purposes of the amount nondiscrimination requirement? The statute refers to "contributions or benefits," but whether logical disjunction or implied parallelism was intended is far from clear. In drafting the regulations, the Treasury opted for flexibility: a cross-testing rule allows defined benefit plans to be tested on a contributions basis, and defined contribution plans on a benefits basis.[133]

The second conundrum regulation drafters had to resolve concerns the meaning of discrimination in circumstances where some but not all rank-and-file employees receive contributions or benefits that represent a smaller proportion of pay than the amount granted one or more HCEs. Contributions or benefits might be based on age or length of service (in whole or in part), and under profit-sharing or stock bonus plans, contributions can be tied to objective measures of profitability or productivity.[134]

---

[133] Treas. Reg. § 1.401(a)(4)-8 (as amended in 2001). The general availability of cross-testing has proven controversial, because it has been exploited by pension consultants to develop age-weighted profit-sharing plans that allocate a share of the employer's annual contribution to the accounts of older HCEs that is a much greater proportion of those HCEs' current compensation than the percentage of pay allocated to the accounts of rank-and-file employees. Tested on a contributions basis, such allocations would clearly violate the uniformity standard for amount nondiscrimination, but with clever planning and careful monitoring the projected benefits that such disproportionate (often wildly disproportionate) contributions hypothetically produce at retirement age can pass the nondiscrimination test. *See generally* Peter Orzag & Norman Stein, *Cross-Tested Defined Contribution Plans: A Response to Professor Zelinsky*, 49 BUFF. L. REV. 629 (2001). Known as "new comparability plans" or "qualified supplemental executive retirement plans" (QSERPs), these programs attracted critical press reports. *E.g.*, Ellen E. Schultz & Theo Francis, *Companies Tap Pension Plans to Fund Executive Benefits*, WALL ST. J. Aug. 4, 2008. Nevertheless, in mid-2016 the IRS and the Treasury Department retracted a proposal that would have curtailed more aggressive QSERPs. Announcement 2016–16, 2016–18 I.R.B. 698 (withdrawing portions of Prop. Reg. §§ 1.401(a)(4)-2(c) and -3 (c), explained at 81 Fed. Reg. 4976, 4980 (Jan. 29, 2016)). This matter is explored further in connection with proposals that would reform or replace the nondiscrimination rules, as part of the discussion of the future of the (semi-) private pension system, *infra* Chapter 10D.

[134] A qualified plan must be "a definite written program or arrangement which is communicated to employees," Treas. Reg. § 1.401-1(a)(2) (as amended in 2014). A pension plan, as the term is used for tax purposes, means a plan designed to provide benefits to employees or their beneficiaries on retirement or for a period of years thereafter, and may be either a defined benefit or a defined contribution arrangement. In either case, discretion in amount is barred because the arrangement will "be considered a pension plan if the employer contribution under the plan can be determined actuarially on the basis of definitely determinable benefits, or, as in the case of money purchase pension plans, such contributions are fixed without being geared to profits." *Id.* -1(b)(1)(i). The employer may retain discretion as to the overall amount contributed to a profit-sharing or stock bonus plan from year to year, but the plan must nevertheless "provide a definite predetermined formula for allocating the contribution made to the plan among the participants." *Id.* -1(b)(1)(ii). The core concept of a "defined benefit" or "defined contribution" plan, in other words, has always been interpreted to bar discretion in setting the amounts earned by individual employees, even though a central tenet of our voluntary employment-based retirement savings system is that the sponsor remains free to set or amend the plan's provisions governing the amount of deferred compensation (the formula governing benefit accrual or contribution allocation). *See supra* Chapter 1C.

Taxes and Retirement Saving

Formulas that take into account such factors can yield a wide range of contribution or benefit accrual rates for both highly compensated and rank-and-file employees. Does the plan "discriminate" if *any* NHCE earns lesser benefits (as a proportion of compensation) than any HCE? The Treasury first proposed just such an extremist or hard-line definition of prohibited favoritism.[135] Plan sponsors, of course, lobbied for a more forgiving standard. Ultimately, the Treasury settled upon a testing approach that accommodates plans that generate a variety of allocation or accrual rates for HCEs and NHCEs, so long as the range of rates for the two groups largely overlaps.[136]

A program that provides retirement savings proportionate to compensation is just what many employers want. By promising a uniform allocation or accrual rate, such a plan is assured of satisfying the amount nondiscrimination test, provided that each participant's contribution or benefit is based on a measure of compensation that does not itself discriminate. That can be accomplished either by using the statute's comprehensive definition of compensation or by consistently excluding certain items of irregular or additional compensation and showing that the resulting

It should be noted that the employer's general freedom to change the amount of retirement savings could be abused. Some oversight of the timing of plan amendments is necessary to prevent the employer from taking advantage of changes in workforce composition to accomplish favoritism by means of plan provisions that, viewed in isolation, appear even-handed. An across-the-board increase in benefits taking effect after most NHCEs have left the plan, and the elimination of an ancillary benefit after most HCEs have already taken advantage of it, are examples of the problem. Therefore, in addition to the requirement that all benefits, rights and features under the plan be made available on a nondiscriminatory basis (qualitative scrutiny) and the amount nondiscrimination test (quantitative scrutiny), the regulations provide that section 401(a)(4) is violated if the timing of a plan amendment or series of amendments has the effect of discriminating significantly in favor of HCEs or former HCEs. Treas. Reg. § 1.401(a)(4)-5 (1993). The timing of the initial establishment or termination of the plan is also subject to review under this rule, but the determination whether the institution, amendment or termination of the plan has the effect of "discriminating significantly" is "based on all the relevant facts and circumstances." *Id.* -5(a)(2). Of particular concern are grants of past service benefits to current employees under a defined benefit plan (whether accomplished by initial establishment or subsequent amendment) where there has been significantly higher turnover among NHCEs than HCEs during the period for which credit is retroactively granted. Under a special safe harbor, however, uniform grants of up to five years of past-service credit under the plan's current benefit formula are deemed nondiscriminatory. *Id.* 5(a)(3).

[135] With respect to contributions, Prop. Treas. Reg. § 1.401(a)(4)-2(c)(1) provided: "A plan satisfies the requirements of this section if no highly compensated employee in the plan has an allocation rate that exceeds that of any nonhighly compensated employee in the plan." 55 Fed. Reg. 19,897, 19,911 (May 14, 1990). The same approach was proposed for testing benefits. Prop. Treas. Reg. § 1.401(a)(4)-3(c)(1)(i), 55 Fed. Reg. at 19,914.

[136] It is noteworthy that the final regulations did not adopt the position advocated by plan sponsors and practitioners, that the amount nondiscrimination test should be limited to a simple comparison of the average rate of contribution or benefits received by the two groups (HCEs and NHCEs). Presumably, the Treasury's concern was that individual allocation rates for the two groups might be distributed in a manner that provided systematically higher benefits to some HCEs. This could happen, for example, if the standard deviation of allocation or accrual rates was larger for HCEs than NHCEs, or if the two distributions were disparately skewed about the means.

362   *Tax Controls: Qualified Retirement Savings*

narrower measure does not systematically favor HCEs.[137] A plan that does so is assured of satisfying the amount nondiscrimination standard. Accordingly, the regulations dispense with annual operational testing for plans that meet stringent uniformity requirements.[138] These design-based safe harbors are often attractive because they reduce plan-administration costs and provide assurance of continuing qualification.

Annual amount nondiscrimination testing is required for plans that do not specify contributions or benefits as a fixed proportion of compensation or a fixed dollar amount. In developing a general test for discrimination, the Treasury hit upon a clever insight: the objective mechanical tests for coverage discrimination could be pressed into service to identify systematic favoritism in the amount of qualified retirement saving. That insight was implemented by requiring that each "rate group" under the plan must satisfy either the ratio percentage test or a modified version of the average benefit test, with those tests applied as if the rate group were a separate plan that benefits only those employees included in the rate group.[139] A rate group for a defined contribution plan is defined as the group of employees who receive allocations of employer contributions or forfeitures under the plan that equal or exceed (either as an absolute dollar amount or as a percentage of plan year compensation) the allocation received by a specific HCE plan member. There is a separate rate group for each HCE in the plan, which is composed of that particular HCE and all other plan members (both HCEs and NHCEs) who have an allocation rate greater than or equal to that HCE. "Thus, an employee is in the rate group for each HCE who has an allocation rate less than or equal to the employee's allocation rate."[140] The general test for nondiscrimination in contributions uses the technique of successive rate group coverage testing to prevent favoritism in the amounts of employer contributions and forfeitures added to participants' accounts during the year.

Rate group testing is best explained by reference to a simple illustration. Assume that Beta Corporation maintains a service-weighted profit-sharing plan.[141] Beta's

---

[137] I.R.C. § 401(a)(5)(B) (2018) (authorizing uniform relationship to compensation "within the meaning of section 414(s)"), *id.* §§ 414(s), 415(c)(3); Treas. Reg. § 1.414(s)-1 (as amended in 2007).

[138] Treas. Reg. § 1.401(a)(4)-2(b)(2) (as amended in 2007) (uniform allocation formula safe harbor for defined contribution plans), § 1.401(a)(4)-3(b) (1993) (uniformity-based safe harbors for certain defined benefit plans).

[139] Treas. Reg. § 1.401(a)(4)-2(c)(1), -2(c)(3)(i) (as amended in 2007).

[140] Treas. Reg. § 1.401(a)(4)-2(c)(1) (as amended in 2007).

[141] The defined contribution plan amount nondiscrimination regulations provide a simplified operational test for certain plans that base contributions in whole or in part on each employee's age or service. This special rule is available only if age or service is taken into account in the manner specified by the definition of a uniform points allocation formula, Treas. Reg. § 1.401 (a)(4)-2(b)(3)(i)(A) (as amended in 2007). The general test is applied in this example, because insufficient facts are presented to know whether Plan B uses a uniform points allocation formula, and because, even if it did, the allocation rates assumed here (see the following table) would not satisfy the simplified operational test for a uniform points plan. That test requires that for the plan year in question, "the average of the allocation rates for the HCEs in the plan must not exceed the average of the allocation rates for the NHCEs in the plan." *Id.* -2(b)(3)(i)(B). The average HCE allocation rate for Plan B is 7.5 percent, while the average allocation rate for "NHCEs *in the plan*" (N1 through N8 only) is only 7.0 percent.

workforce consists of twelve nonexcludible employees, two of whom are highly compensated. Plan B covers both of the company's HCEs and eight of the 10 NHCEs. Assume that Plan B's contribution formula produces the following alloca- tion rates for the year, expressed as a percentage of each employee's plan year compensation, where H1 and H2 are Beta's HCEs and N1–N10 are the NHCEs:

Employee	Allocation Rate (%)
H1	9.00
H2	6.00
N1	9.00
N2	9.00
N3	8.00
N4	7.00
N5	6.00
N6	6.00
N7	6.00
N8	5.00
N9	0.00
N10	0.00

Plan B's ratio percentage (80 percent) easily satisfies the coverage nondiscrimina- tion test, but Plan B plainly does not provide a uniform allocation rate. It will nevertheless pass the amount nondiscrimination test if *each* rate group under the plan satisfies either the ratio percentage test or a modified version of the average benefit test. Plan B has two rate groups, one corresponding to each HCE. Call them rate group 1 (RG1) defined by H1, and rate group 2 (RG2) defined by H2. Each rate group consists of all employees who have an allocation rate at least equal to the allocation rate of the HCE who defines the group. Therefore, RG1 is composed of H1, N1, and N2; RG2 is composed of H1, H2, N1, N2, N3, N4, N5, N6, and N7 (i.e., all employees, whether highly compensated or not, with an allocation rate equal to or greater than the 6 percent received by H2). Treated as if it were a separate plan, the membership of RG2 satisfies the ratio percentage test (both HCEs are included and RG2 also includes seven of ten NHCEs). RG1, however, has a ratio percentage of only 40 percent (= 20 percent of NHCEs divided by 50 percent of HCEs). Consequently, in order for Plan B to pass the general test for nondiscri- mination in contributions, RG1 must satisfy a modified version of the average benefit test.

Recall that there are two components to the average benefit test: the nondiscri- minatory classification test and the average benefit percentage test. For purposes of rate group coverage testing under the section 401(a)(4) regulations, each of these components is adjusted somewhat. The reasonable classification requirement is not applied in testing rate group coverage, and the nondiscriminatory classification test is deemed satisfied if the ratio percentage of the rate group equals or exceeds the midpoint between the safe harbor and prohibited zone ratio percentages for the plan in question (see Figure 10.3), or, if smaller, the ratio percentage of the plan.[142] (Observe that these alterations of the nondiscriminatory classification test eliminate any need for discretionary determinations.) Beta Corporation's NHCE concentration percentage is 83 percent (= 10 NHCEs/12 total nonexcludible employees). At that workforce composition, the midpoint between the safe harbor (32.75 percent) and prohibited zone (22.75 percent) boundaries is 27.75 percent,[143] so RG1's ratio percentage of 40 percent easily passes the modified nondiscriminatory classification test. For purposes of rate group coverage testing, the average benefit percentage test is automatically deemed satisfied by every rate group if it is satisfied by the plan as a whole.[144] Assuming that Plan B is the only qualified plan offered by Beta Corporation, the average benefit percentage of the HCEs is 7.5 percent (= 9 percent + 6 percent, divided by two HCEs), and the average benefit percentage for NHCEs is 5.6 percent (= 9% + 9% + 8% + 7% + 6% + 6% +6% + 5%, divided by ten total NHCEs). The average benefit percentage of the NHCEs (5.6 percent) exceeds 70 percent of the average benefit percentage for the HCEs (70 percent × 7.5 percent = 5.25 percent), so the plan as a whole satisfies the average benefit percentage test, hence RG1 passes the modified average benefit test, and Plan B survives the amount nondiscrimination test. Notice that if N8 were not an active participant (zero contribution, like N9 and N10), Plan B's rate groups would not change (N8 is not included in either RG1 or RG2), but the plan as a whole would fail the average benefit percentage test (5.1 percent average NHCE allocation divided by 7.5 percent average HCE allocation is 68 percent), the coverage of RG1 would not pass muster, and Plan B would face disqualification on the ground that the amounts contributed favor HCEs.[145]

Abstracting from the technical detail and computational gymnastics, a logical pattern emerges. The technique of successive rate group coverage testing to identify amount discrimination is akin to the following protocol: (1) list all plan participants in descending order by rate of employer contribution; (2) identify all the HCEs on the list (by highlighting those names, for example); and (3) check to be sure that the HCEs are not heavily concentrated toward the top of the list. If the HCEs are either dispersed reasonably evenly throughout the list, or disproportionately represented

---

[142] Treas. Reg. § 1.401(a)(4)-2(c)(3)(ii) (as amended in 2007).
[143] Treas. Reg. § 1.410(b)-4(c)(4) (1991), or consult Figure 10.3 *supra*.
[144] Treas. Reg. § 1.401(a)(4)-2(c)(3)(iii) (as amended in 2007).
[145] Two avenues might still be available to Beta Corporation to avoid disqualification. First, the rules governing integration with Social Security (specifically, operational integration via imputation of permitted disparity in testing for amount nondiscrimination) might justify the limited favoritism present here. See *infra* Chapter 10 notes 162–165 and accompanying text. Second, Beta could take advantage of a retroactive correction mechanism to avoid disqualification. See *infra* Chapter 10 notes 171–173 and accompanying text.

Taxes and Retirement Saving 365

toward the bottom, then the plan does not exhibit prohibited favoritism in the amount of retirement savings.

Despite its elegance, from a policy perspective, the technique of successive rate group testing has a couple of shortcomings. As an indicator of discrimination in the amount of qualified plan savings, it is arguably both over- and under-inclusive. First, suppose that H1 in the preceding example had gotten an allocation rate of 10 percent. Observe that if the highest allocation rate for the plan year happens to be received by an HCE, the plan is likely to be disqualified. The rate group defined by that HCE will have a ratio percentage of zero, given that no NHCE gets that much savings, and a ratio percentage below 20 percent is never acceptable under the nondiscriminatory classification test. In some circumstances, the regulation allows actual allocation rates to be grouped within ranges when determining rate group membership, with all rates falling within a given range treated as equal, and that allowance might sometimes be used to bring one or more NHCEs into the top rate group. Yet because the acceptable ranges are quite narrow, in many cases this expedient will prove unavailing.[146]

A second limitation of rate group coverage testing inheres in the fact that no attention is paid to the compensation of the employees within the rate groups. Consequently, the top rate group (meaning the rate group defined by the HCE with the highest allocation rate, which therefore has the smallest membership) might include the most highly paid HCE, and its coverage could pass muster even if the NHCEs included in that rate group were the lowest-paid plan members. The result would be substantial retirement savings by the HCE (highest allocation rate among HCEs applied to highest compensation), while the high allocation rates of the NHCEs in that rate group would not translate into large savings due to their meager compensation levels. Given the redistribution objective, some might view a systematic inverse relationship between NHCE plan members' compensation levels and allocation rates as troubling, if not indicative of abuse. The counterargument, of course, is that the problem is inherent in the mechanical two-group (i.e., HCE versus NHCE) coverage comparison, and a more exacting standard would be too complex and burdensome.

The amount nondiscrimination tests for defined benefit plans are structured like the rules for defined contribution plans described above. There are a number of safe

---

[146] Treas. Reg. § 1.401(a)(4)-2(c)(2)(v) (as amended in 2007). The lowest and highest allocation rates within the range must be within 5 percent (not 5 percentage points) above or below a midpoint allocation rate selected by the employer. Alternatively, if allocation rates are computed as a percentage of plan year compensation, a range of one-quarter of a percentage point above or below the selected midpoint is acceptable. Id. Besides the narrowness of the permitted range of allocation rate grouping, this strategy faces another ill-defined obstacle. The regulation prohibits grouping "if the allocation rates of the HCEs within the range generally are significantly higher than the allocation rates of the NHCEs within the range." Id. -2(c)(2)(v) (A).

harbors for plans that provide uniform benefits.[147] There is also a general test for benefit nondiscrimination that operates by applying the coverage nondiscrimination rules to successive rate groups.[148] But instead of testing allocation rates, the safe harbors and general test for defined benefit plans are applied with reference to *accrual rates* – the increase in each employee's accrued benefit over a selected measurement period.[149] This dependence on accrual rates makes the benefit nondiscrimination regulation considerably more complex, and typically dependent upon actuarial calculations.

Integration with Social Security

Qualified plans encourage the accumulation of savings that will supplement Social Security old-age benefits, so that retired workers will have an adequate standard of living after they leave the labor force. (Recall that Social Security, the mandatory and near-universal public retirement program, provides only a baseline level of retirement income. For a large majority of retirees, Social Security alone is inadequate to maintain their pre-retirement standard of living.)[150] Social Security benefits, however, are not proportionate to pay; they are progressive (or bottom-weighted), meaning that Social Security replaces a larger proportion of low-income workers' pre-retirement earnings than it does for high-income workers. (See Figure 10.1.) Moreover, compensation in excess of the Social Security contribution and benefit base (also known as the taxable wage base; $160,200 in 2023) generates no additional benefits under the public retirement program. Hence highly paid workers need to save a larger proportion of their earnings in order to maintain their standard of living in retirement. This presents a fundamental policy question: should qualified plans, the semi-private retirement savings system, be allowed (or required) to take into account the structure of Social Security in setting the amount of contributions or benefits provided plan members? Arguably, the combination of qualified plan and Social Security benefits should form an integrated support system that delivers adequate retirement resources to all workers, regardless of compensation level. To do so, however, qualified plan coverage or benefits would have to be wrapped around Social Security in a way that *favors* higher-paid workers.

Since 1942, when nondiscrimination requirements were first imposed, Congress has, in one form or another, permitted plan sponsors to take account of Social Security benefits, which necessitates some loosening of the nondiscrimination rules. In the early years, qualified plans were allowed to entirely exclude from coverage any worker whose compensation was less than the Social Security taxable wage base, provided that the plan's contributions or benefits were (1) based solely on that portion of each participant's compensation that exceeded the wage base, and (2)

[147] Treas. Reg. § 1.401(a)(4)-3(b) (1993).
[148] *Id.* § 1.401(a)(4)-3(c).
[149] *Id.* § 1.401(a)(4)-3(d) (including permission to group accrual rates within narrow ranges).
[150] *See supra* text accompanying Figure 10.1.

Taxes and Retirement Saving

not greater than the amount determined by applying a prescribed maximum contribution or benefit rate to that excess compensation. The maximum rates were loosely based on the rate of Social Security contributions and benefits with respect to compensation below the taxable wage base. If those conditions were satisfied, the excluded low-paid workers could be treated as active participants in testing for discriminatory coverage.[151] As Senator Gaylord Nelson complained during the debate on ERISA, "[p]ension benefits given to low-paid employees as an abstraction are taken away in the fine print of the income tax Code."[152]

Hikes in the taxable wage base during the 1970s and 1980s, combined with annual indexing since then, greatly exacerbated this problem. Indeed, the cutoff on Social Security taxes ($160,200 in 2023) now exceeds the compensation threshold for HCE classification ($150,000 in 2023). By way of comparison, in 2021 80 percent of US households received money income from all sources totaling $149,131 or less.[153] Under these circumstances, a rule allowing complete exclusion of employees earning less than the taxable wage base would effectively eviscerate redistribution.

At the Treasury's urging, Congress revised the qualified plan integration rules in 1986 with the enactment of Code section 401(*l*).[154] Social Security integration no longer provides an excuse for the complete exclusion of lower-paid workers from plan membership – the revised approach to integration relaxes the amount non-discrimination standard (specifically, the uniformity rule) but not the coverage

---

[151] Prior to its amendment in 1986, I.R.C. § 401(a)(5) provided in part:

"A classification shall not be considered discriminatory within the meaning of paragraph (4) [the amount nondiscrimination test] or section 410(b) [the prior law coverage nondiscrimination test] merely because it excludes employees the whole of whose remuneration constitutes "wages" under section 3121(a)(1) (relating to the Federal Insurance Contributions Act [FICA, the tax side of social security]) or merely because it is limited to salaried or clerical employees."

That prior law integration rule is elaborated by Treas. Reg. § 1.401-4(b) (as amended in 1993), and illustrated in Rev. Rul. 79-348, 1979-2 C.B. 161 (declared obsolete, Rev. Rul. 93-87, 1993-2 C.B. 124).

[152] 119 CONG. REC. 30,133 (Sept. 18, 1973).

[153] U.S. CENSUS BUREAU, HISTORICAL INCOME TABLES: HOUSEHOLDS, Table H-1. Income Limits for Each Fifth and Top 5 Percent of All Households: 1967–2021 (2019), at www.census .gov/data/tables/time-series/demo/income-poverty/historical-income-households.html.

[154] During the Carter Administration, top Treasury tax policy officials foresaw this problem and urged prompt legislative action. *National Pension Policies: Private Pension Plans: Hearings Before the Subcomm. on Retirement Income and Employment of the House Select Comm. on Aging*, 95th Cong. 228–50 (1978) (statement of Daniel I. Halperin, Tax Legislative Counsel, U.S. Department of the Treasury). The current integration rules largely follow the solution recommended by the Treasury in 1978, but the fix was not adopted until 1986. The top-heavy plan rules enacted in 1982 require that each participant in a top-heavy plan who is not a key employee must get a specified minimum employer contribution or benefit from the plan without regard to Social Security integration. I.R.C. § 416(c), (e) (2018). In large measure, the section 416 top-heavy plan rules were a response to abuses resulting from the laxity of the traditional approach to integration. (Indeed, the top-heavy plan provision can be viewed as a stopgap that ought to have been repealed once integration standards were tightened.)

368   *Tax Controls: Qualified Retirement Savings*

requirement.[155] The integration rules ("permitted disparity") for defined contribution and defined benefit plans necessarily differ due to the different focus of those plan types (money going into the plan versus money paid out), but they share a common theme. An integrated plan must provide some contributions or benefits with respect to employee compensation that is less than the plan's integration level,[156] and the rate at which contributions or benefits are earned on compensation above the plan's integration level cannot exceed the rate applicable to compensation below the integration level by more than (1) 100 percent, or, if smaller, (2) an amount that approximates one-half of the average annual rate of contribution (i.e., taxes) or benefit accrual under the Social Security retirement system.[157] The latter amount is set at 5.7 percent for defined contribution plans (which equals the portion of the employer's 6.2 percent Social Security tax rate that is used to finance old-age benefits), and three-quarters of a percentage point for any year of service taken into account under a defined benefit plan.[158]

---

[155] I.R.C. § 401(a)(5)(C) (2018) now provides: "A plan shall not be considered discriminatory within the meaning of paragraph (4) [requiring that contributions or benefits provided under the plan do not discriminate in favor of HCEs] merely because the contributions or benefits of, or on behalf of, the employees under the plan favor highly compensated employees (as defined in section 414(q)) in the manner permitted under subsection (*l*)." Observe that the prior reference to the section 410(b) coverage rules was dropped. *See supra* Chapter 10 note 151.

[156] The integration level is an amount of compensation specified in the plan (by dollar amount or formula), not greater than the Social Security taxable wage base, at or below which the rate at which contributions or benefits are provided is less than the rate applied above such amount. I.R.C. § 401(*l*)(5)(A) (2018). Typically, defined contribution plans use the taxable wage base as the integration level, while defined benefit plans use covered compensation, which is the average of the Social Security wage base in effect for each of the thirty-five years preceding the year in which the employee attains the Social Security retirement age (computed as if the wage base remains constant in future years). *See id.* § 401(*l*)(4)(C), (*l*)(5)(E). If a plan adopts a different integration level, the maximum permitted disparity (5.7 percent for defined contribution plans or 0.75 percent per year of service for defined benefit plans) might have to be reduced. *See* Treas. Reg. §§ 1.401(*l*)-2(d)(4), -3(d)(9) (as amended in 1993).

[157] I.R.C. § 401(*l*)(2), (*l*)(3)(A), (*l*)(4)(A) (2018). The Federal Insurance Contributions Act (FICA) nominally imposes one-half of the payroll tax that finances the Social Security system on the employer, and one-half on the employee (collected by wage withholding). Starting from the premise that the employer can properly claim credit for only the employer-funded portion of the public retirement program, the maximum permitted disparity for defined contribution plans under section 401(*l*) (i.e., 5.7 percent) is based on one-half of the taxes that finance Social Security old-age benefits, and the maximum permitted disparity for defined benefit plans (0.75 percent per year) is one-half of the approximate average accrual rate of Social Security benefits. Unfortunately, this halfway consideration of Social Security is half-baked. Legal liability has no bearing on the economic incidence of the tax, meaning who suffers its real impact in reduced resources. In a competitive market, the division of the real burden of the payroll tax depends only on the price elasticities of labor supply and demand, regardless of how the tax is collected (whether solely from the employer, solely from the employee, or split between them in some way). For example, in many occupations, employment opportunities are sensitive to labor costs, but the number of hours worked is fairly insensitive to pay rate, and in those circumstances, the burden of the FICA tax would fall largely on labor, despite its 50/50 collection.

[158] I.R.C. § 401(*l*)(2)(A)(ii), (*l*)(4)(A) (2018).

Taxes and Retirement Saving

A plan containing a contribution or benefit formula that complies with I.R.C. § 401(*l*) can automatically satisfy the amount nondiscrimination test. The uniform allocation formula safe harbor (the design-based safe harbor for defined contribution plans) may apply where "a plan satisfies section 401(*l*) in form."[159] So, for example, annual amount nondiscrimination testing would not be required of a money purchase pension plan that promised employer contributions equal to 7 percent of each participant's compensation up to the Social Security wage base plus 12.7 percent of any compensation in excess of the wage base (a formula that takes advantage of the maximum permitted disparity). If instead the plan promised employer contributions of only 5 percent of compensation up to the Social Security wage base, then it could not provide more than 10 percent of any compensation in excess of the wage base (the maximum permitted disparity is the lesser of 5.7 percent or the base contribution percentage). Similarly, the defined benefit safe harbors may be availed of by a plan that "takes permitted disparity into account in a manner that satisfies section 401(*l*) in form."[160] Hence, a unit credit plan could avoid operational testing if it promised a normal retirement benefit of 1.25 percent of each participant's average annual compensation up to covered compensation, plus 2.0 percent of average annual compensation in excess of covered compensation, multiplied by the participant's years of service up to a maximum of thirty-five years.[161]

Suppose that a plan says nothing about integration, and its contribution or benefit formula produces higher allocation or accrual rates for HCEs. The amount nondiscrimination rules do permit such a plan, provided that the higher savings rate for HCEs is no more than the disparity that would have been tolerated if the plan had been properly integrated with Social Security. In computing allocation or accrual rates for purposes of the general tests for discrimination in contributions or benefits, the "disparity permitted under section 401(*l*) may be imputed in accordance with the rules of § 1.401(a)(4)-7."[162] The regulation permitting such operational integration calls for a lot of computation, but the concept is straightforward. "In general, [the regulation] allows permitted disparity to be arithmetically imputed with respect to employer provided contributions or benefits by determining an adjusted allocation or accrual rate that appropriately accounts for the permitted disparity with respect to each employee."[163] In the case of a defined contribution plan, adjusted allocation rates are derived by assuming that the plan takes full advantage of the

---

[159] Treas. Reg. § 1.401(a)(4)-2(b)(2)(ii) (as amended in 2007).
[160] Treas. Reg. § 1.401(a)(4)-3(b)(6)(ii) (1993).
[161] To satisfy the uniform benefit safe harbor for unit credit plans, this plan would also have to define each employee's accrued benefit at any time as the amount determined by applying the plan's formula for the normal retirement benefit to the employee's years of service and average annual compensation determined at the time in question. Treas. Reg. § 1.401(a)(4)-3(b)(3) (as amended in 1993).
[162] Treas. Reg. § 1.401(a)(4)-2(c)(2)(iv) (as amended in 2007), *id.* § 1.401(a)(4)-3(d)(3)(i) (1993).
[163] Treas. Reg. § 1.401(a)(4)-7(a) (1993).

maximum disparity permitted defined contribution plans and uses the Social Security taxable wage base as the integration level.[164] For a defined benefit plan, adjusted accrual rates are derived by assuming that the plan takes full advantage of the maximum disparity permitted defined benefit plans for the first thirty-five years of credited service and uses covered compensation as the integration level.[165] The adjusted (or deemed) allocation or accrual rates so determined for each employee are then evaluated under the general test for discrimination in the amount of contributions or benefits (the successive rate group coverage testing approach). This operational (or de facto) integration technique is called, appropriately enough, imputation of permitted disparity.

By requiring that an integrated plan provide significant savings for rank-and-file employees, section 401(*l*) increases the likelihood that the nondiscrimination rules will actually achieve some level of redistribution. The current integration regime is still subject to criticism, however, because the rules force less redistribution than would be required in their absence. That could be good or bad. If the tax subsidy associated with savings by highly paid employees is not large enough to fund proportionate savings by the rank-and-file, then relaxing the amount nondiscrimination test so that lower-paid workers get some retirement savings is clearly preferable to discontinuance of the plan. But if an unmitigated application of the uniformity test for favoritism would not trigger plan termination, then integration allows the plan sponsor or the HCEs to retain a large share of the tax savings, and to that extent, the qualified plan tax preference is wasted. Which situation applies to a particular enterprise depends on tax rates and workforce composition. Whether on balance integration preserves or inhibits redistribution is an unanswered empirical question. In any event, it is far from clear that integration fits with nondiscrimination, notwithstanding their historical codependence.

It should be understood that integration is no policy panacea – in its current form it achieves only very limited coordination of Social Security and qualified retirement plan benefits. In particular, the permitted disparity rules emphatically will not ensure that workers at all pay levels receive public and private retirement benefits that in combination replace a uniform proportion of their pre-retirement pay. Due to its two-pay-range comparison (i.e., above and below the integration level) integration cannot account for the wide (and continuous) variation in Social Security replacement rates. Figure 10.1 shows replacement rates ranging from 56 percent for "Low" career earnings to 27 percent for "Maximum" earnings (which represents a worker who is paid an amount equal to the taxable wage base each year during her career). To maintain their accustomed lifestyles, each of these workers needs more retirement income than Social Security will provide, but the "Low" earner clearly needs proportionately much less. An integrated qualified plan makes no such

---

[164] *Id.* -7(b)(1).
[165] *Id.* -7(c)(1).

differentiation between these workers, however. Neither of them was paid more than the taxable wage base at any point in their careers, and so each of them would likely earn retirement savings according to the plan's base contribution percentage or base benefit percentage. Consequently, the "Maximum" earner gets the same qualified retirement plan benefits, in proportion to pay, as the "Low" earner. The integration rules, in other words, only allow a higher contribution or benefit rate to be applied to compensation beyond the reach of Social Security; they make no attempt to assure that the combination of Social Security and qualified plan benefits produces a uniform replacement rate over all compensation ranges.[166]

Some argue that avoiding over-pensioning low-paid workers (who receive a higher replacement rate due to the redistributive component of Social Security) constitutes the only justification for curtailing redistribution (i.e., limiting nondiscrimina-tion).[167] The risk of such over-pensioning is generally small because even the lowest-paid workers need to supplement Social Security to maintain an adequate standard of living in retirement. (Recall that the "Low" earnings level depicted in Figure 10.1 is roughly comparable to a career of full-time minimum wage work, which produces a Social Security replacement rate of only 56 percent.) Rank-and-file workers actually covered by qualified plans get even lower Social Security replacement rates. Data reveal that qualified plan participation is strongly correlated with compensation level – coverage is skewed toward workers who earn average wages or higher. In particular, plan membership among the lowest-paid 40 percent of the labor force (those who receive the highest replacement rates under Social Security) is quite rare. Nevertheless, Congress enacted a limited over-pensioning rule in 1986. Notwithstanding the amount nondiscrimination precept, a defined benefit plan is allowed to provide that a participant's accrued benefit shall not exceed the participant's final pay from the employer reduced by half of the Social Security retirement benefits attributable to service with the employer.[168]

---

[166] For a proposal that would coordinate Social Security and qualified plan benefits over all compensation levels, see Nancy J. Altman, *Rethinking Retirement Income Policies: Nondiscrimination, Integration, and the Quest for Worker Security*, 42 TAX L. REV. 433, 494–98 (1987). In developing its integration reform proposal the Carter Administration considered prohibiting integration except where the combination of plan benefits and Social Security would provide substantial retirement security to employees at all income levels, such as by replacing 80 percent of every participant's final compensation. That approach was ultimately abandoned due to its complexity. *See National Pension Policies, supra* Chapter 10 note 154.

[167] Altman, *supra* Chapter 10 note 166, at 495.

[168] I.R.C. § 401(a)(5)(D) (2018); Treas. Reg. 1.401(a)(5)-1(e) (as amended in 1993). Final pay is defined as the highest annual compensation received during the employee's last five years of service with the employer. Note that the final pay limitation takes into account only half of the Social Security primary insurance amount, on the view that the employer can properly claim credit for only the employer-funded portion of the public retirement program. The maximum permitted disparity under section 401(*l*) similarly takes into account only half of Social Security. *See supra* Chapter 10 note 157.

372   *Tax Controls: Qualified Retirement Savings*

Presumably, such a final pay limitation would be triggered by a very low-paid employee (hence, high Social Security replacement rate) who is covered under a generous non-integrated defined benefit plan. The limit allows the plan to cap benefits to avoid an outlandish work disincentive, but under current law the problem appears largely conjectural.

If it were determined that integration could be repealed without causing a net decrease in retirement savings for low-income workers, then an argument could be made that repeal should be accompanied by enactment of a revised limit on qualified plan savings to prevent over-pensioning. The precise limit should be set after consideration of the appropriate target replacement rate. For a defined benefit plan, the limit might look something like 80 percent of final pay reduced by 100 percent of the participant's Social Security primary insurance amount.[169] Under a defined contribution plan, an employer might be allowed to discontinue contributions when the participant's account balance attained a level adequate to purchase an annuity contract that would pay such a benefit. Such a reformed version of the final pay limit would prevent waste from over-pensioning the lowest-paid plan members, but it would do so by allowing the employer or its HCEs to benefit from the waste (i.e., retain rather than redistribute the tax subsidy). In light of nondiscrimination policy, a better approach might prohibit both forms of waste by requiring the employer to take any amount of contributions or benefits that would represent excessive savings for the company's lowest-paid workers (who will have the highest Social Security replacement rates) and redistribute it among other higher-paid NHCEs.

Correction Mechanisms

The primary focus of the nondiscrimination requirements is operational, and so plan sponsors will often be confronted with the situation where changes in work-force composition and compensation levels occurring throughout the year cause the plan to fail the nondiscrimination rules. Sometimes such operational violations may not even be detectable until after the close of the plan year, when complete data become available.[170]

The nondiscrimination regulations provide a retroactive correction mechanism to alleviate this difficulty. If certain conditions are satisfied, the coverage and amount nondiscrimination tests may be satisfied by a retroactive plan amendment that increases the allocations or accruals of employees who benefited under the plan during the plan year being corrected or that grants allocations or accruals to

---

[169] *See* Altman, *supra* Chapter 10 note 166, at 494–98.

[170] Only a plan that grants membership to every nonexcludible NHCE and provides uniform allocations or benefits (i.e., takes advantage of the design-based amount safe harbor) is assured of ongoing compliance with the nondiscrimination standards, come what may.

Taxes and Retirement Saving 373

employees who did not benefit during the year being corrected.[171] In general, four conditions must be met for the corrective amendment to be taken into account in meeting prior-year nondiscrimination obligations: (1) the amendment may not reduce any employee's benefits or options under the plan; (2) the amendment must be given effect for all purposes from the first day of the plan year being corrected; (3) the amendment must be adopted and implemented no later than the fifteenth day of the tenth month after the close of the plan year being corrected (the period is extended further if a determination letter relating to the amendment is requested by that date); and (4) the additional allocations or accruals resulting from the amendment must, when considered alone, benefit a group of employees that satisfies the section 410(b) coverage standards and satisfy section 401(a)(4).[172] The last requirement prevents an employer from retroactively maximizing the coverage rate of HCEs (taking full advantage of the favoritism inherent in the ratio percentage test, for example), or the HCE allocation or accrual rates. (An exception is made for a corrective amendment designed to conform the plan to one of the amount nondiscrimination regulatory safe harbors; such amendments are permitted even if they disproportionately advantage HCEs.) In addition, such corrective amendments must have substance – increasing contributions or benefits of nonvested NHCEs whose employment terminated before the end of the year being corrected will not pass muster because they could not receive any economic benefit from the amendment.[173]

The requirement that each significant benefit, right, and feature provided under the plan be made available in an evenhanded manner (the qualitative component of the ban on discrimination in contributions or benefits) presents a challenge for retroactive correction. After all, if during a particular year a participant was ineligible to elect a lump-sum distribution or obtain a plan loan, amending the plan documents to remove the restriction on access is not going to give her the money when she needed it last year. Nevertheless, prompt plan amendment to correct access problems will sometimes prevent disqualification if the amendment remains in effect for a minimum period going forward.[174]

In recent years, the IRS has come to appreciate that plan disqualification is often an overly harsh and poorly targeted sanction,[175] regardless of whether the fault lies in a violation of the nondiscrimination rules or some other qualification condition. To encourage continuing compliance and prompt correction of problems that occur, the IRS instituted a general administrative process, called the Employee Plans Compliance Resolution System (EPCRS), that allows plan sponsors (1) to self-correct certain operational failures without payment of any fee or sanction,

---

[171] Treas. Reg. § 1.401(a)(4)-11(g)(2) (as amended in 2004).
[172] Id. § 1.401(a)(4)-11(g)(3)(ii)-(v).
[173] Id. § 1.401(a)(4)-11(g)(4).
[174] Id. § 1.401(a)(4)-11(g)(3)(iii), (vi).
[175] See supra Chapter 10 notes 121–127 and accompanying text.

374   *Tax Controls: Qualified Retirement Savings*

(2) to voluntarily correct all qualification failures and obtain the service's approval by paying a limited fee, and even (3) to fix a qualification defect identified on audit by paying a reasonable sanction.[176] EPCRS maintains strong incentives for the plan sponsor to monitor compliance and intervene when necessary, while avoiding the often catastrophic and unproductive consequences of plan disqualification.

Discrimination Tests for 401(k) Plans

Special coverage and amount nondiscrimination tests, including a prohibition on integration with Social Security, are prescribed for cash-or-deferred arrangements, so-called 401(k) plans. The reason is that 401(k) plans are elective contribution programs that allow each employee to choose between taking a portion of her compensation as current cash or directing the employer to contribute it (ordinarily on a pre-tax basis[177]) to the employee's account under a profit-sharing or stock bonus plan. Contributions therefore depend on individual employee elections, and the employer has no direct control over how much, if any, each employee decides to contribute.

The general coverage nondiscrimination tests look to the relative proportions of HCEs and NHCEs who "benefit" under the plan, which in the case of a defined contribution plan means that an employee receives an allocation of employer contributions or forfeitures for the year. Elective contributions under a 401(k) plan are generally treated as pre-tax employer contributions, so under the usual approach satisfaction of the coverage tests would be fortuitous, depending as it would on the outcome of individual employee elections that are largely beyond the employer's control. In deference to this state of affairs, Congress prescribed a special coverage nondiscrimination test for 401(k) plans that treats each employee who is eligible to elect to have a contribution made on his behalf as an employee who benefits under the plan.[178] This relaxed standard only demands that the *opportunity to defer* must not unduly favor HCEs (i.e., satisfy either the ratio percentage test or the average benefit test). Nondiscriminatory *access*, of course, does not assure nondiscriminatory *utilization* of the retirement savings opportunity, much less nondiscrimination in

---

[176] Rev. Proc. 2019-19, 2019-19 I.R.B. 1086. In response to "the ever growing complexity of retirement plan administration," H.R. Rep. No. 117-283, at 126 (2022), in 2022 Congress expanded the availability of EPCRS to several additional type of inadvertent errors. SECURE 2.0 Act of 2022, Pub. L. No. 117-328, Div. T, § 305, 136 Stat. 4459, ____ (2023).

[177] Section 402A permits a 401(k) plan to include a qualified Roth contribution program. Employees utilizing such a program may designate their elective contributions, matching contributions, or nonelective contributions as after-tax contributions, but qualified withdrawals from a designated Roth account are entirely excludible from gross income. I.R.C. § 402A(a)(1)-(3), (c)(1), (d)(1) (2018 & West Supp. 2023). Hence investment returns on the account are tax exempt, just as under a Roth IRA. *See supra* text accompanying Chapter 10 notes 57–63.

[178] I.R.C. §§ 410(b)(6)(E), 401(k)(3)(A)(i) (2018); Treas. Reg. § 1.410(b)-3(a)(2)(i) (as amended in 2004), § 1.401(k)-6 (as amended in 2009) (definition of eligible employee).

Taxes and Retirement Saving

the actual amounts deferred. Because lower-paid employees often cannot afford any reduction in their current cash compensation, broad eligibility provides no assurance that there will be comparable utilization of such elective contribution arrangements by the highly compensated and nonhighly compensated segments of the workforce. As demonstrated earlier, granting tax deferral for retirement savings on an individual basis would do very little to increase saving by low- and middle-income workers, while it would give a windfall to the highly paid, who would simply shift their other savings into the tax-advantaged form.[179] Without something more, a 401(k) plan would be just an employer-mediated IRA shorn of the low IRA contribution limit,[180] and the tax subsidy to high-income savers would not be shifted into retirement savings for rank-and-file workers who cannot afford to save. To implement anti-discrimination policy, therefore, the actual results of employee decision making must somehow be taken into account. A special amount nondiscrimination standard for 401(k) plans, the actual deferral percentage (ADP) test, was designed to accomplish redistribution while accommodating employee choice.[181]

The ADP test limits the actual deferral percentage for the group of eligible HCEs for the current plan year by reference to the actual deferral percentage for the group of eligible NHCEs. For administrative convenience, the actual deferral percentage for the group of eligible NHCEs is ordinarily based on data from the preceding plan year, but at the election of the employer, current year data may be used for NHCEs as well.[182] These actual deferral percentages are defined as the group average (for the groups composed of eligible HCEs and eligible NHCEs) of the ratios, computed separately for each group member for the relevant year, of: (a) elective contributions *plus* qualified matching contributions and qualified nonelective contributions made by the employer; to (b) employee compensation.[183] A qualified matching contribution is an employer contribution made on account of the employee's elective deferral, which is at all times fully vested and subject to certain early distribution restrictions that are applicable to elective deferrals. Similarly, a qualified nonelective contribution is an employer contribution that is neither an elective deferral nor a

---

[179] *See supra* text accompanying Chapter 10 notes 69–74.

[180] Interestingly, the Treasury Department study that initiated the Reagan Administration's tax reform proposals (an effort that culminated in the 1986 Act) recommended repeal of section 401(k) on the ground that "IRAs ... are the appropriate vehicle for receipt of deductible retirement plan contributions by individuals." 2 U.S. DEPARTMENT OF THE TREASURY, TAX REFORM FOR FAIRNESS, SIMPLICITY, AND ECONOMIC GROWTH 357 (1984).

[181] I.R.C. § 401(k)(3)(C) (2018) (contributions under cash-or-deferred arrangement do not discriminate in favor of HCEs if ADP test satisfied).

[182] I.R.C. § 401(k)(3)(A) (2018) (final sentence). The election to use current year data, while not irrevocable, is generally binding for five years. Treas. Reg. § 1.401(k)-2(c)(1) (as amended in 2009). Consequently, the sponsor cannot switch back and forth in computing the NHCE deferral rate baseline, according to which year offers the most favorable number.

[183] I.R.C. § 401(k)(3)(B), (D) (2018); Treas. Reg. § 1.401(k)-2(a)(2), -2(a)(3) (as amended in 2009). Observe that Social Security taxes are not taken into consideration, and so the ADP test is applied without integration with Social Security.

matching contribution and that is subject to the same vesting and distribution rules.[184] An eligible employee who chooses not to make any elective contribution and for whom the employer makes no qualified nonelective contribution for the year is included in the computation of the group average with a deferral rate of zero, which reduces the ADP of the group to which he belongs.[185] In this fashion, the ADP test functions as a kind of combined coverage and amount nondiscrimination test. The ADP limit (or maximum disparity in deferral rates) is as follows[186]:

NHCE ADP	Maximum HCE ADP
0–2%	(NHCE ADP) × 200%
2–8%	(NHCE ADP) + 2 percentage points
8% or more	(NHCE ADP) × 125%

The function defined in the preceding table implies that the ratio of the average contribution rate of eligible NHCEs to the average contribution rate for HCEs under a 401(k) plan is sometimes permitted to be as low as 50 percent (if the NHCE does not exceed 2 percent), but may be required to be as high as 80 percent (if the NHCE ADP is 8 percent or more). If all nonexcludible employees are eligible to choose to defer a portion of their pay, then this ratio of average contribution rates is the same ratio that is computed for purposes of the average benefit percentage test of Code section 410(b)(2)(ii), which requires a relative contribution rate for NHCEs of at least 70 percent.

The inclusion of qualified matching contributions and qualified nonelective contributions in the computation of actual deferral percentages is critical, both to the employer's ability to satisfy the ADP test, and to the accomplishment of the test's purpose (viz., targeting the tax subsidy). If only elective contributions were taken into account, the NHCE actual deferral percentage would be depressed by the many low-paid employees who cannot afford a reduction in their current compensation. (Recall that all eligible employees are included under the ADP test, whether they choose to defer or not; if no contributions are made with respect to an employee, a deferral percentage of zero goes into the corresponding group average.) By offering to match elective deferrals (either dollar-for-dollar or at a specified percentage), the employer can increase the attractiveness of deferral. This should not only induce greater elective deferrals, but the matching contribution, if

---

[184] I.R.C. § 401(k)(3)(D)(ii), (m)(4)(C) (2018).

[185] Treas. Reg. § 1.401(k)-2(a)(3)(i) (as amended in 2009).

[186] *See* I.R.C. § 401(k)(3)(A)(ii) (2018). In the first year of a 401(k) plan's operation, there will be no preceding year NHCE deferrals against which to measure HCE deferrals. In this case, the ADP test is applied by assuming a prior year NHCE average deferral rate of 3 percent, or the employer may elect to use as the baseline for comparison the actual NHCE ADP for the first year. *Id.* § 401(k)(3)(E).

Taxes and Retirement Saving

qualified, will also raise the deferral rate. Unfortunately, however, employee responsiveness to matching contributions cannot be predicted with certainty. For example, workers with pressing current consumption needs may be unwilling to forego part of their pay even if the employer offers to double the value of their savings. But the employer can also increase the NHCE actual deferral percentage by making qualified nonelective contributions on behalf of NHCEs, even if the employees refuse to make any elective contributions. Thus, qualified matching and qualified nonelective contributions give the employer considerable influence over group deferral rates, and such employer contributions are the mechanism by which the tax subsidy associated with savings by the highly paid may be redistributed to those who would not save on their own.

As a special amount nondiscrimination standard, the ADP test has its own fail safe mechanisms. In lieu of the general retroactive correction method described earlier, a violation of the ADP test may be promptly remedied by distributing excess contributions (along with earnings thereon) to the appropriate HCEs or, if the employee elects, by recharacterizing his share of the excess contributions as an after-tax employee contribution to the plan.[187]

Notwithstanding the broad array of mechanisms sponsors have at their fingertips to assure compliance with the ADP test (i.e., qualified matching contributions, qualified nonelective contributions, distribution or recharacterization of excess contributions), employers clamored for design-based safe harbors, and Congress has acquiesced. Instead of complying with the ADP test, a 401(k) plan may be treated as nondiscriminatory if either: (1) the employer matches NHCE deferrals dollar-for-dollar up to 3 percent of compensation and matches NHCE deferrals between 3 and 5 percent of compensation at a rate of 50 percent, and at any level of elective contribution the HCE matching rate is no higher than the rate applicable to NHCEs; or (2) the employer makes a nonelective contribution for each eligible NHCE of at least 3 percent of compensation.[188] The matching contribution safe

---

[187] I.R.C. § 401(k)(8) (2018); Treas. Reg. § 1.401(k)-2(b) (as amended in 2009). The total amount of excess contribution is determined by reducing contributions made on behalf of the HCEs having the highest deferral rates by the amounts necessary to bring the highest HCE deferral rate down to the level that will satisfy the ADP test. The total amount of excess contributions so determined, however, is distributed (or recharacterized as after-tax employee contributions) to those HCEs who deferred the highest dollar amounts, not (as was the case prior to 1997) to those with the highest deferral rates. *Compare* I.R.C. § 401(k)(8)(B)(ii) (2018), *with id.* (k)(8)(C).

Observe that the 401(k) correction devices work by *reducing* qualified plan savings for HCEs, rather than by *increasing* savings for rank-and-file employees, which is the technique applicable to other qualified plans.

[188] I.R.C. § 401(k)(12) (West Supp. 2020).

Even smaller employer contributions are required in the case of a SIMPLE 401(k) plan – the matching contribution need be only 100 percent on the first 3 percent of NHCE elective deferrals with no required match at higher contribution rates, while 2 percent nonelective contributions suffice. I.R.C. § 401(k)(11) (2018). A SIMPLE 401(k) plan, however, can be offered only by a small employer (meaning fewer than 100 employees in the previous plan

harbor demands that each employee eligible to participate be given advance notice each year of her rights under the plan, so that she can make elective deferrals and qualify for the match.[189] The nonelective contribution safe harbor can be utilized even if it is added by plan amendment during the year, so long as the amendment is adopted more than thirty days before the end of the plan year. It can even be invoked by a retroactive plan amendment (made before the close of the following plan year) if nonelective contributions of at least 4 percent of compensation are required.[190] If the plan provides eligible NHCEs with this minimum match or nonelective contribution, then elective deferrals by HCEs are constrained only by the contribution limits imposed by the maximum amount rules. Thus, safe harbor contributions (matching or nonelective) operate as a toll charge for permission to favor highly paid workers in the amount saved for retirement to a degree that would otherwise be wholly unacceptable. Selling indulgences has no doubt increased the popularity of 401(k) plans precisely because it so seriously undermines the redistributive objective of the qualified plan system. While the nondiscrimination rules are admittedly a crude device for targeting the tax subsidy, decoupling the level of obligatory savings on behalf of rank-and-file workers from the amount that executives and highly paid professionals want to save guarantees that much of the subsidy will be wasted rather than redirected to low-paid employees who would not save on their own.

An alternative safe harbor permits a 401(k) plan to include an automatic contribution arrangement under which eligible employees initially defer by default at least 3 percent of pay, and must elect out of participation to receive their full compensation in cash or contribute a lesser amount.[191] The default automatic minimum deferral rate increases in 1 percent increments each succeeding plan year until it reaches 6 percent or compensation.[192] Special notice and election-out requirements apply to such an automatic enrollment feature. Such automatic contribution arrangements are exempt from the ADP test if the employer makes nonelective contributions of 3 percent of compensation or matches employee deferrals at the rate of 100 percent for the first 1 percent of pay and 50 percent for deferrals between 1 and 6 percent of pay.[193]

---

year) and then only if it is the only qualified plan of the employer. *Id.* §§ 401(k)(11)(A), (k)(11)(C), (k)(11)(D)(i), 408(p)(2)(C)(i).

[189] I.R.C. § 401(k)(12)(A)(i), (k)(12)(D) (West Supp. 2020).

[190] I.R.C. § 401(k)(12)(F) (West Supp. 2020). *See* H.R Rep. No. 116-65, Part 1, at 46–49 (2019).

[191] I.R.C. § 401(k)(13) (2018). Some companies introduced automatic enrollment features before the enactment of the statutory safe harbor. The number of 401(k) plans with automatic enrollment increased rapidly between 2004 and 2007. Alicia H. Munnell et al., *An Update on 401(k) Plans: Insights from the 2007 SCF*, at 3 (2009), https://crr.bc.edu/an-update-on-401k-plans-insights-from-the-2007-scf/.

[192] A plan may call for higher default deferral rates than the required minimum described in the text, up to a maximum of 10 percent the first year of default participation and 15 percent thereafter. I.R.C. § 401(k)(13)(C)(iii) (West Supp. 2020).

[193] I.R.C. § 401(k)(13)(D) (2018). Reasonable administrative errors in implementing such an automatic enrollment or automatic escalation feature may be corrected retroactively if specified conditions are satisfied. *Id.* § 414(cc) (West Supp. 2023). Automatic contribution

Taxes and Retirement Saving 379

The newest safe harbor alternative to the ADP test deserves special attention for its breadth and policy implications. Code section 401(k)(16), enacted in 2022, authorizes a new type of plan design, the starter 401(k) deferral-only arrangement (hereafter, "starter 401(k) plan").[194] A starter 401(k) plan is an automatic enrollment cash-or-deferred arrangement that satisfies certain requirements relating to contributions, employer eligibility and employee notices.[195] Contributions must be made for each eligible employee who does not elect out in an amount equal to a uniform percentage of compensation that is not less than 3 percent nor greater than 15 percent (unless the employee affirmatively elects a different contribution level).[196] Importantly, to be eligible to offer the plan the employer must not maintain another qualified plan under which contributions are made or benefits accrued for service during the year, and no employer matching or nonelective contributions are permitted under a starter 401(k) plan.[197] Contributions are subject to an annual dollar limit of $6,000 ($7,000 in the case of an employee who has attained age fifty before the close of the year), inflation indexed.[198] Observe that the starter IRA contribution limits are aligned with IRA contribution limits.[199] That correspondence is revealing: the starter 401(k) plan is apparently intended to function much like an employer-sponsored auto-enrollment IRA program.[200] State-run auto-IRA programs have proliferated since 2017.[201] Starter 401(k) plans differ from state auto-IRA programs in several important respects: (1) employer participation in a starter

arrangements are also provided a safe harbor under ERISA's fiduciary duty rules. ERISA § 404 (c)(5), 29 U.S.C. § 1104(c)(5) (2018); 29 C.F.R. § 2550.404c–5 (2016). *See supra* Chapter 4D.

[194] SECURE 2.0 Act of 2022, Pub. L. No. 117-328, Div. T, § 121, 136 Stat. 4459, ____ (2023) (effective for plan years beginning after 2023).

[195] I.R.C. § 401(k)(16)(B) (West Supp. 2023). Congress also authorized a "starter" 403(b) plan for employees of public schools and tax-exempt charitable organizations, granting a nondiscrimination safe harbor to plans providing only elective deferrals, and subject to conditions corresponding to those governing starter 401(k) plans. *Id.* § 403(b)(16).

[196] *Id.* § 401(k)(16)(C). It is unclear whether an affirmative election could specify a higher contribution level than the uniform "qualified percentage" set by the plan. The safe harbor substitutes for the ADP test, § 401(a)(16)(A), which functions as an amount nondiscrimination standard. Allowing affirmative contributions at rates greater than the uniform qualified percentage arguably conflicts with core antidiscrimination norms.

[197] I.R.C. § 401(k)(16)(D)(i)(I), (k)(16)(E)(i) (West Supp. 2023).

[198] *Id.* § 401(k)(16)(D).

[199] *See* I.R.C. § 219(b)(5) (2018 & West Supp. 2023). The alignment is imperfect because the limit on IRA contributions rose to $6,500 in 2023, IRS Notice 2022-55, 2022-45 I.R.B. 443, 444, while the starter 401(k) plan dollar limit for 2024 is set at $6,000, with inflation indexing in subsequent years. I.R.C. § 401(a)(16)(D)(ii) (West Supp. 2023).

[200] As introduced, the bills proposing starter 401(k) plans did not track IRAs so closely. They would have allowed an employer maintaining a starter 401(k) plan to continue the arrangement even if the employer maintained another qualified plan in a subsequent year and would also have permitted larger catch-up contributions for employees over age fifty. Starter-K Act of 2022, S. 3955, 117th Cong., § 2 (Mar. 30, 2022); H.R. 8125, 117th Cong., § 2 (June 16, 2022).

[201] For an overview of state-sponsored auto-IRA programs, see AARP, State Facilitated Retirement Savings Interactive Map, at www.aarp.org/ppi/state-retirement-plans/savings-plans/; Kathryn L. Moore, *State Automatic Enrollment IRAs after the Trump Election: Are They Preempted by*

401(k) plan is voluntary and brings ERISA into play, including investment responsibilities and fiduciary obligations;[202] and (2) default contributions to an employee's account (treated as deemed elective deferrals) apparently receive pre-tax rather than after-tax (Roth-style) treatment.[203] Starter 401(k) plans can be viewed as a nudge to get employees who are not covered by a qualified plan to open and contribute to an IRA, and from that perspective the initiative appears unobjectionable. If in the future the dollar limit on contributions were stricken or substantially relaxed, however, that apparently unexceptional technical change would open a path around the nondiscrimination rules, and likely spell the end of the central redistributive function of qualified plans.[204]

C LIMITING THE TAX SUBSIDY

In addition to nondiscrimination, which attempts to direct the tax subsidy into additional retirement savings for low-income workers, other tax controls limit the amount of the tax subsidy. These limitations fall into three broad categories: the maximum amount rule, advance funding limits, and distribution timing constraints.

Maximum Amount Rule

The Code caps the amount of tax-subsidized retirement savings that an employer can provide to an employee. To be qualified, the annual benefit of each participant under all defined benefit plans of the employer cannot exceed the smaller of $160,000 indexed for inflation ($265,000 in 2023) or 100 percent of the participant's average compensation for his high three years, where "annual benefit" is defined as the amount of a straight-life annuity commencing between ages sixty-two and sixty-five under a plan that provides no ancillary benefits and that is solely employer-funded (no employee contributions).[205] For a defined contribution plan, the annual addition to a participant's account in any year under all defined contribution plans of the employer is limited to the smaller of $40,000 indexed for inflation ($66,000 in 2023) or 100 percent of the participant's compensation, where "annual addition" is defined as the sum of employer contributions, forfeitures, and (after-tax) employee

---

ERISA?, 27 ELDER L.J. 51, 54–60 (2019); John Chalmers et al., *Do State-Sponsored Retirement Plans Boost Retirement Saving?*, 112 AEA PAPERS & PROC. 142 (2022).

[202] *See* ERISA § 3(2)(A), 29 U.S.C. § 1002(2)(A) (2018); 29 C.F.R. § 2510.3-2(d), -2(f) (2022) (defining employer involvement sufficient to trigger application of ERISA Title I).

[203] Compare I.R.C. § 402(e)(3), (g)(1) (2018) *with* Or. Rev. Stat. §§ 178.210(1), 178.215 (2015), Or. Admin. R. 178-80-0030(1)(d) (2021) (default contributions made to Roth IRA).

[204] *See supra* text accompanying Chapter 10 notes 69–75.

[205] I.R.C. §§ 401(a)(16), 415(a), (b), (f) (2018); IRS Notice 2022-55, 2022-45 I.R.B. 443 (inflation adjustment).

Taxes and Retirement Saving

contributions allocated to the account for the year.[206] The maximum amount rule proceeds from the intuitively appealing principle that "it is appropriate to provide some limitation of corporate pensions out of tax-sheltered dollars which are swollen completely out of proportion to the reasonable needs of individuals for a dignified level of retirement income."[207]

The maximum amount rule is closely related to nondiscrimination. The clearest connection is the compensation cap of Code section 401(a)(17), which provides that the maximum annual compensation that can be taken into account under a qualified plan is $200,000, indexed for inflation ($330,000 in 2023).[208] The compensation cap functions as the link between amount nondiscrimination and the maximum amount of contributions or benefits that may be provided under a qualified plan. Without such a cap, employers could offer their very highly paid executives the maximum amount of tax-subsidized savings while providing only trivial amounts to low- and middle-income workers. For example, the maximum permissible annual addition to an employee's account under a defined contribution plan is $61,000 in 2022. Absent the compensation cap, an executive earning $5 million would receive the maximum permissible employer contribution under a plan calling for uniform contributions at a rate of about 1 percent (specifically, 1.22 percent) of compensation, but such a plan would generate a contribution of only $366 for a rank-and-file employee earning $30,000. Faced with such gigantic disparities in compensation, the proportional amount rule would force insignificant redistribution. With the compensation cap, in contrast, an employer must be willing to offer a 20 percent contribution rate to maximize the executive's savings, which would yield a $6,000 contribution for the rank-and-file employee.

In combination, the maximum amount rule and the compensation cap put some teeth in amount nondiscrimination. Yet from another perspective, the maximum amount rule is founded on a fallacy, and in some circumstances may be deeply discordant with nondiscrimination policy. The fallacy is the premise that generous pensions for corporate executives are necessarily paid "out of tax-sheltered dollars." If the nondiscrimination rules are operating as intended, then executives do not get the tax subsidy; it is instead shifted to pensions for lower-paid workers. Far from being tax-sheltered, in that event, qualified retirement savings for highly paid

---

[206] I.R.C. § 415(a), (c), (f)(1)(B) (2018); IRS Notice 2022-55, 2022-45 I.R.B. 443 (inflation adjustment). *See generally* Martin Fireproofing Profit-Sharing Plan and Trust v. Comm'r, 92 T.C. 1173 (1989).

[207] H.R. REP. NO. 93-807, at 112 (1974), *reprinted in* 2 ERISA LEGISLATIVE HISTORY, *supra* Chapter 1 note 55, at 3115, 3232. The maximum amount rules proved to be the most contentious element of comprehensive pension reform legislation in the Senate. The political controversy surrounded where to draw the line between dignified and excessive levels of tax-subsidized retirement income. William M. Lieber, *An IRS Insider's View of ERISA*, 65 TAX NOTES 751 (1994); *see* Wiedenbeck, *supra* Chapter 10 note 95, at 522–27 (§ 415 grew out of efforts to limit use of pension plans as tax shelter by professionals and small business owners).

[208] I.R.C. § 401(a)(17) (2018); IRS Notice 2022-55, 2022-45 I.R.B. 443 (inflation adjustment).

workers bear an implicit tax that largely captures the benefit of tax deferral and transforms it into higher compensation for rank-and-file employees. Indeed, if the nondiscrimination rules worked optimally, a CEO's \$3 million pension would not be tax preferred because he would have paid for the full value of tax deferral during his working years through a reduction in other forms of compensation. If we limit the CEO's pension to \$265,000 (the 2023 defined benefit plan dollar limit), then we reduce by a factor of eleven the tax benefits available for redistribution to low-paid workers who cannot afford to save on their own.[209] The extent of tax deferral available to high-income savers, in other words, fixes the extent of possible redistribution. We have seen that the efficacy of the nondiscrimination rules depends upon tax rates and workforce composition,[210] and so we should be concerned that capping executives' qualified plan savings will make it uneconomic for some companies to sponsor a plan. In a workforce containing a high proportion of low-paid reluctant savers, the cost of securing sufficient participation by NHCEs to meet nondiscrimination standards may far exceed the compensation cost saving that can be extracted under current law from the few HCEs, and so the employer will make no provision for retirement savings for the rank-and-file. In contrast, if tax-deferred retirement savings by the few HCEs were not confined within the limits set by the maximum amount rule, the tax subsidy associated with increased saving by the HCEs might be sufficient to fund broad coverage. In such situations the maximum amount rule works at cross purposes with nondiscrimination, and actually prevents the establishment of a qualified plan that would benefit low- and middle-income workers. Tax savings at the top supply the fuel that drives the redistributive pump, and by constricting the fuel supply, Code section 415 sometimes shuts down the flow.

Is the maximum amount rule so misguided that it ought to be repealed? That response would be too simplistic. Despite prevailing constraints, many companies sponsor qualified plans (particularly large and mid-sized employers), and at any given time, about half of the American labor force is covered. The current tax subsidy is adequate to fund these existing programs. Because they now satisfy nondiscrimination requirements, uncapping tax-deferred savings by HCEs would not by itself force any additional redistribution – instead of being shifted to employees who would not otherwise save for retirement, the increased subsidy would simply benefit the employer or its HCE-savers. In other words, for plans currently in place,

---

[209] During debate on ERISA, Senator Gaylord Nelson asserted that "it is absurd to maintain that only by allowing highly paid corporate executives such lavish annual pensions will large corporations be willing to establish plans covering most of their workers. I believe that even the highest paid corporate executive would find some value in a much more modest annual pension." 119 CONG. REC. 30,132 (Sept. 18, 1973), *reprinted in* 2 ERISA LEGISLATIVE HISTORY, *supra* Chapter 1 note 55, at 1712. The defect in this reasoning is that, while the executive would find some value in a modest pension, that value might not be large enough to make it worthwhile for the corporation to sponsor a plan due to the high costs imposed by the nondiscrimination requirements.

[210] *See supra* text accompanying Figure 10.2.

Taxes and Retirement Saving 383

the maximum amount rule at least limits the extent of wasted revenue, even though it may block all redistribution within other firms that employ a different mix of personnel. When an intuitively appealing but inflexible anti-abuse rule operates in tandem with a crude redistribution regime, the results are bound to be imperfect.

Yet even if it were justified in principle, the maximum amount rule is deeply flawed in execution. Two defects are especially pernicious. First, the defined benefit and defined contribution plan limits are incomparable and therefore uncoordinated. The defined benefit plan limit is quite logically tied to the life annuity value of retirement savings, but instead of being similarly distribution-based, the defined contribution plan limit restricts the money going into the participant's account rather than the money going out. While simpler to apply, an annual contribution-based limit has no necessary connection to the eventual level of retirement support. A highly paid employee can accumulate far greater qualified retirement savings if she is covered under a defined contribution plan for most of her career than would be permissible if she were under a defined benefit plan for a prolonged period.[211] To be consistent, the defined contribution plan limit should be tied to the projected benefits that the participant's account balance would yield. If a simpler approach that avoids actuarial computation is desired, the limit should at least be geared to the cumulative *total* additions (contributions and forfeitures) allocated to the participant's account to date, rather than to the annual addition for the current year.

The second defect permits an employee to receive both the maximum annual addition under a defined contribution plan and the maximum annual benefit under a defined benefit plan if he is covered under plans of both types. ERISA originally prevented such double-dipping by imposing a combined limit,[212] but Congress repealed the combined limit in 1996, ostensibly as a simplification measure.[213]

---

[211] Using the dollar limits applicable in 2023, for example, a defined contribution plan participant who received annual employer contributions to her account of $66,000 for thirty years beginning at age thirty-five would have an account balance of $5.37 million at age sixty-five, assuming an annual rate of return of 6.0 percent. That accumulation is equivalent to the value of a twenty-year term-certain annuity of about $361,000, assuming that the annuity credits an internal rate of interest of 3 percent. (The average unisex life expectancy at age sixty-five is about twenty years.) In contrast, the defined benefit plan limit for 2023 is $265,000. IRS Notice 2022-55, 2022-45 I.R.B. 443. The disparity increases if the yield on the defined contribution plan is higher.

[212] I.R.C. § 415(e) (1994) (repealed 1996). For an account of the curious origins of the combined limit, see Lieber, *supra* Chapter 10 note 207.

[213] H.R. REP. NO. 104-280, pt. 2, at 417–19 (1995) (combined limit called "one of the most significant sources of complexity relating to qualified pension plans" and an unnecessary deterrent to plan sponsorship). The Clinton Administration went along with the repeal of the combined limit, apparently because it felt that the separate limits were adequately backstopped by I.R.C. § 4980A, which imposed a 15 percent excise tax on the amount by which aggregate annual distributions from all tax-favored retirement savings programs exceeded $155,000 (in 1996 dollars). In 1997, however, Congress proceeded to repeal the section 4980A excise tax. *See* Norman P. Stein, *Simplification and IRC § 415*, 2 FLA. TAX REV. 69 (1994). For background on the former excise tax, see Bruce Wolk, *The New Excise and Estate*

384 Tax Controls: Qualified Retirement Savings

An additional maximum amount rule applies to 401(k) plans and 403(b) tax-sheltered annuities (available to employees of public schools and tax-exempt charitable organizations). While the section 415(c) overall limit on annual additions to defined contribution plans (i.e., the smaller of 100 percent of compensation or $40,000, indexed for inflation) applies to these programs, elective deferrals under such plans are subject to an independent limit of $15,000 (indexed to $22,500 for 2023).[214] An employee making the maximum elective deferral who is age fifty or older is allowed to defer up to an additional $5,000 per year (indexed to $7,500 for 2023), and these so-called catch-up contributions are permitted even if they would otherwise exceed the annual addition limit of section 415(c).[215] The limit on catch-up contributions is doubled for participants aged sixty to sixty-three in 2025.[216] Starting in 2024, however, participants earning more than $145,000 from the employer sponsoring the plan are allowed to make catch-up contributions only if their additional elective deferrals are designated Roth contributions.[217]

Before 2002, the general limit on elective deferrals was set much lower, at $7,000, and catch-up contributions were not permitted. That historically lower elective deferral limit reflected the original congressional view that cash-or-deferred arrangements should serve as supplementary programs offering workers the option to save more than the amount provided under a nonelective employer-funded qualified retirement plan (traditionally a defined benefit plan). The dramatic increase in the elective deferral limit reflects (and reinforces) the trend toward 401(k) plans becoming the primary or sole retirement savings programs for many employers. Rather than

---

Taxes on Excess Retirement Plan Distributions and Accumulations, 9 U. FLA. L. REV. 987 (1987).

    Besides the former combined limit on contributions and benefits, I.R.C. § 415(e) (1994) (repealed 1996), a combined limit on deductible contributions may apply to an employer that sponsors one or more defined benefit pension plans and one or more defined contribution plans if at least one employee is covered under both types of plans. I.R.C. § 404(a)(7)(A), (a)(7)(C)(i) (2018). Despite its long history, that final brake on double dipping was largely removed by the Pension Protection Act of 2006, which exempted PBGC-insured defined benefit plans from the combined limit. *Id.* § 404(a)(7)(C)(iv). If the defined benefit plan is not insured (as in the case of a plan maintained by a professional service employer that has never had more than 25 active participants, see ERISA § 4021(b)(13), 29 U.S.C. § 1321(b)(13) (2018)), the employer can still deduct contributions of up to 6 percent of compensation under a defined contribution plan regardless of combined limit. I.R.C. § 404(a)(7)(C)(iii) (2018).

[214] I.R.C. §§ 401(a)(3), 402(e)(3), (g)(1) (2018); IRS Notice 2022-55, 2022-45 I.R.B. 443.

[215] I.R.C. §§ 402(g)(1)(C), 414(v)(2), (v)(3)(A) (2018). The combination of other elective deferrals and catch-up contributions cannot exceed the participant's compensation, *id.* § 414(v)(2)(A), and so the exemption of catch-up contributions from the limit on annual additions under defined contribution plans has the effect of raising only the section 415(c) dollar limit ($66,000 for 2023). It is the dollar limit that affects middle- and upper-income employees.

[216] I.R.C. § 414(v)(2)(B), (v)(2)(E) (West Supp. 2023).

[217] *Id.* § 414(v)(7). Moreover, if the plan fails to allow participants to make Roth-style catch-up contributions (i.e., does not include a qualified Roth contribution program as defined by § 402A), then no participant is permitted to make any catch-up contribution. *Id.*

Taxes and Retirement Saving

supplementing other programs, today, 401(k) plans frequently substitute for other qualified retirement plans.[218]

Advance Funding Limits

The maximum amount rule, insofar as it is justified,[219] prevents wasted revenue by limiting the amount of tax subsidy associated with savings by HCEs in situations where the nondiscrimination rules would not force redistribution of the subsidy. Tax deferral is the basis of the qualified plan subsidy, and the value of deferral is a function of three factors: the amount of income (here compensation) that escapes current taxation, the tax rate that would apply to that income, and the duration of deferral. The maximum amount rule cabins the subsidy by limiting the amount of compensation eligible for deferral. Alternatively, the extent of the tax subsidy can be controlled by adjusting the duration of deferral. The period of deferral is the time between the employer's deduction of deferred compensation and inclusion of distributions in the recipient's income. The tax Code (perhaps not surprisingly) contains rules that restrict both the beginning and the end of the deferral period. Limits on advance funding prevent the employer from deducting qualified deferred compensation too early, while certain distribution timing rules prohibit employees from delaying distributions for too long.

Subject to certain limits, the employer receives a current deduction for amounts actually contributed to a qualified retirement plan.[220] Prompt payment is required, according to the Supreme Court, because "an objective outlay-of-assets test" ensures "the integrity of the employees' plan and insure[s] the full advantage of any contribution which entitles the employer to a tax benefit."[221] If payment in cash or in-kind were all that was needed to secure the deduction, however, employers could greatly inflate the tax subsidy and shift most of the cost of deferred compensation onto the taxpaying public simply by contributing to a qualified trust sooner, thereby providing a longer accumulation period so that a larger share of future distributions will consist of exempt earnings. Egregious abuses are prevented by the requirement that qualified plan contributions must be "otherwise ... deductible" under the tax Code, which typically means that they must qualify as an ordinary and

---

[218] *See infra* Figure 10.4 and Chapter 10 note 229.

[219] Uncertainty on this point is explained *supra* text accompanying Chapter 10 notes 209–210.

[220] I.R.C. § 404(a)(1)–(3) (2018).

[221] Don E. Williams Co. v. Comm'r, 429 U.S. 569, 579 (1977) (footnote omitted) (accrual basis taxpayer's delivery of fully secured interest-bearing promissory notes to a qualified profit-sharing trust did not constitute payment and so did not qualify for deduction under Code section 404 (a)). Payment before the due date (including extensions) of the employer's tax return is treated as payment on the last day of the taxable year, I.R.C. § 404(a)(6) (2018), and this grace period gives the employer time to gather the data necessary to determine the maximum deductible contribution for the year. *Don E. Williams*, 429 U.S. at 575.

386   *Tax Controls: Qualified Retirement Savings*

necessary business expense.[222] Because the business expense deduction is limited to reasonable compensation for services actually rendered, the employer cannot deduct contributions to a qualified trust made before the employee earns the deferred compensation.[223] But what of a plan that heavily frontloads contributions or benefits? Suppose that a profit-sharing plan provides contributions equal to 100 percent of current compensation for each of an employee's first five years of service, and nothing thereafter? Such contributions are earned by contemporaneous service and would not exceed the current limit set by the maximum amount rule for lower-paid employees. Yet if such frontloaded contributions are invested for twenty or thirty years or longer, an exorbitant share (easily three-quarters or more) of the eventual retirement income distributions would be composed of trust earnings.[224] To prevent such raids on the fisc, Code section 404 imposes limits on the amount allowable as a deduction for contributions to a qualified trust. Contributions in excess of the deduction limit can theoretically be carried forward and deducted in a subsequent year, but practically they are strongly discouraged by a 10 percent penalty tax on nondeductible contributions.[225]

For profit-sharing and stock bonus plans the limit on contributions paid by the employer (under all such plans) is now 25 percent of the compensation otherwise paid or accrued during the taxable year to beneficiaries under such plans.[226] Before 2002, the deduction limit for profit-sharing and stock bonus plans had been set at 15 percent of covered compensation, but if the employer also sponsored a money purchase pension plan (which is a type of defined contribution plan), a combined limit of 25 percent applied.[227] Consequently, deductible contributions of up to

---

[222] I.R.C. § 404(a)(1) (2018) (introductory clause).

[223] I.R.C. § 162(a)(1) (2018). Under general tax timing rules prepaid compensation is a capital expenditure, *id.* § 263, and so would be nondeductible even absent language limiting the business expense deduction to reasonable compensation for services actually rendered.

[224] Invested at a compound annual rate of return of 6 percent, a contribution would quadruple in value in less than twenty-four years. Of course, trust earnings might be higher or the accumulation period longer, and either factor would magnify the effect.

[225] I.R.C. § 404(a)(1)(E), (a)(3)(A)(ii) (2018) (carry forward of excess contributions to pension trusts, and profit-sharing or stock bonus trusts, respectively), *id.* § 4972 (excise tax).

[226] I.R.C. § 404(a)(3)(A) (2018). The compensation cap imposed by section 410(a)(17) ($330,000 for 2023) and the maximum amount rule are applied in computing the deduction limit. *Id.* § 404(j), (*l*).

[227] I.R.C. § 404(a)(3)(A)(i)(I) (2000) (amended 2001), § 404(a)(7)(A)(i) (2018). The 25 percent limit applied to the combination of a money purchase pension plan and a profit-sharing or stock bonus plan because, although it is a defined contribution program, for tax purposes a money purchase plan is classified as a pension plan. Consequently, before 2002, contributions to a money purchase plan were deductible under the pension plan limit of Code section 404(a) (1), rather than under the profit-sharing and stock bonus plan limit of section 404(a)(3). (Recall that money purchase pension plans, unlike profit-sharing and stock bonus plans, are subject to ERISA's minimum funding standards (*supra* Chapter 9A), and so a deduction for the amount of contributions necessary to satisfy the minimum funding standard was allowed by section 404 (a)(1)(A)(i).) The 2001 legislation that increased the limit on deductible contributions from 15 to 25 percent for profit-sharing and stock bonus plans also added I.R.C. § 404(a)(3)(A)(v)

15 percent of covered compensation could be made under the profit-sharing plan (which could be a 401(k) plan) along with deductible annual contributions of 10 percent of pay under the money purchase plan. Once the deduction limit for profit-sharing and stock bonus plans was raised to 25 percent, employers could make the maximum deductible contribution under a profit-sharing plan standing alone; no greater tax benefit could be secured by also sponsoring a money purchase pension plan covering the same workers. In a dramatic demonstration of the force of tax deferral, between 2001 and 2006, the number of money purchase plans declined by 72 percent, as shown in Figure 10.4. This amendment, along with the contemporaneous increase in the elective deferral limit discussed earlier,[228] has no doubt contributed to the recent widespread transformation of 401(k) plans from their former limited role as supplementary savings arrangements to their current exalted status as the exclusive qualified retirement savings program provided by many employers.[229]

From the standpoint of retirement income security, the recent rapid decline in prevalence of money purchase pension plans seems undesirable. To reduce administrative costs, an employer wishing to make the maximum deductible retirement saving contribution would understandably prefer to do so under one plan rather than two. But a money purchase pension plan is the simplest qualified plan and hence the cheapest to maintain (lowest administrative cost). The virtual demise of money purchase plans following the increase in the deduction limit for profit-sharing and stock bonus plans indicates a strong sponsor preference for the latter program types. That preference stems from two factors: benefit cost and funding flexibility. Profit-sharing and stock bonus plans may include a qualified cash-or-deferred arrangement allowing partial funding via elective salary-reduction contributions. The special nondiscrimination rules applicable to 401(k) plans (the ADP test and the safe harbors for minimum matching or nonelective contributions) may in some instances require less redistribution and so entail lower benefit cost than the

---

(2018) and the parenthetical clause in section 404(a)(1)(A), which make contributions to a money purchase plan subject to the deduction limit applicable to profit-sharing and stock bonus plans rather than the limit for defined benefit pension plans.

[228] I.R.C. § 402(g)(1) (2018). *See supra* text accompanying Chapter 10 notes 214–218.

[229] In 2020, 94 percent of 401(k) plans were the only pension plan of the sponsoring employer, and 76 percent of all active participants in 401(k) plans worked for an employer that sponsored no other pension plan. EMPLOYEE BENEFITS SECURITY ADMINISTRATION, PRIVATE PENSION PLAN BULLETIN: ABSTRACT OF 2020 FORM 5500 ANNUAL REPORTS, Table D3, D4 (2022). Craig Copeland, *Retirement Plan Participation: Survey of Income and Program Participation (SIPP) Data, 2006*, 30 EBRI NOTES 6–7 (2009) (in 2006 more than 30 percent of nonagricultural wage and salary workers over age sixteen had a 401(k) plan as their primary retirement savings program, up from 17.4 percent in 1993 and 7.5 percent in 1988). From the standpoint of retirement income adequacy, many experts are troubled by this development. E.g., Munnell, *supra* Chapter 10 note 191, at 10 (2009) ("The time may have come to consider returning 401(k) plans to their original position as a third tier on top of Social Security and employer-sponsored pensions.").

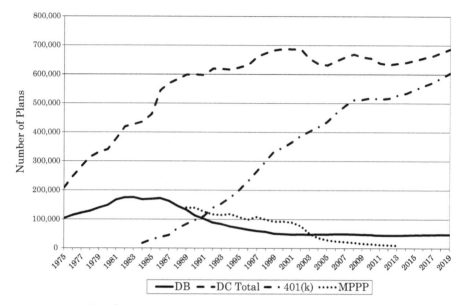

FIGURE 10.4 Number of private pension plans, 1975–2019. By type: DB, DC, 401(k) & MPPP*

* DB = defined benefit; DC = defined contribution; 401(k) = plan containing cash-or-deferred arrangement; MPPP = money purchase pension plan. DC Total includes the number of 401(k) plans and MPPPs each year (graphed separately) as well as other varieties of DC plans.

Source: Employee Benefits Security Administration (EBSA), US Department of Labor, Private Pension Plan Bulletin Historical Tables and Graphs 1975–2019, Tables E1, E7 & E19 (Sept. 2021) (for DB, DC Total and 401(k) data); EBSA, Private Pension Plan Bulletin: Abstract of Form 5500 Annual Reports, Table A1 (annually, 1989–2013) (for MPPP data).

rules applicable to money purchase pension plans.[230] Moreover, annual contributions to a profit-sharing or stock bonus plan are not required – they can be tied to profits or left to the discretion of the employer, which permits reductions in the event the sponsor encounters cash flow problems.[231] A money purchase pension plan, in contrast, entails a contractual commitment to make specified annual contributions (usually a stated percentage of each participant's current compensation). That commitment can be enforced by a suit brought by participants (or, in certain circumstances, by the Labor Department) to remedy a breach of ERISA's minimum funding standards, and so is relatively inflexible.[232] Thus, the lower deduction limit formerly applicable to profit-sharing and stock bonus plans

---

[230] See supra text accompanying Chapter 10 notes 178–193.
[231] See supra Chapter 1A.
[232] ERISA §§ 301(a)(8) (minimum funding rules apply to money purchase pension plans but not other individual account plans), 302(a)(2)(B) (minimum funding standard for single-employer

encouraged employers to provide a portion of each worker's retirement savings in a form (i.e., a money purchase pension) that was less susceptible to cutbacks in difficult economic times. Removing the incentive to provide nondiscretionary baseline savings under a money purchase plan increases the risk that rank-and-file employees will not accumulate sufficient resources for retirement.

The deduction limit applicable to contributions to defined benefit pension plans has similarly been shaped by efforts to control the amount of the qualified retirement plan tax subsidy by limiting excessive prefunding. Consider a unit credit plan that promises an annuity commencing at age sixty-five equal to 1 percent of final average compensation per year of service. Upon hiring a thirty-five-year-old, can the employer deduct an immediate contribution to the plan equal to the present value of 30 percent of the employee's projected final compensation, or must the pension be funded by annual contributions over the new employee's career? Lump-sum advance funding would allow employer contributions to accumulate trust earnings over a longer period, thereby increasing tax deferral and shifting more of the cost of the pension to other taxpayers. Immediate deduction of the present value of the total projected pension cost is obviously inappropriate under a unit credit plan because most of the pension is still unearned, and prepayments or reserves for future expenses are not ordinarily deductible. But what about a flat benefit plan that promises each participant an annuity at age sixty-five of 30 percent of final average compensation without regard to length of service? In this case, a legal obligation accrues upon admission to plan membership, and so an immediate contribution funding the total projected pension cost is arguably deductible.[233] Even in the case of a unit credit plan, substantial (albeit not complete) prefunding of unearned benefits was formerly possible due to the flexibility ERISA originally allowed in the plan's choice of actuarial funding method. Under certain actuarial funding methods (known as cost allocation actuarial methods), the projected total future benefit cost could be allocated between years of service as either a level dollar amount or a fixed percentage of pay, regardless of the rate at which benefits are

---

money purchase pension plan is satisfied if the employer makes the contributions required under the terms of the plan), 502(a)(3), (5) (civil action may be brought to redress violations of ERISA or enforce terms of plan), 29 U.S.C. §§ 1081(a)(8), 1082(a)(2)(B), 1132(a)(3), (5) (2018); see I.R.C. § 412(a)(2)(B), (e)(2) (2018) (tax-law funding rules do not apply to profit-sharing or stock bonus plans). As discussed in Chapter 9A, the minimum funding rules do contain several relief provisions (e.g., waiver in cases of temporary substantial business hardship) that might relax the obligation to contribute to a money purchase plan in exigent circumstances.

[233] *Compare* Jerome Mirza & Assocs. v. United States, 882 F.2d 229 (7th Cir. 1989) (deduction for full cost of immediate prefunding under flat benefit plan disallowed), *with* Citrus Valley Estates, Inc. v. Comm'r, 49 F.3d 1410 (9th Cir. 1995) (immediate deduction of full cost allowed). Under I.R.C. § 415(b)(5) (2018), the dollar limit on defined benefit pensions is now phased in over ten years of *plan participation* (prior to 1986, the phase-in was based on years of service with the employer), which prevents colossal upfront funding of the sort achieved in *Citrus Valley.*

390   *Tax Controls: Qualified Retirement Savings*

actually earned each year under the plan's definition of accrued benefit. Compared to the cost of funding the benefits actually earned each year (known as the benefit allocation actuarial method), level funding required by the cost allocation methods calls for larger contributions in the early years of an employee's plan participation, which has the effect of partially prefunding benefits to be earned in later years of service. That partial prefunding led to concerns about excessive subsidy, to which Congress responded in 1987 by tightening the full funding limit on the employer's contribution deduction.[234]

The Pension Protection Act of 2006 revamped the funding rules and eliminated choice in actuarial funding methods for single-employer defined benefit plans. The minimum funding obligation for single-employer plans is now specified by reference to the funding target and target normal cost for the plan year, and those quantities are determined by the present value of all benefits earned under the plan as of the beginning of the plan year, or expected to be earned during the plan year (respectively).[235] This approach rules out cost allocation actuarial funding methods, which are the level funding methods that permitted substantial prefunding of benefits not yet earned. The maximum deductible contribution is linked to the minimum funding obligation and therefore is also tied to benefits earned to date, which largely precludes excessive subsidization.[236] Congress recognized, however, that there is a trade-off between benefit security, which militates in favor of permitting or even encouraging a certain amount of overfunding, and cost-containment, which supports strict limits on prefunding unearned benefits. To accommodate these competing objectives, the employer is allowed to deduct, in addition to the amount necessary to fully fund all benefits earned during the current and previous plan years, an extra "cushion amount."[237] The cushion amount is defined as (1) one-half of the funding target (i.e., the present value of benefits earned under the plan as of the start of the plan year) plus (2) the amount by which the funding target would increase if the benefits already earned were determined with reference to expected future increases in employee compensation (as where plan benefits are based on final average compensation, for example).[238]

---

[234] I.R.C. § 404(a)(1)(A) (2006) (final sentence as in effect for taxable years beginning before 2008), *id.* § 412(c)(7) (as in effect for taxable years beginning before 2008). H.R. REP. NO. 100-391, pt. II, at 1117–18 (1987) explained:

> "The committee does not believe … that an employer should be entitled to make excessive contributions to a defined benefit pension plan to fund liabilities that it has not yet incurred. Such use of a defined benefit plan is equivalent to a tax-free savings account for future liabilities and is inconsistent generally with the treatment of unaccrued liabilities under the Code." *See* U.S. DEPARTMENT OF THE TREASURY, REPORT TO THE CONGRESS ON THE EFFECT OF THE FULL FUNDING LIMIT ON PENSION BENEFIT SECURITY 4–5 (1991) (study of the impact of the 1987 restrictions on prefunding).

[235] I.R.C. §§ 412(a)(2)(A), 430(a), (b), (c)(1)-(4), (d)(1) (2018). *See supra* Chapter 9A.

[236] I.R.C. § 404(o) (2018).

[237] *Id.* § 404(o)(2)(A).

[238] *Id.* § 404(o)(3). Ordinarily, compensation increases are not anticipated regardless of how reliably they can be projected. Instead, they are taken into account as an increase in target

Distribution Timing

It was noted earlier that ERISA has little to say about the timing of pension plan distributions. Instead, the tasks of discouraging pre-retirement distributions and preventing excessive deferral were left almost entirely to the tax law (see *supra* Chapter 8A). The qualified plan rules have much to say about distribution timing, and with respect to both early and late distributions, two distinct though related policies are in play. First, Congress has sought to target the tax subsidy so as to encourage *retirement* savings, as opposed to savings for other objectives, whether for precautionary purposes, education, home ownership, or bequests. Second, the distribution timing rules also function to influence the *amount* of the tax subsidy.

Late Distributions These dual objectives – controlling the purpose and amount of the tax subsidy – are readily apparent upon a review of the minimum distribution rule of Code section 401(a)(9). The minimum distribution rule forces qualified plans to pay out benefits, regardless of the participant's wishes, over a period that is roughly congruent with the time when most individuals need retirement income. Consequently, distributions cannot be delayed too long, ostensibly to avoid subsidizing intergenerational wealth transfers (bequests or inheritances). Of course, by establishing the maximum duration of accumulation, the minimum distribution rule also limits the duration of tax deferral and fixes the maximum amount of the tax subsidy. As such, it is the counterpart to the advance funding limits explored in the preceding section: the deduction limits set the earliest starting point for tax deferral, while the minimum distribution rule sets the latest endpoint.

Qualified pension, profit-sharing, stock bonus, and annuity plans must all comply with the minimum distribution rule described below, but its reach extends to most other forms of tax-preferred retirement savings, including 403(b) plans for employees of public schools and tax-exempt organizations, eligible deferred compensation plans of state and local governments and tax-exempt organizations, and traditional IRAs.[239] The minimum distribution rule also applies to Roth IRAs, but is relaxed by requiring no distributions while the Roth IRA owner is alive.[240] This breadth of

---

normal cost each year as they occur. *Id.* § 430(b)(2). Thus, the funding target and target normal cost under section 430 reflect termination-based legal liability (as did "current liability" used in the full funding limit of former section 412(c)(7), as in effect before 2008), rather than liability for accrued benefits determined on an ongoing or plan continuation basis. In the event of termination, accrued benefits would be determined based upon compensation history to the date of termination, *see* 29 C.F.R. § 4022.62(b)(2) (2022) (benefits not already in pay status computed according to participant's service and compensation on proposed termination date), while for an ongoing plan, future compensation increases may increase the value of benefits previously earned.

[239] I.R.C. § 401(a)(9) (2018) (pension, profit-sharing, and stock bonus plans); *id.* §§ 403(a)(1), 404 (a)(2) (qualified annuity plans); 403(b)(10) (tax-sheltered annuities); 457(b)(5), (d)(2) (government and exempt-organization plans); 408(a)(6), (b)(3) (individual retirement accounts and annuities).

[240] I.R.C. §§ 408A(c)(4) (West Supp. 2020).

application evinces a seriousness of purpose, as does the sanction for violation. In addition to possible plan disqualification, the minimum distribution rule is enforced by imposing on the payee a 25 percent penalty tax on the amount of any distribution shortfall, or 10 percent if the payee promptly discovers and corrects the shortfall[241]

Distributions must begin by April 1 of the year following the calendar year in which the employee attains age seventy-three or later retires.[242] If the employee's entire interest in the plan is not paid out by that time, then it must in general be distributed in fairly even annual amounts over a period that does not exceed the life (or life expectancy) of the participant, or the joint lives (or joint-life expectancies) of the participant and a designated beneficiary.[243]

Spreading payments over the lives of the participant and the participant's spouse assures both of them a reliable stream of retirement income, consistent with the objective of ERISA's spousal protections (survivor annuity requirements). But does joint-life payout make sense in the case of a non-spouse beneficiary? If an elderly participant selects his infant granddaughter as beneficiary, for example, payment over their joint lives or life expectancies could accomplish a large tax-subsidized intergenerational wealth transfer. Originally, Congress endeavored to curb this by directing the Treasury to develop rules that, instead of cutting short the allowable distribution period, forced more of the total amount to be distributed in the earlier part of that period, during the participant's lifetime.[244] Yet despite that reallocation, with proper planning a wealthy individual (i.e., someone who does not need tax-advantaged savings for retirement support) could obtain tax deferral extending beyond her lifetime by eighty years or more. (Financial planners referred to such

---

[241] I.R.C. § 4974(a), (e) (West Supp. 2023).

[242] For an individual who attains age seventy-four after 2033, the required beginning date becomes April 1 of the year following the calendar year the employee reaches age seventy-five or later retires. I.R.C. § 401(a)(9)(C) (West Supp. 2023). Distributions cannot be delayed past age seventy-three (or seventy-five) if the employee, even if not yet retired, is a 5 percent owner of the employer (as defined under the top-heavy plan rule, § 416(i)(1)(B)), or in the case of an IRA owner. Prior to 2020 the required beginning date was April 1 of the year following the calendar year in which the employee attained age 70½ or retired.

[243] I.R.C. § 401(a)(9)(A) (2018).

[244] I.R.C. § 401(a)(9)(A)(ii) (2018) provides that required distributions shall be made "in accordance with regulations." The regulations impose the "minimum distribution incidental benefit" (a/k/a MDIB) requirement. See id. § 401(a)(9)(G). The MDIB rules imposed a payout rate that forced most of the total distributions into the early years of the permissible distribution period, which is the time when the participant and his or her spouse are alive and can use retirement income. For defined benefit plans, if the employee elects to take distribution in the form of a joint and survivor annuity with a non-spouse beneficiary who is more than ten years younger, the amount payable under the survivor annuity is reduced below the level of the employee's benefit in order to prevent excessive deferral. The survivor benefit, expressed as a percentage of the benefit of the primary annuitant, is required to be smaller as the difference in the ages of the primary annuitant and the survivor annuitant become greater, but the minimum level is 52 percent. Treas. Reg. § 1.401(a)(9)-6 Q&A-2(c) (as amended in 2014); Prop. Treas. Reg. § 1.401(a)(9)-6(b)(2)(iii), 87 Fed. Reg. 10504, 10538 (Feb. 24, 2022).

Taxes and Retirement Saving

strategic choice of beneficiary as "stretch distributions" or a "stretch IRA.") Statutory amendments to the required minimum distribution (RMD) rules which took effect in 2020 curtail deferral much more aggressively by cutting back the permissible distribution period in many instances.[245] The revised RMD rules confine the payout period for defined contribution programs according to the identity of the participant's beneficiary, with different periods applying according to whether the beneficiary is: (1) the participant's spouse; (2) an "eligible" designated beneficiary; (3) a designated beneficiary who is not "eligible"; or (4) a beneficiary that is not a designated beneficiary.[246]

If the beneficiary of the employee is the individual's surviving spouse, distributions may be made over the life or life expectancy of the spouse.[247] If the employee dies before RMDs have begun and the surviving spouse is designated beneficiary then the spouse may elect to be treated as the employee for purposes of determining RMDs, distributions are not required to commence until the year in which the employee would have attained the applicable age for RMDs (rather than within one year of the employee's death), and if the spouse dies before distributions begin, the spouse is treated as the employee for purposes of determining the distribution period.[248]

An "eligible" designated beneficiary may also take distribution over life or life expectancy, beginning within one year of the employee's death. Where distribution is based on life expectancy, the distribution period generally is fixed at the employee's death and then reduced by one for each year that elapses after the year in which it is calculated. Post-2019, individuals eligible for life or life expectancy payouts are limited. In addition to the surviving spouse, the eligible category includes a designated beneficiary who is, as of the date of death of the employee, either disabled, chronically ill, or not more than ten years younger than the employee. Any interest remaining on the death of these non-spouse eligible beneficiaries (for example,

---

[245] The stringent deferral limits enacted in December 2019 notwithstanding, Congress waived the minimum distribution requirements applicable to 2020 without regard to whether the participant or account owner was adversely affected by the coronavirus pandemic. CARES Act, Pub. L. No. 116-136, § 2203, 134 Stat. 282, 343 (2020). That concession has been criticized as lacking any defensible policy justification, amounting to "alms for the affluent." Michael Doran, *Retirement Distributions during the Public Health Crisis*, 167 TAX NOTES FED. 1713, 1716 (June 8, 2020).

[246] I.R.C. § 401(a)(9)(H) (West Supp. 2020), id. § 402(c)(8)(B) (2018). See generally, Voriss J. Blankenship, *Distributions to Beneficiaries of Tax-Favored Retirement Plans, before and after the SECURE Act*, 74 TAX LAWYER 43 (2020); Vorris J. Blankenship, *The SECURE Act: Retirement Plan Distributions after the Death of a Beneficiary*, 74 TAX LAW. 629 (2021). RMDs for defined benefit plans continue to be fixed by reference to the MDIB requirement described *supra* Chapter 10 note 244.

[247] I.R.C. § 401(a)(9)(B)(iii), (E)(ii)(I), (H)(ii) (West Supp. 2020). In addition, a spouse's life expectancy may be redetermined annually, which extends the distribution period. *Id.* § 401(a)(9)(D).

[248] I.R.C. § 401(a)(9)(B)(iv) (West Supp. 2023).

where distributions are made over life expectancy and the beneficiary dies before attaining that mark) must be paid out within ten years. Finally, the category includes a minor child of the employee, but only until the child attains the age of majority, following which any remainder of the child's interest must be paid out within ten years.[249]

A designated beneficiary who is not eligible for life-expectancy-based distributions must receive distribution of his entire interest within ten years after the employee's death, regardless of whether distributions began during the employee's lifetime.[250] Hence, the employee's infant grandchild (who does not meet the statutory definitions of disabled or chronically ill) cannot take distributions from a defined contribution plan based on life expectancy.

If the employee's beneficiary is not a designated beneficiary – as in cases where the person entitled to the interest is not an individual – and the employee dies before starting to take RMDs, then the entire interest of the employee must be distributed within five years of the employee's death.[251] A common situation triggering five-year distribution is where the employee's estate succeeds to his interest.[252]

To backstop the minimum distribution rule, amounts payable to a non-spouse beneficiary after the death of the employee are expressly made ineligible for tax-free rollover to an IRA or another qualified plan.[253]

---

[249] I.R.C. § 401(a)(9)(E)(ii), (iii), (H)(ii) (West Supp. 2020).

[250] I.R.C. § 401(a)(9)(H)(i), (ii) (West Supp. 2020). Proposed regulations distinguish between whether the employee dies before or after her required beginning date (RBD). If the employee dies before the RBD then "the employee's entire interest [must be] distributed by the end of the calendar year that includes the tenth anniversary of the date of the employee's death" but no interim distributions (i.e., payments within the ten-year period) are required. Prop. Treas. Reg. § 1.401(a)(9)-3(c)(3), 87 Fed. Reg. 10504, 10527 (Feb. 24, 2022). In contrast, if the employee dies after the RBD then annual minimum distributions must continue to be made each year within the ten-year period, with the entire remaining balance paid out by the end of the tenth calendar year. *Id.* § 1.401(a)(9)-5(d)(1)(i), (e)(1), (2), 87 Fed. Reg. at 10535, 10536. *See* Required Minimum Distributions, 87 Fed. Reg. at 10514; Richard L. Kaplan, *The Declining Appeal of Inherited Retirement Accounts*, 41 VA. TAX REV. ___ (2023). Financial industry representatives advocate that final regulations require only full payment by the end of the period, with no required interim distributions.

[251] I.R.C. § 401(a)(9)(B)(ii), H)(i) (West Supp. 2020).

[252] Treas. Reg. § 1.401(a)(9)-4 Q&A-3; Prop. Treas. Reg. § 1.401(a)(9)-4(b), 87 Fed. Reg. 10504, 10528 (Feb. 24, 2022).

[253] I.R.C. § 402(c)(1), (4) (eligible rollover distribution requires distribution to the "employee"), (9) (exception for distribution to surviving spouse). Amounts payable to a non-spouse beneficiary of a deceased employee may be transferred tax free in a direct trustee-to-trustee transfer to an IRA established for the designated beneficiary, but the receptacle is tagged as an inherited IRA, § 402(c)(11), and therefore distributions out of that IRA are taxable (i.e., cannot receive rollover treatment), § 408(d)(3)(C). *See* §§ 403(a)(4)(B), (b)(8)(B), 457(e)(16)(B) (corresponding rollover restrictions and inherited IRA treatment prescribed for amounts due non-spouse beneficiary of a deceased employee under qualified annuity plans, 403(b) tax-sheltered annuities, and eligible deferred compensation plans for government and exempt organization employees).

Taxes and Retirement Saving

A major public policy concern of recent years has been encouraging lifetime income distributions from 401(k) plans and other defined contribution programs. Most such plans call for a single sum payout on separation from service, which leaves decisions about the rate at which she can safely spend down retirement savings to the retiring worker. Defined contribution plans can offer life annuities as a distribution option, but many profit-sharing and stock bonus plans do not.[254] Advance commitment of a portion of a retiring worker's account balance to acquisition of a longevity annuity a deferred life annuity purchased on separation from service (or earlier) under which distributions are scheduled to commence at an advanced age, such as eighty or eighty-five – reduces risk that retirement savings will be consumed too rapidly while preserving flexibility in the investment and distribution of the balance of the account. That flexibility, combined with the price discount inherent in a deferred annuity, might make the longevity annuity a popular means to insure against outliving one's savings. The minimum distribution rules, however, present an obstacle to offering longevity annuities under defined contribution plans: prior to the delayed annuity starting date the value of the annuity contract is generally treated as part of the account balance, and so increases required minimum distributions.[255] Therefore, a participant who buys a longevity annuity and early in retirement withdraws a large part of the remainder of her account balance might find that there is not enough left in the account to satisfy minimum distribution obligations. In years before the annuity starting date, the inaccessible value of the longevity annuity contract generates a current minimum distribution obligation, but provides no means to satisfy it. The Treasury amended the section 401(a)(9) regulations in 2014 to alleviate this impediment to broader utilization of longevity annuities by allowing the value of a "qualifying longevity annuity contract" (QLAC) held under a plan to be disregarded in computing required minimum distributions.[256] The problem was not eliminated, however, because the regulatory QLAC definition restricted the premiums that could be paid for the contract to the lesser of $125,000 (adjusted for inflation) and 25 percent of the employee's account balance.[257] In 2022 Congress directed that the regulations be amended to eliminate

---

[254] To encourage broader access to annuities, in 2019 Congress amended ERISA to provide a fiduciary safe harbor for the selection of an annuity provider. If the specified protocol is followed, ERISA's duty of prudence is deemed satisfied. ERISA § 404(e), 29 U.S.C. § 1104 (e) (West Supp. 2020); H.R. Rep. No. 116-65, Part 1, at 84–87 (2019).

[255] Treas. Reg. § 1.401(a)(9)-5, Q&A-3(a) (as amended in 2014); Prop. Treas. Reg. § 1.401(a)(9)-5 (b)(1), 87 Fed. Reg. 10504, 10534 (Feb. 24, 2022).

[256] Treas. Reg. § 1.401(a)(9)-5, Q&A-3(d) (as amended in 2014); Prop. Treas. Reg. § 1.401(a)(9)-5 (b)(4), 87 Fed. Reg. 10504, 10535 (Feb. 24, 2022).

[257] Treas. Reg. § 1.401(a)(9)-6, Q&A-17 (as amended in 2014); Prop. Treas. Reg. § 1.401(a)(9)-5 (b)(4), -6(q), 87 Fed. Reg. 10504, 10535, 10547–48 (Feb. 24, 2022). Purchase of a QLAC does not trigger an obligation to distribute the balance of the account before commencement of annuity payments. Therefore, the dollar and percentage limitations were deemed necessary to prevent utilization of longevity annuities as a device to skew distributions toward the latter portion of the permissible distribution period, in derogation of the minimum distribution

396 *Tax Controls: Qualified Retirement Savings*

the 25 percent limit and increase the dollar limitation on QLAC premiums to $200,000.[258]

Common wisdom holds that the minimum distribution rule targets the tax subsidy on retirement saving, but there is cause for skepticism. A large majority of Americans have no significant assets apart from some home equity and their qualified retirement savings (including IRAs). Low- and moderate-income workers do not need to be *required* to take retirement distributions – they simply couldn't get along without the money. Realistically, only the top 5 percent of households, as ranked by income, have substantial savings besides their interests in a home and qualified retirement programs. Accordingly, the problem of excessive deferral is limited to the very affluent, and this elite group has plenty of other resources from which to make bequests (e.g., life insurance, investments). We can require them to take distributions in old age from their tax-preferred savings, but we cannot force them to use it for consumption. Even if they choose to consume it, any financial advantage they derive from qualified retirement savings just makes other resources available for transfer by gift, bequest, devise or inheritance. Forcing distributions to be contemporaneous with retirement does not prevent the tax subsidy from being passed on to the next generation, it only prevents that disposition from being readily apparent. From this perspective, the minimum distribution feint gives the tax subsidy political cover from popular opposition. Ironically, that misdirection may be needed primarily to protect rank-and-file employees, who may not apprehend that the covert redistribution system embedded in the nondiscrimination rules makes their own retirement income dependent upon the tax benefits accorded the highest-paid participants.

This line of analysis indicates that the principal function of the minimum distribution rule is quantitative rather than qualitative. While we can't control the use to which high-income participants put any financial advantage they derive from qualified retirement savings, limiting the duration of tax deferral surely restricts the amount of the subsidy.[259] The wisdom of that restriction is another matter. As with the maximum amount rule,[260] limiting tax benefits associated with savings by HCEs

---

incidental benefit requirement (see *supra* Chapter 10 note 244). Longevity Annuity Contracts, 77 Fed. Reg. 5443, 5445 (proposed Feb. 3, 2012).

[258] SECURE 2.0 Act of 2022, Pub. L. No. 117-328, Div. T, § 202, 136 Stat. 4459, ____ (2023).

[259] This is dramatically illustrated by the estimated revenue effects of the Setting Every Community Up for Retirement Enhancement Act of 2019, Pub. L. No. 116-94, Div. O, 133 Stat. 2534, 3137–3182. According to estimates by the Joint Committee on Taxation, the provisions of Title I of the bill designed to expand and preserve retirement saving would have a ten-year cost of $14.5 billion, but that aggregate revenue loss would be recouped by tightening the required minimum distribution rules of I.R.C. § 401(a)(9), which was projected to increase revenue over the same period by $15.7 billion. STAFF OF THE JOINT COMM. ON TAX'N, JCX-54R-19, ESTIMATED BUDGET EFFECTS OF THE REVENUE PROVISIONS CONTAINED IN THE HOUSE AMENDMENT TO THE SENATE AMENDMENT TO H.R. 1865, THE FURTHER CONSOLIDATED APPROPRIATIONS ACT, 2020, at 2, 3 (Dec. 17, 2019).

[260] See *supra* text accompanying Chapter 10 notes 209–210.

Taxes and Retirement Saving

(in this case, by limiting the duration rather than the amount of HCE savings) limits the employer's potential compensation cost savings and necessarily caps the extent of potential redistribution. Given the imperfections of the nondiscrimination regime, relaxing or repealing the minimum distribution rule presumably would merely increase wasted revenue (i.e., would force no additional redistribution) associated with existing plans. But some companies do not currently sponsor a plan because their workforce composition is such that the tax savings that could be captured from high-paid participants is insufficient to induce enough rank and file participation to satisfy the nondiscrimination tests. As to these enterprises, a richer tax subsidy might support sufficient compensation cost savings to satisfy the nondiscrimination rules and make plan sponsorship feasible. Relaxing the minimum distribution rule is one way to enrich the subsidy, but there are other available alternatives (for example, permitting greater tax deferral by relaxing the maximum amount rule).

Early Distributions Pre-retirement distributions raise a different set of policy concerns. Unlike late distributions, which present the prospect of excessive deferral by a few very highly compensated employees, the availability of early distributions is particularly important to lower-paid workers. These are the employees who do not save adequately for retirement when left to their own devices and who are therefore the intended beneficiaries of redistribution. The maddeningly intricate system of nondiscrimination rules exists to induce greater retirement savings for rank-and-file employees, and so it might seem that pre-retirement distributions which dissipate those savings are simply anathema and ought to be banned outright. Doesn't proper targeting of the tax subsidy require locking up qualified plan accumulations until retirement? Perhaps, but history and politics have conspired against such a straightforward approach. Moreover, limited pre-retirement access to qualified plan accumulations may be essential to the success of the system, because a flat prohibition on early distributions might cause low-paid workers to place such a low value on qualified plan savings that the available tax subsidy (compensation savings extracted from HCE-savers) would be insufficient to persuade them to cooperate. To mitigate the deterrent effect of locking down retirement plan savings, in 2022 Congress authorized the establishment of limited pension-linked emergency savings accounts for nonhighly compensated employees under most types of tax-favored elective contributions plans, including 401(k), 403(b) and 457(b) plans.[261]

Barring without exception early access to plan savings would cause low-paid workers to more heavily discount the benefit, thereby necessitating a larger bribe (compensation increase) to induce their plan participation. Increasing the bribes needed to satisfy the nondiscrimination rules requires greater redistribution; perhaps more than HCE demand for tax-favored retirement savings could

---

[261] ERISA §§ 3(45), 801–804; 29 U.S.C. §§ 1002(45), 1193–1193c (West Supp. 2023); I.R.C. § 402A(e) (West Supp. 2023). *See supra* Chapter 7A, text accompanying notes 37–44.

finance.[262] Thus there is a trade-off between cost and quality: iron-clad dedication of qualified plan savings to the provision of retirement income might require more redistribution than the system can support, triggering plan terminations. Taking the broad view of timing, limiting late distributions affects high-income savers and reduces the amount of the available tax subsidy, while limiting early distributions impacts cash-strapped rank-and-file workers and increases the amount of subsidy that is required to satisfy nondiscrimination standards.

As mentioned, history and politics (perhaps more than redistribution theory and practice) have shaped the circumstances in which early distributions are permitted. Traditionally, pre-retirement distributions were far more readily available under a profit-sharing or stock bonus plan than under a pension plan. That difference derived from the fact that, by definition, a pension plan is a program "established and maintained by an employer primarily to provide systematically for the payment of definitely determinable benefits to his employees over a period of years, usually for life, *after retirement*."[263] Pension plans may pay a disability pension or provide incidental death benefits, and may permit distribution on severance of employment or upon termination of the plan, but in-service distributions are generally disqualifying.[264] To facilitate phased retirement programs, this rule is relaxed to permit in-service distributions after the employee has attained age 59½.[265]

Profit-sharing and stock bonus plans, in contrast, were originally conceived simply as programs providing *deferred* compensation, not necessarily *retirement* savings, and so in-service distributions were routinely permitted.[266] Specifically, in addition to the circumstances justifying distribution from a pension plan, distributions under a profit-sharing or stock bonus plan are allowed after a fixed number of years (meaning at least two), attainment of a specified age, or in the event of layoff, illness, or hardship.[267] These conditions are so capacious it is a wonder that any balance survived in a profit-sharing or stock bonus account until retirement. Although a 401 (k) plan is ordinarily part of a profit-sharing or stock bonus plan, distribution of amounts attributable to elective contributions are more restricted: in-service distribution after a fixed number of years is not acceptable. Instead, amounts attributable

---

[262] *See supra* Figure 10.2 and accompanying text.

[263] Treas. Reg. § 1.401-1(b)(1)(i) (as amended in 2014) (emphasis added).

[264] Treas. Reg. § 1.401-1(b)(1)(i) (as amended in 2014) (disability pension or incidental death benefits); *see* Rev. Rul. 56-693, 1956-2 C.B. 282 (distribution on severance of employment or termination of plan); Rev. Rul. 74-254, 1974-1 C.B. 91 (same).

[265] I.R.C. § 401(a)(36) (Supp. II 2020). *Compare id. with* ERISA § 3(2)(A), 29 U.S.C. § 1002(2) (A) (2018) (providing, in the pension plan definition itself, that in-service distributions to an employee who has attained age sixty-two "shall not be treated as made in a form other than retirement income or as a distribution prior to termination of covered employment").

[266] Treas. Reg. § 1.401-1(b)(1)(ii), (iii) (as amended in 2014).

[267] *Id.*; Rev. Rul. 71-224, 1971-1 C.B. 124 (hardship distributions allowed); Rev. Rul. 54-231, 1954-1 C.B. 150 (fixed number of years means at least two); Rev. Rul. 68-24, 1968-1 C.B. 150 (qualified profit-sharing plan may allow employees with at least sixty months of participation to withdraw all employer contributions, including those made within the preceding two years).

Taxes and Retirement Saving

to elective contributions, and to qualified matching contributions and qualified nonelective contributions, may be distributed only upon severance of employment, death, disability, plan termination, attainment of age 59½, hardship of the employee, or upon a reservist's call-up to active duty.[268]

After December 28, 2025, a defined contribution plan may also make distributions each year in an aggregate amount that does not exceed the amount paid by the employee during the year for specified long-term care insurance coverage for the employee or the employee's spouse, up to a limit of $2,500 adjusted for inflation.[269] Such distributions will not disqualify a money purchase pension plan (under which in-service distributions are generally prohibited), and may be made from elective contributions, qualified matching or qualified nonelective contributions under a 401(k) plan.[270] Such distributions are also exempt from the additional 10 percent tax on early distributions, discussed below, even though they may be made to young active employees.[271]

To discourage early distributions from qualified plans, an additional 10 percent tax is imposed on the taxable portion of distributions made before the date the employee attains age 59½ unless certain exceptions apply.[272] The exceptions allow early withdrawal without penalty if the distribution is made to the employee upon separation from service after age fifty-five, is made to a beneficiary or the estate of the employee after death, is due to disability, or is paid as an annuity over the life (or life expectancy) of the employee or the joint lives (or joint-life expectancies) of the employee and a designated beneficiary.[273] Distributions to an alternate payee under a qualified domestic relations order and distributions that do not exceed the amount that would be allowed as a medical expense deduction to the employee (regardless of whether the employee itemizes deductions) are also exempt from the 10 percent levy.[274] Up to $5,000 can be distributed penalty-free from a tax-favored retirement program (other than a defined benefit plan) within one year after the birth or adoption of a child of the plan participant or IRA owner.[275] Penalty-free early

---

[268] I.R.C. § 401(k)(2)(B), (k)(3)(D), (k)(12)(E)(i), (k)(13)(D)(iii), (k)(14), (m)(4) (2018 & West Supp. 2023). Corresponding limits on early in-service distributions apply to elective contributions under 403(b) plans and 457 plans. *Id.* §§ 403(b)(7)(A)(i), (b)(7)(D),(b)(11), (b)(17), 457 (d)(1)(A), (d)(4), (2018 & West Supp. 2023).

[269] I.R.C. § 401(a)(39) (West Supp. 2023)

[270] I.R.C. § 401(k)(2)(B)(i)(VII) (West Supp. 2023). Such distributions to cover long-term care insurance costs are also authorized for qualified annuity plans, 403(b) plans and 457(b) plans *Id.* §§ 403(a)(6), 403(b)(7)(A)(i)(VII), (b)(11)(E), 457(d)(1)(A)(v) (West Supp. 2023).

[271] I.R.C. § 72(t)(2)(N) (West Supp. 2023).

[272] I.R.C. § 72(t)(1), (t)(2)(A)(i) (2018). This early withdrawal tax was enacted in 1986 and effectively marks the conversion of profit-sharing and stock bonus plans into *retirement* savings programs.

[273] I.R.C. § 72(t)(2)(A), (t)(3)(B), (t)(4) (2018).

[274] I.R.C. § 72(t)(2)(B), (C) (2018).

[275] I.R.C. § 72(t)(2)(H) (West Supp. 2020). If both parents of the newborn or newly adopted child have their own retirement savings, each can take up to $5,000 in distributions. Moreover, a

Tax Controls: Qualified Retirement Savings

distributions are also permitted to be made to terminally ill employees and in limited amounts from a defined contribution plan (other than a money purchase pension plan) to a participant who is a domestic abuse victim.[276]

Congress has occasionally granted temporary relief from the additional tax on early distributions in response to emergencies causing widespread financial hardship. For example, individuals adversely affected by the coronavirus pandemic were permitted to withdraw up to $100,000 during calendar year 2020 without application of the 10 percent additional tax.[277] Distribution rules were also relaxed in response to Hurricane Katrina.[278] In 2022 Congress adopted a general response. Up to $22,000 may be distributed from a tax-favored retirement plan or IRA to an individual affected by a federally declared disaster.[279] Absent a federally declared disaster, up to $1,000 can be distributed from a tax-favored defined contribution plan or IRA to meet unforeseeable or immediate financial needs relating to necessary personal or family emergency expenses.[280]

The early withdrawal tax applies not only to distributions from a qualified pension, profit-sharing, stock bonus, or annuity plan; it also reaches distributions from 403(b) plan or an individual retirement account or annuity (IRA).[281] In recent years, however, Congress has enacted a raft of additional exceptions that permit early withdrawals from IRAs for various worthy uses, including to pay health insurance

---

special rule provides that if such qualified birth or adoption distributions are subsequently repaid to the plan or IRA the distribution may go entirely untaxed by treating it as a direct trustee-to-trustee rollover. This exception to the early distribution penalty was made to "encourage younger workers to save earlier for their retirement". H.R. Rep. No. 116-65, Part 1, at 70 (2019). *See supra* text accompanying Chapter 10 note 262.

[276] I.R.C. § 72(t)(2)(K), (L) (West Supp. 2023). Distributions due to terminal illness or domestic abuse may be repaid to the plan under rules similar to those governing distributions on account of birth or adoption of a child. *Id.*

[277] CARES Act, Pub. L. No. 116-136, § 2202, 134 Stat. 282, 340 (2020). Moreover, statutory prohibitions that would normally prevent distributions to a participant who is under the age of 59½ and still employed by the plan sponsor were waived, and if the amount distributed were repaid to the plan within three years the distribution was treated as a tax-free direct rollover. *Id.* Concerning the waiver of distribution limits, compare *id.* § 2202(a)(6)(B) with *supra* Chapter 10 note 268 and accompanying text. The CARES Act also temporarily relaxed certain restrictions on plan loans. *See infra* Chapter 10 note 289 and accompanying text. Doran, *supra* Chapter 10 note 245.

[278] *See* Katrina Emergency Tax Relief Act of 2005, Pub. L. No. 109-73, § 101, 119 Stat. 2016, 2017–19 (allowing penalty-free withdrawal of up to $100,000).

[279] I.R.C. § 72(t)(2)(M), (t)(11) (West Supp. 2023). If repaid to the plan within three years the amount distributed is treated as a tax-free direct rollover, and to the extent not repaid is included in gross income ratably over three years. *Id.*

[280] I.R.C. § 72(t)(2)(I) (West Supp. 2023). The plan administrator may rely on an employee's written certification that conditions justifying an emergency personal expense distribution have been met. Repayment within three years is permitted. No additional emergency personal expense distribution may be made during the three calendar years following the distribution unless the distribution is fully repaid or following the distribution the employee makes elective deferrals or employee contributions to the plan at least equal to the amount not repaid. *Id.*

[281] I.R.C. §§ 72(t)(1), 4974(c) (2018).

Taxes and Retirement Saving

premiums while unemployed, to pay higher education expenses of the taxpayer or his spouse, child, or grandchild (or of a child or grandchild of the spouse), to pay certain acquisition costs of first-time homebuyers, and distributions made to a reservist called to active duty.[282] The upshot of all these exceptions is that "individual *retirement* account" has become a misnomer; IRAs are no longer dedicated retirement savings vehicles; they have morphed into tax-preferred savings accounts that may be used to fund a wide range of expenditures that Congress deems laudable. The IRA exceptions have a far broader reach than may at first appear, for they apply to early distributions from a rollover IRA that houses assets accumulated under a qualified plan![283] Indeed, due to the ubiquity of rollovers of qualified plan account balances when workers change jobs, IRAs now hold the largest share of qualified retirement savings,[284] all of which is subject to leakage for various non-retirement purposes. Far from depressing the value of savings by locking them away for decades, after a job change and transfer to an IRA, qualified plan assets, while not quite up for grabs, are at least readily accessible to finance a number of common needs.

Plan Loans Like early distributions, plan loans present similar threats to retirement income security: if the loan is not repaid, the outstanding balance will be set off against the participant's accrued benefit, depleting resources available for support in retirement.[285] On the other hand, a ban on all plan loans might so impair the value of qualified plan savings for young, low-income employees as to make it impossible to satisfy the nondiscrimination rules – the bribes necessary to garner sufficient NHCE participation could become too pricey. Because of ERISA's anti-alienation rule, a credit-constrained participant has nowhere else to turn: by law she cannot use her interest in the plan (frequently the only significant asset of a low-income worker) as security to obtain a loan from another lender.

Not surprisingly, in view of this state of affairs, qualified retirement plans may permit plan loans, but only under circumstances that make it likely that the funds will be available in retirement. There are two distinct requirements. First, to avoid

---

[282] I.R.C. §§ 72(t)(2)(D)-(G), (t)(7), (t)(8), 7701(a)(37) (2018) (definition of individual retirement plan).

[283] *See* McGovern v. Comm'r, T.C. Summary Op. 2003-137 (2003) (payment of qualified higher education expenses with amounts distributed from a qualified plan is subject to 10 percent early withdrawal tax even though additional tax would not have applied if the education expenses had been paid from an IRA, despite the fact that taxpayer had actually transferred the remainder of the qualified plan distribution into a rollover IRA).

[284] At year-end 2021, IRAs held $13.9 trillion out of the total U.S. retirement assets of $39.3 trillion. In comparison, private sector defined contribution plans held about $11.0 trillion, and private sector defined benefit plans held $3.8 trillion. PROQUEST STATISTICAL ABSTRACT OF THE U.S. 2023 ONLINE EDITION, Table 1239. For the contribution of rollovers from qualified plans to IRA balances, see *supra* Chapter 10 note 40.

[285] Recall that an exception to the anti-alienation rule permits plan loans to be secured by the participant's vested accrued benefit. ERISA § 206(d)(2), 29 U.S.C. § 1056(d)(2) (2018); I.R.C. § 401(a)(13)(A) (2018). *See generally supra* Chapter 8 notes 13–14 and accompanying text.

disqualification, plan loans must be available to employees on a nondiscriminatory basis under specific plan provisions calling for reasonable interest and adequate security.[286] Second, the maximum amount of all outstanding plan loans to the employee under all plans of the employer (as defined using the commonly controlled business and affiliated service group workforce aggregation rules) is the smaller of $50,000 or one-half of the present value of the employee's vested accrued benefit (but not less than $10,000).[287] In addition to limiting plan loans to a relatively small amount, they are generally required to be repaid by level amortization over five years. The five-year term requirement does not apply to loans used to purchase a principal residence, presumably because in that case the housing value will be available in retirement even if the loan is not repaid.[288] Plan loan restrictions (relating to both the loan amount and amortization period) have been relaxed on a temporary basis in response to emergencies causing widespread financial hardship, like the coronavirus pandemic.[289] To the extent that a loan to a participant exceeds the limit set by section 72(p), or if the loan does not comply with the term or level amortization requirements, the plan is not disqualified, but receipt of the loan proceeds is treated as a plan distribution. Usually this means that the loan proceeds are taxable, and the 10 percent penalty tax on early withdrawals might also apply.[290]

A study of loan activity under 401(k) plans shows that loan features are common in large plans and that 87 percent of 401(k) plan participants were in plans that permitted loans. Nevertheless, relatively few participants make use of the feature; only 21 percent of those eligible to borrow had loans outstanding at the close of 2013. Moreover, the outstanding loan amount for participants who borrow from the plan tends to be small, averaging only 12 percent of the account balance.[291]

---

[286] I.R.C. §§ 401(a)(13)(A), 4975(d)(1) (2018); Treas. Reg. § 1.401(a)-13(d)(2) (as amended in 1988); Rev. Rul. 89-14, 1989-1 C.B. 111 (reasonable interest rate required even if loan is to an employee who is not a disqualified person).

[287] I.R.C. § 72(p) (2018). Permissible loan amounts are actually specified with reference to the highest outstanding balance of plan loans to the employee within the preceding one-year period. This rule prevents evasion of the five-year term limit via routine extensions or relending.

[288] I.R.C. § 72(p)(2)(B), (C) (2018).

[289] For certain individuals adversely affected by the coronavirus pandemic, CARES Act § 2206(b), 134 Stat. (2020), allows loan amounts of up to $100,000 or 100 percent of the participant's nonforfeitable accrued benefit and grants a one-year delay in repayments.

[290] I.R.C. § 72(p)(1)(A), (t) (2018); Treas. Reg. § 1.72(p)-1, Q&A-11 (as amended in 2006). The repayment requirements (five-year level amortization) must be satisfied in both form and operation, and so an employee-borrower's failure to pay a required installment, if not promptly cured, can trigger a deemed taxable distribution after the loan is made. Id. Q&A-4, -10.

[291] Jack VanDerhei et al., 401(k) Plan Asset Allocation, Account Balances, and Loan Activity in 2016, EBRI ISSUE BRIEF, Sep. 10, 2018, www.ebri.org/content/401(k)-plan-asset-allocation-account-balances-and-loan-activity-in-2016 (19 percent of all 401(k) participants who were eligible for loans had loans outstanding against their 401(k) plan accounts year-end 2016; outstanding loans amounted to 11 percent of the remaining account balance, on average); Geng Li & Paul A. Smith, 401(k) Loans and Household Balance Sheets, 63 NAT'L TAX J. 479, 489,502 (2010) (reporting that the share of eligible households with 401(k) loan balances in

Taxes and Retirement Saving 403

Rollovers Retirement savings may be dissipated if they are distributed during the participant's working years. Americans change jobs frequently, especially younger workers, and qualified plans (even traditional defined benefit pension plans) may permit distribution of the participant's entire interest upon separation from service. If the present value of a participant's vested accrued benefit exceeds $7,000, it cannot be distributed without the consent of the participant (and his or her spouse if married),[292] and in that case, the 10 percent additional tax on early withdrawals may discourage distribution and pre-retirement consumption. But if the present value is less than or equal to $7,000, a qualified plan can require distribution on separation from service, and such mandatory cash-outs are routinely used to avoid the administrative costs associated with maintaining small balances for long periods on behalf of departed former employees. For a number of reasons, even a participant with a larger balance who wants to continue saving for retirement may take distribution in spite of the additional tax. She may want access to the funds as a precaution, as in the situation where an undetermined portion may be needed for support during a period of unemployment. Or a former employee may take distribution because she is not comfortable with the plan's management or investment policies or options and fears her money will not be safe if left there for the long haul. In all of these cases, once the money comes into the hands of the employee, there is a serious risk that it will not actually be preserved for retirement, however responsible one's intentions may be when less flush with cash.

Rather than relying exclusively on the deterrent effect of the early withdrawal penalty tax to safeguard retirement savings, the Code also offers the inducement of continued post-distribution tax deferral through the rollover mechanism. Any distribution from a qualified plan other than a required minimum distribution, a hardship-based distribution, or an annuity distribution, if contributed within sixty days after receipt to an IRA, another qualified plan, a tax-sheltered annuity contract, or an eligible deferred compensation plan of a state or local government, is excluded from gross income under the tax-free rollover rules.[293] The rollover contribution

---

2007 was about 15 percent, and many loan-eligible households carry much more expensive credit card and other consumer debt).

[292] I.R.C. §§ 401(a)(31)(B)(ii), 411(a)(11), 417(e) (2018 & West Supp. 2023); ERISA §§ 203(e) (1), 205(g), 29 U.S.C. §§ 1053(e), 1055(g) (2018 & West Supp. 2023). For distributions before January 1, 2024, the limit on mandatory cash-outs was $5,000.

[293] I.R.C. § 402(c) (2018) (rollovers from qualified pension, profit-sharing or stock bonus plan), *id.* § 403(a)(4) (rollovers from qualified annuity plan). To be eligible for rollover treatment, the disbursing plan must be qualified at the time of the distribution, not simply when the employer made contributions. Treas. Reg. § 1.402(a)-1(a)(1)(ii) (as amended in 2014); Baetens v. Comm'r, 777 F.2d 1160 (6th Cir. 1985); Benbow v. Comm'r, 774 F.2d 740 (7th Cir. 1985).

Distributions under a term-certain annuity that has a period of less than ten years are also eligible for rollover treatment. I.R.C. § 402(c)(4)(A) (2018). Rollovers of distributions under tax-sheltered annuity contracts or eligible deferred compensation plans of state or local governments are also permitted under corresponding rules. *Id.* §§ 403(b)(8), 457(e)(16). Such liberal general rollover rules do not apply to eligible deferred compensation plans of

Tax Controls: Qualified Retirement Savings

need not be of the entire amount distributed – continued tax deferral is granted to any portion of the distribution that is timely transferred to an eligible receptacle.[294] Such a rollover contribution also excuses the amount so contributed from the early distribution penalty tax of section 72(t).[295] Even a distribution of property (e.g., employer stock distributed from a stock bonus plan) is eligible for tax-free rollover if the property received is transferred in-kind to the IRA, qualified plan, or other eligible receptacle,[296] or the property may be sold and the proceeds contributed.[297]

Instead of distribution to the participant followed by contribution to another plan or IRA within sixty days, rollovers may also be accomplished by a direct trustee-to-trustee transfer. In lieu of taking distribution of an amount that would be eligible for tax-free rollover, the plan participant or IRA owner may instruct the trustee to transfer the amount directly to an IRA or qualified plan designated by the participant. Such direct transfers keep retirement savings out of the worker's hands for even the brief period (sixty days) allowed by the rollover rules. By reducing temptation, direct transfers (also known as direct rollovers) might reduce asset leakage out of the

nongovernmental tax-exempt employers, but a tax-free transfer from one eligible deferred compensation plan to another 457 plan (*not* to an IRA, a qualified plan, or a tax-sheltered annuity) is permitted. *Id.* § 457(e)(10).

Distributions from a traditional IRA can be rolled over to another traditional IRA, or to a qualified plan, tax-sheltered annuity, or eligible governmental deferred compensation plan, provided that the distribution is not from an inherited IRA. I.R.C. § 408(d)(3) (2018); *see id.* § 402(c)(11) (inherited IRA includes IRA that receives direct trustee-to-trustee transfer of qualified plan assets on behalf of nonspouse designated beneficiary of deceased employee).

Rollovers to a Roth IRA are subject to special rules because contributions to a Roth IRA must be made out of after-tax income. Distributions from qualified plans and traditional IRAs ordinarily have not been subject to tax and therefore cannot be transferred to a Roth IRA without first being included in income. *Id.* § 408A(c)(6), (d)(3) (rollover contributions to Roth IRA must be included in income but additional 10 percent early withdrawal tax does not apply).

[294] I.R.C. § 402(c)(1)(A) (2018) ("any portion of the balance"), *id.* §§ 402(c)(1) (parenthetical clause), 403(a)(4), (b)(8)(A), 408(d)(3)(D), 457(e)(16)(A). Where a distribution from a qualified plan includes amounts that would be received tax-free (e.g., after-tax employee contributions), then the maximum amount that may be rolled over is the otherwise-taxable portion of the distribution, except in cases where separate accounting for the after-tax portion of a contribution is feasible. *Id.* §§ 402(c)(2), 403(a)(4)(B); *see id.* § 401(a)(31)(C) (direct transfer qualification condition). Where a distribution from a traditional IRA includes amounts that are not subject to tax (i.e., after-tax or nondeductible contributions), the maximum permissible rollover to a qualified plan, tax-sheltered annuity, or eligible governmental deferred compensation plan is the amount of the IRA distribution that would otherwise be includible in gross income. In contrast, if the rollover is made to another IRA, then the contribution can include the nontaxable amount of the distribution. *Compare id.* § 408(d)(3)(A)(i), *with* (d)(3)(A)(ii).

[295] I.R.C. § 72(t)(1) (2018) (additional tax applies to amount included in gross income, while portion of distribution rolled over is excluded from gross income).

[296] I.R.C. §§ 402(c)(1)(C), 403(a)(4)(A)(iii), (b)(8)(A)(iii), 408(d)(3)(A), 457(e)(16)(A)(iii) (2018).

[297] I.R.C. §§ 402(c)(6), 403(a)(4)(B), (b)(8)(B), 457(e)(16)(B) (2018). Special allocation or tracing rules come into play to assure appropriate partial taxation if distributed property is sold and the amount of the rollover contribution is less than the total value of money and property distributed.

Taxes and Retirement Saving

retirement savings system. With that goal in mind, Congress promotes direct rollovers in two ways. First, all qualified pension, profit-sharing, stock bonus, and annuity plans (as well as tax-sheltered annuities and eligible deferred compensation plans of state or local government employers) are required to accept and execute proper direct rollover instructions, and the transfers are expressly excluded from gross income.[298] Second, direct rollovers are encouraged because they avoid the temporary imposition of the 20 percent withholding tax that is otherwise applied to eligible rollover distributions from tax-favored retirement savings programs.[299] The withholding tax is refundable, of course, but a participant who wishes to roll over the entire distribution will have to contribute within sixty days not only the net amount actually received (80 percent of the distribution), but also an additional amount from his or her own resources to make up for the 20 percent withheld. If the distribution is substantial, many workers would find it difficult to finance the additional contribution. If only the amount actually paid to the participant is rolled over, then only 80 percent of the distribution is excludible; the 20 percent that was withheld thus becomes a taxable distribution which (depending on timing) might also be subject to the additional tax on early distributions. Due to the cash flow burden imposed, one might predict that this withholding regime would actually discourage rollover of the full amount distributed, but the freedom from withholding of direct rollovers creates a countervailing incentive that encourages precommitment to the preservation of retirement savings. To promote such precommitment, the plan administrator is required to provide a participant who is scheduled to receive a distribution that is eligible for tax-free rollover with a written explanation of the direct rollover option and the withholding tax that will apply if a direct rollover is not elected.[300]

---

[298] I.R.C. §§ 401(a)(31), 402(e)(6), 403(a)(5), (b)(10), 404(a)(2), 457(d)(1)(C) and (d)(1) (final sentence) (2018). The instructions must specify the IRA or plan to which the direct rollover is to be made, and if the transfer is to a qualified plan, it must be a defined contribution plan, which, by its terms, permits such rollovers. Hence, while all qualified plans (along with 403(b) plans and governmental 457 plans) are required to make direct trustee-to-trustee transfers, they are *not* required to accept them. *Id.* § 401(a)(31)(E). Direct transfer to the participant's IRA is always an available alternative.

[299] I.R.C. § 3405(c), (e)(1), (e)(5) (2018).

[300] I.R.C. § 402(f) (2018). The explanation must be provided within a reasonable time before making the distribution, meaning not more than 180 days nor less than 30 days. Treas. Reg. § 1.402(f)-1, Q&A-2 (as amended in 2007); Pub. L. No. 109-280, § 1102 (2006) (directing that permissible notice period be expanded to 180 days before the date of distribution). The IRS has published a model notice that plan administrators may use to satisfy their advance explanation obligations. I.R.S. Notice 2009-68, 2009-39 I.R.B. 423. The advance explanation requirement applies not only to eligible rollover distributions from qualified pension, profit-sharing, stock bonus plans, but also to distributions from qualified annuity plans, tax-sheltered annuities, and eligible governmental deferred compensation plans. I.R.C. §§ 402(f)(2)(A), 403(a)(4)(B), 403(b)(8)(B), 457(e)(16)(B) (2018).

An empirical study found that the withholding tax and required explanation have led to substantial increases in rollovers, and that the effect was most pronounced for small lump-sum

406 Tax Controls: Qualified Retirement Savings

Experience shows that the likelihood and the amount of a rollover increase with the size of the distribution.[301] Distribution of the participant's full accrued benefit can be required without the participant's consent (mandatory cash-out) if the present value of the accrued benefit is not more than $7,000. Such small accumulations are likely to be spent on current consumption, particularly if the distribution is occasioned by the separation from service of a young employee. In an effort to increase the odds that small retirement savings will be preserved, mandatory distributions in excess of $1,000 are required to be transferred directly into an IRA unless the distributee either designates some other qualified savings program or affirmatively elects to take the distribution herself.[302] This changes the default mode of distribution for mandatory cash-outs exceeding $1,000 from distribution to the departing participant – who may be tempted to spend a small windfall – to direct rollover to an IRA. Another initiative to preserve retirement savings when workers change jobs was enacted in 2022: mandatory cash-outs directly transferred to an IRA may, if specified notice requirements and other conditions are satisfied, subsequently be transferred automatically into an employer-sponsored defined contribution plan in which the IRA owner is an active participant.[303]

D REORIENTING PRIVATE PENSIONS

Nearly fifty years after ERISA's enactment, the indictment against the contemporary private pension system sounds devastating. The project of supplementing Social Security via employer-mediated tax-subsidized deferred compensation programs has become monumentally complex, inordinately expensive, and largely ineffective in

distributions. These findings, the authors conclude, are more consistent with a behavioral than a rational expectations model of decision making. Leonard E. Burman et al., *Effects of Public Policies on the Disposition of Pre-Retirement Lump-Sum Distributions: Rational and Behavioral Influences*, 65 NAT'L TAX J. 863, 883–84 (2018).

[301] Craig Copeland, *Lump-Sum Distributions at Job Change*, 30 EBRI NOTES 2, 8–9 (2009) (analysis of Census Bureau data from the 2004 Survey of Income and Program Participation shows that "the larger the distribution the more likely it was kept entirely in tax-qualified savings"); U.S. GOV'T ACCOUNTABILITY OFFICE, GAO-19-179, RETIREMENT SAVINGS: ADDITIONAL DATA AND ANALYSIS COULD PROVIDE INSIGHT INTO EARLY WITHDRAWALS, Table 5 at 47, at www.gao.gov/assets/700/698041.pdf (2019).

[302] I.R.C. §§ 401(a)(31)(B), 403(b)(10), 404(a)(2), 457(d)(1)(C) (2018). Labor Department regulations provide a safe harbor from ERISA's fiduciary duties for the selection of the rollover IRA provider and the investments products purchased with the funds. 29 C.F.R. § 2550.404a-2 (2022). Even if the automatic rollover does not comply with the safe harbor, the fiduciary of the distributing plan is insulated from liability for losses occurring more than one year after the transfer into the IRA. ERISA § 404(c)(3), 29 U.S.C. § 1104(c)(3) (2018).

[303] I.R.C. § 4975(d)(25), (f)(12) (West Supp. 2023). Such automatic portability transactions were made subject to special regulatory and reporting requirements. SECURE 2.0 Act of 2022, Pub. L. No. 117-328, Div. T, §120, 136 Stat. 4459, ____ (2023). Authorization of automatic portability was pressed by a consortium of large recordkeepers, including Vanguard and Fidelity, presumably because it will help them preserve more assets under management.

Taxes and Retirement Saving

generating additional retirement saving. There is surely evidence to back each count. But is the case against qualified plans compelling?

The preceding review of the tax controls – the qualified plan rules that influence the amount and destination of the tax subsidy – offers convincing proof that the rules have indeed become monumentally complex *for plan sponsors and professionals*. That formidable complexity is largely invisible and irrelevant to plan participants and beneficiaries, the intended objects of the assistance. As has often been noted, the complexity with which tax policy makers should be concerned is the complexity faced by individual taxpayers, who typically navigate the system without professional guidance. The chief decisions presented to the average worker are how much to defer under a 401(k) plan, which investment options to select, and when to take distributions, none of which require a participant to contend with nondiscrimination rules or other daunting qualification conditions.[304] Experts who structure and administer the rules are adept at dealing with complexity and get paid for it, and so we need be concerned with the difficulties faced by specialists only insofar as the resulting transaction costs drag down the system, or the rules are so intricate that results become indeterminate.[305] Complexity, in other words, is primarily relevant to cost, and cost must be evaluated in light of benefit.

Turning to the charge that the retirement savings system is inordinately expensive, two cost components must be assessed. Compliance with ERISA and the qualified plan regime is expensive, especially for defined benefit plans, and some experts conclude that those costs have contributed importantly to the demise of traditional pension plans.[306] Revenue loss must also be considered. The preferential treatment accorded qualified retirement savings represents the first or second largest tax

---

[304] Note that the first two questions, contribution levels and investment choice, are not issues for defined benefit plan participants. These crucial matters have been shifted to individual decision making with the increasing dominance of elective contribution programs (such as 401(k) and 403(b) plans) that give participants control over the selection of investment options under ERISA § 404(c), 29 U.S.C. §1104(c) (2018). *See supra* Chapter 4D. Still, these saving and investment decisions primarily implicate financial planning skills (and may call for increased attention to providing workers with basic financial education), not knowledge of pension law. And importantly, the increasing prevalence of automatic-contribution 401(k) plans, which enroll eligible employees by default (i.e., in the absence of an election out) into salary-reduction contributions that increase over time and invest the contributions in a broadly diversified age-appropriate designated default investment (very commonly target-date funds), alleviates decision making impediments and complexity for many workers. *See* I R C §§ 401(k) (13), 414A (West Sup. 2023); ERISA § 404(c)(5), 29 U.S.C. § 1104(c)(5) (2018); 29 C.F.R. § 2550.404c-5 (2023).

The matter of when to take distributions entails more tax and pension law complications, but the Code demands some advance written explanation of considerations pertinent to this issue. I.R.C. § 402(f) (2018); *see supra* Chapter 10 note 300.

[305] Some experts believe that high transaction costs have been an important driver of the migration away from defined benefit plans by small and medium-sized employers.

[306] John H. Langbein, *ERISA's Role in the Demise of Defined Benefit Pension Plans in the United States*, (Sept. 16, 2022 working paper).

expenditure, estimated at \$229 billion in fiscal year 2022.[307] The magnitude is staggering. Yet this "cost" is mislabeled insofar as the nondiscrimination rules actually redirect the tax subsidy into additional retirement savings for rank-and-file workers. The purpose of the tax allowance is redistribution, and the true cost of accomplishing that goal is only the portion of the subsidy that is *not* shifted (whether retained by HCE-savers, captured by the employer, or used to defray administrative costs).[308]

Thus the case against the private pension system largely comes down to the question of efficacy. How much additional retirement saving (saving that would not otherwise occur) does the tax allowance actually generate, and is it enough? It is difficult to know how efficient our covert redistribution mechanism is in operation.[309] Lacking information on individual propensity to save, the existence of a plan with broad participation does not tell us how much (if any) new saving has been induced. Perhaps plans mostly operate as tax shelters for workers who would have saved anyway. Or perhaps the system is highly efficient, in the sense that foregone tax revenue is transmuted into additional saving with minimal waste. Supposing the latter optimistic assumption were true, still the current system is inadequate. The active participation rate stubbornly hovers around 50 percent of private wage and salary workers aged twenty-one to sixty-four,[310] and that number

[307] This figure includes the tax expenditure associated with traditional and Roth IRAs (\$19.9 billion, total), as well as qualified plans (\$209.4 billion, including defined contribution, defined benefit, and Keogh plans). EXECUTIVE OFFICE OF THE PRESIDENT, ANALYTICAL PERSPECTIVES, BUDGET OF THE UNITED STATES GOVERNMENT, FISCAL YEAR 2023, at 153, 160 (2022), www.govinfo.gov/content/pkg/BUDGET-2023-PER/pdf/BUDGET-2023-PER-5-3.pdf. Congressional estimates are much higher, \$325 billion for FY 2022. See STAFF OF THE JOINT COMM. ON TAXATION, JCX-22-22, ESTIMATES OF FEDERAL TAX EXPENDITURES FOR FISCAL YEARS 2022–2026, at 42 (2022), www.jct.gov/publications/2022/jcx-22-22/.

[308] Redistribution ordinarily entails adverse effects on productivity incentives, of course. When it comes to qualified retirement savings, however, favorable tax treatment mitigates the income tax system's deterrent effect on saving to the extent that HCEs actually benefit.

[309] It is safe to say that the costs associated with the administration of private plans are many times higher than the expense of running the Social Security system, which is about 1 percent of benefits paid. One estimate puts the expense of maintaining a defined benefit plan at 11 percent of benefits paid, and 6 percent on average for defined contribution plans. David M. Cutler, *Reexamining the Three-Legged Stool, in* SOCIAL SECURITY: WHAT ROLE FOR THE FUTURE? 125, 140 (Peter A. Diamond et al. eds., 1996). Of course, if Social Security included a system of private accounts, then program administration expenses would be far higher.

[310] Retirement plan participation among all workers in private industry stood at 52 percent in 2022 (62 percent for full-time workers, but only 20 percent for part-time workers). BUREAU OF LABOR STATISTICS, U.S. DEPARTMENT OF LABOR, NATIONAL COMPENSATION SURVEY: EMPLOYEE BENEFITS IN THE UNITED STATES, MARCH 2022, Table 1, www.bls.gov/ebs/publications/retirement-plan-provisions-for-private-industry-workers-2022.htm. In 2022 Congress enacted a number of initiatives, including mandatory auto-enrollment under most new 401(k) plans, in an attempt to increase participation. I.R.C. § 414A (West Supp. 2023); *see supra* Chapter 7A, text accompanying notes 25–44. Whether or to what extent these measures will move up the needle on retirement plan participation remains to be seen.

Taxes and Retirement Saving

has been basically stagnant since the late 1970s. Yet almost all workers need to supplement Social Security to avoid a sharp drop in their standard of living in retirement.[311] Even for covered workers, many observers fear that the trend away from defined benefit plans to elective contribution programs that leave investment decisions to employees threatens benefit adequacy.[312] Wasteful or not, much is amiss with the modern pension system.

Most experts believe that far-reaching reforms or fundamental overhaul is required to help Americans achieve an adequate level of retirement resources. This section reviews the major components of a number of proposals, ranging from incremental reforms, like adjusting the nondiscrimination regime or sweetening the subsidy to expand coverage, to schemes that would jettison nondiscrimination and substitute a structure designed to attain near-universal coverage.

Calibrating Nondiscrimination

The current nondiscrimination regime, for all its complexity, is a crude device for accomplishing redistribution because both the amount of available subsidy and the aggregate bribes required to satisfy the tests depend upon workforce composition, including factors such as age, compensation level, tax rate, and individual propensity to save. Simply making the nondiscrimination rules stricter, as by raising the acceptable ratio percentage from 70 to 80 percent, for example, would not necessarily increase qualified plan coverage overall. Firms with workforces containing a large proportion of high-income savers (so currently a lot of wasted subsidy) would expand NHCE coverage to meet the new standard, while other companies would terminate existing plans because the enhanced NHCE participation rate would be too costly.

While there is no easy adjustment that will optimize redistribution, a number of modifications seem likely to improve the performance of the nondiscrimination rules. Four candidates are suggested here.

First, plan-by-plan testing for both coverage and amount discrimination accomplishes little beyond inflating compliance costs. Instead, all qualified plans of the employer (as defined under the workforce aggregation rules) could be subjected to a single consolidated application of the average benefit percentage test, with each plan deemed nondiscriminatory if the average benefit percentage of the group of all nonexcludible NHCEs is at least 70 percent of the average benefit percentage for

---

[311] *See supra* Figure 10.1 and accompanying text.

[312] In addition, some observers argue that a recent trend toward more expansive coverage under nonqualified deferred compensation programs (top hat plans) reduces pressure to provide more generous benefits under the company's qualified plan, thereby sidestepping nondiscrimination (redistribution) and suppressing benefits of low and middle income workers. Wiedenbeck & Stein, *supra* Chapter 10 note 19.

the group of HCEs.[313] (Each nonexcludible employee's individual benefit percentage would be computed by summing the contributions and benefits earned by that employee under all plans, and a zero would be included in the group average for each nonexcludible employee who is not an active participant in any plan.) Such a global average benefit test would permit the employer to completely segregate HCEs and NHCEs into different plans having different features (including an HCE contribution or benefit rate that is somewhat higher than is available to any NHCE), and that increased flexibility should yield plans of greater value to their members.[314]

Second, nondiscrimination "safe harbors" of the sort allowed for 401(k) plans should be repealed, except perhaps for small employers. Recall that the ADP test is deemed satisfied if the employer is required to make a qualified nonelective contribution on behalf of each eligible NHCE equal to at least 3 percent of compensation, or if the employer is required to make qualified matching contributions on behalf of each eligible NHCE, dollar-for-dollar on elective contributions up to the first 3 percent of compensation with a 50 percent match of elective contributions between 3 and 5 percent of pay.[315] These safe harbors amount to selling indulgences for discrimination. If an employer makes 3 percent qualified nonelective contributions for all eligible employees, the firm's HCEs may each make the maximum elective deferral ($22,500 in 2023), even if no NHCE elects to defer any portion of her pay. The amendment of existing 401(k) plans to take advantage of the safe harbor is a strong indicator that the toll charge for favoritism is attractively priced, or in other words, that it wastes more subsidy (forces less redistribution) than the ADP test.

Third, the stringency of the nondiscrimination standard might be adjusted to reflect the proportion of the workforce that consists of NHCEs. In general, a workforce containing a high proportion of NHCEs generates little subsidy that could be redistributed (due to few HCE-savers) but contains a large number of low-paid workers who need help saving for retirement. Conversely, a workforce with relatively few NHCEs may be assumed to have a lot of subsidy that could be shifted, but fewer low-paid workers among whom to distribute it. Wasted subsidy might be reduced and qualified plan coverage expanded by calibrating the numerical nondiscrimination standard with the composition of the workforce. Assuming a single consolidated application of the average benefit percentage test (as suggested above), an employer with a workforce that has a low proportion of NHCEs might be

---

[313] See *supra* text accompanying Chapter 10 notes 93–94. An additional anti-abuse rule might be required to assure that retirement savings are broadly distributed among NHCEs, rather than being concentrated in the hands of a favored few. See *supra* Chapter 10 note 93.

[314] This flexibility would be obtained only if testing for qualitative discrimination (testing the availability of benefits, rights, and features; *see* Treas. Reg. § 1.401(a)(4)-5 (as amended in 1993)) were not conducted on a consolidated basis.

[315] I.R.C. § 401(k)(12) (2018); Treas. Reg. § 1.401(k)-3 (as amended in 2009).

required to show that its average benefit percentage for NHCEs is 90 percent (or 110 percent) of the benefit rate for HCEs, for example. In contrast, a firm with a workforce containing few HCEs might be allowed to pass the nondiscrimination standard with an NHCE average benefit percentage that is substantially lower than the 70 percent required by current law. Indeed, as the share of workers who are HCEs gets smaller, the acceptable NHCE average benefit percentage might be decreased to a level that the available compensation cost savings could support – to 40, 30, or 20 percent, for example. Something akin to this is allowed under the nondiscriminatory classification test, where the acceptable plan ratio percentage is reduced (down to as low as 20 percent) as the proportion of NHCEs in the workforce increases, but that test serves only as a gateway to the average benefit percentage test which (under current law) imposes a 70 percent standard regardless of workforce composition.[316] A study of the relationship between plan sponsorship and workforce composition would need to be conducted to estimate how the required NHCE average benefit percentage should vary with NHCE workforce composition, and so set the proposed sliding-scale nondiscrimination standard.[317]

Finally, rather than prescribing a sliding-scale nondiscrimination standard, a fixed numerical benchmark could be imposed, as under current law, but the amount of the subsidy available to employers could be adjusted up or down with variations in workforce composition. While the value of the tax subsidy could be altered in a number of ways, perhaps the most straightforward approach would be to adjust the permissible maximum amount levels under Code section 415. Where a company's workforce is disproportionately composed of HCEs, the caps on the maximum dollar amount of annual benefits and annual additions (for defined benefit and defined contribution plans, respectively) for any participant could be reduced to limit the amount of tax-subsidized savings by highly paid workers, thereby reducing waste (i.e., subsidy in excess of the amount that must be redistributed to satisfy the nondiscrimination standard). Conversely, a firm that employs an unusually low percentage of HCEs could be allowed to give those executives a larger amount of qualified plan savings by raising the dollar caps under the maximum amount rule, so that higher savings levels would still generate enough subsidy to meet the nondiscrimination standard despite the smaller number of HCEs.

Sweetening the Subsidy

The preceding discussion shows that the traditional fixed and invariant nondiscrimination standard can sometimes be satisfied by a plan that accomplishes little

---

[316] See supra Figure 10.3 and accompanying text.
[317] It might be discovered that the simple binary HCE-NHCE classification is too crude to reveal a clear functional relationship to plan sponsorship. If so, a more sophisticated measure of compensation inequality within the workforce, such as the Gini coefficient, might be needed.

redistribution (resulting in much wasted revenue), while in other situations, it cannot be satisfied at all because the compensation cost savings that can be extracted from highly paid workers is insufficient to pay all the bribes that would be needed to induce the requisite level of rank-and-file employee participation. The difference between the two situations (Company A sponsors a qualified plan, Company B does not), as has been shown, is usually attributable to difference in workforce composition (Company A employs predominately HCEs who want to save; Company B overwhelmingly employs low-wage workers who cannot afford to save). Studies confirm that access to a retirement plan at work is not randomly distributed throughout the labor force. Instead, older, higher-paid workers are more likely to be employed by a company that sponsors a plan. Few small firms (meaning those with fewer than 100 employees) sponsor a plan, apparently due to differences in workforce composition. On average, small firm employees have lower earnings, less formal education, and are more likely to work part-time or part year than their counterparts at large firms. The characteristics of workers at small firms that sponsor retirement plans, however, are quite similar to workers at large firms that sponsor plans.[318]

> Although both administrative costs and workforce composition are likely to influence an employer's decision to sponsor a retirement plan, the data suggest that the low sponsorship rate at small firms is more likely due to differences in demand for retirement benefits by the firms' employees than to the fixed costs associated with starting up and administering a plan.[319]

Reduced demand, of course, increases the costs of complying with the nondiscrimination rules (higher bribes required) and so translates into a low qualified plan sponsorship rate. Inducing retirement savings in such circumstances is going to require more public money.

The saver's credit, enacted in 2001, is an effort to provide a larger savings incentive directly to low-income individuals (rather than by boosting the indirect subsidy available through a qualified plan).[320] The saver's credit can be up to 50 percent of the amount of qualified retirement savings contributions for the taxable year not in excess of $2,000. The 50 percent credit rate is available to taxpayers filing a joint return whose adjusted gross income (AGI) does not exceed $43,500 in 2023 ($21,750 for an unmarried individual). At higher incomes, the credit rate is smaller, and no credit is available at all if the AGI on a joint return is over $73,000 in 2023 ($36,500 for single taxpayers). A contribution to a traditional or Roth IRA, or an elective deferral under a 401(k) plan or 403(b) annuity, can qualify

---

[318] Peter Brady & Michael Bogdan, *Who Gets Retirement Plans and Why*, 2012, 19 ICI RESEARCH PERSPECTIVE No. 6, 9 (2013), www.ici.org/system/files/attachments/pdf/per19-06.pdf.

[319] *Id.* at 29.

[320] I.R.C. § 25B (2018).

Taxes and Retirement Saving 413

for the credit. The saver's credit is nonrefundable and it has been little utilized, largely because individuals with incomes low enough to qualify for the credit typically have little or no income tax liability to offset. For taxable years beginning after 2026 the saver's credit is converted into a government matching contribution to the taxpayer's qualified defined contribution plan or IRA.[321] The match is set at 50 percent of up to $2,000 of an eligible individual's qualified retirement savings contributions for the year, but the match phases out for married taxpayers filing jointly with modified AGI between $41,000 and $71,000 ($20,550 to $35,500 in the case of an unmarried individual).

Another measure to increase the subsidy is a credit for pension plan start-up costs of small employers. A 50 percent credit for the costs of establishing and administering a new qualified retirement plan and expenses of providing retirement-related education to employees is granted to employers with no more than 100 workers for the plan's first three years, subject to a maximum credit amount of $5,000 per year.[322] The credit is increased to 100 percent of qualified start-up costs if the employer has fifty or fewer employees.[323] In addition, for the taxable year in which the plan is established and the following four tax years a small employer is allowed a credit for all or a portion of its contributions (other than elective deferrals) to a defined contribution plan on behalf of employees earning $100,000 or less.[324]

Bush Administration Proposals

A different approach to stimulating additional saving is exemplified by the tax recommendations repeatedly put forward by President George W. Bush, which would have expanded Roth-style tax-free savings opportunities in individual accounts of two types, a Retirement Savings Account (RSA), and a Lifetime Savings Account (LSA). At this writing, these unenacted proposals are nearly twenty years old. Critical examination is nonetheless warranted, because the RSA/LSA initiative closely aligns with traditional Republican approaches to savings and tax policy. Something similar is likely to reappear.

The RSA would have allowed contributions of up to $5,000 per year regardless of income or coverage under a qualified retirement plan.[325] As with a Roth IRA,

---

[321] I.R.C. § 6433 (West Supp. 2023).

[322] I.R.C. § 45E (2018).

[323] I.R.C. § 45E(e)(4) (West Supp. 2023).

[324] *Id.* § 45E(f). The credit percentage is 100 percent in the year of plan establishment and the following year, and drops to 75, 50, and 25 percent over the next three tax years.

[325] U.S. DEPARTMENT OF THE TREASURY, GENERAL EXPLANATIONS OF THE ADMINISTRATION'S FISCAL YEAR 2009 REVENUE PROPOSALS 9 (2008) [hereinafter Bush ADMINISTRATION'S FY 2009 REVENUE PROPOSALS], https://home.treasury.gov/system/files/131/General-Explanations-FY2008.pdf. In contrast, deductible contributions to a traditional IRA are subject to a phase-out for workers whose income exceeds specified levels and who are covered by an employer-sponsored retirement plan. I.R.C. § 219(g) (2018). Roth IRA

contributions would be nondeductible (after-tax), but earnings would accumulate tax-free, and qualified distributions would be excluded from gross income. To dedicate RSAs to retirement saving, qualified distributions would be available only after attaining age fifty-eight or in the event of death or disability. (The earnings portion of earlier distributions would be subject to tax, including a 10 percent additional tax.) The RSA would substitute for all current forms of IRAs, other than rollover IRAs created solely to receive qualified plan distributions.

Individuals would also have been allowed to contribute up to $2,000 annually to an LSA, another Roth-style personal account that could be used to save for any purpose. Hence the LSA would not be limited to saving for retirement, health care, or education (for which tax-favored accounts are currently available), but could also be used to save for the purchase of a car or a home or for precautionary purposes. LSA contributions would be allowed whether or not the contributor has earned income and regardless of his total income. The annual contribution limit would apply to all accounts held in a particular individual's name, rather than to the contributor, so that an affluent middle-aged couple could put $2,000 into each of their LSAs and also contribute $2,000 to accounts for each of their children (or grandchildren, etc.).[326]

The RSA-LSA combination was ostensibly designed to both encourage and simplify savings.

> The current list of non-retirement exceptions within IRAs weakens the focus on retirement saving, and the IRA exceptions and special purpose savings vehicles place a burden on taxpayers to document that withdrawals are used for certain purposes that Congress has deemed qualified. In addition, the restrictions on withdrawals and additional tax on early distributions discourage many taxpayers from making contributions because they are concerned about the inability to access the funds should they need them. Consolidating the ... types of IRAs under current law into one account dedicated solely to retirement, and creating a new account that could be used to save for any reason would simplify the taxpayer's decision-making process while further encouraging saving.[327]

From one perspective, the RSA-LSA proposal can be seen as a logical evolutionary step toward rationalizing current savings incentives. Yet the Bush Administration initiative carried with it two indirect effects that some analysts viewed as revolutionary and deeply troubling. First, the new Roth-style accounts would encourage

---

contributions are also subject to an income phase-out, but the income range is higher than for deductible contributions to a traditional IRA. *Id.* § 408A(c)(3).

[326] Unlike the RSA, which would replace traditional and Roth IRAs, the LSA apparently would not replace existing nonretirement tax-advantaged savings vehicles. Hence, health savings accounts, Coverdell educational savings accounts, and section 529 qualified tuition programs would apparently continue to exist alongside LSAs, considerably expanding tax-free savings opportunities.

[327] BUSH ADMINISTRATION'S FY 2009 REVENUE PROPOSALS, *supra* Chapter 10 note 325, at 8.

Taxes and Retirement Saving

individual savings, thereby rendering qualified plan savings relatively less attractive and undermining the nondiscrimination regime. Second, the Bush Administration's savings proposals would also have worked a fundamental transformation of the federal tax system.

The individual tax-favored savings opportunity presented by RSAs and LSAs would weaken interest in qualified retirement plans at all income levels. Low-paid workers, we have seen, derive little benefit from tax deferral and often have little ability to save. To induce their participation in a qualified retirement plan so as to satisfy the nondiscrimination rules, the employer must sweeten the deal by increasing their total compensation. This is done by making a contribution toward retirement savings that is larger than the amount of wages or salary low-paid employees are willing to forgo, which compensation increase (in effect, a bribe to entice participation) is financed by the tax subsidy extracted from highly paid employees who want to save. Limited access to qualified plan savings, particularly the additional tax on early distributions, presents a barrier to participation by low-income workers that the employer must pay to overcome.[328] The LSA, however, offers a vehicle for penalty-free short-term precautionary saving, and for many young or low-paid employees, that alternative might be more attractive than subsidized but restricted qualified plan savings.[329] Middle-income employees who want to save for retirement might conclude that they can save enough individually via the RSA-LSA combination that there is no advantage to be gained from participation in a qualified plan.[330] Moreover, the absence of income limits on RSA and LSA

---

[328] The ban on in-service distributions under pension plans is also a significant barrier (and deterrent to NHCE participation), but profit-sharing and stock bonus plans can allow distribution after as little as two years of participation. In contrast, 401(k) plans cannot permit access to elective deferrals (nor to qualified matching and qualified nonelective contributions) after a stated period of participation or the lapse of a fixed number of years, but that restriction is ameliorated by the authorization of distributions of elective deferrals in the event of the employee's hardship. I.R.C. § 401(k)(2)(B), (k)(3)(D), (m)(4)(C) (2018); Treas. Reg. 1.401 (k)-1(d)(3) (as amended in 2009) (definition of allowable hardship distributions). Hardship distributions are not exempted from the 10 percent additional tax on early distributions, however. I.R.C. § 72(t)(2) (2018).

[329] This comparison holds only for employees who have some federal income tax liability. A worker can always save on his own outside of a qualified plan, IRA, or Roth-style account and retain complete access to his funds, and if his income is low enough, then any pay saved would bear no tax, and the interest or other investment earnings also would not be taxed. For such a worker, the LSA offers no more benefit than "taxable" personal savings.

[330] Under current law, such workers could use an IRA (traditional or Roth) to accumulate $5,000 per year (inflation-indexed to $6,500 in 2023) of tax-favored retirement savings outside of a qualified plan, but with an LSA they could increase the amount of their tax-advantaged individual retirement saving. As described above, the annual LSA contribution limit most recently proposed was only $2,000, but earlier versions of the Administration's LSA proposal would have allowed much higher LSA contributions ($5,000 or $7,500 per year), and if the Bush plan were enacted, there would be continuing political pressure to raise the LSA contribution limit. U.S. DEPARTMENT OF THE TREASURY, GENERAL EXPLANATIONS OF THE ADMINISTRATION'S FISCAL YEAR 2007 REVENUE PROPOSALS 9 (2006)

416   Tax Controls: Qualified Retirement Savings

contributions would reduce demand for more generous employer-sponsored qualified retirement plan benefits among high-income savers – these HCEs, who are the source of the tax subsidy, do not have to share to the extent that they can save through tax-exempt individual accounts.[331] From this perspective, the RSA-LSA proposal has the potential to profoundly exacerbate widely acknowledged problems of the current system: namely, too few low-income people saving too little for retirement and too much of the tax expenditure ending up in the hands of people unlikely to need it.

Beyond these individual tax-favored savings accounts, the Bush Administration also advocated consolidation and simplification of the rules governing all types of tax-favored defined contribution savings programs that permit elective or salary-reduction contributions (including, among others, 401(k) plans, 403(b) annuities, and eligible deferred compensation plans maintained by state or local governments or tax-exempt organizations). A new vehicle, called Employer Retirement Savings Accounts (ERSAs), would be available to all employers and be subject to relaxed nondiscrimination testing. In place of the ADP test applicable to 401(k) plans,[332] the average HCE contribution percentage could be 200 percent of the average NHCE contribution percentage if the average NHCE contribution percentage were 6 percent or less, but if the average NHCE contribution percentage exceeded 6 percent, no limit would apply to HCE contribution rates (other than the Code section 415 maximum annual addition). Under an alternative design-based safe harbor, if each NHCE were eligible to receive fully-vested employer contributions (either matching or nonelective) of at least 3 percent of compensation, no further

---

($5,000 LSA limit), https://home.treasury.gov/system/files/131/General-Explanations-FY2007 .pdf; U.S. Department of the Treasury, General Explanations of the Administration's Fiscal Year 2004 Revenue Proposals 119 (2003) ($7,500 LSA limit), https://home.treasury.gov/system/files/131/General-Explanations-FY2004.pdf. Similarly, the 2005 recommendations of the President's Advisory Panel on Federal Tax Reform included a Roth-style "Save for Family" account to which a taxpayer could contribute up to $10,000 annually in addition to putting $10,000 into a "Save for Retirement" account, and the Save for Family account could be used for retirement (as well as for health care, education, or a down payment on a home). President's Advisory Panel on Federal Tax Reform, Simple, Fair, and Pro-Growth 120 (2005), https://home.treasury.gov/system/files/131/Report-Fix-Tax-System-2005.pdf.

[331] Under current law, a high-income individual who is an active participant in a qualified plan cannot contribute to a Roth IRA or on a tax deductible basis to a traditional IRA due to the income-based limits on contributions to those accounts. I.R.C. §§ 219(g), 408A(c)(3) (2018). Under the Bush Administration proposal, such a high-income active participant could take advantage of the RSA and LSA, which would diminish interest in higher levels of plan contributions or benefits. Apparently, a high-income individual not covered by a qualified plan could contribute $5,000 to an RSA.

This nondiscrimination-avoidance dynamic (the potential to sidestep redistribution) is the same policy concern posed by the recent trend toward broader top hat plan participation. *See supra* Chapter 10 note 312.

[332] *See supra* Chapter 10 notes 181–187 and accompanying text.

nondiscrimination standards would apply.[333] In stark contrast to the proposal to repeal the 401(k) nondiscrimination safe harbors described earlier,[334] the expansion and relaxation of 401(k) rules proposed for ERSAs would say that once certain minimum[335] contributions are provided to NHCEs, no further redistribution is required. Regardless of how much the HCEs saved, they (or their employer) could retain the full value of their favorable tax treatment; none of the tax benefit would have to be shared with rank-and-file employees. Employer-sponsored ERSAs, in common with the proposed RSA and LSA Roth-style individual savings accounts, would achieve simplification by gutting redistribution, allowing tax relief to inure to the benefit of high-income workers and their employers.

From a broader perspective, the Bush Administration's saving proposals also would have pushed the federal tax system farther along the path to a consumption tax base. The $7,000 that anyone could put away in her RSA and LSA each year (more if contributions are made to LSAs for children or others) is more than most Americans save. Consequently, all investment returns – dividends, interest, capital gains, and so forth – would be tax-exempt for a large majority of taxpayers, for whom the federal tax system would become simply a tax on labor income.[336] Many economists and some tax policy experts favor consumption over income as the base for personal taxation on efficiency grounds. As a practical matter, the Bush Administration's savings proposals would have largely accomplished a covert conversion of the federal revenue system to a consumption tax.[337]

Toward Universal Coverage

Each of the reform proposals examined thus far – calibrating the nondiscrimination rules, sweetening the subsidy, and the Bush Administration's individual account

---

[333] Bush Administration's FY 2009 Revenue Proposals, *supra* Chapter 10 note 325, at 15–16.

[334] See *supra* text accompanying Chapter 10 note 315.

[335] Some would say token.

[336] Many consumption-tax features have been engrafted onto the realization-based federal income tax over the years, among the most important being the treatment of qualified retirement savings. The current system is generally understood as a hybrid between an income and a consumption tax. The RSA-LSA proposal, if adopted, would have shifted the balance far closer to a pure consumption tax, but because the accounts would get Roth-style treatment, the resulting consumption tax would be of the prepaid sort. That is, instead of taxing consumption when it occurs (by deducting savings and investments and later taxing the full proceeds when applied to consumption), current taxation of labor income deposited in Roth-type accounts amounts to taxing the present value of future consumption.

[337] See Theodore R. Groom & John B. Shoven, *Deregulating the Private Pension System, in* The Evolving Pension System 123–53 (William G. Gale et al. eds., 2005) ("[E]xpansion of qualified plans can serve as a practical substitute for fundamental tax reform based on a consumption model because pensions are already taxed on that basis and can therefore be expanded without addressing the difficult transitional issues that are involved in converting the entire system to a consumption." *Id.* at 140.)

proposals – recommends incremental change to the existing retirement savings system. While some of these approaches are designed to significantly increase the number of American workers accumulating tax-favored retirement savings, none of them aim at universal coverage. Moreover, all of them depend upon the employment relationship.

The twenty-first century has witnessed the opening of a benefits coverage gap traceable to the decline of traditional employment due to the rapid growth of the so-called gig economy. Internet-based software platforms or smartphone apps connecting drivers with customers (e.g., Uber, Lyft, DoorDash) have become ubiquitous, while online platforms matching users with providers of many other services (including dog walkers, personal caregivers, copywriters, software developers and lawyers) proliferate. The engagement between one service-provider and a particular user is ordinarily an impersonal task-specific short-term (one-off) arrangement, and platform companies take the position that their service providers are independent contractors, not employees. While collecting payment, the platforms do not withhold employment taxes and typically offer few, if any, fringe benefits to their workers. Some service providers, who use the platforms to supplement their income with a part-time "side hustle," may have access to retirement savings or health care through their primary employment. Others work substantially full-time (or more) as freelancers who depend upon the platform as their primary or sole source of income. As long as workers' classification as independent contractors (rather than platform company employees) holds, employer mandates will not extend benefit coverage (either retirement savings or healthcare) to labor sold in the gig economy.[338]

A comprehensive savings program to supplement Social Security has long been understood to require a mandatory system. The 1981 report of the President's Commission on Pension Policy, for example, proposed:

> The Commission recommends that a Minimum Universal Pension System (MUPS) be established for all workers. The system should be funded by employer contributions. The Commission further recommends that a 3 percent of payroll contribution be established as a minimum benefit standard. All employees over the age of 25, with one year of service and 1,000 hours of employment with their employer would be participants in the system. Vesting of benefits would be immediate.
>
> Under a MUPS, current pension plans would be amended to provide the equivalent of what a MUPS would provide. The MUPS benefit would be a supplement to social security benefits and could not be integrated with social security. . . .
>
> Employers should be encouraged to maintain the accumulated funds in pension trusts or through arrangements with insurance companies and other financial

---

[338] In some situations, a plausible claim of employee status can be made. *See* Paul M. Secunda, *Uber Retirement*, 2017 U. Chi. Legal F. 435, 447–52.

institutions. However, those employers who do not wish to administer an employee pension plan could send their contributions to ... a central MUPS portability fund which would be established to invest the funds in the economy. The fund should be administered by an independent Board of Trustees appointed by the President.[339]

Business leaders generally oppose and legislators have shown little interest in a MUPS-type mandate. And as an employer mandate, it fails to address the expanding rift between labor income and employment compensation.

Proposals have been developed that would move toward broader coverage of common law employees in a more politically palatable manner, by using public monies to fund savings on behalf of low-income workers. Two such programs are reviewed below.

Professors Daniel Halperin and Alicia Munnell "think it is time to acknowledge that today's voluntary employer-sponsored pension system is not capable of providing coverage for most of those individuals who end up in the lowest two quintiles of the retirement income distribution .... Reform is also needed to improve coverage and benefit adequacy for the rank and file."[340] Halperin and Munnell propose a two-pronged strategy.[341] First, government would directly fund retirement savings for low-income workers (those earning less than about $20,000 or $25,000 annually), who could be excluded from coverage under employer-sponsored retirement plans. "No longer would employers have to bribe lower-paid workers who have little interest in retirement saving to participate by increasing their total compensation."[342] Second, sponsorship of employer plans would remain voluntary, but if maintained, they would be required to cover virtually all workers not covered by the

---

[339] PRESIDENT'S COMMISSION ON PENSION POLICY, COMING OF AGE: TOWARD A NATIONAL RETIREMENT INCOME POLICY 42–43 (1981). *See* Adam Carasso & Jonathan Barry Forman, *Tax Considerations in a Universal Pension System*, (Urban-Brookings Tax Policy Center Disc. Paper No. 28, 2007), www.urban.org/research/publication/tax-considerations-universal-pension-system-ups.

[340] Daniel I. Halperin & Alicia H. Munnell, *Ensuring Retirement Income for All Workers*, in THE EVOLVING PENSION SYSTEM, *supra* Chapter 10 note 337, at 155, 180.

[341] Halperin & Munnell, *supra* Chapter 10 note 340, at 179–85.

[342] Halperin & Munnell, *supra* Chapter 10 note 340, at 181. In return for diminished employer responsibility for covering low-income workers (reduced cost), Halperin and Munnell propose a 5 percent tax on private pension fund earnings, the revenue from which could be used to help fund the government contributions for low wage workers. *Id.* at 182–83. The publicly funded retirement accounts for individuals earning less than $20,000 or $25,000 would be similar to the Clinton Administration's 1999 Universal Savings Account (USA) proposal, but withdrawals would be prohibited before age sixty-five. The automatic government contribution would be phased out for individuals earning higher incomes, but dollar-for-dollar government matching contributions would apparently be available to workers earning somewhat higher amounts, perhaps up to about twice the income cutoff for the automatic grant (i.e., up to about $40,000 or $50,000 for single individuals). *See* Remarks on the Universal Savings Accounts Initiative (Apr. 14, 1999), *reprinted in* 1 PUBLIC PAPERS OF THE PRESIDENTS OF THE UNITED STATES: WILLIAM J. CLINTON, 1999, at 548 (2000).

public program. As an inducement to do so, the employer would be allowed to provide higher benefits for top earners. If an employer sponsored a plan, all middle- and high-income employees working at least 500 hours per year would have to be covered, and benefits or contributions would have to constitute the same proportion of pay for all workers (without integration with Social Security). Therefore the complex coverage and amount nondiscrimination requirements of current law could be repealed.[343]

The key components of the Halperin and Munnell plan would greatly enlarge the portion of the US labor force that accumulates meaningful retirement savings. Public funding would provide for the lowest-paid workers, while more mid-level earners (rank-and-file employees) would be granted plan membership so that executives could amass higher benefits. Jettisoning the nondiscrimination rules would reduce administrative costs, yielding another inducement to plan sponsorship. (These features figure prominently in some other expert reform proposals.[344]) Yet because qualified plan sponsorship would remain voluntary, some workers would still be left out, including independent contractors (gig workers).

Professor Teresa Ghilarducci suggests a mandatory program that offers government funding for low earners and that preserves significant inducements for employers to offer defined benefit pension plans.[345] Like Halperin and Munnell, Ghilarducci agrees that the old ways aren't working. "To determine what is needed for effective pension reform, it is ... crucial to stop pretending that the tax incentives for defined contribution plans do anything meaningful."[346] Professor Ghilarducci's proposal can be viewed as a version of add-on Social Security individual accounts, but with an important twist. There are three major components of her approach. First, she would repeal favorable tax treatment for all defined contribution plans, whether they are money purchase pension plans, profit-sharing plans, stock bonus plans, employee stock ownership plans (ESOPs), 401(k) plans, 403(b) tax-sheltered

---

[343] Halperin & Munnell, *supra* Chapter 10 note 340, at 183. Current law permits the exclusion of part-time employees working less than 1,000 hours per year. In order to preserve retirement savings by the rank-and-file, Halperin and Munnell would also require full vesting within one year and mandatory rollover of lump-sum distributions to an IRA or another plan. In addition, all plans would have to offer an inflation-indexed annuity as a distribution option.

[344] PAMELA PERUN & C. EUGENE STEUERLE, WHY NOT A "SUPER SIMPLE" SAVING PLAN FOR THE UNITED STATES 8–13 (2008), www.urban.org/sites/default/files/publication/31751/411676-Why-Not-a-quote-Super-Simple-quote-Saving-Plan-for-the-United-States-.PDF.

[345] THERESA GHILARDUCCI, WHEN I'M SIXTY-FOUR 260–93 (2008). The Ghilarducci plan would encompass all common law employees, but it is unclear whether or how it would address independent contractors, including gig workers. Because it builds upon Social Security, independent contractors could presumably be covered by increasing the Self Employed Contributions Act tax on self-employment income by 5 percent. *See* I.R.C. §§ 1401–1403. The plan fails to address the issue, however.

[346] *Id.* at 288.

Taxes and Retirement Saving

annuities, or otherwise.[347] As a substitute for defined contribution plans a "Guaranteed Retirement Account" (GRA) would be established for every worker. Like MUPS, GRAs entail compulsory savings: contributions of 5 percent of pay (up to the Social Security contribution and benefit base) would be required for all employees.[348] The contributions would be collected by withholding from pay and transferred to the Social Security Administration, whence they would be credited to individual accounts and invested by trustees as under the Federal Thrift Savings Plan.[349] GRA balances would earn a guaranteed minimum 3 percent real rate of return. The earliest allowed withdrawal from a GRA would be at the earliest age for claiming Social Security benefits (sixty-two), at which point the balance would be converted to an inflation-adjusted life annuity. (Partial lump-sum payment of up to 10 percent of the account balance would be allowed.[350]) Ghilarducci calculates that the GRA accumulation over a full working career would produce retirement benefits equal to approximately 30 percent of pre-retirement compensation, which in combination with Social Security would yield a retirement income replacement rate for an average wage earner of about 70 percent.[351]

The second component of Ghilarducci's program is a refundable $600 tax credit for every worker contributing to GRA, regardless of income. This credit is set at a

[347] *See Id.* at 264 (proposed $600 tax credit would substitute for current tax breaks granted 401(k) and other individual account plans).

[348] Ghilarducci, *supra* Chapter 10 note 345, at 264. The features of the GRA plan are also explained in Teresa Ghilarducci, *The Plan to Save American Workers' Retirement, in* PENSIONS, SOCIAL SECURITY, AND THE PRIVATIZATION OF RISK 86, 95–101 (Mitchell A. Orenstein ed., 2009). All workers would be allowed to make voluntary additional contributions to their GRA out of after-tax income. This option would allow highly paid employees to contribute some of their earnings that exceed the Social Security contribution and benefit base (such excess earnings would not be subject to the 5 percent contribution requirement), and would also permit middle-income employees who want to replace more than 70 percent of their pre-retirement earnings to use their GRAs to do so.

[349] GHILARDUCCI, *supra* Chapter 10 note 345, at 264–65. Curiously, Professor Ghilarducci does not explicitly address the tax status of the required 5 percent contributions. The assumption seems to be that they would come from the worker's after-tax income (i.e., withheld amounts not excludible from gross income), like the employee's share of Social Security taxes. *See id.* at 264 (voluntary additional contributions would be made with post-tax dollars; refundable tax credit would substitute for tax concessions granted defined contribution plans, presumably including the exclusion of contributions from employee income), *id.* at 276. The tax treatment of GRA distributions is also left entirely unspecified. If contributions are to be included in gross income, then distributions should at least be eligible for tax-free return of capital to that extent, presumably by application of the exclusion ratio approach to annuity taxation. *Cf.* I.R.C. §§ 402(a), 72 (2018). Alternatively, the GRA could be accorded Roth-style preferential tax treatment: contributions subject to tax with an exclusion for all amounts distributed. Because the value of such a yield exemption depends on the employee's tax rate (income level), preferential tax treatment might necessitate the imposition of some limits on voluntary additional contributions. *See supra* Chapter 10 note 348.

[350] GHILARDUCCI, *supra* Chapter 10 note 345, at 265. In lieu of a single life annuity, the GRA owner would be permitted to elect actuarially equivalent (reduced) survivor annuity benefits.

[351] *Id.* at 265.

level that would ensure that the compulsory 5 percent contribution would not impose a reduction in take-home pay on full-time full-year minimum wage workers.[352] The revenue gained from repeal of the favorable treatment of defined contribution plans is projected to be more than enough to fund the tax credits.[353]

Finally, tax-favored defined benefit retirement plans (traditional pension plans) would still be permitted, and Ghilarducci proposes to allow employers to substitute coverage under a defined benefit plan for GRA contributions. An employer contributing at least 5 percent of payroll to a defined benefit plan each year would be excused from the obligation to withhold and pay over 5 percent of each worker's pay as GRA contributions.[354] This continuing role for traditional pension plans is founded upon their superior efficiency and risk allocation characteristics vis-à-vis defined contribution plans.[355] Compared to 401(k) plans and other defined contribution retirement savings programs, large defined benefit plans entail lower per-participant administrative costs, provide better diversification, insulate workers from the adverse effects of sharp market downturns on the eve of retirement, and can be designed to assure that workers do not outlive their savings. These desirable attributes arguably support permitting at least some defined benefit plans to substitute for GRA coverage.

The defined benefit plan opt-out is an intriguing suggestion, but this feature of Ghilarducci's program is not fully developed. Not all defined benefit plans share the desiderata that are crucial to a sound national retirement policy. Presumably, traditional pension coverage would not be an adequate substitute for GRA contributions if the plan permitted pre-retirement[356] or lump-sum distributions, for instance, and the five-year cliff vesting that ERISA currently tolerates could leave a mobile worker with no retirement savings to show for many years of her career. Even if a participant is vested on separation from service, the limited portability of defined benefit pensions would need to be addressed.[357] Perhaps because of these

---

[352] *Id.* at 268.

[353] *Id.* at 276.

[354] *Id.* at 271–72, 292.

[355] The declining prevalence of defined benefit plans, despite their superiority as a means to retirement security, is a main theme of Professor Ghilarducci's book. The same phenomenon is explored from another perspective by Edward A. Zelinsky, *The Origins of the Ownership Society* (2007), which is subtitled, "How the Defined Contribution Paradigm Changed America," and by Langbein, *supra* Chapter 10 note 306.

[356] Under current law, pension plan distributions are permitted upon plan termination or separation from service. I.R.C. § 401(a)(20); *see* Rev. Rul. 56-693, 1956-2 C.B. 282, IRS Gen. Couns. Mem. 39,824 (July 6,1990).

[357] *See* Halperin & Munnell, *supra* Chapter 10 note 340, at 169–73. One approach might be to require that, upon separation from service before attaining Social Security retirement age, a defined benefit plan transfer the actuarial present value of the departing employee's accrued benefits to his GRA.

difficulties, in a subsequent version of the GRA proposal Professor Ghilarducci did not mention the defined benefit plan alternative.[358]

Despite such complications, the defined benefit plan opt-out deserves further study, and for a reason that Professor Ghilarducci does not address. Tax advantages are not the only reason employers sponsor deferred compensation programs. Historically, many qualified plans were instituted in large part to advance the sponsoring company's personnel policy, whether the goal was to reduce turnover, encourage early retirement, offer a productivity incentive, or otherwise. ERISA allows pension plans that satisfy minimum standards of quality to be tailored to serve business objectives; this residual employer flexibility was deliberately preserved to encourage the continued growth of private plans.[359] If designed with care, allowing private plan coverage to substitute for GRA contributions in specified circumstances could benefit both employers and employees. That increased flexibility might reduce business opposition to the GRA proposal and enhance economic efficiency as well.

Some likely features of a composite qualified plan-GRA system can be sketched without getting mired in minutia. First, consider a defined benefit plan opt-out. As indicated earlier, defined benefit plan coverage should be allowed to substitute for mandatory GRA contributions only if plan characteristics provide at least as much savings with comparable security. Retirement distributions should take the form of an inflation-indexed life or joint-life annuity; lump-sum payouts would be barred apart from permitting a single distribution of not more than 10 percent of the actuarial present value of the employee's accrued benefit. Pre-retirement distributions upon separation from service or plan termination could not be made either directly to the participant or to her IRA, but in these circumstances the value of the participant's accrued benefits could be rolled over into the employee's GRA. The requirement that a substitute plan provide savings at least as great as the 5 percent of pay that would otherwise be deposited in a participant's GRA would seem to demand an outright ban on forfeitures, or at least a reduction of the maximum acceptable vesting period to a year or two. Alternatively, however, the vesting schedules currently permitted (five-year cliff or three-to-seven-year graded vesting for defined benefit plans) could still be allowed, but subject to the stipulation that upon separation from service, the plan's forfeiture rules would apply only to the extent that the present value of the participant's accrued benefit under the terms of the plan exceeds the amount that would have accumulated in the participant's GRA but for the plan (i.e., periodic contributions of 5 percent of the wages or salary paid by the sponsor plus the guaranteed investment return of 3 percent thereon). This limited forfeiture would maintain some marginal incentive to continued employment with the plan sponsor, and a benefit formula based on final average

[358] See Ghilarducci, *The Plan to Save American Workers' Retirement, supra* Chapter 10 note 348.
[359] See generally supra Chapter 1C.

compensation could also be used to encourage longer job tenure. Benefits based on final average compensation accrue disproportionately in the later years of a worker's career, inflicting substantial pension losses in the event of mid-career employment change, but so long as the present value of accrued benefits upon separation from service is equal to or greater than the amount that an outgoing participant would have accumulated under a GRA, there is no reason to prohibit an employer from designing a plan to reward service longevity. Early retirement incentives should also be acceptable, provided that the benefits are paid as a life or joint-life annuity, and the actuarial value of benefits that will be paid after the normal retirement date (recall that GRA distributions could commence no earlier than the youngest age for claiming Social Security benefits) is at least equal to the amount that, in the absence of the plan, the participant would have accumulated in her GRA based upon her employment with the plan sponsor.

Allowing coverage under an acceptable defined benefit plan to excuse the employer from making 5 percent contributions to an employee's GRA could be taken even further. One might allow an employer to establish a defined benefit plan that grants past-service credit and also permit the sponsor to immediately fund those retroactive benefits by claiming a refund of prior-year GRA contributions (and earnings thereon) that the employer made on behalf of plan participants in years before the plan was instituted. Prospectively, this retroactive take-up of prior-year GRA contributions would go far toward eliminating underfunding problems with defined benefit plans, and would reduce the exposure of the PBGC.

The GRA compulsory saving system proposed by Professor Ghilarducci is in effect a mandatory federally administered cash balance plan under which every American worker is entitled to annual pay credits of 5 percent of current compensation, along with guaranteed interest credits of 3 percent of the account balance. The cash balance plan is a hybrid design; technically it is categorized as a defined benefit program (because a specified level of benefits is guaranteed regardless of the actual investment performance of the fund), but it promises an accrued benefit that mimics a defined contribution plan (specifically, a 5 percent money purchase pension plan that invests in inflation-protected bonds earning a 3 percent real return).[360]

The androgynous nature of the GRA system offers a hint that some defined contribution plans might also be acceptable substitutes. Historically, defined contribution plans served a number of important employer objectives, many of which have been overlooked as 401(k) plans rose to dominance. In particular, profit-sharing and stock bonus plans were traditionally used to provide a productivity incentive to participating employees. The aggregate annual contribution to a profit-sharing plan could be tied to some measure of business performance, such as profits or sales, for example, with the overall contribution allocated among

---

[360] See *supra* Chapter 7 note 58 and accompanying text.

Taxes and Retirement Saving

participants' accounts in proportion to their current compensation. There appears to be no reason to prohibit an employer from rewarding performance by making productivity-based contributions to its workers' GRAs so long as the minimum annual contribution is 5 percent of pay and the contributions are nondiscriminatory. By using the GRA as the savings vehicle, most of the threats to retirement security often posed by defined contribution plans would be alleviated: funds would obtain low-cost professional management and be broadly diversified, the guaranteed return would protect workers from sharp declines in retirement living standards caused by market volatility, and restrictions on GRA distributions would prevent employees from squandering or outliving their savings.

Replicating the incentives created by investments in employer stock would be antithetical to retirement income security, and so employer contributions under a stock bonus plan or ESOP should not be treated as meeting GRA obligations. Here again, however, the amount going into an employee's broadly diversified and professionally managed GRA could safely be fixed by reference to some measure of enterprise value or stock price movement if the contribution is subject to a 5 percent floor and satisfies nondiscrimination standards. Indeed, even the aversive aspects of investments in employer stock might be partially incorporated in a GRA-based savings program by allowing stock price declines in a given year to reduce or eliminate the employer's required GRA contribution, but only to the extent that the employer's total contributions to an employee's GRA exceed the aggregate minimum required for all of the employee's prior years of service.[361]

The lesson here is that a system of compulsory minimum saving such as Ghilarducci's GRA proposal need not entirely homogenize retirement plans nor displace all work-related incentives. If the savings mandate is thoughtfully coordinated with other employer objectives, then the system could preserve or reclaim many of the personnel management functions that deferred compensation programs traditionally embraced.

E CONCLUSION

Where taxes meet pensions, policies often conflict and law can be unstable. Evaluated exclusively as a problem of income tax policy, the principle of economic neutrality counsels that taxes should not bias the choice between current and deferred compensation. Historically, the matching principle of Code section 404 (a)(5) largely achieved neutrality between current and *nonqualified* deferred

---

[361] Earnings on prior-year *excess* contributions could also be reclaimed (that is, subject to loss in the event of poor stock performance) without jeopardizing baseline GRA protections. Put another way, current year contributions could be reduced (perhaps even below zero) by any amount up to the amount by which the employer's total contributions to date plus guaranteed earnings thereon exceeds the amount that would have been accumulated if the employer had contributed only the minimum each year (5 percent of pay plus earnings thereon).

compensation by suspending the employer's business expense deduction until such time as the employee includes the deferred compensation in gross income. Tax rate changes enacted in 2017 upset the balance by setting the corporate income tax rate well below the top rate applicable to individual income (21 percent versus 37 percent). Moreover, in 2004 Congress enacted rules requiring employees to include nonqualified deferred compensation in advance of receipt unless the program satisfies certain criteria. Such advance inclusion by itself would not undermine tax neutrality, but Congress larded new section 409A with interest and penalty provisions that can upset the balance.

Once pension policy is added to the mix, matters become far more complex. All but the very lowest-paid workers must save to supplement Social Security if they are to have more than a subsistence-level standard of living in retirement. Low and moderate-income workers, however, simply do not save adequately when left to their own devices. Consequently, Congress encourages retirement saving by deliberately tilting the balance between current and deferred compensation, granting preferential tax treatment to qualified deferred compensation and to savings that are committed to an individual retirement account. The tax preference takes the form of deferral (which under certain conditions is equivalent to exemption from tax of the investment yield), which makes the value of the subsidy depend on the worker's marginal tax rate. Because individual income tax rates are progressive, tax deferral (or yield exemption) by itself provides the largest saving incentive to the highest income employees, and offers no assistance to the many American workers (almost 40 percent of US households) whose income is low enough that they incur no federal income tax liability. Left undisturbed, this state of affairs would clearly produce a perverse distribution of tax benefits: low- and middle-income workers who most need help saving would get little or no incentive, while highly paid workers who can and do save on their own would get a substantial tax reduction simply by shifting their saving into a tax-advantaged account. Under such circumstances, tax deferral is not an effective incentive that induces additional retirement saving – rather than offering assistance to those who need it, the tax concession is so much wasted revenue. There should be little wonder that year after year, IRA contributions are overwhelmingly made by high-income individuals.

Many analysts assail the "upside-down" nature of our retirement savings tax subsidy,[362] but in doing so they overlook the impact of the qualified retirement plan nondiscrimination rules, which are intended to mitigate the perverse distribution of tax benefits that would otherwise occur. When they operate correctly, the nondiscrimination rules funnel the tax benefits from highly paid workers who wish

---

[362] E.g., GENE SPERLING, THE PRO-GROWTH PROGRESSIVE 183–88 (2005) (taking no notice of the nondiscrimination rules, author asserts that the "reason our system is so upside-down is that the only way we encourage savings is through tax deductions"); THERESA GHILARDUCCI, WHEN I'M SIXTY-FOUR 275–77 (2008) (asserting that 70 percent of the tax subsidy goes to those in the top 20 percent of the income distribution).

Taxes and Retirement Saving

to save into additional retirement saving by middle- and low-paid employees who cannot afford the reduction in their current take-home pay that unassisted plan participation would otherwise entail. Often, highly paid workers must give up a portion of their tax benefits by allowing the employer to reduce their compensation; that compensation cost savings is then used to finance additional compensation for rank-and-file employees whose participation is necessary to satisfy the nondiscrimination rules and who would not otherwise be willing to save. In this way, the nondiscrimination rules create a covert redistribution mechanism that is generally underappreciated or misunderstood. The common assertion that the $100+ billion annual tax expenditure for qualified retirement plans overwhelmingly benefits high-income employees is at best misleading, because it ignores the fact that a large share of the tax savings may be recaptured from the apparent beneficiaries (high-income plan participants) by means of an implicit tax exacted by the employer via a reduction in their compensation.[363] To get any tax benefit from retirement savings, executives may have to consent to earning less than they would in the absence of a qualified plan, while low-wage workers may be getting paid more than they otherwise would. As has been shown, one can fairly criticize the efficacy of the non-discrimination rules in shifting the tax subsidy from a windfall for highly paid executive and professional employees into retirement savings for rank-and-file workers. Yet even though the existing nondiscrimination regime is admittedly a makeshift, haphazard, and clunky redistribution device, it should not be dismissed or ignored. Indeed, under an income tax, the preferential treatment of qualified plan savings could not be justified without some such means of targeting the subsidy.

The future of qualified retirement plans largely depends upon the future of the income tax, which can no longer be taken for granted. Under a consumption tax base, the whole complex edifice would crumble because there would be no special advantage to employer-sponsored programs – all saving would be taxable only when withdrawn and applied to consumption. (If low-income workers needed help saving for retirement under a consumption tax, then forthright redistribution in the form of direct government assistance would be necessary. Social Security benefits might be made more generous for the low-income elderly, or a system of federal matching contributions to restricted retirement savings accounts might be established.) Assuming the income tax abides in something like its current (hybrid) form, the effectiveness of the nondiscrimination regime could be enhanced with a number of

---

[363] *See supra* Chapter 10 note 362. Leonard E. Burman et al., *Distributional Effects of Defined Contribution Plans and Individual Retirement Accounts*, 8 (Tax Policy Center Disc. Paper No. 16, 2004), http://webarchive.urban.org/UploadedPDF/311029_TPC_DP16.pdf (authors "do not make any adjustments for the presence or operation of nondiscrimination rules" in estimating distributional effects). *But see* Halperin & Munnell, *supra* Chapter 10 note 340, at 159 (due to nondiscrimination rules "plan sponsors may have to use some of the tax benefits to increase the total compensation of 'reluctant savers,' those [employees] who do not much value this deferred compensation").

incremental reforms. Those refinements, however desirable, would not solve the central problem of national retirement policy, namely, the stubborn fact that at any time, only about one-half of the American labor force is covered by any kind of employment-based retirement savings program. This coverage gap is concentrated among lower-paid workers and small business employees. Something more than rejiggering intra-firm compensation levels is needed to make long-term investors out of these reluctant savers. Quite a number of proposals have been advanced, but they mostly boil down to either contributing public monies to retirement accounts for low-wage workers, or imposing a compulsory minimum savings requirement on all American workers, or both.

PART V

Health Plan Content Controls

11

Employment-Based Health Care

In 2010 the United States Congress enacted the Patient Protection & Affordable Care Act (ACA),[1] the most significant health care reform in a generation. To say the ACA was controversial is to put it mildly: in the decade after its passage it spawned major litigation that came before the Supreme Court on multiple occasions.[2] While the ACA preserved ERISA, it altered the federal landscape for employment-based health plans, imposing multiple requirements where ERISA had not, partially filling the regulatory gap that ERISA's broad preemption had largely blocked states from filling.[3]

Accordingly, the current statutory reality is that employment-based health insurance is chiefly regulated by the ACA, ERISA, and saved state law, as well as a raft of pertinent provisions in the Internal Revenue Code. The entire foundation of that body of law rests upon certain assumptions about the merits of employer involvement in the provision of health care. This chapter provides a conceptual overview of employment-based health insurance under ERISA and the ACA, focusing on the rationales offered in support of the employment link. The chapter will not comprehensively survey the many ACA rules and regulations that shape employment-based health benefits after the landmark statute's enactment. Instead, it will highlight the

---

[1] The Patient Protection and Affordable Care Act, Pub. L. No. 111-148, 124 Stat. 119 (2010), as amended by the Health Care and Education Reconciliation Act, Pub. L. No. 111-152, 124 Stat. 1029 (2010). Herein we refer to the two pieces of legislation collectively as "ACA."

[2] "The ACA is the most challenged statute in American history. The first lawsuits were filed moments after the law was enacted – on March 23, 2010 – alleging that the ACA was unconstitutional. Ten years later, the ACA is still under attack, being litigated in three Supreme Court cases within [2020] alone – for a collective total of seven Supreme Court challenges in a decade." Abbe R. Gluck, Mark Regan & Erica Turret, *The Affordable Care Act's Litigation Decade*, 108 GEO. L.J. 1471, 1472 (2020).

[3] *See* Brendan S. Maher, *Regulating Employment-Based Anything*, 100 MINN. L. REV. 1257, 1314–19 (2016) (hereinafter *REBA*).

431

432   *Health Plan Content Controls*

key statutory and judicial rules, from both ERISA and ACA, which now define the
landscape of health insurance in the United States.

A HEALTH CARE FINANCE AND EMPLOYMENT

Apart from public programs like Medicare and Medicaid, there are three common
ways to finance the cost of medical care: one may participate in an employment-
based group health care plan; one may purchase an individual health insurance
policy; or one may agree to pay for health care expenses as they are incurred.[4] The
first, a method largely unique to the United States, is our focus.

The provision of employment-based health benefits has a long history. In the late
1800s, industrial enterprises, such as railroad and mining companies, began to
experiment with programs where employer-funded physicians provided care to
workers who were injured on the job or afflicted with a prevalent illness.[5] By the
early twentieth century, retailer Montgomery Ward provided something analogous
to contemporary disability insurance to its workers: payment for wages lost because
of sickness.[6] In 1929, a group of teachers in Dallas contracted with a local hospital to
provide needed care for a fixed fee per group member – the start of Blue Cross.[7]
When World War II arrived, wage and price controls limited pay increases but did
not limit fringe benefits like health insurance, which contributed to its spread and
stoked labor's postwar expectation that health benefits should be a standard component of a good compensation arrangement.[8] By 1970, roughly 150 million
workers and their dependents had access to hospitalization insurance, and some
75 million had access to major medical insurance.[9] By 2010, almost 70 percent of
working-age Americans had access to employment-based health insurance through
their own job or a family member's.[10] But the historical details matter less than the

[4] *Id.* at 1274–75. Many Americans have insufficient salary, savings, or other resources to pay
medical expenses as they arise, and therefore medical debt is a major component of consumer
debt and a substantial contributor to consumer bankruptcies. CONSUMER FIN. PROT.
BUREAU, MEDICAL DEBT BURDEN IN THE UNITED STATES 5–6 (2022) (estimating that
in 2021 approximately 20 percent of households had past-due medical debt totaling about
$88 billion).
[5] Laura A. Scofea, *The Development and Growth of Employer-Provided Health Insurance*, 117
MONTHLY LAB. REV. 3, 3 (1994).
[6] *Id.* at 4.
[7] *Id.* at 5.
[8] Clark C. Havighurst, *American Health Care and the Law*, in THE PRIVATIZATION OF
HEALTH CARE REFORM: LEGAL AND REGULATORY PERSPECTIVES 1, 3–4 (M. Gregg
Bloche ed., 2003).
[9] Walter W. Kolodrubetz, *Two Decades of Employee-Benefit Plans, 1950–70: A Review*, 35 SOC.
SEC. BULL. 10, 10 (1972).
[10] Beth Levin Crimmel, *STATISTICAL BRIEF #360: Employer-Sponsored Health Insurance
Offers, Eligibility, and Enrollment Rates for Civilian Employees within the Private and the
State and Local Government Sectors, by Census Division*, 2010, AGENCY FOR HEALTHCARE
RESEARCH AND QUALITY (2012), https://meps.ahrq.gov/data_files/publications/st360/stat360

Employment-Based Health Care

details of insurance economics, which supply the chief reason employment-based insurance became widespread in the United States.

Health insurance is subject to adverse selection, the phenomenon that those who *seek* insurance are more likely to need to use it, and are thus more costly to the insurer.[11] On its face that does not seem problematic. The insurance company, after all, could simply charge a higher premium to account for the increased risk. The problem is asymmetric information.[12] Even for insurance companies, it is difficult to predict the actual risk of an individual insured, because most individuals have *un*ascertainable characteristics that correlate with risk.[13] Thus, based on the reasonably ascertainable characteristics of a given potential insured, an insurance company may conclude that a premium of X is sufficient to make extending insurance profitable.[14] Adverse selection suggests that those who are seeking insurance are likely to have unascertainable characteristics that make the actuarial risk they pose to the insurance company high, and high in a way that the insurance company cannot reliably predict.[15] While the insurance company may defend its interests by simply raising premiums across the board, that makes insurance even less attractive to healthy people, requiring the insurance company to raise premiums still higher, and so on.[16] The result is that, without some mechanism to combat adverse selection, health insurance markets will function poorly, if at all.[17] When health care is so expensive that few can afford it out of pocket, that becomes a social problem.[18]

Employment-based insurance combats adverse selection by in effect making the insurable unit a group rather than an individual.[19] Writing a policy for a group that exists for some reason other than to buy insurance poses far less adverse selection risk

---

.pdf) (explaining that 88.4 percent of workers' employers in the United States offered health insurance plans, and 78.1 percent of those workers were eligible for the plans offered).

[11] *See e.g.*, George A. Akerlof, *The Market for "Lemons"*, 84 Q. J. Econ. 488, 492–94 (1970) (formal explanation of adverse selection theory).

[12] Maher, *REBA*, *supra* Chapter 11 note 3, at 1281.

[13] Louis Kaplow, *An Economic Analysis of Legal Transitions*, 99 Harv. L. Rev. 509, 543 (1986).

[14] 43 Am. Jur. 2d Insurance § 2 (2022) (detailing the process of underwriting, generally). The process by which an insurer gathers information about the potential insured and calculates a fair premium for such a person is called "risk underwriting." David A. Hyman & Mark Hall, *Two Cheers for Employment-Based Health Insurance*, 2 Yale J. Health Pol'y L. & Ethics 23, 32 (2001).

[15] Brendan S. Maher, *Unlocking Exchanges*, 24 Conn. Ins. L.J. 125, 129 (2017) (hereinafter *UE*).

[16] Maher, *REBA*, *supra* Chapter 11 note 3, at 1281.

[17] Maher, *UE*, *supra* Chapter 11 note 15, at 130. *See also* Akerloff, *supra* Chapter 11 note 11, at 492–94.

[18] *Id.*

[19] Maher, *REBA*, *supra* Chapter 11 note 3, at 1275–90.

than writing a policy for an individual.[20] The more people in the group, the more likely the group's actuarial risk approaches the risk of the entire community (which includes both healthy and unhealthy people).[21] This is far from the only rationale in favor of employment-based insurance, but it exerts a powerful effect, particularly in the United States, where (before the ACA was enacted) the only meaningful choice for most workers was between obtaining health insurance through employment or buying individual (or family) coverage.[22] Medicare and Medicaid did not exist until 1965, and those programs were not options for workers who are neither elderly nor needy.[23] That left the individual market for health insurance, which was plagued by strict medical underwriting criteria and high premiums necessary to respond to the problem of adverse selection.[24]

As a result of those realities, health insurance through the workplace was a desirable option for employers because it meant their workers were more likely to be able to obtain care and not miss work; for employees because infirmities in the individual market meant employment-based insurance was either the cheaper or only option for many of them; and for the government, which saw a way to make health insurance available to a significant part of the population without the creation of a new government program.[25] Favorable tax treatment for employer-provided health insurance was enacted in 1954 and has continued ever since.[26] Such preferential tax treatment for employment-based health insurance is an

[20] Maher, *UE*, *supra* Chapter 11 note 15, at 136 n.30 ("This assumes that the group is assembled for some reason other than to buy insurance; that is obviously the case with employee groups, who are assembled by dint of their decision to work for a given employer.") *See also* John Aloysius Cogan Jr., *Does Small Group Health Insurance Deliver Group Benefits? An Argument in Favor of Allowing the Small Group Market to Die*, 93 WASH. L. REV. 1121, 1151 (2018) (noting reduction of adverse selection risk in group insurance); Allison K. Hoffman, *Oil and Water: Mixing Individual Mandates, Fragmented Markets, and Health Reform*, 36 AM. J. L. & MED. 7, 28 (2010) (explaining there is "little concern of adverse selection with respect to large, employer-sponsored group insurance").

[21] *See* Maher, *REBA*, *supra* Chapter 11 note 3, at 1280–83; *see also* Maher, *UE*, *supra* Chapter 11 note 15, at 136.

[22] Maher, *UE*, *supra* Chapter 11 note 15, at 144 ("Thus, prior to the [ACA], heath care was reliably available only to those that had access to private or public insurance, namely the elderly (through Medicare), the poor (through Medicaid), or the employed (through EB coverage). Those outside those categories could only obtain insurance through the individual market, which was not accessible to most people.").

[23] Social Security Act Medicare Amendments of 1965, Pub. L. 89–97, 79 Stat. 286 (1965) (Medicare amendment).

[24] Maher, *UE*, *supra* Chapter 11 note 15, at 144 ("[I]ndividual markets are plagued with administrative and adverse selection problems.").

[25] *See* Maher, *UE*, *supra* Chapter 11 note 15, at 136.

[26] *See, e.g.*, 26 U.S.C. § 106 (2018). *See also* Eileen J. O'Connor et. al., *2008 Federalist Society Tax Policy Conference Panel: "How Our Tax Laws Affect How Health Is Paid for and Delivered"*, 9 ENGAGE: J. FEDERALIST SOC'Y PRAC. GRPS. 8, 10 (2008) (Professor Monahan discussing differential tax treatment of health care expenditures, pre-ACA); Stephen Utz, *The Affordable Care Act and Tax Policy*, 44 CONN. L. REV. 1213, 1233–34 (2012) (explaining, post-ACA, the differential tax treatment of health expenditures).

Employment-Based Health Care

alternative to the direct expenditure of government funds to subsidize health insurance.[27] The magnitude of the indirect subsidy is enormous: recent Treasury estimates calculate the tax-expenditure for employment-based health insurance to be in excess of $220 billion – the single largest tax break in the federal budget.[28]

Some observers have long argued that employment-based insurance is a historical accident arising from the United States' early twentieth century political failure to adopt broad-based public health insurance.[29] Alternate approaches to providing health care, this argument goes, would deliver more value per dollar spent, or would be fairer, or would have some other policy advantage.[30] While those arguments may very well be true – in the end employment-based insurance may indeed be less efficient or less fair than alternative forms of health care financing – an important clarification is needed. That employment-based health insurance is a historical accident does *not* mean that employment-based health insurance has nothing to recommend it.

One should not assume that the sole justification for employment-based insurance is the political calculation that a great many voters are sufficiently happy with their employment-based insurance (and tax burden) and will punish politicians who endanger continuance of the current system. This is not to deny entirely the political aspect of the staying power of employment-based health insurance – there is little doubt that social inertia and status quo bias do indeed cut meaningfully in favor of it.[31] Yet there are also policy reasons to think that employment-based health insurance is more than an artifact of the failure of Progressive Era and New Deal politicians to adopt a national health insurance program.

Many of the policy rationales for employment-based insurance are more easily recognized when compared to a world in which the only option is to purchase insurance on the individual market. That contrast allows for a starker description of employment-based insurance's justifications. Using employment as a fulcrum for health care delivery does, as explained above, leverage the natural fact that employee

---

[27] *See generally* STANLEY S. SURREY, PATHWAYS TO TAX REFORM (1973); STANLEY S. SURREY & PAUL R. MCDANIEL, TAX EXPENDITURES (1985).

[28] OFF. OF MGMT. & BUDGET, ANALYTICAL PERSPECTIVES, BUDGET OF THE U.S. GOVERNMENT, FISCAL YEAR 2023 153, 160 (2022), www.govinfo.gov/content/pkg/BUDGET-2023-PER/pdf/BUDGET-2023-PER.pdf.

[29] David Blumenthal, *Employer-Sponsored Health Insurance in the United States: Origins and Implications*, 355 NEW ENG. J. MED. 82, 82 (2006) (describing how many have described the American embrace of employment-based insurance as "an accident of history").

[30] *Cf.* ERIC SCHNEIDER ET. AL., MIRROR, MIRROR 2017: INTERNATIONAL COMPARISON REFLECTS FLAWS AND OPPORTUNITIES FOR BETTER U.S. HEALTH CARE 4 (2017) https://interactives.commonwealthfund.org/2017/july/mirror-mirror/assets/Schneider_mirror_mirror_2017.pdf.

[31] *See* Maher, REBA, *supra* Chapter 11 note 3, at 1317; *see also* Ross Douthat, Opinion, *A Hidden Consensus on Health Care*, N.Y. TIMES (July 6, 2013) www.nytimes.com/2013/07/07/opinion/sunday/douthat-a-hidden-consensus-on-health-care.html (arguing that political and social calculations favor continuing existence of employment-based insurance).

groups are largely insulated from adverse selection. But there are other aspects about employment-based insurance that provide additional reason to think a government may be justified in encouraging or requiring that employers play a meaningful role in health care purchasing.

First, employers are group purchasers, which, in addition to the adverse selection benefits, has two further ones.[32] Bulk purchases, in insurance as with other goods, are cheaper than individual ones, and thus large employers can purchase insurance policies at a lower unit cost than individuals. Employer group purchases are also a simple place to deploy a cross-subsidy: some workers are going to be more costly to insure than others, because of their underlying health status.

The administrative ease of writing a group policy with a group-average premium meant there were few objections when, years after ERISA was originally passed, Congress barred medical underwriting within an employment group.[33] While insurers remained able to charge different companies different group rates (a law firm can be charged less than a trucking company, for example), few bemoaned the loss of the ability to charge some employees *within* a company a higher premium. Whether that cross-subsidy was tolerated by the public as part of a sense of worker solidarity or an inability to understand what was happening is unknown, but few of the feverish complaints later leveled against the ACA's use of cross-subsidies to "make the healthy pay for the sick" were made with the same level of vigor against Congress's application of the very same practice at the employer level.[34]

A second policy advantage is that with employment-based insurance, the insurance consumer is in essence the company, which often has resources and specialist employees who have developed sophistication with respect to making insurance purchases. Employment-based insurance thus offers the promise of more sophisticated purchasers – the employer's professional administrators – serving as agents for

---

[32] Maher, *UE*, *supra* Chapter 11 note 15, at 136–37.

[33] ERISA § 702(b)(1), 29 U.S.C. § 1182(b)(1) (2018) (barring, as a part of HIPAA's enactment in 1996, premium discrimination within group). HIPAA added Part 7 to Title I of ERISA in 1996, of which section 702(b)(1) was one meaningful part. Health Insurance Portability and Accountability Act, Pub. L. 104–191, 110 Stat. 1936 (1996). *See also* Colleen E. Medill, *HIPAA and Its Related Legislation: A New Role for ERISA in the Regulation of Private Health Care Plans?*, 65 TENN. L. REV. 485, 497 (1998) (discussing in detail various HIPAA amendments to ERISA).

[34] *Cf.* David Cutler, *Should Healthy People Have to Pay for Chronic Illnesses?*, WASH. POST (Mar. 17, 2017), www.washingtonpost.com/posteverything/wp/2017/03/17/should-healthy-people-have-to-pay-for-chronic-illnesses/ (noting ACA opponent Paul Ryan's view that the "fatal conceit of Obamacare" is that "the people who are healthy pay for people who are sick"); Complaint at ¶19, Virginia ex rel. Cuccinelli, v. Sebelius, 2010 WL 1038397, ¶19 (E.D. Va.) ("Requiring citizen-to-citizen subsidy or redistribution is contrary to the foundational assumptions of the constitutional compact.").

less sophisticated employees in narrowing down a wild variety of potential insurance options to actionable choices.[35]

A third policy advantage relates to behavioral economic insights that have made clear humans are beset with cognitive biases that frustrate optimal decision making, especially with respect to purchasing insurance.[36] For example, humans are poor estimators of long-term risk; make decisions based on snippets of salient information recently encountered rather comprehensively evaluating a large body of complex information; and frequently avoid making tough decisions, that is, they procrastinate.[37] None of those infirmities are helpful with respect to the optimal purchase of health insurance. Employment-based arrangements can defeat or diminish some of these cognitive biases, not only by transferring an important part of health insurance decision making to company administrators with appropriate expertise, but also by requiring that employees make *some* choice with respect to health insurance, as opposed to simply never purchasing it because they never get around to it. Virtually all workers are familiar with filling out company paperwork in connection with benefit elections and payroll deductions; the choice regarding health insurance is one that is scheduled, compartmentalized, and presented as "here are the specific choices you must make about segregating a portion of your salary to purchase health insurance" (and indeed sacrificing the employer contribution if you choose not to purchase it). That framing has the virtue of making it more likely that individuals will get health insurance than if they were in the same financial position but left entirely to their own wits. Indeed, that the acquisition of insurance through the workplace is a forced, structured choice filtered through the work of human resources professionals reduces considerably the likelihood that individuals will sub-optimally underinsure.[38]

All of the above can be accomplished, moreover, without triggering government intervention in personal affairs. Certainly there are reasons to question these purported advantages, both on their own terms and in comparison to alternative ways to pay for and deliver care. But the case for employment-based health insurance is not quite as flimsy as is sometimes suggested. Before considering the degree to which the enactment of ACA changed the employment-based health landscape, it will be instructive to tour the world of ERISA health care *prior* to the passage of the ACA.

---

[35] Maher, REBA, *supra* Chapter 11 note 3, at 1278–80 (explaining benefit of sophisticated actors).

[36] Maher, *UE, supra* Chapter 11 note 15, at 137–38.

[37] As Professor Brian Galle put it, "there is now extensive evidence that most people are disproportionately sensitive to small, immediate costs; that is one of the reasons we procrastinate even essential tasks." Brian Galle, *Hidden Taxes*, 87 Wash. U. L. Rev. 59, 83–84 (2009) (describing various cognitive biases and listing research studies). *See generally* Daniel Ariely, Predictably Irrational: The Hidden Forces That Shape Our Decisions (2008); Daniel Kahneman, Thinking Fast and Slow (2011).

[38] *See* Maher, *UE, supra* Chapter 11 note 15, at 137–39.

B ERISA AND HEALTH REGULATION

ERISA is first and foremost a pension statute, then a retirement statute, then a benefits statute. It was never a health care financing statute. That it is called the Employee Retirement Income Security Act of 1974 was no accident; it was conceived and written as a Congressional response to well-known failures and abuses of traditional pension promises.[39] Nonetheless, ERISA from its inception has regulated employment plans that offer "welfare benefits" – of which the classic and most costly example is health care benefits.[40] Prior to the ACA's enactment, however, it provided very little substantive regulation of what an employer's health care promise to its employees need contain.[41]

Nonetheless, ERISA's impact upon health care regulation has been substantial, for at least two reasons. First, because of the sheer number of people who obtain health insurance through their employers, ERISA's rules govern the overwhelming majority of people who have private health insurance.[42] Second, because ERISA's preemptive reach is very broad, ERISA's lack of substantive health care regulation created a regulatory vacuum: enormous numbers of Americans had their health care bargains governed by a federal statute that provided little substantive rules at all, and states were profoundly constrained in their ability to fill that space. Preemption is discussed in greater detail in Chapter 6, but some principles are rehearsed and contextualized here, to highlight the role preemption played in shaping health care reform and regulation efforts in the United States prior to the enactment of the ACA.

Affirmative Regulation

One can readily imagine health insurance regulation that involves legislative specification of what a health insurance policy *must* cover for it to be permissibly sold, and at what price. Health insurance, after all, is chiefly useful to beneficiaries on the

---

[39] ERISA § 2, 29 U.S.C. § 1001 (2018) (explaining Congress's purpose for enacting ERISA); *see supra* Chapter 1.

[40] ERISA § 3(1), 29 U.S.C. § 1002(1) (2018) (defining "welfare plan" as one providing "medical, surgical, or hospital care or benefits, or benefits in the event of sickness, accident, disability, death or unemployment, or vacation benefits, apprenticeship or other training programs, or day care centers, scholarship funds, or prepaid legal services").

[41] ERISA's pre-ACA mandated benefit requirements included hospital delivery of newborns, mental health parity, and mastectomies. ERISA §§ 711-13, 29 U.S.C. §§ 1185–1185b (2018). *See generally* Medill, *supra* Chapter 11 note 33 (noting ERISA's original lack of substantive health care regulation and describing pre-ACA amendments to ERISA such as COBRA, HIPAA and the Newborns' and Mothers' Health Protection Act as modest, limited, non-comprehensive reforms).

[42] Katherine Keisler-Starkey & Lisa N. Bunch, U.S. Census Bureau, Health Insurance Coverage in the United States 3 (2020), www.census.gov/content/dam/Census/library/publications/2020/demo/p60-271.pdf ("In 2019, the percentage of people with employer-provided coverage at the time of interview was slightly higher than in 2018, from 55.2 percent in 2018 to 55.4 percent in 2019.").

Employment-Based Health Care

basis of *what* it covers, and then only useful if it is affordable. A policy purporting to be health insurance that offers no more than coverage for knee injuries costing less than $100 is functionally worthless, and a policy offering coverage for all imaginable conditions at the world's finest facilities would cost so much that virtually anyone who actually needs insurance could not afford it. Yet ERISA (with minor exceptions) regulated neither benefit coverage nor price – and, prior to the ACA, neither did any other federal statute.[43]

ERISA's rules for health care plans are largely rules of procedure, review, and remedy that apply to *all* ERISA benefit promises, not just those relating to health care. They consist of rules about how and when a plan must notify beneficiaries about their benefits,[44] obligations of loyalty and care in plan administration,[45] rules about what causes of action are available to enforce a participant's or beneficiary's rights,[46] rules about the standard of review a judge must use in considering such a claim,[47] rules about the availability of a jury,[48] rules about available damages,[49] and rules about when and how much a plan can recoup from an injured beneficiary who has successfully recovered in tort against a negligent third party.[50] Moreover, several of these rules are either judge-made or have been meaningfully affected by judicial interpretation and largely tilt in favor employers and payers, with the animating idea being that one of Congress's primary aims in passing ERISA was

---

[43] *Id.*

[44] *See e.g.*, ERISA §§ 101–05, 29 U.S.C. §§ 1021–25 (2018) (disclosure requirements).

[45] ERISA § 404, 29 U.S.C. § 1104 (2018).

[46] ERISA § 502, 29 U.S.C. § 1132 (articulating ERISA's civil enforcement scheme); Pilot Life Ins. Co. v. Dedeaux, 481 U.S. 41 (1987) (state law claims for benefit denials are preempted).

[47] Firestone Tire & Rubber Co. v. Bruch, 489 U.S. 101 (1989) (deferential review to administrator when plan awards discretion to administrator); Metro. Life Ins. Co. v. Glenn, 554 U.S. 105 (2008) (deferential review even when structural conflict of interest present); Conkright v. Frommert, 559 U.S. 506 (2010) (deferential review due even in the aftermath of arbitrary and capricious determination by administrator); 29 C.F.R. § 2590.715–2719(b)(2)(F)(1) (2022) (deference lost in health care denials if administrator did not substantially comply with federal regulations governing internal review). *See also supra* Chapter 5B.

[48] Brendan S. Maher, *The Affordable Care Act, Remedy, and Litigation Reform*, 63 Am. U. L. Rev. 649, 660 n.53 (2014) (collecting federal courts of appeal decisions denying a jury right in benefit denial cases).

[49] Mass. Mut. Life Ins. Co. v. Russell, 473 U.S. 134, 144 (1985) (extracontractual damages arising from delay in paying benefits are not available under ERISA); Mertens v. Hewitt Assocs., 508 U.S. 248, 256 (1993) (available relief under (a)(3) is limited only to relief that was "typically available in equity" and thus does not include compensatory damages); Cigna Corp. v. Amara, 563 U.S. 421 (2011) (not overruling *Mertens* but holding that equitable relief such as surcharge, reformation, and estoppel can result in the awarding of monetary damages); *see also supra* Chapter 5D.

[50] Indeed, the Supreme Court has four times addressed the scope of the subrogation right that payers hold under ERISA against injured insureds who have recovered something from a third-party tortfeasor. *See* Great-West Life & Annuity Ins. Co. v. Knudson, 534 U.S. 204 (2002); Sereboff v. Mid Atl. Med. Servs. Inc., 547 U.S. 356 (2006); US Airways, Inc. v. McCutchen, 569 U.S. 88 (2013); Montanile v. Bd. of Trs. of the Nat'l Elevator Indus. Health Benefit Plan, 577 U.S. 136 (2016).

440 *Health Plan Content Controls*

to provide uniform rules that would make employers feel comfortable in offering benefit plans.[51] Accordingly, judicial readings of ERISA's text that would impose upon plans additional cost or liability obligations, as well as procedural glosses likely to have that effect, have long been disfavored by the Supreme Court, notwithstanding the repeated and sometimes vociferous denunciations of scholarly commentators.[52]

While the Supreme Court has on multiple occasions stated that its interpretations of ERISA were motivated by a confidence that its rulings were consistent with Congress's goal of making the cost of offering benefit plans uniform and predictable,[53] there is little agreement about whether or not employer-friendly judicial interpretations of ERISA have impacted employers' decisions to offer health benefits.

Two areas in which ERISA's lack of affirmative regulation with respect to health plans is likely to surprise the uninitiated involve vesting and funding of health benefits. Unlike pension plans, ERISA does not require a welfare plan, including a health plan, to be funded, nor does it grant participants any statutory vesting rights.[54] Under ERISA, an employer can terminate or modify a health plan at any time, just so long as the termination or modification complies with ERISA's minimal procedural requirements and does not offend some other federal law.[55]

Two post-1974 additions to ERISA nicely illustrate both the advantages and limitations of employer-provided health insurance. Due to the adverse selection problem, by the mid-1980s health insurance was often practically unaffordable to an individual who lost employer group coverage, even if access to the group terminated

[51] *See* Varity Corp. v. Howe, 516 U.S. 489, 497 (1996) (noting importance of not making the burden of ERISA's legal rules so high as to "unduly discourage employers from offering welfare benefit plans in the first place").

[52] *See e.g.*, George Lee Flint, Jr., *ERISA: Extracontractual Damages Mandated for Benefit Claims Actions*, 36 ARIZ. L. REV. 611, 617–20 (1994) (criticizing the Supreme Court's ERISA benefit denial jurisprudence); Judith Resnik, *Constricting Remedies: The Rehnquist Judiciary, Congress, and Federal Power*, 78 IND. L.J. 223, 256–58 (2003) (criticizing the Supreme Court's view of "appropriate equitable relief" under ERISA); Paul M. Secunda, *Sorry, No Remedy: Intersectionality and the Grand Irony of ERISA*, 61 HASTINGS L.J. 131, 133 (2009) (criticizing the Supreme Court's ERISA remedies jurisprudence); *see generally* John H. Langbein, *What ERISA Means by "Equitable": The Supreme Court's Trail of Error in Russell, Mertens, and Great-West*, 103 COLUM. L. REV. 1317 (2003).

[53] Pilot Life Ins. Co. v. Dedeaux, 481 U.S. 41, 54 (1987) (explaining that ERISA "set forth a comprehensive civil enforcement scheme that represents a careful balancing of the need for prompt and fair claims settlement procedures against the public interest in encouraging the formation of employee benefit plans"); Aetna Health Inc. v. Davila, 542 U.S. 200, 209 (2004) (quoting *Pilot Life*'s "careful balancing" language); Conkright v. Frommert, 559 U.S. 506, 507 (2010) (again, quoting *Pilot Life*'s "careful balancing" language).

[54] Curtiss-Wright Corp. v. Schoonejongen, 514 U.S. 73, 78 (1995) ("Employers or other plan sponsors are generally free under ERISA, for any reason at any time, to adopt, modify, or terminate welfare plans .... Nor does ERISA establish any minimum participation, vesting, or funding requirements for welfare plans as it does for pension plans.").

[55] *Id.* at 78–79.

through no fault of her own. Worse still, the employee or family member who lost group coverage would typically discover that substitute coverage obtained on the individual market or from a new employer contained preexisting condition exclusions that operated to exclude payment of benefits based on a physical or mental health condition that was present before the date of enrollment in the new insurance. Consequently, people with costly medical conditions frequently found that preserving access to their previous employer group coverage was essential to obtaining continued care.

This desperate reality moved Congress to adopt continuation coverage requirements in 1986, adding a new Part 6 to ERISA Title I, commonly known as the COBRA rules.[56] These rules give individuals insured under most group health plans who lose coverage due to certain qualifying events an option to continue their coverage under the plan for a specified period, typically eighteen to thirty-six months, on condition that they pay the full premium cost of the coverage.[57] The employer is not required to contribute to (subsidize) that cost – indeed, to reflect administrative expenses the employer is allowed to charge 102 percent of the actuarially determined group premium – but the beneficiary who elects such continuation coverage does not have to pay the much higher rates demanded for an individual health insurance policy and does not forfeit coverage for preexisting conditions.[58] The right to elect continuation coverage is granted if the employee loses coverage due to termination (other than for gross misconduct), reduction of hours, or becoming eligible for Medicare, and also applies to beneficiaries of the employee who would lose coverage for these reasons or due to divorce or legal separation from the employee or a child no longer qualifying as a dependent under the plan's rules.[59]

COBRA continuation coverage protects workers and insured family members for a limited time from the consequences of actually losing employer group coverage. But as health care costs continued to escalate in the 1990s, Congress became increasingly concerned that the prospect of losing coverage was causing "job lock" – that workers were deterred from voluntarily *changing* jobs because the *new* employer's health plan excluded coverage for preexisting conditions (and thus meant some new employees or their beneficiaries who had coverage at the first employer were not eligible for coverage at the new firm). That drag on economic efficiency spawned initial limitations on group health plan preexisting condition exclusions

---

[56] Consolidated Omnibus Budget Reconciliation Act of 1985, Pub. L. No. 99-272, §§ 10,001–03, 100 Stat. 82, 222–37 (1986) (codified as amended in scattered sections of 26 U.S.C., 29 U.S.C., and 42 U.S.C.).

[57] ERISA §§ 601–09, 29 U.S.C. §§ 1161–69 (2018). The continuation coverage rules do not apply to a firm that normally employs fewer than twenty employees on a typical business day in the preceding calendar year. *Id.* at § 1161(b).

[58] ERISA § 602(1), (3), 9 U.S.C. §§ 1162(1), (3) (2018).

[59] ERISA § 603, 29 U.S.C. § 1163 (2018).

442 *Health Plan Content Controls*

with the enactment of ERISA Part 7 as part of the Health Insurance Portability and Accountability Act of 1996 (HIPAA).[60] As described below, the Affordable Care Act imposed more robust prohibitions on coverage exclusions, but HIPAA's stopgap move in that direction highlights another vulnerability of employment-based coverage.

Negative Regulation

ERISA's lack of affirmative regulation would have mattered less were it not paired with the statute's enormous preemptive reach. ERISA's preemptive scope is attributable to *both* expansive express preemption and implied preemption, because courts sometimes conclude that state laws not expressly preempted nonetheless fall because they conflict with or frustrate ERISA's objectives.[61]

Section 514 of ERISA lays out ERISA's three-pronged express preemption inquiry.[62] First, it preempts all laws that "relate to" employee benefit plans.[63] Second it "saves" from preemption all state laws that regulate banking, securities, or insurance.[64] Third, it bars states from "deeming" an employee benefit plan to be an insurance or banking company subject to a state's saved laws.[65] ERISA's implied preemptive reach is (unsurprisingly) more challenging to define, but it unquestionably captures state laws that supplement ERISA's (1) causes of action or (2) available remedies.[66] Predictably, litigation over ERISA's preemptive reach has occurred frequently in the decades since ERISA was first enacted, and often reaches the Supreme Court.[67] In health care terms, the statute has undermined or blocked numerous state efforts to fill the substantive gaps left by ERISA, a few examples of which are explored below.

Mandated benefits laws. One key set of preemption cases arises from the traditional primacy of states in regulating insurance.[68] Many states have "mandated

---

[60] Health Insurance Portability and Accountability Act of 1996, Pub. L. No. 104-191, §§ 101, 102, 110, Stat. 1936, 1939–55 (1996).

[61] ERISA § 514, 29 U.S.C. § 1144 (2018) (setting forth ERISA's express preemptive provision). *See supra* Chapter 6 for an involved discussion of ERISA's preemptive reach.

[62] ERISA § 514, 29 U.S.C. § 1144 (2018).

[63] *Id.* at § 1144(a).

[64] *Id.* at § 1144(b)(2)(A).

[65] *Id.* at § 1144(b)(2)(B).

[66] Rush Prudential HMO, Inc. v. Moran, 536 U.S. 355, 378–80 (2002).

[67] *See supra* Chapter 6 (discussing and categorizing ERISA preemption cases to have come before the Court).

[68] "When the States speak in the field of 'insurance,' they speak with the authority of a long tradition. For the regulation of 'insurance,' though within the ambit of federal power ... has traditionally been under the control of the States." Sec. & Exch. Comm'n v. Variable Annuity Life Ins. Co. of Am., 359 U.S. 65, 68–69 (1959). State primacy in insurance is statutorily embodied in the McCarran-Ferguson Act, 15 U.S.C. §§ 1011–15. (2018) *See id.* at § 1012(b) ("No Act of Congress shall be construed to invalidate, impair, or supersede any law enacted by

Employment-Based Health Care

benefits" laws – laws that, tracking natural intuitions about the role of a health insurance regulator, define what conditions or categories of condition must be covered by any health insurance policy sold in the state.[69]

In virtually all cases there is little dispute that such laws "relate to" employee benefit plans, which are, functionally speaking, in the business of offering health insurance.[70] The question is whether such laws are saved by the savings clause, and the degree to which such saved state laws can operate upon employee benefit plans without violating the deemer clause.[71] The doctrinal interpretation adopted by the Supreme Court has turned upon *how* a health plan is financed.[72] If a health plan pays a third-party insurer to directly insure its beneficiaries, then a state, by virtue of its saved powers to regulate insurance, may pass mandated benefits laws that govern health insurers in the state.[73] Such law is saved, and targeted as it is at health insurers, not plans, it does not run afoul of the deemer clause.[74] But if a plan that chooses to self-insure, that is, to back its health promises to employees with its own general revenues, it cannot be reached by state mandated benefits law, because of the deemer clause.[75] Even though such self-insured employer plans are unquestionably serving as insurers in a conceptual sense, the deemer clause explicitly bars states from regulating those plans.[76]

A consequence is that ERISA's preemptive scheme allows plans to *choose* whether or not to be subject to state regulation. If a state has mandated benefits regulation (or other saved law) that a plan deems too costly, the plan sponsor can simply self-insure, entirely freeing the plan from the costs of complying with state regulation. If the plan chooses not to self-insure, then the health benefits offered to employees will be indirectly subjected to a state's mandated benefits rules by virtue of the health insurer issuing the policy being so bound.[77]

A further insurance practice made an employer's ability to distance itself from state health insurance regulation even more complete. Companies the size of Apple or Google have more resources than insurance companies and are functionally indifferent to the risk that is associated with a health benefits promise; no matter how

---

any State for the purpose of regulating the business of insurance, or which imposes a fee or tax upon such business, unless such Act specifically relates to the business of insurance.").

[69] Metro. Life Ins. Co. v. Massachusetts, 471 U.S. 724, 727–31 (1985) (explaining the prevalence of mandated-benefit laws throughout insurance such as car and health insurances).

[70] *Id.* at 739 (explaining the expansive reach of ERISA's "relate to" clause).

[71] *Id.* at 740–41.

[72] FMC Corp. v. Holliday, 498 U.S. 52, 61–63 (1990) (explaining that self-insured employee benefit plans cannot be regulated by states and are thus subject to ERISA regulations).

[73] *Metro. Life*, 471 U.S. at 739–43.

[74] *Id.* at 746–47.

[75] FMC, 498 U.S. at 61.

[76] *Id.*

[77] *Id.* at 64 ("Our interpretation of the deemer clause makes clear that if a plan is insured, a State may regulate it indirectly through regulation of its insurer and its insurer's insurance contracts; if the plan is uninsured, the State may not regulate it.").

costly an individual claim, or how many high-dollar claims happen to occur in a given year, Google's resources will be adequate to cover them.[78] On the other end of the scale are small employers for whom even one costly sickness of an employee (or a member of her family) could bankrupt the business. Thus a company's size and risk tolerance serves as a natural barrier to employers opting to self-insure to avoid saved state regulation.

The existence of "stop-loss" insurance diminishes that natural barrier significantly. Stop-loss insurance is a form of reinsurance, in which the employer who has self-insured its health benefits promise arranges with an insurer to transfer risk above a certain "attachment point," namely, an amount of dollars above which the stop-loss insurer reimburses the *employer* for monies paid out on a claim or set of claims.[79] Such policies permit employers too small to tolerate the financial risk of truly self-insuring health benefits to facially self-insure while offloading the segment of risk they are unable to bear.[80]

In the late 1990s, Maryland attempted to act when its insurance regulators concluded that too many small employers were using stop-loss insurance as an expedient to avoid Maryland's mandated benefits laws.[81] The state declared that stop-loss policies employing a low attachment point (at first $25,000 and later $10,000) would be treated as health insurance policies subject to Maryland's mandated benefits laws (and thus denied approval by the state if such policies failed to meet mandated benefits requirements).[82] In the case of *American Medical Security v. Bartlett*, various plaintiffs challenged Maryland's actions as being pre-empted by ERISA, in particular the statute's "deemer clause."[83] The plaintiffs included employers whose self-insured packages of benefits, propped up by stop-loss policies with low attachment points, were narrower than Maryland's mandated requirements.[84]

The case went to the Fourth Circuit Court of Appeals, where the court sided with the plaintiffs. It reasoned that, while stop-loss regulation was saved under the savings

---

[78] Both Google and Apple have market capitalizations well in excess of one *trillion* dollars, larger than any insurer. *Compare* ALPHABET MARKET CAP, MACROTRENDS, www.macrotrends .net/stocks/charts/GOOGL/alphabet/market-cap (last visited Nov. 12, 2022), *and* MARKET CAPITALIZATION OF APPLE, https://companiesmarketcap.com/apple/marketcap/, *with* LARGEST INSURANCE COMPANIES BY MARKET CAP, https://companiesmarketcap.com/insur ance/largest-insurance-companies-by-market-cap/ (last visited Nov. 12, 2022).

[79] *Cf.* Bill Gray Enters., Inc. Emp. Health and Welfare Plan v. Gourley, 248 F.3d 206, 214–15 (3d Cir. 2001), *abrogated on other grounds by* US Airways, Inc. v. McCutchen, 663 F.3d 671 (3d. Cir. 2011), *vacated on other grounds by* US Airways, Inc. v. McCutchen, 569 U.S. 88 (2013) (explaining stop-loss insurance generally).

[80] Am. Med. Sec., Inc. v. Bartlett, 111 F3d 358, 362 (1997) (citing *In re* Md. Stop Loss Ins. Litig., No. MIA–370–12195 at 4 (Dec. 8, 1995)).

[81] *Id.*

[82] *Id.* at 360.

[83] *Id.* at 360–61.

[84] *Id.* at 360.

Employment-Based Health Care

clause, Maryland's effort to fashion stop-loss regulation in the way it had amounted to an attempt to improperly "deem" an employee benefit plan an insurer.[85] The court's reasoning relied on a purposive analysis of the deemer clause, which was, in the court's view, enacted by Congress to ensure that "at bottom state insurance regulation may not directly or indirectly regulate self-funded ERISA plans."[86] Since the employer, rather than an insurer, still retained legal responsibility for paying for claims, the court of appeals thought it was proper to view the employer as maintaining the type of self-insured plan that the Supreme Court had held could not be reached by saved insurance laws.[87] Scholarly observers criticized the decision,[88] and while the Supreme Court denied certiorari, the opinion served to chill state efforts to constrain the use of stop-loss insurance to evade saved state insurance laws.[89] By the time of the Affordable Care Act, roughly 60 percent of covered persons were believed to be in self-insured plans.[90]

General health reform. Another set of controversial health care preemption cases turns on state efforts to pursue health reform more generally. Prior to the Affordable Care Act, both a city (San Francisco) and a state (Maryland) attempted to enact broad-based health reform styled as "pay or play" reforms – a conceit that the ACA would later itself adopt.[91] In both cases the idea was roughly that employers who did not offer health insurance to their employees would owe the local government

---

[85] *Id.* at 363–65.

[86] *Id.* at 361 (citing FMC Corp. v. Holliday, 498 U.S. 52, 62 (1990)).

[87] *See id.* at 364.

[88] *See generally* Russell Korobkin, *The Battle over Self-Insured Health Plans, or "One Good Loophole Deserves Another"*, 5 YALE J. HEALTH POL'Y, L. & ETHICS 89 (2005).

[89] Am. Med. Sec. Inc., v. Bartlett, 111 F.3d 358 (4th Cir. 1997), *cert denied*, Larsen v. Am. Med. Sec., Inc., 524 U.S. 936 (1998). Not all states were deterred. After its defeat in court, Maryland itself promulgated a revised version of its preempted regulation that was never challenged, likely because insurance company behind the original litigation withdrew from the Maryland market. *See* Korobkin, *supra* Chapter 11 note 88, at 128 (2005) (discussing aftermath of *Bartlett*). In addition, the US Department of Labor later released technical guidance on stop-loss insurance regulation specifically criticizing *Bartlett* and taking the position that "States may regulate insurance policies issued to plans or plan sponsors, including stop-loss insurance policies, if the law regulates the insurance company and the business of insurance .... Thus, a State law that prohibits insurers from issuing stop-loss contracts with attachments points below specified levels would not, in the Department [of Labor's] view, be preempted by ERISA." I.R.S. TECH. RELEASE NO. 2014-01, GUIDANCE ON STATE REGULATION OF STOP-LOSS INSURANCE (Nov. 6, 2014), www.dol.gov/agencies/ebsa/employ ers-and-advisers/guidance/technical-releases/14-01

[90] National Totals for Enrollees and Cost of Health Insurance Coverage for the Private and Public Sectors, MEDICAL EXPENDITURE PANEL SURVEY (2010) https://meps.ahrq.gov/data_ stats/summ_tables/insr/national/series_4/2010/ic10_iva_b.pdf).

[91] "Pay or play" is health reform shorthand for the idea that employers need either offer health benefits to employees or, in the alternative, pay money to the government. The ACA used that mechanism with respect to large employers, who either needed to offer suitable health insurance to their employees or make a "shared responsibility" payment to the federal government. I.R.C. § 4980H (2018). *Cf. Employer Shared Responsibility Provisions*, IRS (Sept. 29, 2022), www.irs.gov/affordable-care-act/employers/employer-shared-responsibility-pro

446   *Health Plan Content Controls*

additional monies, monies the government would then use to fund a public health insurance program.[92] Both efforts were challenged in federal court as being preempted by ERISA.

In *Retail Industry Leaders Association* v. *Fielder*, the Fourth Circuit concluded that Maryland had run afoul of ERISA's preemption provisions.[93] The Maryland law in question required very large employers to spend at least 8 percent of their total payroll on employee health care.[94] Failure to do so meant the employer had to pay the shortfall to the state, which the state intended to use to fund a broad-based public health insurance program.[95] The court concluded that such a law "relate[d] to" employee benefit plans by forcing employers to offer health benefits to their employees.[96] Choosing to not offer health benefits meant the employer had to pay 8 percent of its payroll to the state, to fund a program available to many more people than the company's employees.[97] Choosing to offer benefits, in contrast, meant such monies would be spent directly on the company's employees.[98] Faced with a choice between spending 8 percent of payroll on their employees' health benefits or spending the same amount on a state program that would benefit a population far larger than their employees, the court concluded that no rational employer would choose to dilute its resources by doing anything other than spending its monies on employee health care.[99] That functionally compelled choice meant the Maryland law "relate[d] to" employee benefit plans, as it amounted to a state order to offer health benefits.[100]

The city of San Francisco enacted a similar "pay or play" scheme requiring employers to devote a certain amount of revenue to employee health care costs (the amount varied depending on whether the employer was a nonprofit or for-profit enterprise) or pay any shortfall to the city.[101] In *Golden Gate Restaurant Association* v. *City and County of San Francisco*, the Ninth Circuit concluded that the city's law was not preempted by ERISA, reasoning that the law did not formally dictate to any employer whether it should offer health benefits or how it should structure them.[102] The court took pains to distinguish the case from *Fielder*, arguing that, in contrast to

---

visions (acknowledging that the relevant ACA provisions are often referred to as the "pay or play provisions").

[92] Retail Indus. Leaders Ass'n v. Fielder, 475 F.3d 180, 184–85 (4th Cir. 2007); Golden Gate Rest. v. City & Cnty. of San Francisco, 546 F.3d 639, 642–45 (9th Cir. 2008).

[93] *Fielder*, 475 F.3d at 183.

[94] *Id.* at 184.

[95] *Id.* at 184–85.

[96] *Id.* at 193–94.

[97] *Id.* at 184–85.

[98] *Id.* at 193.

[99] *Id.* at 193.

[100] *See id.* at 197.

[101] Golden Gate Rest. Ass'n v. City & Cnty. of San Francisco, 546 F.3d 639, 644–45 (9th Cir. 2008).

[102] *Id.* at 655–56, 661.

Employment-Based Health Care

Fielder, an employer still had an actual choice, because choosing not to offer benefits (and thus pay the City) would secure for the employer meaningful benefits.[103] In "elect[ing] to pay the City," the court explained, the "employer's employees are eligible for free or discounted enrollment in [the City health care program], or for medical reimbursement accounts."[104] As such, San Francisco's ordinance did not amount to a functional diktat that employers offer health benefits; it presented employers with an actual, permissible choice.[105]

Neither *Fielder* nor *Golden Gate* reached the Supreme Court.[106] In 2010, the importance of those rulings was diminished by the passage of the Affordable Care Act. But even post-ACA, the threat of ERISA preemption of state health care initiatives still stands, as explained in Part D below.

C THE ACA AND EMPLOYMENT-BASED HEALTH REGULATION

While some characterizations of the ACA in the aftermath of its passage were regrettably intemperate and inaccurate, the legislation did unquestionably instantiate meaningful health reform, including with respect to health benefits offered at the workplace. Unfortunately, as a consequence of the unusual way the ACA became law (through reconciliation), it is not a cleanly written statute.[107] Beyond inartful drafting, the ACA is also a naturally complex piece of legislation; whether or not a given ACA rule applies often depends on whether the financing mechanism in question is, for example, individual insurance, small group insurance, large group insurance, a self-insured plan, or a grandfathered plan.[108] A comprehensive summary of which ACA reforms reach which type of plan is beyond the scope of this

---

[103] *Id.* at 660 (distinguishing *Fielder* because "the City-payment option under the San Francisco Ordinance offers employers a meaningful alternative that allows them to preserve the existing structure of their ERISA plans.").

[104] *Id.*

[105] *Id.*

[106] Golden Gate Rest. Ass'n.v. City & Cnty. of San Francisco, Cal., 561 U.S. 1024, 1024 (2010) (denying certiorari). Certiorari was not sought in *Fielder*.

[107] As Chief Justice John G. Roberts, Jr., wrote: "Congress passed much of the Act using a complicated budgetary procedure known as 'reconciliation,' which limited opportunities for debate and amendment, and bypassed the Senate's normal 60–vote filibuster requirement . . . . As a result, the Act does not reflect the type of care and deliberation that one might expect of such significant legislation." King v. Burwell, 576 U.S. 473, 491–92 (2015) (internal citation omitted). *See also* John Cannan, A *Legislative History of the Affordable Care Act: How Legislative Procedure Shapes Legislative History*, 105 L. LIB. J. 131, 159–167 (2013) (describing the unusual nature of the ACA's enactment).

[108] 42 U.S.C. § 300gg–91(a)(1) (2018) (defining group health plan and referencing ERISA); *id.* at (b)(2) (defining health insurance issuer and referencing ERISA); *id.* at (b)(4) (defining group health insurance coverage); *id.* at (b)(5) (defining individual insurance coverage); *id.* at (e)(1) (A) (defining individual market); *id.* at (e)(2) (defining large employer); *id.* at (e)(3) (defining large group market); *id.* at (e)(4) (defining small employer); *id.* at (e)(5) (defining small group market). *See also infra* Chapter 11 note 111 (explaining how different provisions affect different types of insurance plan).

448 *Health Plan Content Controls*

work, but several particular reforms will be examined to illuminate the principles animating them.

Conceptual Highlights

The ACA amended ERISA directly and by reference. The ACA directly added section 715(a) to ERISA, which was codified at 29 U.S.C. § 1185d.[109] The ACA likewise substantively amended the Public Health Service Act (PHSA), and the ACA-added Section 715(a) of ERISA incorporated by reference a portion of those ACA-PHSA amendments,[110] which are now codified at 42 U.S.C. §§ 300gg to 300gg-28.[111]

A "grandfathered plan" is one that existed prior to March 23, 2010, and has not since made certain changes; grandfathered plans need not comply with many of the Act's requirements, including the contraceptive mandate. 42 U.S.C. §§ 18011(a), (e) (2018). Because continually writing "non-grandfathered" is cumbersome, the reader should assume that any reference herein to how the ACA treats a particular type of plan is referring to a "non-grandfathered" version of that plan.

[109] Patient Protection and Affordable Care Act, Pub. L. No. 111-148, tit. I, § 1563(e), 124 Stat. 119, 270.

[110] "[T]he provisions of part A of title XXVII of the Public Health Service Act (as amended by the [ACA]) shall apply to group health plans, and health insurance issuers providing health insurance coverage in connection with group health plans, as if included in this subpart [of ERISA]." ERISA § 715, 29 U.S.C. § 1185d(a)(1) (2018).

[111] Those provisions and their titles (as of 2022) are:

§ 300gg. Fair health insurance premiums;

§ 300gg–1. Guaranteed availability of coverage;

§ 300gg–2. Guaranteed renewability of coverage;

§ 300gg–3. Prohibition of preexisting condition exclusions or other discrimination based on health status;

§ 300gg–4. Prohibiting discrimination against individual participants and beneficiaries based on health status;

§ 300gg–5. Non-discrimination in health care;

§ 300gg–6. Comprehensive health insurance coverage;

§ 300gg–7. Prohibition on excessive waiting periods;

§ 300gg–8. Coverage for individuals participating in approved clinical trials;

§ 300gg–9. Disclosure of information;

§ 300gg–11. No lifetime or annual limits;

§ 300gg–12. Prohibition on rescissions;

§ 300gg–13. Coverage of preventive health services;

§ 300gg–14. Extension of dependent coverage;

§ 300gg–15. Development and utilization of uniform explanation of coverage documents and standardized definitions;

§ 300gg–15a. Provision of additional information;

§ 300gg–16. Prohibition on discrimination in favor of highly compensated individuals;

§ 300gg–17. Ensuring the quality of care;

§ 300gg–18. Bringing down the cost of health care coverage;

§ 300gg–19. Appeals process;

§ 300gg–19a. Patient protections;

§ 300gg–19b. Information on prescription drugs;

§ 300gg–21. Exclusion of certain plans;

Employment-Based Health Care 449

The ACA's intention, however, was to do far more than amend ERISA; its central aim was to reform the provision of health insurance in the United States, including private insurance, whether that insurance was provided through the employer or not.[112] We accordingly discuss some of the ACA's major individual market reforms as a baseline, as a point of comparison, and as a way to consider what effects those reforms might indirectly have on employer-provided insurance.

The Act's most well-known set of reforms specifically targeted individual insurance, where adverse selection, high prices, and consumer cognitive biases had long crippled the market.[113] The thrust of the ACA's individual market reforms was to make the individual market stable, affordable, and intelligible.[114] It aimed to accomplish that through the use of community rating, guaranteed issue, and individual mandate reforms, as well as through the creation of insurance "exchanges" bolstered by tax credits.[115]

§ 300gg–22. Enforcement;

§ 300gg–23. Preemption; State flexibility; construction;

§ 300gg–25. Standards relating to benefits for mothers and newborns;

§ 300gg–26. Parity in mental health and substance use disorder benefits;

§ 300gg–27. Required coverage for reconstructive surgery following mastectomies;

§ 300gg–28. Coverage of dependent students on medically necessary leave of absence.

A reader should note, however, a few things. First, section 715 itself provides that sections 300gg-16 (relating to highly compensated individual nondiscrimination) and 300gg-18 (relating to reporting and medical loss ratios) do *not* apply to self-insured plans. ERISA § 715(b), 29 U.S.C. § 1185d(b) (2018). Second, by its terms it applies to "group health plans" and "health insurance issuers." *Id.* at (a)(2). ERISA defines both of those terms. ERISA § 733, 29 U.S.C. § 1191b (2018). A group health plan is "an employee welfare benefit plan to the extent that the plan provides medical care ... to employees or their dependents ... directly or through insurance, reimbursement, or otherwise." ERISA § 733(a)(1), 29 U.S.C. § 1191b(a)(1). That definition *includes* self-insured plans, as self-insured plans are necessarily welfare benefit plans. In contrast, a "health insurance issuer" is defined by ERISA as "an insurance company, insurance service, or insurance organization (including a health maintenance organization, ...) which is licensed to engage in the business of insurance in a State and ... does not include a group health plan." ERISA § 733(b)(2), § 1191b(b)(2). Accordingly, when analyzing a specific provision of the PHSA that ERISA section 715(a) now incorporates, i.e., 42 U.S.C §§ 300gg to 300gg-28, one must pay careful attention to whether the provision targets group health plans, health insurance issuers, or both (or uses some other limiting language). If a provision applies only to "health insurance issuers," then it does *not*, by its own definition, apply to self-insured plans. If a provision applies to group health plans, then the provision *does*, by its own definition, reach self-insured plans. Finally, a given individual 300gg provision may have additional language that further narrows its reach. For example, the ban on premium variation does not reach self-insured or large group plans, 42 U.S.C. § 300gg(a)(1) (2018). And the provision that requires the offering of "essential health benefits," § 300gg-6(a), likewise does not apply to self-insured or large group plans.

[112] *See generally* Remarks on Signing the Patient Protection and Affordable Care Act, 1 Pub. Papers 400 (Mar. 23, 2010).

[113] *See* Maher, *UE, supra* Chapter 11 note 15, at 144–45; Jonathan Gruber, *Covering the Uninsured in the United States*, 46 J. Econ. Literature 571, 574–77 (2008) (discussing problems in individual insurance market).

[114] Maher, *UE supra* Chapter 11 note 15, at 144–45.

[115] King v. Burwell, 576 U.S. 473, 493 (2015) (explaining ACA reform scheme).

450 *Health Plan Content Controls*

Community rating refers to the requirement that all insurance policies sold use premiums based on the actuarial community risk, with premium variation permitted only based on geographic area, age, tobacco use, and whether the policy is individual or family.[116] Guaranteed issue requires insurers to sell policies to individuals who seek to buy them (with narrow exceptions).[117] The individual mandate refers to the obligation of all persons to maintain qualified insurance (whether through employment, the government, or individually) if doing so would cost less than a specified percentage of their income.[118] The insurance exchanges are online marketplaces where individuals can purchase ACA-regulated health insurance in a consumer-friendly format.[119] Tax credits are available to those whose income is from 100 percent to 400 percent of the federal poverty level, with the amount of the available credit decreasing in proportion to income.[120] Although the individual mandate was effectively repealed as of January 2019,[121] the other reforms have successfully if imperfectly created a reasonably stable individual market.

Notably, the ACA does *not* envision giving individuals real freedom to choose between individual insurance and employment-based insurance. While individuals are not barred from doing so, tax law favors the latter and certain employers face penalties for not offering health insurance.[122] If an employer offers insurance that meets specified standards, an individual's choice to purchase insurance on the exchanges is not eligible for tax credits and ordinarily does not qualify as a purchase that can be financed with pre-tax dollars.[123] In contrast, the purchase of employment-based insurance is generally permitted to be made with pre-tax dollars.[124]

---

[116] 42 U.S.C. §§ 300gg(a)(1)(A) (permissible premium variations), 300gg-4(b) (2018) (barring premium adjustment based on health status).

[117] 42 U.S.C. §§ 300gg-1 (guaranteed availability), 300gg-2 (2018) (guaranteed renewability, with limited exceptions).

[118] 26 U.S.C. § 5000A (2018) (individual mandate provision).

[119] 42 U.S.C. § 18031 (2018) (creating exchanges). *See also* Brendan S. Maher, *Some Thoughts on Health Care Exchanges: Choice, Defaults, and the Unconnected*, 44 CONN. L. REV. 1099, 1105–10 (2012) (reviewing insurance exchange implementation).

[120] 26 U.S.C. § 36B(b)(3)(A)(i) (2018).

[121] Tax Cuts and Jobs Act of 2017, Pub. L. No. 115-97, §11081(a)(2), 131 Stat. 2054, 2092 (2017) (amending I.R.C. § 5000A(c)(3)(A) to set mandate payment to zero).

[122] 26 U.S.C. § 4980H (2018) (employer "shared responsibility" obligations and penalties); Burwell v. Hobby Lobby Stores, Inc., 573 U.S. 682, 720 (2014) (explaining employer penalties).

[123] 26 U.S.C. § 36B(c)(2)(B)–(C) (ACA tax credit eligibility); *Id.* at § 213(a), (d) (2018) (expenses for medical care, including the cost of health insurance coverage, deductible only to the extent they exceed 10 percent of adjusted gross income). Moreover, the medical expense deduction can be claimed only if the taxpayer itemizes deductions. *See* U.S.C. §§63(b), 62(a) (2018). *But see infra* Chapter 11 note 132 (explaining recent changes in the law that could serve to "unlock" the exchanges for employed persons).

[124] 26 U.S.C. § 106(a) (2018) (employee's gross income does not include employer-provided health coverage). *See also* Stephen Utz, *The Affordable Care Act and Tax Policy*, 44 CONN.

Employment-Based Health Care

In terms of employer incentives, companies with more than fifty full-time employees are subject to what is commonly called the "employer mandate."[125] To avoid tax penalties such employers must provide health insurance that is "affordable" and provides "minimum value."[126] The former requirement turns on whether the cost of insurance offered exceeds a certain percentage of the employee's household income, and the latter turns on whether the offered insurance will cover at least 60 percent of costs expected to be incurred under the plan.[127] An observer might worry that a cost-conscious large employer looking to avoid tax penalties might circumvent the spirit of the ACA by offering a plan that covered more than 60 percent of expected costs under the plan, but defined covered benefits so narrowly that the plan does not really offer the protection that is generally understood as health insurance. While labor market pressures significantly reduce the likelihood that employers might succumb to that temptation, subsequent federal regulations further curbed that possibility by making clear that plans need offer a substantial scope of benefits.[128]

An employer that fails to meet the required conditions owes the federal government a "shared responsibility payment." Generally speaking, if fewer than the required percentage (in most cases 95 percent) of employees are offered affordable, minimum value coverage, and if at least one employee purchases exchange insurance and receives a premium tax credit, then a shared responsibility payment (penalty) is due for every full-time employee in the company beyond the first thirty,[129] not just the employees who received premium tax credits. If a company offers minimum value coverage to at least the minimum percentage of employees, then the shared responsibility payment the company owes is based only on the number of full-time employees who actually purchase exchange insurance with the use of premium tax credits (which are not available to employees who have access to affordable, minimum value coverage through the workplace).[130]

L. REV. 1213, 1233 (2012) (explaining and criticizing disparate tax treatment of health care expenditures).

[125] 26 U.S.C. § 4980H(c)(2)(A) (2018) (defining "applicable large employer").

[126] *Id.* at § 4980H(a)–(b) (2018); *Id.* at § 36B(c)(2)(C)(i)–(ii) (2018) (defining "affordable" and "minimum value"). Section 36B is relevant because the employer penalties in section 4980H are triggered by at least one employee ultimately enrolling in a "qualified health plan with respect to which an applicable premium tax credit or cost-sharing reduction is allowed or paid with respect to the employee." *Id.* at § 4980H(a)(2), (b)(1)(B) (2018). An employer who is offered employment-based coverage that is both affordable and of minimum value is not eligible to do so. *Id.* at § 36B(c)(2)(B)–(C) (2018).

[127] *Id.* at § 36B(c)(2)(C)(i)(II); *Id.* at § 36B(c)(2)(C)(ii).

[128] *See infra* Chapter 11 note 134 and accompanying text.

[129] 26 U.S.C. § 4980H(a)(2) (2018); *id.* at (c)(2)(D). *See generally Employer Shared Responsibility Provisions*, IRS, at www.irs.gov/affordable-care-act/employers/employer-shared-responsibility-provisions (last updated Sept. 29, 2022) (explaining how IRS generally assesses shared responsibility penalties).

[130] 26 U.S.C. § 4980H(b)(1)(B). *See generally* IRS, *supra* Chapter 11 note 129.

Unlike the individual mandate, the justification for the employer mandate has nothing to do with adverse selection. Instead, it reflects a political and policy judgment favoring continued involvement of employers in health insurance. In political terms, many beneficiaries of employment-based health insurance were and are quite happy with their coverage; many lacked enthusiasm for doing anything to threaten the employment-based system.[131] But the ACA's successful creation of an individual market was just such an implicit threat. With all individuals able to purchase insurance on the exchange, had ACA's architects chosen to make exchange insurance eligible for purchase with pre-tax dollars (or otherwise tax-favored), many businesses, it was feared, would have been tempted to stop offering health insurance. The potential chaos of that change – employed individuals losing coverage and seeking refuge in the newly created exchanges – was both politically undesirable as well as a policy risk, because whatever the theoretical merit of the exchanges, few concepts work flawlessly in their first iteration. Tens of millions of voters being immediately dumped from their reliable employment-based plans onto the new exchanges was a bridge too far.

Today, that fear is eroding somewhat. Recent changes to the law – perhaps motivated by implicit recognition that the exchanges are now fairly affordable and stable – have given both small and large employers more options to permit employees to buy (with pre-tax dollars) individual health insurance on the exchanges and elsewhere.[132] Whether those options will be taken up by employers (and/or whether

[131] E.g., David Gamage, *Perverse Incentives Arising from the Tax Provisions of Healthcare Reform: Why Further Reforms Are Needed to Prevent Avoidable Costs to Low- and Moderate-Income Workers*, 65 TAX L. REV. 669, 692 (2012) (discussing fears of Obama dministration and ACA draftsmen regarding "whether employers would stop offering health insurance after the ACA came into effect"); Linda Bergthold, *ACA: Threat to Employer-Sponsored Plans?*, HEALTHINSURANCE.ORG (Feb. 14, 2014), www.healthinsurance.org/blog/aca-threat-to-employer-sponsored-plans/ (responding to post-enactment but pre-implementation concerns that ACA would undermine employer based insurance). Indeed, the reason for including "grandfathered plans" in the ACA was to reassure voters frightened that reform would destroy their then-current plans. *Cf.* Sarah Kliff & Ezra Klein, The Lessons of Obamacare, VOX (Mar. 15, 2017, 6:00 AM), www.vox.com/policy-and-politics/2017/3/15/14908524/obamacare-lessons-ahca-gop (discussing the inclusion of grandfathered plans in ACA).

[132] *See* Maher, *UE*, *supra* Chapter 11 note 15, at 149. Changes in the law effected by the 21st Century Cures Act, Pub. L. No. 114-255, § 18001, 130 Stat. 1033 (2016), now allow small employers to set up health reimbursement accounts that permit employees to freely purchase a qualifying policy with pre-tax dollars. 26 U.S.C. § 9831(d) (2018); I.R.S. Notice 2017–67, 2017-47 I.R.B. (explaining QSEHRA accounts).

A later change in the law permits the creation of Individual Coverage Health Reimbursement Accounts (ICHRA), which allow *any* employer (large or small) to set up a reimbursement account that employees can use to purchase qualifying insurance. *See* I.R.S. Notice 2018-88, 2018-49 I.R.B. 817; Treas. Reg. § 54.9802-4(a)–(c) (2022). Employees do not have to purchase insurance, but if they do not, no reimbursement money will be paid out, i.e., the money that would have been available for reimbursement of health insurance premiums is retained by the company. *Id.* -4(c)(1)(ii). Importantly, among other conditions, if the reimbursement promise is sufficiently generous (i.e., if it consists of an employer contribution of a certain amount, namely an amount that permits the employees to purchase a self-only silver

Employment-Based Health Care 453

labor will push back) will provide additional insight into the value of the practical role employers serve in the health insurance arena.

Differing Substantive Requirements

Interestingly, the ACA's substantive requirements do *not* all apply equally to individual versus employment-based insurance. Indeed, one of the ACA's best-known requirements – the requirement that insurance policies cover ten categories of "essential health benefits" – does *not* apply to large group plans.[133] The presumption of ACA's drafters was that market forces would motivate large employers to offer comprehensive coverage without a legislative mandate. Thus, even after the passage of the ACA, large employers have genuine freedom to construct their benefit offerings as they see fit. The chief duty they must observe is the duty to offer "minimum value" coverage – which is largely a cost-based test that, even with the implementing regulations, could be satisfied by offering fewer categories of coverage than the ten essential health benefits categories.[134] That said, while large employers

---

plan without requiring an employee use more than a certain percentage of his income), the creation of the ICHRA satisfies the employer mandate. See I.R.S. Notice 2018-88, 2018-49 I.R.B. 817, 821; Treas. Reg. § 1.36B-2(c)(5) (2022). Past versions of health reimbursement accounts, in contrast, were – unless coupled with employer-offered health insurance – not held to satisfy the employer mandate. Thus, in effect both the QSHERA and the ICHRA operate to, in a limited way, "unlock" the exchanges by allowing employers to send employees there to purchase insurance with pre-tax dollars. *Cf.* Maher, *REBA*, *supra* Chapter 11 note 3; *see also* Maher, *UE*, *supra* Chapter 11 note 15. Whether this approach will be on balance salutary – and/or widely adopted by employers – remains to be seen; at a minimum, some of the particulars may need tweaking.

[133] *See supra* Chapter 11 note 111.

[134] 26 U.S.C. § 36B(c)(2)(C)(ii) (2018) (defining minimum value). Subsequent regulations have clarified that "[a]n employer-sponsored plan provides minimum value (MV) only if the percentage of the total allowed costs of benefits provided under the plan is greater than or equal to 60 percent, *and* the benefits under the plan include substantial coverage of inpatient hospital services and physician services." 45 C.F.R. § 156.145(a) (2022) (emphasis added). HHS explained its rationale as follows:

"That the [minimum value] standard may be interpreted to require that employer-sponsored plans cover critical benefits is evident in the structure of the Affordable Care Act, the context in which the grant of the authority to the Secretary to prescribe regulations under section 1302 was enacted, and the policy underlying the legislation. Section 1302(b) authorizes the Secretary of HHS to define EHB to be offered by individual market and small group health insurance plans, provided that this definition include at least 10 specified categories of benefits, and that the benefits be equal to the scope of benefits provided under a typical employer plan. To inform this determination as to the scope of a typical employer plan, section 1302(b)(2)(A) provides that the Secretary of Labor shall conduct a survey of employer-sponsored coverage to determine the benefits typically covered by employers, including multiemployer plans, and provide a report on such survey to the Secretary [of HHS]. These provisions suggest that, while detailed requirements for EHB in the individual and small group health insurance markets were deemed necessary, the benefits covered by typical employer plans providing primary coverage at the time the Affordable Care Act was enacted were seen as sufficient to satisfy the Act's objectives for the breadth of benefits needed for health plan coverage and, in fact, to serve

454   *Health Plan Content Controls*

retain some flexibility in the scope of care they may choose to cover, empirical studies nonetheless suggest that employer plans are comparatively generous in terms of coverage, without any indication that important categories of care are being excluded.[135]

In contrast, the essential health benefits (EHB) requirement *does* apply to small group plans as well as policies sold on the individual exchanges.[136] While the ACA itself broadly enumerates the ten minimum categories of EHB that must be covered, it gives the HHS Secretary discretion to further define the scope and content of EHBs.[137] To date, HHS has chosen a federalism-friendly approach with respect to that task, by allowing states to play a large role in defining what essential health benefits are within their borders. In essence the Secretary has allowed the states to define EHBs with reference to a "benchmark plan" for that state (of which one example is one of the three largest benefit plans the State offers to its employees) as chosen in a process that involves both HHS and the State.[138]

Other major ACA coverage requirements apply to all health insurance, including large group and self-insured plans. Among these general requirements are the prohibition on lifetime or annual limits,[139] the barring of preexisting condition

> as the basis for determining EHB. They also suggest that any meaningful standard of minimum coverage may require providing certain critical benefits.
>
> Employer-sponsored plans in the large group market and self-insured employers continue to have flexibility in designing their plans. They are not required to cover all EHB. Providing flexibility, however, does not mean that these plans can offer whatever benefits they choose and automatically meet MV requirements. A plan that excludes substantial coverage for inpatient hospital and physician services is not a health plan in any meaningful sense and is contrary to the purpose of the MV requirement to ensure that an employer-sponsored plan, while not required to cover all EHB, nonetheless must offer coverage with minimum value at least roughly comparable to that of a bronze plan offered on an Exchange.
>
> For these reasons, the Secretary has concluded that the provisions of section 1302(d)(2) of the Affordable Care Act – requiring that the regulations for determining the percentage of the total allowed costs of benefits that apply to plans that must cover all EHB also be applied as a basis for determining minimum value – reflect a statutory design to provide basic minimum standards for health benefits coverage through the MV requirement, without requiring large group market plans and self-insured plans to meet all EHB standards. Given the scope of benefits covered by typical employer plans, the MV requirement is properly viewed as a means of ensuring that employer-sponsored plans satisfy basic minimum standards while also accommodating flexibility in the design of those plans." Patient Protection and Affordable Care Act; HHS Notice of Benefit and Payment Parameters for 2016, 80 Fed. Reg. 10,750, 10,827–28 (Feb. 27, 2015), www.govinfo.gov/content/pkg/FR-2015-02-27/pdf/2015-03751.pdf. *See also* I.R.S. Notice 2014-69, 2014-48 I.R.B. 903 (setting forth concurring IRS view).

[135] Maher, *UE*, supra Chapter 11 note 15, at 150 n.77-78 (examining research regarding generosity of coverage of employer plans versus exchange plans).

[136] 42 U.S.C. § 300gg-6(a) (2018).

[137] 42 U.S.C. § 18022(b)(1) (2018).

[138] 45 C.F.R §§ 156.100–.155 (2022); *id.* at §156.100 (benchmarking options pre-2020); *id.* at §156.111 (benchmarking options in or after 2020).

[139] 42 U.S.C. § 300gg-11(a) (2018). That large group and self-insured plans are not obligated to offer essential health benefits does not save them from this provision. If they offer benefits that fall within the ten essential health benefits categories, they cannot impose lifetime limits on

Employment-Based Health Care

exclusions,[140] the requirement that dependent coverage for children be available until age twenty-six,[141] and the requirement that "preventive care" be provided without cost-sharing.[142]

That last requirement sparked litigation that reached the Supreme Court. In *Burwell* v. *Hobby Lobby Stores, Inc.*, the Court concluded that the Religious Freedom Restoration Act (RFRA) protected the rights of religious employers to refuse to provide contraception through their benefits plan.[143] At the time of *Hobby Lobby*, regulations promulgated by the Obama Administration provided that the "preventive care" required by the ACA included contraception and thus required that nonexempt employers offering health coverage provide cost-free contraception as a part of that coverage.[144] HHS also promulgated a regulatory "accommodation" for certain religious employers that exempted those employers from covering contraception while nonetheless requiring an insurer or third-party administrator to provide contraception to the affected women.[145] The *Hobby Lobby* Court reasoned that such an accommodation could also be extended to secular, for-profit corporations run by persons (such as the *Hobby Lobby* plaintiffs) with religious beliefs offended by the provision of certain types of contraception, and that the government's failure to do so constituted a violation of the RFRA.[146]

After *Hobby Lobby*, other aggrieved plaintiffs pursued litigation on the grounds that the Obama-era contraceptive accommodations process impermissibly burdened their religious beliefs. Their theory was that the relevant accommodation – which required a party to submit a notice of their religious objection to either their insurer or the government in order to trigger an alternative means of providing contraception – violated the RFRA by making the objectors functionally complicit in supplying contraception they found religiously objectionable.[147] In *Zubik* v. *Burwell*, the Supreme Court granted certiorari on the question and heard oral argument, but then, after supplemental briefing, issued a per curiam opinion remanding the issue

---

those benefits. All insurers can, however, impose lifetime or annual benefit limits on those benefits that are not essential health benefits. *Id.* at § 300gg-11(b).

[140] 42 U.S.C. § 300gg-4 (2018).

[141] 42 U.S.C § 300gg-14 (2018).

[142] 42 U.S.C § 300gg-13 (2018). Litigation regarding the preventive care requirement is ongoing. *See* Braidwood Mgmt. Inc. v. Becerra, No. 4:20-CV-00283-O, 2023 WL 2703229 (N.D. Tex. Mar. 30, 2023)(striking down part of the requirement). At time of press, the matter is on appeal.

[143] Burwell v. Hobby Lobby Stores, Inc., 573 U.S. 682, 690 (2014).

[144] While section 300gg-13 requires that preventive care be provided without cost-sharing, it only defines "preventive care" by reference to external determination. 42 U.S.C. § 300gg-13(a)(1)–(5)(2018). Based on the recommendation of Health Resources and Services Administration, the Obama era HHS promulgated a rule requiring "coverage, without cost sharing for all Food and Drug Administration approved contraceptive methods, sterilization procedures, and patient education and counseling." *Burwell*, 573 U.S. at 697 (cleaned up).

[145] *Burwell*, 573 at 698–99.

[146] *Id.* at 692.

[147] Zubik v. Burwell, 578 U.S. 403 (2016).

Health Plan Content Controls

to the lower courts, based on the view of both *Zubik* parties that a new form of accommodation could be written that did not violate the plaintiff's religious freedom by making them complicit in providing contraception while also ensuring cost-free access to contraception by covered women.[148]

Federal regulators proved unable to draft such a regulation, and the Trump Administration took a different approach. It expanded the group of people who could religiously or morally object to (and thus be free from providing in a benefit plan) contraception, while also abandoning any requirement that such plans provide, through insurers or third parties, cost-free contraception to women.[149] Litigation over the Trump regulations reached the Supreme Court in *Little Sisters of the Poor Saints Peter and Paul Home v. Pennsylvania*.[150] In *Little Sisters*, the Supreme Court upheld the Trump Administration's contraceptive-mandate exemption rule.[151] Justice Ginsburg wrote a stinging dissent, decrying in particular the fact that the relevant exemption upheld by the Court "contains no alternative mechanism to ensure affected women's continued access to contraceptive coverage."[152]

The contraceptive-mandate cases troubled scholarly observers.[153] While a potential benefit of an employment-based approach might be to leverage the superior expertise of the employer's administrative professionals to choose or design health benefit packages tailored to the needs of the workforce, the involvement of the employer also provides an additional veto point on the provision of care, a veto point that could be avoided if health insurance is provided by non-employer means.[154]

---

[148] *Id.* at 408.

[149] 45 C.F.R. § 147.132 (2022) (expanding religious exemption and providing no required alternative means to ensure cost-sharing). Section 147.131 provides for a voluntary alternative mechanism to provide contraception, at the discretion of the objecting employer.

[150] 140 S. Ct. 2367 (2020).

[151] *Id.* at 2373.

[152] *Id.* at 2403 (Ginsburg, J., dissenting).

[153] *E.g.*, Elizabeth Sepper, *Free Exercise Lochnerism*, 115 Colum. L. Rev. 1453, 1495–1507 (2015) (criticizing reasoning in, and regulatory implications of, *Hobby Lobby*); Naomi Cahn, June Carbone, *Uncoupling*, 53 Ariz. St. L.J. 1, 52–52 (2021) (criticizing implications of *Little Sisters*).

[154] Maher, *REBA*, *supra* Chapter 11 note 3, at 1302. The *Hobby Lobby* dispute also revealed a continuing public misconception about who "pays" for health benefits. Although employers marginally benefit from having a healthier workforce (and thus from offering benefits), the overwhelming benefit of having health insurance is enjoyed by employees and their families. Health benefits are thus not "paid" for by the employer as some form of gratuity; they are "paid" for by the collective foregone wages of the employees. Albert de Roode, *Pensions As Wages*, 3 Am. Econ. Rev. 287, 287 (1913). Indeed, labor and health economists have repeatedly analyzed how the increasing cost of health care (and thus health insurance) has depressed wages, as a large and larger portion of wages "pays" for health benefits rather than finding its way into weekly paychecks. *See generally* Gary Burtless & Sveta Milusheva, *Effects of Employer-Sponsored Health Insurance Costs on Social Security Taxable Wages*, 73 Soc. Sec. Bull. (2013), www.ssa.gov/policy/docs/ssb/v73n1/v73n1p83.html. Yet various mainstream descriptions on *Hobby Lobby* styled the issue as whether religious bosses should have to "pay" for benefits they objected to. Maher, *REBA*, *supra* Chapter 11 note 3, at 1307–08.

D STATES IN THE POST-ACA WORLD

The ACA's amendments to ERISA did not directly alter ERISA's preemptive provision, that is, section 514.[155] The ACA generally leaves in place ERISA's broad ouster of state law.[156][157]

As discussed above, ERISA's broad preemptive reach was a challenge for health care reformers because its expulsion of states from the field was coupled with a federal failure to regulate health benefits. The ACA addressed that failure, rendering the need for state action less pressing than before the ACA's passage. Yet although the ACA imposed a variety of content requirements that now bind employment-based plans as matter of federal law, a state's ability to engage in additional regulation beyond what the ACA contains remains constrained by ERISA and, in an important way, by the ACA itself.

ACA Preemption. The ACA's general preemption provision is by its terms lenient; it displaces only those state laws that "prevent the application" of a part of the ACA.[158] Thus, unlike ERISA (in which even laws that supplement or extend ERISA are preempted) the ACA does the opposite – only state laws that block the ACA are generally preempted. But that regulatory freedom is less than advertised. First, large employer plans are *not* subject to ACA's essential health benefits requirement,[159] and thus, unlike small group plans, cannot be reached by a state's soft "benchmarking" power to define EHBs.[160] Nor can a state's mandated benefit laws regulate such plans if they self-insure, because of ERISA.[161] Thus, large employer plans that self-insure have flexibility regarding the core benefits offered while staying entirely free

---

[155] 29 U.S.C. § 1144 (2018). *See also* 42 U.S.C. § 300gg-23(a) (2018).

[156] The specifics as to how the ACA alters ERISA's preemptive power, if at all, are unsettled and the Supreme Court explicitly declined to address the issue in *Gobeille*. Gobeille v. Liberty Mut. Ins. Co., 577 U.S. 312, 326 (2016). That the ACA might have a potentially indirect effect on the practical scope of ERISA preemption is possible and a subject on which we do not here speculate.

[157] One minor exception is the ACA's requirement that insureds have access to independent external review for claims denied on medical necessity grounds; there the ACA invokes *federal* power to adopt certain *state* rules to flesh out the federal guarantee of external review. A 2004 dispute about Illinois's power to impose independent review requirements on employment-based health plans led to the Supreme Court narrowly finding, in *Rush Prudential*, that Illinois had such power to do so. Rush Prudential HMO, Inc. v. Moran, 536 U.S. 355, 361–62 (2002) (holding that the Illinois law imposing the independent review requirement was not preempted by ERISA). The ACA in effect imposes a federal obligation that independent external review must be provided by all plans and insurers but, in a somewhat convoluted fashion, borrows certain state rules for the particulars of the review. 42 U.S.C. § 300gg-19(b) (2018).

[158] 42 U.S.C. §18041(d) (2018).

[159] 42 U.S.C. § 300gg-6 (2018).

[160] *See supra* Chapter 11 note 138 and accompanying text.

[161] *See supra* Chapter 11 notes 72–77 and accompanying text.

of state regulation on the subject.[162] Second, even for the small group plans that are obligated to provide essential health benefits (as defined by a state-specific benchmarking process), if the state wishes by legislative mandate to require *additional* benefits beyond EHBs, then the ACA requires the state to fund that additional requirement, either by making payments to individuals that purchase such policies or to insurers that sell them.[163]

ERISA Preemption Redux. While some subjects at which reformers took aim were resolved by the ACA – for example, the prohibition on preexisting condition exclusions – other state reform initiatives are still constrained by ERISA preemption.

As discussed in Chapter 6, in *Gobeille* v. *Liberty Mutual* the Supreme Court held that Vermont's effort to construct an all-payer claims database was preempted insofar as it compelled self-insured plans to report claims information to the state.[164] Such databases were and are popular in many states, as the ability to track and analyze who is paying how much for what across the state is valuable for understanding and regulating health care activities and expenditures.[165] The *Gobeille* decision accordingly raised concerns that, given the prevalence of self-insured plans, the decision would severely limit the ability of regulators to gather health care expense and utilization information needed to improve the delivery and cost of care.[166] In his *Gobeille* concurrence, Justice Breyer expressed the hope that state and federal regulators could work together with the aim of having federal regulators use their power to obtain the information the states wanted.[167]

In the aftermath of *Gobeille*, however, Congress acted. As a part of the No Surprises Act, Congress amended ERISA, adding section 735 (codified at 29

---

[162] *See supra* Chapter 11 note 134 and accompanying text. While it does not appear at current time that a meaningful number of large employers are taking advantage of this flexibility to exploit employees, were they to do so, states would be powerless.

[163] 42 U.S.C. § 18031(d)(3)(B)(i)-(ii) (2018). The reason for this rule is so that states did not take advantage of federal subsidies regarding ACA insurance to provide overly generous benefits. As of 2020, no state ran afoul of this provision. HHS, however, expressed concern that "that there may be states that are not defraying the costs of the state-required benefits in accordance with federal requirements" and tightened the relevant regulations. Patient Protection and Affordable Care Act; HHS Notice of Benefit and Payment Parameters for 2021; Notice Requirement for Non-Federal Governmental Plans, 85 Fed. Reg. 29,164, 29,219 (July 1, 2020).

[164] Gobeille v. Liberty Mut. Ins. Co., 577 U.S. 312, 315–19, 321–24 (2016).

[165] *Id.* at 315, 333 n.1. (detailing the twenty other states in addition to Vermont who have implemented APCD databases).

[166] E.g., Nicholas Bagley, *The Supreme Court's Wrongheaded Decision in Gobeille*, THE INCIDENTAL ECONOMIST (Mar. 3, 2016), https://theincidentaleconomist.com/wordpress/the-supreme-courts-wrongheaded-decision-in-gobeille/ (criticizing *Gobeille*); Sarah H. Gordon, *Using All-Payer Data to Conduct Cross-State Comparisons of Health Insurance Enrollment*, HEALTH AFFS. BLOG (July 12, 2019), www.healthaffairs.org/do/10.1377/hblog20190708.605861/full/ (noting that *Gobeille* limited the data to be gleaned from existing all payer claim databases).

[167] *Gobeille* at 331 (Breyer, J., concurring).

Employment-Based Health Care

U.S.C. §1191d).[168] That provision authorizes HHS to develop "a standardized reporting format" for voluntary reporting by plans to state all-payer claims databases with regard to the type of health care cost information sought by Vermont in *Gobeille*.[169] The hope is that standardized format will increase the likelihood that self-insured plans will elect to report their claim and cost information to the states with databases. For good or ill, that amendment to ERISA confirms that the 116th Congress approved of the view of the *Gobeille* court. States lack the power to collect health information within their own borders, depending on who holds it, and ERISA is the reason why.[170]

As discussed in Part B of this chapter, the circuit courts of appeals have taken differing views regarding the degree to which "pay or play" health reform schemes adopted by states or municipalities violate ERISA.[171] The enactment of the ACA has not mooted the question. In *ERISA Industry Committee* v. *Seattle*, the plaintiff challenged a Seattle law requiring hotels and ancillary hotel businesses to supplement the pay for certain low wage employees by making "healthcare expenditures" on behalf of those employees.[172] Covered employers were given three options for making the required healthcare expenditures. They could pay the required sums to the employees directly; to a third party, such as an insurance carrier, for the purpose of providing health care; or into a self-funded program to be used to pay for employee medical care.[173] The district court, relying on the preemption analysis in *Golden Gate*, dismissed the plaintiff's complaint, and the Ninth Circuit affirmed.[174] The plaintiff sought certiorari, but after the Court called for the views of the Solicitor General, it declined to take the case.[175] The lesson is that ACA's substantive reforms, however salutary, are not nearly so far-reaching as to render state or local health reform initiatives redundant, and that reformers acting in that space would be wise to pay careful attention to ERISA's preemptive shadow.

---

[168] Pub. L. 116-260, div. BB, tit. I, § 115(b), 134 Stat. 2877 (2020).

[169] ERISA § 735, 29 U.S.C. § 1191d (2018). The section requires an advisory committee be convened and deliver a report to the Secretary, § 1191d(b). See U.S. DEP'T OF LAB., State All Payer Claims Databases Advisory Committee Report with Recommendations Under Section 735 of the Employee Retirement Income Security Act of 1974 (2021), www.dol.gov/sites/dolgov/files/ebsa/about-ebsa/about-us/state-all-payer-claims-databases-advisory-committee/final-report-and-recommendations-2021.pdf.

[170] *See supra* Chapter 6 note 58 and accompanying text. *See infra* Chapter 11 notes 169–171 and accompanying text.

[171] *See supra* Chapter 11 notes 91–105 and accompanying text.

[172] ERISA Indus. Comm. v. City of Seattle, No. C18–1188 TSZ, 2020 WL 2307481, at *1 (W.D. Wash. May 8, 2020), *aff'd*, 840 F. App'x 248 (9th Cir. 2021).

[173] *Id.*

[174] *Id.* at *4–6; ERISA Indus. Comm. v. City of Seattle, 840 Fed. App'x 248 (9th Cir. 2021), *cert. denied sub nom.* The ERISA Indus. Comm. v. City of Seattle, 143 S. Ct. 443 (2022).

[175] The ERISA Indus. Comm. v. City of Seattle, 143 S. Ct. 443 (2022). The Solicitor General had recommended a denial of certiorari. Brief for the United States as Amicus Curiae at 1, The ERISA Indus. Comm. v. City of Seattle, 143 S. Ct. 443 (2022) (No. 21-1019).

E FUTURE HEALTH REFORM

Past reform episodes have all included marked enthusiasm for concepts – such as managed care, consumer-driven care, and increased disclosure – that were expected to promote health care quality while reducing (or at least holding steady) costs. Those concepts are all still with us, although the bloom is off the rose. In practice all of them displayed significant shortcomings that proved to limit the salutary work that scholars, policy experts, and the public expected them to accomplish. Calls for more health reform therefore remain common.[176]

Today's health reform discussions intersect with the employment-based system by questioning more insistently than in the past whether employers and insurers have a role to play *at all* in the American health care system. Among the Democrats who ran for President in the 2020 election, every leading candidate proposed expanding public insurance, either through the adoption of a "Medicare for All" proposal, or through proposals for a "public option," wherein all or some percentage of Americans would have the option to purchase coverage from a public health insurance program like Medicare or Medicaid.[177] Republicans questioned the wisdom of both proposals.[178]

The vices and virtues of a national health system are well-known, exhibited, as they are, by the widespread adoption of such approaches in other advanced economies. Asserted virtues include fewer overall dollars spent, better results per dollar spent, and true universal access to care. Asserted vices include longer waiting times, slower medical advances, loss of skilled doctors as promising young professionals emigrate or switch fields, and objections to the large government role in intensely personal decisions. Those arguments won't be assayed here, as adoption of a program like Medicare for All would effectively terminate employment-based health insurance.

A world with some form of public option would pose interesting questions about what role employment-based health insurance would play in such a system.[179] Critics of the public option assert that the existence of a public option would quickly compete private payers out of business because of the government's cost advantages

---

[176] *E.g.*, Brendan S. Maher, *The Private Option*, 2020 Mich. St. L. Rev. 1043, 1045 nn.1 & 2 (2020) (listing reform ideas debated in the run-up to the 2020 election) [hereinafter *PO*].

[177] Kevin Uhrmacher et al., *Where 2020 Democrats Stand on Health Care*, Wash. Post, www .washingtonpost.com/graphics/politics/policy-2020/medicare-for-all/ (last updated Apr. 8, 2020).

[178] In addition to their long-standing opposition to "Medicare for All" type national health insurance, Republicans also sharply criticized "public option" approaches. Seema Verma, *I'm the Administrator of Medicaid and Medicare. A Public Option Is a Bad Idea.*, Wash. Post (July 24, 2019, 4:37 PM), www.washingtonpost.com/opinions/a-public-option-for-health-insur ance-is-a-terrible-idea/2019/07/24/fb651c1a-ae2e-11e9-8e77-03b30bc29f64_story.html [https://perma.cc/ 6C22-4TX4].

[179] *See generally* Maher, *PO*, *supra* Chapter 11 note 176 (extended consideration of how the availability of a public option might influence the overall provision of care).

(including greater purchasing power and lack of a profit imperative).[180] Yet a public option reform could conceivably block that possibility by barring individuals with access to employment-based insurance from choosing the public option at an affordable price.

If we assume, however, that those with access to employment-based insurance could select the public option, then the question becomes more interesting. In what ways might the existence of a public option serve to affect employment-based health insurance? Perhaps such a reform would totally eviscerate employment-based insurance. Freed from any employer mandate to provide insurance and relieved of labor pressure to provide health benefits (because workers can avail themselves of the exchanges or the public option), employers might terminate health benefits *en masse*. Yet for self-interested reasons employers might not be so inclined. Competitive pressure to provide benefits, and benefits in some way "better" than those available under a public option, might drive some employers to retain and improve the health benefits they offer. It would likely be difficult for employers and their insurers to compete on price with a public option. But one can imagine private payers competing along other dimensions, such as attracting a network of better doctors, offering concierge-style medical services, promising reduced waiting times for treatment, or providing cutting-edge personalized treatments not covered by the public option. That development could make the decision to choose the public option over the company's plan a close question for many employees. Hence, a public option might not compete employment-based health plans out of existence, if plans are restructured to offer a premium product, allowing participants to avoid shortcomings of the public system.[181]

A second potential reason that employment-based insurance might survive in a public option world is that it provides an attractive middle ground. Many Americans profess to distrust social insurance programs and oppose increased government involvement in their lives. Yet those same people often find the task of investigating and securing their own insurance daunting and unpleasant. Employment-based insurance could spare them the effort of making difficult insurance trade-offs while at the same time avoiding the philosophical angst of reliance on government.[182] Conversely, a massive flight to a public option might reveal that purported philosophical objections to government involvement in health care are *far* less widely held than many commentators and politicians have claimed.

---

[180] E.g., Janet Trautwein, *A Public Option Wouldn't Just Compete with Private Insurance – It Would Destroy It*, DESERT SUN (June 4, 2021, 6:00 AM), www.desertsun.com/story/opinion/contributors/2021/06/04/public-option-would-destroy-private-health-insurance/7527231002/.

[181] Maher, *PO, supra* Chapter 11 note 176, at 1078–91.

[182] Maher, *REBA, supra* Chapter 11 note 3, at 1290–91.

F CONCLUSION

The Affordable Care Act fundamentally changed health insurance in the United States, including employment-based health insurance. And while not all of the ACA's reforms reached all employment-based plans, some did, partially filling the regulatory vacuum that ERISA had created. But the ACA was not, as critics claimed, a "federal takeover of health care."[183] ERISA long ago made the largest form of private health insurance – employment-based health insurance – a field of federal dominion, drastically curtailing the states' ability to regulate via far-reaching pre-emption. The ACA simply started to build within the vast territory ERISA had already appropriated. As US health care costs continue to escalate, absorbing an ever-higher share of economic output (GDP), one expects more changes to follow. Content regulation of private health care plans has likely only just begun.

---

[183] *Examining Obamacare Transparency Failures: Hearing before the H. Comm. on Oversight & Gov't Reform*, 113th Cong. 93 (2014) (statement of Rep. Scott DesJarlais, Member, H. Comm. on Oversight & Gov't Reform).

APPENDIX

ERISA's Legislative History

BACKGROUND

James A. Wooten, *"The Most Glorious Story of Failure in the Business": The Studebaker-Packard Corporation and the Origins of ERISA*, 49 BUFF. L. REV. 683 (2001).

Michael S. Gordon, *Overview: Why Was ERISA Enacted?, in* S. SPEC. COMM. ON AGING, 98TH CONG., THE EMPLOYEE RETIREMENT INCOME SECURITY ACT OF 1974: THE FIRST DECADE 1 (Comm. Print 1984).

MERTON C. BERNSTEIN, THE FUTURE OF PRIVATE PENSIONS (Free Press of Glencoe 1964).

ERISA PRECURSORS (IN CHRONOLOGICAL ORDER)

U.S. DEPARTMENT OF LABOR, LEGISLATIVE HISTORY OF THE WELFARE AND PENSION PLANS DISCLOSURE ACT OF 1958, *as Amended by* Pub. L. 87-420 of 1962 (Washington, D.C., GPO; 1962). Compilation includes the legislative history of the 1962 amendments.

PRESIDENT'S COMM. ON CORPORATE PENSION FUNDS AND OTHER PRIVATE RETIREMENT AND WELFARE PROGRAMS, PUBLIC POLICY AND PRIVATE PENSION PROGRAMS, A REPORT TO THE PRESIDENT ON PRIVATE EMPLOYEE RETIREMENT PLANS (Washington, D.C., GPO; 1965).

S. COMM. ON GOVERNMENT OPERATIONS, DIVERSION OF UNION WELFARE-PENSION FUNDS OF ALLIED TRADES COUNCIL AND TEAMSTERS LOCAL 815, S. REP. NO. 89-1348 (1966).

Private Pension Plans: Hearings before the Subcomm. on Fiscal Policy of the J. Econ. Comm., 89th Cong. (1966) (background study of pension plans).

S. 1024, 90th Cong. (1967). This is the Johnson Administration fiduciary responsibility bill, the principal provisions of which are described at 113 CONG. REC. 3924–25 (1967) (statement of Sen. Yarborough).

S. 1103, 90th Cong. (1967). This is the original comprehensive pension regulatory proposal of Senator Jacob Javits (R–N.Y.). The proposal is printed, together with Senator Javits's introductory statement and explanatory notes, at 113 CONG. REC. 4650–61 (1967). According to those notes, the proposal was in large measure derived from the Ontario

464 *Appendix*

Pension Benefits Act, 1965, S.O. 1965, ch. 96, 4 R.S.O. 1970, ch. 342, See the remarks of Senator Javits at pp. 4–27 of the 1966 Joint Economic Committee hearings.

H.R. 16462, 91st Cong. (1970). This is the Nixon Administration fiduciary responsibility bill, which is printed, together with an introductory statement and section-by-section analysis, at 116 CONG. REC. 7566–78 (1970).

S. 2, 92d Cong. (1971). This is a revised version of Senator Javits's comprehensive regulatory proposal, which is printed, together with introductory and explanatory statements, at 117 CONG. REC. 274–84 (1971), and in *Private Welfare and Pension Plan Study, 1971: Hearings Before the Subcomm. on Labor of the S. Comm. on Labor and Public Welfare*, 92d Cong. 11–92 (1971).

S. 3598, 92d Cong. (1972). This is a comprehensive reform bill jointly sponsored by Senators Williams and Javits, chair and ranking minority member, respectively, of the Senate Committee on Labor and Public Welfare, which is printed, together with introductory statements, at 118 CONG. REC. 16904-22 (1972).

S. REP. NO. 92-1150 (1972) (Comm. on Labor and Public Welfare report on S. 3598).

S. REP. NO. 92-1224 (1972) (Finance Comm. report on S. 3598, stripping the bill of its coverage, vesting, funding, termination insurance, and portability provisions, leaving only fiduciary standards and additional disclosure requirements).

ERISA IN THE 93D CONGRESS

JAMES A. WOOTEN, THE EMPLOYEE RETIREMENT INCOME SECURITY ACT OF 1974: A POLITICAL HISTORY (University of California Press 2004).

SUBCOMM. ON LABOR OF THE S. COMM. ON LABOR AND PUBLIC WELFARE, 94TH CONG., LEGISLATIVE HISTORY OF THE EMPLOYEE RETIREMENT INCOME SECURITY ACT OF 1974 (Washington, DC, GPO; Comm. Print 1976) (3 volumes) (ERISA LEGISLATIVE HISTORY).

Richard M. Nixon, Recommendations for Pension Reform, H.R. DOC. NO. 93-82, (Apr. 11, 1973) (presidential message outlining the components of bills subsequently introduced as S. 1557 and S. 1631, 93d Cong. (1973)). Although the bills introduced in the 93d Congress, together with introductory and explanatory statements, are reprinted in the compiled ERISA LEGISLATIVE HISTORY (preceding source), the presidential message does not appear therein.

James A. Wooten, *A Legislative and Political History of ERISA Preemption*, published in the JOURNAL OF PENSION BENEFITS in four parts, as follows:

Part 1, vol. 14:31 (2006);

Part 2, vol. 14:5 (2007);

Part 3, vol. 15:15 (2008);

Part 4, vol. 22:3 (2014).

Symposium: *ERISA at 40: What Were They Thinking?*, DREXEL L. REV. vol.6, no. 4 (2014).

Index

ABLE accounts 332–33
abuse and mismanagement, prevention of 17–18, 32, 36, 39, 49n116, 57, 61
abuse of discretion
  conflicts of interest 171–74
  denial of benefits as 171–72
  factfinding 66, 169–70
  standard of review 32, 100–2, 114, 167–70
ACA See Affordable Care Act
accounting methods 317, 319
accumulation of pension savings
  benefit accrual 237–50, 261–62
    age discrimination 238–41
    anti-cutback rule 245–49
    backloaded accrual 241–45, 261
    cash balance plans 239–40
    defined benefit plans 226, 237–42, 244–45
    defined contribution plans 237–40, 242
    fractional rule variances 242–45
    grounds for stopping 239
    plan amendments and 182, 245–50
    service conditions 237–38
  forfeiture conditions 227
  overview 227
  plan participation
    administration costs 232
    age and service conditions 228–36
    barriers to 231–32, 235, 408–9
    breaks in service 228–29
    expanding coverage 231–36
    minimum standards 228–30
    part-time workers 231–34, 418
    rates 3, 408–9
    standards 163–64, 237–38
    unionized workers 353n107

vesting
  enforcement 255–57
  minimum standards approach 18–19, 228–29, 251–54, 259, 261–62
  overview 227
  policy 257–60
  statutory standards 228, 231, 250–55
  See also pension plans
actual deferral percentage (ADP) test 375–80
actuarial funding methods 291–92, 389–90
actuarial reports 70, 70n43
ADEA See Age Discrimination in Employment Act
administrative deviation approach 154n158
administrative exhaustion 175–76
adoption leave 229
ADP test See actual deferral percentage (ADP) test
advance funding limits 385–90
Affordable Care Act (ACA)
  administrative/judicial review 176
  children of beneficiaries, extension of services for 225n1
  community rating 449–50
  content controls, generally 27, 59, 447–56
  contraceptive services 447n108, 455–56
  disclosure obligations 63
  employee freedom of choice 450
  employer mandate, justification for 452–53
  essential health benefits requirement 453–55, 457–58
  guaranteed issue 449–50
  impact of 431, 442, 447–48, 462
  individual mandate 449–50, 452
  insurance 'exchanges' 449–50, 452–53
  large group plans, applicability to 453–55, 457
  lawsuits 431n2, 455–56
  lifetime/dollar limits, restrictions on 225n1

Index

Affordable Care Act (ACA) (cont.)
  limitations 450
  minimum value requirement 451, 453–55
  preemption provisions 457–59
  preventative health services 225n1, 455–56
  purpose 449
  reforms, scope of 449
  religious conflicts 447n108, 455–56
  scope of provisions 448
  shared responsibility payments 451
  state laws, influences on 457–59
  summary of benefits and coverage (SBC) 63
  tax credits 449–51
  tax incentives 450–51
age and service requirements
  discrimination regarding pension plans, and 13,
    238–41
  normal retirement age 237–38
age discrimination 13, 238–41
Age Discrimination in Employment Act (ADEA)
    238–39
annuity plans 7, 9, 279–85, 300–1, 308, 343–44,
    389, 395–96
anti-alienation 265–79, 286
  bankruptcy, and 267
  conflicts of interest, and 267–68
  exceptions 266–68
  involuntary assignments 267
  IRS, and 267n15
  minimum standards 13
  overriding beneficiary designations 273–79
  plan loans 266–67, 401
  purpose of provisions 265–66, 269, 285
  qualified domestic relations orders 269–73, 286
anti-cutback rule 245–49
anti-inurement rule 133
anti-reduction rule See anti-cutback rule
anti-retaliation rule and plan amendments 179–82
association retirement plans 232–33
average benefit percentage test 344–50, 354n109, 364

backpay claims and awards 188
bankruptcy
  company stock, and 320n15
  PBGC's liens 298, 305–6
  rabbi trusts, and 321–22, 324
  retirement savings, and 267
  underfunded plans 7n21, 289
beneficiaries See plan participants and
    beneficiaries
beneficiary designation
  killer laws 216–17, 273, 276n55
  overriding beneficiary designations 273–79
  preemption, and 205–6, 215–16

benefit accrual 237–50, 261–62
  age discrimination 239–41
  anti-cutback rule 245–49
  backloaded accrual 241–45, 261
  cash balance plans 239–40
  defined benefit plans 226, 237–42, 244–45
  defined contribution plans 237–40, 242
  fractional rule variances 242–45
  generally 227
  grounds for stopping 239
  money purchase pension plans 239–40
  plan amendments, and 245–50
  service conditions 237–38
benefit overpayments, recovery of 249
benefit plans See employee benefit plans
benefits gap 418
binding obligations 69
blackout periods, advance notice 66–67
Blue Cross 432
bonus payments 47n106
Bush Administration reform proposals 413–17
Bush, George W. 334n67, 413
business partners, ERISA applicability 40–41,
    43n87, 44

cash balance plans 239–40
cash-basis accounting 317, 319
cash-or-deferred arrangements (CODA) See 401(k)
    plans
catch-up contributions 384–85
causation
  'but for' test, enforcement standing 165–66
  estoppel 83–84, 83n100, 83n101
causes of action
  equitable enforcement of plan or ERISA 75–87
    estoppel 79–87, 90–92
    reformation 76–77, 93
    surcharge 78–79, 93–94
  fraud and misrepresentation 177–78
  interference with protected rights 160n3, 179–82,
    188, 255–56
  overview 176–77
  participation in fiduciary breach 178–79
  private rights of action under ERISA 176–77
  retaliation or wrongful discharge 179–82
  specific intent requirement 180
  unlawful purpose 180
charitable organizations 25
children
  COBRA continuation coverage eligibility 441
  health care plans, coverage under 26, 225n1
  maternity/paternity/adoption benefits 229
  medical child support orders 26, 27n107
  overriding beneficiary designations 273–79

Index

penalty-free early distributions after birth/
adoption 399
qualified domestic relations orders (QDRO)
269–73, 286, 307
choice-of-law provisions 213
church plans
control or association requirement 56
definition 57n148
establishment or maintained, interpretation
56–57
exemption 12–13, 12n34, 25, 53–54, 56–58, 290
ministers, employee status 56–57
nondiscrimination rules, exemption from 342
vesting 54n134
civil actions *See* enforcement
Civil Rights Act (Title VII) 180
COBRA *See* Consolidated Omnibus Budget
Reconciliation Act
CODA *See* 401(k) plans
cofiduciaries 125–27
collective bargaining agreements 353
government plans 55–56
Commerce Clause 28
commerce, defined 28
community property 205, 284–85, 287
community rating 449–50
compensation cap 381
conduct controls overview 59
See also disclosure obligations; enforcement;
fiduciaries; preemption
conflicts of interest
abuse of direction, and 171–74
administrative law approach 173–74
anti-alienation, and 267–68
corporate takeovers 131, 135–37
enforcement 171–76
exclusive benefit rule, and 132–33, 135–37
fiduciary impartiality, and 130–31
fiduciary prohibited transactions 116, 140–42
improper motivation 135–36
investment decision-making, ESG
considerations 138–39
plan participants and beneficiaries 130–35
procedural prudence 138–39
totality of the circumstances approach 172–73
trust law, and 134–35, 142, 172n52
Consolidated Omnibus Budget Reconciliation
Act of 1985 (COBRA) 26, 27n106, 225n1,
438n41, 441n56, 441–42
continuation coverage
eligibility for 441
equivalent tax rules 27
requirement to offer 225n1
scope of 26–27, 441–42

health insurance portability 225n1
tax penalties for failure to offer services 225n1
constructive notice 106
constructive ownership rules 301–2, 351, 354
consumption tax 427–28
content controls
Affordable Care Act, generally 27, 59, 447–56
Congressional policy 14, 20n75, 21, 21n79, 197–98
generally 18–19, 196–97, 225–26
health care plans 225
minimum standards approach 4, 13, 16–21, 51,
54n134, 59, 179, 197, 213, 226, 227, 230,
238n58, 238n59, 242, 244, 252, 254, 260, 288,
423, 453n134
participant control over investments 21
pension plans 196–97, 225–26
purpose 18–19
welfare plans 197, 225
See also accumulation of pension savings;
distribution of pension benefits; security of
pension benefits
continuation coverage *See* Consolidated Omnibus
Budget Reconciliation Act
contraceptive services 447–48, 455–56
contractors, independent 41–43, 57, 418
controlled group, definition 350–51
Coronavirus 297n40, 393n245, 400, 402n289
corporate takeovers
fiduciary impartiality 131
plan participant conflicts of interest 131, 135–37
severance payments, and 30–32
Coverdell education savings accounts (ESAs) 332,
414n326

damages 183–84
de novo review 168–69, 169n43
death
beneficiary designation 217–18
COBRA continuation coverage 26
community property rights 205, 284–85, 287
divorce and death benefits 26, 217–18, 274
early distribution of benefits, and 46, 264n3
fixed-term deferred compensation 46
forfeiture of benefits at 279n66, 279n68, 286–87
killer laws 216–17, 273, 276–77
pension plans, and 46, 46n105
plan participant status 164
pre-retirement, family law creditor access to
benefits 271–72
spousal protection 13, 26, 287
survivor benefits 26, 253, 268, 273–77, 287
welfare plans 48
will revocation on divorce, default rule 274
wrongful death 183, 192

deferred compensation, generally
company stock 318–19
definition 361–62
foreign corporations 323n25
nonqualified 22–23, 317–24
property transfers, and 317–22
substantial risk of forfeiture 318n11–12
deferred compensation plans
advance funding 317–18, 320
anti-cutback rule, and 248
benefit distribution, timing of 248, 324
complexity of 327, 406
conditional requirements 317–18
content controls, generally 226
emergency in-service distributions 264
employer's deductions 323
excluded benefits 50
government or church plans 54
in-service deferred compensation 50
interest liabilities 324
law reforms 324
noncompliance penalties 324
nonqualified deferred compensation 22–23,
317–24
preferential tax treatment for 22–25
'primarily' requirement 321, 322n22
profit sharing plans 264
qualified *vs.* nonqualified 5–6
rabbi trusts, and 320–22, 324
security for payment 320–22
tax-exempt employers, and 323n25
taxation, and 5–6, 317–18, 324
unfunded plans exception 39–40, 51–53, 290–91,
317, 319–20
welfare benefits 49–50
See also pension plans; top hat plans
defined benefit plans
administrative costs 232
advance funding methods 291
annuity due formulae 9
backloaded accrual 241–45, 261
benefit accrual 226, 237–38, 241–45, 366
blackout periods 66–67
cash balance plans 239–40
compensation cap 381–82
contribution formula 6, 9
deduction limits 389–90
defined contribution plans, vs. 6–7, 9, 312, 424–25
defined in ERISA 6
distribution of funds 263, 392n244
early distribution 263
employee *vs.* employer risk 6–7
funding 9, 13–14, 289–90, 292–93
grounds for stopping benefit accrual 239

integration with Social Security 368–70
legislative limits on standing, and 162–63
maximum amount rule 380, 383, 411
minimum coverage requirement 355–56
minimum funding standards 13, 162, 289–90,
292–93, 390
nondiscrimination requirement 359–66
number of 312, 388
opt-out, reform proposal 422–24
PBGC termination insurance 299–306
proposed plan for 422–24
remedies 189
retroactivity of benefits 9
sponsorship trends 289
stringent regulation 13–14
survivor protection 287
termination 162n10
vesting 241–42, 251
defined contribution plans
backloaded accrual 242
benefit accrual 237, 239, 242
compensation cap 381–82
contribution formulae 6, 8–9, 361
defined benefit plans, vs. 6–7, 9, 312, 424–25
defined in ERISA 6, 162n11
disclosure obligations 66–67
distribution of funds 263–64
early distribution 263–64, 399–400
employee *vs.* employer risk 6–7
enforcement incentives 162
grounds for stopping benefit accrual 239
integration with Social Security 369–70
maximum amount rule 380–81, 383, 411
nondiscrimination requirement 359–66
number of 388
plan coverage, encouraging 232–33
pooled employer plans 233
survivor protection 280, 287
vesting 251
denial of benefits
abuse of discretion, whether 171–72
administrative exhaustion 175–76
compensation, limitations 183–84, 190
information disclosure requests 67
review and claims mechanisms 65–66
SPD inaccuracies, and 73–74, 77n79
dependent care benefits 50, 50n119
depreciation 291–92
disability insurance 432
disability pensions 46, 300
disaster relief, emergency distributions 400
disclosure obligations
civil penalties for non-compliance 67, 70n45,
160n3

Index

469

fiduciary disclosure
  fiduciary silence 97–98, 110–11
  liability 93–94, 97–98
  misleading information 107–8, 110–11
  financial decision making, and 15–17, 61, 118
  funded status of pension plans 65, 298
  individual status 65–67
  lifetime income equivalent 66n26
  mandatory disclosures 13, 15–16, 26, 69
  material omissions approach 98–103
  minimum funding standards 298
  optimal disclosure 71–73, 100–2
  overview 13, 15–17, 62
  participant-directed investments 66–67
  PBGC 63–65, 289, 306
  permitted limitations 69–70
  plan funding notices 65
  regarding future benefits 89–91, 107–9
  regime triggers 33
  statutory
    individual status 65–67
    plan finances 63–65
    plan instruments 67–70
    plan terms 63
  summary annual report (SAR) 64, 64n17
  summary of benefits and coverage (SBC) 63
  summary of material modifications (SMM) 63,
    95–96, 105n185
  summary plan descriptions (SPD) 15–16, 63,
    71–103
  See also informal communications; summary
    plan description (SPD)
discretionary benefits 35–36
discrimination
  adverse employment acts as cause in action
    180–82
  age discrimination 13, 238–41
  cash balance plans 239–40
  NHCEs *vs.* HCEs
    discrimination in contributions or benefits
     358–66
    discrimination in coverage 343–50, 354n109
    nondiscrimination principle 23–24, 26–27,
     33/–42
    preferential tax treatment, and 230
disqualified person, definition 144
distribution of pension benefits
  anti-alienation 265–79, 286
    bankruptcy, and 267
    conflicts of interest, and 267–68
    exceptions 266–68
    involuntary assignments 267
    IRS, and 267n15
    minimum standards 13

  overriding beneficiary designations
    273–79
  plan loans 266–67, 401
  purpose of provisions 265–66, 269, 285
  qualified domestic relations orders 205,
    269–73, 286
emergency in-service distributions 264n3
emergency savings accounts 50, 236, 397
excess distributions, recovery 249
involuntary assignments 267
mandatory cash-outs 406
overriding beneficiary designations 273–79
overview 263
phased retirement programs 7n24, 264, 264n1
plan loans 266–67, 283, 401–2
pre-retirement distributions
  emergency/disaster relief 400
  family law creditor access to benefits 271–72
  nondiscrimination rules, and 397
  tax-free distributions to alternate payee
    399–400
  tax penalties 399–400
  timing of 264, 268–69, 286, 397–401
profit-sharing plans 264
qualified domestic relations orders (QDRO)
  205, 269–73, 286, 307, 399
required minimum distribution (RMD)
  393–94
rollovers 248, 325–26, 400n277, 403–6
Roth IRAs 236, 328–33, 391–92, 403n293, 417
spousal rights 268, 273–77, 279–84
  beneficiary designation, and 205–6, 215–16
  community property 205, 284–85, 287
  consent requirement 274, 283
  crimes committed by spouse, and 217, 273,
    276
  minimum requirements 287
  prenuptial agreements 281n78
  qualified domestic relations order (QDRO)
    205, 269–73, 286, 307, 399
  qualified joint and survivor annuity (QJSA)
    279–83, 392–93
  qualified pre-retirement survivor annuity
    (QPSA) 279–82
  remarriage after participant's death 281
  survivor benefits for former spouse,
    restrictions on 269–77, 271n33
  survivor protection 13, 26, 253, 268, 273–77,
    279–84, 287, 392–93
  waiver of pension benefits 281–82
state and local laws 25
stock bonus plans 264
timing of plan distributions
  anti-cutback rule, and 248

distribution of pension benefits (cont.)
early distribution 263–64, 286
generally 286
late distribution 265, 286, 391–92
lifetime distribution 392–94
minimum distribution rule 391–92
penalty taxes 264, 264n3, 286, 392
pre-retirement distributions 264, 268–69, 286, 397–401
qualifying longevity annuity contracts (QLACs) 395–96
required minimum distribution (RMD) 393–94
rollovers 248, 286, 394, 400n277, 403–6
tax rule restrictions 24n89
diversification rule 128
divorce
beneficiary designation, and 205–6, 215–18
COBRA continuation coverage eligibility 441
divorced spouses eligibility for coverage 13, 205–6, 215–18
medical child support orders 26, 27n107
overriding beneficiary designations 273–79
qualified domestic relations order (QDRO) 205, 269–73, 286
qualified joint and survivor annuity (QJSA) 279–83
state laws regarding 205–6, 215–18, 274
survivor benefits for former spouse, restrictions on 269–77
will revocation, default rule 274
domestic abuse, victims of 399–400

early retirement 238, 241, 301
economic neutrality principle 55n141, 425–26
education assistance programs 6, 50
educational organization employees 25n99, 25n100
elective contribution schemes 233–35
automatic enrollment 235
barriers to participation 231–32, 235, 408–9
contribution caps 236
Labor Department investment rules 235
matching principle 236, 323
student loans and 235
See also 401(k) plans; 403(b) plans
emergency in-service distributions 264, 400
emergency savings programs 50, 236, 397
employee benefit plans
apparent authority to institute or amend plans 110n107
claims procedures 192
content controls, generally 225–26
discretionary benefits 35–36
employee evaluation 61, 266, 407

employer right to amend 76, 88–92, 181–82, 360n134
ERISA applicability overview 44
ERISA definition 5–6, 28, 33, 44
ERISA exemptions 12–13, 53–58
ERISA policy interactions, and 21, 442
ERISA's pattern of regulation 14–15
federal fiduciary standards 14–15, 32, 116, 128–29
federal revenue, and 23
minimum standards approach 13, 18–21, 213
multiple rights and obligations 58
non-ERISA fringe benefits 48
overview of varieties of 10f
participant status 163–64
'pay-or-play' health care reforms 445–47
pension-welfare dichotomy 44–50, 58
plan instruments 67–70
plan prerequisites 28–29, 57
failure to satisfy reporting standards, and 34n38, 36–38
indefiniteness, and 33–37, 57
restricted coverage, and 37–40
standard of proof 34–35
transience, and 29–33, 57
preemption of mandated state laws 442–43
varieties of 5–12
Employee Plans Compliance Resolution System (EPCRS) 373–74
employee stock ownership plans (ESOP) 47n107, 70n44
See also employer stock funds
employees
adverse employment actions 179–82
church ministers or clergy, employee status 56–57
civil actions under ERISA 179–82
decision making, informed 61, 266, 407
defined 41–42, 57–58, 350–51
educational organizations, in 25n99, 25n100
enforcement standing 164, 191
ERISA definition 40–41, 43
ERISA exclusion criteria 43, 43n89, 352–54
expectations of 37, 37n52, 57
freelancers 43n88, 418
gig economy, influences of 418
independent contractors 41–43, 57, 418
individual employment contracts 39, 40
leased employees 351
nonresident aliens 353
part-time workers 231, 233–34, 351, 418
partners/nominal partners 44
pension/ welfare plan evaluation by 61, 266, 407
planning interests 21

Index

471

reasonable expectation of returning to covered
employment 164–65
status 40–44, 56–57
tax allowance benefits for 23–24
unionized workers 353
working owners 40–41, 43, 58
wrongful discharge or retaliation 179–82
See also highly compensated employees
(HCEs); nonhighly compensated
employees (NHCEs)
Employer Retirement Savings Accounts (ERSAs)
proposal 416–17
employer stock funds
applicability criteria 152–53
fiduciary obligations 153–57
loss aversion 153–54
Moench presumption 154–57
stock drop cases 153, 156
taxation 318
See also employee stock ownership plans
(ESOP)
employers
autonomy of 19–21
business owners' benefit programs 40–41
compensation costs for 3
constructive ownership rules 301–2, 351, 354
contributions matching principle 22–23, 236,
323, 357, 425–26
controlled group, definition 350–51
cost controls 21
interests of 134
limits on contributions 325
non-compliance with disclosure rules 67, 70n45,
160n3
overfunded plans, and 289
plan beneficiaries, as 134
right to amend plans 76, 76n70, 88–92, 168,
181–82
self-insured plans 218–19, 443–45, 454n139,
458–59
underfunded plans 298
workforce aggregation rules 351
employment-based health care
ACA reforms 447–56
access to 432–33
benefits for employers of 434–37
contraceptive services 447n108, 455–56
ERISA impacts on health regulation 438–47
generally 438
preemption rules 442–43
grandfathered plans 447–48
group health care plans 433–34
health care reform debates 460–61
historical development 432–33

lifetime limits, prohibition 225n1, 454–55
mandated state benefits laws 442–43
'pay or play' health care 445–47, 459
preemption, and
mandated state benefits laws 442–43
'pay or play' health care reforms 445–47, 459
rules, scope of 442–43
preexisting medical conditions 26, 225n1, 441–42,
454–55
preventative health services 225n1, 455–56
public option reform proposal 460–61
religious conflicts 447n108, 455–56
state laws, influences of ACA on 457–59
tax incentives 434–35
employment-based health insurance
actuarial risk 434
benefits for employers of 434–37
employer mandate, justification for 452
ERISA preemption, and 442
essential health benefits requirement 453–55,
457–58
generally 433–34
historical influences on 434–35
Individual Coverage Health Reimbursement
Accounts (ICHRA) 452n132
insurance 'exchanges' 449–50, 452–53
mandated benefits laws 442–43
minimum value requirement 451, 453–55
preexisting medical conditions 26, 225n1, 441–42,
454–55
religious conflicts 447n108, 455–56
self-insured plans 218–19, 443–45, 454n139,
458–59
shared responsibility payments 451
stop-loss insurance 444–45
tax credits 449–51
tax expenditure 434–35
tax incentives 450–51
enforcement
causes of action *See* causes of action
civil actions under ERISA 4n7, 73, 176–82,
188–92
civil penalties
non-disclosure, for 67, 70n45, 160n3
prohibited-transactions, for 144–45
conflicts of interest 171–74
generally 61, 191–92
informal (non-SPD) communications, of
103–12, 114–15
applicable circumstances 106–10
objections to 102–6
plan amendments 103–6
plan clarification 106–7
minimum funding contributions 297–98

enforcement (cont.)
PBGC termination insurance 162, 305–6
plaintiff eligibility criteria 161–64
remedies
compensation, limitations 183–84, 190–92
equitable relief 61, 74–75, 75n68, 93–94, 96, 144, 180, 184–88, 268
ERISA's remedial balance 175–77, 188–91
estoppel 74–75, 78–87, 104–6, 187
fiduciary breach, for 78, 183–84, 189–90, 189n144
individual vs. plan injuries 189
prohibited transactions 143–44
reformation 75–77, 79n86, 95
restitution 185–86, 188, 255
supplemental remedies, preemption of 207–8
surcharge 78–79, 79n85, 79n86, 93–94, 187
tort-like damages 183–84
scope of review
abuse of discretion 66, 167–75
under ACA 176
administrative exhaustion requirement 175–76
conflicts of interest 171–74
de novo review 168–69, 169n43
factfinding 66, 169–70
generally 167
limitations 192
plan interpretations 167–69
SPDs 71–103, 112–14
standing 161–67, 191, 255
assignees 166–67
'but for' test 165–66
definition of participant 163–65, 191
reasonable expectation of returning to covered employment 164–65
under-enforcement, effects of 82–83, 98
vesting 164, 166, 255–60
environmental, social or governance (ESG) factors in investment decision making 138–39
EPCRS 373–74 See Employee Plans Compliance Resolution System (EPCRS)
equitable relief 61, 74–75, 75n68, 93–94, 96, 113, 144, 180, 184–88, 268
ERISA, general considerations
civil actions under 4n7, 176–82
see also causes of action
compliance investigations, authority for 63–64
exemption of church or governmental plans 12–13, 12n34, 25, 53–57
four-tiered system of regulation under 12–15
higher than market quality standards, imposition of 172–73
increase in retirement savings since passage of 3

informed financial decision making component of 15–17, 266
labor provisions vs. tax provisions 4, 54–55
minimum standards approach 13, 18–21, 213
policy interactions 21
private actions under 176–77
promotion of plan sponsorship 121, 191
protective policy 18–19, 39, 121, 165
purpose 15, 19, 57–58, 67–68, 83, 121, 175–76, 191, 439–40
tax Code qualification criteria, and 22–25, 315n2, 316
ERSAs See Employer Retirement Savings Accounts proposal
ESAs See Coverdell education savings accounts
essential health benefits requirement 453–55, 457–58
establishment requirement for plan/benefit arrangements 33–37
employee reliance/belief in existence 37, 37n52, 57
failure to satisfy reporting standards 34n38, 36–37
informal policies 35–36
standard of proof 34–35
estoppel
causation 83–84, 83n100, 83n101
detrimental reliance 79–87, 79n87, 90, 98, 104n184
essential elements 79n87, 187
extraordinary circumstances condition 85–87, 85n109, 85n111, 85n112
informal communications 79–80, 103–6
likely harm standard 86–87
oral modifications 104–5, 105n186
reliance -or-prejudice test 84, 86
standard of proof 74–75, 76n76, 78, 82, 86–87
excise tax 144–45
exclusive benefit rule 127–28, 133–39
exculpatory clauses 17, 116, 131–33
executive compensation, ERISA exclusions 39–40
existence of plans/arrangement, challenges to
establishment requirement 33–37
restricted coverage 37–40
transience 29–33
express terms, standardization of 17

factfinding, abuse of discretion 65–66, 169–70
family law claims
qualified domestic relations orders (QDRO) 269–73, 286, 399
federal common law, preemption 216–18
federal fiduciary standards 17–18

Index

473

federal revenue, and qualified retirement plans 23, 325

Federal Thrift Savings Plan 421

fiduciaries

abuse and mismanagement, prevention of 17–18, 32, 36, 39, 57, 61

abuse of discretion
  conflicts of interest 171–75
  factfinding 66, 169–70
  standard of review 32, 100–2, 101n176, 114, 167–70

advisory functions 117

apparent authority 110–11

conflicts of interest 130–33
  prohibited transactions 116, 140–42

de facto fiduciaries 119

definition 17, 32, 116–19

delegation of duties 124–27

discretionary authority 32, 35–36, 100–1, 119–21

dual status (multi hat) situations 121–23, 132–33

fiduciary disclosure 110–12, 197
  advice or instruction, regarding 69, 93–94
  fiduciary silence 97–98, 110–11
  liability 93–94, 97–98
  misleading information 107–8, 110–11
  top hat plans 51–53
  triggers for 111

fiduciary duties
  benefit overpayment recovery 249
  cofiduciary liability 125–27
  diversification rule 128
  employer stock funds 153–57
  exclusive benefit rule 127–28, 133–39
  exculpatory clauses 17, 116, 131–33
  federal fiduciary standards 17–18
  fiduciary acts 95–98, 111, 122–23
  generally 13–15, 117–19, 127–29, 157–59
  impartiality 121, 129–31
  improper motivation 135–36
  informal communications 103, 107–10, 114–15
  joint or divided responsibilities 124–27
  limitations on 112
  loyalty 111–12, 118, 127, 129–30
  mandatory nature 128
  ministerial duties 120–21
  named fiduciaries 124
  participant-directed investments 124, 145–52, 158
  prudence/reasonable care 127–28, 137–39
  remedies for breach of 78, 183–84, 188–91, 189–90, 189n144
  settlor *vs.* trustee functions 121–22
  trust 78

fiduciary silence 97–98, 110–11

financial decision making, and 15–17, 61, 118–21

funding, and 119–21

general principles 117–18

impartiality 121, 128–31

insider dealing 116

liabilities of 13, 75n63, 93–94, 107–10, 125–27

multiple fiduciaries 124–27

multiple roles of 121–23, 133–34

participant-directed investments
  employer stock funds 152–57
  limited options 150–52

plan administrators, as 75n63, 124–27

plan interpretation function of 101n176

plan participants, as 122

prohibited transactions 116, 140–42

representation of the plan's future status 89–94, 107–9

SPDs content, liability for 93–94, 97, 101–2n176

See also plan administrators

fiduciary breach
  enforcement incentives 162–63
  liabilities 125–27
  loyalty 111
  participation in, as cause in action 178–79
  remedies for 78, 183–84, 188–91, 189n144
  trust 78

financial limits in health care plans, prohibition 225n1

first-in-time rule 271

529 plans 332, 414n326

flat benefit plans 8–9

forfeiture conditions
  limitations on 227, 253, 261
  multiple conditions 254–55
  nonforfeitable, definition 253–54
  reasonable service periods, and 227
  vesting, and 250–55, 257–60

Form 5500 (IRS/DOL/PBGC) 63–64

401(k) plans
  ADP test 375–80
  automatic contribution arrangement 378
  catch-up contributions 384
  deduction limits 385–90
  defined 8
  discrimination tests for 374–80
  distribution rules 377
  elective deferrals 384–85, 412–13
  employee evaluation and decision-making 407
  employer contributions 374–80
  excess contributions, treatment of 377
  GRAs, compared with 422
  lifetime income distributions 395–96

474 Index

401(k) plans (cont.)
  maximum amount rule 384–85
  nondiscrimination rules, and 374–80, 387–88, 410
  number of 159, 388
  plan loans 402
  proposed rules for 416–17
  qualifying longevity annuity contracts 395–96
  safe harbor rules 410, 416–17
  saver's credit scheme 412–13
  starter 401(k) plans 379–80
  stock fund as alternative to 153
  See also individual retirement accounts (IRA)
403(b) plans
  catch up contributions 384
  early distributions 400
  elective deferrals 331–32, 384–85, 412–13
  maximum amount rule 384
  minimum distribution rules 391
  rollovers 405n298
  saver's credit scheme 412–13
  tax deferral 405n298
404(c) plans 147–48
fraud and misrepresentation 192
  'but for' test, enforcement standing 165–66
  cause in action, as 177–78
  fiduciary duties 110–11
  informal communications, and 107–9
  SPDs, and 76–77, 76n76, 77n80, 93–94, 96–98, 177–78
freedom of contract 211–14, 216, 223
funding notices 65
funding targets, attainment 65
funds, definition 33, 36

garnishment law 200–1, 215
genetic information 27
Georgia garnishment law 201n29, 215
gig economy 418
golden parachutes 30–32
good faith principle 79n87
governmental plans
  agency and control criteria 54–55
  collective bargaining agreements 55–56
  cost implications 54
  defined 54–55
  exemption 12–13, 12n34, 25, 53–56, 58, 290
  Indian tribal governments 25n98, 54n137
  minimum distribution rule, and 391
  nondiscrimination rules, exemption from 342
  rollovers 405n298
  tax rule interpretation 54–55, 54n138
  vesting 54n134
grandfathered plans 447–48, 447n108

guaranteed benefits 300–5
Guaranteed Retirement Account (GRA) proposal 421–25

Hawaii law mandated health insurance benefits law 212
health care, generally
  employer spending 3, 24–25
  ERISA's remedial balance, and 175n67, 190
  financing methods 432
health care plans
  ACA *See* Affordable Care Act (ACA)
  child health care benefits 26, 225n1
  COBRA reforms *See* Consolidated Omnibus Reconciliation Act (COBRA)
  continuation coverage 26, 225n1
  costs, compared with other welfare benefits 5
  eligibility conditions 88–89
  employer right to amend 88–92
  employer spending on 3, 24–25
  equitable remedies 185–88
  funding requirement 440
  health reimbursement arrangements (HRA) 185–87, 452n132
  health savings accounts (HSA) 414n326
  lifetime limits, prohibition 225n1, 454–55
  limitations of 440–41
  managed care 122
  participant status 163–67
  plan amendments 440
  portability 225n1
  preexisting condition coverage 26, 225n1, 441–42, 454–55
  preventative health services 225n1, 455–56
  regulation of 26–27
  rescission, restrictions on 225n1
  retirees, for 49–50
  tax penalties for failure to offer services 225n1
  vesting 440
  workers covered by 3
  See also Consolidated Omnibus Reconciliation Act (COBRA); employment-based health care; employment-based health insurance; taxes and health care; welfare plans
health care spending 3, 24–25
health information, collection 458–59
health insurance, generally
  adverse selection problem 433–34, 436, 440–41
  development 432
  group policies, advantages of 436–37
  insurance premiums 433
  See also employment-based health insurance
health maintenance organizations (HMOs)
  fiduciary acts 96, 111, 122–23

Index

preemption 207n61–3, 209–10
supplemental remedies, preemption of
   207n61–3
health reimbursement arrangement (HRA) 185–87,
   452n132
health savings accounts (HSA) 414n326
highly compensated employees (HCEs)
   average benefit percentage test 345–50
   defined 53, 354–55
   discrimination in contributions or benefits
      358–66
   discrimination in coverage 343–50
   disqualified plans and tax consequences
      356–58
   401(k) plans 374–80
   income limits and tax exempt IRAs 416n331
   IRA contributions by 329–30
   maximum amount rule 380–85
   minimum coverage requirement 343, 346–47,
      355–56
   minimum distribution rule 396–97
   nondiscrimination and redistribution 337–42,
      409–13
   proposed plans for 413–17
   retirement savings 335–36, 366–68, 370–71
   Social Security, and 366–71
   unfunded deferred compensation plans, ERISA
      exception 39–40
   See also employees; nonhighly compensated
      employees (NHCEs); top hat plans
HRA. See health reimbursement arrangement
HSA. See health savings accounts
human judgment, limitations of 18–19

Illinois insurance discretionary clause law 221
impartiality, fiduciary 121, 128–31
implied terms, standardization of 17
imputation of permitted disparity 349
income tax
   accounting methods 317
   company stock transfers 318
   constructive receipt 317, 324
   early distributions 263–64, 264n3
   economic neutrality principle, and 55n141
   household income tax liability 335–36
   in-kind compensation 317–18
   incentives for nonqualified arrangements 323
   incentives for qualified arrangements 327
   independent contractors 43n88, 418
   nonlapse restrictions 318n10
   plan classification, and 7–8
   property, definition 319–20, 321n16
   retirement plans, future of relationship with
      427–28

taxable income, timing of 317
   See also taxes and health care; taxes and
      retirement saving
independent contractors 41–43, 57, 418
Indian tribal governments 25n98, 54n137
individual account plans. See defined contribution
   plans
Individual Coverage Health Reimbursement
   Accounts (ICHRA) 452n132
individual retirement accounts (IRA) 327–33
   assets held in 326n40
   contributions limits 327–28, 379
   direct deposit with default contributions
      330–32
   distributions 264
   early withdrawals 400–1
   Lifetime Savings Accounts, vs. 334n67, 413–16
   maximum allowable tax-deductible
      contributions 328
   minimum distribution rule, and 391
   participation in 234
   preemption 234
   purpose 327, 400–1
   rollovers 280, 331–32, 400n277, 401, 403–6
   Roth IRAs 236, 328–33, 391–92, 403n293, 412–14,
      417
   saver's credit, and 412–13
   starter 401(k) plans, vs. 379–80
   state-mandated initiatives 234, 379–80
   tax deferral, and 22–23, 328–32
   tax-free rollovers 400n277, 403–6
   See also 401(k) plans; 403(b) plans
individual status, disclosure obligations 65–67
informal communications
   deference, appropriateness in 101n176
   enforcement 114–15
   estoppel, and 80–81, 104–6
   fiduciary obligations 107–10, 115–16
   fraud and misrepresentation, and 107–9
   future status of plan, regarding 107–9
   inconsistent statements 104–6
   liability for 101n176, 103, 106, 114–15
   plan amendments 103–6
   plan clarification 106–7
   reliance on 114–15
   vesting language 90n128
   written 105–6
   See also disclosure obligations; summary plan
      description (SPD)
information overload 16, 19, 71
insider dealing 116
insurance regulation
   discretionary clauses, prohibition of 221
   federal preemption 218–20

476   *Index*

insurance regulation (cont.)
  generally 442*n*68
  risk pooling arrangements 220–21
  state laws 25, 218–21
insurance savings clause 195, 200, 218–21, 443
Internal Revenue Code
  advance funding contributions 385
  anti-alienation rule 267*n*15
  compliance incentives 315–16
  constructive ownership rules 301–2
  deferred compensation plans 6–8
  duplication of ERISA pension content controls
    315–16
  minimum funding standards
    actuarial funding methods, choice of 390
    plan amendments 296–97
    qualified plan provisions funding
      requirements 298, 327*n*41
    waivers 296–97
  plan loans under 266–67
  property, definition 319–20, 321*n*16
  qualification criteria for preferential tax
    treatment 22–25, 315*n*2, 316
  qualified plan provisions funding requirements
    298
  qualified retirement plan provisions 286, 325–27
Internal Revenue Service
  actuarial assumptions for minimum funding
    obligations, on 295, 389–90
  governmental and church plans, on 54–55
  plan disqualification, on 356–58, 373–74
investment advisers 124
IRAs *See* individual retirement accounts

judicial review 36, 167
  de novo review 168–70, 169*n*43
  expertise, relevance 170, 170*n*45
  plan interpretations 167–69

Kentucky insurance provider law 221
Keogh plans 38*n*63
killer laws 216–17, 273, 276, 276*n*53–55

labor mobility 258
lifetime benefits
  limits in health care plans, prohibition 225*n*1,
    454–55
  SPD representations 89–92, 90*n*128
lifetime income equivalent 66*n*26
Lifetime Savings Accounts (LSA) proposal 334*n*67,
  413–16
loans (plan) 266–67, 283, 401–2
long-term disability plans 70*n*45
longevity annuities 395–96

Louisiana community property law 205, 284–85
low-income workers *See* nonhighly compensated
  employees (NHCEs)
lump sum payments 29–33

Maine severance payment law 29–30, 32–33, 211–12
mandatory cash-outs 406
mandatory disclosure rules 13, 15–16, 26
Maryland 'pay or play' health care reforms 445–47
Maryland stop-loss insurance law 444–45
Massachusetts severance payments/'tin parachute'
  law 31–32
matching principle 22–23, 236, 323, 357, 425–26
material omissions approach 98–103
maternity leave 229
Medicaid 432, 434
medical child support orders 26, 27*n*107
Medicare 432, 434
Medicare for All, proposal 460
minimum coverage requirement 343, 346–47,
  355–56
minimum distribution incidental benefit (MDIB)
  392*n*244
minimum funding standards
  actuarial assumptions 291–96, 312
  actuarial methods 291–94, 389–90
  advance funding 291, 385–90
  Congressional intention 288–90
  cushion amount 390
  deductibility of advance funding contributions
    293
  depreciation 291–92
  disclosure of funded status 298
  enforcement 162, 297–98
  exempt plans 14, 51, 290–91
  funding overview 290–94
  generally 226, 288–89
  minimum funding waivers 296–97, 304
  money purchase pension plans 287
  partly insurer-guaranteed pension benefits
    14–15
  past-service credits 289–90, 293–94
  plan amendments 296–97
  plan default, risks of 290
  profit-sharing plans 280, 287, 290*n*7
  qualified plans, for 298, 327*n*41
  relief provisions 296–97
  stock bonus plans 280, 287, 290
  tax penalties for failure to satisfy 327*n*41
  top hat plans 51–53, 290–91
  underfunded plans 297–98
  vesting 288
Minimum Universal Pension System (MUPS)
  418–19

Index

misrepresentation *See* fraud and misrepresentation
Moench presumption 154–57
money purchase pension plans
  advantages of 387
  benefit accrual 239–40, 249
  contributions to 250n97
  deduction limits 385–90
  defined 8
  discrimination in coverage 239–40
  minimum funding standards 287
  nondiscrimination testing 344
  number of 387–88
  plan amendments 63
  survivor protection 287
  vesting 251n103
moral hazard 301n65, 302, 312
multiemployer plans 12, 25–26, 232–33

New Jersey worker compensation statute 212–13
New York health plan administration law 209–10
NHCEs *See* nonhighly compensated employees
  (NHCEs)
Nixon Administration reform proposals 327n43
nondiscrimination principle 23–24, 26–27
  average benefit percentage test 344–50, 354n109,
    364
  nondiscriminatory classification test 344–50
  plan aggregation rule 343–44, 347–50, 355–56
  ratio percentage test 343–50, 355, 365
nonfiduciaries, civil actions against 178–79
nonforfeitable benefits, definition 300
nonhighly compensated employees (NHCEs)
  access to workplace retirement plans 353–54, 418
  defined 354–55
  discrimination in contributions or benefits
    358–66
  discrimination in coverage 343–50, 354n109
  disqualified plans and tax consequences 356–58
  emergency in-service distributions, and 264, 400
  401(k) plans, and 374–80
  minimum coverage requirement 343, 346–47,
    355–56
  minimum distribution rule 396
  minimum eligibility conditions, and 353–54
  Minimum Universal Pension System (MUPS)
    proposal 418–19
  nondiscrimination and redistribution 337–42,
    409–11
  over-pensioning, risk of 371–72
  pension-linked emergency savings programs 50,
    236, 397
  plan loans 401
  plan membership rates 370–71
  pre-retirement distributions, and 397–98

  proposed plans for 415–17
  retirement savings 236, 334–36, 370–72, 396
  Social Security, and 366–72
  See also employees; highly compensated
    employees (HCEs)
nonqualified arrangements
  nonqualified deferred compensation plans
    317–24
  qualified deferred compensation plans,
    compared with 5–6
  tax incentives 323
nonresident alien employees 353
normal retirement age (NRA) 237–38

Obama Administration reforms 455–56
  See also Affordable Care Act (ACA)
133 1/3 percent rule 242–43
over-pensioning 371–72
overfunded plans
  during 1980s and 1990s 289
  advance funding contributions 293
  distribution of excess to participants 309
  diversion of overfunding 310–11
  employer access to excess assets 289, 309–10
  lack of injury as result of 162n9
  notice of noncompliance 308
  notice of plan benefits 307
  spin-off termination 310
  termination 7n21, 289, 306–11

parol variance claims 104–6
part-time workers 231, 233–34, 351, 418
partial disability 98–100
participant-directed investments
  fiduciary obligations
    liability, limits of 124, 145–52, 158
    limited options 150–52
  increase in 146
  informed decision making, information
    provision for 147–48
  investment alternatives, provision of 147–48
  plan disclosure obligations 66–67
  prohibited transaction exception, and 142–43
  remedies 189
  risks of 158–59
  status reports 66–67
party in interest, definition 140, 142–43
past service credits 9, 289–90, 293–94
paternalism 18–19, 21, 50, 132–33, 286
paternity leave 229
Patient Protection and Affordable Care Act *See*
  Affordable Care Act (ACA)
'pay or play' health care reforms 445–47, 459
payments, specification of basis for making 36

478 *Index*

payroll tax exemptions 325*n*32
PBGC *See* Pension Benefit Guaranty Corporation
Pension Benefit Guaranty Corporation (PBGC)
  bankruptcy, PBGC's liens 298, 305–6
  compliance with 13–14
  disclosure obligations 63–65, 289, 306
  exceptions 299
  Form 5500 63–64
  insurance premiums 312
  insurance requirement 14, 45
  losses 298
  minimum funding waivers, and 296–97, 304
  overfunded plans, and 7*n*21, 289, 306–11
  plan funding notice, and 65
  risk from plan termination, and 299–300, 306
  standing for 162–63, 191
  termination insurance program
    asset allocation priority schedule 302–5
    exemptions 299
    generally 162, 299–300
    guaranteed benefits 300–5
    monitoring and enforcement 305–6
    professional service employers 299
    single employer plans 65, 288–89, 302
    top hat plans, and 299
    underfunded plans 303–4
  top hat plans exemption 299
  underfunded plans and bankruptcy of employer
    7*n*21, 289, 305–6
pension overpayments 249
pension plans
  age and service conditions 228–31, 353–54
  barriers to coverage 231–32
  benefit payments, methods of 45–46
  benefit statements 66–67
  bonus payments 47*n*106
  classification 10
  content controls 196–97, 225–26
  death benefits 46
  deferral of compensation, and 45–47
  defined in ERISA 5, 7–8, 33, 45–46
  disability pensions 46
  disclosure obligations 62
  disclosure regarding future benefits 89–91
  eligibility conditions 227
  employee stock purchase plans, as 47*n*107
  under ERISA 7–8, 28–29, 45–47, 51–53, 290–91,
    322
  ERISA *vs.* IRS meaning 7–8
  expensive nature of 406–8
  forfeiture conditions 227
  informed decisions, and 16, 266
  minimum standards 13–14, 18–21, 226–30
  number of private plans 232

participation standards 163–64, 237–38
pension-linked emergency savings accounts 50,
  236, 397
plan amendments 248–49
preemption 196–97
reform proposals
  Bush Administration 413–17
  calibrating nondiscrimination 409–11
  relaxed nondiscrimination test alternatives
    416–17
  saver's credit scheme 412–13
  subsidy incentives 411–13
  universal coverage 417–25
severance payments, and 47
Social Security, and 366–72
start-up cost credits 413
stringent regulation of 13–14, 47*n*109
surrounding circumstances, as result of 46–47
tax treatment 249
term as used for tax purpose 7–8
top hat plans exemption 51–53, 290–91, 322
vesting requirement 45, 227, 230
See also accumulation of pension savings;
  content controls; distribution of pension
  benefits; minimum funding standards;
  money purchase pension plans;
  overfunded plans; security of pension
  benefits; underfunded plans
plan administrators
  authority for investment decision making 124
  delegation of duties 124
  disclosure obligations 67, 124, 249–50
  discretionary authority 119–21
  enforcement standing 164–65
  role of 75*n*63, 124, 249–50
  See also fiduciaries
plan aggregation rule 343–44, 347–50, 355–56
plan amendments
  advance notice requirement 63, 67, 249–50
  adverse employment actions, and 181–82
  anti-cutback rule 245–49
  authority to amend plans 248–49
  benefit accrual, and 182, 245–50
  employer right to amend 76, 76*n*70, 88–92, 168,
    181–82, 360*n*134
  financial decision making, and 16*n*55, 248
  funding notice requirement 65
  health care plans 440
  inconsistent with SPD 76–77, 88–90
  informal 103–6, 181
  minimum funding standards 296–97
  nondiscrimination obligations, and 372–74
  oral representations 104–5, 104*n*182, 105*n*186
  reservation of rights clauses 88–92, 92*n*133

Index

479

section 510, and 181–82
for single or few employees 181
vesting 90n129, 252–53
welfare plans 105n187, 440
plan funding notices 65
plan instruments, disclosure obligations 67–70
plan interpretations
express grant of fiduciary discretion 168
judicial review 167–69
plan participants and beneficiaries
active participants 343
assignees 166–67
children of, coverage extensions 225n1
civil enforcement actions by 179–82
compensation, availability of 183–84
conflicts of interest 130–31
definition of beneficiary 273, 283–84
definition of participant 40–41, 43n87, 163–65, 191
duty of impartiality 130–31
duty to consult SPD 104
employers as 134
enforcement, plaintiff eligibility criteria 161–66
ERISA protections extension to beneficiaries 40–41
identification 205–6
improper motivation 135–36
inquiries by 111
inter-participant conflicts 130–31
party in interest, definition 140
standing 255
See also disclosure obligations
plan termination
overfunded plans 289, 306–11
partial termination 256–57
spin-off termination 310
termination insurance program *See* Pension Benefit Guarantee Corporation (PBGC)
underfunded plans 7n21, 162n10, 289, 303–4
vesting, and 256–57
plans, definition 33, 36–38
plant shutdown benefits 301, 304
pooled employer plans 233
portability of health insurance/care plans 225n1
precautionary saving 50, 236, 336, 415
preemption
Affordable Care Act provisions 457–59
ambiguity of statutory provisions 196
beneficiary designation, laws affecting 205–6, 215–16
categories of preempted laws 203–8
mandated coverage requirements 204, 442–43
supplemental remedies, laws providing for 207–8

uniform administrative practices, laws affecting 205–7
categories of statutory preemption 195–96
civil claims approaches, and 72
conflict preemption 195, 199, 209
Congressional objectives 198–99, 217, 223
costs and preemption policy 195, 197, 210–16
cost control principle, scope of 214–16, 222
indirect costs of plans 211
uniformity vs freedom of contract approaches 211–14
deemer clause 232–33, 443–45
early approach to 199–203
express preemption clause
breadth and ambiguity of 196–99, 201, 222
deemer clause 232–33, 443–45
generally 194–95, 222–23
legislative history 197–98
'relate to' 195–99, 201–3, 208, 222
savings clause 195, 200, 218–21, 443
statutory basis 195–96
federal common law and 216–18
field preemption 195–96, 198, 204, 208
implied preemption 195, 198, 442
insurance savings clause 195, 200, 218–21, 443
judicial interpretation
early approach 199–203
generally 194–95
purposive approach 208–10
litigation 442
obstacle preemption 195, 198–99, 205, 208–9
'pay-or-play' health care reforms 445–47
pension plans 196–97
purposive approach 197–98, 208–10
'relate to' 195–99, 201–3
savings clause 195, 200, 218–21, 443
state and local laws
anti-alienation rules, and 269, 276
benefits, comparison of 197–98
cost controls 211
criminal law, and 200
exemptions, interpretation 12–13, 200–1, 222–23
freedom of contract, and 213–14, 216, 223
indirect economic effects 209–10, 222–23
less or more demanding standards, imposition 213–14
mandated benefits laws 442–43
obstacle or conflict preemption 208–9
supplemental remedies 207–8
state-mandated IRAs 234
uniformity, and 195, 211–14
welfare benefits 200–1, 215
welfare plans 48, 196–98, 202, 204, 442

preexisting medical conditions 26, 225n1, 441–42, 454–55
preferential tax treatment
  company stock 318n12
  deferred compensation plans 22–25, 325–27
  employer-provided health insurance 434–35
  net costs of tax deferral 23
  penalty taxes for prohibited transactions 145
  plan service conditions, and 230
  qualified retirement plans 325–27
  vesting, and 256–57
  welfare benefits, for 6
prenuptial agreements 281n78
President's Advisory Panel on Tax Reform 415n330
President's Commission on Pension Policy 418–19
presumption of prudence 155–57
preventative health services 225n1, 455–56
private retirement plans
  costs *vs.* efficacy 408–9
  worker participation in 3, 232, 408–9
professional service employers 299
profit-sharing plans
  deduction limits 386–89
  defined 8
  ERISA pension plan, classification as 7–8
  limitations on employer contributions 386–87
  minimum distribution rule, and 391
  minimum funding standards 280, 287, 290
  nondiscrimination 360n133
  plan aggregation rule 343–44
  pre-retirement distributions, and 264, 398, 400
  vesting 250n97
program, as employee benefit plan 33
prohibited transactions 32, 139–45
  civil actions under ERISA 178–79
  civil penalties 144–45
  duty to avoid 179
  employer-investment transactions 140–41
  excise taxes 144–45
  exemptions 143–44
  fiduciary conflict transactions 116, 140–42
  nonfiduciary party participation 178–79
  participant-directed investments, and 142–43
  party in interest, definition 140, 142–43
  remedies 143–44
property
  community property rights 205, 284–85, 287
  deferred compensation 317–22
  definition 319–20, 321n16
prudence rule 125–27, 137–39

QDRO *See* qualified domestic relations order
QJSA *See* qualified joint and survivor annuity

QLACs *See* qualifying longevity annuity contracts
QPSA *See* qualified pre-retirement survivor annuity
QSERPs *See* qualified supplemental executive retirement plans
QSHERA *See* qualified small employer health reimbursement arrangement
QSLOBs *See* qualified separate lines of business
qualified domestic relations orders (QDRO) 205, 269–73, 286, 307, 399
qualified joint and survivor annuity (QJSA) 279–83
qualified plans, definition 22, 360n134
qualified pre-retirement survivor annuity (QPSA) 279–82
qualified separate lines of business (QSLOBs) 352–53
qualified small employer health reimbursement arrangement (QSHERA) 453n132
qualified supplemental executive retirement plans (QSERPs) 360n133
qualified tuition program (529 plans) 332, 414n326
qualifying longevity annuity contracts (QLACs) 395–96

rabbi trusts 320–22, 324
ratio percentage test 343, 347–50, 355, 365
Reagan Administration reforms 375n180
reasonable expectation of benefits 37, 37n52, 57
reasonable service periods 227
redistribution and nondiscrimination rules 337–42
reformation 75–77, 79n86, 95
reinstatement 188
reliance, detrimental
  estoppel 79–87, 79n87, 90, 104–6, 104n184
  inaccurate SPD, on 74–75, 76n76, 77n80, 78, 81–82, 113–14
Religious Freedom Restoration Act (RFRA) 455–56
remedies
  appropriate remedies, definition 182–83
  backpay claims 188
  compensation, limitations 183–84, 190–92
  damage multipliers 82n97
  equitable relief 61, 74–75, 75n68, 93–94, 96, 113, 144, 180, 184–88, 268
  ERISA's remedial balance 175–77, 182–83, 188–91
  estoppel 74–75, 78–87, 104–6
  fiduciary breach, for 78, 183–84, 189–90, 189n144
  inaccurate SPD, for 74–75
  individual *vs.* plan injuries 189
  prohibited transactions 143–44
  reinstatement 188
  reformation 75–77, 79n86, 95

Index

restitution 185–86, 188, 255
section 510 cases 188, 255–56
statutory limitations 182–83
supplemental remedies, preemption of 207–8
surcharge 78–79, 79n85, 79n86, 93–94, 187
tort-like damages 183–84
rescission of plan benefits, restrictions 225n1
reservation of rights clauses 88–92, 92n133
restitution 185–86, 188, 255
restricted coverage, scope of 37–40
retaliation 179–82
retirement
early 238, 241, 265, 301
health care 49–50
normal retirement age 237–38
phased retirement programs 7n24, 264, 264n1
public safety employees 238
See also retirement savings
retirement income, definition 45n98
retirement savings
bankruptcy, and 267
complexity of 406–7
Congressional efforts to increase 19, 23–24, 50
costs of preferential tax treatment 23, 407–8
elective contribution schemes 233–35
expensive nature of system 406–8
low-income workers 236
part-time workers 231, 233–34, 418
participation rates 3, 232, 408–9
pre-retirement standard of living, and 334–35, 409
precautionary saving programs 50, 236
preferential tax treatment 23, 407–8
saver's credit scheme 412–13
state law initiatives 234
subsidy incentives 411–13
See also retirement; taxes and retirement saving
Retirement Savings Account (RSA) proposal 334n67, 413–16
Return/Report of Employee Benefit Plan 63–64
rollovers 248, 280, 286, 325–26, 331–32, 400n277, 403–6
Roth IRAs 236, 328–33, 391–92, 403n293, 412–14, 417

safe harbor rules 410, 416–17
San Francisco 'pay or play' health care reforms 445–47
SAR *See* summary annual report
saver's credit scheme 412–13
SBC *See* summary of benefits and coverage (SBC)
Seattle healthcare expenditures law 459
Secretary of Labor
civil enforcement actions by 176, 298
disclosure obligations, and 62

minimum funding requirements enforcement by 298
SECURE 2.0 Act
automatic enrollment in elective contribution schemes 235n32
automatic portability transactions 406n303
emergency savings accounts 236n38
Employee Plans Compliance Resolution System (EPCRS) 374n176
involuntary cash-out limit 308n105
multiple employer 403(b) plans 233n23
qualified longevity annuity contract (QLAC) limits 396n258
recoupment of pension overpayments 185n121
starter 401(k) plan 379, 379n194
security of pension benefits
minimum funding standards 162
actuarial assumptions 291–96, 312
actuarial methods 291–94
disclosure of funded status 298
enforcement of 162, 297–98
exempt plans 14, 290
funding overview 290–94
relief provisions 296–97
PBGC termination insurance
disclosure obligations 63–65, 289
generally 162, 289, 299–300
guaranteed benefits 300–5
monitoring and enforcement 162, 305–6
rabbi trusts 320–22, 324
self-employment
single-employee pension arrangements 38
tax obligations 420n345
self-insured plans 218–19, 443–45, 454n139, 458–59
separate interest approach 271–72
service conditions
benefit accrual, and 237–38
breaks in service 228–29, 252
gig economy 418
imposition of 13
maternity/paternity/adoption leave 229
minimum service conditions 353–54
part-time workers 231, 233–34, 418
pension plans 228–36
reasonable service conditions 227
vesting 252–53
year of service, definition 228
severance payments 29–33, 37n50, 37n52, 47, 49, 49n115, 201n29
shared payment approach 271–72
shared responsibility payments 451
silence
fiduciary silence 97–98, 110–11
SPD coverage 98–99

Index

single employer plans 12, 38–39, 65, 288–89, 302
small-scale plans
  ERISA applicability 37–40
  exemptions, legislative history 37–38
  plan start-up cost credits 413
SMM *See* summary of material modifications
Social Security
  adequacy of 334–35, 366, 370–71
  age benefits may be claimed 241n64
  bridge payments 241, 241n64
  401(k) plans and 374
  401(l) rules 367–72
  Guaranteed Retirement Account (GRA),
    proposal 421–25
  Minimum Universal Pension System (MUPS),
    proposal 418–19
  nondiscrimination rules 366–72
  nonhighly compensated employees (NHCEs),
    and 366–68
  payroll tax exemptions 325n32
  pension plans, and 366–67
    complexity of supplementing via 406
    qualified plans, integration with 366–72
  proposed plan for 418–25
  standard of living provided by 23, 366, 370–71, 409
  taxable wages 335, 366–67
  uniformity rule 367–70
SPD *See* summary plan description
spendthrift protection clauses 265–66, 269
spousal rights
  beneficiary designation, and 205–6, 215–16
  community property 205, 284–85, 287
  consent requirement 274, 283
  crimes committed by spouse, and 216–17, 273, 276
  distribution of pension benefits 268, 273–77,
    279–84, 393–94
  prenuptial agreements 281n78
  qualified domestic relations orders (QDRO)
    205, 269–73, 286, 307, 399
  qualified joint and survivor annuities (QJSA)
    279–83
  qualified pre-retirement survivor annuity
    (QPSA) 279–82
  remarriage after participant's death 281
  survivor protection 13, 26, 253, 268, 276, 279–84,
    287
  waiver of pension benefits 281–82
  working owners, of 40–41, 58
  See also divorce
standard of proof
  detrimental reliance on SPD 74–75, 76n76,
    77n80, 78, 82, 86–87, 98
  establishment requirement for plan/benefit
    arrangements 34–35

standard of review
  abuse of discretion 32, 100–2, 101n176, 114,
    167–70
    conflicts of interest, and 171–75
    factfinding 66, 169–70
standing *See* enforcement
start-up cost credits 413
starter 401(k) plans 379–80
state and local laws
  beneficiary designation 205–6, 215–16, 274–77
  community property 205, 284–85
  divorce, survivor benefits 205–6, 215–18,
    273–77
  federal fiduciary standards, differences from 17
  health care information disclosure 206–7
  health plan administration 209–10
  insurance regulation 25, 220–21, 444–45
  killer laws 216–17, 273, 276, 276n55
  mandatory health insurance benefits 212
  'pay or play' health care reforms 445–47
  preemption
    anti-alienation rules 269
    benefits, comparison of 197–98
    cost controls 211
    criminal law, and 200
    exemptions, interpretation 12–13, 200–1,
      222–23
    freedom of contract, and 213–14, 216, 223
    indirect economic effects 209–10, 222–23
    less or more demanding standards, imposition
      213–14
    obstacle or conflict preemption 208–9
    supplemental remedies 207–8
  relevance for welfare and pension plans 25, 41
  retirement savings initiatives 234
  severance payments 29–30, 32–33, 211–12
  stop-loss insurance 444–45
  worker compensation 212–13
stock bonus plans
  deduction limit for 386–89
  defined 8
  ERISA *vs.* IRC meaning 7–8
  limits on employer contributions 386–87
  minimum distribution rule, and 391
  minimum funding standards, and 280, 287
  plan aggregation 343–44
  pre-retirement distributions, and 264, 398, 400
  rollovers 404–5
  stock value drops 153, 156
  income tax law 7–8, 318–19
stop-loss insurance 444–45
student loans 235
substantial owners 299
summary of benefits and coverage (SBC) 63

Index

summary annual report (SAR) 64, 64*n*17

summary of material modifications (SMM) 63, 95–96

summary plan description (SPD)

  amendment or reformation of 76–78

  conflicts with plan documents 80–81, 98–99

  contradictory SPDs 87–94, 104–5, 112–14

  controlling legal effect of 74–75, 81

  detrimental reliance on 74–75, 76*n*76, 77*n*80, 78, 90, 98, 113–14

  disclosure obligations 71–72, 114

  enforcement 112–14

  failure to warn 94–99, 102–3, 114

  fraud or misrepresentation 76–77, 76*n*76, 77*n*80, 93–94, 96–98, 177–78

  future benefits, representations regarding 89–91, 89*n*124

  generally 15–16, 63, 71–74, 112–13

  inaccurate SPDs 73–87, 102–3, 113

  incomplete SPDs 94–103, 114

  material omissions approach 98–103

  negligent drafting 78

  optimal disclosure as objective of 71–73, 100–2, 114

  plan amendments inconsistent with 76, 88–90

  plan term information, and 63

  purpose 80–81, 95, 103–4

  reasonable expectation of accuracy and content 80–81

  remedies for disclosure harms 74–87

  See also disclosure obligations; informal communications

surcharge 78–79, 79*n*85, 79*n*86, 93–94, 187

Taft-Hartley Act

  abuse of discretion standard application 167

  appropriate equitable relief 268

  influences on ERISA benefits lists 48–49

  welfare plans, amendment 48–49

tax, income *See* income tax

tax sheltered annuity plans 9*n*29, 25*n*99, 25*n*100

tax subsidies and economic growth 23–24

taxes and health care

  cost-containment 122

  cost sharing 451*n*126

  disability insurance 432

  employer financing generally 23

  health reimbursement arrangements 185–87, 452*n*132

  health savings accounts 414*n*326

  preferential tax treatment for employer-provided health insurance 434–35

  tax exemptions 6

  See also employment-based health care; health care plans

taxes and retirement saving

  ABLE accounts 332–33

  advance funding limits 385–90

  annual value of tax subsidy 326

  complexities of 407

  Coverdell education savings accounts (ESAs) 332, 414*n*326

  distribution timing

    early/pre-retirement distribution 264, 264*n*3, 268–69, 286, 397 401

    late distribution 265, 286, 391–92

    lifetime distribution 392–94

    minimum distribution rule 391–92

    penalty taxes 264, 264*n*3, 286, 392

    profit-sharing/stock bonus plans 264, 264*n*3, 287

    qualifying longevity annuity contracts (QLACs) 395–96

    required minimum distribution (RMD) 393–94

    rollovers 248, 286, 325–26, 331–32, 394, 400*n*277, 403–6

    shortfall penalty tax 392

    survivor protection 392–93

    tax-free emergency distributions 400

    tax rule restrictions 24*n*89

  economic growth, influences on 333–34

  employee choice, influences on 337–40, 407

  encouraging savings 19, 23–24, 232, 333, 356

  favorable tax treatment of qualified plans 325–27

  529 plans 332, 414*n*326

  IRAs 327–33

  maximum amount rule 380–85, 411

  nondiscrimination rules

    annual amount nondiscrimination testing 361–62

    average benefit percentage test 344–50, 354*n*109, 364

    calibrating 409–11

    correction mechanisms 372–74

    discrimination in contributions or benefits 358–66

    discrimination in coverage 343–50, 354*n*109

    effectiveness of 337–38

    employees defined 350–55

    exemptions 342, 352–54

    401(k) plans 374–80, 387–88, 410

    integration with Social Security 366–72

    limitations of 342, 349–50

    maximum amount rule 380–85, 411

    minimum coverage requirement 343, 346–47, 355–56

    nondiscrimination and redistribution 337–42, 409–13

    nondiscriminatory classification test 344–50

484 Index

taxes and retirement saving (cont.)
    permitted disparity rules 368–72
    plan aggregation rule 343–44, 347–50,
        355–56
    purpose 337, 349–50
    rate group nondiscrimination testing 361–66
    ratio percentage test 343, 347–50, 355, 365
    safe harbors 410, 416–17
    sanctions for deficient coverage 356–58
    pension reform proposals
        Bush Administration 413–17
        calibrating nondiscrimination 409–11
        relaxed nondiscrimination test alternatives
            416–17
        saver's credit scheme 412–13
        subsidy incentives 411–13
        universal coverage 417–25
    pre-retirement earnings, replacement of 334–35
    proportion of disposable of income 333–34
    qualified retirement plans 286, 325–27
    tax controls, categories of 333
    tax deferral
        advance funding limits 385–90
        IRAs 22–23, 328–32
        net costs 23
    See also income tax; retirement savings
terminal illness 399–400
termination of employment
    standing 164
    vesting, and 256
    wrongful discharge 179–82
3 percent rule 242–43
tin parachutes 31–32
top hat plans
    bargaining power, relevance of 53, 53n133
    classification 51, 321
    definition 52
    disclosure obligations 51
    exemption of 51–53, 58, 290–91, 322
    forfeiture requirement 52–53, 52n130, 52n131
    minimum funding standards 51, 290–91
    PBGC termination insurance, and 299
    'primarily' definition 52
tort-like damages 183–84
transience of plan/benefit arrangements 29–33
Treasury Department, tax reform 360n133, 375n180
trust law
    administrative deviation approach 154n158
    applicability to pension plans 17n58
    beneficial interests, tax liability 319–20
    breach of trust by fiduciary 78
    conflicts of interest 134–35, 142, 172n52
    de novo review 168
    diversification rule 128

duties
    disclosure 64
    impartiality 129–31
    loyalty 127, 129–31
    prudence/reasonable care 127–28, 131, 138
influences on ERISA fiduciary rules 116–17,
    128–29, 192
investment decision making, delegation 124
no further inquiry rule 142
plan interpretation 168
rabbi trusts 320–22, 324
self-dealing restrictions 142
trustees
    disclosure obligations 71, 111n212
    fiduciary liabilities 125–26

underfunded plans
    actuarial assumptions 295–96
    bankruptcy 7n21, 289, 305–6
    disclosure of funded status, and 298
    enforcement of minimum funding standards
        297–98
    government plans 12n34
    grants of past-service credits, and 290, 293
    liability-increasing amendments 297
    minimum funding standards 297–98
    notification requirements for defined benefit
        plans, and 65
    oral modifications 105n186
    plan amendments 297
    plan termination 7n21, 162n10, 289, 303–4
    single employer plans 297–98, 302
    See also Pension Benefit Guaranty Corporation
        (PBGC)
unfunded executive deferred compensation plans
    See top hat plans
Uniform Partnership Act 44
unionized workers 49n116, 353
unit credit plans 8–9, 244–45, 369, 389
'usual and customary charges' limitation 69–70

Vermont health care information law 206–7,
    458–59
vesting
    accrued benefits 228–29, 231, 250–55
    adverse employment actions and 180–81
    breaks in service 252–53
    church plans 54n134
    cliff *vs.* graded conditions 252–55
    conditions required for 227
    Congressional policy 259–60
    cost implications of mandatory vesting
        258n126
    defined benefit plans 241–42, 251

Index

defined contribution plans 251
delays 252–53
disclosure obligations 66, 255
employee contributions 250
employee termination 256–57
employer contributions 250–51
enforcement 164, 166, 255–57
forfeiture of benefits 250–54, 258–59
401(k) plans 357, 376
governmental plans 53n134
health care plans 49
interference with 255–56
lack of vesting provisions 18, 18n64, 49, 259
language, in informal communications 90n128
mandatory vesting 256n126, 260
minimum standards approach 18–19, 228–29, 251–54, 259, 261–62, 288
money purchase pension plans 251n103
participant status, and 163
pension plans 45, 227, 230
plan amendments 90n129, 252–53
plan termination 256–57
policy 257–60
profit-sharing plans 250n97
rule variances 242–45, 251
section 510 liability 255–56
service conditions 252–53
statutory standards 228–29, 231, 250–55
term standardization 19
welfare plans 49, 166, 181, 440
vicarious liability 126

Washington state beneficiary designation law 205–6, 215–16, 274–77
Welfare and Pension Plans Disclosure Act 1958 (WPPDA) 38, 48–49
welfare benefits
benefits in kind 44
classification, overview 11f

garnishment 200–1, 215
interference with, cause in action 181–82
preemption 200–1, 215
preferential tax treatment 6
vesting 166, 181
welfare plans
assignment of benefits 166–67
content controls 197, 225
deferred welfare benefits 49–50
defined 5, 28–29, 33, 44, 48–50
disclosure obligations 14, 48–49, 62
disclosure regarding future benefits 48, 89–91
emergency savings programs 50, 397
employer right to amend 76, 88–92, 181–82
enforcement incentives 162n11, 166
excluded benefits 50, 58
fiduciary authority 119–20
funding requirement 440
grandfathered plans 447–48, 447n108
informal communications 105n187
insurance-funded plans, ERISA modifications for 14–15
plan amendments 105n187, 440
plan instruments 67–70
preemption 48, 196–98, 202, 204
protection of rights 181–82
regulatory basis 14
retiree health care benefits 49–50
severance pay arrangements 47, 49, 49n115
Taft-Hartley Act amendments 48–49
tax treatment 4
unionized workers 49n116
vesting 49, 166, 181, 440
workforce aggregation rules 351–52
WPPDA See Welfare and Pension Plans Disclosure Act 1958
wrongful discharge 179–82

year of service, definition 228

Printed in the USA
CPSIA information can be obtained
at www.ICGtesting.com
LVHW011631230824
789095LV00003B/254